# CHEMISTRY

## Students' book

## Fourth edition

D1428572

**Nuffield Advanced Chemistry**
**Published for the Nuffield Foundation by Pearson Education**

Nuffield Advanced Chemistry
4th edition

**General editor**
Michael Vokins

**Editors**
Alan Furse
Robin Hillman
Glyn James

**Contributors**
John Apsey
Pamela Butler
David Craggs
Elwyn Davies
Douglas Snowden

**Safety adviser**
Peter Borrows

**Nuffield Curriculum Projects Centre**
Sarah Codrington
Andrew Hunt

**Advisers**
Paul Barber
Suzanne Barrett
Jeannette Bartholemew
Alexander Burford
John Carleton
Roger Chambers
Celia Douse
Malcolm Evetts
Alastair Fleming
Graham Hall
Ros Hay
Peter Jackson
Paul Lear
Colin Osborne
Bryan Stokes
Geoff Wake
Penelope Wilson
Rita Woodward

This edition of Nuffield Advanced Chemistry is dedicated to
Michael Vokins

Pearson Education Limited
Edinburgh Gate
Harlow
Essex
CM20 2JE
England

© 1970, 1984, 1994, 2000 The Nuffield Foundation

The right of The Nuffield Foundation to be identified as author of this Work has been asserted by them in accordance with the Copyright, Designs and Patents Act of 1988.

All rights reserved. No part of this publication may be reproduced, stored in a retrieval system, or transmitted in any form or by any means, electronic, mechanical, photocopying, recording or otherwise without the prior written permission of the Publishers or a licence permitting restricted copying in the United Kingdom issued by the Copyright Licensing Agency Ltd., 90 Tottenham Court Road, London W1P 0LP.

ISBN 0 582 32835 7

First published 1970
Revised edition published 1984
Third edition published 1994
Fourth edition published 2000
Fifth impression 2004

Printed in China
GCC/05

The Publisher's policy is to use paper manufactured from sustainable forests.

**Note**
All references to the **Book of data** are to the Nuffield Advanced Science book published by Longman

**Title page** Fireworks displays are coloured by the use of metal compounds, produce large amounts of energy, and change from an orderly firework to disordered debris: all themes that we will be developing in this book. On display are the flame colours of Groups 1 and 2 metals.

# CONTENTS

Copper oxides were used to make this coloured glass, depicting a devil. This shows colours due to transition metal ions in the solid (or semi-liquid) state. What other transition metal ion colours do you know already?

Gold was used to make this funeral mask, from ancient Greece. This shows the colour of the metal itself. What other coloured metals are there?

The first iron bridge in the world, at Coalbrookdale. Why was a large-scale iron structure so long in coming (eighteenth century) when iron has been known for a very long time?

# Metal compounds: an introduction to inorganic chemistry

**IRON**

*Fe fi fo fum*
*As hard as nails*
*As tough as they come*

I'm the most important
Metal known to man
(though aluminium
is more common
do we need another can?)

Five per cent of the earth's crust
I am also the stone at its centre
Iron fist in iron glove
Adding weight to the system
I am the firma in the terra

*Fe fi fo*
*Don't drop me on your toe*

My hobbies are space travel
And changing the course of history
(they even named an Age after me
– eat your heart out Gold)

And changing shape of course
From axe heads and plough shares
To masks maidens and missiles
I am malleable
I bend to your will
I am both the sword and the shield
The bullet and the forceps

I am all around you
And more much more
You are all around me 2, 3, 4 ...

You've got me
Under your skin
I'm in your blood
What a spin that I'm in
Haemoglobin
You've got me
Under your skin

So strike while I'm hot
For if I'm not there
What are you?
Anaemic that's what

*Fe fi*
*High and mighty*
*Iron*

Gregarious and fancy free
Easy going that's me
No hidden depths
I'm not elusive
To be conclusive
You get what you see
*fe      Fe*

*Roger McGough*

Over 100 elements have been identified by chemists and about 80 can be found in the minerals that make up the Earth's crust, of which 21 also occur in plants and animals; the other 20 elements have been produced in nuclear experiments and are radioactive.

**Most elements are metals** and the compounds that they form with non-metals are known as **inorganic compounds**. Compounds of the non-metal carbon with other non-metals are known as **organic compounds**.

As you do the various activities in the first two topics of the course, try to be aware of the general characteristics of the compounds you are using. In Topic 1 these will be **inorganic**, whereas many of those in Topic 2 are **organic**. You will notice a number of differences in the nature of the materials themselves and in the ways in which they are used.

Learning how to manufacture and use metals has marked important stages in the history of civilisation, such as the Bronze age and the Iron age. Only after centuries of development did we learn how to manufacture iron in the large quantities which were the key to the Industrial Revolution in the eighteenth and nineteenth centuries. Today, understanding the elements used in semiconductors is the key to the development of computers and Information Technology. And iron still has a contribution to make as one of its oxides is the coating on floppy disks.

**Figure 1.1**
**Iron occurs everywhere!**
- The red colour in bricks is due to an iron compound. Which one?
- Meteorite from Mars – contains iron.
- The red colour of blood is due to an iron compound. What is its name?

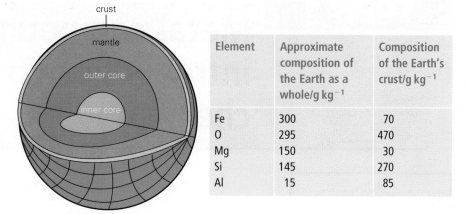

Figure 1.2 **Composition of the Earth and the Earth's crust**

| Element | Approximate composition of the Earth as a whole/g kg$^{-1}$ | Composition of the Earth's crust/g kg$^{-1}$ |
|---|---|---|
| Fe | 300 | 70 |
| O | 295 | 470 |
| Mg | 150 | 30 |
| Si | 145 | 270 |
| Al | 15 | 85 |

Iron is particularly interesting because it occurs everywhere. The Earth's core behaves as if it is iron; the Earth as a whole is about 30% iron, while the Earth's crust contains about 5% of iron; meteorites are composed mostly of iron; ploughed fields are red to brown in colour because of the iron compounds in the soil; red pottery contains iron; a red-brick wall contains iron; red paints are usually based on iron compounds; haemoglobin contains iron and you will have about 3.5 g of iron in your body and need 10 mg of iron in your food each day.

## 1.1 Types of inorganic reaction

In this first section we shall examine some types of reaction which are frequently encountered in inorganic chemistry. When you have finished the section you should be able to recognise each type and be able to describe it with the aid of an equation. Help with equations, if needed, is given in section 1.3. Section 1.3 is the first of what we shall call the 'chemists' toolkits', which are specially designed to explain the formal ways in which some procedures are carried out.

## Thermal decomposition reactions

Many compounds break down into a number of different simpler compounds when they are heated. This type of reaction is known as 'thermal decomposition', and is usually accompanied by the evolution of gases such as water vapour, oxygen, carbon dioxide and nitrogen dioxide.

- *Any hydrated compound* – decomposes with relatively gentle heating, releasing water vapour.
- *Metal **carbon**ates* – decompose (with varying degrees of ease) into metal oxides and **carbon** dioxide gas.
- *Metal **sulph**ates* – usually decompose into metal oxides and a mixture of different oxides of **sulph**ur.
- *Metal **nitr**ates* – usually decompose into metal oxides and a mixture of **nitr**ogen dioxide and oxygen gases; however, some nitrates decompose to a lesser extent, where oxygen is the only gas evolved.

In Experiment 1.1a you are going to heat small samples of some common laboratory substances all of which decompose in some way when heated. Whilst

---

**SIMPLE 'TESTS' FOR GASES LIKELY TO BE EVOLVED**

**Water vapour**
*When cooled down, condenses into droplets of liquid water.*

**Carbon dioxide**
*Bubble through lime water. The solution turns cloudy.*

**Oxygen**
*Use a glowing splint. This will burst into flame.*

**Oxides of sulphur**
*Are colourless (sometimes produce misty fumes when moist) and are strongly acidic, so use moist Full-range Indicator paper or blue litmus paper.*

**Nitrogen dioxide**
*Is a brown acidic gas, so observe its colour and use moist Full-range Indicator paper or blue litmus paper.*

Figure 1.3   **Compounds for Experiment 1.1a**

you are heating the solids you or a partner should note down as many observations as you can and test for any gases evolved. The compounds which you are going to use are:

- cobalt(II) chloride
- copper(II) nitrate
- iron(II) sulphate
- zinc carbonate
- sodium nitrate.

✎   **In your notes:** First design a table – something similar to the one shown below.

| Name | Formula | Appearance | Observations on heating | Names of any gases evolved |
|---|---|---|---|---|
| cobalt(II) chloride | | | | |
| etc. | | | | |

# Thermal decomposition reactions

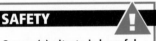

## SAFETY

Copper(II) nitrate is harmful and oxidising.
Iron(II) sulphate is harmful.
Nitrogen dioxide is *very* toxic.
Oxides of nitrogen and oxides of sulphur are toxic by inhalation and can cause burns. **Carry out these experiments on a very small scale in a fume cupboard or well-ventilated laboratory.**

Before you start the test tube reactions described below, note down in your table the name, formula and appearance of each chemical.

In each experiment take a clean, dry, hard glass test tube, and use only a small amount of the solid. If you need to repeat an experiment, you must wait for the tube to cool and then add another spatula-full of solid before re-heating. **You must carry out these experiments in a well-ventilated laboratory or fume cupboard.**

In each case, heat the solid gently at first and then more strongly. If a liquid appears in the tube, continue heating until no further change occurs. Watch carefully to observe all changes. If working in a pair, one of you can concentrate on heating while the other notes down the observations. The sodium nitrate in particular will need prolonged and intense heating for any decomposition to occur, so be patient! Remember to carry out any tests for the gases *which you are expecting to be evolved.*

✎   **In your notes:**

1   Which of your compounds changed permanently?

2   What does this suggest has happened to these compounds?

3   Which substance was yellow when hot but became white on cooling?

4   What does this suggest? (Think about this – there is both a physical and a chemical change happening here.)

5   Some solids appear to melt when heated. In fact they give off so much water when heated that the solid dissolves in it. Which of your substances behaved in this way? Look up the formula for the substances which did this (*Book of data* or bottle label) and check that the explanation is reasonable.

6   Were the gases given off the ones you expected?

7   What laboratory use could be made of the cooled solid which remained after you heated the hydrated cobalt chloride?

Figure 1.4   **Nitrogen dioxide gas is produced when copper(II) nitrate is heated (in a fume cupboard)**

**SAFETY**

Ammonium dichromate(VI) is explosive and toxic by inhalation. It is a category 2 carcinogen. It must be heated only in an efficient fume cupboard, or in a vessel with a mineral wool plug to prevent particles escaping.

# Demonstration: the thermal decomposition of ammonium dichromate(VI)

**In your notes:** Write down exactly what you observed.

1 Is there evidence to suggest whether the reaction is endothermic or exothermic?

2 What evidence is there that a gas has been evolved?

3 What can you say about the density of ammonium dichromate(VI) compared with the solid residue left behind?

Figure 1.5 **An ammonium dichromate(VI) 'volcano' (in a fume cupboard)**

# Precipitation reactions

The next type of chemical change to be studied is ionic precipitation. In order to do this you will need to know the basic 'solubility rules' for inorganic compounds. The first part of the next experiment tests some of these rules.

---

**'SOLUBILITY RULES'**

1. Sodium, potassium and ammonium compounds are always soluble in water

2. All nitrates are soluble in water

3. Most chlorides are soluble in water; lead chloride and silver chloride are common exceptions to this rule

4. Most sulphates are soluble in water; lead sulphate and barium sulphate are common exceptions to this rule

5. Most oxides, hydroxides and carbonates are insoluble in water; those of sodium and potassium are soluble. Calcium hydroxide is slightly soluble in water

---

Figure 1.6 **Compounds for Experiment 1.1b**

**In your notes:** First design a table using the following headings: name, formula, appearance, solubility, colour of solution. Add an extra column which you will need for an extension to the first experiment. You will need a row for each of the following substances:

| copper(II) chloride | iron(II) sulphate | magnesium carbonate |
| iron(III) nitrate | iron(III) oxide | potassium carbonate |

As you carry out the experiments enter your observations in the table as you go along, otherwise you will forget important details which need to be recorded.

**EXPERIMENT 1.1b**

## Solubility and precipitation reactions

**SAFETY**

Copper(II) chloride is toxic.
Iron(II) sulphate is harmful.
Iron(III) nitrate is irritant.
0.4 M sodium hydroxide is an
irritant.

Choose one of the compounds supplied. Write down its formula and appearance.

Next use a spatula to transfer a tiny quantity of it to a test tube, enough to cover just the end of the spatula. Add about $5 \, cm^3$ of de-ionised (or distilled) water and shake the tube, and stir using a glass rod if necessary, to see whether the solid is capable of dissolving in water. If you use too much solid it may be hard to tell whether any has dissolved.

Note the colour of any solution formed. You may need to hold a test tube of water alongside for comparison, because some of the solutions may be very pale in colour. If the solid does not dissolve record this fact in your table.

Keep any solutions formed for the next experiment, otherwise dispose of your mixture down the sink.

✎ **In your notes:**

1 Were any of the metal compounds you used coloured? If so, whereabouts in the Periodic Table do the metals occur?

2 Did the formula for any of the compounds include the formula for water? If so, what does this tell you about the solid?

3 Did the compounds obey the solubility rules?

Four of the experiments carried out above should have produced solutions: the ones with **copper(II) chloride, iron(II) sulphate, iron(III) nitrate** and **potassium carbonate**.

To each of these four solutions now add a few drops of dilute (0.4 M) sodium hydroxide solution. Use a glass rod to stir the mixtures obtained.

✎ **In your notes:** Enter your results in the final column of the table, labelled 'addition of NaOH', noting the production of any cloudiness, which indicates the formation of an insoluble solid, known as a 'precipitate'. Record the colour of any precipitate.

# Interpretation of the experiments

It is important that you understand exactly what is going on when a precipitate is formed. In all the experiments which you have just carried out, the chemicals were ionic and in solution, so, before mixing, the ions were totally mobile and independent of each other. Consider the experiment above – the one between aqueous copper(II) chloride and aqueous sodium hydroxide.

● The solution of copper(II) chloride contains $Cu^{2+}(aq)$ and $Cl^-(aq)$ ions.
● The solution of sodium hydroxide contains $Na^+(aq)$ and $OH^-(aq)$ ions.

You will have noticed already that a blue precipitate was formed in this reaction, so presumably two of the ions must have been attracted to each other in very large numbers and created a three-dimensional ionic lattice. If you inspect the four ions above, and assume that the interaction must have been between oppositely charged ions, then the precipitate must have been formed either between the $Na^+(aq)$ and $Cl^-(aq)$ ions or between the $Cu^{2+}(aq)$ and $OH^-(aq)$ ions. This reaction **cannot** have been between the $Na^+(aq)$ and $Cl^-(aq)$ ions, because sodium chloride is a soluble substance according to the 'solubility rules' and based on previous experience. However, copper(II) hydroxide is insoluble, as

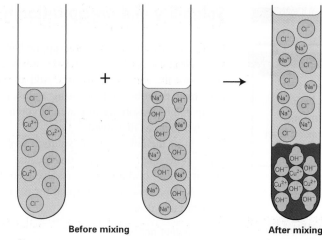

**Before mixing**

The $Cu^{2+}$ and $Cl^-$ ions are totally mobile and move about randomly in solution

The $Na^+$ and $OH^-$ ions are totally mobile and move about randomly in solution

**After mixing**

The $Cu^{2+}$ and $OH^-$ ions come together to form a precipitate of solid copper(II) hydroxide;

The $Na^+$ and $Cl^-$ ions are still moving about freely and have not taken part in the reaction: these are the 'spectator ions'

**Figure 1.7  Formation of copper(II) hydroxide from copper(II) chloride and sodium hydroxide solutions**

are most hydroxides, so this must be the identity of the blue precipitate. Its formula is **$Cu(OH)_2$** and it was created when the copper(II) ions in the copper(II) chloride solution combined with the hydroxide ions in the sodium hydroxide solution in a $1:2$ ratio, i.e.

$$Cu^{2+}(aq) + 2OH^-(aq) \longrightarrow Cu(OH)_2(s)$$

Notice that the sodium ions, **$Na^+(aq)$**, and the chloride ions, **$Cl^-(aq)$**, do not feature in the reaction at all. They are present in the mixture, of course, but they do not interact in any way, and at the end of the reaction they are still present and as mobile as they ever were. For this reason they are often known as **'spectator ions'**. If you had filtered the mixture, they would have passed through the filter paper and formed the filtrate as a solution of sodium chloride, whereas the solid blue copper(II) hydroxide would have been the residue on the filter paper.

**The type of equation above is known as an 'ionic equation'** because it involves the interaction of ions. **Spectator ions are always omitted in ionic equations,** because the intention is to illustrate precisely what is happening in the solution, ignoring any ions which do not change.

The 'full' equation for the reaction is in fact:

$$CuCl_2(aq) + 2NaOH(aq) \longrightarrow Cu(OH)_2(s) + 2NaCl(aq)$$

but the ionic equation given earlier is more useful because it represents the chemical change occurring.

## STUDY TASK

Use the space below your table to copy down the ionic equation between copper(II) and hydroxide ions, given above.

Next construct ionic equations for the other precipitation reactions which occurred.

Why was it that there was no precipitate with potassium ions?

If you study your table you will observe that coloured precipitates were formed with $Cu^{2+}(aq)$, $Fe^{2+}(aq)$ and $Fe^{3+}(aq)$ ions:

- $Cu^{2+}(aq)$ ions form a **blue** precipitate with aqueous sodium hydroxide
- $Fe^{2+}(aq)$ ions form a **'dirty' green** precipitate with aqueous sodium hydroxide
- $Fe^{3+}(aq)$ ions form a **'rusty' brown** precipitate with aqueous sodium hydroxide.

The different colour of precipitate formed by $Fe^{2+}(aq)$ and $Fe^{3+}(aq)$ ions when added to aqueous sodium hydroxide is a very useful means of distinguishing between them. Try to remember these colours, because you will need this information in a later experiment.

EXPERIMENT 1.1b (cont.)

## Further precipitation reactions

### SAFETY ⚠

0.4 M sodium hydroxide is an irritant.
Aqueous lead(II) nitrate is toxic.

Mix the following solutions in pairs and use the ideas encountered in the previous experiment to interpret what happens. If a precipitate is formed, use the 'solubility rules' to decide what it is, and write an ionic equation for the reaction.

✎   **In your notes:** You may find it convenient to set out your results in a table with six columns. You will need a row for each of the following substances.

| sodium chloride | sodium hydroxide | lead(II) nitrate |
| sodium sulphate | copper(II) sulphate | sodium carbonate |

At the end of this section you should make a note of the 'solubility rules' in your notebook and then learn them.

## Redox reactions (1)

'Redox' is a made-up word derived from **red**uction and **ox**idation. Originally 'oxidation' meant a process in which a material gained oxygen and 'reduction' meant the opposite, the loss of oxygen. For example, aluminium can be oxidised by a reaction with iron(III) oxide. This reaction is called the **Thermit reaction**.

When doing this reaction it is important to work out suitable quantities by using the mole concept. Help with this, if needed, is given in section 1.4, which is the second of the 'chemists' toolkits'.

### COMMENT

The reactivity series of the metals lists them in descending order of reactivity. The strongest reducing agents are at the beginning of the list. Here is a selection of metals in reactivity series order:

- potassium, K
- sodium, Na
- calcium, Ca
- magnesium, Mg
- aluminium, Al
- iron, Fe
- lead, Pb
- copper, Cu
- silver, Ag

# Demonstration of the Thermit reaction

Figure 1.8    The Thermit reaction

This demonstration uses a variety of metals from different positions in the reactivity series to try to produce iron from iron(III) oxide.

If iron(III) oxide and aluminium react, the balanced equation should be:

$$Fe_2O_3(s) + 2Al(s) \longrightarrow 2Fe(s) + Al_2O_3(s)$$

and the amounts to mix will be:

| 1 mol of $Fe_2O_3$ | | 2 mol of Al | |
|---|---|---|---|
| 2Fe | 112 g | 2Al | 54 g |
| 3O | 48 g | | |
| | 160 g | | 54 g |

For an ordinary laboratory experiment we must scale down the quantities and use no more than $\frac{1}{20}$ mol of $Fe_2O_3$.

## SAFETY

Powdered aluminium and magnesium and magnesium ribbon are highly flammable, and the dust produced by the aluminium powder is harmful.

Do not attempt to investigate any other mixtures using aluminium powder.

Zinc powder is flammable.

**Safety screens should be used for this experiment.**

## Procedure

0.05 mol of dry iron(III) oxide, $Fe_2O_3$, is weighed out and mixed with 0.1 mol of aluminium, Al, in the form of fine powder. They are mixed by stirring them together on a sheet of paper and then poured into a cone of filter paper to form a conical pile. The cone needs to be stood in a tray of sand because of the great energy evolved.

Magnesium is used as a 'fuse'. A depression at the top of the pile is filled with a little magnesium powder and a 10 cm length of magnesium ribbon is inserted into it. When the fuse has been lit your teacher must stand back and must not approach the experiment if the ignition seems to have failed, as it can be delayed.

The mixtures of iron(III) oxide with copper and zinc can be tested by the same technique, using the appropriate molar ratios.

 In your notes:

1    Which mixtures react?

2    Is much energy given out?

3    How could you show that metallic iron has been formed?

# Interpretation of the experiments

These reactions are redox (reduction–oxidation) reactions:

- The aluminium has **gained oxygen** and has therefore been **oxidised**.
- The iron(III) oxide has **lost oxygen** and therefore the iron has been **reduced**.

Notice that the two processes have gone on simultaneously: whenever oxidation occurs there will be a balancing reduction. This is why the total process is one of 'redox'.

You should have seen that aluminium and zinc are high enough in the reactivity series to reduce iron(III) oxide to iron with the release of a considerable

COMMENT

When chemicals react and give off energy to their surroundings we say an **exothermic reaction** has taken place. Some reactions 'pull in' energy from their surroundings and in these cases we say an **endothermic reaction** has occurred.

amount of energy. However, copper is not reactive enough to take part in this redox process.

For the reduction of 1 mole of iron(III) oxide, the equations and matching amounts of energy are

$$Fe_2O_3(s) + 2Al(s) \longrightarrow 2Fe(s) + Al_2O_3(s) \quad -851.5\,kJ \text{ (highly exothermic)}$$
$$Fe_2O_3(s) + 3Zn(s) \longrightarrow 2Fe(s) + 3ZnO(s) \quad -220.7\,kJ \text{ (exothermic)}$$
$$Fe_2O_3(s) + 3Cu(s) \longrightarrow 2Fe(s) + 3CuO(s) \quad +352.3\,kJ \text{ (endothermic)}$$

**By convention the amount of energy in an exothermic change is given a negative value, and that in an endothermic change is given a positive value.**

We can see from these values why there was no dramatic flare-up with the copper–iron(III) oxide mixture: the reaction is endothermic, so we would have to heat the mixture to a very high temperature indeed if there was to be any chance of a reaction. In practice, even at high temperature, the reaction does not take place.

In Topic 5 you will learn how to measure the energy given off or absorbed by reactions.

## The Thermit process

The aluminium–iron(III) oxide reaction is known as the **Thermit reaction** and is used in industry in situations where it is not practicable to weld iron by the use of gas or electric heating. For example, the Thermit process is regularly used on the railways to produce the continuous rail system. To weld normal grade rail, a significant amount of molten iron is needed and the rails to be welded have to be heated to a high temperature as part of the process. The Thermit welding process uses 10 kilograms of Thermit mixture plus about 3 kilograms of alloying mixture, which varies with the type of rail being welded. The reaction is all over in 15 seconds and produces 7 kilograms of iron. Enough energy is released to produce molten iron at a temperature of 2050 °C.

**Figure 1.9  Tapping molten iron from a furnace**

## COMMENT

Roman numerals (I, II, III, etc) in a name indicate the degree of oxidation of the iron. The uncombined element is sometimes described as iron(0), because the iron atoms are not oxidised at all.

In iron(II) oxide, FeO, there are two oxygen ions to every two ions of iron, whereas in iron(III) oxide, $Fe_2O_3$, there are three oxygen ions to every two ions of iron.

Iron(II) compounds used to be known as 'ferrous compounds', and iron(III) compounds were known as 'ferric compounds', and you can still see these names on medicines.

Oxidation and reduction are studied in more detail in Topic 6.

# Redox reactions (2)

We have mentioned already that iron can form two different series of compounds. One of these contains $Fe^{2+}$ ions and the other $Fe^{3+}$ ions. **Transition metals such as iron frequently form more than one type of ion.** This section is concerned with the conversion of one type of iron ion into the other.

The process of converting an atom or ion into one having a greater positive charge (or smaller negative charge) is called **oxidation**. This change involves the loss of electrons from the ions. One way of doing this is to make an element or compound react with oxygen; the process of changing iron(II) oxide, **FeO**, into iron(III) oxide, $\mathbf{Fe_2O_3}$, for example, would be an example of oxidation. However, the reaction with oxygen is not the only way of making the change. **Any substance which is capable of bringing about oxidation is known as an oxidising agent.**

**The reverse of oxidation is called reduction, and the substances which cause reduction to occur are known as reducing agents.**

Whenever oxidation occurs, reduction must also take place. If one particular species loses electrons (oxidation), then, logically, another species must gain these electrons (reduction). These two processes go hand-in-hand in **redox** reactions.

---

**EXPERIMENT 1.1d**

## Redox reactions

### SAFETY ⚠️

The sodium hydroxide solution used is an irritant. '20-volume' hydrogen peroxide is an irritant. The acidified potassium manganate(VII) solution is an irritant. Concentrated nitric acid is corrosive and oxidising. Sodium disulphate(IV) solution is harmful.

### Oxidation

First you are going to oxidise an iron(II) compound (containing $Fe^{2+}$ ions) into an iron(III) compound (containing $Fe^{3+}$ ions). Use a fresh dilute solution of iron(II) sulphate to which an equal volume of dilute sulphuric acid has been added; some reactions take place more readily in acidic conditions. The difference in colour of iron(II) hydroxide and iron(III) hydroxide which you recorded at the end of Experiment 1.1b should help you to decide whether a reaction has taken place.

Mix small volumes of the acidified iron(II) sulphate solution with the following oxidising agents:

* hydrogen peroxide solution
* potassium manganate(VII) solution
* 5 **drops** of concentrated nitric acid and warm **gently**.

To the resulting mixture in each case add dilute sodium hydroxide solution until a precipitate forms. Avoid adding too much of the manganate(VII) solution since the strong colour may mask later colour changes.

 **In your notes:** Design a table in which to record the results from this experiment and the next. Write the formulae of as many compounds as you can, and name as many products as you can. Write down in your table all the colour changes: in each case describe the colour **before** and **after** the reaction has occurred.

### Reduction

You are now going to try to reduce an iron(III) compound (containing $Fe^{3+}$ ions) into an iron(II) compound (containing $Fe^{2+}$ ions). Use a freshly made dilute solution of acidified iron(III) sulphate.

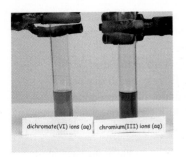

Figure 1.10 **Different colours of dichromate(VI) and chromium(III) ions**

Mix small volumes of acidic iron(III) sulphate solution with the following reducing agents, followed by drops of sodium hydroxide solution until a precipitate is obtained:

- a small piece of zinc; warm and leave for 2 minutes before adding the sodium hydroxide
- a slightly larger volume of either sodium disulphate(IV) or sodium sulphite solution; warm carefully until the reddish colour fades.

In Topic 2 you will be using another oxidising agent, acidified sodium dichromate(VI). Its orange colour is due to the ion $Cr_2O_7^{2-}$(aq). After acting as an oxidising agent chromium ions $Cr^{3+}$(aq) are formed, which are green.

# Redox reactions (3)
# The reaction of iron with copper(II) sulphate

### COMMENT

Whichever equation is correct, it should be clear that displacement reactions involve oxidation and reduction: the iron is **oxidised** because its atoms **lose electrons**; the copper ions are **reduced** to copper metal by **gaining electrons**.

You may find the following mnemonic useful:

**OIL RIG**
**O**xidation **I**s **L**oss
**R**eduction **I**s **G**ain

This is a displacement reaction in which one metal 'displaces' another metal from a solution. Iron is more reactive than copper so, when some metallic iron is added to copper(II) sulphate solution, the products of the reaction will be copper and iron sulphate. There are, however, two iron sulphates and it is not immediately obvious which one is formed. Expressed in the form of ionic equations, the two possible reactions are:

$$Fe(s) + Cu^{2+}(aq) \longrightarrow Fe^{2+}(aq) + Cu(s)$$

and

$$2Fe(s) + 3Cu^{2+}(aq) \longrightarrow 2Fe^{3+}(aq) + 3Cu(s)$$

In the first equation, 1 mole of iron produces 1 mole of copper, but in the second equation 1 mole of iron produces 1.5 moles of copper. By weighing the iron used and the copper produced it should be possible to find out which of the two equations correctly represents the reaction.

**EXPERIMENT 1.1e**

## Deciding which equation is correct

### SAFETY ⚠

1 M aqueous copper(II) sulphate is harmful.
Propanone is highly flammable.
Iron sulphate which is formed is harmful.

### Procedure

Weigh a dry piece of filter paper, fold it, place it inside a filter funnel, and stand this inside a conical flask ready for a filtration which will be necessary near the end of this experiment.

Weigh exactly 0.56 g of iron powder into a 100 cm³ beaker and add to it at least 15 cm³ of 1 M copper(II) sulphate solution. Heat the mixture to boiling, stirring well all the time, and allow it to boil for 1 minute. Now allow the contents of the beaker to cool and the precipitate of copper to settle. Pour off as much of the liquid as you can, being careful not to lose any copper.

Add pure water until the beaker is about one third full, and stir the mixture. Allow the copper to settle and pour off as much liquid as possible. Repeat this process with more pure water, and after two or three 'washings' carefully pour off as much water as you can, without losing any of the copper down the sink. Now add about 20 cm³ of propanone and stir the mixture.

Filter the mixture through the apparatus you set up at the start of the experiment, and leave the residue of copper in the filter paper to dry naturally as the propanone evaporates. Next, drive off the remainder of the propanone by removing the funnel and heating it in an oven at 100 °C for about 5 minutes. Allow the funnel to cool, remove the filter paper carefully and weigh it, together with the residue of copper which it contains.

   **In your notes:**

**1**   How many moles of iron powder were used?

**2**   How many moles of copper were produced?

**3**   Which equation for the reaction is correct?

**4**   What was the purpose of using propanone in this experiment?

## 1.2   Making salts

In this section you are going to learn more about how to calculate the reacting amounts needed to prepare some ionic compounds. You will also be developing your laboratory skills and finding out more about the chemistry of metals and their compounds.

**EXPERIMENT 1.2a**

## The preparation of nickel sulphate, $NiSO_4.7H_2O$

### SAFETY

Nickel(II) carbonate is harmful. 1 M sulphuric acid is an irritant.
The product is also harmful, and the solution may cause sensitisation by skin contact.

The carbonates of metals are typically basic, which means that they are able to react with acids. These acid–base reactions can be used to make salts, compounds in which there are positive ions from a metal and negative ions from an acid. In this preparation you will make nickel sulphate from nickel carbonate and sulphuric acid.

### Procedure

Using a measuring cylinder, transfer 25 cm³ of 1 M sulphuric acid into a 100 cm³ beaker. 25 cm³ of 1 M sulphuric acid contains $\frac{1}{40}$ mol of sulphuric acid, and the equation for the reaction is:

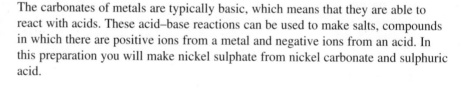

$$NiCO_3(s) + H_2SO_4(aq) \longrightarrow NiSO_4(aq) + CO_2(g) + H_2O(l)$$

Calculate the mass of nickel carbonate to use and weigh out enough to give a very slight excess. Add a little of your calculated amount of nickel carbonate to the sulphuric acid and heat the beaker and its contents on a tripod and gauze. The mixture should be heated until it just boils, stirring continuously. When the nickel carbonate dissolves, stop heating for a short time, add a little more of the nickel carbonate and heat again. Continue in this way until all of the nickel carbonate has been added.

**Be careful to use the minimum of heating so as not to lose too much water by evaporation at this stage. Do not add nickel carbonate when the liquid is actually boiling, because it may boil up suddenly if you do.**

Figure 1.11   Crystals of annabergite, $Ni_3As_2O_8.8H_2O$

Filter the hot mixture into a clean beaker or evaporating basin to remove the excess nickel carbonate. Boil the solution of nickel sulphate until about half of the water has evaporated. This concentrates the solution but does not remove all of the water. Some water is necessary to provide the 'water of crystallisation' which is part of the formula for the crystals ($NiSO_4.7H_2O$). Transfer the hot concentrated solution into a Petri dish or other shallow container and allow to cool and crystallise. Depending on the extent to which you have evaporated the solution, it may begin to crystallise quite quickly or it may need to be left covered (to keep out dust etc.) for a few hours. When crystals have formed, pour away what remains of the solution and dry the crystals on absorbent paper.

✎ **In your notes:** Calculate the mass in grams of hydrated nickel sulphate which could theoretically have been prepared. Use a Periodic Table as a source of data.

What is the main reason why the actual yield of crystals will be much lower than this in practice?

---

**EXPERIMENT 1.2b**

## The preparation of ammonium iron(II) sulphate (Mohr's salt), $(NH_4)_2SO_4.FeSO_4.6H_2O$

When solutions of ammonium sulphate and iron(II) sulphate are mixed and allowed to evaporate, the crystals which form contain the two salts in an exact one-to-one ratio by moles. The two sets of ions can pack together in a regular pattern that results in crystals of constant composition. The crystalline product is known as a '**double salt**'. Its solution behaves just like a mixture of ammonium sulphate and iron(II) sulphate.

$$(NH_4)_2SO_4(aq) + FeSO_4(aq) \longrightarrow (NH_4)_2SO_4.FeSO_4.6H_2O(s)$$

This double salt was introduced into general use by the chemist Mohr because it is less reactive with oxygen in the air than iron(II) sulphate.

You are first going to prepare iron(II) sulphate by reacting iron with dilute sulphuric acid:

$$Fe(s) + H_2SO_4(aq) \longrightarrow FeSO_4(aq) + H_2(g)$$

Use this equation to calculate the amount of iron that will react with 25 cm$^3$ of dilute sulphuric acid ($\frac{1}{20}$ mol). Increase the amount of sulphuric acid by 10% when doing the experiment to make sure all the iron reacts. The dilute sulphuric acid solution (and the dilute aqueous ammonia) should contain 2 moles per cubic decimetre of solution.

You are then going to prepare ammonium sulphate by reacting dilute ammonia with dilute sulphuric acid:

$$2NH_3(aq) + H_2SO_4(aq) \longrightarrow (NH_4)_2SO_4(aq)$$

Use this equation to calculate the volume of ammonia solution which will react with 25 cm$^3$ of dilute sulphuric acid ($\frac{1}{20}$ mol). Measure out 10% more ammonia to allow for loss due to evaporation while stored.

**COMMENT**

In laboratories the preferred units for volume are the cubic centimetre, cm$^3$, and the cubic decimetre, dm$^3$. Shops sell liquids in packages marked with different units:

1 litre = 1000 cm$^3$ = **1 dm$^3$**
1 cl = **10 cm$^3$**
1 ml = **1 cm$^3$**

The cubic centimetre and the cubic decimetre are preferred because they are related to the metre, one of the 'base' units. See page 2 in the *Book of data* for a description of the base units used in Science.

**SAFETY**

2 M sulphuric acid is corrosive.
Ammonia gas formed is toxic.

Figure 1.12 1 mol of iron, 1 mol of iron(II) sulphate, and 1 mol dm⁻³ of iron(II) sulphate solution

## Procedure

Measure out $50 \, cm^3$ of 2 M sulphuric acid and divide into two equal portions.

### Making the iron(II) sulphate

Heat the first $25 \, cm^3$ portion of acid to boiling in a conical flask at least $250 \, cm^3$ in size, remove the source of heat and stand the flask on a heat resisting mat.

Add your calculated amount of iron filings in **small** portions. The energy given out by the reaction will keep the solution close to boiling. Keep a plug of cotton wool in the mouth of the conical flask as much as possible **to reduce the escape of acid spray**.

When all the iron filings have been added leave the mixture to continue reacting slowly. When the reaction slows down add an extra 10% of acid ($2.5 \, cm^3$). Meanwhile prepare the ammonium sulphate.

### Making the ammonium sulphate

Put the other $25 \, cm^3$ portion of dilute sulphuric acid into a beaker and add sufficient dilute ammonia to neutralise the acid. Add the final portions of your calculated volume of ammonia solution in $5 \, cm^3$ portions until a drop of the mixture turns red litmus paper to blue. Boil the solution briskly to drive off the excess of ammonia as a gas (TAKE CARE: ammonia gas is toxic). Concentrate the solution by leaving it boiling.

Separate the iron(II) sulphate solution from undissolved impurities and excess iron by filtering; collect the solution in a beaker containing $5 \, cm^3$ of dilute sulphuric acid to keep the solution acidic. Wash the filter paper with a small portion of water in order to collect all your iron(II) sulphate.

### Making the double salt

Now add the iron(II) sulphate solution to the ammonium sulphate solution. If the ammonia was not neutralised completely the mixture will go cloudy and you will need to add a little more acid. Boil until the volume is reduced to about $40 \, cm^3$, then remove the source of heat and wait until the beaker is cool enough to handle.

Pour your concentrated solution of Mohr's salt into a dust-free, flat-bottomed crystallising dish, cover with a watch glass, label the apparatus and set aside. Crystals may appear within an hour, but will probably take several days to form properly.

✎ **In your notes:**

1 What colour are the crystals you obtain?

2 Leave some crystals exposed to see whether they are stable in the air. What happens?

3 What ions are present in a solution of Mohr's salt?

4 Calculate the theoretical (maximum) yield of crystals which could be made.

5 List all the reactions used in this preparation. Which of them is/are:
    a neutralisation?
    b redox?

# 1.3   The chemists' toolkit: writing formulae and balancing equations

**COMMENT**

This toolkit is presented as an aid to revising the ideas and not as a full introduction. If the ideas are unfamiliar your teacher has a full version, which includes supporting practical work.

Pharmacists, food scientists and chemical engineers all use special ways of planning their work and solving their problems. Similarly, for hundreds of years chemists have been devising names for their discoveries and methods.

We are going to call these procedures the 'chemists' toolkit'. You will need to learn these aspects of chemistry with care, otherwise chemical reactions will pass before you as no more than a colourful parade. So, take careful note of these toolkit sections: they are all listed together in the index. This first toolkit starts with the names and symbols given to the elements.

Some of the names and methods you will meet in your study of chemistry will seem straightforward and others oddly named. For example, you need to be able to construct and analyse chemical formulae with complete accuracy; most symbols for elements are a straightforward two-letter abbreviation of their names, but some are unexpected:

**BACKGROUND**

| Sodium | Na, from the Arabic for soda, natrun |
| Potassium | K, from an Arabic word for burnt ashes |
| Silver | Ag, from the Latin name for the metal |
| Copper | Cu, from the Latin name for the metal |
| Iron | Fe, from the Latin name for the metal |

| magnesium | **Mg** | |
| aluminium | **Al** | |
| lead | **Pb** | as in 'plumber' |
| iron | **Fe** | as in 'chemin de fer' (railway) |

## Writing formulae

The composition of compounds is recorded in their formulae, using procedures developed over the years. Thus, for copper(II) chloride the chemical formula records:

**COMMENT**

A formula is a shorthand way of describing a chemical substance using symbols. The empirical formula is the simplest formula. It shows the ratio of numbers of each type of atom in a compound.

- the elements present                                      **Cu** and **Cl**
- the number of atoms of each element                 **1** Cu and **2** Cl
- their arrangement into cations and anions        $Cu^{2+}$ $2Cl^{-}$, that is, $CuCl_2$

The proportion of one Cu atom to two Cl atoms is fixed; when you need to record 2 formulae of copper(II) chloride you write **$2CuCl_2$**, and not $Cu_2Cl_4$.

Additional information can be added to the formula of a compound. When the solid contains 'water of crystallisation' in a fixed proportion the number of molecules of water is recorded after the formula of the salt using a **dot** as in:

| hydrated copper(II) nitrate | $Cu(NO_3)_2.6H_2O$ |
| hydrated cobalt(II) sulphate | $CoSO_4.7H_2O$ |

**The general rule about writing the formulae of ionic compounds is that the numbers of each ion are such that the positive and negative charges balance to zero.** When you are familiar with the Periodic Table you will find it helps you recall the charges on the various ions. But essentially you have to memorise this information:

| Charge on the ion | Periodic Table group | Other examples |
|---|---|---|
| $1+$ | Group 1 $Li^+$ $Na^+$ $K^+$ | $H^+$ $NH_4^+$ $Ag^+$ |
| $2+$ | Group 2 $Mg^{2+}$ $Ca^{2+}$ $Sr^{2+}$ $Ba^{2+}$ | $Co^{2+}$ $Cu^{2+}$ $Fe^{2+}$ |
| $3+$ | Group 3 $Al^{3+}$ | $Fe^{3+}$ |
| $2-$ | Group 6 $O^{2-}$ $S^{2-}$ | $SO_4^{2-}$ $CO_3^{2-}$ |
| $1-$ | Group 7 $Cl^-$ $Br^-$ $I^-$ | $OH^-$ $NO_3^-$ |

✎   **In your notes:** Copy this table and add other examples as you meet them.

## Balancing equations

To write the **balanced equation** of a reaction you need to go through a careful sequence of steps. **You must make sure that there is no change in the elements present or in the number of atoms as you alter them from reactants into products.** And you have to make sure you get the formulae right. Consider the reaction of iron with dilute hydrochloric acid.

**Step 1**: identify the reactants and products by name

**iron** and **hydrochloric acid** $\longrightarrow$ **iron(II) chloride** and **hydrogen**

**Step 2**: write down their correct formulae

**Fe** and **HCl** $\longrightarrow$ **FeCl$_2$** and **H$_2$**

**Step 3**: balance the numbers of atoms of each element by adjusting the number of formulae of each compound

$$Fe + 2HCl \longrightarrow FeCl_2 + H_2$$

**Step 4**: arrive at a complete balanced equation by adding information about the physical state of the compounds

$$Fe(s) + 2HCl(aq) \longrightarrow FeCl_2(aq) + H_2(g)$$

An equation either records an experiment we have done or can be used to predict the amounts to mix in an investigation.

COMMENT

The state symbols are: (s) solid, (g) gas, (l) liquid, (aq) aqueous solution in water (from 'aqua').

**1.4**

# The chemists' toolkit: the mole, molar mass and molar volume

## Relative atomic mass

A single atom of an element weighs a tiny fraction of a gram, as you can see from the masses given in the note in the margin. Masses as small as this are very difficult to work with so chemists use a simpler way of comparing the masses of atoms.

The first step is to choose a standard atom – one with which other atoms can be compared. **The standard atom chosen is that of the isotope of carbon with 6 protons and 6 neutrons in it, $^{12}$C. This isotope is said to have a relative atomic mass of 12.**

A magnesium atom is, on average (allowing for the existence of isotopes), about twice as heavy as a carbon atom and, therefore, has a relative atomic mass of 24. The masses of other atoms can be placed on this scale by the use of an instrument called a *mass spectrometer* (see Topic 21 for details). On the Periodic Table at the end of this book you will find the relative atomic mass of most elements given to the nearest whole number (for most elements this is sufficiently accurate for practical purposes).

Using a list of relative atomic masses, it is easy to work out the **relative formula mass** of any molecule or group of atoms in a compound. For example, the formula mass of the water molecule, $H_2O$, is 18, two hydrogen atoms at 1 each and an oxygen atom counting 16.

BACKGROUND

| Element | Mass of 1 atom/g |
| --- | --- |
| Hydrogen | $0.166 \times 10^{-23}$ |
| Carbon-12 | $1.99 \times 10^{-23}$ |
| Cobalt | $9.78 \times 10^{-23}$ |
| Lead | $34.4 \times 10^{-23}$ |

BACKGROUND

Relative atomic mass of an element

$$= \frac{\text{average mass of 1 atom}}{\frac{1}{12} \times \text{mass of 1 atom of } ^{12}\text{C}}$$

1 mole of carbon atoms, C(s), 12g

Figure 1.13

# Moles

The relative atomic mass of carbon is 12. **Figure 1.13 shows what 12 g of carbon looks like. This quantity of carbon is called 1 mole of carbon atoms and its mass is called the molar mass of carbon atoms.** In the same way, the relative atomic mass of sodium is 23 and the molar mass of sodium atoms is $23\,\text{g mol}^{-1}$.

It is just as easy to measure out 1 mole of water molecules; the relative formula mass of water is 18, so the molar mass of water molecules is $18\,\text{g mol}^{-1}$. You can do the same with any pure substance whose formula you know; you can even do it with ions, because the mass of electrons is so small that the charge on an ion can be ignored. The mass of 1 mole of sulphate ions, for example, is found by first working out its relative formula mass:

$$SO_4^{2-}: \quad (1 \times 32) + (4 \times 16) = 96$$

The molar mass of sulphate ions is $96\,\text{g mol}^{-1}$.

Here are the molar masses, symbol $M$, of some substances:

| Substance | Formula | Molar mass, $M$/g mol$^{-1}$ |
|---|---|---|
| ammonium ions | $NH_4^+$ | 18 |
| chloride ions | $Cl^-$ | 35.5 |
| methane molecules | $CH_4$ | 16 |
| silver nitrate formulae | $AgNO_3$ | 170 |

> **COMMENT**
>
> The units of molar mass are 'grams per mole', written as '$\text{g mol}^{-1}$'.

# The Avogadro constant

**Figure 1.14**   Amedeo Avogadro was an Italian nobleman, Count of Quaregna and Cerreto, who trained as a lawyer before turning to science. His recognition that gaseous elements might occur as molecules rather than atoms was published in 1811. He was the first to suggest that equal volumes of gases contain equal numbers of molecules. This in time led to the idea of the constant named after him. Find out what else Avogadro worked on – an internet search might help.

The pile of carbon shown in figure 1.13 has a very large number of atoms in it. An Austrian schoolmaster called Loschmidt was the first to estimate this number and later measurements have confirmed that it is close to $6.02 \times 10^{23}$. The Avogadro constant, given the symbol $L$ in honour of Loschmidt, is said to be $6.02 \times 10^{23}\,\text{mol}^{-1}$ or, in words, $6.02 \times 10^{23}$ 'items' per mole.

Next comes a most important fact. **Not only does 1 mole of carbon atoms have $L$ atoms, but 1 mole of atoms of any other element also has $L$ atoms in it.**

In the same way, 1 mole of molecules of water (18 g) contains $L$ water molecules and so does 1 mole of particles of all other substances.

It is important to state clearly what sort of particles we are talking about; to say '1 mole of oxygen', for example, is to be incomplete. We need to know whether we are discussing oxygen *atoms* or oxygen *molecules*. A mole of oxygen atoms has $L$ atoms and weighs 16 g but a mole of oxygen molecules, $O_2$, has $2L$ atoms and weighs 32 g.

# Using moles

When you are doing experiments and wish to work out how much of a particular substance to use, 1 mole may be an inappropriately large quantity, so you might prefer to use some other number of moles. To work out the mass of a number of moles of material you use the following relationship:

mass to use (g) = number of moles (mol) $\times$ molar mass (g mol$^{-1}$)

There are also occasions when you need to know how many moles of material you are dealing with when you know its mass. The relationship then is

$$\text{number of moles (mol)} = \frac{\text{mass of material (g)}}{\text{molar mass (g mol}^{-1})}$$

# Moles of gases

**COMMENT**

A close approximation to 24 dm³ is a cube with each side a little shorter than a 30 cm ruler.

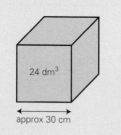

24 dm³

approx 30 cm

Figure 1.15 **The volume of 1 mole of gas molecules**

The volumes of gases are particularly easy to work out. 1 mole of molecules of any gas, whatever it is, always has about the same volume. At ordinary temperatures and pressures this volume, called **the molar volume of a gas, is approximately 24 dm³** (which is the same as 24 litres or 24 000 cm³). In the preparation of Mohr's salt in Experiment 1.2b the equation for one of the reactions was

$$Fe(s) + H_2SO_4(aq) \longrightarrow FeSO_4(aq) + H_2(g)$$

The equation shows that 1 mole of sulphuric acid formulae produces 1 mole of hydrogen molecules. In the experiment, you used $\frac{1}{20}$ mol of sulphuric acid formulae, so you produced $\frac{1}{20}$ mol of hydrogen molecules. So

$$\text{volume of hydrogen produced} = 24\,000 \times \tfrac{1}{20}\ \text{cm}^3$$
$$= 1200\ \text{cm}^3$$

This is more than enough to fill the conical flask you used.

Figure 1.16 **Chemists use aspects of the toolkit in real life. Name all the pieces of equipment in use here.**

**QUESTIONS**

You should find that these questions are a straightforward review of the ideas presented in this toolkit on the mole. When you have looked up the relative atomic mass of helium in the Periodic Table at the end of this book you should be able to do the calculations by mental arithmetic.

1 Calculate the mass in grams of
   **a** 1 mole of helium atoms
   **b** 2 moles of helium atoms
   **c** 0.3 moles of helium atoms.

2 Calculate the number of moles of helium atoms in
   a  4 g of helium
   b  100 g of helium
   c  0.001 g of helium.

3 Calculate the volume of
   a  1 mole of helium atoms
   b  100 moles of helium atoms
   c  4 g of helium
   d  100 g of helium.

4 How many moles of protons are there in 1 mole of helium atoms?

Now attempt some of the questions at the end of this topic.

# 1.5 Background reading: a golden opportunity

## QUESTIONS

Figure 1.17  Mercury is used to recover gold particles, causing river pollution. What are the symptoms of mercury poisoning, and what is the connection with Minemata in Japan?

Read the passage below straight through, and then more carefully, in order to answer the following questions.

1  How does gold occur in refractory minerals?

2  Why is cyanidation difficult in the traditional process for extracting gold?

3  State TWO reasons why roasting concentrate is not permitted on National Park property.

4  Why is fresh water needed for the BacTech process for gold extraction?

5  What other factor contributes to the profitability of the BacTech operation, apart from the extraction of gold?

6  Write a summary in continuous prose, in no more than 100 words, describing the BacTech process of extracting gold from its ore.

## 'There's gold in them thar hills!'

And plenty of volunteers to help dig for it, it seems. Few people strike it lucky, however; more fortunes were lost than were ever won in the famous nineteenth century gold rushes of California, Ballarat and the Klondike.

Gold mining today may not be quite so frenetic, but it is still a risky business. Even after finding reliable deposits, extracting the gold from them is no mean feat. Between 15 and 30% of the world's gold reserves occur as refractory minerals – microscopic particles of gold encapsulated in a mineral matrix; well known examples include arsenopyrite (FeAsS), iron pyrites ($FeS_2$) and chalcopyrite ($CuFeS_2$).

Gold is usually obtained by crushing and grinding ore from the mine and separating these refractory minerals from the oxide ore and other non-metallic minerals by froth flotation to produce a sulphide concentrate. This is then roasted to liberate the gold, which is extracted by treating the resulting mixture with an aerated solution of sodium cyanide. The process is not without problems; roasting converts any sulphur in the refractory minerals to sulphur dioxide and any arsenic to arsenic(III) oxide, both of which have undesirable environmental and economic implications. In some cases, roasting traps the gold in fused silicate minerals and fails to liberate all the metal. Cyanidation is also difficult. The mineral matrix acts as an impervious physical barrier and shields most of the gold particles from attack by cyanide ions. Despite being used for over 100 years, cyanidation of refractory ores yields only a fraction of the contained gold.

And so it might have continued, if it had not been for a chance coincidence that resulted as part of the reorganisation of the University of London. At the time, a team of Chelsea students was carrying out a final-year project on the mineralogy of a refractory sulphide concentrate produced from a gold deposit at the Clogau St David's mine in North Wales. The group quickly hit upon a problem. Since roasting the concentrate to liberate the gold was not permitted on the National Park property where the mine was located, they were only able to extract 10% of the gold by conventional cyanidation. As an alternative to roasting, the students investigated various ways of making the gold in the concentrate more soluble by using acidic solutions of thiourea with different oxidants. They showed that gold could be made more soluble, but not to an extent that would be economic.

Instead, the answer to the problem arose from existing interests at Queen Elizabeth College on metal–microbe interactions. For the Chelsea researchers, this work suggested a possible solution and the two groups soon combined forces. The researchers treated the concentrate with the thermophilic (heat-loving) bacterium *Sulpholobus acidocalderius*.

This is a bacterium which catalyses two processes. It helps atmospheric oxygen to oxidise sulphide minerals and it helps to make the products of oxidation water-soluble. Fresh water contains sufficient dissolved oxygen to carry out the oxidation. The bacteria, concentrate and fresh water were mixed together in stirred tanks. When the oxidation process was complete, the pH of the mixture was adjusted by the addition of lime. Sodium cyanide solution was now added. Gold was then extracted from the resulting solution by reaction with zinc shavings. The extract increased the gold recovery from 10 to 100%. BacTech have patented the process and have been using it at the Youanmi Mine, 500 km north-east of Perth in Western Australia.

The recovery of base metals during gold extraction is also high. BacTech researchers have recovered between 95 to 99% Cu and Ni, 89 to 99% Co and 91 to 96% Zn, all of which contribute to the profitability of plant operations. In fact, recent work has shown that bacterial recovery of the base metals alone, whether or not gold is present in the concentrate, is feasible and economically competitive with conventional processes.

BacTech has recently managed to raise more funds, which will help to accelerate the development of its technology and establish its presence in the US. The company has also joined forces with the South African company Mintek to pool and jointly market bacterial oxidation technology.

## KEY SKILLS

### Communication

Reading about the extraction of gold (background reading, section 1.5) and summarising the information gives you an opportunity to develop your skills of selecting and synthesising information from a document.

### Application of number

Experiments 1.2a and 1.2b provide opportunities for you to develop the skills involved in planning, carrying through and interpreting a complex activity.

## TOPIC REVIEW

Now that you have completed the first topic of the course, you will probably find that you have made a variety of notes. In their present form they may or may not be very useful. It is important that, at this point, you consider how to organise your work with an eye to future, related topics and, of course, examinations. You need a systematic way of working.

Here are some ideas as they might be applied to Topic 1.

1  **List key words or terms with definitions**

It is important that you **recognise and understand the terms** listed below when you come across them in a different context. Exam questions rarely ask you about the exact experiment(s) that you carried out.

- element, compound, atomic number, mass number, isotope
- thermal decomposition
- exothermic and endothermic
- solvent, solute, solution and soluble
- precipitation reaction and spectator ions
- redox reaction
- acid, base, neutralisation and salt
- the mole, molar mass and molar volume
- Avogadro constant, $L$

2  **Summarise the key principles as simply as possible**

This could mean, for example, drawing a **summary chart** or a 'spider diagram' as a means to easy learning. You might use some **mnemonic** or **rhyme** to help you remember an important principle or idea. Whatever you do, **the emphasis must be on patterns or types of behaviour** that you can apply to other, new situations. Remember that the specific detail of the work covered should be reflected in the notes you have made during the topic; the point of the topic review is a focused summary of what you must take with you into future topics.

You must be able to:

- determine relative atomic masses and the relative abundance of isotopes from simple mass spectra
- recognise different types of chemical change as well as predict and test for the possible outcomes of such changes (*list them, know tests for gases, learn the solubility rules and colours of ions*)
- write balanced molecular and ionic equations for such changes with state symbols
- use the mole concept to calculate amounts of substance (*write some examples to act as templates for the future*).

When you have done the above you should be able to answer the end-of-topic questions. Alternatively, you may choose to use them whilst compiling your review.

# REVIEW QUESTIONS

✻ Indicates that the *Book of data* is needed.

**1.1**   Name the compounds which have the formulae given below.
Pay careful attention to spelling names accurately.

| | | | | | | | | |
|---|---|---|---|---|---|---|---|---|
| a | $H_2SO_4$ | (1) | f | $KHCO_3$ | (1) | k | $(NH_4)_2SO_4$ | (1) |
| b | $HNO_3$ | (1) | g | $NH_4Cl$ | (1) | l | $MnCO_3$ | (1) |
| c | $NH_3$ | (1) | h | $AgNO_3$ | (1) | m | $CoBr_2$ | (1) |
| d | $Na_2CO_3$ | (1) | i | $Ca(OH)_2$ | (1) | n | $Cr_2O_3$ | (1) |
| e | $K_2SO_4$ | (1) | j | $H_2O_2$ | (1) | o | $CaF_2$ | (1) |

**(15 marks)**

**1.2** Write down the formulae for the following elements, adding the appropriate state symbol for the element at 25 °C and 1 atm. *Learn the formulae if you do not know them.*

| | | | | | | | | | |
|---|---|---|---|---|---|---|---|---|---|
| **a** | hydrogen | (1) | **e** | chlorine | (1) | **h** | iodine | (1) |
| **b** | helium | (1) | **f** | potassium | (1) | **i** | mercury | (1) |
| **c** | nitrogen | (1) | **g** | bromine | (1) | **j** | sulphur | (1) |
| **d** | oxygen | (1) | | | | | | |

**(10 marks)**

**1.3** Write formulae for the following compounds:

| | | | | | | |
|---|---|---|---|---|---|---|
| **a** | copper(II) sulphate | (1) | **f** | ammonium nitrate | (1) |
| **b** | potassium nitrate | (1) | **g** | iron(II) iodide | (1) |
| **c** | calcium chloride | (1) | **h** | aluminium nitrate | (1) |
| **d** | zinc oxide | (1) | **i** | iron(III) sulphate | (1) |
| **e** | potassium carbonate | (1) | **j** | magnesium hydroxide | (1) |

**(10 marks)**

**1.4** Write balanced chemical equations, including state symbols, for the following thermal decomposition reactions:

**a** mercury(II) oxide, producing metallic mercury and oxygen gas (2)

**b** zinc(II) nitrate, producing solid zinc(II) oxide, gaseous nitrogen dioxide ($NO_2$) and oxygen gas (2)

**c** lithium carbonate, producing solid lithium oxide and carbon dioxide gas (2)

**d** sodium hydrogencarbonate, producing solid sodium carbonate, carbon dioxide gas, and water (2)

**e** aluminium hydroxide, producing aluminium oxide and water. (2)

**(10 marks)**

**1.5** A precipitate is formed when the following pairs of solutions are mixed together. In each case,

**i** write down the formulae of the ions present in the solutions

**ii** identify the pair of ions which will produce an insoluble substance and hence record the formula and name of the precipitate

**iii** write a balanced **ionic** equation for the reaction.

**a** sodium carbonate and calcium chloride (4)

**b** magnesium sulphate and potassium hydroxide (4)

**c** zinc nitrate and sodium hydroxide (4)

**d** aluminium sulphate and potassium hydroxide (4)

**e** lead(II) nitrate and potassium chromate ($K_2CrO_4$) (4)

**(20 marks)**

**1.6**    The following equations represent reactions of various types. State the type of reaction in each case, giving a reason for each answer.

a    $CaCO_3(s) \xrightarrow{heat} CaO(s) + CO_2(g)$    (2)

b    $ZnSO_4(aq) + 2NaOH(aq) \longrightarrow Zn(OH)_2(s) + Na_2SO_4(aq)$    (2)

c    $Fe_2O_3(s) + 3CO(g) \longrightarrow 2Fe(s) + 3CO_2(g)$    (2)

d    $Pb^{2+}(aq) + 2I^-(aq) \longrightarrow PbI_2(s)$    (2)

e    $2FeCl_2(aq) + Cl_2(g) \longrightarrow 2FeCl_3(aq)$    (2)

(**10 marks**)

**1.7**    Write balanced equations, including state symbols, for the following reactions:

a    a mixture of powdered magnesium metal and iron(III) oxide, heated in a crucible and producing magnesium oxide and iron metal    (2)

b    sodium hydroxide solution reacting with dilute hydrochloric acid, producing sodium chloride solution and water    (2)

c    metallic zinc reacting with dilute hydrochloric acid, producing zinc chloride solution and hydrogen gas    (2)

d    metallic aluminium reacting with dilute sulphuric acid, producing aluminium sulphate solution and hydrogen gas    (2)

e    ammonia gas reacting with dilute nitric acid, producing a solution of ammonium nitrate    (2)

(**10 marks**)

**\* 1.8**    Calculate the molar masses of the following compounds:

a    nitric acid, $HNO_3$    (1)

b    anhydrous iron(III) chloride, $FeCl_3$    (1)

c    hydrated iron(III) chloride, $FeCl_3.6H_2O$    (1)
       (Note: the full name for this compound is iron(III) chloride-6-water)

d    sodium carbonate-10-water, $Na_2CO_3.10H_2O$    (1)

e    ammonium iron(III) sulphate-24-water, $(NH_4)_2SO_4.Fe_2(SO_4)_3.24H_2O$    (1)

(**5 marks**)

**\* 1.9**    Calculate the mass of each of the following amounts of substance, giving each answer to 2 significant figures:

a    0.10 mol of zinc atoms, Zn    (1)

b    0.20 mol of magnesium atoms, Mg    (1)

c    1.0 mol of potassium hydrogencarbonate, $KHCO_3$    (2)

d    0.10 mol of lead(II) nitrate, $Pb(NO_3)_2$    (3)

e    0.05 mol of aluminium oxide, $Al_2O_3$    (3)

(**10 marks**)

**\* 1.10**    Calculate the number of moles of each of the following masses of substance, giving each answer to 2 significant figures:

a    80 g of bromine molecules, $Br_2$    (2)

b    3.0 g of magnesium metal, Mg    (2)

c    8.5 g of silver nitrate, $AgNO_3$    (2)

d    2.0 g of sodium hydroxide, NaOH    (2)

e    2.0 kg of sodium hydroxide, NaOH    (2)

(**10 marks**)

* **1.11**    Use the equations you wrote in answer to question **1.4** or **1.7** (as appropriate) when answering this question. Calculate the following, setting out your method clearly:

    **a**    the mass of magnesium needed to react with 8.0 g of iron(III) oxide    (3)

    **b**    the mass of mercury and the volume of oxygen gas (measured at room temperature and pressure) obtained by heating 4.34 g of mercury(II) oxide    (5)

    **c**    the volume of hydrogen gas (measured at room temperature and pressure) produced when 15.0 g of zinc reacted with an excess of dilute hydrochloric acid    (3)

    **d**    the mass of aluminium which would be needed to generate 4.8 dm$^3$ of hydrogen (measured at room temperature and pressure) by reaction with excess dilute sulphuric acid    (3)

    **e**    the mass of ammonium nitrate obtained when 600 cm$^3$ of ammonia gas (measured at room temperature and pressure) reacted with an excess of nitric acid.    (3)

    **(17 marks)**

* **1.12**    A student was asked to make crystals of hydrated magnesium chloride, $MgCl_2.6H_2O$ (its full name is magnesium chloride-6-water), starting with solid magnesium oxide and dilute hydrochloric acid.

    **a**    Write a balanced equation, including state symbols, for the reaction.    (2)

    **b**    The student was provided with a solution containing 0.100 mol of HCl. What mass of magnesium oxide would be needed to react with this amount of acid?    (2)

    **c**    In theory, what mass of the crystals could be made from these amounts of reactants?    (2)

    **d**    Why, in practice, would the yield of crystals be lower than this?    (2)

    **(8 marks)**

# EXAMINATION QUESTIONS

Questions of the summary and comprehension type are found in the background reading section (section 1.5).

**1.13**    **a**    When zinc reacts with dilute sulphuric acid the balanced equation is:

$$Zn(s) + H_2SO_4(aq) \longrightarrow ZnSO_4(aq) + H_2(g)$$

Rewrite this equation omitting the sulphate ions, $SO_4^{2-}$, giving the equation in its ionic form with state symbols.    (2)

    **b**    What practical steps should be taken to obtain dry crystals of hydrated zinc sulphate from the solution of zinc sulphate?    (3)

    **c**    What mass of hydrated zinc sulphate, $ZnSO_4.7H_2O$, would result from the complete reaction of 2.0 g of zinc with excess dilute sulphuric acid?    (3)

    **(8 marks)**

**1.14**    This question is about a laboratory preparation of the vanadium alum, $K_2SO_4.V_2(SO_4)_3.24H_2O$. Two salts, whose formulae are $K_2SO_4$ and $V_2(SO_4).3H_2O$, were weighed out and dissolved together in hot water. The solution was then allowed to cool.

   **a**    What is the formula of the vanadium ion in the compounds mentioned?    (1)

   **b**    What mass of anhydrous potassium sulphate would be required to react with 4.44 g of the hydrated vanadium sulphate to form the vanadium alum?    (3)

   **c**    Vanadium forms several oxides, including $VO_2$, $V_2O_5$, $V_2O_3$. In which of these is the vanadium least highly oxidised? Give TWO reasons for your answer illustrating different interpretations of the term 'oxidised'.    (3)

             **(7 marks)**

**1.15**    The metallic element manganese, Mn, reacts with reagent **A** forming a solution of manganese(II) sulphate and evolving hydrogen gas:

$$Mn(s) + A \longrightarrow MnSO_4(aq) + H_2(g)$$

   **a**    **i**    Name reagent **A**.    (1)

       **ii**    State TWO observations you would expect to make during this reaction.    (2)

   **b**    A student carried out this reaction to try to prepare 0.1 mole of crystals of manganese(II) sulphate, $MnSO_4.4H_2O$. The exact quantity of reagent **A** needed was calculated and measured into a beaker. 6.0 g of powdered manganese was added. When the reaction had finished the solution was filtered, concentrated by evaporation and set aside to crystallise. The crystals were removed, dried and weighed.

       **i**    How many moles of manganese are contained in 0.1 mole of hydrated manganese(II) sulphate crystals, $MnSO_4.4H_2O$?    (1)

       **ii**    How many moles of atoms of manganese were weighed out?    (1)

       **iii**    Compare your answers to **i** and **ii** and comment on any difference.    (1)

       **iv**    Why was the solution filtered after the reaction had finished?    (1)

       **v**    Why was the solution not evaporated to dryness after filtering?    (1)

       **vi**    Calculate the mass of 0.1 mole of manganese(II) sulphate crystals, $MnSO_4.4H_2O$.    (2)

       **vii**    The student's actual yield of crystals was less than 0.1 mole. Suggest ONE reason for this.    (1)

   **c**    Some types of steel contain a small proportion (less than 1%) of manganese.

       **i**    Suggest ONE physical property of steel which might usefully be changed by the addition of manganese.    (1)

       **ii**    The manganese is added to the steel in the form of ferromanganese, an alloy consisting of 80% Mn and 20% Fe, both measured by mass. Ferromanganese is made by heating a mixture of the oxides $MnO_2$ and $Fe_2O_3$ with carbon in a furnace. What kind of chemical reaction do these oxides undergo in the furnace?    (1)

       **iii**    Show by calculation that ferromanganese contains approximately 4 manganese atoms for every iron atom.    (1)

             **(14 marks)**

# Alcohols: an introduction to organic chemistry

CH₃   OH

Carbon atoms have an amazing ability to join together in chains, rings, balls and networks. So many of the molecules in living organisms are carbon compounds that we call the study of carbon chemistry **organic chemistry**.

Figure 2.1 a   **Linalool, found in lavender**

b   **Nylon, the synthetic polymer**

In the past people found almost all the carbon compounds they needed in living things. They found ways to extract drugs, perfumes and dyes from plants and animal tissues.

One aroma still extracted on a commercial scale is oil of lavender. The flower heads are harvested in July and the oil extracted from 0.25 tonne of flower heads at a time by steam distillation.

Figure 2.2 a   **Growing lavender commercially**

b   **Extracting oil of lavender**

Nowadays we get most of our carbon chemicals from oil, gas and coal. **The petrochemical industry starts with crude oil, refines it, processes it and produces the huge variety of chemicals needed to manufacture plastics, fibres, drugs, pesticides and so on**

In this topic you will:

- be introduced to some of the rules for naming carbon compounds
- investigate the reactions of simple alcohols like ethanol
- learn about some of the special apparatus used in experiments with organic compounds.

## 2.1   The chemists' toolkit: naming carbon compounds

Chemists have identified or prepared over five million carbon compounds in laboratories around the world. In this course, you will meet numerous compounds with up to six carbon atoms and several with 200 or more (not that you have to learn these formulae). For instance:

$C_6H_3OCl_3$          TCP, an antiseptic
$C_{254}H_{377}N_{65}O_{75}S_6$     insulin, a hormone

We can make the study of such a huge number of carbon compounds more manageable by grouping them in families. You may already be familiar with some of the simpler members of the hydrocarbon family, which we call the **alkanes**.

The simplest alkane is methane, $CH_4$, which makes up most of natural gas (see figure 2.3). The next three members of the alkane family are also used as fuels:

$CH_4$       methane, found in natural gas
$C_2H_6$      ethane
$C_3H_8$      propane, in Calor gas
$C_4H_{10}$     butane, in Camping Gaz

**The carbon atoms in the molecules of these compounds form four bonds. The hydrogen atoms each form one bond.**

The family of alkanes is an example of a **homologous series**: a series of compounds of the same type with the same general formula. The general formula for the alkanes is $C_nH_{2n+2}$.

$CH_4$          The formula

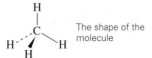

H—C—H        The chemical bonds

The shape of the molecule

The space filled by the molecule

**Figure 2.3   Drawings representing methane**

### COMMENT

When elements react together to form uncharged molecules the number of bonds, —, formed between the atoms depends on the number of pairs of electrons available. This can be deduced from their positions in the Periodic Table, at least for simple molecules.

| Group | Element | Number of covalent bonds | Examples |
|---|---|---|---|
| – | H | 1 | $H_2$ |
| 4 | C | 4 | $CH_4$ |
| 5 | N | 3 | $NH_3$ |
| 6 | O | 2 | $H_2O$ |
| 7 | Cl, Br, I | 1 | HCl |

---

### REVIEW TASK

Working in groups, make a list of what you can recall about covalent compounds and the properties that distinguish them from ionic compounds. Then answer these questions:

1  Are the bonds in hydrocarbon molecules ionic or covalent?

2  Draw a diagram to show the number and arrangement of electrons in carbon and hydrogen atoms.

3  Draw a diagram to show how the electrons in carbon and hydrogen atoms form the bonds in methane.

---

The carbon atoms are arranged in chains, and each molecular formula differs from the one next to it in the homologous series by a $CH_2$ unit.

These are the ways of representing the formulae of organic compounds:

- **Molecular formulae** show the number of atoms in a single molecule:

    $CH_4$          $C_2H_6$              $C_3H_8$                      $C_4H_{10}$

- **Structural formulae** show how the atoms are grouped in the molecule:

    $CH_4$          $CH_3—CH_3$        $CH_3—CH_2—CH_3$      $CH_3—CH_2—CH_2—CH_3$

- **Displayed formulae** show all the atoms and all the bonds:

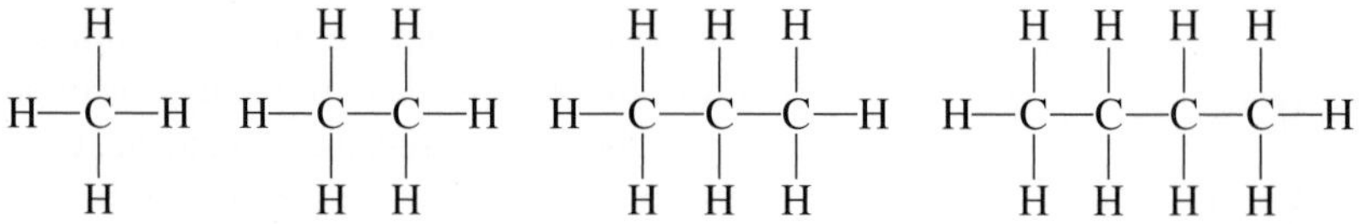

methane        ethane          propane          butane

**Isomers are compounds that have the same molecular formula but different structures.** For example, chemists have found **two** compounds with the formula $C_4H_{10}$. One boils at $-1\,°C$ while the other boils at $-12\,°C$. The displayed and structural formulae of the two compounds are shown below.

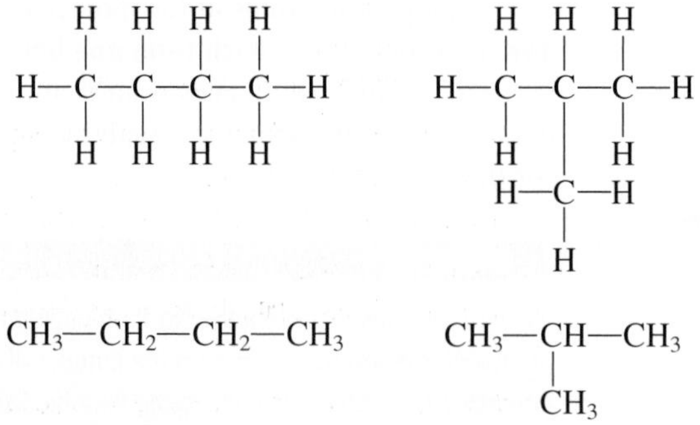

$CH_3—CH_2—CH_2—CH_3$          $CH_3—CH—CH_3$
                                                          |
                                                        $CH_3$

butane                              2-methylpropane

The rules for naming compounds have been settled by international agreement amongst chemists. We need only a few rules to start with, so here we will deal only with some simple compounds of carbon and hydrogen, and some alcohols.

# Names for compounds containing carbon atom chains

COMMENT

| Number of carbon atoms in chain | Molecular formula | Name |
|---|---|---|
| 1 | $CH_4$ | methane |
| 2 | $C_2H_6$ | ethane |
| 3 | $C_3H_8$ | propane |
| 4 | $C_4H_{10}$ | butane |
| 5 | $C_5H_{12}$ | pentane |
| 6 | $C_6H_{14}$ | hexane |
| $n$ | $C_nH_{2n+2}$ | |

Compounds in which the molecules are made up of straight chains of carbon atoms with C—C bonds and combined with hydrogen only, have the general name **alkanes**. Names for individual compounds all have the ending '**-ane**'. For example,

$$CH_3—CH_2—CH_2—CH_3 \quad \text{but}\textbf{ane}$$

The names of the first four hydrocarbons in the series, containing 1, 2, 3 and 4 carbon atoms respectively, are methane, ethane, propane and butane. These do not follow any logical system and must be learned. The rest of the hydrocarbons in the series are named by using a Greek numeral root and the ending '-ane', for example, pentane (five carbon atoms in an unbranched chain), hexane (six carbon atoms). The roots are the same as those used in naming geometric figures (pentagon, hexagon, etc.).

# Names for alkanes containing a ring of carbon atoms

These are named from the corresponding straight-chain hydrocarbon by adding the prefix '**cyclo-**'. An example is cyclohexane, which can be represented as:

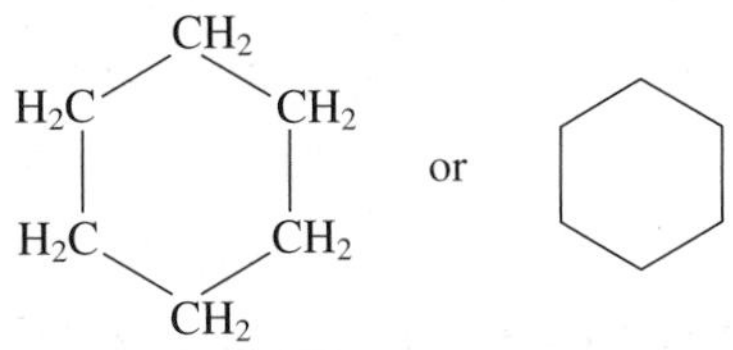

## STUDY TASK

For this activity you will need a set of molecular models or a computer with software for molecular modelling.

1  Make models of the molecules of the first five members of the alkane family.

2  Draw up a table with four columns showing the names of the alkanes, their formulae, drawings of their molecular shapes, and their physical states at room temperature. You will find their physical properties listed in table 5.5 of the *Book of data*.

3  Make models of the isomers with the formula $C_5H_{12}$. You should be able to make three different models. Write down the displayed and structural formulae corresponding to the structures.

4  Why are hexane and cyclohexane NOT isomers?

# Names for primary alcohols

Most people think of drinks of various kinds when they read or hear the word alcohol. But for chemists alcohol, or ethanol, is only one of another homologous series of similar compounds.

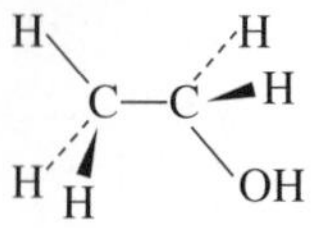

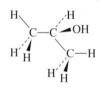

Figure 2.4 **Ethanol**

**Alcohols have a hydroxyl group, —OH, attached to a carbon atom by a covalent bond**. The —OH group is an example of what is called a **functional group**.

The first three members of the alcohol series are methanol, ethanol and propanol. We name them by changing the end of the name of the corresponding alkane to '**ol**'.

$CH_4$ methane $\qquad$ $CH_3$—OH metha**nol**
$CH_3$—$CH_3$ ethane $\qquad$ $CH_3$—$CH_2$—OH etha**nol**
$CH_3$—$CH_2$—$CH_3$ propane $\qquad$ $CH_3$—$CH_2$—$CH_2$—OH propan-1-**ol**

When the —OH group of an alcohol is attached to a carbon atom which is attached directly to only **one** other carbon atom as in our examples, the compound is known as a **primary** alcohol.

## Naming more complicated alcohols

When the —OH group is attached to a carbon atom which is attached directly to **two** other carbon atoms, the compound is a **secondary** alcohol, and when to **three** other carbon atoms, it is a **tertiary** alcohol. Make sure that you understand this naming by looking carefully at the following structural formulae, which are all isomers of $C_4H_{10}O$.

$CH_3$—$CH_2$—$CH_2$—$CH_2$—OH $\qquad$ butan-1-ol, a primary alcohol

$CH_3$—$CH_2$—CH—$CH_3$ $\qquad$ butan-2-ol, a secondary alcohol
$\qquad\qquad$ |
$\qquad\qquad$ OH

$\qquad\qquad$ $CH_3$
$\qquad\qquad$ |
$CH_3$—C—$CH_3$ $\qquad$ 2-methylpropan-2-ol, a tertiary alcohol
$\qquad\qquad$ |
$\qquad\qquad$ OH

Figure 2.5 **Propan-2-ol**

When alcohols contain more than one hydroxyl group they are known as **di**ols or **tri**ols, etc, after the number of hydroxyl groups they contain.

$CH_2$—$CH_2$
| $\qquad$ | $\qquad$ ethane-1,2-diol (glycol)
OH $\quad$ OH

$CH_2$—CH—$CH_2$
| $\qquad$ | $\qquad$ | $\qquad$ propane-1,2,3-triol (glycerol)
OH $\quad$ OH $\quad$ OH

**BACKGROUND**

The freezing point of an insect is the temperature at which some of its body water can be frozen. For most insects this would normally be about −1 °C but it depends upon the concentration and nature of the solute in the tissues. Just as wise motorists protect their car radiators by the addition of antifreeze in which the important component is ethane-1,2-diol (glycol), so it appears that some insects accumulate propane-1,2,3-triol (glycerol) in their body water during the autumn (figure 2.6, opposite). In this way the insects can withstand low temperatures and avoid the danger of cell damage by the formation of ice crystals. If they contain 15% propane-1,2,3-triol the eggs of the moth *Alsophila pometaria* can be cooled to −45 °C before ice crystals form.

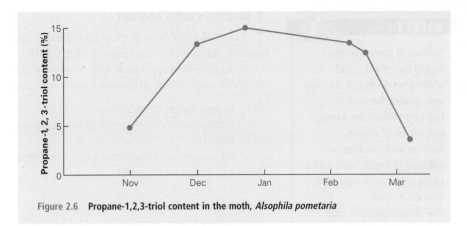

Figure 2.6    Propane-1,2,3-triol content in the moth, *Alsophila pometaria*

## 2.2    Reactions of alcohols

**COMMENT**

You will find a table of functional groups in Topic 8, section 8.1. These are the functional groups which you must be able to recognise and recall.

In organic chemistry we use the term **functional group** to describe the atom, or group of atoms, which gives a compound its characteristic properties.

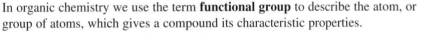

Alcohols are more reactive than alkanes because C—O and O—H bonds break more easily than C—H and C—C bonds in reactions with aqueous reagents. The alcohols share similar properties because they all have the C—OH group of atoms in their molecules.

Water also contains the O—H bond and you should be able to predict some of the properties of alcohols by considering the reactions of water.

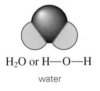

$H_2O$ or H—O—H
water

### EXPERIMENT 2.2a

## Experiments with alcohols

These reactions will introduce you to the reactions of the alcohol functional group and you will be able to see how the whole family of alcohols behaves.

### Procedure

#### 1 Solubility in water

To 1 cm$^3$ of ethanol in a test tube add 1 cm$^3$ of water. Do the two liquids mix? Test the mixture with Full-range Indicator.

Repeat with a range of alcohols, increasing the volume of water used if mixing does not occur.

✎    **In your notes:** How does the solubility of alcohols compare with the solubility of alkanes? What is the trend in solubility in water in the series methanol to pentan-1-ol? Suggest an explanation for the trend.

**SAFETY**

Remember that alcohols are highly flammable, and toxic or harmful.
You must wear eye protection at all times.

## SAFETY ⚠

Sodium is corrosive and highly flammable, and undergoes a violent reaction with water; fumes from burning sodium are highly irritant to all tissues.

Sodium dichromate(VI) solution is highly toxic and a category 2 carcinogen; it is also an irritant.

The dilute sulphuric acid (1.0 M) is an irritant.

## 2 Reaction with sodium

To 1 cm³ of ethanol in an evaporating basin add one small piece of freshly cut sodium the size of a rice grain (TAKE CARE). Is there any sign of reaction?

Repeat the experiment with a range of alcohols. Add ethanol to dissolve all traces of sodium before throwing away the reaction mixture.

✎    **In your notes:** What do you see on adding sodium to an alcohol? What are the products? Is this what you would predict by comparing alcohols to water? Which bond in the alcohol breaks?

What is the trend in rate of reaction from methanol to pentan-1-ol? Can you suggest an explanation for the trend?

## 3 Oxidation

To 5 cm³ of dilute sulphuric acid in a boiling tube add a few drops of sodium dichromate(VI) solution. Next add 2 drops of ethanol and heat the reaction mixture until it **just** boils. Is there any sign of reaction? Is there any change of smell suggestive of a new organic compound?

Repeat the experiment with a range of alcohols.

✎    **In your notes:** Record the colour changes and smells. Refer to the colours of chromium compounds in the *Book of data*, table 5.3 page 71, to see if this gives you any clues to what may be happening.

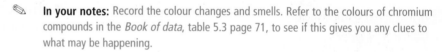

**EXPERIMENT 2.2b**

# Preparations using propan-1-ol

In these experiments you will be collecting the products of the reactions in order to study their properties. Carry out **1** and **either 2 or 3** and share your product with someone who carried out the alternative experiment.

## Procedure

### 1 The dehydration of propan-1-ol

## SAFETY ⚠

Both propan-1-ol and the products of this reaction are highly flammable. The bromine water you will use is harmful and an irritant.

Put propan-1-ol in a test tube to a depth of 1 cm. Push in some loosely packed ceramic fibre until all the propan-1-ol has been soaked up. Now add a 2 cm depth of aluminium oxide granules and arrange the apparatus for the collection of a gas, as shown in figure 2.7.

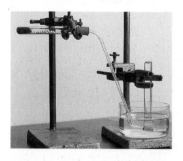

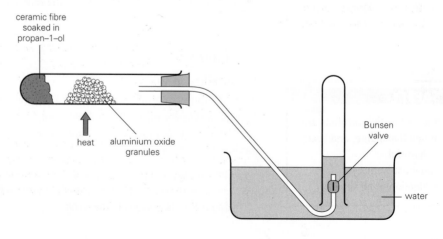

Figure 2.7  **A photograph and a drawing of the apparatus you will be using for the dehydration experiment**

Heat the granules gently and collect three or four test tubes of gas, discarding the first one which will contain mainly air.

Carry out the following tests on the gas:

**a** Add 1 cm³ of bromine water. Shake the test tube and look for any colour changes that suggest a reaction.

**b** Add 1 cm³ of a very dilute, acidified solution of potassium manganate(VII).

✎ **In your notes:** Note what you can see at each stage.

What do the tests **a** and **b** tell you about the nature of the product from the dehydration of propan-1-ol?

## 2 The oxidation of propan-1-ol

This experiment uses approximately equal quantities (0.02 mole) of propan-1-ol and an oxidising agent, and they are refluxed together in order to oxidise the propan-1-ol as fully as possible under these conditions.

Measure 5 cm³ of water into a boiling tube. Add 6 g of sodium dichromate(VI) (WEAR GLOVES), shake and set aside to dissolve.

Put about 1.5 cm³ propan-1-ol into a 50 cm³ pear-shaped flask and add about 5 cm³ of water and two or three anti-bumping granules. Put a condenser on the flask for reflux, as shown in figure 2.8.

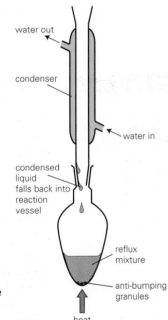

water out

condenser

water in

condensed liquid falls back into reaction vessel

reflux mixture

anti-bumping granules

heat

Figure 2.8 **A photograph and a drawing of the apparatus for refluxing**

Add 2 cm³ of concentrated sulphuric acid (TAKE CARE) down the condenser **in drops** from a dropping pipette. While the mixture is still warm start to add your sodium dichromate(VI) solution down the condenser **in drops** from a dropping pipette. The energy released from the reaction should make the mixture boil. **Add the solution a drop at a time** so that the mixture continues to boil without any external heating.

When all the sodium dichromate(VI) solution has been added, use a low Bunsen burner flame to keep the mixture boiling for 10 minutes, not allowing any vapour to escape. At the end of that time remove the Bunsen burner and arrange the apparatus for distillation, as shown in figure 2.9 (overleaf). Gently distil 2–3 cm³ of liquid into a test tube.

There is a microscale alternative to this experiment

**SAFETY** ⚠

You must wear gloves when handling solid sodium dichromate(VI) since it is highly toxic and a category 2 carcinogen; it is also an irritant. Avoid inhaling any dust.

Concentrated sulphuric acid is corrosive.

If your reaction mixture does not boil spontaneously, stop adding the sodium dichromate(VI), otherwise the energy released may cause sudden and violent boiling. Seek your teacher's advice.

Because of the unpredictable chemical splash, eye protection (goggles) should be worn by **all** in the laboratory as long as anyone is carrying out this reaction.

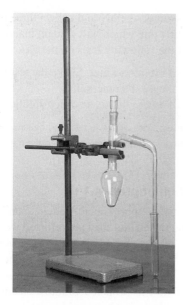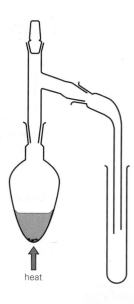

heat

Figure 2.9 **A photograph and a drawing of the apparatus for distilling your product**

BACKGROUND

Benedict's solution contains a copper(II) compound and is used to test for organic reducing agents. An alternative reagent is Fehling's solution.

The liquid that collects is an aqueous solution of the product. Carry out the following tests on it, recording your results in a table. Leave two columns in your table in which to record the results of each test when performed on propan-1-ol and the product of the next reaction.

**a**   Note the smell of the product.
**b**   Will it neutralise **an appreciable volume** of sodium carbonate solution? How much do you have to add before the effervescence stops?
**c**   Add a few drops of the product to 2 cm³ of Benedict's solution and 1 cm³ of dilute sodium hydroxide, then boil gently.

✎   **In your notes:** Compare these results with those obtained using propan-1-ol, and the product made in the next experiment.

### 3 The partial oxidation of propan-1-ol

This experiment uses only half the quantity of oxidising agent (0.01 mol) that the previous experiment used and the product is distilled from the reaction mixture immediately it is formed. In this way we hope to achieve a partial oxidation of propan-1-ol.

Place about 10 cm³ of dilute sulphuric acid in a flask and add about 3 g of sodium dichromate(VI) and 2 or 3 anti-bumping granules. Shake the contents of the flask until solution is complete (do not warm).

Add 1.5 cm³ of propan-1-ol in drops from a dropping pipette, shaking the flask so as to mix the contents, and then assemble the apparatus as shown in figure 2.9.

Gently and slowly distil 2 cm³ of liquid into a test tube, taking care that none of the reaction mixture splashes over.

Carry out the tests **2a, b** and **c** above, comparing the results.

There is a microscale alternative to this experiment

# Interpretation of the reactions of alcohols

## Behaviour with water

Alcohols will mix with water but **as the hydrocarbon chain gets longer the solubility gets less**

The solutions are neutral: this shows that the functional group does not form either hydrogen ions or hydroxide ions with water.

## Reaction with sodium

The reaction of sodium with alcohols is very similar to the reaction of the metal with water. Alcohols react less vigorously than water.

$$2Na + 2CH_3-CH_2-CH_2OH \longrightarrow 2CH_3-CH_3-CH_2-CH_2O^- Na^+ + H_2$$
sodium propoxide

$$2Na + 2HOH \longrightarrow 2HO^- Na^+ + H_2$$
sodium hydroxide<br>(usually written NaOH)

In both these reactions each sodium atom loses an electron forming a positive ion while the hydrogen atoms in the —OH groups combine to form hydrogen gas. The organic product is called an **alkoxide**, and is an ionic compound.

## Oxidation

Sodium dichromate(VI) is an oxidising agent. It oxidises alcohols such as propan-1-ol first to compounds called **aldehydes** and then to acids, called **carboxylic acids**.

**Aldehydes** are a group of compounds, all with the same functional group and names that end in '**-al**', such as ethan**al** and propan**al**. An example is shown in the margin. You will have to read the names of alcohols and aldehydes carefully to avoid muddling them.

**Carboxylic acids** are also a related group of compounds and are named by altering the names of alkanes, for example ethan**oic acid** and propan**oic acid** (see the margin).

The functional group $C=O$ is known as the **carbonyl group**.

An aldehyde is obtained if the product is separated from the reaction mixture as it forms, as in Experiment 2.2b(3). This prevents further oxidation to the acid.

An aldehyde (ethanal)

A carboxylic acid (ethanoic acid)

$$CH_3-CH_2-CH_2OH \xrightarrow{\substack{\text{warm with acidified} \\ \text{sodium dichromate(VI)}}} CH_3-CH_2-CHO$$
propanal (an aldehyde)

Note the way this reaction is written. Often, in the case of organic reactions, it is convenient to write unbalanced equations which show the main reactants and products and state the conditions for the change above the reaction arrow. State symbols are usually omitted.

Heating the alcohol with excess acidified sodium dichromate(VI) takes the process a stage further, as in Experiment 2.2b(2). Heating in a flask fitted with a reflux condenser helps to make sure there is no loss of volatile reactants or products.

$$CH_3-CH_2-CH_2OH \xrightarrow{\substack{\text{heat with excess acidified} \\ \text{sodium dichromate(VI)}}} CH_3-CH_2-CO_2H$$
propanoic acid (a carboxylic acid)

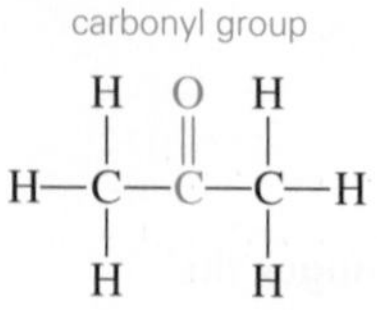

carbonyl group

$$CH_3 - CO - CH_3$$

Figure 2.10 **Displayed and structural formulae of the ketone, propanone**

# Oxidation of secondary alcohols

The oxidation of secondary alcohols also results in a product with a carbonyl group, C=O. Compounds in which a carbonyl group is bonded to two alkyl groups are known as **ketones** and their names end in '**-one**', as in propan**one** and butan**one**.

A typical reaction is the oxidation of propan-2-ol to propanone:

$$CH_3CH(OH)CH_3 \xrightarrow[\text{sodium dichromate(VI)}]{\text{heat with acidified}} CH_3COCH_3$$
propanone (a ketone)

# Dehydration

Propan-1-ol loses water when its vapour passes over a catalyst such as aluminium oxide at about 400 °C. **This is an example of an elimination reaction**, in which the elements of water, —H and —OH, are removed from neighbouring carbon atoms.

$$CH_3 - CH_2 - CH_2OH \longrightarrow CH_3 - CH=CH_2 + H_2O$$
propene (an alkene)

The product is propene, a molecule with a double bond. Propene belongs to the family of hydrocarbons called **alkenes**.

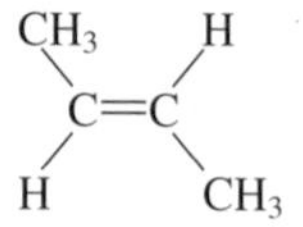

Other alcohols behave in a similar way.

Another way to dehydrate an alcohol is to heat the liquid alcohol with concentrated phosphoric acid or sulphuric acid. You will have an opportunity to try this reaction in Experiment 2.3.

An alkene (butene)

## STUDY TASK

1 Make molecular models of ethene, ethanal and ethanoic acid.

2 a Write an equation to show what happens when butan-1-ol reacts with sodium.

  b Name the organic product and write out its displayed formula.

3 Use a set of molecular models to show what happens in each of the following reactions. For each example name the main organic product and write down its displayed formula.

  a passing ethanol vapour over aluminium oxide at 400 °C

  b passing butan-1-ol vapour over hot aluminium oxide, $Al_2O_3$

  c refluxing ethanol with excess acidified sodium dichromate(VI)

## QUESTIONS

A model kit will help you here.

1 Write the displayed formula for an isomer of propan-1-ol.

2 Write the displayed formula for one other isomer with the formula $C_4H_{10}O$ and decide whether it is a primary, secondary or tertiary alcohol.

## 2.3 How much?

Read a cookery recipe and you will see that it tells you how much you need of each ingredient. It will probably also tell you how many people the meal will feed. The recipe answers the question 'How much?'.

Chemists also need to answer this question when making new chemicals both on a laboratory scale and in industry. In this section you are going to find out how to calculate chemical recipes with the help of the ideas about chemical amounts which you met in Topic 1.

### The chemists' toolkit: molar masses of organic compounds

Working out the molar masses of organic compounds should not be a problem provided you organise your work neatly. This also helps when you want to check a calculation. You could try organising your calculations like these two examples:

COMMENT

Molar masses of the elements:
$H = 1$; $C = 12$; $O = 16$;
$Cl = 35.5\,g\,mol^{-1}$

| Molar mass of ethanol | Molar mass of TCP |
|---|---|
| $C_2H_5OH$ | $C_6H_3OCl_3$ |
| $2C = 24$ | $6C = 72$ |
| $6H = 6$ | $3H = 3$ |
| $10 = 16$ | $10 = 16$ |
| $\overline{46\,g\,mol^{-1}}$ | $3Cl = 106.5$ |
| | $\overline{197.5\,g\,mol^{-1}}$ |

When an organic compound is liquid it is often convenient to measure it by volume rather than mass, using the relationship:

$$\text{volume/cm}^3 = \frac{\text{mass/g}}{\text{density/g cm}^{-3}}$$

QUESTIONS

1 Try working out the molar mass of linalool from the formula on page 26.

2 Work out the volumes of the liquids in figure 2.11. Their densities to two significant figures (from table 5.5 in the *Book of data*) are: water 1.00, ethanol 0.78, cyclohexanol 0.96 g cm$^{-3}$.

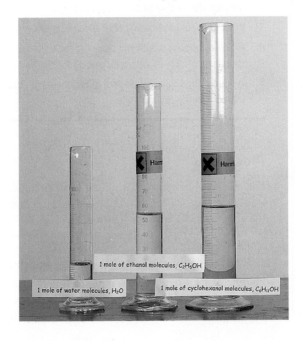

1 mole of ethanol molecules, $C_2H_5OH$

1 mole of water molecules, $H_2O$

1 mole of cyclohexanol molecules, $C_6H_{11}OH$

Figure 2.11 **One mole of each liquid**

# Stages in a laboratory preparation

When setting out to make an organic compound you have to go through several stages.

1   Find out the equation for the reaction and calculate the amounts of reactants to use.

2   Measure out the reactants in the right proportions.

3   Mix the reagents in a suitable apparatus and keep them in the right conditions for long enough to complete the reaction; this often means heating and perhaps adding a catalyst.

4   Separate the product from the reaction mixture.

5   Purify the product.

6   Weigh the purified product and calculate the yield.

7   Carry out tests to check that the process has produced the required product.

---

**EXPERIMENT 2.3**

There is a microscale alternative to this experiment

## How much cyclohexene can you get from cyclohexanol?

We can illustrate these stages with the preparation of cyclohexene from cyclohexanol. Instead of passing the vapour over hot aluminium oxide, as in Experiment 2.2b(1), here we use concentrated phosphoric acid as the dehydrating agent.

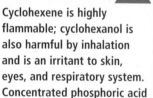

**SAFETY**

Cyclohexene is highly flammable; cyclohexanol is also harmful by inhalation and is an irritant to skin, eyes, and respiratory system. Concentrated phosphoric acid is corrosive.
Calcium chloride is an irritant to the eyes.
The fumes from this experiment are most unpleasant; either use tubing to carry the vapour below bench level or preferably do the reaction in a fume cupboard.
Do not store your product; it will eventually form unstable by-products.

### QUESTIONS

1   What do the words 'dehydration' and 'dehydrating agent' mean?

2   Write the structural formulae of cyclohexanol and cyclohexene. Show how dehydration converts the alcohol to the cycloalkene.

3   What are your predictions about the solubilities of cyclohexene and cyclohexanol in water?

4   Which compound would you expect to have the lower boiling point: cyclohexene or cyclohexanol? Check with the *Book of data*, table 5.5.

5   Work out the volume of 0.1 mol of cyclohexanol. You will find its density and molar mass in table 5.5 in the *Book of data*.

### Procedure

Place 0.1 mol of cyclohexanol in a flask and add, **dropwise**, while shaking the flask, 4 cm³ of concentrated phosphoric acid from a dropping pipette. Assemble the apparatus as shown in figure 2.12.

Heat the flask gently and distil very slowly, collecting the liquid which comes over between 70 and 90 °C.

Pour the distillate into a separating funnel (see figure 2.13) and add an equal volume of a saturated solution of sodium chloride. Shake the funnel and allow the two layers to separate. Run off the lower aqueous layer and then run the top layer (cyclohexene, density 0.81 g cm⁻³) into a small conical flask.

COMMENT

Wash and dry your distillation apparatus as you will need it again.

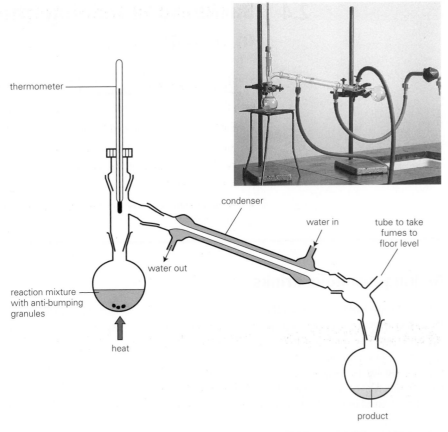

thermometer

condenser

water in

tube to take fumes to floor level

water out

reaction mixture with anti-bumping granules

heat

product

Figure 2.12   **A photograph and a drawing of the apparatus for distillation at a known temperature**

To the crude alkene, add two or three pieces of anhydrous calcium chloride and stopper the flask. Shake for a few minutes until the liquid is clear.

Decant the alkene into a clean flask and redistil it, collecting the liquid distilling between 81–85 °C in a preweighed sample tube. If your volume of alkene from the first stage is small, it would be better to combine your product with another student's and carry out the redistillation together. Weigh the sample tube with your product.

Carry out test tube tests on your product to show that it is an alkene and not an alcohol. Look at your results for Experiment 2.2b(1) for some ideas.

**In your notes:** Describe this preparation using the seven stages listed on page 38 as a guide to what to include.

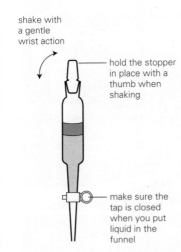

shake with a gentle wrist action

hold the stopper in place with a thumb when shaking

make sure the tap is closed when you put liquid in the funnel

Figure 2.13   **Using a separating funnel**

- What are the conditions for converting cyclohexanol to cyclohexene? Write an equation for the reaction.
- How is the product separated from the reaction mixture and why does the method work?
- There are three stages to the purification of the product. What are they and how do they work?
- Calculate the theoretical yield from 0.1 mol of cyclohexanol, based on 100% yield according to the equation. What percentage of the theoretical yield did you actually get?
- What test did you carry out on the product? What were the results?

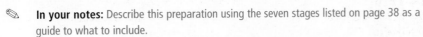

## 2.4 Background reading: the history of alcohol

QUESTIONS

Read the passage below in order to answer the following questions.

1 Give TWO conditions needed for food to be turned into alcohol on storing.

2 How do yeast cells get the energy they need to stay alive and replicate?

3 Explain why it is possible for someone to be convicted of drink-driving on the day after a night of heavy drinking.

4 Write a summary in continuous prose, in no more than 100 words, describing the process of wine-making.

## Making alcoholic drinks

We do not know when or how the first alcoholic drinks were made; the processes were worked out independently all over the world and before written records were being kept. All that was needed was foods with a good sugar content, such as fruit or honey, that had gone mouldy, probably stored so that only a little air was present. With a bit of luck the waste food turned into liquids that tasted good, could be stored without further decay, and acted as narcotics, causing stimulation, intoxication, or even death, depending on the amount consumed.

What started as home-brewing must have rapidly become a specialist trade and is today a world-wide industry, based on a thorough understanding of the chemical and biochemical changes that are involved.

Figure 2.14 **The equipment for brewing beer 300 years ago**

It was only in 1858, some 5000 years after people started making beer and wine, that the French scientist Louis Pasteur published his research and the process of fermentation began to be understood. Before Pasteur, the process was believed to be chemical only, but Pasteur was able to show that the yeasts which cause fermentation are living, single-celled moulds. When the supply of oxygen is limited, they convert glucose into ethanol and carbon dioxide, at the same time getting the energy to stay alive and form new yeast cells.

$$C_6H_{12}O_6 \longrightarrow 2C_2H_5OH + 2CO_2$$

glucose      ethanol     (energy given out 210 kJ mol$^{-1}$)

We will use the process of wine-making to illustrate some of the chemical and biochemical changes involved in fermentation. Grapes are crushed to separate the juice as soon as possible after picking. Damaged grapes can start to ferment spontaneously using the wild yeasts on their skins. The juice, called *must*, is mainly water, containing about 20% sugars (glucose and fructose), 1% complex organic acids (tartaric, malic and citric acids), some inorganic salts and biochemicals in small amounts, such as proteins.

Before fermentation is started, wild yeasts may have to be killed by the addition of a little sulphur dioxide, and sugar or tartaric acid is added to get the best balance. Without careful chemical analysis, adding these ingredients would be a matter of guesswork.

Fermentation can be started by the addition of a yeast selected for its properties or, if suitable, the natural yeasts that were on the grape skins do the work of fermentation. At the early stage some oxygen is necessary to encourage the multiplication of the yeast cells. The temperature at which fermentation takes place has to be controlled – about 20 °C is suitable – and this is not easy as the process is exothermic. A low temperature results in a slower fermentation and this has two advantages; there is time for desirable flavour products to be produced in other reactions and the final concentration of alcohol will be high. There is a limit to the concentration that can be achieved by fermentation because alcohol is actually toxic to yeast cells and kills them at concentrations much above 15%.

However the wine is not yet ready for drinking; over the next year it is allowed to 'age'. It was Pasteur who identified the chemical change involved at this stage – a slow oxidation. The wine has to be allowed controlled access to limited air – too much will ruin it. Finally, the wine is filtered free of substances that have precipitated during the year and is bottled ready for drinking.

## Alcohol as a drug

The ethanol in alcoholic drinks is absorbed and distributed throughout the drinker's body without any chemical change; that is why ethanol is readily detected on the breath and in the urine after being consumed.

Ethanol acts as a narcotic, depressing some of the control systems in the brain, reducing muscular co-ordination and, eventually, causing unconsciousness. There can also be excess water excretion caused by the action of ethanol on some hormones.

What happens to the ethanol consumed? The problem is that the chemical reactions that remove ethanol from our systems (our metabolism) depend on a catalyst (an enzyme) that is only present in small amounts. It takes 5 hours or more to metabolise the alcohol in 2 pints of beer. There is no acknowledged remedy except time.

The long-term effects of excessive alcohol consumption are very serious. A significant number of deaths each year are related to alcohol consumption, far more than are due to the consumption of drugs like heroin and cocaine. People under the influence of drink are involved in 10 fatal road accidents every week. In hospitals, including specialist children's hospitals, 8 out of 10 people treated in accident departments have injuries related to alcohol consumption, ranging from broken limbs to facial injuries, where the victim may be scarred for life. Part of the problem is that people think of the consumption of alcoholic drinks as just a recreational activity, whereas in fact they are consuming a drug that has powerful and dangerous side effects.

## KEY SKILLS

### Communication

Reading about the history of alcohol (background reading section 2.4) and summarising the information gives you an opportunity to develop your skills of selecting and synthesising information from a document.

## TOPIC REVIEW

The organic chemistry studied in Topic 2 seems very different from the inorganic chemistry in Topic 1. However, you should take a similar approach to reviewing and summarising organic chemistry.

Remember that you are looking for **patterns within the key words, terms, principles and ideas** and you need **ways of helping you learn and understand these patterns** so that you will be confident when applying them in new situations.

1   **List key words or terms with definitions.**

Make sure that, whenever possible, you give an example to support your understanding and learning.

- hydrocarbon, alkane, alkene
- homologous series
- molecular formula
- structural formula
- displayed formula
- isomers
- functional group
- primary, secondary and tertiary alcohols
- aldehyde, ketone, carboxylic acid
- carbonyl group

2   **Summarise the key principles as simply as possible.**

A **summary chart** or 'spider diagram' can help you to learn the basic reactions of the **alcohols**. This type of summary is of particular use in organic chemistry.

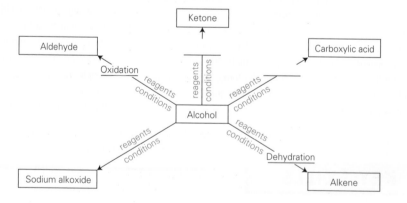

Draw this spider diagram out on a large scale so that you can include details of the **reagents** used, the **reaction conditions** and the **type of reaction** involved for the reactions of ethanol. You must know how to name alkanes and alcohols with up to six carbon atoms.

# REVIEW QUESTIONS

**✱** Indicates that the *Book of data* is needed.

**2.1 and 2.2**   Draw the displayed formulae (showing all the bonds) for the following compounds:

| **2.1** | | | | **2.2** | | | |
|---|---|---|---|---|---|---|---|
| | a | propan-1-ol | (1) | | a | ethane | (1) |
| | b | butan-1-ol | (1) | | b | butane | (1) |
| | c | butan-2-ol | (1) | | c | 2-methylbutane | (1) |
| | d | propan-2-ol | (1) | | d | cyclopropane | (1) |
| | e | 2-methylbutan-2-ol | (1) | | e | heptane | (1) |
| | | | **(5 marks)** | | | | **(5 marks)** |

**2.3 and 2.4**   Name the compounds having the following structural formulae:

**2.3**
a  $CH_3OH$   (1)
b  $(CH_3)_2CHCH_2OH$   (1)
c  $(CH_3)_3COH$   (1)
d  $CH_2OH$
   |
   $CH_2OH$   (1)
e  $CH_3CH_2O^-Na^+$   (1)
**(5 marks)**

**2.4**
a  $CH_3CH_2CH_3$   (1)
b  $CH_3CH_2CH_2CH_2CH_3$   (1)
c  $CH_3CHCH_2CH_2CH_3$   (1)
   |
   $CH_3$
d  $CH_2{-}CH_2$
   |       |
   $CH_2{-}CH_2$   (1)
e  $CH_3CH{=}CH_2$   (1)
**(5 marks)**

**2.5**   Write balanced equations, including state symbols, for the following reactions:

a   methanol with sodium                           (2)
b   ethanol with sodium                            (2)
c   propan-1-ol with sodium                        (2)
d   the dehydration of ethanol                     (2)
e   the dehydration of propan-1-ol                 (2)
f   the dehydration of cyclopentanol               (2)
**(12 marks)**

**2.6**   Draw the displayed formulae and give the names of the organic compounds formed in the following reactions:

a   the partial oxidation of methanol              (2)
b   the full oxidation of methanol                 (2)
c   the partial oxidation of propan-1-ol           (2)
d   the full oxidation of propan-1-ol              (2)
e   the partial oxidation of butan-1-ol            (2)
f   the partial oxidation of butan-2-ol            (2)
**(12 marks)**

**2.7**   Propan-1-ol and propan-2-ol are *isomers*. Use their molecular formulae and structural formulae to explain what this means.   **(3 marks)**

**2.8**    The structural formulae of three alcohols, isomers of $C_4H_{10}O$, are shown on page 30. Draw the structural formula of the fourth isomer and state whether it is a primary, secondary or tertiary alcohol.    **(2 marks)**

**✱ 2.9**    Calculate the molar masses of the following compounds:

a    $CH_3CH_2CHOHCH_3$    (1)
b    $(CH_3)_2CHCH_2OH$    (1)
c    $CH_3CH_2CH_2CHOHCH_2CH_3$    (1)
d    $CH_3CH_2CH_2CO_2H$    (1)
e    $(CH_3)_2CHCH=CH_2$    (1)
                                                    **(5 marks)**

**✱ 2.10**    Draw the structural formulae and calculate the molar masses of each of the following compounds:

a    methanal    (2)
b    sodium methoxide    (2)
c    cyclopentanol    (2)
d    cyclopentene    (2)
e    propanone    (2)
                                                    **(10 marks)**

**✱ 2.11**    In an experiment 3.7 g of butan-1-ol was heated with excess concentrated phosphoric acid. The main product of the reaction was obtained in a yield of 1.8 g after purification.

a    Name the product and write a balanced equation for the reaction.    (2)
b    Calculate the maximum theoretically obtainable yield of the product.    (3)
c    Calculate the percentage yield of product obtained.    (2)
d    Suggest TWO reasons why the actual yield was significantly lower than the theoretical yield.    (2)
e    What was the function of the concentrated phosphoric acid in the reaction?    (1)
                                                    **(10 marks)**

**2.12**    Benedict's solution is used to test for the presence of a specific functional group in an organic compound.

a    What is the original colour of Benedict's solution?    (1)
b    Give the formula of the ion responsible for this colour.    (1)
c    What conditions are needed for the reaction to take place?    (1)
d    Draw the displayed formula and give the name of a compound containing three carbon atoms which you would expect to give a positive reaction with Benedict's solution.    (2)
e    Draw the displayed formula and give the name of an *isomer* of the compound you suggested in **d**, which would not react with Benedict's solution.    (2)
f    What is the name and colour of the solid product you see when the test is positive?    (2)
g    What term is used to describe a solid formed from a solution during a reaction?    (1)
                                                    **(10 marks)**

**2.13** The following substances all have the same molecular formula, $C_7H_{15}OH$.

A $CH_3-\overset{\overset{\displaystyle H}{|}}{\underset{\underset{\displaystyle CH_3}{|}}{C}}-\overset{\overset{\displaystyle CH_3}{|}}{\underset{\underset{\displaystyle H}{|}}{C}}-\overset{\overset{\displaystyle H}{|}}{\underset{\underset{\displaystyle H}{|}}{C}}-\overset{\overset{\displaystyle H}{|}}{\underset{\underset{\displaystyle H}{|}}{C}}-OH$

B $H-\overset{\overset{\displaystyle CH_3}{|}}{\underset{\underset{\displaystyle CH_3}{|}}{C}}-\overset{\overset{\displaystyle H}{|}}{\underset{\underset{\displaystyle H}{|}}{C}}-\overset{\overset{\displaystyle OH}{|}}{\underset{\underset{\displaystyle CH_3}{|}}{C}}-CH_3$

C $CH_3-\overset{\overset{\displaystyle H}{|}}{\underset{\underset{\displaystyle CH_3}{|}}{C}}-\overset{\overset{\displaystyle OH}{|}}{\underset{\underset{\displaystyle CH_3}{|}}{C}}-C_2H_5$

D $CH_3-\overset{\overset{\displaystyle OH}{|}}{\underset{\underset{\displaystyle CH_2CH_3}{|}}{C}}-CH(CH_3)_2$

a Which substance is identical with **C**? (1)
b Which substances are tertiary alcohols? (2)
c Which substance is 2,4-dimethylpentan-2-ol? (1)
d Which substance could be oxidised to an aldehyde? (1)
e Which substance could be oxidised to a carboxylic acid containing the same number of carbon atoms? (1)

**(6 marks)**

# EXAMINATION QUESTIONS

Questions of the summary and comprehension type are found in the background reading section (section 2.4).

**2.14** Properties of some organic compounds containing three carbon atoms per molecule are summarised on the following chart.

$$C_3H_6 \overset{\text{Reaction 1}}{\longleftarrow} C_3H_7OH \overset{\text{Reaction 2}}{\longrightarrow} \underset{\textbf{Y}}{C_3H_6O}$$

$$\downarrow \text{Na}$$

$$\textbf{X}$$

a i What **type** of reaction is Reaction 1? (1)
  ii Name or give the formula of a suitable reagent for carrying out Reaction 1. (1)
  iii What type of hydrocarbon is the compound $C_3H_6$? (1)

b i Write the structural formula for the ionic solid **X** which may be isolated from the reaction involving sodium, showing the ionic charges clearly. (2)
  ii What gas is produced at the same time as **X**? (1)

c i What **type** of reaction is Reaction 2? (1)
  ii Give the names or formulae of TWO reagents which, when mixed together, would be suitable for carrying out Reaction 2. (2)

d The compound **Y** is found not to react with Benedict's solution. Draw **displayed** formulae for **Y** and for the alcohol from which it is made. (4)

e If your laboratory had run out of this alcohol, what other alcohol could be used to carry out Reaction 1? Justify your answer. (2)

**(15 marks)**

**2.15**   This question is about butan-1-ol, $C_4H_9OH$, some of whose reactions are shown below:

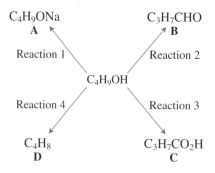

a   Draw the displayed formula for butan-1-ol.   (1)

b   Name the reactant which must be added to butan-1-ol to bring about **Reaction 1**.   (1)

c   In **Reaction 2** the same reagents can be used as in **Reaction 3**, but under different conditions.

   i   What is the general name given to this type of reaction?   (1)

   ii   Give the names or formulae of two reagents which, when mixed together, would be suitable for carrying out **Reaction 2**.   (2)

   iii   What conditions would be used to bring about **Reaction 2**?   (1)

   iv   What conditions would be used to bring about **Reaction 3**?   (1)

d   How could you distinguish between pure samples of substances **B** and **C** in your school laboratory? Give a different test for each substance and describe the expected result.   (4)

e   Which reaction will result in the formation of an ionic organic product?   (1)

f   i   Draw a labelled diagram to show how you would carry out **Reaction 4** in the laboratory to collect a sample of substance **D**.   (4)

   ii   What would you expect to see when substance **D** is shaken with an acidified solution of potassium manganate(VII)?   (2)

   iii   Write a balanced equation, including state symbols, for the complete combustion of substance **D** in air.   (2)

**(20 marks)**

**2.16**    Methanol may be oxidised catalytically using the following apparatus:

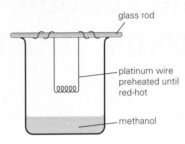

glass rod

platinum wire
preheated until
red-hot

methanol

When placed in position, the wire continues to glow and the pungent odour of methanal is noticed.

**a**    Draw the displayed formula for the pungent-smelling product, methanal.  (1)

**b**  **i**  What is the oxidising agent in this reaction?                                   (1)
      **ii**  What can be deduced from the fact that the wire continues to glow?  (1)

**c**    The reaction can be carried out by an alternative method.
      **i**  What oxidising mixture might be used in an alternative method?     (2)
      **ii**  When an alternative method is used, a possible problem is that the
          methanal might be oxidised further to methanoic acid.
          Suggest TWO ways of minimising this problem.                           (2)

**d**    What colour change is expected when methanal is warmed with
      Benedict's solution (with added sodium hydroxide if necessary)?       (2)
                                                                        **(9 marks)**

# The Periodic Table and atomic structure

In this topic we shall look at atomic structure and especially what we know about the arrangements of electrons in atoms. **Chemists base many of their explanations on their knowledge of atomic structure.** They use the Periodic Table to make sense of all that is known about the 110 or so different elements and their compounds. We shall see how atomic theory can help to make sense of two of the types of strong bonding which hold together the atoms or ions in crystals.

The aims of the topic are to:

- summarise the main features of the Periodic Table
- establish a model of the atom
- relate the model of the atom to the key features of the Periodic Table
- examine the nature of ions
- look briefly at bonding in metals.

## 3.1 The Periodic Table

The Periodic Table is one of the great achievements of chemical science, as it brings order and system to the enormous amount of information which is known about the chemical elements and their compounds. The first successful table to group elements according to their chemical behaviour was devised by the Russian chemist Mendeleev in 1869. Mendeleev based his table on the 60 or so elements then known. Since that time, the table has grown to accommodate over 100 elements. It has also been rearranged to take account of the electronic structures of the atoms, which were quite unknown to Mendeleev. That the original concept has proved capable of absorbing this new knowledge, shows the value of Mendeleev's original proposal.

### Mendeleev's Table

Dmitri Mendeleev was Professor of Chemistry at St Petersburg. He arranged the elements according to their relative atomic masses but he left gaps for elements which, he said, had not yet been discovered; and he listed separately some 'odd'

Figure 3.1   **An unusual presentation of the Periodic Table!**

**Figure 3.2** Dmitri Mendeleev, who produced the first Periodic Table in 1869, similar to those used today

elements (for example, cobalt and nickel) whose properties did not fit in with those of the main groups. Apart from the fact that it contained only about 60 elements, Mendeleev's Periodic Table is much the same as the one we use today. In other words, the outline of the jigsaw was complete, although a number of the pieces were still missing.

Perhaps the most important feature of Mendeleev's work was that he left gaps in his Table where he thought the 'missing' elements should be. This was important because, if a theoretical idea in science is to be really useful, it should not only explain the known facts but also enable new information to be *predicted*. In this way, the theory can be tested by seeing whether or not the predictions prove to be correct.

With Mendeleev's Table – and this was what drew attention to his ideas in the first place – not only were elements discovered which fitted the gaps, but their properties agreed remarkably well with his predictions.

Take one example. When Mendeleev was arranging his Table, he left a gap for an element between silicon and tin. He predicted that the atomic mass of this element would be 72 and its density 5.5 g cm$^{-3}$, basing his predictions on the properties of other known elements which surrounded the gap. Seventeen years later the element was discovered. It had a relative atomic mass of 72.6 and a density of 5.35 g cm$^{-3}$. It was given the name germanium. Mendeleev made other predictions about it too. The table below shows how closely he was able to predict the properties of this new element, and provides confirmation of the correctness of his ideas.

| Mendeleev's predictions | Observed properties |
|---|---|
| Colour will be light grey | Colour is silvery grey |
| Will combine with two atoms of oxygen to form a white powder (the oxide) with a high melting point | Combines with two atoms of oxygen to form a white powder (the oxide) with a melting point above 1000 °C |
| The oxide will have a density of 4.7 g cm$^{-3}$ | Density of the oxide is 4.2 g cm$^{-3}$ |
| Will combine with four atoms of chlorine to form a chloride which will have a boiling point of less than 100 °C | Combines with four atoms of chlorine to form a chloride which boils at 84 °C |
| The density of this chloride will be 1.9 g cm$^{-3}$ | The density of this chloride is 1.8 g cm$^{-3}$ |

## The modern Periodic Table

**When the elements are listed in order of increasing atomic number, elements with similar properties appear in a regular pattern in the list**. These patterns are particularly well demonstrated when the elements are arranged in the form known as the **long form of the Periodic Table**.

Look at the outline Periodic Table in figure 3.3 (overleaf).

**A vertical column is called a group.** The groups are numbered from 1 to 7, with the last column called Group 0 (zero). Several groups have names as well as numbers.

**A horizontal row is called a period.** Periods are numbered from the top downwards.

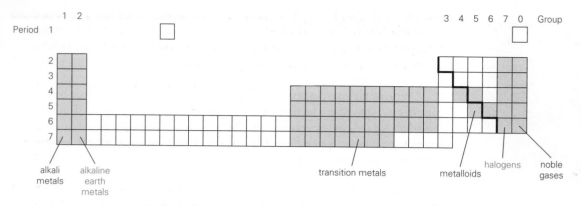

Figure 3.3    **The long form of the Periodic Table of the elements (in outline)**

| Group number | Name | | Period number | Elements |
|---|---|---|---|---|
| 1 | alkali metals | | 1 | H and He (two elements) |
| 2 | alkaline earth metals | | 2 | Li to Ne (eight elements) |
| 7 | halogens | | 3 | Na to Ar (eight elements) |
| 0 | noble gases | | 4 | K to Kr and so on |

Three horizontal regions of the Table also have names: these are the **transition elements**, the **lanthanides** and the **actinides**:

| Name of region | Elements |
|---|---|
| transition elements | titanium (Ti) to copper (Cu) |
| lanthanides | cerium (Ce) to lutetium (Lu) |
| actinides | thorium (Th) to lawrencium (Lr) |

| Particle | Symbol | Charge |
|---|---|---|
| proton | p | + |
| neutron | n | zero |
| electron | e | − |

COMMENT

Isotopes of an element are written:

$^{n+p}_{p}$Symbol

e.g. $^{54}_{26}$Fe and $^{56}_{26}$Fe

The data included in the Periodic Table for each element are typically its atomic number and its molar mass. **The number of protons in an atom is its atomic number, Z.** Each element has a unique number of protons in its nucleus: a different number of protons in an atom means it is a different element.

**The number of protons plus the number of neutrons in an atom is its mass number.** An element can have more than one mass number because different atoms of the same element can have different numbers of neutrons in their nuclei.

**Atoms with the same number of protons but different numbers of neutrons are called isotopes of an element.** The **molar mass** of an element refers to the naturally occurring mixture of isotopes and is determined by an instrument known as a **mass spectrometer**.

The mass spectrometer is described in Topic 21. Topic 21 is for reference. You will study mass spectrometry in the second year of this course; however, this particular use of the mass spectrometer must be covered now. You should, therefore, read section 21.1 as far as the first study task on page 509. Then answer the following questions.

| Relative mass of silicon isotopes | Percentage abundance |
|---|---|
| 28.0 | 92.2 |
| 29.0 | 4.7 |
| 30.0 | 3.1 |

QUESTIONS

Naturally-occurring silicon is a mixture of three isotopes. Its atomic number is 14.

1  Give symbols to represent atoms of the three isotopes.

2  How many neutrons and protons are there in the nuclei of each of the three isotopes of silicon?

3  Calculate the mean relative atomic mass of silicon.

Atoms of elements, when not combined with other elements, have no overall electrical charge and this controls the number of electrons around a nucleus. To produce electrically uncharged atoms, the number of negatively charged electrons must equal the number of positively charged protons in the nucleus. As an example, the commonest iron atom consists of:

- 26 protons, $p^+$
- 30 neutrons, $n$
- 26 electrons, $e^-$

From the normal behaviour of electric charge we might expect the atoms to consist of a tightly compacted ball of the three types of particle. Scientists now accept a model of the atom which consists of a tiny nucleus of protons and neutrons surrounded by an external 'cloud' of electrons.

Figure 3.4  **Scanning electron micrograph (SEM) of crystals of the metal palladium (metal giant structure)**

# Periodicity of physical properties

**Periodicity** is the name given to the regular occurrence of similar features. A school timetable exhibits periodicity; the same lessons recur at periodic intervals, usually every week. In the same way, the Periodic Table shows periodicity.

**The electrical conductivities show a repeating, or periodic, pattern. Metals (which are good conductors of electricity) lie to the left of the 'staircase' line in figure 3.3; metalloids (with some conductivity) straddle the line, and non-metals (which are poor conductors) lie to the right of the line.**

Some interesting information about periodicity amongst the elements can be obtained by comparing the change in various physical properties with change in atomic number. These comparisons can be seen by assembling the data in tables or more readily by plotting charts using a spreadsheet on a computer.

Figure 3.5  **Scanning electron micrograph (SEM) of the tip of a dental drill showing numerous diamond particles encrusted on its surface (non-metal giant structure)**

STUDY TASK

1  Use the *Book of data* to look up the molar masses and densities of the first 18 elements. Calculate their atomic volumes and draw a bar chart from your data: if a computer is available use a spreadsheet program to produce a bar chart automatically.

2  Use the *Book of data* to look up the melting and boiling points of the first 18 elements ($T_m$ and $T_b$ in kelvins). Draw a bar chart from your data.

a  What patterns can you detect in the data?

b  Is there a clear change in the pattern from metals to non-metals?

Figure 3.6    Native sulphur crystals (non-metal with molecular structure)

## 3.2    The story of the atom

Although the idea that matter is composed of small particles is rooted in thinking that goes back over 2000 years, it is only in comparatively recent times that scientists have been able to carry out experiments to test their ideas. In 1827, Robert Brown observed the movement of pollen grains on the surface of water and found the movement to be completely random. This motion came to be known as **Brownian motion** and is caused by bombardment of the pollen grains by molecules in the liquid. Later, in 1908, Perrin showed that particles in gases behaved with the same random motion.

Modern instruments such as the **scanning tunnelling microscope (STM)** even allow us to see the positions of individual atoms.

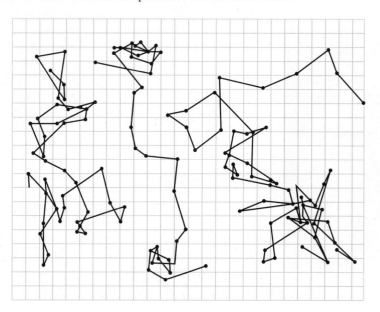

Figure 3.7    Brownian motion is good evidence for the existence of small particles (the position of the particles is marked every 5 seconds)

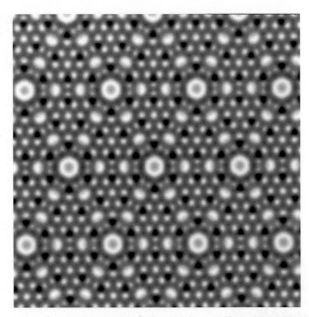

Figure 3.8  **Electronmicrograph of a silicon crystal. The position of individual atoms in complicated compounds can be deduced using various techniques – in this case the pictures were obtained using a high resolution electron microscope**

There is no one correct model of the atom, and there never can be. Matter behaves as if it were made of our model atoms, but our mental models only *represent* matter and correspond to it in the way that a map corresponds to the town it represents.

In everyday life we make use of the model which is most convenient for us. For example, if you were on holiday in Paris and wanted to use the Métro to get from one point to another, you would get hold of a map of the Métro; this would be a model of the underground system showing how the lines and stations are

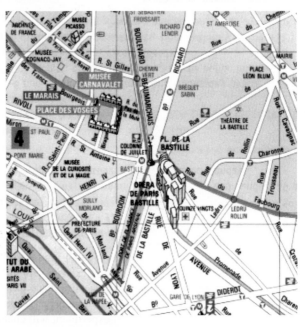

Figure 3.9 a   **A map of part of the Paris Métro; when you want to catch a bus you need a different map**

b   **A map of bus routes in central Paris. Chemists use different models (like maps) depending on what it is that they are studying**

arranged in relation to each other. If you were going to travel by bus, you would use a different model showing the bus routes. If you were going to walk, you would choose another sort of map showing the detailed relationships of each street to the next. They are all maps of Paris – all models of the structure of the city, but all different and emphasising different aspects.

So it is with models of the atom. Simple kinetic theory, in which we consider each atom to be a small sphere, helps us to understand the differences between solids, liquids and gases. This is not a detailed model of the atom itself, so much as describing how atoms are packed together and able to move relative to each other. It does not tell us much about the nature of each atom. In order to explain chemical changes, a more detailed model is required. The most suitable model for this was developed mainly in the years between 1895 and 1940. More detailed models have been developed since then, but on the whole they contribute to our understanding of the nucleus rather than of chemical reactions.

Figure 3.10  **Lise Meitner and Otto Hahn in their laboratory. Why did Meitner leave Germany for Sweden in the late 1930s?**

## STUDY TASK

As a member of a small group, use a range of books and other resources to study **one** of the stages in the development of our model of the atom (these are listed below). In your group, find out about the people involved, their experiments and the key ideas they proposed.

1   Democritus to Dalton, the first ideas about atoms

2   Faraday to J.J. Thomson, evidence for electrons

3   Marie Curie to Rutherford, radioactive particles and the proton

4   Geiger and Rutherford, the idea of the nuclear atom

5   Moseley, the idea of atomic number

6   Chadwick, Otto Hahn and Lise Meitner, the neutron and atomic fission (see figure 3.10)

Summarise your findings. Produce a poster or OHP transparency to present to the other groups and give a talk of about 5 minutes.

You will find collected biographies and the Internet helpful; also check whether your library has an appropriate CD-ROM.

In the next section of this topic we shall examine some of the evidence which has helped chemists to find out more about the arrangements of electrons in atoms. It is the electrons on the outsides of atoms which determine how atoms bond together and react.

## 3.3   Flame colours and emission spectra

One way to study the arrangement of electrons in atoms is to disturb the electrons and then observe what happens as they go back to their original arrangement.

A good way to do this is to heat compounds in a Bunsen burner flame and study the characteristic colours produced. These colours are caused by electrons losing the energy they have gained from the Bunsen burner flame. The next experiment will enable you to gather some information about these colours.

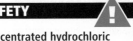

## The flame colours of the elements of Groups 1 and 2

All compounds of a particular element give the same flame colour, but the chlorides are the best to use because they vaporise relatively easily in a Bunsen burner flame.

You can see the patterns in the spectra by looking at flame colours with a hand spectroscope.

### Procedure

**SAFETY**

Concentrated hydrochloric acid is corrosive.
Some barium salts are toxic; others are harmful if inhaled or swallowed.

Clean a platinum or nichrome wire by heating it in a non-luminous Bunsen burner flame, dipping it into a little concentrated hydrochloric acid on a watch glass (TAKE CARE) and heating it again. Continue this until the wire produces little or no colour in the flame.

Pour the impure acid away and take a fresh portion. Dip the clean wire into the acid and then into a small portion of powdered compound on a watch glass. Use chlorides where possible, otherwise use nitrates or carbonates.

Hold the wire so that the powdered solid is in the edge of the flame and note any colour in the flame which results. The colour disappears fairly quickly but can be renewed by dipping the wire into acid and chloride again and reheating.

Observe the flame through a diffraction grating or direct vision spectroscope and look for the coloured lines that make up the spectrum. (You may need to take a fresh sample of solid for this and to do the experiment in a darkened corner of the laboratory.)

When you want to examine the flame colours of other elements it is easier to exchange apparatus with other students. Cleaning your own wire thoroughly for each new sample is time-consuming.

✎   **In your notes:** Record the coloured lines that you see for each element which you examine. Use colour plate C.2 in the *Book of data* to compare with your observations.

## Interpretation of the emission spectra of elements

When atoms of an element are supplied with sufficient energy they emit light. This energy may be provided in several ways. If the element is a gas, it may be placed in an electric discharge tube at low pressure; neon signs work on this principle. Certain easily vaporised metals also emit light under these conditions; an example is the yellow street lamps which are sodium discharge tubes. When the light which is emitted is examined through a spectroscope, it is found not to consist of a continuous range of colours like part of a rainbow, but to be made up of separate coloured lines. The energy which has been supplied to the atoms is not re-emitted all in one go but in 'packets' of energy which give rise to the lines.

**Each element has its own characteristic set of lines, and these enable elements to be identified by examination of their spectra.** Indeed, spectroscopic examination of the Sun revealed the existence of an element which, at that time, had not been discovered on Earth; it was named helium, from the Greek word helios, meaning the Sun.

**The type of spectrum produced is known as a line emission spectrum.** We can explain this by assuming that electrons in an atom can exist only in definite energy levels; they cannot possess energies of intermediate size. It is as if they

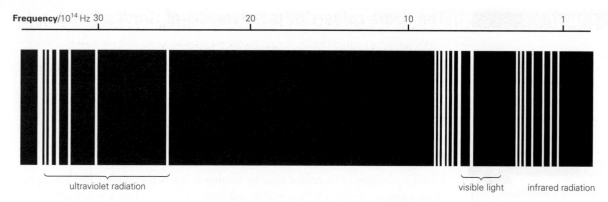

**Frequency**/$10^{14}$ Hz    30          20          10          1

ultraviolet radiation                    visible light    infrared radiation

Figure 3.11 **The line emission spectrum of hydrogen (note that the scale used refers to frequency in units of $10^{14}$ Hz)**

were on a set of steps, rather than a slope, and that when energy is lost an electron moves from one step to another. Sometimes the electron moves one step at a time, sometimes two steps or sometimes more. Since there are millions of atoms present, vast numbers of electrons are moving in each of the different possible ways, giving rise to each of the possible lines in a uniform way.

In the flame test, some electrons in an atom are given sufficient energy to make them jump from a lower energy to a higher energy level. This is known as **excitation**. The electrons then fall back in one step, or a series of steps, from the higher energy level to the lower energy level. The energy is lost as light of a certain frequency, depending on the amount of energy given out. This gives the flame a characteristic colour for each element.

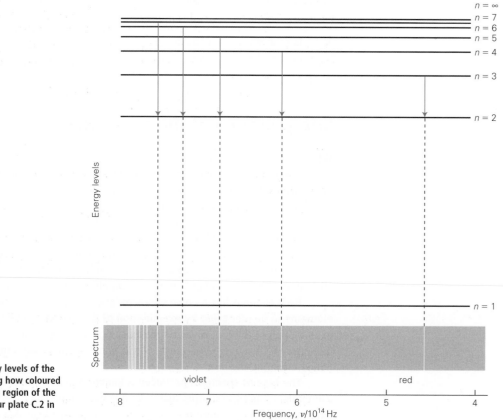

Figure 3.12 **The energy levels of the hydrogen atom, showing how coloured lines occur in the visible region of the spectrum (see also colour plate C.2 in the *Book of data*)**

BACKGROUND

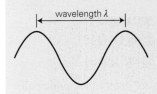

wavelength $\lambda$

Visible light is one form of electromagnetic radiation. Electromagnetic radiation behaves like a wave with a characteristic wavelength and frequency. Electromagnetic radiation always travels at the same speed (symbol $c$) in the same medium – in a vacuum, at a speed of nearly $3 \times 10^8 \, \mathrm{m \, s^{-1}}$. A wave of light, therefore, always travels the distance between two points in a certain time. Wavelength (symbol $\lambda$) measures the distance in metres travelled by the wave in one cycle, while frequency tells us how many cycles a wave goes through per second. Frequency (symbol $\nu$) is, therefore, measured in units of $\mathrm{s^{-1}}$, often termed hertz and abbreviated to Hz. The speed, frequency and wavelength of electromagnetic radiation are related very simply by the equation:

$$c = \lambda \nu$$

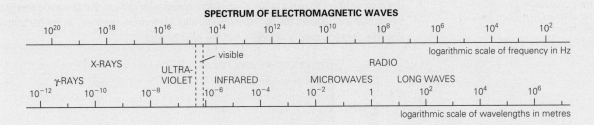

SPECTRUM OF ELECTROMAGNETIC WAVES

In order for atoms to form positive ions, electrons must be removed completely. An atom, therefore, has to be given enough energy to promote an electron *beyond* the outermost energy level of the atom ($n = \infty$ in figure 3.12). **This ionisation requires an input of energy known as the ionisation energy which is given the symbol $E_m$.** It is important to know the amount of energy which is needed to remove an electron from an atom if we are to understand the energy changes involved in chemical bonding.

The *first* ionisation energy of an element is the energy required to remove *one mole of electrons* from *one mole of atoms* of the element in the gaseous state, to form gaseous ions, and is given the symbol $E_{m1}$.

$$M(g) \longrightarrow M^+(g) + e^- \qquad \text{First ionisation energy } E_{m1}$$

The values of ionisation energies are given in kilojoules per mole, $\mathrm{kJ \, mol^{-1}}$. Some values are:

$$Na(g) \longrightarrow Na^+(g) + e^- \qquad \text{First ionisation energy} = 496 \, \mathrm{kJ \, mol^{-1}}$$

$$Mg(g) \longrightarrow Mg^+(g) + e^- \qquad \text{First ionisation energy} = 738 \, \mathrm{kJ \, mol^{-1}}$$

$$Al(g) \longrightarrow Al^+(g) + e^- \qquad \text{First ionisation energy} = 578 \, \mathrm{kJ \, mol^{-1}}$$

## 3.4 The arrangement of electrons in atoms

A knowledge of ionisation energies provides valuable information about the arrangement of electrons within atoms.

So far we have considered the removal of one electron only; but if an atom containing several electrons is treated with sufficient vigour, more than one electron may be removed from it. A succession of ionisation energies is, therefore,

possible and is represented by the symbols $E_{m2}$, $E_{m3}$ and so on.
For example in the case of lithium:

$$Li(g) \longrightarrow Li^+(g) + e^- \qquad\qquad E_{m1} = 520 \text{ kJ mol}^{-1}$$
$$Li^+(g) \longrightarrow Li^{2+}(g) + e^- \qquad\qquad E_{m2} = 7298 \text{ kJ mol}^{-1}$$
$$Li^{2+}(g) \longrightarrow Li^{3+}(g) + e^- \qquad\qquad E_{m3} = 11815 \text{ kJ mol}^{-1}$$

The values for the successive ionisation energies are determined principally from spectroscopic measurements: a table of successive ionisation energies for a number of elements is given in the *Book of data*.

## STUDY TASK

1  Use a spreadsheet to plot a graph of ionisation energies for sodium. Put ionisation energy on the vertical axis, against the corresponding number of electrons removed, on the horizontal axis. The data you need is in table 4.1 of the *Book of data*.

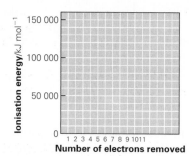

a  What do you notice, first about the general trend in values, and second about their magnitude?
b  Why do you think a general increase in values occurs?

2  Now plot a graph of the logarithm (to base 10) of the ionisation energy against number of electrons removed. Use the log button on your calculator or the log function in the spreadsheet.
a  Does this give any information about groups of electrons which can be removed more readily than others?
b  How many electrons are there in each group?

3  Using the same table in the *Book of data*, study the change in the first ionisation energy of the elements for the first 20 elements. Plot the value of the first ionisation energy for each element on the vertical axis, against its atomic number on the horizontal axis. When you have plotted the points, draw lines between them to show the pattern, and label each point with the symbol for the element.
a  Where do the alkali metals, lithium, sodium and potassium, appear?
b  Where do the noble gases appear?
c  Do you notice any groups of points in the pattern? How many elements are there in each section?
d  Do the numbers of elements in each section bear any relation to the numbers of electrons in the pattern you found in the successive ionisation energies for sodium?

# Interpretation of the patterns in the ionisation energies

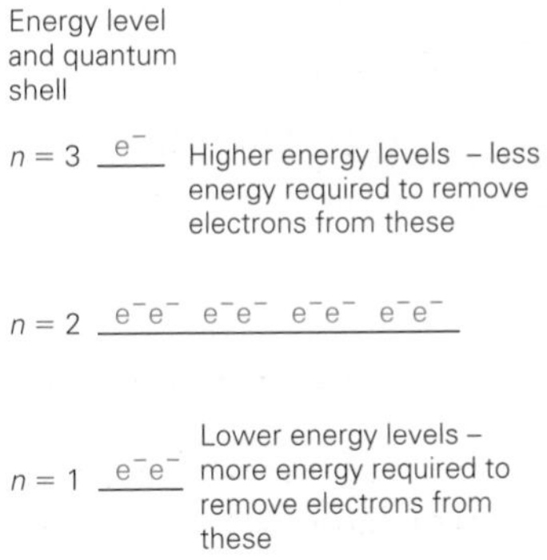

Energy level
and quantum
shell

$n = 3$ ___e⁻___ Higher energy levels – less energy required to remove electrons from these

$n = 2$ ___e⁻e⁻ e⁻e⁻ e⁻e⁻ e⁻e⁻___

$n = 1$ ___e⁻e⁻___ Lower energy levels – more energy required to remove electrons from these

**Figure 3.13 Energy levels of ground-state electrons in an isolated sodium atom ('ground-state' means that the electrons are all in the lowest possible energy state)**

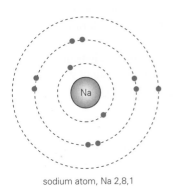

sodium atom, Na 2,8,1

**Figure 3.14 Quantum shells of electrons in an isolated sodium atom**

You should be able to see that your graph of the successive ionisation energies of sodium shows that one electron needs much less energy for its removal than do the others. It must, therefore, be in a higher energy level relative to the nucleus; eight electrons required much more energy, and must be in a lower energy level; the last two electrons must be in a still lower energy level.

The lowest energy level is called the $n = 1$ level; the next level up is called the $n = 2$ level, and so on. Thus, for sodium there would appear to be:

- 2 electrons in the lowest energy level, $n = 1$
- 8 electrons in an intermediate energy level, $n = 2$
- 1 electron in the highest energy level, $n = 3$

We can represent this on an energy level diagram, as in figure 3.13, using e⁻ to represent one electron.

The two electrons in the $n = 1$ energy level are closer to the nucleus than the other electrons, and they are said to be in the **first quantum shell**. The eight electrons in the $n = 2$ energy level are further from the nucleus, and are said to be in the **second quantum shell**. The single electron in sodium is further still from the nucleus and is said to be in the **third quantum shell**. This is represented in figure 3.14.

## COMMENT

When considering diagrams such as figure 3.14, you may be misled into thinking that the electrons occupy specific positions in circular orbits. They do not. Such representations are very simple models with considerable value for counting the number of electrons in each quantum shell but, as we shall see later, they are not very accurate representations of electron behaviour.

**Thus there are two ways of looking at electrons in atoms: from the point of view of their energy levels, $n = 1, 2, 3, 4$, etc., and from the point of view of how far from the nucleus they are on average, that is, in the first, second, third or fourth, etc., quantum shell.**

The successive ionisation energies for potassium have a pattern in which 1 electron is most easily removed, followed by 8 which are difficult, followed by 8 which are even more difficult, followed by 2 which are extremely difficult to remove (see figure 3.15, overleaf).

By looking at the pattern of successive ionisation energies of a particular element, it is possible to assess which Periodic Table group the element is in. Thus a particular element has as its first six ionisation energies (all in kJ mol⁻¹) the values:

789    1577    3232    4356    16091    19785

You will notice the big jump between the fourth and fifth ionisation energies. Four electrons are, therefore, relatively easily removed, suggesting that they are located in the outer quantum shell. The element is, therefore, in Group 4.

Now let us look at the graph of the first ionisation energies of the elements plotted against atomic number (see figure 3.16).

Figure 3.15 **Ionisation energy and energy levels of electrons in an isolated potassium atom**

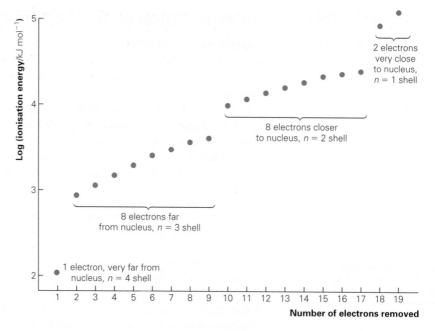

Energy level

$n = 4$ $\underline{e^-}$ Highest energy level – electrons easily removed

$n = 3$ $\underline{e^-e^-}$ $\underline{e^-e^-}$ $\underline{e^-e^-}$ $\underline{e^-e^-}$

$n = 2$ $\underline{e^-e^-}$ $\underline{e^-e^-}$ $\underline{e^-e^-}$ $\underline{e^-e^-}$

$n = 1$ $\underline{e^-e^-}$ Lowest energy level – electrons very difficult to remove

**Across a period you will notice that the general trend is for the first ionisation energies to increase**. This is a result of the greater force of attraction being experienced by electrons in the same quantum shell as a result of greater nuclear charge.

Notice from the graph of the first ionisation energies of the elements that the groups of eight (e.g. from Li to Ne and from Na to Ar) are made up of groups of two, three and three points. This indicates that the eight electrons are not all exactly the same as far as their energies are concerned.

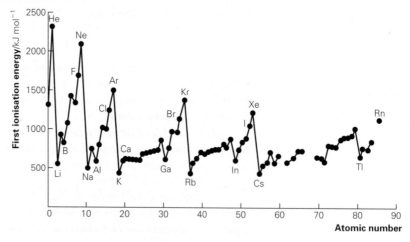

Figure 3.16 **Periodic patterns in the first ionisation energies of the elements**

---

## STUDY TASK

How does the first ionisation energy change on going down a group in the Periodic Table? Suggest reasons for any patterns you observe.

COMMENT

- s sub-levels can contain 2 electrons
- p sub-levels can contain 6
- d sub-levels can contain 10
- f sub-levels can contain 14.

From this type of evidence, and also from studies of spectral lines, it has been concluded that the energy levels are split so that the $n = 2$ level has two electrons in a sub-level known as 2s (slightly more difficult to remove) and six electrons in a sub-level known as 2p (slightly less difficult to remove).

From similar evidence, it has been concluded that the $n = 3$ level is split into s, p, and d sub-levels.

The $n = 4$ level has an additional f sub-level, and so on.

Look again at the figures of energy levels (figures 3.13, 3.14, 3.15). You will see that the electrons have been grouped in pairs. Evidence from spectra suggests that electrons are paired and spin in opposite directions, represented as ↑↓. It is believed that both electrons in a pair have the same energy. This is illustrated in figure 3.17.

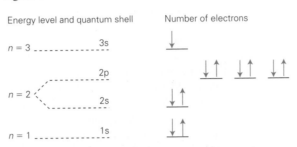

Figure 3.17  **Energy levels of electrons in a sodium atom, showing sub-levels**

Now let us look a little more closely at the way in which electron configurations are written.

The arrangement of the $n = 1$ to $n = 4$ energy levels is shown in figure 3.18.

The atomic number of neon is 10, and its atom, therefore, contains 10 electrons. These are arranged as follows:

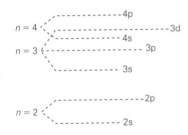

Energy level and quantum shell

Figure 3.18  **Energy levels of electrons in atoms**

- 2 are in the $n = 1$ level, and are in the s sub-level, $1s^2$
- 2 are in the $n = 2$ level, and are in the s sub-level, $2s^2$
- 6 are in the $n = 2$ level, and are in the p sub-level, $2p^6$

So, the electronic structure of neon is written $1s^2 2s^2 2p^6$.

The next element, sodium, atomic number 11, has one electron in the $n = 3$ level, and it is in an s sub-level, since this is the lowest $n = 3$ level. The electronic structure of sodium is, therefore, $1s^2 2s^2 2p^6 3s^1$.

## QUESTIONS

From figure 3.16 you will see that after calcium, atomic number 20, the 2,3,3 pattern is broken.

1   How many elements produce the break?

2   What might this indicate in terms of electrons?

3   What is the name of this set of elements in the Periodic Table?

After calcium, a new energy level belonging to the $n = 3$ quantum shell becomes occupied; the electrons are known as d electrons. A d sub-level can hold 10 electrons when full. You will notice from figure 3.18 that the 3d level is just above the 4s level and just below the 4p level. This is of great importance in the chemistry of the transition elements.

Electrons occupy the orbital with the lowest energy, so when the 4s sub-level is full, electrons are added to the 3d sub-level. The electron configuration of scandium, for example, is $1s^2 2s^2 2p^6 3s^2 3p^6 3d^1 4s^2$.

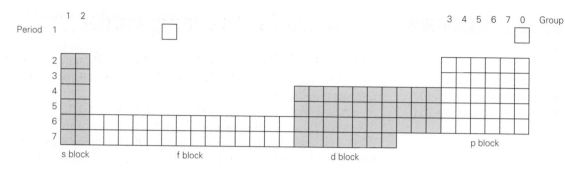

Figure 3.19  **Part of the Periodic Table, showing the pattern of blocks**

Each major peak in the ionisation energy curve in figure 3.16 represents an element with a completed quantum shell. The element concerned is a noble gas. The pattern of electronic structure is mirrored in the Periodic Table.

When the final electron to be added to an electron configuration is added to an s sub-level, the element is said to be in the s block; if added to a p sub-level it is said to be in the p block, and so on.

This pattern of blocks is illustrated in figure 3.19.

Within a particular group of the Periodic Table, the ground-state electron configurations of the atoms are similar. For the elements of Group 1, for instance, the configurations are:

lithium     $1s^22s^1$
sodium     $1s^22s^22p^63s^1$
potassium  $1s^22s^22p^63s^23p^64s^1$
rubidium   $1s^22s^22p^63s^23p^63d^{10}4s^24p^65s^1$
caesium    $1s^22s^22p^63s^23p^63d^{10}4s^24p^64d^{10}5s^25p^66s^1$

**The chemical similarities which exist among members of a group of elements are the result of their similar electron arrangements.**

The group number of a particular element corresponds to the *total number of outer shell s and p electrons*. For example, fluorine has the configuration $1s^22s^22p^5$ so is in Group 7 $(2 + 5 = 7)$.

The period number of a particular element corresponds to the number of quantum shells which are occupied. For example, potassium is in the fourth period as its atoms have the configuration $1s^22s^22p^63s^23p^64s^1$. There are electrons present in the first four quantum shells.

## Electron affinity

So far this section has looked at the loss of electrons and the energy involved. But, for non-metals such as the halogens, *gaining* an electron to form an anion is normal behaviour in some chemical reactions. **The energy change which takes place when each of the atoms in a mole of gaseous atoms acquires an electron to become a singly-charged negative ion is known as the electron affinity, $E_{aff}$**

$$Cl(g) + e^- \longrightarrow Cl^-(g) \qquad E_{aff} = -349 \text{ kJ mol}^{-1}$$

Note that the definition relates to the energy change for a mole of *atoms*, Cl, and not molecules, $Cl_2$.

# 3.5    Evidence for the ionic model

Understanding electron configurations can help to explain what happens when atoms turn into ions. The bonding in chemical substances depends on how the electrons are distributed within them.

Chemical elements and compounds can be divided on the basis of their structures into two main types: **giant** and **molecular**. The properties of a substance are greatly influenced by its structure, for example, as a rough 'rule of thumb', giant structures have boiling points above 500 °C and molecular structures have boiling points below 500 °C.

There are three types of strong chemical bonding: **metallic bonding**, **covalent bonding** and **ionic bonding**.

All molecular substances are held together by covalent bonds (see Topic 7). Giant structures can have ionic, covalent or metallic bonding. For example sodium chloride crystals have a giant, ionically-bonded structure while diamond and sand (silicon dioxide, $SiO_2$) have giant, covalently-bonded structures. All metals have giant structures with metallic bonding.

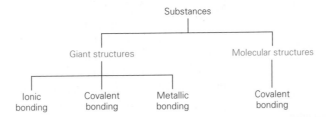

Sodium chloride is a very familiar compound, but its properties reveal the importance of ion formation and ionic bonding. A violently reactive metal combines with a pungent, toxic gas and they are transformed into a safe material: fish live in its solution and our blood contains it in solution.

## REVIEW TASK

From your previous science course you should be familiar with the effects of electrolysis and the evidence it provides for the existence of charged particles in solutions. In groups, list all you can recall about the properties of ionic compounds.

---

**EXPERIMENT 3.5**

## Properties of ionic compounds

Since we cannot see ions and watch their behaviour, we have to rely on experimental observations to build a theoretical model to explain their properties. This is typical of chemistry – it is essentially an experimental science.

### Procedure

#### 1 The electrical conductivity of solutions

In this experiment we shall be attempting to examine the properties of some solutions without decomposing them.

**SAFETY** ⚠

Potassium chlorate is oxidising.

Copper(II) sulphate solution is harmful.

Solid potassium manganate(VII) is harmful and oxidising.

Sodium hydroxide, used in part 1, is irritant at 0.1 M.

You are going to look at the electrical properties of solutions using a simple AC circuit. You will need a low voltage power pack, a torch bulb and carbon rods to dip into the test solutions. Your teacher will tell you the maximum AC voltage that you should not exceed. Test the following solutions, whose concentrations should all be about 0.1 M, to find out if they conduct electricity:

a hydrochloric acid
b sodium hydroxide
c sodium chloride
d magnesium sulphate
e aluminium nitrate.

 **In your notes:** Did all the solutions conduct electricity? What was the reason for using AC rather than DC current?

## 2 Migration of ions

You may try either or both of the following experiments.

### a Using copper(II) sulphate

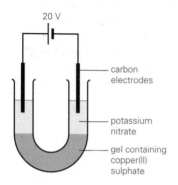

Figure 3.20 **Experiment using copper(II) sulphate**

Measure the volume of your U-tube and divide by four. Prepare a 'quarter volume' of 10% solution of gelatin by adding gelatin to boiling water.

While the gel is still hot add a 'quarter volume' of dilute copper(II) sulphate and pour the mixture into the U-tube. Cool the U-tube in ice, and when the gel has set add a concentrated solution of potassium nitrate to each limb of the U-tube. Place carbon electrodes in each limb of the U-tube and connect to a 20 V DC power supply for about 30 minutes.

 **In your notes:** Note which electrode the coloured ion moves towards. Which ion is responsible for this colour? What does this tell you about the nature of the charge on the ion?

### b Using potassium manganate(VII)

Cut a strip of chromatography paper to the width, but slightly longer than a microscope slide. Mark the middle with a pencil line, moisten with tap water and place on a slide. Use tweezers to place a small crystal of potassium manganate(VII) in the centre of the paper, and cover with another slide to reduce evaporation. Connect the paper to a 20 V DC power supply using crocodile clips and leave for about 20 minutes.

**In your notes:** Note which electrode the coloured ion moves towards. Which ion is responsible for this colour? What does this tell you about the charge on the ion?

## STUDY TASK

Summarise all the evidence which you have encountered for the existence of ions. Look up the melting and boiling points of some of the ionic compounds you have been working with.

Figure 3.21 **Large potassium nitrate crystals. Do you think the saturated solution from which they were crystallising was being cooled slowly or quickly?**

## 3 Examination of ionic crystals

If you have time, you could grow your own ionic crystals of salts like sodium chloride, ammonium chloride and potassium chloride.

Examine your crystals under a light microscope and draw what you see. Try splitting some crystals of rock salt (sodium chloride – see figure 3.23) or calcite (calcium carbonate) using a penknife and tapping with a small hammer. Be sure to wear eye protection in case fragments fly up. You should find that the crystals split into regular shapes. This is due to the regular packing of ions which may be seen most clearly in a model of the crystal structure.

## Interpretation of the experiments

The electrical conductivity of solutions is the most obvious evidence for the existence of charged particles in the solutions of salts; and the experiment on migration shows that metals form positively charged cations while non-metals form negatively charged anions in salts. This is equally true when salts are molten.

One consequence of ionic compounds consisting of charged ions is their solubility in liquids such as water, and their insolubility in hydrocarbon solvents.

In addition, because there are large forces of attraction between the oppositely charged ions, ionic compounds have high melting and boiling points.

## The shape of ions

Forming an ion has a dramatic effect on the size of an atom and some examples are shown for cations and anions in figure 3.22.

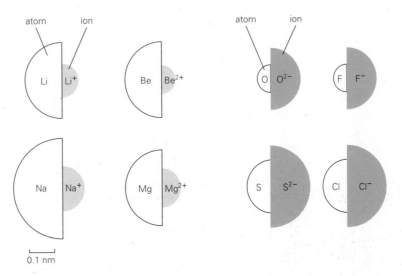

Figure 3.22    **Atoms and ions drawn to scale**

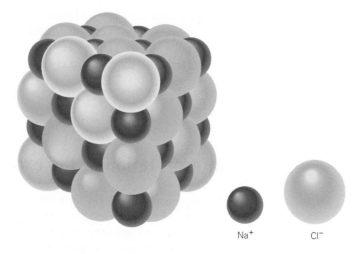

Figure 3.23 **Sodium chloride crystals and a model of its ionic structure**

Within a crystal, the ions are held in place by strong forces of attraction between oppositely charged ions, and by the repulsions of the similarly charged ions. These forces are non-directional, unlike the forces in a covalent bond, which are directional. **So the ions are arranged in giant crystal lattices, in which attractive and repulsive forces are balanced.** (See figure 3.23.)

When building models of ionic structures, those ions which are formed from single atoms are usually represented as spheres. You might think that, as ions possess a complete outer electron shell, the electron distribution is spherical. There is some experimental evidence for this view, based on a study of electron density maps, obtained by X-ray diffraction measurements. X-ray diffraction is described in Topic 21.

The electron density maps which are obtained resemble contour maps used in geography to indicate points of equal height above sea level. Each contour on an electron density map joins points of equal electron density and so, just as hills can be identified on geographical maps, so can atoms and ions on electron density maps.

Figure 3.24 shows electron density maps for sodium chloride and calcium fluoride. Do the maps suggest that these ions exist as distinct and separate entities? Do the ions appear to be spherical?

In Topic 16 we will look at how the spherical model does not apply to large anions combining with small, densely charged cations.

### STUDY TASK

Try to measure the radius of a sodium ion and a chloride ion using figure 3.24.

1   What difficulty is involved? Suggest one method of overcoming it.

2   What do you think limits the accuracy of the ionic radii shown on electron density maps?

3   What distance can you measure more accurately using the electron density map?

This task is designed to introduce you to the problem of deciding exactly how large ions are.

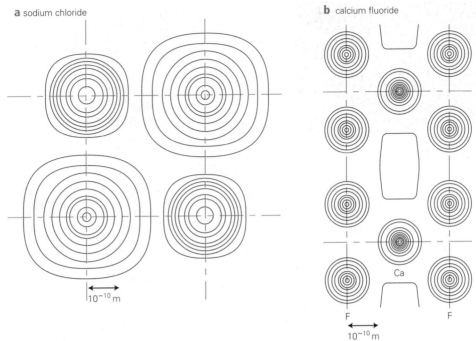

**a** sodium chloride

**b** calcium fluoride

$10^{-10}$ m

Ca

F          F

$10^{-10}$ m

Figure 3.24   **Electron density maps for a sodium chloride and b calcium fluoride**

# Electron arrangements in ions

COMMENT

Typical cations:
$Li^+$, $Na^+$, $K^+$
$Mg^{2+}$, $Ca^{2+}$, $Ba^{2+}$
$Al^{3+}$

Typical anions:
$F^-$, $Cl^-$, $Br^-$, $I^-$
$O^{2-}$, $S^{2-}$
$N^{3-}$ (uncommon)

You should memorise the charges carried by each of these ions and be able to relate them to their Periodic Table group.

We know, from their typical properties of electrical conductance and high melting and boiling points, that **most compounds formed between metallic and non-metallic elements are ionic**, with the metals forming positively charged cations and the non-metals forming negatively charged anions.

The diagrams in figure 3.25 (overleaf) show how the transfer of electrons from one atom to another gives ions. In these diagrams the nucleus of each atom is represented by its symbol, and the shells of electrons are represented by groups of dots and crosses around the nucleus. The shell of lowest energy is nearest to the nucleus, and successively higher energy levels are shown at increasing distances.

Notice that the electronic structures of the ions that are formed are identical to those of a noble gas.

Remember that in such 'dot and cross' diagrams, dots and crosses are used for the electrons in different atoms so that transfers of electrons are easily followed. The individual electrons are not, however, distinguishable. Also remember when drawing 'dot and cross' diagrams that the dots and crosses are a means of counting electrons, and showing the number present; they do not show the positions of the electrons. The electrons are actually distributed in space as diffuse negative charge clouds.

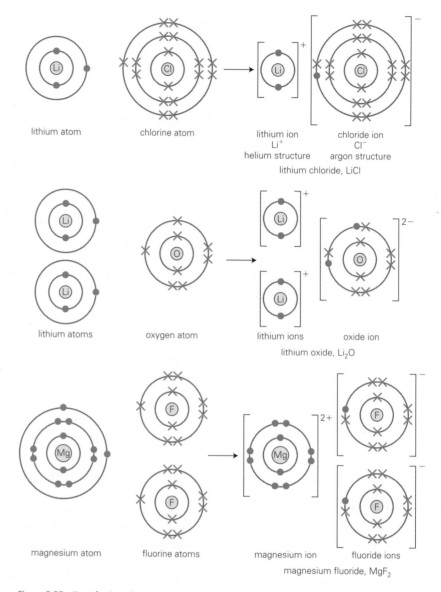

**Figure 3.25 Transferring electrons to form ions**

**Figure 3.26 The proposal that ions had a 'noble gas' electronic structure was put forward by G. N. Lewis in 1916**

## QUESTIONS

Draw similar diagrams to show how the following compounds might be formed by electron transfer: sodium fluoride, magnesium oxide, calcium chloride, aluminium oxide. Add the names of the noble gases whose electronic structures are formed in your diagrams.

You will notice that making up the noble gas structure leads to the experimentally determined empirical formula.

So far this topic has covered only simple ions derived from single atoms of the elements involved. Other ions exist that consist of a group of atoms linked by covalent bonds (discussed in detail in Topic 7), and the charge is associated with the group of atoms as a whole. Examples are the ammonium cation and the hydroxide anion.

$$\begin{bmatrix} & H & \\ & | & \\ H-\!\!\!&N&\!\!\!-H \\ & | & \\ & H & \end{bmatrix}^{+} \qquad O-\!\!\!-H^{-}$$

Other examples which should be familiar are the carbonate anion, $CO_3^{2-}$, and the nitrate and sulphate anions, $NO_3^-$ and $SO_4^{2-}$

## 3.6 Metallic bonds

Metallic bonding is one of the three types of strong chemical bonding.

Significant properties of metals are their high melting points (compared with most non-metals), their high electrical conductivities, and their high thermal conductivities. Any model of the nature of bonding in metals must be able to account for these properties. **A simple model of bonding in a solid metal consists of positive metal ions surrounded by a sea of mobile electrons** (see figure 3.27).

The sea of electrons bonds the metal ions tightly into the lattice, and generally results in a high melting point. Since the strong bonding forces are still present in the liquid, many metals have a wide temperature range over which they remain liquid. The mobility of the electrons provides a means of conducting electricity and heat.

In contrast, non-metals have low melting points and only a narrow temperature range before the liquid boils.

The model of metallic structure is a simplification and it does not account for all of the properties of metals.

Figure 3.27 **Electron density map of aluminium (*right*), and the 'sea of electrons' model of metallic structure (*below*)**

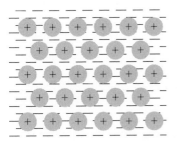

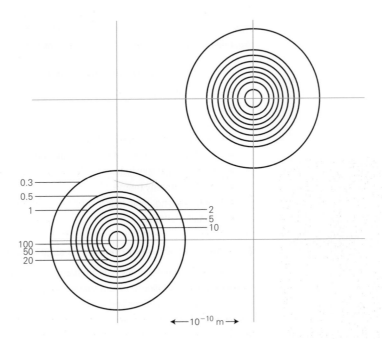

(Contours are labelled in electrons per $10^{-30}$ m$^3$.)

## KEY SKILLS

### Communication

The study task on page 54 provides an opportunity to select and synthesise information from a range of sources and then make a presentation with images in an appropriate language and style for your audience.

### Application of number

The study task on page 51 gives you the chance to extract information from large data sets, present your findings in charts to show trends, and make comparisons.

### IT

You could choose to search for the data you need for the study task on page 51 from a CD-ROM and then use appropriate software, such as a spreadsheet, to display your findings. You could develop and refine the display of information to meet your purpose of looking for patterns in the data.

## TOPIC REVIEW

In this topic you have met a large number of new ideas. These ideas have been presented to you with much scientific evidence to support them. It is important not only that you understand the ideas, but also that you appreciate how scientists derived them from the evidence collected. When tackling this topic review, start with what you know about the Periodic Table and use the experiment to produce flame colours as the link with the more theoretical ideas.

1   **List key words or terms with definitions**
    - group, period, periodicity
    - protons, neutrons, electrons
    - ionisation energy
    - quantum shells and sub-shells
    - electronic arrangement of atoms and ions
    - line emission spectrum
    - electron density maps
    - ionic bonding, ionic radius
    - metallic bonding

2   **Summarise the key principles as simply as possible**

    This topic is more densely packed than the previous two, and you should expect to spend quite some time digesting and summarising all the important ideas. To summarise the events and evidence you might find a summary chart helpful. Diagrams of all kinds will make learning these ideas easier.

    You must:
    - be able to interpret the sequence of ionisation energies for an element
    - know the origin of flame colours and the colour for each element studied

- be able to show, diagrammatically, how an ionic compound is formed
- be able to recognise the nature of an element and the bonding in its compounds from given data
- be able to interpret trends in atomic and ionic radii and ionisation energies down a group and across a period.

# REVIEW QUESTIONS

✱ Indicates that the *Book of data* is needed.

✱ **3.1**  Copy and complete the following table showing the numbers of protons, neutrons and electrons in the atoms and ions shown.

| Atom or ion | Protons | Neutrons | Electrons |
|---|---|---|---|
| Iodine atom, $^{127}_{53}I$ | | | |
| Iodide ion, $^{127}_{53}I^-$ | | | |
| Scandium atom, $^{45}_{21}Sc$ | | | |
| Scandium ion, $^{45}_{21}Sc^{3+}$ | | | |
| Hydride ion, $^{2}_{1}H^-$ | | | |

**(15 marks)**

✱ **3.2**  **a**  Explain why a mass spectrometer trace for fluorine shows only one peak whilst that for bromine shows two peaks.  (2)

**b**  A mass spectrometer trace for a sample of titanium showed the following five peaks:

| Mass/charge ratio | Height of peak/cm |
|---|---|
| 46 | 0.80 |
| 47 | 0.73 |
| 48 | 7.40 |
| 49 | 0.55 |
| 50 | 0.52 |

Use this data to calculate the relative atomic mass of titanium, giving your answer to two significant figures.  (3)

**c**  Using graph paper, make a scale drawing of the mass spectrometer trace you would expect to be produced by a sample of molybdenum.  (5)

**(10 marks)**

✱ **3.3**  **a**  Use a spreadsheet to produce a graph of the melting points of the elements in Periods 4 and 5 of the Periodic Table, plotted against group number. (Exclude the d-block elements Sc to Zn and Y to Cd.) (Alternatively, tabulate the values and plot the graph manually.)  (4)

**b**  Compare the pattern of melting points of the elements on your graph with that shown by the elements of Periods 2 and 3 (see the study task on page 51). What are the main similarities and differences?  (4)

**(8 marks)**

**✷ 3.4**   **a**   Referring to the *Book of data*, write down the formulae of the fluorides of the elements in Period 3 from sodium to sulphur. (Where an element forms two fluorides, choose the one having the higher proportion of fluorine.)   (2)

**b**   Write a sentence describing the pattern shown by these formulae.   (2)

**c**   Compare this pattern with that shown by the oxides of these elements (listed on page 392). What difference is there between the two patterns?   (1)

**d**   Try to explain the difference.   (2)

**(7 marks)**

**3.5**   Do you think the following are correct statements? Justify your answer in each case.

**a**   All metallic elements are transition elements.   (2)

**b**   A group in the Periodic Table consists either of metallic or of non-metallic elements, never both.   (2)

**(4 marks)**

**3.6**   Flame tests carried out on some compounds of Group 1 and 2 elements gave the following results. Identify the elements as precisely as possible, from their flame colours.

**a**   yellow   (1)

**b**   lilac   (1)

**c**   brick-red   (1)

**d**   green   (1)

**e**   no colour   (1)

**(5 marks)**

**3.7**   Give brief, clear explanations of the following:

**a**   When the red flame produced by a strontium compound is viewed through a direct-vision spectroscope a number of coloured lines are seen.   (3)

**b**   There are more lines in the emission spectrum of strontium than in that of sodium.   (1)

**c**   Some Group 2 elements do not produce a flame colour.   (2)

**(6 marks)**

**✷ 3.8**   How much energy (measured in $kJ\ mol^{-1}$) is needed to bring about each of the following conversions, starting with 1 mole of atoms of the element in each case?

**a**   **i**   $Na(g) \longrightarrow Na^+(g) + e^-$   (1)

   **ii**   $Mg(g) \longrightarrow Mg^{2+}(g) + 2e^-$   (1)

   **iii**   $Al(g) \longrightarrow Al^{3+}(g) + 3e^-$   (1)

   **iv**   $Si(g) \longrightarrow Si^{4+}(g) + 4e^-$   (1)

**b**   Suggest a reason why the compounds of sodium are ionic whilst those of silicon are covalent.   (1)

**c**   Do you think magnesium and aluminium are likely to form ionic or covalent compounds? Give reasons for your answer.   (2)

**(7 marks)**

**3.9** The electron energy levels of a certain element can be represented by:

$$1s^2 2s^2 2p^6 3s^2 3p^1$$

Sketch a graph showing the general form which you would expect for the first five ionisation energies of the element. **(5 marks)**

**3.10** The outermost electrons in the atoms of some elements are shown below. Place each element in its correct group in the Periodic Table.

a    $2s^2 2p^6$        (1)
b    $3s^2 3p^3$        (1)
c    $3d^{10} 4s^2 4p^1$        (1)
d    $3d^{10} 4s^2 4p^6 5s^2$        (1)
e    $5s^2 5p^5$        (1)
       **(5 marks)**

**3.11** Write the names and formulae for all the possible compounds in which the ions listed below can be combined together.

$Na^+$      $Br^-$
$Mg^{2+}$    $O^{2-}$
$Al^{3+}$     $N^{3-}$        **(9 marks)**

**3.12** A 'migration of ions' experiment, similar to Experiment 3.5, 2a (page 64) was carried out using a solution of copper(II) chromate(VI), $CuCrO_4$, instead of copper(II) sulphate. The solution around the anode ($+ve$) gradually became yellow, whilst that around the cathode ($-ve$) became blue.

a    Write down the formula of the ion responsible for:
    i    the blue colour        (1)
    ii   the yellow colour.        (1)

b    What colour would you expect the original copper(II) chromate(VI) solution to have? Give a reason for your answer.        (2)
       **(4 marks)**

**3.13** Draw 'dot and cross' diagrams for the following ionic compounds, showing *all* electrons (i.e. not just the outer shells). Show the charge on each ion in your diagrams.

a    lithium fluoride        (2)
b    calcium chloride        (2)
c    sodium oxide        (2)
d    potassium sulphide        (2)
e    magnesium nitride        (2)
       **(10 marks)**

# EXAMINATION QUESTIONS

**3.14** When magnesium burns in air, the metal not only combines with the oxygen to give magnesium oxide, MgO, but also with the nitrogen, giving magnesium nitride, $Mg_3N_2$. Similar reactions happen when lithium is burned.

a Write the electronic configuration of the nitride ion, $N^{3-}$. Use the s, p, d, f notation. (2)

b Draw a 'dot and cross' diagram for the nitride ion, showing all the electrons present. (1)

c What is the formula for lithium nitride? (1)

d Some atomic and ionic radii for nitrogen and oxygen are given below.

| Atomic radius/nm | Ionic radius/nm |
|---|---|
| N 0.075 | $N^{3-}$ 0.171 |
| O 0.073 | $O^{2-}$ 0.140 |

Suggest ONE reason in each case why:

i the ions are larger than the corresponding atoms (1)

ii the oxide ion is smaller than the nitride ion. (1)

e When a metal burns, the flame often shows a colour typical of the ion of the metal.

i What flame colour is typical of the lithium ion? (1)

ii Explain how flame colours result from electronic transitions. (2)

iii Why does the magnesium ion not have a flame colour? (1)

**(10 marks)**

**3.15** Bauxite, impure aluminium oxide, is the main industrial source of aluminium. It must be purified before the aluminium is extracted from it and this is done by boiling it with a concentrated aqueous solution of sodium hydroxide. The reaction may be represented by the equation:

$$Al_2O_3(s) + 2NaOH(aq) \longrightarrow 2NaAlO_2(aq) + H_2O(l)$$

Solid impurities, mainly iron(III) oxide, are filtered off and aluminium hydroxide, $Al(OH)_3$, is precipitated from the filtrate. This precipitate is then heated strongly to give pure aluminium oxide.

a Write a balanced equation, including state symbols, for the decomposition of aluminium hydroxide. (2)

b i What mass of sodium hydroxide would be needed to react with 5.10 g of aluminium oxide? (2)

ii Why in practice would more than this be required? (1)

c i Using the Periodic Table, write down the atomic number of aluminium. (1)

ii Complete the electronic configuration of the aluminium atom by giving the values of $x$ and $y$:

$$1s^2 2s^2 2p^6 3s^x 3p^y$$

(2)

d i Sodium compounds might be present in small quantities in the purified aluminium oxide. Describe how the flame colour due to sodium ions might be demonstrated practically. (3)

    **ii** What is the flame colour associated with sodium? (1)

    **iii** How, in principle, might the production of its flame colour be used to make an estimate of the percentage of sodium in the aluminium oxide? (2)

**(14 marks)**

**3.16** The first ionisation energies of several elements of consecutively increasing atomic number are shown below. The letters are not the symbols for the elements.

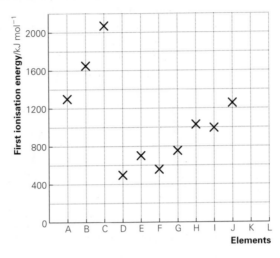

**a** What are your estimates of the first ionisation energies of the elements **K** and **L**? (2)

**b** **i** Which elements, from **A** to **L**, are noble gases? (1)

    **ii** Which elements are alkali metals? (1)

    **iii** Which of the elements **A** to **D** consist of small molecules? (1)

    **iv** Which element could have the electron configuration $1s^2 2s^2 2p^6 3s^2 3p^1$? (1)

    **v** **E** and **J** form an ionic compound of formula **EJ₂**. Give the formulae of two further ionic compounds of **E** with other elements from **A** to **L**. (2)

**c** Explain why there is a general rise in first ionisation energy from element **D** to element **J**. (2)

**(10 marks)**

**3.17** Ionisation energies in kJ mol⁻¹ of three elements **R**, **S**, **T**, which are consecutive in atomic number, are:

| | 1st | 2nd | 3rd | 4th | 5th | 6th | 7th |
|---|---|---|---|---|---|---|---|
| **R** | 1251 | 2297 | 3822 | 5158 | 6542 | 9362 | 11018 |
| **S** | 1521 | 2666 | 3931 | 5771 | 7238 | 8781 | 11996 |
| **T** | 419 | 3051 | 4412 | 5877 | 7975 | 9649 | 11343 |

**a** In which group of the Periodic Table would **T** be found? Justify your answer. (2)

**b** Estimate the 8th ionisation energy of the element **S** to 2 significant figures. (2)

**c**    What type of electron (s, p, etc.) is removed when an atom of **R** is ionised by the removal of 1 electron? (1)

**d**    Write an equation, with state symbols, to represent the reaction accompanied by the second ionisation energy of **T** (use **T** as the symbol for the element). (2)

**e**    The sketch graph below shows the first ionisation energies of **R**, **S** and **T**. Copy and continue the sketch so as to show the pattern of the first ionisation energies of the next three elements of the Periodic Table, **U**, **V** and **W**, assuming that transition elements are not involved. (3)

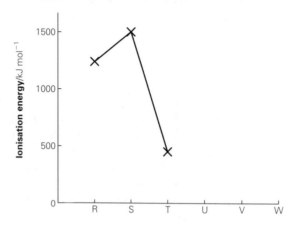

**f**    The first six ionisation energies of another element **M** are shown in the following sketch graph.

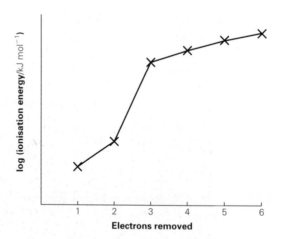

Explain why **M** cannot have an atomic number less than 12. (3)

**(13 marks)**

# Acid–base reactions and the alkaline earth elements

In this topic we extend your understanding of the behaviour of acids and bases. The study of acid–base behaviour is linked to the chemistry of the Group 2 elements and their compounds.

Traditionally the Group 2 elements are called **alkaline earth elements**. The compounds of some of the Group 2 elements can readily be seen in the countryside. Calcium carbonate is found as chalk, limestone and marble in very large quantities. Limestone rock, being basic, is attacked by the natural acidity of rain and this can result in spectacular underground rivers and caves (see figure 4.1). It is also commonly used by animals for their skeletons or shells: egg shells are made of calcium carbonate in the crystalline form known as calcite. Calcite is also used by molluscs for their tough shells, but cuttlefish use a form called aragonite because they need a very buoyant skeleton.

So, in this topic you should expect to increase your understanding of acids and bases and, through an extensive series of experiments, learn about the Group 2 elements and their compounds.

Figure 4.1   Exploring a limestone cave. How are the ions arranged in a crystal of calcite? Is there any similarity to the structure of sodium chloride?

## 4.1 Acids and bases

Acids and bases account for eight of the top 15 chemicals that are manufactured in very large quantities. You should already have some knowledge of the behaviour of acids and bases and in this section we will be looking at a definition of wide application.

Figure 4.2 **Electroplating a sieve using an acidic electrolyte**

---

**STUDY TASK**

Working in groups, make a list of the typical properties of acids and bases, for example hydrochloric acid and sodium hydroxide.

---

**EXPERIMENT 4.1**

### What is an acid?

These experiments are intended to raise questions about the use of the term 'acid' and lead to a useful method of interpreting acid–base reactions.

### Procedure

1 Use a selection of indicators to check the neutralisation of acids by bases. Suitable **dilute** solutions to test are acids such as hydrochloric acid, sulphuric acid and ethanoic acid, and bases such as sodium hydroxide, calcium hydroxide and ammonia. Remember that, even when dilute, some acids are corrosive or irritant to your skin.

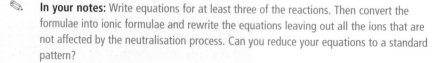

**In your notes:** Write equations for at least three of the reactions. Then convert the formulae into ionic formulae and rewrite the equations leaving out all the ions that are not affected by the neutralisation process. Can you reduce your equations to a standard pattern?

---

**SAFETY** ⚠

The solution of hydrogen chloride in the hydrocarbon solvent is flammable.
The vapour of this liquid can cause headaches and nausea.
8 M ammonia is corrosive. Remember to wear eye protection.
0.1 M sodium hydroxide is an irritant.
Indicator solutions made up in ethanol are highly flammable.
Anhydrous sodium carbonate is an irritant.

COMMENT

Ions that are present in reagents but are not altered by a reaction are known as 'spectator ions' (see section 1.1). In the reaction

$$Na_2CO_3(aq) + 2HCl(aq) \longrightarrow 2NaCl(aq) + H_2O(l) + CO_2(g)$$

the ionic form is:

$$CO_3^{2-}(aq) + 2H^+ \longrightarrow H_2O(l) + CO_2(g)$$

2  Test samples of a solution of hydrogen chloride in a dry hydrocarbon solvent with magnesium metal, anhydrous sodium carbonate, and dry indicator paper; test for electrical conductivity.

  Add the same small amount of water to each sample and notice any differences in reactivity.

3  Allow ammonia gas to drift across a small basin containing hydrogen chloride in hydrocarbon solvent (TAKE CARE – irritant gases).

✎  **In your notes:** Write an equation for the reaction between the two gases. How can hydrogen ions be involved in this reaction?

COMMENT

To obtain carbonic acid solution exhale through a sample of water using a drinking straw.
Throw away the straw as soon as you have used it.
Lime water is a saturated solution of calcium hydroxide in water.

4  Measure the pH of some aqueous solutions of acids and bases of concentration $\frac{1}{100}$ mol dm$^{-3}$, using indicators or a pH meter. Suitable acids include carbonic, ethanoic, phosphoric, and hydrochloric acids. Suitable bases include sodium hydroxide, calcium hydroxide, ammonia and urea.

✎  **In your notes:** The solutions of acids and bases have the same amount of substance in solution, so why do these solutions have such varied pH values?

# Interpretation of acid–base reactions

You should have found that most of the **neutralisation reactions** between acids and bases in aqueous solution follow a common pattern

$$\text{acid} + \text{base} \longrightarrow \text{salt} + \text{water}$$

and **can be summarised in one ionic equation**

$$H^+(aq) + OH^-(aq) \longrightarrow H_2O(l)$$

This common pattern of behaviour was recognised by Arrhenius and his definitions of acids and bases were:

**An Arrhenius acid is a compound containing hydrogen which will form hydrogen ions in water.**

**An Arrhenius base is a compound which will form hydroxide ions in water.**

However, experiments have shown that the Arrhenius definitions are limited to behaviour in water. A better definition would be based on features common to reactions between gases and reactions in solvents other than water, for example,

$$H{-}Cl(g) + NH_3(g) \longrightarrow NH_4^+Cl^-(s)$$

and even reactions we have not thought of as acid–base reactions:

$$H{-}OH(l) + NH_3(g) \longrightarrow NH_4^+(aq) + OH^-(aq)$$

This approach led to a theory of acid–base behaviour that was put forward independently in 1923 by the Danish chemist Brønsted and the British chemist Lowry. In their theory, an acid is a substance which can provide protons (hydrogen ions) in a reaction; a base is a substance which can combine with protons.

**An acid is a proton donor; a base is a proton acceptor.**

In the reaction of hydrogen chloride gas with water,

$$\overset{\overset{\displaystyle \longrightarrow H^+ \longrightarrow}{}}{\underset{\text{acid}}{H{-}Cl(g)} + \underset{\text{base}}{H_2O(l)} \longrightarrow Cl^-(aq) + H_3O^+(aq)}$$

the water behaves as a base by accepting a proton. **The $H_3O^+$ ion is called the oxonium ion**

But water can also act as an acid. In aqueous ammonia, for example, the water is donating a proton in the acid–base reaction:

$$\overset{\overset{\displaystyle \longrightarrow H^+ \longrightarrow}{}}{\underset{\text{acid}}{H_2O(l)} + \underset{\text{base}}{NH_3(aq)} \longrightarrow OH^-(aq) + NH_4^+(aq)}$$

It is this property that gives water its special importance in acid–base behaviour.
**We can say that acid–base reactions are essentially a competition for protons between two bases.**

## COMMENT

Not all the hydrogen atoms in a compound need be acidic: they are in $H_2CO_3$, $H_3PO_4$, but only one is acidic in $CH_3CO_2H$ and none is acidic in ethanol, $CH_3CH_2OH$.
Bases need not contain hydroxide groups, but they do produce hydroxide ions when they react with water:

$$CaO(s) + H_2O(l) \longrightarrow Ca^{2+}(aq) + 2OH^-(aq)$$
$$NH_3(g) + H_2O(l) \longrightarrow NH_4^+(aq) + OH^-(aq)$$

# Strong and weak acids and bases

You will have seen in the experiments that the pH of solutions is not directly related to the number of protons that the molecules can accept or donate; if that was the case, $H_3PO_4$ would have a smaller pH value than $HCl$.

The pH of a solution depends on the extent to which the available protons are actually transferred to water to form oxonium ions:

$$HCl(g) + H_2O(l) \xrightarrow{100\%} Cl^-(aq) + H_3O^+(aq)$$

or

$$CH_3CH_2CO_2H(l) + H_2O(l) \xrightarrow{\text{less than } 1\%} CH_3CH_2CO_2^-(aq) + H_3O^+(aq)$$

**Acids that donate their acidic protons almost completely to water are classified as strong acids; acids that interact very little with water are classified as weak acids.** There is no sharp dividing line between strong and weak acids but there is a continuous spectrum of acid strength (figure 4.3). The same sort of

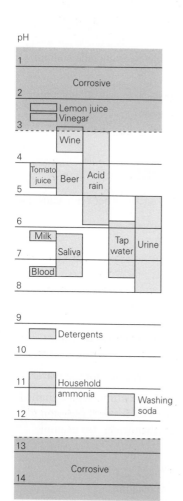

Figure 4.3   **pH values of strong and weak acids and alkalis**

relationship is true for strong and weak bases. Weak bases only release low concentrations of hydroxide ions.

$$NH_3(aq) + H_2O(aq) \rightleftharpoons NH_4^+(aq) + OH^-(aq)$$

In Topic 14 we shall look at the quantitative basis of the Brønsted–Lowry theory.

## 4.2   The chemists' toolkit: solution concentration

In Topic 1 we introduced amounts in moles and molar masses. This is fine for solids and pure liquids, but it is often far more convenient to carry out reactions in aqueous solution. Reactions between ionic compounds often only work in solution, where the ions are mobile and able to interact successfully. Some compounds, such as hydrogen chloride and ammonia, are gases at room temperature, and are therefore only usually found in a laboratory in solution.

We have already seen that **the mole is the standard unit of amount in chemistry**, so it is perhaps not surprising that the concentration of solutions is measured by how many moles ($n$) of the substance are present in a given volume. The standard volume in chemistry is one cubic decimetre, written as $1\,dm^3$, but in measuring out solutions in the laboratory it is much more convenient to measure in $cm^3$ ($V$). Concentrations are measured in moles per cubic decimetre, $mol\,dm^{-3}$, and these units are usually abbreviated to M.

**Thus a solution containing 2.00 mol of solute per cubic decimetre of solution is described as having a concentration of $2.00\,mol\,dm^{-3}$, or simply 2.00 M.** We can also use the word 'molar' to indicate concentration, so this particular solution would be described as being 2.00 molar.

When we wish to refer to a compound in a solution of known concentration, the way to write it down is to enclose the formula in square brackets, [ ]. For example, the concentration of a solution of sodium carbonate containing 1.50 moles in one cubic decimetre of solution would be written as:

$$[Na_2CO_3(aq)] = 1.50\,mol\,dm^{-3} = 1.50\,M$$

Since two moles of sodium ions and one mole of carbonate ions are set free into solution for each mole of sodium carbonate used, it follows that the concentration of sodium ions is 3.00 M and that of the carbonate ions is 1.50 M:

$$[Na^+(aq)] = 3.00\,M \quad \text{and} \quad [CO_3^{2-}(aq)] = 1.50\,M$$

The majority of solutions are aqueous, meaning that water is the solvent, but, of course, solutions can be made up in any solvent, providing the solute dissolves in it.

> **COMMENT**
>
> A relationship you can use is
>
> $$c\;(mol\,dm^{-3}) = \frac{1000\,n\;(moles)}{V\;(cm^3)}$$

> **COMMENT**
>
> M is an abbreviation for '$mol\,dm^{-3}$'. It is *not* short for 'mole'.

> **COMMENT**
>
> The approximate concentrations of some typical laboratory reagents are:
>
> | | |
> |---|---|
> | Concentrated sulphuric acid (pure) | $[H_2SO_4(l)] = 18\,M$ |
> | Concentrated nitric acid | $[HNO_3(l)] = 16\,M$ |
> | Concentrated hydrochloric acid | $[HCl(aq)] = 10\,M$ |
> | Dilute acids, e.g. dilute sulphuric acid | $[H_2SO_4(aq)] = 1\,M$ |
> | Dilute alkalis, e.g. dilute sodium hydroxide | $[NaOH(aq)] = 0.4\,M$ |

# Making a 'standard' solution of known concentration

It is possible to prepare a solution with a known concentration, and to do this we use a volumetric flask, sometimes known also as a standard or graduated flask. Flasks range in size from $50 \, cm^3$ to $5000 \, cm^3$, depending on the volume of solution required.

A solution of known concentration is made by weighing out the appropriate mass of the solute, often a solid, dissolving it in a small volume of solvent in a beaker and transferring the solution to a graduated flask. The beaker has to be washed with additional pure solvent to make sure no solute is left behind. Finally more solvent is added to 'make up to the mark'. The flask is stoppered and then inverted several times to make sure that the solution is well mixed.

For example, assume that you wish to make $250 \, cm^3$ of an aqueous solution of sodium carbonate, $Na_2CO_3$, containing $0.800 \, mol \, dm^{-3}$.

Since only $250 \, cm^3$ of solution are required, you need:

$$\left(\frac{250}{1000}\right) \times 0.800 = 0.200 \, mol$$

Next the molar mass of sodium carbonate is needed:

| | | |
|---|---|---|
| Na | $2 \times 23$ | 46 |
| C | | 12 |
| O | $3 \times 16$ | 48 |
| | | $\overline{106} \, g \, mol^{-1}$ |

$0.200 \, mol$ of sodium carbonate weighs $0.200 \times 106 = 21.2 \, g$, and so the mass to weigh out accurately is $21.2 \, g$. When this is dissolved in exactly $250 \, cm^3$ of solution, this results in a **standard solution** of sodium carbonate of concentration $0.800 \, M$.

## BACKGROUND

You are not often expected to make up your own standard solutions, but it is helpful to understand the procedure used.

## QUESTIONS

1   Calculate the number of moles of:
    a   sodium hydroxide in $25 \, cm^3$ of $1.5 \, mol \, dm^{-3}$ sodium hydroxide solution
    b   sodium carbonate in $10 \, cm^3$ of $3.0 \, mol \, dm^{-3}$ sodium carbonate solution.

2   Calculate the mass of:
    a   hydrogen chloride in $500 \, cm^3$ of $2 \, M$ hydrochloric acid
    b   ammonia present in $20 \, cm^3$ of a solution of $8 \, M$ ammonia.

3   Calculate the concentration in $mol \, dm^{-3}$ of:
    a   a solution made by dissolving $2.92 \, g$ of sodium chloride in $400 \, cm^3$ of solution
    b   a solution which contains $6.95 \, g$ of hydrated iron(II) sulphate, $FeSO_4.7H_2O$, in $250 \, cm^3$.

# Titrations

It may be necessary to find the concentration of a substance in a solution. For example, if a river has been contaminated with acidic material, environmental authorities will need to analyse a sample to find out the concentration of acid in the water. One way to do this is to react a certain volume of the river water with an alkali to find out the volume of alkali required to neutralise the sample.

Finding out the volume ratio in which two solutions react is carried out using a technique known as 'titration', and the usual laboratory process involves the use of a burette, a pipette, and a conical flask. It is important to realise that titrations can be carried out with any two solutions which react together. The only requirement is that there should be a method of determining when one solution has completely reacted with the other.

In the case of a titration between an acid and an alkali, it is usual to fill the burette with the acid, and have the alkali in the conical flask. An indicator is used to detect the 'end-point' of the reaction. Two common indicators used in titrations are methyl orange and phenolphthalein, though there are others which you will find in table 6.6 of the *Book of data*.

|  | Methyl orange | Phenolphthalein |
|---|---|---|
| In alkali (in the flask) | yellow | pink |
| At the end-point | orange | *just* colourless |
| In acid | red | colourless |

# Titration procedure

Assume that you have a solution of sulphuric acid of unknown concentration and a **standard** solution of sodium hydroxide. The titration procedure is as follows: the burette is rinsed with pure water and then with a small amount of the solution with which it is going to be filled, in this case, the sulphuric acid. Then the burette is filled up to a specific graduation mark with more of the acid, ensuring that the jet at the base of the burette contains no air bubbles.

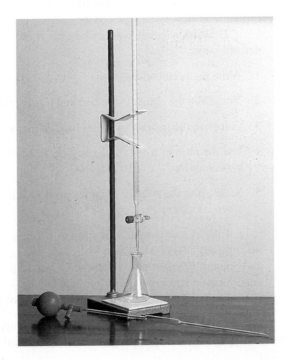

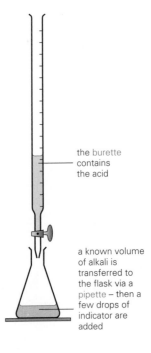

the burette contains the acid

a known volume of alkali is transferred to the flask via a pipette – then a few drops of indicator are added

Figure 4.4   **A photograph and a drawing of the titration of an alkali with an acid**

Secondly, a pipette is rinsed with a small amount of the solution which is going to be used, in this case, the sodium hydroxide solution. This pipette is used to transfer a known volume of the sodium hydroxide solution to a clean conical flask, using a pipette-filler for safety. The usual size of pipette is one of capacity $10.0 \, cm^3$, but a $20.0 \, cm^3$ or $25.0 \, cm^3$ pipette can be used instead. Next, one or two drops of indicator are added to the alkali in the flask and mixed well.

The acid is now run in from the burette, with continual swirling of the flask to ensure thorough mixing, until there is a sudden change in colour. With methyl orange the change should be from yellow to orange, but it is easy to 'overshoot' the end-point, and the colour of the mixture will be red.

Note the reading on the burette. This volume is almost certainly inaccurate, but represents a useful 'range-finder', so that next time you know when to proceed more carefully and add the acid drop by drop.

The mixture in the flask is disposed of, the flask washed with pure water and a fresh volume of alkali is transferred to the flask using the pipette and filler. One or two drops of indicator are added again, and the titration is repeated. This time you must proceed rather more cautiously as the end-point nears. It should be possible to add the acid from the burette drop by drop, until there is a sudden colour change to orange (one drop is about $0.05 \, cm^3$).

On this second occasion, it should be possible to find the volume of acid required more precisely. The burette reading is taken for the second time, and you have now established the volume of acid required to neutralise all the alkali in the flask.

This titration is repeated again, so as to obtain a minimum of two consistent readings; that is, volume readings which agree to within $0.1 \, cm^3$.

## Titration calculations

There are mathematical formulae which can be used to help with titration calculations. However, it is very likely that you will not remember their exact format. The step-by-step procedure outlined below will always work.

Titration calculations *are* straightforward, provided you follow five well-defined steps:

1 Write the balanced equation.

2 Note from the equation the reacting ratio of the reacting species.

3 Calculate the number of moles used of the standard solution.

4 Use the ratio to work out the number of moles in the sample of unknown concentration.

5 Scale up to the number of moles per $1000 \, cm^3$. Convert to grams per $1000 \, cm^3$ when necessary.

Take as an example, a titration in which a $25.0 \, cm^3$ pipette was used to measure out a $0.060 \, M$ sodium hydroxide standard solution. Assume that the end-point of the titration was reached when $12.8 \, cm^3$ of sulphuric acid of unknown concentration had been added from the burette.

The aim is to calculate the concentration of the sulphuric acid.

A good start is to draw a sketch of the titration apparatus and label it with the data you are given. It usually helps to be able to visualise a problem.

1   **Write the balanced equation for the reaction between sodium hydroxide and sulphuric acid.**

$$2NaOH(aq) + H_2SO_4(aq) \longrightarrow Na_2SO_4(aq) + 2H_2O(l)$$

2   **Use the equation to deduce the mole ratio in which sodium hydroxide and sulphuric acid react.**

A 2:1 ratio in this case.

3   **Calculate the number of moles of the standard solution used in the titration, in this case the number of moles measured out by the pipette.**
Since the sodium hydroxide solution has a concentration of 0.060 M this means that 1000 cm$^3$ of sodium hydroxide solution contains 0.060 mol, so 25 cm$^3$ of this solution will contain:

$$\left(\frac{25}{1000}\right) dm^3 \times 0.060 \ mol \ dm^{-3} = 0.0015 \ mol$$

4   **Calculate the number of moles of the other substance used, in this case the number of moles of H$_2$SO$_4$ run in from the burette.**
Since we know that the mole ratio of NaOH to H$_2$SO$_4$ is 2:1 and that 0.0015 mol of sodium hydroxide was used (stage 3), the number of moles of sulphuric acid required must have been:

$$\tfrac{1}{2} \times 0.0015 \ mol = 0.00075 \ mol$$

5   **Calculate the concentration of the other substance used.**
0.000 75 mol of sulphuric acid must have been in the 12.8 cm$^3$ of acid run in from the burette. To determine its concentration in mol dm$^{-3}$ we must calculate how much acid there was in 1000 cm$^3$:

$$[H_2SO_4(aq)] = 0.00075 \ mol \div \left(\frac{12.8}{1000}\right) dm^3$$

$$= 0.0586 \ mol \ dm^{-3} \ (0.059 \ M \ to \ 2 \ significant \ figures)$$

To calculate the concentration of acid in g dm$^{-3}$, the molar mass of H$_2$SO$_4$ is needed (98 g mol$^{-1}$). So

$$[H_2SO_4] = 98 \ g \ mol^{-1} \times 0.0586 \ mol \ dm^{-3}$$

$$= 5.74 \ g \ dm^{-3} \ (5.7 \ g \ dm^{-3} \ to \ 2 \ significant \ figures)$$

**All titration calculations can be carried out in a similar fashion, however complicated the reaction.** Always start your calculation by considering the substance for which you know the volume and the concentration (stage 3). Together with the equation and mole ratio (stages 1 and 2) you will be able to work out the number of moles of the other substance, and then you can calculate whatever the question demands.

Titration calculations need lots of practice and you will find several examples in the end-of-topic questions.

# The solubility of calcium hydroxide

We can use an acid–base neutralisation reaction to measure the solubility of calcium hydroxide.

TOPIC 4

# To find the solubility of calcium hydroxide in water by titration

**SAFETY**

Calcium hydroxide is strongly alkaline.
Wear eye protection.

## Procedure

1   Put about $100\,cm^3$ of pure water in a conical flask and add one spatula measure of solid calcium hydroxide (irritating to eyes). Fit the flask with a cork or rubber stopper and agitate the mixture thoroughly. Allow the mixture to stand for at least 24 hours so that the water becomes saturated with the calcium hydroxide.

     Carefully decant the solution into a filter funnel and filter paper over a second conical flask, so as to collect the saturated solution of calcium hydroxide. Measure the temperature of the solution obtained.

2   Titrate $10.0\,cm^3$ portions of this solution with $0.050\,M$ hydrochloric acid, using methyl orange as indicator. Repeat the titrations until two successive results agree to within $0.1\,cm^3$. If you are not familiar with how to use a burette and pipette, ask for help.

✎   **In your notes:** Write a short account of the procedure for this experiment and record your results in a table like the one below. Carry out the calculation set out below either with your own results, or with those shown here.

Titration of $10.0\,cm^3$ portions of saturated calcium hydroxide solution with $0.050\,M$ hydrochloric acid solution

|  | Range-finding titration /cm³ | Run 1 /cm³ | Run 2 /cm³ |
|---|---|---|---|
| **Second** burette reading | 9.60 | 9.30 | 18.50 |
| **First** burette reading | 0.00 | 0.00 | 9.30 |
| Volume delivered | 9.60 | 9.30 | 9.20 |
| Volume of acid used | 9.60 | 9.30 | 9.20 |

## Calculation

1   Write the equation for the reaction between calcium hydroxide and hydrochloric acid, checking the formulae and balancing carefully.

2   Use this equation to deduce how many moles of calcium hydroxide reacted with one mole of hydrochloric acid.

3   From the average volume of $0.050\,M$ hydrochloric acid used, calculate the number of moles of hydrochloric acid used in the titration.

4   This number of moles of calcium hydroxide must have been in $10.0\,cm^3$, so how many moles of calcium hydroxide would have been in $1000\,cm^3$?

5   From this, calculate the mass of calcium hydroxide in $1000\,cm^3$ of saturated solution. You will need to look up the molar mass of calcium hydroxide, or of the elements it contains.

6   Complete the sentence: 'The solubility of calcium hydroxide is therefore … $g\,dm^{-3}$ at … °C.'

COMMENT

The solubility of most substances varies with temperature, so the temperature of the saturated solution of calcium hydroxide should be recorded along with its solubility.

# 4.3 The properties of the alkaline earth elements

**Group 2:**

- Beryllium, Be
- Magnesium, Mg
- Calcium, Ca
- Strontium, Sr
- Barium, Ba
- Radium, Ra

In this first section on Group 2 you will be gathering some information about the alkaline earth metals (excluding radium), and then trying to find any trends that might exist in their properties.

 **In your notes:** The information is best recorded in your notebook in a series of tables. Suggested table formats are given as you work through this section. Questions are given after each blank table; you should write the answers to these questions in your notebook after your own table, in such a way as to make clear what the questions were.

## The physical appearance of the elements

> **COMMENT**
>
> The *Book of data* gives these temperatures in kelvins. To change them to °C, subtract 273 from the kelvin value.

Draw up a table like the one shown below. Describe the appearance of each element, using samples of the elements where possible. Look up the melting points and boiling points and the densities of the elements in table 5.2 in the *Book of data* and record these.

| Element | Appearance | Melting point/°C | Boiling point/°C | Density/g cm$^{-3}$ |
|---|---|---|---|---|
| Beryllium | | | | |
| Magnesium | | | | |
| Calcium | | | | |
| Strontium | | | | |
| Barium | | | | |

 **In your notes:** What trends are there in these physical properties of the metals?

> **COMMENT**
>
> A trend is a general direction, or a tendency. The melting points of the Group 1 alkali metals get lower going from lithium to caesium, so the *trend* is for melting points to get lower going down the group.

Figure 4.5   **Barium, an element of Group 2. Why is barium stored under oil but magnesium is not? What other metals are stored in this way?**

# The radii of the atoms and ions of the elements

COMMENT

1 nm = $10^{-9}$ metre

Use a table like the one given below. Look up the atomic and ionic radii, and the formulae of the ions, in the *Book of data*. Use the value $r_m$, radius of an atom in the metal, for the first quantity, and $r_i$, the radius of the ion, for the second. Note that the values are given in nanometres, nm.

| Element | Atomic radius $(r_m)$ /nm | Cation formed | Radius of cation $(r_i)$ /nm | Electronic structure of the atoms (from Topic 3) |
|---------|---------|---------|---------|---------|
| Beryllium | 0.112 | $Be^{2+}$ | 0.027 | |
| | | | | |

 **In your notes:** What generalisation can be made about the size of the ions of these metals, relative to the size of their atoms, and the trends down the group?

The relative sizes of these atoms and ions are shown in figure 4.6.

# The reactions of the metals with oxygen and with water

Your teacher will show you the reactions of some of these metals with oxygen and with water (or steam for magnesium), or you may be able to carry out some of the experiments yourself. Students no longer handle beryllium because it is so toxic.

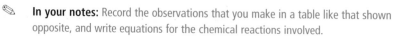 **In your notes:** Record the observations that you make in a table like that shown opposite, and write equations for the chemical reactions involved.

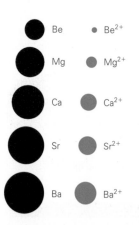

Figure 4.6   **Scale drawings showing the relative sizes of the atoms and ions of the elements of Group 2 (scale 1 mm = 0.04 nm)**

| Element | Reaction with water | Reaction with oxygen |
|---|---|---|
| | | |
| | | |

✎  **In your notes:** What trends are noticeable in the vigour of these reactions?

---

### COMMENT

The equation for the reaction of calcium with water is:

$$Ca(s) + 2H_2O(l) \longrightarrow Ca(OH)_2(aq) + H_2(g)$$

This is typical of the alkaline earth metals.
Magnesium burns in oxygen (or air) to give magnesium oxide:

$$2Mg(s) + O_2(g) \longrightarrow 2MgO(s)$$

The other Group 2 metals react similarly.

---

## 4.4 Some compounds of the elements of Group 2

In this section you will study the properties of oxides, some salts and the action of heat on the carbonates and nitrates.

### EXPERIMENT 4.4a

## The action of water on some Group 2 oxides

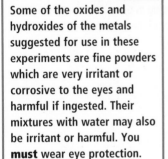

**SAFETY**

Some of the oxides and hydroxides of the metals suggested for use in these experiments are fine powders which are very irritant or corrosive to the eyes and harmful if ingested. Their mixtures with water may also be irritant or harmful. You **must** wear eye protection.

Oxides of metals are normally basic, and so they react with acids to give salts. When a basic oxide is mixed with water, it is possible that it may react to form a hydroxide, and when the hydroxide is soluble, the solution will be alkaline.

### Procedure

1  To a **tiny** spatula sample of calcium oxide add about 5 cm$^3$ of pure water. Find the pH of the mixture, using Full-range Indicator paper.  Then add 1 M hydrochloric acid until the mixture is just acidic. Enter the result in a table like the one that follows.

| Name of oxide | Formula | pH of mixture with water | Observations on adding 1 M hydrochloric acid |
|---|---|---|---|
| | | | |
| | | | |

2  Repeat the experiment with magnesium oxide and any other Group 2 oxides available.

**In your notes:** Here are some questions about the results of the experiments. Write the answers into your notebook in such a way as to make it clear what each question was.

1   What signs were there that reactions occurred when water was added to the oxides?

2   What was the evidence that the oxides are basic?

3   Since the mixtures of the oxides with water were alkaline, hydroxides were presumably formed. Write an equation for ONE reaction of an oxide with water.

4   Write an equation for ONE of the reactions of a hydroxide with hydrochloric acid.

5   What can be said about the solubility in water of the chlorides of each of the metals whose oxides you used?

6   What differences, if any, would you expect to find if you had used dilute sulphuric acid in this experiment?

Use table 5.3 in the *Book of data* to find the solubilities of the sulphates of the metals. All the nitrates are soluble, as are the chlorides.

---

**EXPERIMENT 4.4b**

**SAFETY**

Some of these salts may also be irritant or harmful.

## Formulae and flame colours of some salts

### Procedure

Examine the chlorides and sulphates of the elements and record in a copy of the table below their appearance and chemical formulae, including any water of crystallisation.

Formulae may be printed on the labels of the bottles containing the various compounds, or they may be found from table 5.3 in the *Book of data*.

| Element | Chloride | Sulphate | Flame colour (from Topic 3) |
|---------|----------|----------|------------------------------|
|         |          |          |                              |
|         |          |          |                              |

 **In your notes:** Are all the formulae consistent with being in Group 2 of the Periodic Table? What connection is there between the tendency of these compounds to be hydrated and the positions of the metals in the group?

---

**EXPERIMENT 4.4c**

**BACKGROUND**

Experiments 4.4c and 4.4d are difficult to carry out in a laboratory. Viewing the results from a CD-ROM may be more effective.

## Heating the carbonates

You will now be looking at the effect of heat on the carbonates of the elements of Group 2, and looking for any trends that can be seen in the ease with which they decompose.

When carbonates are heated, they may decompose, and when they do, carbon dioxide is evolved and the oxide of the metal remains. Copper carbonate, for example, decomposes according to the equation:

$$CuCO_3(s) \longrightarrow CuO(s) + CO_2(g)$$

**SAFETY**

Barium carbonate is harmful.

## Procedure

Devise and use a technique for estimating the comparative readiness with which the carbonates of the Group 2 elements decompose. Record your results in the form of a table.

| Carbonate | Effect | Ionic radius of cation/nm |
|-----------|--------|---------------------------|
| $MgCO_3$  |        |                           |
| $CaCO_3$  |        |                           |
| $SrCO_3$  |        |                           |
| $BaCO_3$  |        |                           |

✎ **In your notes:** There is a connection between the trend of behaviour down the group and the ionic radius of the cation. Discuss with your teacher the reasons for the connection and record in your notebook the outcome of your discussion.

Write an equation for one of the decompositions that took place.

---

**EXPERIMENT 4.4d**

## Heating the nitrates

When metal nitrates decompose, one of two things can happen:

1  Oxygen is evolved and the nitrite of the metal (containing the ion $NO_2^-$) is formed.

2  Oxygen and the brown gas nitrogen dioxide are evolved and the oxide of the metal remains. Lead nitrate, for example, decomposes according to the equation

$$2Pb(NO_3)_2(s) \longrightarrow 2PbO(s) + 4NO_2(g) + O_2(g)$$

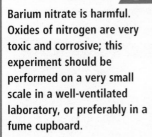

**SAFETY**

Barium nitrate is harmful. Oxides of nitrogen are very toxic and corrosive; this experiment should be performed on a very small scale in a well-ventilated laboratory, or preferably in a fume cupboard.

## Procedure

Investigate the effect of heat on the nitrates of the Group 2 elements, planning your own experiment. Get your teacher to check your plans.

✎ **In your notes:** Draw up a similar table to the one that you made for the carbonates and, once again, compare the results with the trends in the ionic radii of the metal ions. Write equations for any decompositions that took place.

## 4.5    Background reading: the role of calcium in agriculture

---

### QUESTIONS

Read the passage below in order to answer the following questions.

1    Why are calcium compounds added to agricultural land?

2    How does the soil pH affect the growth of plants?

3    Summarise the information about the effect of soil pH on the growth of particular plants.

4    Explain how the calcium content of soil can vary.

---

Calcium compounds are the principal factor in controlling the pH of the soil. Soil pH affects the ability of plants to absorb nutrients because it affects both the concentration of nutrients in the soil solution and the growth of roots.

For example at a pH of about 5 the concentrations of aluminium and manganese (generally toxic to plant roots) are higher than at a pH of 7. However, some plants grow best at a low soil pH and are checked at higher values. Tea is a well-known example of a crop which thrives in very acid soils and it contains far more aluminium than most plants.

Some species of forest trees do not thrive in soils of high pH. Sitka Spruce, for example, was found to make the best growth at pH 5 and failed to grow well on neutral and alkaline soils, but growth was depressed below pH 5 – a narrow range of optimum pH. On the other hand, sugar beet does not grow well under acid conditions and the optimum pH for this crop is around 6.5 to 7.0.

Crops are roughly graded in their tolerance for soil acidity: lucerne, sugar beet and barley are only considered suitable for neutral soils (pH 7.0 to 6.5); wheat grows well on slightly acid soils (pH 6.5 to 6.0); and potatoes and rye prefer soils of pH 5.0 – too acid for sugar beet and barley.

Rain water, which contains carbonic acid, $H_2CO_3$, leads, as it percolates through the soil, to the replacement of cations such as $Ca^{2+}$ by $H^+$ and so to soil acidification (the more exchangeable $H^+$ present, the more acid the soil). Fertilisers such as ammonium sulphate, $(NH_4)_2SO_4$, are also involved in cation exchange with calcium.

$$Ca^{2+}\text{-soil} + 2NH_4^+(aq) \longrightarrow (NH_4^+)_2\text{-soil} + Ca^{2+}(aq)$$

The $NH_4^+$ ions held in the soil are converted first to $NO_2^-$ and then to $NO_3^-$ as the result of bacterial action. Hydrogen ions are produced simultaneously to balance these anions and these replace ammonium ions in the exchange complex, making the soil more acid.

Calcium is an essential plant nutrient. Exchangeable calcium and other ions are removed from the soil by growing crops. Some examples of the quantities involved are given in the following table (1 hectare = 10 000 m².)

| Crop | Yield /tonnes ha$^{-1}$ | Calcium removed /kg ha$^{-1}$ | Magnesium removed /kg ha$^{-1}$ |
|---|---|---|---|
| Potatoes | 50 | 10 | 7 |
| Hay | 10 | 70 | 25 |
| Wheat (grain) | 8 | 25 | 18 |

Except in chalk soils, the weathering of mineral fragments in the soil is generally not enough to replace the calcium that is lost in these various ways, and the deficiency has to be made good by the addition of compounds such as calcium hydroxide (slaked lime) or calcium carbonate (ground limestone) – a process, therefore, known as 'liming'.

Figure 4.7    Barley on an unlimed plot: the soil has a low calcium content; it has become acid in reaction and the barley crop has failed. The neighbouring plot has been well limed, has a good calcium content and a pH of about 6.5; the barley crop is doing well

# KEY SKILLS

## Application of number

A titration is a complex activity which breaks down into a series of tasks. Once you have learnt the practical skills you can use a titration in an investigation which involves planning, interpreting information, carrying out multi-stage calculations, working to appropriate levels of accuracy, interpreting results and presenting findings.

The study of Group 2 elements gives you an opportunity to gather numerical information from different sources and then present your findings in ways which show trends and make comparisons.

# TOPIC REVIEW

In Topic 4, some of the terms and ideas that you learnt in Topics 1 and 3 have been incorporated into the study of acid–base theory and Group 2 elements, for example, the use of ionic equations. This emphasises the way in which chemical knowledge constantly builds and how important it is to have a secure understanding of one topic before moving on to another.

1   **List key words or terms with definitions**

Make sure that you **give examples or equations** where appropriate.

- acid, base
- oxonium ion
- strong and weak acids and bases
- standard solution
- titration, neutralisation

2   **Summarise the key principles as simply as possible**

Once again many of the ideas to be understood involve **recognising patterns of behaviour**.

You must know:

- what all acid–base reactions have in common
- how to find the concentration of a given acid or base using a standard solution (this includes the practical work and the subsequent processing of the results collected)
- some important uses of Group 2 compounds.

You must be able to:

- use evidence/data to describe trends in the chemistry of Group 2 metals (utilising ideas learnt in Topics 1 and 3).

# REVIEW QUESTIONS

**✱** Indicates that the *Book of data* is needed.

**4.1**   **a**   Explain why $H^+$ is a correct representation of a proton. (2)

**b**   'Bare', uncombined protons are thought unlikely to exist in aqueous solutions. Suggest a reason for this and state what is likely to happen to any such protons. (2)

**(4 marks)**

**4.2**   Write equations for the donation of one proton to one molecule of water by each of the following acids:

**a**   nitric acid, $HNO_3$ (1)
**b**   sulphuric acid, $H_2SO_4$ (1)
**c**   hydrogensulphate ion, $HSO_4^-$ (1)
**d**   phosphoric acid, $H_3PO_4$ (1)
**e**   methanoic acid, $HCO_2H$ (the final H provides the donated proton) (1)
**f**   carbonic acid, $H_2CO_3$. (1)

**(6 marks)**

**4.3**   Identify the acids and the bases on the left-hand side of each of the following equations:

**a**   $HCN(g) + H_2O(l) \rightleftharpoons H_3O^+(aq) + CN^-(aq)$ (2)
**b**   $NH_4^+(aq) + H_2O(l) \rightleftharpoons H_3O^+(aq) + NH_3(aq)$ (2)
**c**   $HCO_3^-(aq) + H_3O^+(aq) \rightleftharpoons H_2CO_3(aq) + H_2O(l)$ (2)
**d**   $HCO_3^-(aq) + H_2O(l) \rightleftharpoons H_3O^+(aq) + CO_3^{2-}(aq)$ (2)
**e**   $H_2O(l) + H_2PO_4^-(aq) \rightleftharpoons HPO_4^{2-}(aq) + H_3O^+(aq)$ (2)
**f**   $NH_4^+ + NH_2^- \rightleftharpoons NH_3 + NH_3$ (2)
(in liquid ammonia) **(12 marks)**

**4.4**   Write balanced equations, including state symbols, for the reactions which occur between the following pairs of substances under standard laboratory conditions:

**a**   barium and oxygen (2)
**b**   strontium and chlorine (2)
**c**   calcium and water (2)
**d**   barium hydroxide solution and dilute sulphuric acid (2)
**e**   a precipitate of strontium hydroxide and dilute nitric acid. (2)

**(10 marks)**

**✱ 4.5**   **a**   Some compounds undergo thermal decomposition when heated. Explain the meaning of this term. (1)

**b**   Write balanced equations, with state symbols, for the thermal decomposition of:
  **i** strontium carbonate (2)
  **ii** anhydrous magnesium nitrate (2)
  **iii** magnesium nitrate-6-water. (1)

**(6 marks)**

**\* 4.6**    What mass of each of the following is dissolved in 250 cm$^3$ of a solution of concentration 0.100 mol dm$^{-3}$?

    **a**    hydrochloric acid, HCl    (2)
    **b**    sulphuric acid, $H_2SO_4$    (2)
    **c**    sodium hydroxide, NaOH    (2)
    **d**    potassium manganate(VII), $KMnO_4$    (2)
    **e**    sodium thiosulphate-5-water, $Na_2S_2O_3.5H_2O$    (2)

    **(10 marks)**

**\* 4.7**    How many moles of each solute are contained in the following solutions? Give your answers to three significant figures.

    **a**    25.0 cm$^3$ of 0.100 M sodium chloride    (2)
    **b**    10.0 cm$^3$ of 2.00 M sodium hydroxide    (2)
    **c**    20.0 cm$^3$ of 0.050 M sulphuric acid    (2)
    **d**    17.5 cm$^3$ of 0.200 M nitric acid    (2)
    **e**    30.0 cm$^3$ of 0.040 M barium hydroxide.    (2)

    **(10 marks)**

**\* 4.8**    What is the concentration, in mol dm$^{-3}$, of each of the following solutions?

    **a**    5.85 g of sodium chloride, NaCl, in 100 cm$^3$ of solution    (2)
    **b**    1.70 g of silver nitrate, $AgNO_3$, in 250 cm$^3$ of solution    (2)
    **c**    3.16 g of potassium manganate(VII), $KMnO_4$, in 2.00 dm$^3$ of solution    (2)
    **d**    5.04 g of ethanedioic acid, $H_2C_2O_4.2H_2O$ in 500 cm$^3$ of solution    (2)
    **e**    7.15 g of sodium carbonate, $Na_2CO_3.10H_2O$, in 250 cm$^3$ of solution.    (2)

    **(10 marks)**

**\* 4.9**    **a**    Use the *Book of data* to find the density of pure nitric acid, $HNO_3$. Include the units.    (1)
    **b**    Use the density and molar mass to calculate the volume of 1 mole of pure nitric acid.    (2)
    **c**    What volume of pure nitric acid would you need to measure out in order to prepare 250 cm$^3$ of 1.0 M nitric acid?    (1)

    **d**    What pieces of apparatus would you use to measure:
      **i**  the pure nitric acid    (1)
      **ii**  the 250 cm$^3$ of solution?    (1)

    **(6 marks)**

**\* 4.10**    Using the same sequence of operations as in question **4.9**, calculate the volume of pure sulphuric acid, $H_2SO_4$, you would need to prepare 5 dm$^3$ of 1.0 M sulphuric acid.

    **(4 marks)**

**✻ 4.11**  Calculate the concentration, in $mol\,dm^{-3}$, of the following. (Assume that all the compounds are fully ionised.)

a  hydrogen ions in $1.00\,dm^3$ of solution containing 3.65 g of hydrogen chloride (2)

b  barium ions in $1.00\,dm^3$ of solution containing 17.1 g of barium hydroxide, $Ba(OH)_2$ (2)

c  hydroxide ions in the solution in **b** (2)

d  sulphate ions in a solution of aluminium sulphate-12-water, $Al_2(SO_4)_3.12H_2O$ of concentration $0.1\,mol\,dm^{-3}$ (2)

e  aluminium ions in the solution in **d**. (2)

**(10 marks)**

**✻ 4.12**  $10.0\,cm^3$ of a saturated solution of strontium hydroxide at 20 °C was exactly neutralised by $13.0\,cm^3$ of 0.100 M hydrochloric acid in a titration.

a  What indicator would be suitable for the titration and what would be its colour change? (2)

b  Write a balanced equation for the reaction. (2)

c  Calculate the number of moles of HCl in $13.0\,cm^3$ of 0.100 M solution. (1)

d  Use your answers to **b** and **c** to calculate the number of moles of strontium hydroxide in the $10.0\,cm^3$ of saturated solution. (2)

e  Hence, calculate the concentration, in $mol\,dm^{-3}$, of the saturated solution of strontium hydroxide. (1)

f  Calculate the solubility (at 20 °C) of strontium hydroxide in $g\,dm^{-3}$. (2)

**(10 marks)**

**4.13**  In a similar experiment to that described in question **4.12**, $25.0\,cm^3$ of another saturated solution of strontium hydroxide (also at 20 °C) was exactly neutralised by $16.3\,cm^3$ of 0.100 M sulphuric acid.

Write a balanced equation for the reaction and carry out a similar sequence of calculations to determine another value for the solubility of strontium hydroxide at 20 °C. **(8 marks)**

**4.14**  You should begin each of the following questions by writing a balanced equation for the reaction concerned.

a  Calculate the volume of 0.10 M hydrochloric acid needed to neutralise $20.0\,cm^3$ of 0.050 M sodium hydroxide. (3)

b  Calculate the volume of 0.050 M nitric acid needed to neutralise $25.0\,cm^3$ of 0.08 M potassium hydroxide. (3)

c  Calculate the volume of 0.020 M sulphuric acid needed to neutralise $50.0\,cm^3$ of 0.010 M sodium hydroxide. (3)

d  $10.0\,cm^3$ of a solution of sodium hydroxide was neutralised by $12.5\,cm^3$ of 0.10 M HCl. Calculate the concentration, in $mol\,dm^{-3}$, of the alkali. (3)

e  $25.0\,cm^3$ of a 0.050 M solution of sodium hydroxide was neutralised by $20.0\,cm^3$ of sulphuric acid. Calculate the concentration, in $mol\,dm^{-3}$, of the acid. (3)

**(15 marks)**

# EXAMINATION QUESTIONS

Questions of the summary and comprehension type are found in the background reading section (section 4.5).

**4.15**    Beryllium and barium are in the same group in the Periodic Table.

a    What is the electronic configuration, in terms of s, p and d electrons, of:
  i   the beryllium atom    (1)
  ii  the barium atom?    (1)

b   i   What is the formula for a barium ion in its compounds?    (1)
  ii  Explain, in terms of ionisation energies, the ionic charge of barium in its compounds.    (1)

c   i   Which of the two elements has the higher first ionisation energy? Give a reason for this.    (2)
  ii  Would their ions be smaller or larger than their atoms? Give a reason for this.    (2)

**(8 marks)**

**4.16**    Strontium oxide is made from the mineral celestine (which contains strontium sulphate) by strongly heating it with carbon to form a sulphide.

$$SrSO_4(s) + 4C(s) \longrightarrow SrS(s) + 4CO(g)$$

The sulphide formed is reacted with sodium hydroxide solution.

$$SrS(s) + 2NaOH(aq) \longrightarrow Sr(OH)_2(s) + Na_2S(aq)$$

Sodium sulphide is removed with water, and thermal decomposition of the strontium hydroxide is used to produce the oxide.

a    Suggest ONE safety precaution which should be taken when heating celestine with carbon in the laboratory. Give a reason for the precaution.    (2)

b    Outline the practical procedure you would use to remove sodium sulphide and obtain pure, dry strontium oxide.    (3)

c   i   Write a balanced equation, including state symbols, for the thermal decomposition of strontium hydroxide.    (2)
  ii  1.3 g of strontium oxide was obtained from 4.6 g of strontium sulphate. Calculate the percentage yield.    (3)

d   i   Write out the electronic configuration of a strontium atom in its ground state.    (1)
  ii  How does the electronic configuration of a strontium ion differ from that of a strontium atom?    (1)
  iii Draw a 'dot and cross' diagram to show the electronic structure of strontium oxide, showing only the outer electron shells.    (1)

e   i   Using a sample of strontium oxide, what procedure would you use to observe the flame colour of strontium?    (2)
  ii  What is the flame colour of strontium?    (1)
  iii What is the origin of flame colours?    (2)

f    Strontium hydroxide is slightly soluble in water, giving a solution containing hydroxide ions. Both water and hydroxide ions are Brønsted–Lowry bases. Give the formulae for the species formed when each accepts a proton.    (2)

**(20 marks)**

**4.17**  **a**  What mass, in grams, of methanoic acid, $HCO_2H$, would be needed to make $100\ cm^3$ of a solution of concentration $1.0\ mol\ dm^{-3}$? (2)

**b**  Write a balanced equation, including state symbols, showing the ions which form when methanoic acid dissolves in water. (2)

**c**  In a solution of methanoic acid of concentration $1\ mol\ dm^{-3}$, between 1% and 2% of the acid molecules donate protons to the water. What does this indicate about the strength of methanoic acid? (1)

**(5 marks)**

**4.18**  A student carried out an experiment to try to find the concentration of a sample of concentrated sulphuric acid supplied by a chemical manufacturer.

**a**  $1.00\ cm^3$ of the acid was added to pure water and then diluted to a total volume of $250\ cm^3$.
Suggest suitable apparatus which could have been used to measure the $250\ cm^3$ of solution. (1)

**b**  The student then measured out $25.0\ cm^3$ portions of this diluted acid and titrated them with $0.200\ M$ sodium hydroxide solution, using a suitable indicator. The average volume of sodium hydroxide required was $18.5\ cm^3$.
  **i** Write a balanced equation, including state symbols, for the reaction which occurred during the titration. (1)
  **ii** Calculate the number of moles of sodium hydroxide in $18.5\ cm^3$ of the $0.200\ M$ sodium hydroxide solution. (1)
  **iii** Calculate the number of moles of sulphuric acid in $25.0\ cm^3$ of the dilute solution. (1)
  **iv** Calculate the number of moles of sulphuric acid in $1000\ cm^3$ of the original concentrated acid. (1)

**c**  'Universal Indicator' used for the first titration was found to be unsuitable.
  **i** Why is 'Universal Indicator' unsuitable for this titration? (1)
  **ii** Suggest a more suitable indicator. (1)

**d**  **i** Sulphuric acid has a density of $1.84\ g\ cm^{-3}$ and a molar mass of $98\ g\ mol^{-1}$.
Calculate the number of moles of pure sulphuric acid in $1000\ cm^3$. (1)
  **ii** Compare the answer with your answer to **b iv** and suggest a reason for any difference. (1)

**e**  Chemists believe that dilute sulphuric acid contains ions. Give ONE piece of evidence which supports this idea. (1)

**f**  **i** Phosphoric acid, $H_3PO_4$, is used industrially for making fertilisers. It is produced by the reaction between calcium phosphate, $Ca_3(PO_4)_2$, and sulphuric acid.
Write down the formulae of the ions present in calcium phosphate. (2)
  **ii** Write a balanced equation for the reaction between calcium phosphate and sulphuric acid. Calcium sulphate is produced as well as phosphoric acid. (1)
  **iii** In carrying out this process on a large scale, a company will buy raw materials as cheaply as possible, minimise operating costs and try to obtain the best possible price for the phosphoric acid.
Suggest ONE other way in which the company might try to increase profitability. (1)

**(14 marks)**

**4.19**    An impure sample of magnesium carbonate, $MgCO_3$, was dissolved in $30.0 \, cm^3$ of $0.100 \, M$ hydrochloric acid. The magnesium carbonate reacted with this acid according to the equation:

$$MgCO_3(s) + 2HCl(aq) \longrightarrow MgCl_2(aq) + CO_2(g) + H_2O(l)$$

leaving some of the acid unreacted. This excess acid was titrated with $0.100 \, M$ sodium hydroxide solution and $12.3 \, cm^3$ was required for neutralisation. The results were used to find the percentage purity of the magnesium carbonate.

a    Name a suitable indicator to use for the titration and give its colour change.    (3)

b    i    What volume of $0.100 \, M$ HCl actually reacted with the magnesium carbonate?    (1)
    ii    How many moles of hydrochloric acid were in this volume?    (1)
    iii    How many moles of magnesium carbonate reacted with this hydrochloric acid?    (1)
    iv    What mass of magnesium carbonate was in the sample?    (1)
    v    The impure sample weighed $0.124 \, g$. What was the percentage by mass of magnesium carbonate in it?    (1)

c    The carbonate ion in magnesium carbonate can be said to act as a Brønsted–Lowry base:

$$2H_3O^+(aq) + CO_3^{2-}(s) \longrightarrow 2H_2O(l) + H_2CO_3(aq)$$

The carbonic acid, $H_2CO_3$, immediately decomposes into carbon dioxide and water.
    i    Explain why the carbonate ion is regarded as a Brønsted–Lowry base.    (2)
    ii    Write an equation, with state symbols, to show how hydrogen chloride gas, HCl(g), reacts as a Brønsted–Lowry acid when it dissolves in water.    (2)

d    The hydrogencarbonate ion, $HCO_3^-$, can behave either as an acid or as a base, using the Brønsted–Lowry definitions.
    Write down the formula of the ion or molecule produced in each case.    (2)
    **(14 marks)**

**4.20**    A $0.20 \, M$ solution of calcium nitrate was added separately to $0.20 \, M$ solutions of sodium carbonate, $Na_2CO_3$, and sodium ethanedioate, $Na_2C_2O_4$.

a    Calculate the mass of hydrated calcium nitrate, $Ca(NO_3)_2.4H_2O$ that would be needed to make $100 \, cm^3$ of $0.20 \, M$ calcium nitrate solution.    (2)

b    In both cases a white precipitate was formed. Give the names of the two precipitates.    (2)

c    Write balanced ionic equations, including state symbols, for the two reactions.    (2)

d    Calculate the volume of $0.20 \, M$ sodium carbonate solution that would be needed to react completely with $20.0 \, cm^3$ of $0.20 \, M$ calcium nitrate solution.    (2)
    **(8 marks)**

# TOPIC 5

# Energy change and reactions

Figure 5.1 **Where does the energy come from?**

There is an energy change when all chemical reactions take place. In some reactions energy is absorbed by the substances involved, but more usually energy is given out, which is why a car engine becomes hot as the fuel burns, why our bodies are kept warm by the food we eat, and why fireworks become dangerously hot as they burn. **The study of these energy changes is as much a part of chemistry as the study of changes in composition or structure that result from reactions.**

In this topic you will:

- learn what is meant by **enthalpy changes** and how they can be measured
- start using the enthalpy values given in table 5.3 in the *Book of data*.

## 5.1 Energy from chemical reactions

We shall be looking at reactions for which the energy changes lead to heating or cooling rather than the production of light or electric power. Your teacher may show you some energy changes of reactions to start you thinking about energy in chemistry.

### EXPERIMENT 5.1 Measuring some energy changes

These experiments are designed to give you a first impression of how energy changes can be measured. To calculate the total energy change in a chemical reaction we need to know the amounts (in moles) that react, and we have to measure any temperature change that takes place.

You are going to look at an oxidation–reduction reaction and a neutralisation. For each reaction you have to calculate the mass of solid reagent to use. The molar amounts are stated in the procedure below. Have your calculations checked before you start the experiment.

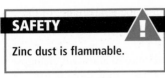

SAFETY

Zinc dust is flammable.

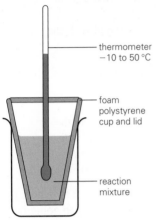

thermometer
−10 to 50 °C

foam
polystyrene
cup and lid

reaction
mixture

**Figure 5.2   A simple method of measuring energy changes**

## Procedure

### 1   The reaction between copper(II) sulphate and zinc

$$Cu^{2+}(aq) + Zn(s) \longrightarrow Cu(s) + Zn^{2+}(aq)$$

Measure $25.0\,cm^3$ of 0.2 M copper(II) sulphate solution into a well insulated container and then measure its temperature. Add 0.01 mol (an excess) of zinc powder, Zn. Stir gently and continuously and note the highest temperature reached. Work out the temperature change to the nearest 0.1 °C.

### 2   The reaction between citric acid and sodium hydrogencarbonate

$$C_6H_8O_7(aq) + 3HCO_3^-(s) \longrightarrow C_6H_5O_7^{3-}(aq) + 3CO_2(g) + 3H_2O(l)$$

Repeat part **1** using $25\,cm^3$ of 1.0 M citric acid and 0.1 mol (an excess) of sodium hydrogencarbonate, $NaHCO_3$. Record the temperature change as before.

✎   **In your notes:** Record the equations of the reactions and whether they were exothermic or endothermic.

From your results calculate the energy change in kilojoules per mole for 1.0 mol of copper(II) sulphate, $CuSO_4$, and 1.0 mol of citric acid, $C_6H_8O_7$, respectively.

## How to do the calculation

We are going to assume that all the energy produced in the reactions is exchanged between the reactants and the water in the calorimeter, and no energy is transferred to the air, the glass of the thermometer, the material of the calorimeter, or even the products of the reaction. We are also going to assume that $1\,cm^3$ of a dilute aqueous solution weighs 1 g and therefore needs 4.18 joules to change in temperature by 1 °C (as does $1\,cm^3$ of water).

The relationship we are going to use is:

$$\begin{array}{c} \text{energy exchanged between} \\ \text{reactants and surroundings, } Q/J \end{array} = \begin{array}{c} \text{specific heat capacity} \\ \text{of the solution, } c/J\,g^{-1}\,K^{-1} \end{array} \times \begin{array}{c} \text{mass of the} \\ \text{solution, } m/g \end{array} \times \begin{array}{c} \text{temperature} \\ \text{change, } \Delta T/K \end{array}$$

$$Q = cm\Delta T$$

which, with our assumptions, becomes:

$$Q = 4.18\,J\,cm^{-3}\,K^{-1} \times \text{volume of solution}/cm^3 \times \text{temperature change}/K$$

To complete the calculation you need to work out how much energy would have been exchanged if you had used 1 mol of copper(II) sulphate, $CuSO_4$, and 1 mol of citric acid, $C_6H_8O_7$.

## Recording energy changes

When we investigate energy changes, we must state the conditions under which the changes are measured, so that the results of different experiments can be compared.

The energy change that we shall be measuring in this topic is the **enthalpy change**. This can be considered as the energy that would be exchanged with the

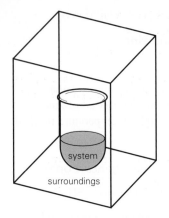

Figure 5.3 **The system is the sample or reaction mixture. Outside the system are the surroundings, which include the apparatus**

**surroundings** if the reaction occurred in such a way that the temperature of the **system** before and after the reaction were the same. **The reaction mixture is referred to as the system.**

The reaction must also take place at constant pressure to allow for changes in volume between the reactants and products, such as the carbon dioxide gas produced.

**The enthalpy change of a reaction is the energy exchanged with the surroundings at constant pressure.**

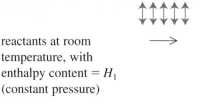

energy exchanged with the surroundings

reactants at room temperature, with enthalpy content $= H_1$ (constant pressure) $\longrightarrow$ products returned to the same temperature, with enthalpy content $= H_2$ (constant pressure)

The symbol $\Delta$ (Greek capital delta, equivalent to our D) is used to denote the change in the value of a physical quantity. So the change in enthalpy in going from reactants to products is given by:

$$\Delta H = H_2 - H_1$$

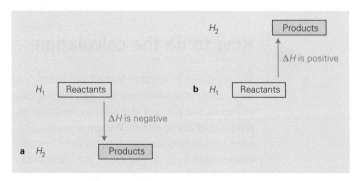

Figure 5.4 a **An exothermic reaction,** b **an endothermic reaction**

For the reaction:

$$Mg(s) + Cl_2(g) \longrightarrow MgCl_2(s) \qquad \Delta H = -641.3 \, kJ \, mol^{-1}$$

The value of $\Delta H$ is for the amounts shown in the equation, that is, for one mole of magnesium atoms, Mg, one mole of chlorine molecules, $Cl_2$, and one mole of magnesium chloride, $MgCl_2$,. Normally, a **standard** enthalpy change is quoted and it is then given the symbol $\Delta H^{\ominus}$. This means that the enthalpy change was measured in conditions fixed by convention.

**The standard enthalpy change for a reaction, symbol $\Delta H^{\ominus}$, refers to the amounts shown in the equation, at a pressure of 1 atmosphere, at a temperature of 298 K, with the substances in the physical states normal under these conditions. Solutions must have a concentration of 1 mol dm$^{-3}$.**

For the Thermit reaction and a neutralisation, for example:

$$Fe_2O_3(s) + 2Al(s) \longrightarrow 2Fe(s) + Al_2O_3(s) \quad \Delta H^{\ominus}_{reaction} = -851.5 \, kJ \, mol^{-1}$$
$$NH_3(g) + HCl(g) \longrightarrow NH_4Cl(s) \qquad \Delta H^{\ominus}_{reaction} = -176.0 \, kJ \, mol^{-1}$$

For important reactions we have a shorthand which saves us from having to write the full equation. The magnesium chloride reaction is an example; the

**COMMENT**

The standard conditions ($^{\ominus}$) for measuring enthalpy changes are:

- physical state of reagents: normal state (solid, liquid, gas) at 298 K and 1 atmosphere
- solutions: 1.0 M
- experimental conditions: the energy exchange with the surroundings is at 298 K (25 °C) and 1 atmosphere pressure

From now on $\Delta H^{\ominus}(298)$ will be referred to as $\Delta H^{\ominus}$, as all our standard values will be for 298 K.

COMMENT

The standard temperature is stated in **kelvins** (symbol K). The lowest temperature that is possible is 0 K, which is −273 °C. As the kelvin was chosen to be the same size (or temperature interval) as the degree celsius (or centigrade), it follows that

0 °C is  273 K

25 °C is  298 K

and in general $t$ °C is $(273 + t)$ K

enthalpy change is called the **standard enthalpy change of formation** of magnesium chloride. It is given the symbol $\Delta H_f^\ominus$ [MgCl$_2$(s)].

$$Mg(s) + Cl_2(g) \longrightarrow MgCl_2(s) \qquad \Delta H_f^\ominus = -641.3 \text{ kJ mol}^{-1}$$

**The standard enthalpy change of formation of a compound, symbol $\Delta H_f^\ominus$, is the enthalpy change that takes place when one mole of the compound is formed from its elements under the standard conditions.**

For example:

$$2Fe(s) + 1\tfrac{1}{2}O_2(g) \longrightarrow Fe_2O_3(s) \qquad \Delta H_f^\ominus [Fe_2O_3(s)] = -824.2 \text{ kJ mol}^{-1}$$

$$\tfrac{1}{2}H_2(g) + \tfrac{1}{2}Cl_2(g) \longrightarrow HCl(g) \qquad \Delta H_f^\ominus [HCl(g)] \;\; = -92.3 \text{ kJ mol}^{-1}$$

## 5.2 Hess's Law

As the law of conservation of energy applies to chemical processes just as much as to any other process, then, when one set of substances is converted to another set, by whatever route, the total energy change must be the same.

**The First Law of Thermodynamics states that energy is always conserved.**

If this were not so, it would be possible to go from A + B to C + D by one route and then back again by a different route with an overall gain of energy. The law of conservation of energy tells us that this is impossible: the energy change must be the same by whatever route we travel from A + B to C + D (see figure 5.5).

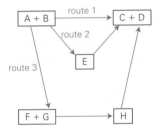

Figure 5.5    **A Hess cycle by three alternative routes**

In 1840 Germain Hess discovered this particular application of the law of conservation of energy experimentally, and it is generally referred to as **Hess's Law**.

**Hess's Law states that the total enthalpy change accompanying a chemical change is independent of the route by which the chemical change takes place.**

The correctness of Hess's Law can be illustrated by the following example. You should have determined the enthalpy change $\Delta H$ for the displacement of copper by zinc:

$$Cu^{2+}(aq) + Zn(s) \longrightarrow Cu(s) + Zn^{2+}(aq) \qquad \Delta H^\ominus = -219 \text{ kJ mol}^{-1}$$

If the copper obtained is used to displace silver from a solution of silver ions, we would find that $\Delta H$ is:

$$2Ag^+(aq) + Cu(s) \longrightarrow 2Ag(s) + Cu^{2+}(aq) \qquad \Delta H^\ominus = -146 \text{ kJ mol}^{-1}$$

But if zinc is to displace silver directly, we find that $\Delta H$ is:

$$2Ag^+(aq) + Zn(s) \longrightarrow 2Ag(s) + Zn^{2+}(aq) \qquad \Delta H^\ominus = -365 \text{ kJ mol}^{-1}$$

You can see that the overall enthalpy change in kilojoules per mole is the same whichever route you take:

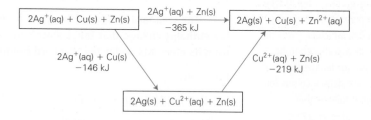

**The great value of Hess's Law is that it can be used to calculate enthalpy changes that cannot be determined by experiment.** For example $\Delta H_f^{\ominus}$ values have been determined directly for many oxides but for some this is not possible. $\Delta H_f^{\ominus}$ for magnetic iron oxide, $Fe_3O_4$, is an example of a standard enthalpy change of formation which cannot be measured directly. This is because when iron is burnt completely in oxygen it is impossible to prevent iron(III) oxide, $Fe_2O_3$, forming.

In these, and in many hundreds of other instances, values for the standard enthalpy changes of formation have been obtained in indirect ways, by means of calculations using Hess's Law.

## Determining standard enthalpy changes of reaction

In Topic 1 we quoted an enthalpy (energy) of reaction for a change that does not actually occur:

$$Fe_2O_3(s) + 3Cu(s) \longrightarrow 2Fe(s) + 3CuO(s)$$

How was the value found when no experimental measurement is possible? The answer is that a Hess cycle was constructed using standard enthalpy changes of formation:

$$2Fe(s) + 1\tfrac{1}{2}O_2(g) \longrightarrow Fe_2O_3(s) \quad \Delta H_f^{\ominus}[Fe_2O_3(s)] = -824.2 \text{ kJ mol}^{-1}$$

$$Cu(s) + \tfrac{1}{2}O_2(g) \longrightarrow CuO(s) \qquad \Delta H_f^{\ominus}[CuO(s)] \;\; = -157.3 \text{ kJ mol}^{-1}$$

The balanced equations of the three reactions were combined in a Hess cycle:

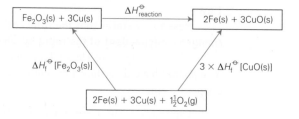

From this diagram it is possible to deduce the value of $\Delta H_{\text{reaction}}^{\ominus}$ as follows:

$$\Delta H_f^{\ominus}[Fe_2O_3(s)] + \Delta H_{\text{reaction}}^{\ominus} = 3\Delta H_f^{\ominus}[CuO(s)]$$

$$-824.2 \text{ kJ mol}^{-1} + \Delta H_{\text{reaction}}^{\ominus} = 3(-157.3 \text{ kJ mol}^{-1})$$

$$\Delta H_{\text{reaction}}^{\ominus} = +352.3 \text{ kJ mol}^{-1}$$

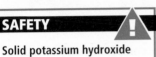

## EXPERIMENT 5.2

# Measuring the enthalpy change of acid-base reactions

**SAFETY**

Solid potassium hydroxide and solid sodium hydroxide are very corrosive indeed and cause severe burns. Solutions of potassium hydroxide and sodium hydroxide 0.5 M or more are corrosive. Solutions of potassium hydroxide and sodium hydroxide 0.05 M to 0.49 M are irritant. Solutions of hydrochloric acid 6.5 M or more are corrosive. Solutions of hydrochloric acid 2.0 M to 6.4 M are irritant.

**You must make a Risk Assessment for the practical work which you propose, and have it checked by your teacher before you start any practical work.**

The procedure we have provided for this experiment is unusual because it is incomplete. All experiments require **planning** and often many trial experiments are carried out before the best procedure is arrived at: in this experiment you are expected to decide for yourself what might be a good procedure.

## Procedure

### 1 The reaction between hydrochloric acid and a solution of sodium hydroxide

$$HCl(aq) + NaOH(aq) \longrightarrow NaCl(aq) + H_2O(l)$$

You should plan to use the same type of apparatus as you used in Experiment 5.1.

- What concentrations of hydrochloric acid and sodium hydroxide solution would you consider safe to use?
- What volumes of solution would be suitable?
- Does it matter which solution you put in the calorimeter and which you add?

You must have your plan checked, and if necessary altered, before you do this experiment.

### 2 The reaction between hydrochloric acid and a solution of potassium hydroxide

$$HCl(aq) + KOH(aq) \longrightarrow KCl(aq) + H_2O(l)$$

**In your notes:** Using the method of Experiment 5.1, calculate the enthalpy change when 1 mole of hydrochloric acid is neutralised by 1 mole of sodium hydroxide, and by 1 mole of potassium hydroxide.

Allowing for the accuracy of your experiment, are the results similar?

Write an **ionic equation**, for both experiments, cancelling out the 'spectator ions'.

How do the ionic equations help to explain the results of the experiments?

## 5.3   Uses of standard enthalpy changes of formation

Standard enthalpy changes of formation of inorganic compounds are given in the *Book of data*.

We can use standard enthalpy changes of formation to find the enthalpy change that takes place in a reaction, without doing an experiment in every case.

As an example let us look at the reaction of ammonia gas with hydrogen chloride gas to give ammonium chloride. $\Delta H^{\ominus}_{\text{reaction}}$ can be calculated as follows.

First write down the equation for the reaction:

$$NH_3(g) + HCl(g) \longrightarrow NH_4Cl(s)$$

The standard enthalpy changes of formation that you need are:

$$\Delta H_f^{\ominus}[NH_3(g)] = -46 \text{ kJ mol}^{-1}$$
$$\Delta H_f^{\ominus}[HCl(g)] = -92 \text{ kJ mol}^{-1}$$
$$\Delta H_f^{\ominus}[NH_4Cl(g)] = -314 \text{ kJ mol}^{-1}$$

Then draw a Hess cycle showing the formation of the compounds on both sides of the equation from their elements:

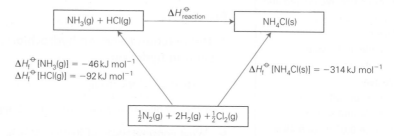

The total enthalpy change must be the same by whatever route the ammonium chloride is formed (whether it is formed direct from its elements, or through the intermediates of ammonia and hydrogen chloride).

Therefore,

$$\Delta H_f^{\ominus}[NH_4Cl(s)] = \Delta H_f^{\ominus}[NH_3(g)] + \Delta H_f^{\ominus}[HCl(g)] + \Delta H_{reaction}^{\ominus}$$

That is:

$$-314 \text{ kJ mol}^{-1} = -46 \text{ kJ mol}^{-1} - 92 \text{ kJ mol}^{-1} + \Delta H_{reaction}^{\ominus}$$

So,

$$\Delta H_{reaction}^{\ominus} = (46 + 92 - 314 \text{ kJ mol}^{-1}) = -176 \text{ kJ mol}^{-1}$$

This example shows that standard enthalpy changes of chemical reactions can be calculated from the standard enthalpy changes of formation of the reactants and products. This is the great value of standard enthalpy changes of formation; they make it possible to calculate enthalpy changes which cannot otherwise be found.

By using a similar procedure we can use Hess's Law to calculate most other enthalpy changes which cannot be determined directly.

$$\Delta H_{reaction}^{\ominus} = \Delta H_f^{\ominus} \text{ [products]} - \Delta H_f^{\ominus} \text{ [reactants]}$$

## STUDY TASK

1   Look up the following compounds in the *Book of data*, and write in your notes their names, formulae, and standard enthalpy changes of formation. This will give you an idea of the range and pattern of values that exist.

| | | | |
|---|---|---|---|
| Lithium chloride | Sodium oxide | Hydrogen chloride | Carbon dioxide |
| Sodium chloride | Magnesium oxide | Hydrogen bromide | Nitrogen dioxide |
| Potassium chloride | Aluminium oxide | Hydrogen iodide | Water |

2   Use the following steps to calculate the standard enthalpy change of reaction for the reaction:

$$BaO(s) + CO_2(g) \longrightarrow BaCO_3(s)$$

a   Draw a Hess cycle showing the formation of the reactants and the formation of the products from their elements.

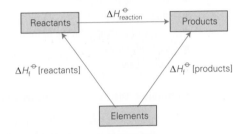

b   Look up in the *Book of data* the standard enthalpy changes of formation of the compounds $BaO$, $CO_2$, and $BaCO_3$.

c   Calculate your answer for the standard enthalpy change of reaction from the relationship:

$$\Delta H^{\ominus}_{reaction} = \Delta H_f^{\ominus}[products] - \Delta H^{\ominus}[reactants]$$

Include a sign and units in your answer. Is the reaction exothermic or endothermic?

3   In Topic 1 you probably heated some hydrated cobalt chloride, $CoCl_2.6H_2O$ and it decomposed. You should now be able to calculate the standard enthalpy change of the reaction, assuming that liquid water is formed at room temperature.

a   Use your notes for Topic 1 to write a balanced equation for the decomposition; use your equation and the *Book of data* to calculate the standard enthalpy change of the reaction. Include a sign and units in your answer.

b   In the experiment you had to heat continuously. Does this suggest that the reaction is exothermic or endothermic?

# KEY SKILLS

## Application of number

In Experiment 5.2 you have to work out the quantities to use. So you have to start by planning your experiment. Then you have to carry out a multi-stage calculation, working to appropriate degrees of accuracy with the help of formulae. Finally you draw an appropriate conclusion and discuss how possible sources of error might have affected your results.

# TOPIC REVIEW

The new vocabulary encountered in this topic is very important for your future work. All **definitions and standard notation** given in this topic **must be learned** so that they may be **used precisely**. In addition, **equations, state symbols and units** are extremely important.

1   **List key words or terms with definitions**

Wherever relevant give the appropriate notation.

- system and surroundings
- enthalpy change
- specific heat capacity
- standard conditions
- standard enthalpy change of formation and reaction
- signs of $\Delta H$ values
- Hess's Law

2   **Summarise the key principles as simply as possible**

The calculations in this topic offer many opportunities for careless workers to make mistakes. The challenge is to stay in **control** of **signs, values, units** and **amounts** of substance.

You should know:

- how to use Hess's Law
- what data you need to collect to calculate the enthalpy change of a reaction
- how to process this data
- about the practical errors you must overcome.

# REVIEW QUESTIONS

✱ Indicates that the *Book of data* is needed.

**5.1**   In this question you are given the results of some experiments in which acids were neutralised by alkalis in insulated polystyrene cups. In each case the temperature rise accompanying neutralisation was measured.

| Experiment | Acid | Alkali | Temperature rise /°C |
|---|---|---|---|
| 1 | 50 cm$^3$ 1.0 M HCl | 50 cm$^3$ 1.0 M NaOH | 6.9 |
| 2 | 20 cm$^3$ 2.0 M HNO$_3$ | 20 cm$^3$ 2.0 M KOH | 13.8 |
| 3 | 20 cm$^3$ 1.0 M H$_2$SO$_4$ | 20 cm$^3$ 2.0 M NaOH | 13.8 |

a   For Experiment 1, calculate the heat evolved (assume that the heat produced was used only to heat the solution, that the density of both solutions was $1.0 \, \text{g cm}^{-3}$ and that the specific heat capacity of the solutions was $4.2 \, \text{J g}^{-1} \, \text{K}^{-1}$).

(2)

**b** From your answer to **a**, calculate the enthalpy change of the reaction, per mole of acid. Include the correct sign and units in your answer. (1)

**c** Use the results of Experiments 2 and 3 to calculate the enthalpy changes per mole of acid for these reactions. (4)

**d** Compare the values for the three enthalpy changes of neutralisation and try to explain the relationships between them. (3)

**(10 marks)**

**5.2** $100 \, cm^3$ of 0.02 M copper(II) sulphate solution was put in a calorimeter and an excess of magnesium powder was added. The temperature of the solution rose by 2.5 °C.

**a** Write a balanced equation for the reaction, including state symbols. (1)

**b** Calculate the number of moles of copper(II) ions used. (1)

**c** Calculate the heat evolved per mole of copper ions. Assume that the heat produced was used only to heat the solution; also that the density and the specific heat capacity of the solution are the same as those of water, as in part **a** of question **5.1**. (2)

**d** Rewrite the equation for the reaction as an ionic equation, together with the enthalpy change, giving the correct sign and units. (2)

**(6 marks)**

**5.3** $50 \, cm^3$ of 0.05 M silver nitrate solution was put in a calorimeter and an excess of copper powder was added. 184 J of energy was produced.

**a** Write a balanced equation for the reaction, including state symbols. (1)

**b** Calculate the number of moles of silver ions used in the experiment. (1)

**c** Calculate the number of moles of copper atoms which reacted. (1)

**d** Calculate the enthalpy change for the reaction, per mole of copper atoms. (2)

**e** Rewrite the equation for the reaction as an ionic equation, together with the enthalpy change, giving the correct sign and units. (1)

**(6 marks)**

**\* 5.4** Write balanced equations, including state symbols, for the formation of one mole of each of the following compounds from their elements under standard conditions. Add to each equation the standard enthalpy change of formation, including the appropriate sign and units.

**a** calcium oxide (2)
**b** potassium bromide (2)
**c** sodium hydroxide (2)
**d** ethanol (2)
**e** magnesium carbonate (2)

**(10 marks)**

**\* 5.5** One mole of ammonia reacted under standard conditions with one mole of hydrogen bromide, forming solid ammonium bromide.

$$NH_3(g) + HBr(g) \longrightarrow NH_4Br(s)$$

a   Draw a Hess cycle showing the formation of the reactants and products from their elements and also the above reaction. (3)

b   Look up the appropriate standard enthalpy changes of formation and add them to your Hess cycle. (3)

c   Calculate the standard enthalpy change for the reaction, including its correct sign and units. (2)

**(8 marks)**

**\* 5.6** Calculate $\Delta H^\ominus(298)$ for the following reactions.

a   $N_2O(g) + Cu(s) \longrightarrow CuO(s) + N_2(g)$   (2)

b   $NH_4Cl(s) \longrightarrow NH_3(g) + HCl(g)$   (2)

c   $MgCO_3(s) \longrightarrow MgO(s) + CO_2(g)$   (2)

d   $CO_2(g) + 2Mg(s) \longrightarrow 2MgO(s) + C(s)$   (2)

e   $2Al(s) + Fe_2O_3(s) \longrightarrow 2Fe(s) + Al_2O_3(s)$   (2)

f   $2NaNO_3(s) \longrightarrow 2NaNO_2(s) + O_2(g)$   (2)

g   $2Cu(NO_3)_2.3H_2O(s) \longrightarrow 2CuO(s) + 4NO_2(g) + O_2(g) + 6H_2O(l)$   (2)

**(14 marks)**

**5.7** In answering this question, you will need to use your answers from questions **5.2** and **5.3**. Your task is to calculate the standard enthalpy change for the reaction between magnesium metal and silver nitrate solution by working through steps **a** to **d** below.

a   Write a balanced equation, including state symbols, for the reaction. (1)

b   Draw a Hess cycle which puts together this reaction and the reactions in questions **5.2** and **5.3**. (3)

c   Use your Hess cycle to calculate the standard enthalpy change for the reaction between magnesium metal and silver nitrate solution. (2)

d   Rewrite the equation for the reaction as an ionic equation, together with its enthalpy change, which should have its correct sign and units. (2)

**(8 marks)**

**5.8** Suppose you were given the enthalpy changes for the following reactions:

$$2Fe(s) + 1\tfrac{1}{2}O_2(g) \longrightarrow Fe_2O_3(s)$$
$$Ca(s) + \tfrac{1}{2}O_2(g) \longrightarrow CaO(s)$$

What further information, if any, would you need in order to calculate the enthalpy changes of each of the following reactions?

a   $3Ca(s) + Fe_2O_3(s) \longrightarrow 3CaO(s) + 2Fe(s)$   (1)

b   $Ca(s) + CuO(s) \longrightarrow CaO(s) + Cu(s)$   (1)

c   $2Fe(s) + 3CuO(s) \longrightarrow Fe_2O_3(s) + 3Cu(s)$   (1)

**(3 marks)**

# EXAMINATION QUESTIONS

**5.9** The enthalpy change of precipitation of magnesium carbonate was investigated by mixing magnesium nitrate solution with sodium carbonate solution. In a first experiment $10.0\,cm^3$ of $1.0\,M$ magnesium nitrate solution at $20.0\,°C$ was placed in a plastic beaker and an equal volume of $1.0\,M$ sodium carbonate solution at $20.0\,°C$ was added. The temperature rose to $22.1\,°C$. The experiment was performed a second time, using $50.0\,cm^3$ of $1.0\,M$ solution, and then performed a third time, using $50.0\,cm^3$ of $0.20\,M$ solution.

a  What range and what sensitivity should you select for the thermometer to be used in this experiment? (2)

b  Calculate the temperature rise you would expect in:
   i  the second experiment (1)
   ii  the third experiment. (1)

c  Which of the three experiments is likely to lead to the most accurate determination of a temperature rise? Justify your answer. (2)

d  Which of the three experiments is likely to lead to the least accurate determination of a temperature rise? Justify your answer. (2)

e  Write an ionic equation, including state symbols, for the reaction. (2)

f  Using the data from the first experiment, calculate the standard enthalpy change for the reaction.
   (Assume that both solutions are of density $1.0\,g\,cm^{-3}$ and specific heat capacity $4.18\,J\,g^{-1}\,K^{-1}$) (2)

**(12 marks)**

**5.10** The enthalpy change for the decomposition of calcium carbonate

$$CaCO_3(s) \longrightarrow CaO(s) + CO_2(g)$$

is impossible to determine directly so the following method was devised:

Two pieces of natural chalk, calcium carbonate, were chosen, each of mass $1.25\,g$. One piece, **A**, was put into $20.0\,cm^3$ of dilute hydrochloric acid, the temperature of which rose by $2.0\,°C$. The other piece of chalk was heated in the hottest flame available for 10 minutes to decompose it to calcium oxide. It was then allowed to cool to room temperature before it was added to $20.0\,cm^3$ (an excess) of dilute hydrochloric acid. The temperature of the acid rose by $12\,°C$.
(Molar mass of $CaCO_3 = 100\,g\,mol^{-1}$)

a  i  Calculate the energy produced by the reaction of each solid sample with the acid. Use the relationship:

   energy produced in joules $= 4.18 \times$ mass of solution $\times$ temperature rise (2)

   ii  State TWO assumptions that have to be made when using the relationship in **i**. (2)

   iii  How many moles of chalk were there in each of the original pieces? (Assume the chalk was pure calcium carbonate.) (1)

   iv  Use your answers to **a i** and **a ii** to calculate enthalpy changes for the two reactions with the acid, $\Delta H_A$ (from $CaCO_3$) and $\Delta H_B$ (from $CaO$). Your answers should be given to 2 significant figures and include signs and units. (4)

**b**    A Hess cycle based on these reactions is:

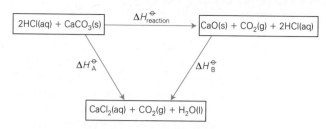

Use this and your answers in **a** to calculate a value for $\Delta H^{\ominus}_{reaction}$.
Your answer should be given to 2 significant figures and include sign and
units.                                                                                                    (2)

**c**    The value for $\Delta H^{\ominus}_{reaction}$ obtained from the *Book of data* is $+178.3\,\text{kJ mol}^{-1}$.
Suggest THREE reasons for the difference between this value and the value
you calculated in **b**.                                                                        (3)

                                                                                                    **(14 marks)**

**5.11**    A student was using yeast to ferment glucose and wished to work out whether
there would be a significant temperature change during the process. The reaction
is:

$$C_6H_{12}O_6(aq) \longrightarrow 2C_2H_5OH(aq) + 2CO_2(g)  \quad \Delta H = -97.9\,\text{kJ mol}^{-1}$$

$18.0\,\text{g}$ $(0.100\,\text{mol})$ of glucose was dissolved in $250\,\text{g}$ of water and yeast was
added.

**a   i**  How much heat energy was produced in the experiment?                    (1)
  **ii**  Use the expression

       energy produced in joules $=$ mass of water $\times 4.18 \times$ rise in temperature

       to calculate the rise in temperature. Ignore the masses of glucose
       and yeast.                                                                                   (2)

**b   i**  Would this temperature rise prove to be a serious problem in the laboratory-
       scale process? Justify your answer.                                                 (2)
  **ii**  Suggest whether the exothermic nature of the reaction would be a
       problem in the large-scale brewing of beer in batches of 50 000 litres.
       Justify your answer.                                                                     (2)

                                                                                                    **(7 marks)**

**5.12** Sodium hydrogencarbonate, $NaHCO_3$, decomposes on heating. The decomposition products are sodium carbonate, carbon dioxide and water. The equation for the reaction is:

$$2NaHCO_3(s) \longrightarrow Na_2CO_3(s) + CO_2(g) + H_2O(l)$$

The standard enthalpy changes of formation at 298 K of the four compounds are listed below:

| Compound | $\Delta H_f$/kJ mol$^{-1}$ |
|---|---|
| $NaHCO_3(s)$ | −951 |
| $Na_2CO_3(s)$ | −1131 |
| $CO_2(g)$ | −394 |
| $H_2O(l)$ | −286 |

**a** Copy and complete the following Hess cycle by filling in the empty box.

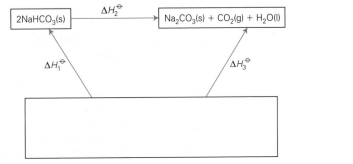

(2)

**b** Use your completed cycle to calculate the standard enthalpy change (in kJ) accompanying the thermal decomposition of 2 moles of sodium hydrogencarbonate.
(Remember to include the appropriate sign in your answer.) (2)

**(4 marks)**

# Redox reactions and the halogens

This topic is about the halogens, the elements of Group 7 of the Periodic Table. You will be considering the reactivity of both the elements and some of their compounds, and how that **reactivity is related to their electronic structure and their position in the Periodic Table**. You will also be using 'oxidation numbers', which are very useful when looking for patterns in **oxidation and reduction (redox)** reactions.

All the halogens are in use commercially, either as the free element or in compounds. For example, chlorine is used as a disinfectant, both as the element and in compounds; halogens and their compounds are important as anaesthetics and solvents. Halogen compounds have in the past been used as coolants in refrigerators and as propellants in aerosols but we are now aware of their danger to health and the environment. Knowledge of their chemistry enables us to find substitutes for them.

Figure 6.1   A film of ptfe in the joint prevents the microscale distillation unit sticking to the flask. ptfe is the non-stick polymer of tetrafluoroethene consisting just of carbon and halogen atoms.

# 6.1 Sources of the halogens

The halogens are obtained from a variety of sources and extracted by a number of different methods depending on convenience and cost. Some information is summarised in the table below.

| Halogen | Abundance (parts per million by mass) | | Source | Relative cost of sodium halide (laboratory grade) | Chemical process to obtain the free element |
|---|---|---|---|---|---|
| | in rocks | in the sea | | | |
| Fluorine | 700 | 1.4 | fluorite, $CaF_2$, eg Derbyshire 'Blue John' | 8 | Electrolysis of a solution of potassium fluoride in anhydrous hydrogen fluoride |
| Chlorine | 200 | 19 000 | rock salt, NaCl, and sea water | 1 | Electrolysis of an aqueous saturated solution of sodium chloride |
| Bromine | 3 | 67 | sea water | 4 | Oxidation of bromide solution by chlorine |
| Iodine | 0.3 | 0.05 | underground brines and caliche, $NaNO_3$, containing $NaIO_3$ | 20 | Reduction of iodate solution by sodium hydrogensulphite |

Iodine, with much the lowest overall abundance of the halogens, occurs in extensive deposits in northern Chile between the Pacific ocean and the Andes mountain range. The rock is called **caliche** and the principal mineral is sodium nitrate, but it also contains iodine compounds in varying proportions, usually enough to make the extraction of the element economically possible. For example, one sample of caliche analysed was found to contain 500 g of sodium iodide per tonne and 1500 g of sodium iodate(V), $NaIO_3$, per tonne.

Figure 6.2 **Extraction of sodium chloride from sea water is carried out on a large scale by natural evaporation. Most salt is used in solution. Why go to the trouble of obtaining solid salt rather than just using sea water?**

Figure 6.3 *Laminaria saccharina* seaweed extracts iodine from sea water

Sea water is a good source of chemicals, and chlorine and bromine are among the elements whose compounds are obtained from it. However, by far the most important source of chlorine compounds is rock salt, which is mainly sodium chloride. Rock salt deposits are formed by the evaporation of sea water, a process that has produced vast rock salt deposits in many parts of the world, including Britain, and is still doing so today in places like the Dead Sea.

The occurrence of hydrogen fluoride and hydrogen chloride gases in nature is surprising, as they are so reactive. They are usually associated with volcanic action; in the Valley of Ten Thousand Smokes in Alaska, for example, eruptions early this century produced over one million tonnes of hydrogen chloride and nearly a quarter of a million tonnes of hydrogen fluoride per year.

A number of plants and animals concentrate halogen compounds from their environment to a remarkable extent. The *Laminaria* seaweeds (see figure 6.3) can contain 800 parts per million of iodine in fresh wet weed, taken in as iodide ions from the sea where iodine is present at a concentration of only 0.05 part per million.

Certain species of marine snail, called *Murex brandaris*, found principally in the Eastern Mediterranean, take in bromide ions to produce compounds which are fine dyes, such as Tyrian purple (dibromoindigo). The tea plant, *Camellia sinensis*, takes in fluoride ions from the soil to the extent that dried tea leaves contain about 100 parts per million of fluorine, which results in a concentration of about 1 part per million in a cup of tea.

## STUDY TASK

1   The passage above gives details of the iodine compounds in one sample of caliche. How many tonnes of caliche of this composition would be needed for the extraction of one mole of iodine molecules, $I_2$?
    What assumptions have you made in your calculation?

2   Find out how the UK obtains its supplies of the halogens, including sources, the methods of extraction used and some idea of the annual quantities produced. This may be done as a group activity, with each group presenting findings about one of the halogens to the rest of the class as, for example, a poster or an OHP transparency.

---

**EXPERIMENT 6.1**

# The extraction of iodine from seaweed

For this experiment you need a *Laminaria* seaweed that has been dried: other varieties of seaweed contain much less iodine. After releasing the iodine by oxidation you will concentrate it by a process called 'solvent extraction'.

## Procedure

Burn about 5 g of dried seaweed to ash on a tin lid in a fume cupboard (because of the smell). Transfer the ash to a small beaker and boil with 25 cm$^3$ of water for about 3 minutes.

Filter into a boiling tube, and add 3 cm$^3$ of dilute sulphuric acid and 10 cm$^3$ of dilute (20 volume) hydrogen peroxide to the solution.

Pour your mixture into a separating funnel and add 10 cm$^3$ of hydrocarbon

**SAFETY**

Dilute sulphuric acid is an irritant.
Hydrogen peroxide solution is an irritant.
The hydrocarbon solvent is highly flammable.

BACKGROUND

'20 volume' hydrogen peroxide when fresh will give off 20 cm$^3$ of oxygen gas per 1 cm$^3$ of solution.

solvent. Stopper the funnel and mix the contents well by inverting the funnel several times – release any build-up of pressure by opening the tap when the funnel is upside down. Run the upper layer into a small conical flask and label it as 'Iodine extract in hydrocarbon solvent'.

✎ **In your notes:** How might you obtain iodine from your solution? Write a description of solvent extraction, using diagrams where you think they will be helpful.

## 6.2   Redox reactions and oxidation numbers

REVIEW TASK

Working in groups, list the main features of redox reactions.

In Topic 1 you were shown how restricting redox reactions to reactions involving oxygen was too limiting; in this section we will develop a more general definition and use it to introduce the idea of oxidation numbers.

EXPERIMENT 6.2

### The reactions between halogens and halide ions

This experiment investigates the relative reactivity of the halogen elements towards the halide anions.

Use the halogen elements chlorine, bromine and iodine in solution: chlorine and bromine are dissolved in water, and iodine is dissolved in aqueous potassium iodide, as the solubility of iodine in water is low.

### Procedure

SAFETY ⚠

Handle the solutions with care; chlorine is toxic, aqueous bromine is harmful. Avoid inhaling any vapours, and do not allow the solutions to come into contact with your skin or clothing.
Fluorine is too hazardous for use under ordinary laboratory conditions.
Remember to wear eye protection.

1   Set up four test tubes containing about 1 cm$^3$ each of solutions of potassium chloride, potassium bromide and potassium iodide, and 1 cm$^3$ of water as a control.
   **a** Add two or three drops of chlorine solution to each.

✎ **In your notes:** Have reactions taken place? What are the products? Use the colour changes as a guide.

Write equations for any reactions you see. Would the addition of a hydrocarbon solvent help you in reaching a decision?

   **b** Add an equal volume of hydrocarbon solvent to each test tube, stopper the test tubes and shake.

✎ **In your notes:** Record the colours of each layer. Why do you think the halogens are more soluble in hydrocarbon solvent than in water?

2   Now repeat the experiment, using in turn bromine solution and iodine solution. Is a definite trend in reactivity observable in this experiment?

✎ **In your notes:** Write an ionic equation for each reaction that took place.

Draw up a table for recording your results. A suitable table is shown overleaf.

| | Action on | | | |
|---|---|---|---|---|
| Solution added | water | potassium chloride solution | potassium bromide solution | potassium iodide solution |
| Chlorine solution | | | | |

# Oxidation and reduction by electron transfer

You should have realised from the equations you have just written that the reactions involved the transfer of an electron from one halogen to another.

When the reactions are analysed into component reactions such as

$$2Br^-(aq) \longrightarrow Br_2(aq) + 2e^-$$
and
$$2e^- + Cl_2(aq) \longrightarrow 2Cl^-(aq)$$

> **COMMENT**
>
> These are known as **half-reactions**.

you can see how the reactions involve the transfer of electrons.

In the first half-reaction, each bromide ion loses an electron when it is oxidised; in the second half-reaction each chlorine atom gains an electron when it is reduced. In the complete reaction, bromide ion is the reducing agent and chlorine is the oxidising agent.

$$2Br^-(aq) + Cl_2(aq) \longrightarrow 2Cl^-(aq) + Br_2(aq)$$

reducing agent    oxidising agent

To summarise:

> **COMMENT**
>
> The mnemonic OIL RIG 'Oxidation Is Loss, Reduction Is Gain' will help you remember this.

**Loss of electrons is an oxidation process.**

And the opposite:

**Gain of electrons is a reduction process.**

It follows from these definitions that compounds that gain electrons in reactions are acting as oxidising agents; those that lose electrons are acting as reducing agents.

# The chemists' toolkit: oxidation numbers

The halogens combine with almost all other elements, as well as with each other, and so have a large number of compounds. It is not easy to name halogen compounds in a way that is both unambiguous and chemically helpful. **One way in which they can be classified is according to the 'oxidation number' of the halogen atom in the compound.**

When you look at formulae by Periodic Table groups you can see definite patterns. This can be seen, for example, when comparing the formulae of the chlorides and oxides of the elements of Period 3:

> **COMMENT**
>
> In some cases only one of several possible compounds has been selected.

| | | | | | |
|---|---|---|---|---|---|
| NaCl | $MgCl_2$ | $AlCl_3$ | $SiCl_4$ | $PCl_3$ | $SCl_2$ |
| $Na_2O$ | MgO | $Al_2O_3$ | $SiO_2$ | $P_2O_3$ | $SO_2$ |

We will begin by considering ionic compounds. In ionic compounds such as those just listed, the charge on the ion of each element is taken as the oxidation number of that element. In NaCl, therefore, the oxidation number of sodium is $+1$ and that of chlorine is $-1$, and in sodium monoxide, $Na_2O$, sodium and oxygen have oxidation numbers of $+1$ and $-2$ respectively.

Just as the overall positive and negative charges of an ionic compound balance and their sum is zero, so the sum of the oxidation numbers in any compound is zero.

With the oxidation number of oxygen fixed as $-2$ in all its common compounds, the use of oxidation number can be extended to molecular compounds. For example, in the molecular compound $CO_2$ the oxidation number of carbon must be $+4$ for the total sum of the oxidation numbers to be zero.

**Extensions of this sort enable one to assign an oxidation number to any element in any compound, once the empirical formula of that compound has been determined experimentally.**

## Rules for assigning oxidation numbers

1   The oxidation number of any uncombined element is zero.

2   The oxidation number of each of the atoms in a compound counts separately, and their algebraic sum is zero.

3   The oxidation number of an element existing as a monatomic ion is the charge on that ion.

4   In a polyatomic ion, the algebraic sum of the oxidation numbers of the atoms is the charge on the ion.

5   Many elements have invariable oxidation numbers in their common compounds, including:

| | |
|---|---|
| Group 1 metals | $+1$ |
| Group 2 metals | $+2$ |
| Al | $+3$ |
| H | $+1$ except in metal hydrides (where it is $-1$) |
| F | $-1$ |
| Cl, Br, I | $-1$ except in compounds with oxygen or fluorine |
| O | $-2$ except in peroxides and compounds with fluorine |

**BACKGROUND**

Hydrogen is $-1$ in $LiAlH_4$.
Chlorine is $+1$ in $Cl_2O$.
Oxygen is $-1$ in $H_2O_2$ (the structure is H—O—O—H).
Transition metals each have a range of oxidation numbers.

The application of these rules is relatively straightforward. For example, in binary compounds of one metal with one non-metal, there is no difficulty in deciding which sign should be given to which element; the metal is given a positive sign and the non-metal a negative one. For many other compounds the signs can be decided by using the invariable oxidation numbers given in rule **5**. The signs are always relative to other elements. For example, the oxidation number of sulphur in sodium sulphide, $Na_2S$, is $-2$; its oxidation number in sulphur dioxide, $SO_2$, however, is $+4$.

As an example of the rule about polyatomic ions, consider the $SO_4^{2-}$ ion: the oxidation number of oxygen is fixed as $-2$, the total for oxygen is therefore $-8$, so the oxidation number of sulphur must be $+6$ for the algebraic sum to be the charge on the ion ($-2$).

QUESTIONS

1   Work out the oxidation numbers of each element in the compounds below.

KBr    BaO    $Al_2S_3$    $NO_2$    $NH_3$    $SO_3$    $NaNO_3$    $Na_2CO_3$    $NaClO_4$

2   Work out the oxidation numbers of vanadium in $VO_2^+$ and $VO_3^-$. Try to write an equation involving protons that shows that these ions are related by an acid–base reaction rather than a redox reaction.

BACKGROUND

It has been suggested that anti-oxidants in food help to protect us from diseases like cancer. Vegetables and fruit with red pigments are good sources of anti-oxidants: tomato skin, red onion, red lettuce and red wine.

# Oxidation and reduction

A change in the oxidation number of an element in a reaction can be used to discover whether the element has been oxidised or reduced. In a particular reaction, **a substance which increases the oxidation number of an element is called an oxidising agent, whereas one which decreases the oxidation number of an element is called a reducing agent**. The word 'increases' is taken to mean 'makes more positive or less negative'.

# Oxidation numbers and the Stock notation

The Roman numerals used in the naming of compounds of metals are, in fact, the oxidation numbers of these elements. This system of naming is known as the **Stock notation**, after the chemist who devised it. It is usually only used when it is useful to have a simple way of distinguishing between similar compounds. For example, in the oxide of copper, CuO, the oxidation number of copper is $+2$ and the compound is known as copper(II) oxide. In the oxide $Cu_2O$ the oxidation number of copper is $+1$ and the compound is known as copper(I) oxide.

Stock notation is used less widely for distinguishing between the compounds of non-metals. Compounds such as NO and $NO_2$ are referred to by the names nitrogen monoxide and nitrogen dioxide, rather than nitrogen(II) oxide and nitrogen(IV) oxide.

When naming oxoacids, the oxidation number of the central atom in the acid is written after the rest of the name, which always ends in '**-ic**'. For example, $H_3PO_4$ is phosphoric(V) acid.

The salts and ions of oxoacids are named by writing the oxidation number of the central atom after the rest of the name, which always ends in '**-ate**'. For example, in $Na_2SO_3$ (anion $SO_3^{2-}$), sulphur has an oxidation number of $+4$ and can be called sodium sulphate(IV) as well as sodium sulphite.

The salts of the common acids are usually named without including the appropriate oxidation number: $Na_2SO_4$ is sodium sulphate, not sodium sulphate(VI) and $NaNO_3$, sodium nitrate, is not called sodium nitrate(V).

# The chemists' toolkit: balancing redox equations

It is sometimes helpful to use oxidation numbers in balancing the equation for a redox reaction.

In a simple example, the oxidation number method is not really necessary:

$$2Br^-(aq) + Cl_2(aq) \longrightarrow 2Cl^-(aq) + Br_2(aq)$$
$$2 \times (-1) \qquad (0) \qquad\qquad 2 \times (-1) \qquad (0)$$

COMMENT

To balance a redox equation:

1   write down oxidation numbers

2   calculate the changes in oxidation numbers that occur

3   balance to give a total oxidation number change of zero

4   balance for oxygen by adding water to the equation when necessary

5   balance for hydrogen by adding hydrogen ions when necessary

6   check that any $+$ and $-$ charges balance.

We can use the volcano experiment as an example of how oxidation numbers can be applied to equation balancing in a more complex situation. This is a reaction that you met in Topic 1.

$$(NH_4)_2Cr_2O_7 \longrightarrow N_2 + H_2O + Cr_2O_3 \qquad \text{(unbalanced)}$$

First you have to identify the elements which actually change in oxidation number. The nitrogen has changed from $-3$ to $0$ and the chromium has changed from $+6$ to $+3$: the hydrogen and oxygen are unchanged.

The total change of oxidation numbers is therefore an increase of 6 for the two nitrogen atoms and a decrease of 6 for the two chromium atoms. **The total change in oxidation number is zero**.

Any remaining balancing numbers may now be inserted, so that the balanced equation, together with state symbols is

$$(NH_4)_2Cr_2O_7(s) \longrightarrow N_2(g) + 4H_2O(l) + Cr_2O_3(s) \qquad \text{(balanced)}$$

There are examples for you to try in the questions at the end of the topic. They make more use of oxidation numbers than our examples, and you should find many of them fairly straightforward.

## 6.3  The properties of the halogens

✎   **In your notes:** Write a general account of the halogens in your notes, using the outline below as a guide. You should begin by explaining what a halogen is and then list the characteristic properties with carefully selected examples in each case. Use the *Book of data* and a spreadsheet program if one is available to display your data as bar charts. This should make trends and patterns in the data easier to recognise.

### 1  Trends in physical properties

The physical properties of the halogens show considerable variation down their Periodic Table group.

Include in your survey of their properties a description of their appearance and their hazardous properties, together with data on molar masses, and melting and boiling points. Report any trends that you can identify in the data. The data you need are in table 5.2 of the *Book of data*.

We suggest you use a table to record your findings, similar to this one.

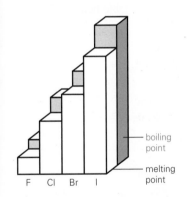

Figure 6.4  **Trends in melting and boiling points**

COMMENT

You may prefer to record temperatures in °C in which case convert the temperatures in kelvins in the *Book of data* into °C by subtracting 273.

| Name | Formula | Appearance of element | Hazardous properties | Melting point/°C | Boiling point/°C | Molar mass /g mol$^{-1}$ |
|------|---------|----------------------|---------------------|------------------|------------------|-------------------------|
| Fluorine | F$_2$ | yellow gas | | | | |
| Chlorine | Cl$_2$ | | | | | |
| Bromine | Br$_2$ | | | | | |
| Iodine | I$_2$ | | | | | |

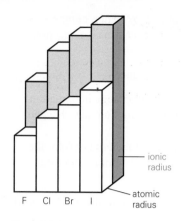

Figure 6.5 **Trends in size**

COMMENT

Atomic radii are quoted in nanometres, $1\ nm = 10^{-9}$ metre.

| | | | |
|---|---|---|---|
| +7 | $Cl_2O_7$ | $HClO_4$ | $K^+IO_4^-$ |
| +6 | $Cl_2O_6 \rightleftharpoons 2ClO_3$ | | |
| +5 | | $HClO_3$ | $K^+ClO_3^-$ |
| +4 | $ClO_2$ | | |
| +3 | | $HClO_2$ | $K^+ClO_2^-$ |
| +2 | | | |
| +1 | $Cl_2O$ | $HClO$ | $K^+ClO^-$ |
| 0 | $Cl_2$ | | |
| −1 | | $HCl$ | $K^+Cl^-$    $PCl_3$ |

Figure 6.6 **Oxidation number chart for chlorine**

## 2 Electronic structure of the halide ions

Look up the electronic configurations of the halogens in table 4.2 in the *Book of data*. Write out the electronic configuration of the **anions**.

Also record the sizes of the atoms and anions as their radii; to get a feel for the relative sizes you should make scale drawings. The data you need are in table 4.4 (use covalent radii for the atomic radii).

| Name | Symbol | Electronic configuration of: | | Atomic radius /nm | Ionic radius /nm |
|---|---|---|---|---|---|
| | | the atom | the anion | | |
| Fluorine | F | | | | |
| Chlorine | Cl | | | | |
| Bromine | Br | | | | |
| Iodine | I | | | | |

## 3 Variable oxidation numbers

Oxidation numbers are invariable for some elements, but those of a number of elements, such as the halogens, may have different values in different compounds. **The range of oxidation numbers of such elements is very well shown by constructing an oxidation number chart.** The formulae of the various compounds can be written on the chart, as shown in figure 6.6.

In this book the Stock names for these compounds will be used, but as the old names may still be found, both names are included in the table below. The potassium salts are given as examples.

| Formula of compound | Oxidation number of chlorine | Stock name | Old name |
|---|---|---|---|
| $KClO_4$ | +7 | potassium chlorate(VII) | potassium perchlorate |
| $KClO_3$ | +5 | potassium chlorate(V) | potassium chlorate |
| $KClO_2$ | +3 | potassium chlorate(III) | potassium chlorite |
| $KClO$ | +1 | potassium chlorate(I) | potassium hypochlorite |
| $KCl$ | −1 | potassium chloride | potassium chloride |

Work out the oxidation numbers of a variety of halogen compounds and draw up a table similar to the one above; do not bother to list the old names.

## 4 Sources and uses

Record at least one source from which each halogen can be manufactured, one industrial use and one example of a use made by plants or animals. You will need to read the background reading section (section 6.9) in order to complete this task.

# 6.4    Oxidation number −1: the halides

The halides of many elements are toxic or corrosive. There are, however, some properties of halides that can be investigated with relative safety using compounds of the alkali metals, and they are included in the next experiment.

## EXPERIMENT 6.4

### Some reactions of the halides

#### Procedure

##### 1  The silver halides

Use 0.1 M solutions of potassium (or sodium) chloride, bromide and iodide. Where you can, attempt to estimate roughly the proportions of the solutions needed for complete reaction.

a    To 1 cm³ portions of each of the halide solutions, add a few drops of 0.1 M silver nitrate solution.

b    To the precipitates obtained in part **a** add 8 M ammonia solution.

c    Obtain a second set of silver halide precipitates and leave them exposed to the light for a few minutes.

✎    **In your notes:** Record your results in a table, noting similarities and differences between the reactions.

##### 2  The action of concentrated sulphuric acid on the potassium salts

a    Put about 0.1 g of the solid salt into a test tube (about enough to fill the rounded end of the tube if it is 100 × 16 mm) and add about 10 drops of concentrated sulphuric acid (TAKE CARE). Warm the reaction mixture gently if necessary.

✎    **In your notes:** Identify as many products as you can (test with strips of filter paper moistened with lead(II) ethanoate, potassium dichromate(VI) and ammonia solutions). Note the similarities and differences between the reactions. Record and explain your observations as fully as you can.

b    Repeat part **a**, using phosphoric acid (TAKE CARE) in place of sulphuric acid. Note any difference.

##### 3  The properties of the hydrogen halides

Use the reactions in **2** to prepare and collect samples of hydrogen chloride, hydrogen bromide, and hydrogen iodide. The apparatus shown in figure 6.7 is convenient for this purpose. A good yield of gas is obtained if solid 100% phosphoric acid is used, but you must use **dry** test tubes to collect your samples of gas.

Mix about 2 g of halide with an equal quantity of solid phosphoric acid (TAKE CARE) in the side-arm test tube. Stopper it securely. Put a **dry** test tube round the delivery tube and warm the mixture gently until gas is evolved. Collect at least three tubes of gas, sealing them with a dry stopper when full. Clouds of misty, white fumes will first form at the mouth of the test tube when it is less than half full of hydrogen halide gas. Let the fumes form for at least 10 seconds before sealing with a dry stopper.

**SAFETY**

8 M ammonia is corrosive. Concentrated sulphuric acid and solid phosphoric acid are corrosive. Use **solid** potassium (or sodium) chloride, bromide, and iodide in part 2. **You MUST wear eye protection.** Do part 3 in a fume cupboard as toxic and corrosive gases are formed.

COMMENT

The photochemical change which occurs when silver bromide is exposed to sunlight is used in black-and-white photography. The silver ions are converted to silver metal which remains as an opaque image on the photographic film.

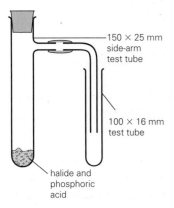

150 × 25 mm side-arm test tube

100 × 16 mm test tube

halide and phosphoric acid

Figure 6.7    **Apparatus for making the hydrogen halides**

Use the tubes of gas to investigate:

**a**  *The solubility of the gas in water.* Invert a tube of gas in a beaker of water and remove the stopper.

✎    **In your notes:** If the water rises rapidly the gas is readily soluble. Is there a residue of undissolved gas and, if so, what do you suppose it is?

**b**  *The reaction of the gas with ammonia gas.* Hold a drop of fairly concentrated ammonia solution in the mouth of an open test tube, using a glass tube or rod.

✎    **In your notes:** What do you observe, and what do you suppose is formed?

**c**  *The stability of the gas towards heat.* Heat the end of a length of nichrome wire or a glass rod to dull red heat, and plunge it into a tube of gas; if no change occurs in the gas, try again with the wire hotter.

✎    **In your notes:** What do you observe?

Record the properties of these hydrogen halides in a table in your notes, and write equations for the reactions you have seen.

# 6.5    Oxidation number 0: the halogens

The reactions of the halogens with metallic and non-metallic elements have similarities to the combustion of elements in oxygen. Your teacher may show you a few typical examples. In this section you are going to study one particular reaction: the reaction of the halogen elements with alkalis.

## EXPERIMENT 6.5

## The reactions of halogens with alkalis

### Procedure

**SAFETY**

0.4 M sodium hydroxide solution is harmful and irritant.

Take 2 cm$^3$ samples of solutions of each of the halogens in water and add a few drops at a time of 0.4 M sodium hydroxide solution. It should be easy to see what happens to the bromine and iodine because the solutions are coloured; the chlorine is less easy to observe.

✎    **In your notes:** Record your observations as follows.

| Halogen solution | Observations on adding alkali | Equation |
|---|---|---|
|  |  |  |
|  |  |  |

# An interpretation of the reactions of the halogens with alkalis

Halogens react with cold sodium hydroxide solution according to the pattern set by chlorine:

$$Cl_2(g) + 2NaOH(aq) \longrightarrow NaCl(aq) + NaClO(aq) + H_2O(l)$$

The compound with formula NaClO is called sodium chlorate(I) or sodium hypochlorite.

## QUESTIONS

1    Turn the equation into an **ionic equation**, leaving out the sodium ions since these do not undergo chemical change.

2    What changes of oxidation number does the chlorine undergo?

---

**A reaction in which the same element both increases and decreases in oxidation number is called a disproportionation reaction** – we say that chlorine 'disproportionates' when it reacts with alkalis.

When the solution is hot, chlorate(I) ions themselves disproportionate so that the overall reaction between chlorine and hot sodium hydroxide is

$$3Cl_2(aq) + 6NaOH(aq) \longrightarrow 5NaCl(aq) + NaClO_3(aq) + 3H_2O(l)$$

or, ionically,

$$3Cl_2(aq) + 6OH^-(aq) \longrightarrow 5Cl^-(aq) + ClO_3^-(aq) + 3H_2O(l)$$

## QUESTIONS

3    What changes of oxidation number does the chlorine now undergo?

4    What is the equation for the reaction between iodine and hot potassium hydroxide solution?

---

# 6.6    Oxidation number +1: sodium chlorate(I)

Sodium chlorate(I) is stable only in solution, and is made by reaction between chlorine and cold sodium hydroxide solution. It is alternatively known as sodium hypochlorite, and is sold in solution as 'bleach', or as a very dilute solution used as a sterilising agent for babies' feeding bottles.

$$Cl_2(aq) + 2NaOH(aq) \longrightarrow NaCl(aq) + NaClO(aq) + H_2O(l)$$

On standing, particularly in sunlight, the solution evolves oxygen. Because of this, bleach solutions are normally supplied in opaque plastic containers or in brown bottles.

$$2NaClO(aq) \longrightarrow 2NaCl(aq) + O_2(g)$$

What type of reagent would you expect sodium chlorate(I) to be in redox reactions?

TOPIC 6

**SAFETY**

Handle sodium chlorate(I) solution with care. It is corrosive. **You MUST wear eye protection.**

## Some reactions of sodium chlorate(I)

### Procedure

### 1 Reaction with iron(II) ions, $Fe^{2+}(aq)$

Add some sodium chlorate(I) solution to a solution of iron(II) sulphate. Test to find out the oxidation number of the iron in the product.

✎ **In your notes:** Record your observations and try to write a balanced equation for the reaction.

### 2 Reaction with iodide ions, $I^-(aq)$

Add **one drop** of sodium chlorate(I) solution to a solution of potassium iodide.

✎ **In your notes:** Record your observations and try to write a balanced equation for the reaction.

### QUESTIONS

1 What changes of oxidation number occur during these reactions?

2 Use the rules in section 6.2 to help you balance the equations of the reactions you have just carried out.

3 In the second experiment you should have seen the colour diminish in intensity a moment or two after it appeared: try to work out why.

## 6.7 Oxidation number +5: the potassium halates(V)

The halates(V) are vigorous oxidising agents which must be handled with great care. Potassium and sodium chlorate(V) are very dangerous indeed, and mixtures of the solids with many other substances explode in a violent and unpredictable manner. Because of this it is essential to check the names of the various compounds of the halogens with great care before carrying out any experiments.

Remember that when the words chlorate, bromate or iodate in a name are **not** followed by a Roman numeral, the names are probably the old names for chlorate(V), bromate(V), and iodate(V).

EXPERIMENT 6.7

# Some reactions of the potassium halates(v)

The three potassium halates(v) which are used in this set of experiments have the formulae $KClO_3$, $KBrO_3$, and $KIO_3$.

## Procedure

### 1 Reaction with iron(ii) ions, Fe²⁺(aq)

Make a solution of each of the halates(v) in turn and acidify each with 1 M sulphuric acid. Add the acidified solutions to samples of iron(II) sulphate solution and warm gently.

✎    **In your notes:** Describe and try to explain what you see.

### 2 Reaction with iodide ions, I⁻(aq)

Add acidified samples of each of the halates(v) to portions of potassium iodide solution.

✎    **In your notes:** Which species have been oxidised and which reduced in the reactions that occurred?

---

**SAFETY**

All three potassium halates(v) are oxidising and can be explosive with combustible materials. Potassium chlorate(v) is also harmful.
Potassium bromate(v) is toxic and is a category 2 carcinogen.

---

## 6.8  The preparation and analysis of potassium iodate(v)

The reaction between the halogens and alkalis that you studied in section 6.5 can be used to prepare potassium iodate(v) from iodine. Potassium iodide is formed as an additional product at the same time.

$$3I_2(s) + 6KOH(aq) \longrightarrow KIO_3(aq) + 5KI(aq) + 3H_2O(l)$$

You are going to use 10 cm³ of 4 M potassium hydroxide solution. Calculate the maximum yield, in grams, you can expect of potassium iodate(v) and potassium iodide.

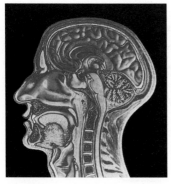

Figure 6.8    **Use of iodine in medical scanning**

**BACKGROUND**

One use for potassium iodate is in a tablet issued to people living near nuclear power stations. In the event of radioactive gases escaping from the nuclear power station the tablet can be swallowed to give some emergency protection against damage by X-rays from radioactive decay.

The iodine atoms in the potassium iodate can absorb X-rays, turning the energy into harmless heat energy, whereas the DNA in cells can suffer permanent damage, which might not be apparent until years later.

The same property of iodine is used in hospitals to obtain images of parts of the body such as the brain and kidneys. Normally these are transparent to X-rays but injecting an iodine compound into the blood results in it being carried very rapidly to all the cells. A computer scan enables doctors to see the detailed structure of the organs to help with their diagnosis.

**EXPERIMENT 6.8a**

# The preparation of potassium iodate(v)

**SAFETY** ⚠️

The concentrated potassium hydroxide solution used in this experiment is very corrosive; it causes severe burns and is particularly dangerous to the eyes. **You MUST wear goggles** (not just safety glasses) and take great care. Wear protective gloves when clearing up any spillages. Iodine is harmful so do not touch any.

The mixture has a tendency to 'spit' towards the end of the evaporation.

Potassium iodate(v) formed in this reaction is oxidising and may be harmful if ingested.

## Procedure

1  Take about $10\,cm^3$ of 4 M potassium hydroxide solution (TAKE CARE) in a boiling tube and heat it in a beaker of boiling water. Cautiously add solid iodine (TAKE CARE), very slowly **in small pieces**, until there is a very slight excess, that is, until the iodine colour is visible. Cool to below room temperature in a water bath containing a little ice, then add the minimum quantity of 4 M potassium hydroxide solution (a drop or two) to react with the excess of iodine to give a solution which is a very pale yellow colour.

2  The solution contains both potassium iodate(V) and potassium iodide dissolved in water. The solubility of these two substances varies with temperature as shown in figure 6.9. Use the graph to predict the identity of the crystals formed by cooling the hot solution.

   Allow the solution to cool to room temperature and filter off the crystals, using suction filtration with a Buchner funnel (see figure 6.10). Wash the crystals with about $5\,cm^3$ of water and transfer them to fresh filter paper to dry them.

3  Transfer the solution in the Buchner flask to an evaporating basin and cautiously evaporate the solution to dryness, using a water bath for heating if necessary.

 **In your notes:** Write up this experiment, explaining how you used the graph in figure 6.9 to identify your products. Label your products and keep them. When you have completed the next sections you should be able to devise tests to confirm your deductions from the graph. Consider whether your tests will work if your products are impure.

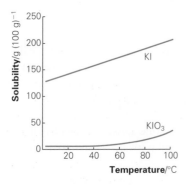

Figure 6.9  **The change in solubility of potassium iodate(v) and potassium iodide with temperature**

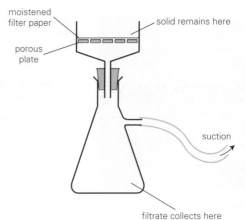

Figure 6.10  **Photograph and drawing of a Buchner flask prepared for use**

# The reaction between iodine and sodium thiosulphate

The reaction to be investigated in this section has a practical value in the quantitative analysis of oxidising agents. You will first be investigating the reaction itself and then using it to analyse the samples you obtained in Experiment 6.8a.

### Procedure

Titrate 10 cm$^3$ samples of 0.010 M iodine, $I_2$, solution with 0.010 M sodium thiosulphate, $Na_2S_2O_3$, solution. You can measure the iodine solution using a burette or a pipette; if the latter, you must use a pipette filler to fill it. The sodium thiosulphate solution must be delivered from a burette.

You will probably be able to do these titrations without using an indicator because the iodine solution is yellow–red in colour and the products of the reaction are colourless. Nevertheless the end-point can be 'sharpened' considerably by adding a few drops of 1% starch when the iodine colour has become very pale. A very dark blue colour is produced which suddenly disappears at the end-point of the titration.

✎   **In your notes:** Record the details of the experiment and give your titration results in the form of a table as on page 86.

Show that your titration results are consistent with the equation for the reaction, which is

$$2Na_2S_2O_3(aq) + I_2(aq) \longrightarrow 2NaI(aq) + Na_2S_4O_6(aq)$$

or, ionically,

$$2S_2O_3^{2-}(aq) + I_2(aq) \longrightarrow 2I^-(aq) + S_4O_6^{2-}(aq)$$

Record these equations in your notes.

Work out the oxidation number of sulphur in sodium thiosulphate, $Na_2S_2O_3$, and in sodium tetrathionate, $Na_2S_4O_6$. It is interesting that the oxidation number of sulphur in sodium tetrathionate contains a fraction. This does not invalidate the use of the oxidation number and the situation is not unusual, particularly in organic chemistry.

This reaction may be used to estimate the concentrations of oxidising agents which will oxidise iodide ions to iodine. Either or both of the following experiments may now be done.

# To determine the purity of samples of potassium iodate(v)

# Part 1

You are going to find the percentage purity of the potassium iodate(V) from Experiment 6.8a. It is quite possible that this contains small amounts of other substances. This experiment is intended to find out how much of a weighed sample of your product is actually potassium iodate(V) and to express this as percentage purity.

## Procedure

1   Weigh out accurately between 0.05 and 0.10 g of your potassium iodate(V) (oxidising), dissolve it in pure water in a beaker, and transfer the solution through a funnel to a 100 cm$^3$ volumetric flask. Rinse out the beaker several times with water and add the rinsings to the flask. Then make up the volume of the solution to the mark on the neck of the flask with pure water. Mix the contents of the flask well.

2   To 10.0 cm$^3$ portions of this potassium iodate(V) solution, taken with a pipette and pipette filler or with a burette, add about 10 cm$^3$ of approximately 0.1 M potassium iodide and about 10 cm$^3$ of 1 M sulphuric acid (irritant). The effect of this is to liberate iodine according to the equation:

$$IO_3^-(aq) + 5I^-(aq) + 6H^+(aq) \longrightarrow 3I_2(aq) + 3H_2O(l)$$

3   Titrate each sample with 0.010 M sodium thiosulphate, using 1% starch as indicator.

✎   **In your notes:** Record your results in a table.

Use your results to calculate the percentage purity of your potassium iodate(V) as follows.

1   How many moles of sodium thiosulphate, $Na_2S_2O_3$, were used in an average titration?

2   How many moles of iodine molecules did these react with? (See the equation in the previous experiment.)

3   How many moles of iodate(V) ions are involved in producing this iodine? (See the equation above.)

4   What mass of potassium iodate(V) is this?

5   The mass of pure potassium iodate(V) in 100 cm$^3$ of solution is 10 times this.

6   Calculate the percentage purity of the potassium iodate(V) according to the relationship:

$$\text{percentage purity} = \frac{\text{mass of KIO}_3 \text{ as calculated in } \mathbf{5}}{\text{mass of crude KIO}_3} \times 100$$

# Part 2

You are going to find the percentage of potassium iodate(V) remaining in the potassium iodide from Experiment 6.8a. The principal impurity in the potassium iodide is likely to be potassium iodate(V). When this mixture is acidified, iodine will be liberated according to the equation:

$$IO_3^-(aq) + 5I^-(aq) + 6H^+(aq) \longrightarrow 3I_2(aq) + 3H_2O(l)$$

## Procedure

Weigh out accurately about 0.5 g of crude potassium iodide and dissolve it in water, making up the solution to 100 cm$^3$ as in part 1. Acidify 10 cm$^3$ portions of the solution with 10 cm$^3$ of 1 M sulphuric acid (irritant), titrate with 0.010 M sodium thiosulphate using starch as indicator, and record your results in a table.

✎   **In your notes:** Calculate the percentage of potassium iodate(V) in the sample in the same way as in part 1.

# 6.9   Background reading: the halogens in human metabolism

QUESTIONS

Read the passage below in order to answer the following questions.

1   Explain why the halogens are toxic to life.

2   In which parts of the body is fluoride found at relatively high concentrations?

3   Give TWO reasons why the concentration of fluoride ion must be carefully controlled when it is added to drinking water.

4   What is an 'antibacterial solution'?

5   Calculate the concentration of chloride ions (in $mol\,dm^{-3}$) in blood plasma.

6   Which halide ion can be oxidised in the body to halogen? Suggest why only this ion is oxidised.

7   List the halogens in order of increasing importance in our diet. Justify the order in terms of their functions.

8   Summarise in about 100 words the role of the halogens in human metabolism.

The halogens are powerful oxidising agents. In all living cells there are a large number of complex organic molecules which are extremely sensitive to even mild oxidising systems, and for this reason the halogens in general are toxic to life, except at very low concentrations. However, their reduction products, that is the halides, occur in many living systems at varying concentrations.

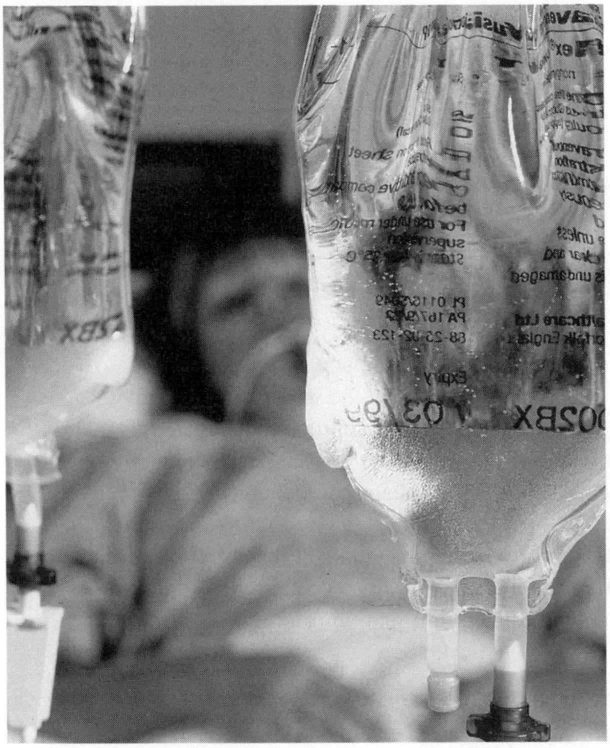

The element fluorine is too powerful an oxidising agent to occur free in nature and it is extremely toxic to all living systems. On the other hand, the fluorides are widely distributed in the plant and animal kingdoms. They are present in some of the food that we eat, and the fluoride ion is easily absorbed and slowly excreted. It becomes concentrated in the supporting structures such as the bones. In humans, there is a high concentration in teeth, especially in the enamel. At present there appears to be no known specific role for the fluoride ion in metabolism.

A large number of dental studies have shown that fluoride ions in low concentrations in drinking water can effectively arrest the development of tooth decay in children. As a result of these studies, fluoride ions are now added to the drinking water supply in certain areas in Great Britain. However, the concentration of the fluoride ion must be critically controlled because at slightly higher concentrations the ion causes mottling of the dental enamel, and at much higher concentrations the ion is toxic to life. But at the correct concentration in drinking water it is beneficial to the healthy development of teeth.

Chlorine, like fluorine, is very toxic to living systems and was used as a chemical weapon in the First World War. This halogen is sufficiently soluble in water to be useful as an antibacterial solution and for this reason it is often added to the drinking water at concentrations of 0.1 to 0.5 part per million.

The chloride ion is the principal anion found in the fluid which bathes our body cells (the extracellular fluid); blood plasma forms a

Figure 6.11   **An intravenous drip includes chlorides in solution.**

significant proportion of this fluid. In this extracellular fluid the chloride ion plays an important role in the maintenance of the water potential between the intracellular fluid and the extracellular fluid. The concentration of chloride ions in the blood plasma is about 365 mg per 100 cm$^3$ which closely resembles the concentration of chloride in sea water. From this fact attempts have been made to draw conclusions that life originated in the sea.

Apart from the abundance of the chloride ion in blood plasma, it is also present in sweat and saliva. Consequently, during bouts of hard physical activity, or if we have to live in a hot climate, situations in which we would sweat more than usual, it is essential that we increase the intake of salt to compensate for the increased losses of sodium and chloride ions. Muscular cramp is one of the first symptoms of this salt deficiency.

Bromine is also too powerful an oxidising agent to be encountered in living systems but the bromide anion occurs in small amounts. This ion is readily absorbed from the diet and, unlike the fluoride or the chloride ion, the bromide ion exhibits a highly specific effect on the central nervous system. Bromides depress the higher centres of the brain so that at the correct dosage the effect is one of sedation, but at higher dosages the effect is drowsiness and sleep. Bromides, unlike the fluorides, are not concentrated in any one tissue in the body and are eliminated in much the same way as the chlorides, namely by urinary excretion.

The element iodine is essential for humans and all other mammals, and we derive much of our daily requirement from small amounts of iodide ions which are present in common salt as a trace contamination. In mammals the iodide is concentrated by a small endocrine gland which is located in the neck and called the thyroid. The iodide-trapping mechanism in the thyroid is not fully understood but after the anion is concentrated it is subjected to an oxidation–reduction reaction and converted from iodide to iodine. The iodine is then involved in a series of reactions which eventually yield the hormone thyroxine. This hormone is secreted by the thyroid gland and circulates via the blood; it is picked up by almost all cells and tissues. Thyroxine influences the rate of metabolism in body tissues, in particular the rate of oxygen uptake. In certain communities where the drinking water is low in iodide and the diet does not contain any other sources of iodide, there is the possibility of iodine deficiency disease developing. This can be prevented by supplying such communities with common salt to which iodide has been added.

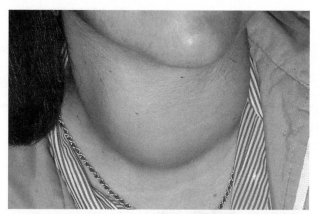

Figure 6.12   **Goitre is a malfunction of the thyroid gland. It is caused by iodine deficiency.**

## KEY SKILLS

### Communication

Finding out about the sources and uses of the halogens is an opportunity to select information from a range of sources and to bring the information together as a coherent report. In your report you can select an appropriate form for presenting the information, write in a suitable style, organise your material coherently and, if necessary, re-draft your document to ensure that your meaning is clear and accurate.

Reading about the halogens in human metabolism (background reading, section 6.9) and summarising the information gives you an opportunity to develop your skills of selecting and synthesising information from a document.

# TOPIC REVIEW

**A detailed knowledge of the practical work in this topic is essential** in addition to a sound understanding of balancing equations using oxidation numbers. Remember OIL RIG from Topic 1.

**1   List key words or terms with definitions**

Give **examples** to help you remember the following terms:

- oxidation number
- Stock notation
- disproportionation
- percentage purity.

**2   Summarise the key principles as simply as possible**

You must know:

- the rules for assigning oxidation numbers
- how to make compounds of specific oxidation state.

You might draw a **summary chart** here or a 'spider diagram' showing how one compound might be converted into another, with a different oxidation number. (See the spider diagram at the end of Topic 2.)

# REVIEW QUESTIONS

✶ Indicates that the *Book of data* is needed.

**6.1**   Consider the first element in each of the following reactions. Write down its initial and final oxidation numbers and state whether it has been oxidised, reduced or neither.

| | | | |
|---|---|---|---|
| **a** | $Ag^+(aq) + e^-$ | $\longrightarrow Ag(s)$ | (2) |
| **b** | $Zn(s) + 2H^+(aq)$ | $\longrightarrow Zn^{2+}(aq) + H_2(g)$ | (2) |
| **c** | $2Sr(s) + O_2(g)$ | $\longrightarrow 2SrO(s)$ | (2) |
| **d** | $2Na(s) + Cl_2(g)$ | $\longrightarrow 2NaCl(s)$ | (2) |
| **e** | $Cl_2(g) + 2Na(s)$ | $\longrightarrow 2NaCl(s)$ | (2) |
| **f** | $2Co^{2+}(aq) + Cl_2(g)$ | $\longrightarrow 2Co^{3+}(aq) + 2Cl^-(aq)$ | (2) |
| **g** | $H_2(g) + Cl_2(g)$ | $\longrightarrow 2HCl(g)$ | (2) |
| **h** | $2I^-(aq) + Br_2(aq)$ | $\longrightarrow I_2(aq) + 2Br^-(aq)$ | (2) |
| **i** | $O_2(g) + 2H_2(g)$ | $\longrightarrow 2H_2O(g)$ | (2) |
| **j** | $Cu^{2+}(aq) + Cu(s)$ | $\longrightarrow 2Cu^+(aq)$ | (2) |

**(20 marks)**

**6.2** Give the Stock names of the compounds whose formulae are shown below. Remember that you must include the oxidation number of the metal in each case.

| | | | | | | | | |
|---|---|---|---|---|---|---|---|---|
| a | $CuO$ | f | $PbCl_4$ | k | $Mn_2O_7$ | p | $Ag_2O$ |
| b | $Cu_2O$ | g | $CrBr_2$ | l | $UF_6$ | q | $V_2O_5$ |
| c | $Fe(OH)_3$ | h | $Mn_2O_3$ | m | $CuSO_4.5H_2O$ | r | $Sr(NO_3)_2$ |
| d | $FeS$ | i | $MnO_2$ | n | $TiI_4$ | s | $OsO_4$ |
| e | $PbCO_3$ | j | $MnO_3$ | o | $NiO$ | t | $BiCl_3$ |

**(20 marks)**

**6.3** Identify the element which has been oxidised, and also the oxidising agent in each of the following reactions:

a $\quad 2Fe(s) + 3Cl_2(g) \longrightarrow 2FeCl_3(s)$ (2)

b $\quad 2Br^-(aq) + Cl_2(aq) \longrightarrow Br_2(aq) + 2Cl^-(aq)$ (2)

c $\quad 2I^-(aq) + H_2O_2(aq) \longrightarrow 2H^+(aq) + I_2(aq) + 2H_2O(l)$ (2)

d $\quad I_2(aq) + 2S_2O_3^{2-}(aq) \longrightarrow 2I^-(aq) + S_4O_6^{2-}$ (2)

e $\quad Cu(s) + 4HNO_3(aq) \longrightarrow Cu(NO_3)_2(aq) + 2NO_2(g) + 2H_2O(l)$ (2)

**(10 marks)**

**6.4** Identify the element which has been reduced and also the reducing agent in each of the following reactions:

a $\quad CuO(s) + H_2(g) \longrightarrow Cu(s) + H_2O(l)$ (2)

b $\quad 2I^-(aq) + Br_2(aq) \longrightarrow I_2(aq) + 2Br^-(aq)$ (2)

c $\quad Mg(s) + 2Ag^+(aq) \longrightarrow Mg^{2+}(aq) + 2Ag(s)$ (2)

d $\quad 2Fe^{2+}(aq) + Cl_2(g) \longrightarrow 2Fe^{3+}(aq) + 2Cl^-(aq)$ (2)

e $\quad Br_2(aq) + H_2S(g) \longrightarrow 2HBr(aq) + S(s)$ (2)

**(10 marks)**

**✱ 6.5** Write balanced chemical equations, including state symbols, for reactions between the following, under standard conditions:

a sodium and chlorine (1)

b aluminium and iodine (1)

c magnesium and bromine (1)

d phosphorus and chlorine, forming phosphorus(III) chloride (1)

e hydrogen and fluorine (1)

**(5 marks)**

**6.6** Use the oxidation number method to balance the following equations:

a $\quad Zn(s) + Fe^{3+}(aq) \longrightarrow Zn^{2+}(aq) + Fe^{2+}(aq)$ (2)

b $\quad Al(s) + H^+(aq) \longrightarrow Al^{3+}(aq) + H_2(g)$ (2)

c $\quad Fe(s) + Fe^{3+}(aq) \longrightarrow Fe^{2+}(aq)$ (2)

d $\quad CuO(s) + NH_3(g) \longrightarrow Cu(s) + H_2O(l) + N_2(g)$ (2)

e $\quad Sn(s) + HNO_3(l) \longrightarrow SnO_2(s) + NO_2(g) + H_2O(l)$ (2)

f $\quad SO_2(aq) + Br_2(aq) + H_2O(l) \longrightarrow H^+(aq) + SO_4^{2-}(aq) + Br^-(aq)$ (2)

g $\quad As_2O_3(s) + I_2(aq) + H_2O(l) \longrightarrow As_2O_5(aq) + H^+(aq) + I^-(aq)$ (2)

h $\quad MnO_4^-(aq) + Fe^{2+}(aq) + H^+(aq) \longrightarrow Mn^{2+}(aq) + Fe^{3+}(aq) + H_2O(l)$ (2)

i $\quad Cr_2O_7^{2-}(aq) + I^-(aq) + H^+(aq) \longrightarrow Cr^{3+}(aq) + I_2(aq) + H_2O(l)$ (2)

j $\quad BrO_3^-(aq) + N_2H_4(aq) \longrightarrow Br^-(aq) + N_2(g) + H_2O(l)$ (2)

**(20 marks)**

**\* 6.7**  24.8g of sodium thiosulphate-5-water, $Na_2S_2O_3.5H_2O$, was dissolved in water and made up to $1.00 \, dm^3$. $23.6 \, cm^3$ of this solution reacted exactly with $25.0 \, cm^3$ of an aqueous solution of iodine.

**a**  Name suitable pieces of apparatus which you would use to measure
  **i** $1.00 \, dm^3$ of solution                                                      (1)
  **ii** $25.0 \, cm^3$ of iodine solution                                              (1)
  **iii** $23.6 \, cm^3$ of sodium thiosulphate solution                                (1)

**b**  Calculate the molar mass of sodium thiosulphate-5-water.                          (1)

**c**  Calculate the concentration, in $mol \, dm^{-3}$, of thiosulphate ions, $S_2O_3^{2-}(aq)$, in the solution.                                                           (1)

**d**  Calculate the number of moles of thiosulphate ions in $23.6 \, cm^3$ of solution.   (1)

**e**  Write a balanced equation, including state symbols, for the reaction between thiosulphate ions and iodine molecules.                                                 (1)

**f**  Use the equation and your answer to **d** to calculate the number of moles of iodine molecules, $I_2(aq)$, in $25.0 \, cm^3$ of solution.                              (1)

**g**  From your answer to **f**, calculate the concentration of iodine, $I_2(aq)$, in $mol \, dm^{-3}$.                                                                       (1)

**h**  Calculate the concentration of iodine, $I_2(aq)$, in $g \, dm^{-3}$.               (1)
                                                                          **(10 marks)**

**6.8**  $20 \, dm^3$ of air, contaminated with chlorine, was bubbled through an excess of aqueous potassium iodide. The iodine so formed reacted exactly with $45.0 \, cm^3$ of $0.100 \, M$ sodium thiosulphate solution, $Na_2S_2O_3$. Calculate the mass of chlorine in the sample of air.                                                          **(6 marks)**

**6.9**  When acidified sodium chlorate(V) is added to an acidified solution containing tin(II) ions, the chlorine is reduced to oxidation number $-1$ and the tin is oxidised to tin(IV) ions, $Sn^{4+}(aq)$.

**a**  What is meant by the term 'reducing agent'?                                       (2)

**b**  What is the reducing agent in the reaction described?                             (1)

**c**  **i** By how many units does each atom of chlorine go down in oxidation number?   (1)
  **ii** By how many units does each tin ion go up in oxidation number?                  (1)
  **iii** How many tin ions react with one chlorate(V) ion?                             (1)
  **iv** How many $H^+(aq)$ ions are required to react with one chlorate(V) ion, assuming that all the oxygen atoms in the chlorate ion are converted into water molecules?                                                                       (1)
  **v** Hence write the ionic equation for the reaction.                                 (3)
                                                                          **(10 marks)**

## EXAMINATION QUESTIONS

Questions of the summary and comprehension type are found in the background reading section (section 6.9).

**6.10**  **a**  An aqueous solution of silver nitrate is added to an aqueous solution of potassium iodide in a test tube.
  **i**  State what you would observe.  (2)
  **ii**  Write a balanced equation, including state symbols, for the reaction that occurs.  (2)

**b**  The reaction in **a** is repeated using potassium bromide instead of potassium iodide. The reaction mixture is allowed to stand in sunlight for a few minutes.
  **i**  State what you would observe after a few minutes.  (1)
  **ii**  Suggest a useful application of this reaction.  (1)
  **iii**  Concentrated ammonia solution is added to the reaction mixture in **b**. State and explain what you would observe.  (2)

**c**  A few drops of concentrated sulphuric acid are added to some potassium bromide in a test tube. At first a colourless gas is given off which fumes at the mouth of the test tube and gives dense white fumes with ammonia.
  **i**  Name the gas given off.  (1)
  **ii**  Write a balanced equation for the reaction between the gas and ammonia.  (1)
  **iii**  After a short time reddish-brown fumes are observed in the test tube. Name this reddish-brown substance.  (1)
  **iv**  During this time, a piece of filter paper soaked in acidified potassium dichromate(VI) is held at the end of the test tube. The colour changes from yellow to green. Name the gas which produces this change.  (1)
  **v**  Concentrated sulphuric acid has reacted in two ways in these reactions. Classify its behaviour in reaction **c i** and in reaction **c iii**.  (2)

  **(14 marks)**

**6.11**  Persulphate ions, $S_2O_8^{2-}$, react with iodide ions in aqueous solution to form iodine and sulphate ions, $SO_4^{2-}$.

**a**  What are the oxidation numbers of iodine in:
  **i**  iodine molecules, $I_2$  (1)
  **ii**  iodide ions, $I^-$?  (1)

**b**  Assuming that the oxidation number of sulphur is $+6$ in both sulphate and persulphate ions, give the oxidation numbers of oxygen in:
  **i**  sulphate ions, $SO_4^{2-}$  (1)
  **ii**  persulphate ions, $S_2O_8^{2-}$.  (1)

**c**  Identify the oxidising agent in the reaction.  (1)

**d**  Write a balanced equation for the reaction between persulphate ions and iodide ions.  (1)

  **(6 marks)**

**6.12**   **a**   Iodine reacts with hot concentrated sodium hydroxide solution according to the equation:

$$3I_2(aq) + 6NaOH(aq) \longrightarrow 5NaI(aq) + NaIO_3(aq) + 3H_2O(l)$$

   **i** What are the oxidation numbers of iodine in $I_2$, NaI and $NaIO_3$?   (3)
   **ii** What is the name given to this type of redox reaction?   (1)

   **b**   An experiment was carried out to determine the purity of a sample of sodium iodate, $NaIO_3$, made by the reaction described in **a**. 0.060g of the sample was dissolved in pure water to make $100\,cm^3$ of solution. A $10.0\,cm^3$ portion of this solution was taken and added to an excess of acidified potassium iodide solution. The iodine liberated was titrated with 0.0100 M sodium thiosulphate solution.

   **i** What piece of apparatus would you use to measure out the $10.0\,cm^3$ sample?   (1)
   **ii** Name a suitable indicator to use for this titration and give the colour change expected.   (3)
   **iii** The volume of sodium thiosulphate solution required in the titration was $16.7\,cm^3$. Calculate the number of moles of sodium thiosulphate used.   (1)
   **iv** The equation for the reaction between iodine, $I_2$, and thiosulphate ions, $S_2O_3^{2-}$, is:

$$I_2(aq) + 2S_2O_3^{2-}(aq) \longrightarrow 2I^-(aq) + S_4O_6^{2-}(aq)$$

   Calculate the number of moles of iodine molecules, $I_2$, which reacted with the sodium thiosulphate solution.   (1)
   **v** The equation for the reaction between sodium iodide and sodium iodate, $NaIO_3$, is:

$$NaIO_3(aq) + 5NaI(aq) + 3H_2SO_4(aq) \longrightarrow 3I_2(aq) + 3H_2O(l) + Na_2SO_4(aq)$$

   Calculate the number of moles of sodium iodate, $NaIO_3$, in the original sample.   (1)

   **vi** Calculate the mass of sodium iodate, $NaIO_3$, in the original sample and hence calculate the percentage purity of the sample to 2 significant figures. (Molar mass of $NaIO_3 = 198\,g\,mol^{-1}$)   (2)

   **c**   When a similar experiment is used to make and analyse potassium iodate, $KIO_3$, a higher percentage purity is obtained. Suggest a reason for this.   (1)

   **(14 marks)**

**6.13**   Standard solutions containing thiosulphate ions are used to measure the amount of iodine in a solution. The result can be used to find the reacting quantities in some redox reactions.

   $20.0\,cm^3$ of 0.100 M copper sulphate solution was reacted with an excess of potassium iodide. The iodide formed reacted with exactly $40.0\,cm^3$ of 0.0500 M sodium thiosulphate solution.

   **a**   Calculate the number of thiosulphate ions, $S_2O_3^{2-}$, used in the reaction.   (1)
   **b**   Write the ionic equation for the reaction between iodine and thiosulphate ions.   (1)
   **c**   Calculate the number of moles of iodine molecules, $I_2$, in the reaction mixture.   (1)

**d** Calculate the number of moles of copper(II) ions, $Cu^{2+}(aq)$, in $20.0 \, cm^3$ of $0.100 \, M$ copper sulphate solution which reacted with the potassium iodide. (1)

**e** Use oxidation numbers and your answers to **c** and **d** to complete the equation for the reaction between copper(II) ions and iodide ions.

$$Cu^{2+}(aq) + I^-(aq) \longrightarrow I_2(aq) +$$

Justify your balancing of the equation. (2)

**(6 marks)**

**6.14** This question is about some of the reactions of the halogens.

**a** Chlorine solution, $Cl_2(aq)$, is added to potassium bromide solution and potassium iodide solution in separate test tubes.
To help identify the products an equal volume of hydrocarbon solvent is shaken with the contents of each test tube.

**i** State the colour of the hydrocarbon solvent at the end of each reaction with chlorine. (2)

**ii** Write the equation, including state symbols, for the reaction between chlorine solution and potassium bromide solution. (2)

**b** Concentrations of oxidising agents which will oxidise iodide ions to iodine can be measured by titrating the resulting iodine with a standard sodium thiosulphate solution.

$10.0 \, cm^3$ samples of a solution containing $0.0100 \, mol \, dm^{-3}$ of iodine, $I_2$, were found to react with exactly $20.0 \, cm^3$ of a $0.0100 \, mol \, dm^{-3}$ aqueous solution of sodium thiosulphate.

Calculate the number of moles of iodine and sodium thiosulphate that react together and write the equation for the reaction between iodine and sodium thiosulphate.

Show how your equation is consistent with your calculation. (3)

**c** **i** What is the biological action that is common to all three solutions of chlorine, bromine and iodine? (1)

**ii** Give ONE everyday application of one of these solutions acting in this way. (1)

**(9 marks)**

# Covalency and bond breaking

In Topic 3 you met two of the three types of strong chemical bonding: **ionic** and **metallic** bonding. This topic concentrates on the third type: **covalent** bonding. **It is covalent bonding which holds together the atoms in molecules.** Covalent bonds break and new ones form whenever molecules react. An understanding of covalent bonding helps to explain why some reactions are fast while others are slow. Chemists are also interested in the study of reversible reactions and how we can control the conditions to affect the direction and extent of chemical change.

The aims of the topic are:

- to establish the nature of covalent bonds
- to use ideas of electron pair repulsion to establish the shapes and bond angles of simple molecules
- to extend the idea of covalency to include dative covalent bonds
- to introduce the idea of electronegativity, leading to a realisation that covalent bonds between atoms of different elements are not pure covalent bonds but also have some degree of ionic character
- to study bond energies as a method of comparing the strengths of bonds
- to establish links between bond energies and rates of reaction, introducing the concepts of collision theory and activation energy
- to introduce the idea that reactions may be reversible and that, in a closed system, this can lead to a state of equilibrium
- to establish how the equilibrium state responds to changes in its conditions.

## 7.1 Electron density maps

Any model of the bonding in molecules must be able to account for the formula of the molecule, its structure, and the forces which hold the atoms together. One way of looking at molecules is to examine their electron density maps (which were introduced in section 3.5). This section begins by comparing an electron density map for a molecular substance with one for an ionic substance.

The electron density map, determined by X-ray diffraction (see section 21.4), for ionic sodium chloride is shown in figure 7.1 (overleaf), and the map for an organic molecule, 4-methoxybenzoic acid, is shown in figure 7.2.

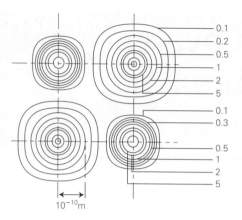

Figure 7.1 Electron density map for sodium chloride (contours are labelled in electrons per $10^{-30}$ m$^3$)

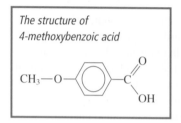

The structure of
4-methoxybenzoic acid

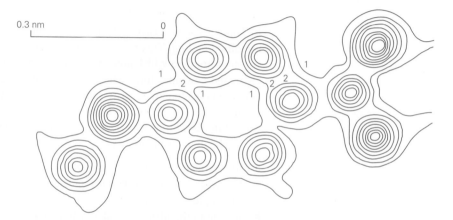

Figure 7.2 Electron density map for 4-methoxybenzoic acid (contours are labelled in electrons per $10^{-30}$ m$^3$)

## QUESTIONS

1   Identify the sodium and chloride ions in figure 7.1, and the carbon and oxygen atoms in figure 7.2. The structural formula of the organic acid is shown in the margin.
Use the number of electrons associated with the different types of atoms as a guide. Justify your choices.

2   What can you say about the electron density between adjacent ions in sodium chloride?

3   What do you notice about the contours in the organic compound that is different from the contours in ionic compounds?

4   What does this tell you about the electron density between the nuclei of the atoms in the molecule?

The maps in figures 7.1 and 7.2 show that, in structures consisting of ions, the electron density drops to zero between the ions. The ions are discrete particles. In molecules there is a substantial electron density *between* the two bonded atoms. Thus it seems that **in molecules bonds consist of electrons shared between nuclei** These bonds formed by electron sharing are known as **covalent bonds**.

## 7.2 Electron sharing in covalent molecules

Covalent bonding exists between atoms when electrons are shared, usually in pairs. In many cases, the result of covalent bonding is such that a noble gas electron structure is built up around each atom. Figure 7.3 shows how this is done for methane, $CH_4$, ammonia, $NH_3$, water, $H_2O$ and hydrogen chloride, HCl. These are examples of 'dot and cross' diagrams.

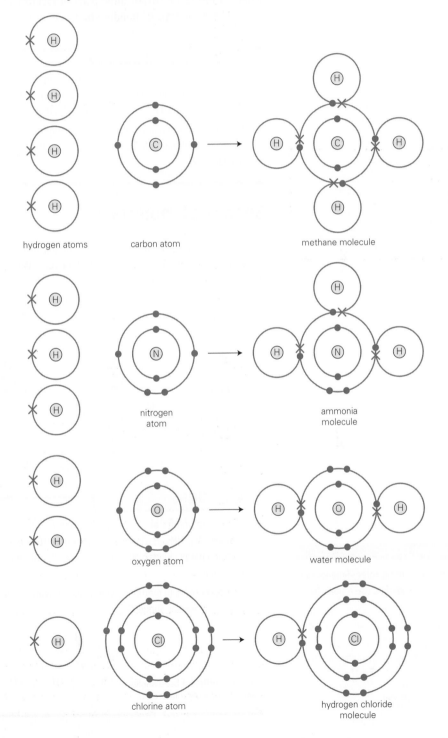

**Figure 7.3 The formation of covalent bonds**

The hydrogen atoms in methane have a share in the electrons from the carbon atom, thus acquiring the same electron arrangement as a helium atom. The carbon atom has acquired the same electron arrangement as a neon atom by sharing electrons from the hydrogen atoms.

Now look carefully at the 'dot and cross' diagrams for ammonia, $NH_3$, water, $H_2O$ and hydrogen chloride, $HCl$. In all three molecules there are only single covalent bonds. In some molecules there can be double or triple bonds where atoms share two or three pairs of electrons between them.

The usual type of bonding between atoms of non-metals is covalent bonding.

## QUESTIONS

1   Try to draw 'dot and cross' diagrams showing the arrangement of electrons in some molecules with only single bonds: hydrogen, $H_2$; chlorine, $Cl_2$; hydrogen fluoride, $HF$; chloromethane, $CH_3Cl$; methanol, $CH_3OH$; ethane, $CH_3CH_3$.

2   Now draw 'dot and cross' diagrams showing the arrangement of electrons in some molecules with multiple bonds: oxygen, $O_2$; nitrogen, $N_2$;. ethene, $CH_2{=}CH_2$; carbon dioxide, $CO_2$.

# Shapes of molecules

Look at the shapes of the molecules shown in figure 7.4 and the arrangement of their clouds of negatively-charged electrons. Why do you think that the molecules have the shapes that they do?

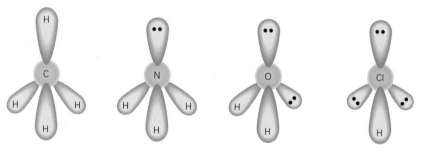

**Figure 7.4   Electron cloud models of $CH_4$, $NH_3$, $H_2O$ and HCl**

## QUESTIONS

1   What do you notice about the spatial arrangements of the bonds in the molecules of the hydrides $CH_4$, $NH_3$, $H_2O$ and HCl? What does this suggest about the interaction between electron charge clouds? Why are the molecules of ammonia and water *not* planar and linear respectively?

2   The bond angles in methane, ammonia, and water molecules are given in figure 7.5. What do these diagrams suggest?

### COMMENT

In representing three-dimensional shapes, chemists use a bond like this:

going away from you — out of plane of paper

coming towards you

**Figure 7.5   Different bond angles in similar, tetrahedral molecules**

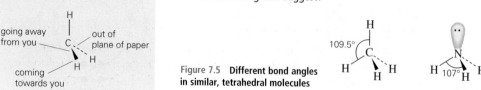

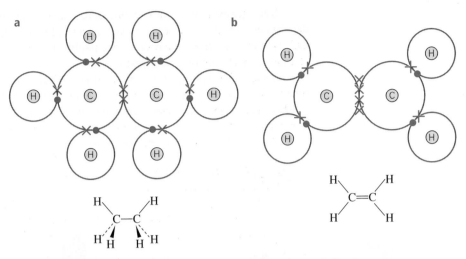

Figure 7.6 Representations of a ethane, b ethene, showing outer electron shells only

From your consideration of the shapes of molecules containing single bonds, and the changes in the bond angles from one hydride to another, you should have come to the following conclusions:

- **Pairs of electrons in an atom tend to get as far away from each other as they can. This results in a tetrahedral distribution when there are four electron pairs.**
- **Non-bonding pairs of electrons in an atom, that is, pairs of electrons not shared with another atom, repel one another more strongly than shared pairs do.** This causes some distortion of the tetrahedral arrangement. Chemists describe non-bonding pairs of electrons as 'lone pairs' of electrons.

If you did not come to these conclusions, you may like to go back over the evidence to see how well they account for the observations.

In three dimensions, the electron density of each of the bonds so far mentioned is symmetrical about the axis of a line joining the centres of the atoms forming the bond. Bonds of this type are known as $\sigma$ bonds (sigma bonds). Another important example of a $\sigma$ bond is the single bond between carbon atoms, as in the ethane molecule, $CH_3$—$CH_3$ (figure 7.6a). Topic 8 looks at the carbon–carbon $\sigma$ bond in more detail.

## Multiple bonds

Predictions about the shapes of molecules can be extended to cover multiple bonds.

### QUESTION

Look again at the 'dot and cross' diagrams you drew for ethene. Suggest a shape for an ethene molecule, $CH_2$=$CH_2$.

A double bond, as in ethene, consists of two pairs of shared electrons. However, it does not follow that a double bond can be thought of as two single bonds, although it might seem so from our usual method of representing double bonds (figure 7.6b).

Evidence from both chemical properties and structural studies suggests that the electron density in a double bond is **asymmetric** about the axis joining the two nuclei. In the case of the carbon–carbon double bond, the electron density distribution corresponds to a σ bond (sigma bond) *plus* what is described as a π bond (pi bond). The π bond consists of two electron clouds, as shown in figure 7.7b, which are not symmetrical about the axis joining the carbon nuclei. A σ bond between carbon nuclei is shown in figure 7.7a.

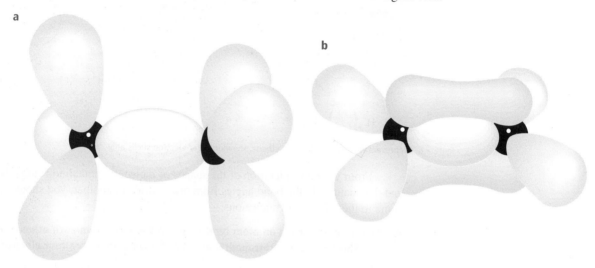

a

b

Figure 7.7   **Models showing the electron density distribution in** a **ethane,** b **ethene**

The ideas developed above enable us to predict correctly the shapes of a surprisingly large number of molecules and other structures; but the models are subject to some limitations. Some of these will be discussed later.

## Covalent giant structures

Covalent bonding is not limited to molecules. There are important elements and compounds in which non-metal atoms join together by covalent bonding to form giant lattices of atoms. Examples are diamond, graphite and silicon dioxide.

In diamond, carbon atoms are arranged so that each atom has a single covalent bond to four neighbouring atoms arranged around it in a tetrahedral pattern. This basic structure builds up to form a three-dimensional giant structure (figure 7.8, opposite) in which billions of atoms are joined together, all by strong bonds, to form the hardest natural material known.

Carbon atoms can also stack together in another way. Each carbon atom can join by a covalent bond to three neighbours to give a two-dimensional sheet with a honeycomb pattern. The sheets then stack together to form crystals of graphite (figure 7.9). Although it looks very different from diamond, it has a giant structure and, like diamond, has a very high melting point. Diamond does not conduct electricity because all the electrons are in fixed positions, shared between pairs of carbon atoms.

The atoms *within* each sheet of graphite are joined by strong, covalent bonds but *between* the sheets, bonding is relatively weak. As a result, the layers of atoms can slide over each other – graphite is a very soft substance with a greasy feel to it. Whenever you write with a pencil you are rubbing off layers of carbon atoms onto the paper.

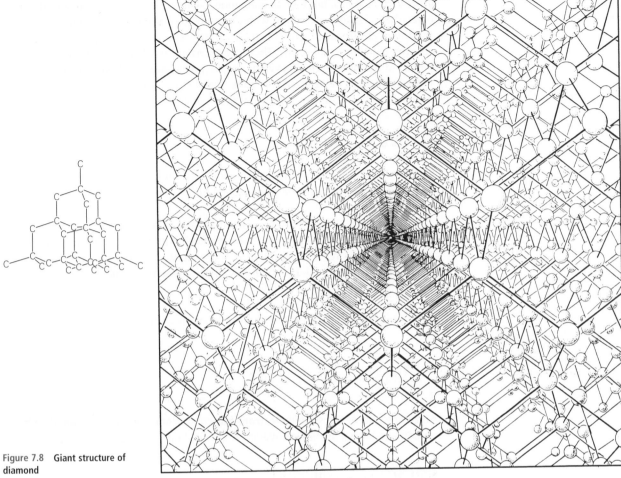

Figure 7.8 Giant structure of diamond

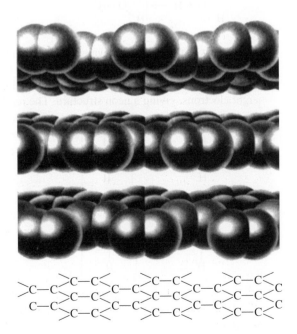

Figure 7.9 Giant structure of graphite

Notice that each carbon atom in graphite is bonded covalently to only three other carbon atoms, not four as in diamond. This means that only three of the four outer-shell electrons are paired with electrons from neighbouring atoms. The remaining electrons are shared between all the atoms in the sheet. They form an electron cloud over the atoms. **These electrons are not fixed (localised) between a pair of atoms as in normal covalent bonding. They are free to move. Chemists describe them as delocalised electrons.** This helps to explain why graphite can conduct electricity, unlike most other non-metals.

## Dative covalency

The two electrons which form a covalent bond between two atoms do not necessarily have to come one from each atom; both may come from one of the atoms.

Look back at the electronic structure of water in figure 7.3. Four of the eight electrons around the oxygen atom are not shared with any other atom. Water molecules readily react with protons to form oxonium ions, as described in section 4.1, the Brønsted–Lowry theory of acid–base behaviour.

$$H_2O + H^+ \longrightarrow H_3O^+$$

This can be interpreted in terms of electron sharing as follows:

$$\text{H}\overset{\text{O}\times}{\underset{\times\times}{\text{O}}}\text{H} + \text{H}^+ \longrightarrow \left[\text{H}\overset{\text{O}\times}{\underset{\times\times}{\text{O}}}\text{H} \quad \text{H}\right]^+$$

**Since one pair of the shared electrons has come from one atom, the bonding is sometimes known as dative covalency,** and the bond is indicated by an arrow:

$$\overset{\text{H}}{\underset{\text{H}}{\diagdown}}\text{O} + \text{H}^+ \longrightarrow \left[\overset{\text{H}}{\underset{\text{H}}{\diagdown}}\text{O} \rightarrow \text{H}\right]^+$$

Another example of dative covalency occurs in the ammonium ion, $NH_4^+$. As the next diagram shows, in the ammonium ion the hydrogen atoms each have a share in two electrons, giving a helium structure; and the nitrogen atom has a share in eight electrons, giving a neon structure. The ion has an overall +1 charge:

$$\text{H}\overset{\text{O}\times}{\underset{\times\text{O}}{\text{N}}}\text{H} + \text{H}^+ \longrightarrow \left[\text{H}\overset{\text{O}\times}{\underset{\times\text{O}}{\text{N}}}\text{H}\right]^+$$

$$\text{H}\!-\!\overset{\text{H}}{\underset{\text{H}}{\text{N}}} + \text{H}^+ \longrightarrow \left[\text{H}\!-\!\overset{\text{H}}{\underset{\text{H}}{\text{N}}}\!\rightarrow\!\text{H}\right]^+$$

The charge came originally from the proton; now it is distributed all over the ion, and is not located on any particular atom. As all the N—H bonds are the same length, and the hydrogen atoms are indistinguishable, this suggests that the ammonium ion could be represented as:

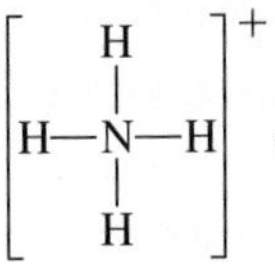

$$\left[ \begin{array}{c} H \\ | \\ H—N—H \\ | \\ H \end{array} \right]^{+} \quad \text{or} \quad NH_4^{+}$$

In the same way, the hydroxonium ion could be represented as:

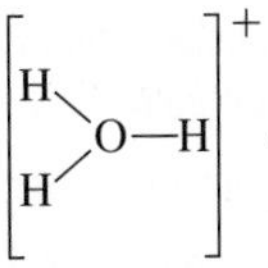

$$\left[ \begin{array}{c} H \\ \diagdown \\ O—H \\ \diagup \\ H \end{array} \right]^{+} \quad \text{or} \quad H_3O^{+}$$

The carbon monoxide molecule and the nitric acid molecule also have dative covalent bonds.

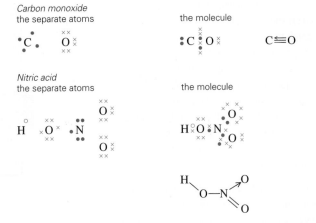

*Carbon monoxide*
the separate atoms

the molecule

*Nitric acid*
the separate atoms

the molecule

The nitric acid molecule apparently contains two different types of bonds between nitrogen and oxygen atoms. In fact, this is *not* the case and is discussed further in section 7.6.

## STUDY TASK

1   Use the information in this section to draw the three-dimensional shapes of these molecules and ions: $H_2O$, $NH_3$, $H_3O^{+}$, $NH_4^{+}$, $HNO_3$. Show the non-bonding lone pairs in your diagrams.

2   Suggest an explanation to account for the fact that the H—O—H bond angle in an $H_3O^{+}$ ion (107°) is larger than the H—O—H bond angle in a water molecule (104°). Refer back to figure 7.5 to help you.

## 7.3 Background reading: growing diamonds

QUESTIONS

Read the passage below in order to answer the following questions.

1   Give TWO reasons why alchemists tried to make gold from copper, rather than diamonds from graphite.

2   a   State the physical property of diamond which suggested that high pressure would be needed in its synthesis from graphite.
   b   Explain why high pressure is needed in the synthesis of diamond from graphite.
   c   Suggest a reason why high temperatures are needed to make diamond from graphite.
   d   Where do many scientists believe that the conditions of pressure and temperature for making diamonds occur naturally?

3   Explain why large natural diamonds, rather than synthetic ones, are still used in jewellery.

4   Describe in no more than 100 words how diamonds can be made from graphite.

From the fabled Golconda mines of ancient India to Paul Simon's 'Diamonds on the Soles of her Shoes', diamonds have been a source of fascination to men and to women. Had medieval alchemists known that graphite and diamond are merely different forms of the same element, carbon, they might have spent as much time attempting to synthesise diamonds as they did attempting to transmute base metals into gold. But copper at least looks something like gold, whereas graphite and diamond could scarcely be more dissimilar; one is dull, black, and soft enough to rub off on paper, the other is brilliant, transparent, and hard enough to drill granite. It was not until 1954 that modern alchemists learned how to synthesise diamonds from graphite.

The first steps towards the successful synthesis of diamond came from theoretical arguments and from considerations of the circumstances under which diamonds are found in nature. Diamond has a density of $3.51 \, \text{g cm}^{-3}$ whereas the density of graphite is only $2.26 \, \text{g cm}^{-3}$. Thus, very high pressure is required to squeeze the graphite carbons into the tighter packing arrangement of the diamond crystal. Many scientists believe that natural diamonds are formed under such conditions, 100 or 200 miles below the surface of the Earth, and are later brought by volcanic action closer to the surface where they can be mined.

Laboratory duplication of these harsh conditions was finally accomplished in 1954 by four General Electric scientists, Francis Budy, Tracy Hall, Herbert Strong, and Robert Wentorf. The team of General Electric scientists developed a small chamber that could maintain temperatures up to 2500 °C and pressures of $1.0 \times 10^5$ atm.

Their first attempts not only failed to produce diamond but also failed even to melt the graphite. The melting temperature of graphite is above 4000 °C, far beyond the chamber's maximum of 2500 °C.

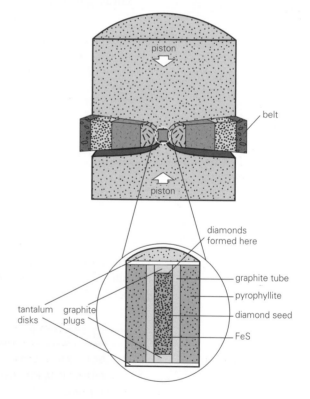

Figure 7.10   **Making diamonds**

The researchers finally hit upon the idea of adding small amounts of a metal that does melt below 2500 °C, in the hope that some of the graphite might dissolve in the molten metal and then crystallise out as diamond. The strategy worked beautifully with many metals: chromium, manganese, iron, cobalt, nickel, tantalum, ruthenium, rhodium, palladium, iridium, and platinum. When the mixture reached 1200–2400 °C under a pressure of $1.0 \times 10^5$ atm small diamond crystals began to form at a significant rate. At last, a practical synthesis of diamond had been achieved.

The crystals – usually yellow or green and less than 1 mm across – were not gem quality, but they were as hard as natural diamond and were useful as an industrial abrasive.

Today, the same method is used. It is called the high-pressure,

high-temperature method (HPHT). Annual worldwide production of synthetic diamonds is measured by the ton, far outstripping natural diamond production from mines. Synthetic HPHT diamonds as large as 8 mm across have been made, but the long heating and pressing time they require – seven days – makes them more costly than natural diamonds of the same size. Therefore, the large diamonds used in jewellery are still natural diamonds.

# 7.4 The chemists' toolkit: electronegativity

*shared two e⁻ = covalent bond*

Two electrons shared between two atoms constitute a covalent bond between these atoms. It is reasonable to ask whether the electrons are always shared equally *some are not shared equally* between the two atoms, or whether some elements are more 'electron-attractive' than others. It is found that elements do differ considerably in their electron-attractiveness. The term used for this is **electronegativity**.

*electronegativity = how much the e⁻ in bond are repelled to each atom.*

**The electronegativity of an atom represents the power of an atom in a molecule to attract electrons to itself.**

Many attempts have been made to allot numerical values to the electronegativities of the elements, but so far no wholly satisfactory method has been devised; the most widely used values are based on the method of the American chemist Linus Pauling. But whatever numerical scale is used, the trends in the values of the electronegativities of the elements in the Periodic Table are clear.

Figure 7.11
a **Trends in electronegativity in the Periodic Table**
b **The electronegativities of the halogens decrease steadily down the group**

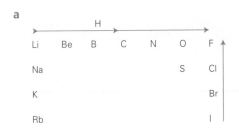

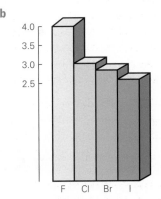

It can be seen, from figure 7.11, that the most electronegative element is fluorine; oxygen, chlorine, and nitrogen are also very electronegative.

When two atoms bonded covalently are atoms of the same element, then the attractions of their nuclei for the bonding electrons are the same, and the bonding electrons will be shared equally between them. But if the atoms are not of the same element, the two nuclei exert different degrees of attractive force on the bonding electrons, and these electrons are displaced towards one atom. Figure 7.12 illustrates this.

**This unequal sharing of electrons is known as bond polarisation.** It represents the departure of the bond from being purely covalent, and it introduces some ionic character into the bond.

One important conclusion is that wholly ionic and wholly covalent bonds are extreme types, and examples occur over the whole range of intermediate types: bonds can be partially ionic and partially covalent in character.

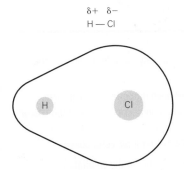

$\delta+ \quad \delta-$
H — Cl

Figure 7.12 **One of the atoms in this molecule is more electronegative than the other. δ+ and δ− show partial charges on the atoms.**

# Electronegativity and polar molecules

Figure 7.12 actually represents the shape of the HCl molecule. Turn back to the figure and then attempt the questions below.

$$O=C\begin{matrix} CH_3 \\ \\ CH_3 \end{matrix}$$

$$CH_3-CH_3$$

$$Cl-CH_3$$

Are these molecules polar?

---

## QUESTIONS

1  Copy figure 7.12 into your notebook and draw in, by means of a + and a −, the relative positions of the centre of positive charge and the centre of negative charge. What implications do you think this has for the properties of the molecule?

2  Suggest relative positions for the centre of positive charge and the centre of negative charge in the molecules shown in the margin. What elements in addition to oxygen and chlorine would be likely to produce these effects?

---

In asymmetric molecules such as HCl and $CH_3CH_2Cl$, the centre of positive charge does not coincide with the centre of negative charge, and a permanent **dipole** results. Such molecules are said to be **polar**. Highly electronegative elements such as F, O, Cl and N cause polarity in molecules. They do so partly by virtue of the bond polarisation which they produce, and partly by virtue of their lone pairs of electrons.

Polarity in molecules has important effects on the physical and chemical properties of the substances, and on the mechanisms by which they undergo reaction.

---

## QUESTION

Look back to the charge cloud diagrams for the molecules shown in figure 7.4. Decide which of these molecules are polar and which are non-polar. Draw them and label them.

---

**7.5**  # Background reading: electron spectroscopy for chemical analysis

---

## QUESTIONS

Read the following passage straight through, and then more carefully, in order to answer the following questions.

1  a  In ammonia, $NH_3$, the ionic character of the bond between nitrogen and hydrogen (N—H) is 18%. State the charge on each hydrogen atom and hence calculate the charge on the nitrogen atom.

   b  Explain why liquid ammonia is likely to be a good solvent for ionic compounds.

2  Use the results given for the sulphate ion to calculate the charge on the sulphate ion.

3  Describe the shape of the thiosulphate ion with an appropriate diagram.

4  **a**  Using the normal rules, calculate the oxidation number of sulphur in the thiosulphate ion, $S_2O_3^{2-}$.

  **b**  Suggest a reason why oxidation numbers are not always the same as the true electric charge on atoms in molecules or ions consisting of several atoms.

5  Describe the process of electron spectroscopy for chemical analysis (ESCA) and explain how it can be used to give important information about atoms in molecules, in not more than 100 words.

# ESCA – a practical method for determining charges on atoms in molecules

It is often useful to know actual charges on atoms in polar molecules. Such knowledge can help in the predictions of physical properties of compounds like the melting point, boiling point and solubility. It is also an aid to predicting and understanding chemical reactions.

In molecules like HCl, $H_2O$ or $NH_3$, determining the distribution of electric charge on the atoms is simple. The degree of ionic character of the bonds can be found by calculating the difference in electronegativity between the elements and then consulting an appropriate table of data.

Consider the example of water, $H_2O$. The difference in electronegativity gives 39% ionic character for the bond between oxygen and hydrogen. This means that the charge on each hydrogen atom is $+0.39$, and the charge on the oxygen atom is $-0.78$.

$$
\begin{array}{c}
-0.78 \\
\text{O} \\
+0.39 \ \diagup \ \diagdown \ +0.39 \\
\text{H} \quad \text{H}
\end{array}
$$

Figure 7.13   **Charges on the atoms in a water molecule**

This calculation shows that the oxygen atom in water has a very significant negative charge. This helps to explain the solubility of ionic compounds in water. Positive ions will be powerfully attracted to negative oxygen atoms in water molecules, and negative ions to the positive hydrogen atoms.

The calculation of charge distribution becomes much more difficult when the molecules contain multiple or delocalised bonds, or the molecule is non-symmetrical. It is more convenient to use experimental data instead of relying on theoretical calculations.

The main source of experimental data about charge distribution in molecules is the permanent dipole moment, which is based on measurements of the effect of a substance on an applied electric field. Unfortunately, the interpretation of such data is still difficult for complex molecules.

However, in the last 20 years the method of X-ray spectroscopy has opened up new horizons in determining the distribution of charge in molecules and ions. There are three branches of spectroscopy which involve the interaction of X-rays with molecules: ESCA (electron spectroscopy for chemical analysis), Auger spectroscopy and X-ray fluorescence spectroscopy.

When X-rays of known energy are absorbed by an atom, an electron from an inner shell is expelled and the atom becomes a positive ion in a high energy state. ESCA is concerned with measuring the kinetic energy of the expelled electrons using an electron spectrometer.

The kinetic energy of emitted electrons depends upon their binding energy within the atom. When electrons are held tightly the energy needed to release them is greater, and the kinetic energy of electrons released is less. The kinetic energy of emitted electrons, $E_k$, is related to the energy of the X-rays, $h\nu$, and the binding energy of the electrons, $E_b$, by the equation:

$$E_b = h\nu - E_k$$

The binding energy of an electron depends on the attractive force exerted by the positive nucleus on the negative electron. This is often referred to as the Coulombic force of attraction. The Coulombic attractive force is dependent on the effective charge on

Figure 7.14   **Operation of an ESCA machine**

the nucleus; the higher the effective nuclear charge, the stronger the force of attraction. The effective charge on the nucleus is related to the partial charge on the atom. So the binding energy of an electron depends on the partial charge on an atom.

A more detailed analysis shows that there is a linear relationship between electron binding energies and partial charges on atoms.

Thus by measuring kinetic energies of electrons, it is possible through calculating electron binding energies to find partial charges on atoms relatively easily.

The reason ESCA is so important is that it enables the charge on the individual atoms within molecules or ions to be calculated.

Examples of ions where ESCA helps us to understand their electronic structure are the sulphate ion and the thiosulphate ion.

In the sulphate ion ESCA shows that the ion consists of a sulphur atom with a charge of $+1.12$, and four oxygen atoms with equal charges of $-0.78$.

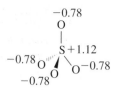

Figure 7.15 Charges on the sulphate ion as determined by ESCA

In the thiosulphate ion, $S_2O_3^{2-}$, the oxygen atoms carry the same charge of $-0.83$, but one sulphur atom has a charge of $-0.50$, and the other has a charge of $+0.99$.

These results are interesting and are quite different from the values which would be assigned to sulphur and oxygen using the concept of oxidation number in these ions. They suggest that oxidation number, while useful as a concept, is not a good indicator of the true pattern of electric charge in an ion consisting of several atoms.

## 7.6 Bond energies

Hess's Law (see section 5.2) makes it possible to calculate the energy involved in the making and breaking of covalent bonds. The results allow comparisons between the strengths of different bonds. This is helpful when trying to explain how molecules react (the mechanism) and how fast they react (the rate).

The first step is to determine the enthalpy changes of combustion of the compound, and of the separate elements. The next step is use Hess's Law to calculate the enthalpy change of formation of the compound.

**The standard enthalpy change of combustion of a substance, symbol $\Delta H_c^\ominus$ (298), is defined as the enthalpy change that occurs when one mole of the substance undergoes complete combustion under standard conditions.**

For a compound containing carbon, for example, complete combustion means the conversion of the whole of the carbon to carbon dioxide, as shown in the following equation.

$$C_{12}H_{22}O_{11}(s) + 12O_2(g) \longrightarrow 12CO_2(g) + 11H_2O(l) \qquad \Delta H_c^\ominus = -5639.7\,\text{kJ mol}^{-1}$$
sucrose

The enthalpy change of formation of sucrose can then be calculated from the enthalpy change of combustion by the use of a Hess cycle of the form:

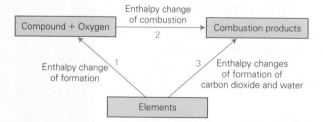

It follows from Hess's Law that the sum of the enthalpy changes for processes 1 and 2 is equal to the enthalpy change for process 3.

BACKGROUND

The standard enthalpy changes of formation of water and of carbon dioxide can be measured directly by calorimetry experiments, and these two values are known to a very high degree of accuracy.

$$C(graphite) + O_2(g) \longrightarrow CO_2(g) \qquad \Delta H_f^{\ominus}(298) = -393.5 \, kJ \, mol^{-1}$$

$$H_2(g) + \tfrac{1}{2}O_2(g) \longrightarrow H_2O(l) \qquad \Delta H_f^{\ominus}(298) = -285.8 \, kJ \, mol^{-1}$$

Let us therefore take methane as an example.

First, write down the equation for the standard enthalpy change of formation of methane (that is, from its constituent elements in their standard states). Thus:

$$C(graphite) + 2H_2(g) \xrightarrow{\Delta H_f^{\ominus}} CH_4(g)$$

Now write down the equations for burning, separately, each of the constituent elements and the product, methane, in oxygen:

$$C(graphite) + O_2(g) \xrightarrow{\Delta H_f^{\ominus}} CO_2(g)$$

$$2H_2(g) + O_2(g) \xrightarrow{2 \times \Delta H_f^{\ominus}} 2H_2O(l)$$

$$CH_4(g) + 2O_2(g) \xrightarrow{\Delta H_c^{\ominus}} CO_2(g) + 2H_2O(l)$$

The data for these reactions are

$$\Delta H_f^{\ominus}[CO_2(g)] \quad = -393.5 \, kJ \, mol^{-1}$$
$$2 \times \Delta H_f^{\ominus}[H_2O(l)] = -571.6 \, kJ \, mol^{-1}$$
$$\Delta H_c^{\ominus}[CH_4(g)] \quad = -890.3 \, kJ \, mol^{-1}$$

We may now substitute the methane example in the general Hess cycle, given earlier.

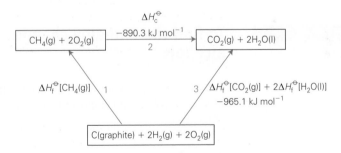

The overall energy change in going from elements to combustion products must be the same whatever the route. Equating the two routes, we have:

enthalpy change for process 3 = sum of enthalpy changes for processes 1 and 2

Therefore:

$$-965.1 \, kJ \, mol^{-1} = \Delta H_f^{\ominus}[CH_4(g)] + (-890.3 \, kJ \, mol^{-1})$$
$$\Delta H_f^{\ominus}[CH_4(g)] = -74.8 \, kJ \, mol^{-1}$$

Determining the enthalpies of formation of compounds is the first step in determining individual bond energies.

---

STUDY TASK

The compound methanol, $CH_3OH$, cannot be prepared directly from its elements. Given that the standard enthalpy change of combustion of methanol, $\Delta H_c^{\ominus}$, is $-726.0\,kJ\,mol^{-1}$, calculate the standard enthalpy change of formation of the compound.

$$C(graphite) + 2H_2(g) + \tfrac{1}{2}O_2(g) \longrightarrow CH_3OH(l)$$

The other standard enthalpy changes that you need have been given earlier in this topic.

---

How can enthalpy changes of combustion give information about the energy required to break individual bonds?

One way of attempting to answer this question would be to find a series of substances which are closely related to each other, and which differ from each other by some fixed unit of structure. Then by studying such substances it might be possible to see whether that fixed unit of structure makes any consistent contribution to the overall energy situation.

A possible example is the series of alcohols:

- $CH_3CH_2CH_2OH$                propan-1-ol
- $CH_3CH_2CH_2CH_2OH$           butan-1-ol
- $CH_3CH_2CH_2CH_2CH_2OH$       pentan-1-ol
- $CH_3CH_2CH_2CH_2CH_2CH_2OH$    hexan-1-ol
- $CH_3CH_2CH_2CH_2CH_2CH_2CH_2OH$    heptan-1-ol
- $CH_3CH_2CH_2CH_2CH_2CH_2CH_2CH_2OH$   octan-1-ol

Each compound differs from the next by one $—CH_2—$ unit.

In this series, the question 'Does the $—CH_2—$ group make a specific contribution to the enthalpy change of combustion of alcohols?' can be posed. One method of finding out is to burn the alcohols and measure the enthalpy change per mole of each.

---

EXPERIMENT 7.6

# To find the enthalpy changes of combustion of some alcohols

In this experiment, you will find the enthalpy change of combustion of one of the series of alcohols and compare your results with those obtained by other members of the class.

## Procedure

There are different types of combustion calorimeter; the heat energy losses from the calorimeter in figure 7.16 (opposite) are too great for accurate work, but acceptable **comparisons** can be made for similar compounds provided the calorimeter is first **calibrated**.

### Calibration of the apparatus

1   Make sure the outside of your calorimeter is clean, then half fill with water. Fit the lid with the thermometer in place. Stir and record the temperature of the water.

---

**SAFETY** ⚠️

The alcohols in the series propan-1-ol to octan-1-ol are highly flammable and harmful.

(Ethanol and methanol are even more flammable, and methanol is at least harmful.)

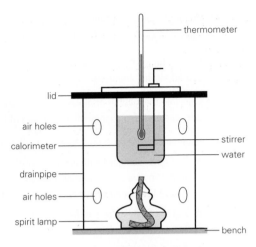

Figure 7.16 A simple combustion calorimeter

2 Take a small spirit lamp that is almost full of propan-1-ol and light the wick. The flame needs to be 1–2 cm high and the wick itself should not be burning: adjust the wick if necessary. Place the metal (or glass) cap on the lamp to extinguish the flame. Allow to cool, wipe any condensation off the cap, and weigh the complete spirit lamp with the cap in place.

3 Check the temperature of the water and record it as the starting temperature.

4 In quick succession on a level and draught-free surface, light the wick of the spirit lamp, place the 'chimney' around the spirit lamp, and fit the lid and calorimeter on top of the chimney. Start a stop watch.

5 Stir continuously, gently and slowly.

6 When there has been a temperature rise of at least 5 °C, record the temperature and immediately lift the chimney and calorimeter, as one piece, off the spirit lamp and **at once put the cap on to extinguish the flame and trap any alcohol vapour**.

7 Then reweigh the complete spirit lamp with the cap in place.

### Determination of the enthalpy change of combustion of an alcohol

Repeat the experiment with an alcohol from the series butan-1-ol to octan-1-ol, making sure that the class covers the whole series at least once. Aim to get the same temperature rise in each experiment so that the heat losses involved in each experiment are approximately the same.

✎ **In your notes:**

1 Use the results from burning propan-1-ol to calculate the heat capacity of the apparatus. In this way you use the results for one alcohol to calibrate the apparatus.

First look up the molar mass and enthalpy change of combustion of propan-1-ol in the *Book of data* and then calculate the energy produced by burning the alcohol:

$$\text{energy produced, } Q/\text{kJ} = \frac{\text{mass of propan-1-ol burned/g}}{\text{molar mass of propan-1-ol/g mol}^{-1}} \times \text{enthalpy change of combustion of propan-1-ol/kJ mol}^{-1}$$

Use your value for the energy released on burning and the measured temperature rise to calculate the heat capacity of the apparatus:

$$\text{energy produced, } Q/\text{kJ} = \text{heat capacity of the apparatus, } c/\text{kJ K}^{-1} \times \text{temperature rise/K}$$

**COMMENT**

The suggested temperature change, of 5 °C, is only a guide, and may need to be altered for different sizes of apparatus.

2 Again use the relationship:

energy produced, $Q/kJ$ = heat capacity of the apparatus, $c/kJ\ K^{-1} \times$ temperature rise/K

but this time determine a value for $Q$, the heat energy produced by burning the second alcohol you used.

3 Calculate the number of moles of alcohol burned in the second experiment and hence $\Delta H_c$, the enthalpy change of combustion of the alcohol in kilojoules per mole.

4 Comment on the procedure to examine the likely uncertainty in your results.

a The term 'standard enthalpy change of combustion' implies complete combustion, in this instance to carbon dioxide and water. Can we be sure that this has taken place? What might have been formed instead, to some extent?

b List the main sources of heat loss and the precautions you took to reduce heat losses.

c Do you think the various sources of error will tend to make your value more or less negative than the true one?

d Compare your results with those of others in the class, and see whether they provide any answer to the question: does the $CH_2$ group make a specific contribution to the enthalpy change of combustion of alcohols?

---

## STUDY TASK

Using a spreadsheet, plot a graph of $\Delta H_c$ for the alcohols from methanol to octan-1-ol against the number of carbon atoms. Use your own values and those of other members of your class, or take values from the *Book of Data*.

---

You should have found that the difference in value between successive alcohols in the series is about the same; and, of course, the structural difference between successive alcohols is the $CH_2$ group of atoms.

When one extra $CH_2$ group burns, extra energy must be supplied to break more bonds; but even more energy is released by the formation of extra $C{=}O$ bonds and $O{-}H$ bonds. This is demonstrated below for the burning of the two simplest alkanes, with highlighting in green to show the extra bonds broken and the extra bonds formed.

### COMMENT

The first step in a reaction is always the supply of energy to break bonds. Energy is only released when the new bonds are formed.

Experimentally, a fixed amount of energy is associated with this number of bonds broken and bonds formed. It seems likely, therefore, that each individual bond has its own energy that must be supplied to break it, or that will be released when it is formed.

## Bond energies in other compounds

Consider now the alkane series of hydrocarbons and begin with the first member, methane, $CH_4$. It seems reasonable to assume that the energy associated with the C—H bonds must be reflected in the total amount of energy required to break the molecule into its constituent atoms.

$$CH_4(g) \longrightarrow C(g) + 4H(g)$$

Notice that breaking a molecule into its atoms results in the atoms being in the gaseous state, $C(g)$ and not $C$(graphite), together with $H(g)$ and not $H_2(g)$.

To construct a Hess cycle in which an element goes from its standard state (solid, liquid, or gaseous molecules) to gaseous atoms we need to know a special enthalpy change: the **enthalpy change of atomisation** of an element, $\Delta H_{at}$.

**The standard enthalpy change of atomisation of an element, symbol $\Delta H_{at}^{\ominus}$, is the enthalpy change that takes place when one mole of gaseous atoms is made from the element in its standard state under standard conditions.**

| Equation | Enthalpy change of atomisation/kJ mol$^{-1}$ |
|---|---|
| $C$(graphite) $\longrightarrow$ $C(g)$ | +716.7 |
| $\frac{1}{2}O_2(g) \longrightarrow O(g)$ | +249.2 |
| $\frac{1}{2}H_2(g) \longrightarrow H(g)$ | +218.0 |

We can now calculate the enthalpy change of atomisation of methane by constructing the appropriate Hess cycle. The equation is

$$CH_4(g) \longrightarrow C(g) + 4H(g)$$

The enthalpy changes are shown on the diagram:

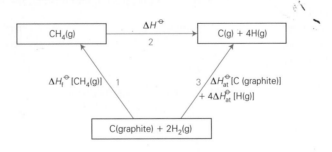

$$2 + 1 = 3$$

$$\Delta H^{\ominus} + \Delta H_f^{\ominus}[CH_4(g)] = \Delta H_{at}^{\ominus}[C\text{(graphite)}] + 4\Delta H_{at}^{\ominus}[H(g)]$$

Putting in the values:

$$\Delta H^{\ominus} = -(-74.8 \text{ kJ mol}^{-1}) + 716.7 \text{ kJ mol}^{-1} + (4 \times 218 \text{ kJ mol}^{-1})$$
$$= +1663.5 \text{ kJ mol}^{-1}$$

So, for the reaction,

$$H-\underset{\underset{H}{|}}{\overset{\overset{H}{|}}{C}}-H(g) \longrightarrow C(g) + 4H(g) \quad \Delta H^{\ominus} = +1663.5 \text{ kJ mol}^{-1}$$

Although $CH_4$ is tetrahedral in shape, it is often printed for convenience as:

$$H-\underset{\underset{H}{|}}{\overset{\overset{H}{|}}{C}}-H$$

Do not be led into thinking that the bond angles in methane are all $90°$.

If the bonds are equal in strength, then the bond energy of one C—H bond should be:

$$\frac{1663.5}{4} = +415.9 \text{ kJ mol}^{-1}$$

Denoting the bond energy of the C—H bond by $E(C—H)$ we have

$$E(C—H) = +415.9 \text{ kJ mol}^{-1}$$

Now consider ethane, $C_2H_6$. A similar calculation to the one above shows that the reaction

$$C_2H_6(g) \longrightarrow 2C(g) + 6H(g) \qquad \Delta H^{\ominus} = +2826.1 \text{ kJ mol}^{-1}$$

involves the breaking of six C—H bonds and one C—C bond. Denoting the bond energy of the C—C bond by $E(C—C)$, we have:

$$+2826.1 = E(C—C) + 6E(C—H)$$

Substituting the value 415.9 for $E(C—H)$:

$$+2826.1 = E(C—C) + (6 \times 415.9)$$

So,    $E(C—C) = +330.7 \text{ kJ mol}^{-1}$

The bond energy $E(C—Cl)$ has been determined using several compounds. The table below shows the compounds and the values obtained for them.

| Compound | | E(C—Cl) /kJ mol$^{-1}$ |
|---|---|---|
| $Cl-\underset{\underset{Cl}{|}}{\overset{\overset{Cl}{|}}{C}}-Cl$ | tetrachloromethane | + 327 |
| $H-\underset{\underset{H}{|}}{\overset{\overset{H}{|}}{C}}-Cl$ | chloromethane | + 335 |
| $H-\underset{\underset{H}{|}}{\overset{\overset{H}{|}}{C}}-\underset{\underset{H}{|}}{\overset{\overset{H}{|}}{C}}-Cl$ | chloroethane | + 342 |

**COMMENT**

From the examples shown in the table, it can be seen that the C—Cl bond energy value is approximately the same in each case, though it depends upon the compound from which it was determined, to some extent; that is, the environment of the bond affects the value. The X—Y bond energy will vary somewhat, depending upon the nature of the other atoms or groups of atoms which are attached to X and Y. But if an average bond energy is taken this can often be very useful. Tables have therefore been prepared giving average bond energies.

| Bond | E/kJ mol$^{-1}$ |
|---|---|
| C—H | 413 |
| C—C | 347 |
| C—O | 358 |
| C—Cl | 346 |
| O—H | 464 |

A fuller table is given in the *Book of data*, table 4.6.

An approximate value for the enthalpy change involved in the atomisation of a compound from the gaseous state can be obtained by adding up the average bond energies for all the bonds in the molecule of that compound.

## QUESTIONS

1 Using the bond energies listed work out an approximate value for the energy needed to atomise one mole of gaseous propan-1-ol, $CH_3CH_2CH_2OH$. (Propan-1-ol is, of course, normally a liquid.)

2 Make a table showing the bond energies for the hydrides across the Periodic Table, C—H, N—H, O—H, and F—H, and then insert the vertical series F—H, Cl—H, Br—H, and I—H (listed as H—I in Table 4.6 in the *Book of data*). What are the trends in the ease of breaking the bonds, and what information can you deduce from them?

# Bond lengths and bond energies

The greater electron density between nuclei joined by multiple bonds causes a greater force of attraction between the nuclei and is reflected in shorter bond lengths and greater bond energies. Examine the figures given in the table below to confirm this. Are the bond energies of multiple bonds simple multiples of the bond energies of single bonds?

| Bond | Compound(s) | Bond length/nm | Bond energy/kJ mol$^{-1}$ |
|---|---|---|---|
| C—C | alkanes | 0.154 | 347 |
| C=C | alkenes | 0.134 | 612 |
| C≡C | alkynes | 0.120 | 838 |
| C—N | amines | 0.147 | 286 |
| C=N | (average) | 0.130 | 615 |
| C≡N | nitriles | 0.116 | 887 |
| C—O | alcohols | 0.143 | 336 |
| C=O | ketones | 0.122 | 749 |
| C≜O | carbon monoxide | 0.113 | 1077 |

# Bond energies and rates of reaction

In gases and liquids, molecules are in constant motion. Even when using very small quantities of reactants, many millions of collisions happen between molecules every second. If a collision occurs between molecules of substances which are capable of reacting with each other, the reaction may happen with great force or very gently, depending on how quickly the molecules are moving at the moment of collision and in what directions the molecules are travelling when the impact occurs. **The fundamental idea is that a reaction will happen between the two molecules only if the collision occurs with enough energy to break bonds in either or both of the molecules.**

Not all collisions occur with sufficient energy to break bonds even when the molecules are moving quickly. A simple analogy would be damage caused in a road traffic accident. Two cars each travelling at 30 mph in a head-on collision will cause each other massive damage; a car going at 31 mph hitting another one, going at 29 mph, in the back would be a much less traumatic experience.

Unlike the interaction between colliding cars, molecular collisions can sometimes only be effective if they happen between *particular atoms* in the molecules concerned. A useful example here is the reaction between bromoethane and aqueous hydroxide ions. The overall equation for this reaction (which you will study in Topic 10 and again in more detail in Topic 11) is:

$$
\underset{\substack{| \ \ |\\ H \ H}}{\overset{\substack{H \ H\\ | \ \ |}}{H-C-C-Br}} + OH^{-} \longrightarrow \underset{\substack{| \ \ |\\ H \ H}}{\overset{\substack{H \ H\\ | \ \ |}}{H-C-C-OH}} + Br^{-}
$$

There is evidence that in this reaction the oxygen atom of the hydroxide ion has to hit the carbon atom which is attached to the bromine atom in bromoethane:

$$
HO \rightsquigarrow \underset{\underset{H}{\overset{|}{H}}}{\overset{CH_3}{\overset{|}{C}}} \overset{\delta+}{\phantom{C}}\!\!\!-\overset{\delta-}{Br}
$$

We will be examining the evidence for this in Topic 11.

The reaction between a hydroxide ion and a bromoethane molecule goes through an in-between 'transition state'. A bond starts to form between the oxygen atom and the carbon atom while the bond between the carbon atom and the bromine atom is breaking. **The point where the old bond has not quite broken and the new bond has not quite formed is the point of maximum energy and represents the transition state at the top of an energy barrier between reactants and products**

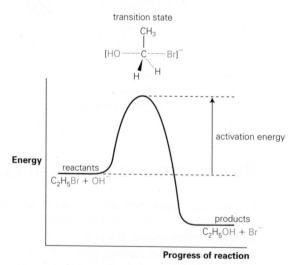

Figure 7.17   **An energy profile for the reaction**

**The difference in energy between the reactants and the transition state is the activation energy, $E_a$.** The greater the activation energy the more difficult it is to form the transition state and therefore the slower the reaction. One important factor in the value of the activation energy is the bond energy of the bonds which have to be broken, though of course the activation energy will always be less than this because a new bond is being formed at the same time.

Raising the temperature of the reaction mixture increases the kinetic energy of the molecules and so increases the number of collisions which occur with sufficient energy to reach the transition state.

Another way of increasing the rate of reaction is to provide a suitable **catalyst. A catalyst accelerates a reaction by making possible an alternative mechanism involving a different transition state and lower activation energy.** The effect of this is that more molecular collisions have the energy needed to reach the transition state.

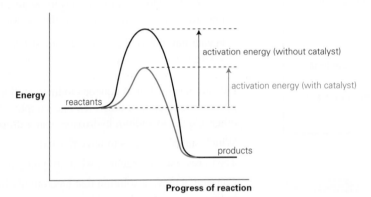

Figure 7.18   **An energy profile showing the effect of a catalyst**

There is no single theory to explain how catalysts work. Some solid catalysts adsorb molecules of reactant, that is to say the molecules stick to the surface of the catalyst. The creation of the forces of attraction between the reactant molecules and the catalyst surface can have the effect of weakening the bonds which have to be broken during the reaction which is being catalysed. Enzymes are very important catalysts in living systems and their action depends on an exact fit between their molecules and those of the substance upon which they are acting.

Here are some examples to show the effect of catalysts:

- $H_2O_2(aq) \longrightarrow H_2O(l) + \frac{1}{2}O_2(g)$

  | | |
  |---|---|
  | Without a catalyst, | activation energy $= +79$ kJ mol$^{-1}$ |
  | With a platinum catalyst, | activation energy $= +49$ kJ mol$^{-1}$ |
  | With an enzyme as catalyst, | activation energy $= +36$ kJ mol$^{-1}$ |

- $2HI(g) \longrightarrow H_2(l) + I_2(g)$

  | | |
  |---|---|
  | Without a catalyst, | activation energy $= +183$ kJ mol$^{-1}$ |
  | With a gold catalyst, | activation energy $= +105$ kJ mol$^{-1}$ |
  | With a platinum catalyst, | activation energy $= +58$ kJ mol$^{-1}$ |

## 7.7  Reversible reactions

In section 7.6 we considered the link between the rate of a reaction and the energies of the bonds which had to be broken. Implicit in the argument was the assumption that a reaction would go to completion. But do all reactions do so?

We are going to start thinking about some examples of reversible processes in order to be clear about what is happening at the molecular level. In the experiment below several of the reactions involve ions as well as molecules. These reactions are easier, quicker and safer to study than reactions just between covalent molecules. The principles, however, are the same.

# Reversible reactions

## Procedure

**SAFETY**

**!**

0.01 M iodine solution is harmful.

0.1 M sulphuric acid is an irritant.

0.1 M sodium hydroxide is corrosive.

The indicator solutions are flammable.

**COMMENT**

Look up your notes from Topic 6 if you need help.

1    Place a small amount of ammonium chloride, $NH_4Cl$, in a boiling tube and heat it gently. Do not allow fumes to escape. Perform this test in a fume cupboard or place a loose plug of glass wool in the mouth of the boiling tube.

✎    **In your notes:** Record your observations. Did the ammonium chloride decompose? Did it re-form?

2    Put samples of 0.01 M aqueous iodine solution (in potassium iodide solution) into two separate test tubes. To one sample add 0.1 M sulphuric acid and to the other add 0.1 M sodium hydroxide, using dropping pipettes.

Which sample appears to have reacted?

Try to reverse the reaction: what are you going to add?

Can you achieve a solution that has roughly half the original concentration of iodine?

✎    **In your notes:** Record your observations and the conditions needed to make the reaction go one way and the change in conditions needed to make it go the other way.

3    Take three small Petri dishes. Adding enough liquid to cover the bottom of a dish, add 0.1 M hydrochloric acid to the first dish, 0.1 M sodium hydroxide to the second, and pure water to the third. Using a dropping pipette add 1 cm³ of an indicator to the acid and alkali, and 2 cm³ of indicator to the water.

Place the dishes on a white tile or piece of paper, with the acid and alkali dishes in a stack and the neutral water dish alongside.

Compare the colours by looking down through the dishes.

✎    **In your notes:** Is the acid plus alkali colour the same as the neutral water colour? How does altering the conditions affect the indicator? What is the reversible change you are studying in this example?

4    Put 5 cm³ of 0.1 M cobalt(II) sulphate solution into a test tube. Add concentrated hydrochloric acid using a dropping pipette (TAKE CARE) until the colour change is complete.

Can you get the mixture to return to the original pink colour by adding water cautiously? Now try adding concentrated hydrochloric acid again.

✎    **In your notes:** Describe the sequence of colour changes. Can you make any suggestion about the reaction occurring?

# Interpretation of the reversible processes

## 1 Ammonium chloride

You will see the white solid vaporising at the bottom of the test tube as it decomposes into gaseous ammonia, $NH_3$, and gaseous hydrogen chloride, $HCl$.

Further up the tube where it is cooler you will see white solid re-forming as the gaseous products recombine to form ammonium chloride. This is an example of a reaction which takes place in both directions – a reversible reaction – and it can be summed up in the chemical equations:

$$NH_4Cl(s) \xrightarrow{\text{on heating}} NH_3(g) + HCl(g)$$

$$NH_4Cl(s) \xleftarrow{\text{on cooling}} NH_3(g) + HCl(g)$$

## 2 Iodine and alkali

As you should recall from Topic 6, iodine reacts with cold, dilute sodium hydroxide solution.

$$I_2(aq) + 2NaOH(aq) \longrightarrow NaI(aq) + NaIO(aq) + H_2O(l)$$

As this reaction proceeds, the reactants are used up and the products are simultaneously formed. **This process is called the forward reaction.**

The experiment you carried out showed that the iodine solution can be recovered by adding dilute acid.

$$NaI(aq) + NaIO(aq) + H_2SO_4(aq) \longrightarrow I_2(aq) + Na_2SO_4(aq) + H_2O(l)$$

**This process is called the reverse reaction.**

At a suitable intermediate pH you can imagine a position of *balance* being reached between these two processes occurring in opposite directions – in other words **the reaction reaches a state of equilibrium**.

The reaction can be more readily understood when it is written in the form of an ionic equation.

$$I_2(aq) + 2OH^-(aq) \rightleftharpoons I^-(aq) + IO^-(aq) + H_2O(l)$$

The sodium ions and the sulphate ions are 'spectator ions' and do not undergo chemical change in either direction. They have, therefore, been left out so that we can look at what actually reacts.

## 3 Indicators

As you saw in Topic 4, indicators readily and reversibly change from their acidic to their alkaline colour. When carried out carefully, this experiment demonstrates that their neutral colour is a mixture of their colours in acidic and alkaline solutions.

Indicators are complex molecules and we therefore represent them by the formula HIn.

$$HIn(aq) \rightleftharpoons H^+(aq) + In^-(aq)$$

gives colour in acidic conditions    gives colour in alkaline conditions

COMMENT

The symbol $\rightleftharpoons$ indicates that we are considering a reversible reaction.

## 4 The colour of cobalt ions

This experiment also illustrates the effect on a reversible reaction of changing the concentration of some of the reactants. Leaving out the 'spectator' ions, the equation for the reaction is:

$$Co(H_2O)_6^{2+}(aq) + 4Cl^-(aq) \rightleftharpoons CoCl_4^{2-}(aq) + 6H_2O(l)$$

pink                                  blue

Notice that cobalt ions in solution are hydrated. The ions $Co(H_2O)_6^{2+}(aq)$ and $CoCl_4^{2-}(aq)$ are examples of **complex ions**, which you will study in more detail in Topic 19.

When you first added concentrated hydrochloric acid, chloride ions from the acid started displacing water molecules bonded to the cobalt(II) ion. This resulted in a colour change from pink to blue as the forward reaction occurred.

Adding water caused the reverse reaction to occur and the pink colour reappeared.

## QUESTIONS

A concentrated solution of bismuth(III) chloride is clear and colourless but when water is added it becomes cloudy. The equation is:

$$BiCl_3(aq) + H_2O(l) \rightleftharpoons BiOCl(s) + 2HCl(aq)$$

1   What could you add to the cloudy mixture to make it go clear again?

2   Having made the mixture clear, how could you re-form the precipitate?

3   What do you imagine an intermediate state would look like?

4   Repeating **1** and **2** as a cycle gets progressively more difficult to carry out. Why do you think this is?

---

**EXPERIMENT 7.7b**

# Dynamic equilibrium

**SAFETY**

Hydrocarbon solvent is flammable.

## Procedure

1   Iodine, $I_2$, is only slightly soluble in water but much more soluble in aqueous potassium iodide solution. It is also soluble in organic solvents such as hydrocarbons.

   **a** Use a spatula or tweezers to put one very small piece of iodine into a test tube. Add 5 cm³ of a hydrocarbon solvent and shake the test tube gently (TAKE CARE and do not put your thumb over the mouth of the test tube). Note the colour of the solution and its intensity.
   Now add 5 cm³ of potassium iodide solution and shake again. How is the iodine colour distributed between the two solvents?

   **b** Repeat **a** using a piece of iodine of similar size but add the solvents in the reverse order. Note the colours and their intensity.

   **In your notes:** Is the final effect the same in both **a** and **b**? Do you think that iodine molecules are on the move even when no colour changes can be seen? Describe what you think is happening in terms of the movement of iodine molecules between the solvents when they are first added to the test tubes.

# Interpretation of dynamic equilibrium

We already know of a number of changes which, when allowed to start, do not proceed to completion. That is, not all the reactants are changed into new forms or new substances.

Shaking a solution of iodine in a hydrocarbon with potassium iodide solution leads to an equilibrium state. The same equilibrium state is achieved by shaking a solution of iodine in potassium iodide with the hydrocarbon.

This state of equilibrium is represented by:

$$I_2(\text{hydrocarbon}) \rightleftharpoons I_2(\text{aq})$$

**The equilibrium state can be approached from either direction.**

In the equilibrium mixtures there is nothing to stop iodine molecules continuing to move from the hydrocarbon to the aqueous layer. There is also nothing to stop iodine molecules moving back from the aqueous layer to the hydrocarbon solvent.

The two processes must be going on simultaneously but at the same rate, otherwise the properties of the system would alter. This possibility can be investigated by using a radioactive isotope as a tracer. Using the radioactive isotope [131]I it is possible to detect the interchange of iodine between the aqueous solution and the hydrocarbon solution even when they are at equilibrium and do not appear to be changing.

It is not only equilibria between solutions which reach a state of equilibrium in which forward and backward processes cancel each other out because they are happening at the same rate. The same thing happens with chemical reactions at equilibrium. **This means that chemical equilibria are dynamic states**

# The effect of changes of concentration on an equilibrium system

It would seem likely that reversible reactions would respond to a change in the conditions of the equilibrium system by counteracting the change which is being made: increasing the concentration of a product would result in the equilibrium reversing in favour of the reactants, and vice versa.

Do equilibrium systems behave similarly when changes in temperature and pressure are made? We shall investigate this in the next experiment. This time the example involves only covalent molecules.

**EXPERIMENT 7.7c** — ## The $N_2O_4 \rightleftharpoons 2NO_2$ equilibrium

The oxides of nitrogen produced from the thermal decomposition of lead(II) nitrate can be collected in a gas syringe. Both gases are present at room temperature; nitrogen dioxide is brown and dinitrogen tetroxide is colourless. This experiment will be demonstrated to you by your teacher because of the hazardous nature of oxides of nitrogen.

## SAFETY ⚠

Nitrogen oxides are very toxic and corrosive; this experiment must be carried out in a fume cupboard. Migraine sufferers should take particular care not to breathe in the fumes.

## Procedure

### 1 Effect of change of temperature

Have two beakers of water available, one cooled to less than 10 °C with ice, and the other warmed to about 50 °C.

Note the colour of the gas mixture at room temperature, and what the changes are on cooling and warming the gas mixture when it is immersed alternately in the beakers of hot and cold water.

✎    **In your notes:** Remembering that $N_2O_4$ is colourless and $NO_2$ is brown, how do you interpret the changes in colour?

### 2 Effect of change of pressure

Note the colour change when the pressure is suddenly altered by pushing in the piston of the syringe; and when the piston is pulled out as far as possible.

✎    **In your notes:** How do you interpret the colour changes with pressure?

The colour changes with pressure change are not so easy to interpret because the volume change will alter the colour anyhow. And the final colour changes obtained do not happen instantly, as the rate of the reaction is quite slow.

## Effect of temperature change

When the syringe was placed in the beaker of warm water, the mixture became a rich dark brown, showing that more $NO_2(g)$ molecules had formed. The equilibrium had adjusted to the increase in temperature.

In the beaker containing cold water, the mixture became much lighter because the concentration of $N_2O_4(g)$ molecules increased. Thus:

$$N_2O_4(g) \xrightarrow{\text{on heating}} 2NO_2(g)$$

$$2NO_2(g) \xrightarrow{\text{on cooling}} N_2O_4(g)$$

To understand this further we need more information: specifically, we need to know the **enthalpy change of reaction**.

$$N_2O_4(g) \rightleftharpoons 2NO_2(g) \qquad \Delta H^\ominus = +58.0 \, \text{kJ mol}^{-1}$$

**The reaction in the forward direction is endothermic, so it is favoured when additional heat energy is supplied,** as the change takes in the extra energy given to the system.

The opposite is true for the exothermic reactions, which are favoured by lowering the temperature.

## COMMENT

When an enthalpy change of reaction is quoted alongside an equilibrium system, it refers to the **forward reaction**, that is from left to right of the equation. Remember that a reaction which is exothermic in one direction must be endothermic in the other.

## Effect of pressure change

You should have seen that, when the pressure of the system was increased, initially it became darker as the concentration of the brown $NO_2$ molecules increased. However, this is quickly followed by a lightening of colour as the equilibrium readjusts to a new position. The final colour is in fact lighter than the original mixture, showing that the reaction has formed a higher proportion of colourless $N_2O_4(g)$.

$$2NO_2(g) \xrightarrow{\text{increasing pressure}} N_2O_4(g)$$

The move is, therefore, towards the existence of fewer molecules. This tends to reduce the pressure and, thus, counteracts the increase in the applied pressure.

When the pressure on the gas is reduced, after an initial lightening in colour the gas mixture ends up darker than it was originally. Therefore:

$$N_2O_4(g) \xrightarrow{\text{decreasing pressure}} 2NO_2(g)$$

So, once again, the applied change is opposed. In this case there is an increase in the total number of molecules, which tends to counteract the decrease in the applied pressure.

**Increased pressure, therefore, moves a reaction towards the side of the equation which has fewer molecules. Decreased pressure has the reverse effect.**

In the case of reactions such as

$$H_2(g) + Cl_2(g) \rightleftharpoons 2HCl(g)$$

a change in pressure does not shift the equation either way since there is no change in the total number of molecules when reaction occurs.

# The effect of a catalyst on an equilibrium system

A common misunderstanding is to suppose that a catalyst increases the amount of product obtained in an equilibrium reaction. It does not.

A catalyst speeds up the *rate at which equilibrium is reached* but does not affect the amounts of products and reactants present at equilibrium. A catalyst affects both the forward reaction and the reverse reaction to the same extent.

It is not usual in industry to allow a reaction to go fully to equilibrium. The addition of a catalyst to a process ensures that there is a greater yield of product per hour. An industrial plant has to be run in accordance with the best economic principles at all times.

# Le Chatelier's Principle

There has been a common thread running through this discussion of the effects of a change in concentration, pressure or temperature on an equilibrium system. The position of equilibrium shifts in the direction which opposes the change in the conditions. We can, therefore, make an equilibrium system go the way we want by suitably adjusting the conditions under which it is carried out.

We can shift the position of equilibrium in favour of more product using the general guidelines:

1 raise the temperature when the reaction is endothermic

2 lower the temperature when the reaction is exothermic

3 raise the pressure when there are fewer gaseous product molecules than gaseous reactant molecules

4 lower the pressure when there are fewer gaseous reactant molecules than gaseous product molecules.

The appropriate procedure is to do the opposite to the natural effect of the reaction. These guidelines were first recognised by the French scientist, Henri Le Chatelier, in 1888 and are summed up in the principle which bears his name.

**When a system in equilibrium is subjected to a change, the processes which take place are such as to tend to counteract the change.**

This principle has been, and continues to be, of great significance in the study of chemical equilibria: many important industrial processes are based on reversible reactions.

## KEY SKILLS

### Communication

Reading about growing diamonds and about electron spectroscopy (background reading, sections 7.3 and 7.5) and summarising the information in each passage gives you opportunities to develop your skills of selecting and synthesising information from documents.

### Application of number

Experiment 7.6 involves a multi-step calculation. It is important to show your methods clearly and work to appropriate levels of accuracy. You have to use and rearrange formulae. You have to interpret your results, assess possible sources of error and explain how your results relate to the purpose of your activity.

### IT

In this topic you could use chemical modelling software from a CD-ROM or the Internet to study the shapes of covalent molecules. This would allow you to compare the advantages and limitations of using software, physical models and textbook diagrams to study molecular shapes.

## TOPIC REVIEW

Topic 7 has introduced you to an interrelated set of ideas. The unifying theme of 'covalent bonding' has been used to interpret a number of important aspects of chemistry. Keep this in mind as you summarise the topic.

1 **List key words or terms with definitions where necessary**

Give **examples** to help you remember the following terms:

- electron density maps
- covalent bonds
- $\sigma$ and $\pi$ bonds
- lone pairs of electrons
- dative bonds
- bond lengths and bond angles
- electronegativity

- polar molecules
- delocalised electrons
- bond energy
- $\Delta H_f^{\ominus}$ (you must be able to write the definition for this term)
- standard enthalpy change of atomisation (you must know the notation for this term)
- activation energy
- catalyst
- reversible reaction
- dynamic equilibrium.

**2   Summarise the key principles as simply as possible**

This topic requires **clear explanations** of the different **ideas** and **how they relate one to the other**. You must be able to describe these relationships and give examples:

- the reasons for the shapes of different covalent molecules
- the relationship between the physical properties of an element or compound and its structure and bonding
- the use of Hess's Law to determine bond energies
- bond energies in relationship to reactivity
- the effect of bond breaking and making on rates of reaction
- Le Chatelier's Principle and the effects of changing concentrations, pressures and temperatures on systems at equilibrium.

# REVIEW QUESTIONS

✱ Indicates that the *Book of data* is needed.

**7.1**   Draw 'dot and cross' diagrams to show the electron arrangements in the following, showing outer shell electrons only:

| | | | | | | |
|---|---|---|---|---|---|---|
| a | bromine, $Br_2$ | (1) | f | methanal, HCHO | (1) |
| b | hydrogen fluoride, HF | (1) | g | hydrogen cyanide, HCN | (1) |
| c | hydrogen sulphide, $H_2S$ | (1) | h | hydrogen peroxide, $H_2O_2$ | (1) |
| d | carbon dioxide, $CO_2$ | (1) | i | the ammonium ion, $NH_4^+$ | (1) |
| e | silane, $SiH_4$ | (1) | j | the hydroxide ion, $OH^-$ | (1) |

**(10 marks)**

**7.2**   **c–i**   Sketch the shapes of the molecules and ions in question **7.1** parts **c** to **i** inclusive, using 'stick' diagrams. Estimate the bond angles and mark them on your diagrams.

(2 marks each, **14 marks in total**)

**7.3**   Write balanced equations, including state symbols, for the complete combustion in air or oxygen, of the following compounds:

| | | |
|---|---|---|
| a | pentane | (2) |
| b | octane | (2) |
| c | cyclopentane | (2) |
| d | methanol | (2) |
| e | ethanol | (2) |

**(10 marks)**

**✱ 7.4** Cyclohexane burns in excess air or oxygen, forming carbon dioxide and water. Calculate its standard enthalpy change of formation in the following way:

a   Write the equation for the complete combustion of cyclohexane. (2)

b   Draw a Hess cycle showing the following three changes, all under standard conditions:
   - the formation of cyclohexane from its elements,
   - the combustion of cyclohexane in oxygen,
   - the formation of the corresponding amounts of carbon dioxide and water from the elements. (4)

c   Using the *Book of data*, find the standard enthalpy change of combustion of cyclohexane, and the standard enthalpy changes of formation of the appropriate amounts of carbon dioxide and water. Insert them in the correct places on your Hess cycle. (3)

d   Use the cycle to calculate the standard enthalpy change of formation of cyclohexane. Give your answer to an appropriate number of significant figures, and include its sign and units. (2)

e   Compare your answer to that given in the *Book of data*. (1)

**(12 marks)**

**✱ 7.5** Use the method set out in question **7.4** to calculate the standard enthalpy change of formation of propan-1-ol, $CH_3CH_2CH_2OH(l)$. **(10 marks)**

**✱ 7.6** The table below shows the quantity of heat energy produced when 1.00 g of each of the alcohols listed was burned in a combustion calorimeter.

| Alcohol | Heat produced/kJ |
| --- | --- |
| Methanol, $CH_3OH$ | 22.34 |
| Ethanol, $CH_3CH_2OH$ | 29.80 |
| Propan-1-ol, $CH_3CH_2CH_2OH$ | 33.50 |
| Butan-1-ol, $CH_3CH_2CH_2CH_2OH$ | 36.12 |

a   Calculate the standard enthalpy change of combustion of each alcohol. (4)

b   What pattern can you see in the values you calculated in **a**? (1)

c   Plot a graph of standard enthalpy change of combustion against number of carbon atoms in the alcohol. Choose scales which will allow you to predict the value for pentan-1-ol. (3)

d   Use your graph to predict the standard enthalpy change of combustion of pentan-1-ol and compare your prediction with the value given in the *Book of data*. (2)

**(10 marks)**

**\* 7.7**     With the help of the *Book of data*, evaluate $\Delta H^{\ominus}(298)$ for each of the following reactions. You need to look up only one data item in each case.

  **a**   $C(graphite, s) \longrightarrow C(g)$     (1)
  **b**   $H_2(g) \longrightarrow 2H(g)$     (1)
  **c**   $\frac{1}{2}O_2(g) \longrightarrow O(g)$     (1)
  **d**   $CH_4(g) + 2O_2(g) \longrightarrow CO_2(g) + 2H_2O(l)$     (1)
  **e**   $CH_4(g) \longrightarrow C(g) + 4H(g)$     (1)

**(5 marks)**

**\* 7.8**     **a**   Construct a Hess cycle showing the standard enthalpy change of formation of hydrogen fluoride and the standard enthalpy changes of atomisation of its elements.     (3)

  **b**   Use the cycle to calculate the enthalpy change for the reaction:

$$HF(g) \longrightarrow H(g) + F(g)$$     (2)

  **c**   Compare your answer to **b** with the H—F bond energy from the *Book of data*.     (1)

  **d**   Use the *Book of data* to find the bond energies H—Cl, H—Br and H—I. Identify the pattern shown by the H—Hal bond energies and suggest an explanation for it.     (4)

**(10 marks)**

**7.9**     Given that

$$P(g) + 3Cl(g) \longrightarrow PCl_3(g) \qquad \Delta H = -983 \text{ kJ mol}^{-1}$$

$$P(s) + 1\tfrac{1}{2}Cl_2(g) \longrightarrow PCl_3(g) \qquad \Delta H = -305 \text{ kJ mol}^{-1}$$

$$P(s) \longrightarrow P(g) \qquad \Delta H = +314 \text{ kJ mol}^{-1}$$

calculate the following bond energies:

  **a**   P—Cl in $PCl_3$     (2)
  **b**   Cl—Cl in $Cl_2$     (2)

**(4 marks)**

**7.10**     Use the general trends in electronegativity to explain the following:

  **a**   Sodium hydride is not covalent but consists of the ions $Na^+$ and $H^-$.     (2)
  **b**   Methane ($CH_4$) has a covalent molecular structure and the electrons are evenly shared in the bonds between the carbon and hydrogen atoms in the methane molecules.     (2)
  **c**   Hydrogen chloride gas has a covalent molecular structure but the molecule has a dipole:

$$\overset{\delta^+}{H}\text{—}\overset{\delta^-}{Cl}$$     (3)

  **d**   Lithium forms a crystalline fluoride, $Li^+ F^-$, whereas oxygen forms a gaseous fluoride, $OF_2$.     (3)

**(10 marks)**

**7.11**   Draw up a table showing how (if at all) you would expect the rate of each of the reactions 1, 2 and 3 below to be affected by the following changes:

**a**   increased temperature
**b**   increased total pressure of gas
**c**   increased surface area of solid
**d**   increased concentration of solution.

Reaction 1:   the reaction of zinc with dilute sulphuric acid

$$Zn(s) + H_2SO_4(aq) \longrightarrow ZnSO_4(aq) + H_2(g)$$

Reaction 2:   the reaction of sulphur dioxide with oxygen in the presence of a platinum/rhodium metal catalyst

$$2SO_2(g) + O_2(g) \longrightarrow 2SO_3(g)$$

Reaction 3:   the decomposition of an aqueous solution of hydrogen peroxide, catalysed by solid manganese(IV) oxide

$$2H_2O_2(aq) \longrightarrow 2H_2O(l) + O_2(g)$$

**(12 marks)**

**7.12**   Draw up a table showing how the position of equilibrium in reactions 1, 2 and 3 below would be affected by the following changes:

**a**   increased temperature
**b**   increased pressure.

Reaction 1:   the reaction of sulphur dioxide with oxygen in the presence of a platinum/rhodium catalyst

$$2SO_2(g) + O_2(g) \rightleftharpoons 2SO_3(g) \qquad \Delta H = -197\,kJ\,mol^{-1}$$

Reaction 2:   the reaction between hydrogen and iodine forming hydrogen iodide, all in the gaseous state

$$H_2(g) + I_2(g) \rightleftharpoons 2HI(g) \qquad \Delta H = +53.0\,kJ\,mol^{-1}$$

Reaction 3:   the equilibrium between dioxygen ($O_2$) and trioxygen ($O_3$, ozone)

$$3O_2(g) \rightleftharpoons 2O_3(g) \qquad \Delta H = +285.4\,kJ\,mol^{-1}$$

**(6 marks)**

**✱ 7.13**   **a**   Use table 6.2 in the *Book of data* to find the activation energy for the reaction

$$2H_2O_2(aq) \longrightarrow 2H_2O(l) + O_2(g)$$

when uncatalysed, when catalysed by colloidal (finely divided) platinum and when enzyme-catalysed. (1)

**b**   Comment on the values you have quoted in **a**. (3)

**c**   What volume of oxygen (measured at 20 °C and 1 atm) would you expect to be produced as a result of the uncatalysed decomposition of 50 cm$^3$ of a 2.0 M solution of hydrogen peroxide? (3)

**d**   Would the volume of oxygen produced be different if the reaction was catalysed? Justify your answer. (2)

**(9 marks)**

# EXAMINATION QUESTIONS

Questions of the summary and comprehension type are found in the background reading sections (sections 7.3 and 7.5).

**7.14**   Cyanogen, $(CN)_2$, behaves like the halogens in its chemical reactions. Its hydride, hydrogen cyanide, HCN, is similar to the hydrogen halides.

   **a**  **i** Draw 'dot and cross' diagrams of hydrogen chloride, hydrogen cyanide and cyanogen molecules. You need include only outer shell electrons.    (3)

      **ii** Draw the displayed formula for cyanogen, showing the CCN bond angle.  (2)

   **b**  Use the following Hess cycle and data (at 298 K) to calculate the standard enthalpy change of formation of cyanogen, including its sign and unit.

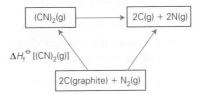

$$\Delta H_{at}[(CN)_2(g)] = +2121 \text{ kJ mol}^{-1}$$
$$\Delta H_{at}[C(graphite)] = +717 \text{ kJ mol}^{-1}$$
$$\Delta H_{at}[\tfrac{1}{2}N_2(g)] = +473 \text{ kJ mol}^{-1}$$

                                                                        (3)

   **c**  Potassium cyanide, KCN, reacts with concentrated sulphuric acid in a similar way to potassium iodide. Suggest THREE possible gaseous products.    (3)

   **d**  Chlorine reacts with cold sodium hydroxide solution in a disproportionation reaction.

$$Cl_2(aq) + 2NaOH(aq) \longrightarrow NaCl(aq) + NaClO(aq) + H_2O(l)$$

      **i** State the oxidation numbers of chlorine in $Cl_2$, NaCl and NaClO.    (2)

      **ii** What is meant by the term 'disproportionation'?    (1)

     **iii** Suggest a balanced chemical equation for the reaction between cyanogen and cold sodium hydroxide solution.    (1)

   **e**  Suggest a reason why there are no experiments on the chemistry of cyanogen in Advanced Level chemistry courses.    (1)

                                                             **(16 marks)**

**7.15**   The bond energy of the C—O bond can be found by using the atomisation energy of the compound methoxymethane whose displayed formula is:

               H      H
               |       |
          H—C—O—C—H
               |       |
               H      H

The atomisation energy of methoxymethane is $+3194 \text{ kJ mol}^{-1}$.
The bond energy of the C—H bond is $+413 \text{ kJ mol}^{-1}$.

   **a**  Draw a 'dot and cross' diagram for methoxymethane.    (1)

   **b**  Write a balanced equation, including state symbols, to show the complete atomisation of methoxymethane (which is a gas at room temperature).    (2)

   **c**  Calculate the bond energy of the C—O bond.    (2)

**d**    The atomisation energy of methoxymethane can be found from a Hess cycle involving its enthalpy change of formation $\Delta H_f$ and the enthalpies of atomisation of graphite, $\Delta H_{at}$[graphite], hydrogen, $\Delta H_{at}[\frac{1}{2}H_2(g)]$ and oxygen, $\Delta H_{at}[\frac{1}{2}O_2(g)]$. Construct such a Hess cycle, indicating clearly which enthalpy changes correspond to which reactions.    (4)

**e**    Suggest ONE reason why atomisation energies determined as in **d** are not very accurate.    (1)

**(10 marks)**

**7.16**    **a**    The following results were obtained from an experiment to determine the enthalpy change of combustion of propanone, $CH_3COCH_3$:

     Heat capacity of the apparatus $= 3.34\,kJ\,°C^{-1}$
     Loss of mass of burner      $= 2.90\,g$
     Temperature rise         $= 25.3\,°C$

   **i** Calculate the quantity of heat (kJ) produced in the experiment.    (2)
   **ii** Calculate the enthalpy change of combustion of propanone.
     (Molar mass of propanone $= 58\,g\,mol^{-1}$).    (2)

**b**    Construct a thermochemical (Hess) cycle to determine the enthalpy change of atomisation, $\Delta H_{at}$, of propanone, given the following data:

     $\Delta H_f^{\ominus}$ [propanone(l)]      $= -248\,kJ\,mol^{-1}$
     $\Delta H_{at}^{\ominus}$ [carbon(graphite)] $= +715\,kJ\,mol^{-1}$
     $\Delta H_{at}^{\ominus}$ [hydrogen(g)]      $= +218\,kJ\,mol^{-1}$
     $\Delta H_{at}^{\ominus}$ [oxygen(g)]        $= +249\,kJ\,mol^{-1}$

     (The enthalpy change of atomisation refers to the formation of 1 mole of gaseous atoms of the element concerned.)    (4)

**c**    Use the average bond energies, $E$, given below to calculate another value for the enthalpy change of atomisation of propanone.

     $E(C\!-\!C) = +346\,kJ\,mol^{-1}$
     $E(C\!-\!H) = +413\,kJ\,mol^{-1}$
     $E(C\!=\!O) = +749\,kJ\,mol^{-1}$    (3)

**d**    Comment on the agreement, or disagreement, between the two values calculated in **b** and **c**.    (1)

**(12 marks)**

**7.17**    This question is about a series of salts: sodium chlorate(I), sodium chlorate(III), sodium chlorate(V) and sodium chlorate(VII).

**a**    Draw 'dot and cross' diagrams to show the electronic structures of the chlorate(I) ion, $ClO^-$, and the chlorate(V) ion, $ClO_3^-$.    (4)

**b**    Draw diagrams to show the molecular shapes of the chlorate(III) ion, $ClO_2^-$, and the chlorate(VII) ion, $ClO_4^-$.
     Mark on the diagrams your estimate of any bond angles.    (4)

**(8 marks)**

**7.18**    Antimony (symbol Sb) is a p-block element in Group 5 of the Periodic Table. It forms a chloride of formula $SbCl_3$.

**a**   **i**   Draw a 'dot and cross' diagram (outer electron shells only) of a molecule of antimony(III) chloride.    (2)

    **ii**   Sketch the shape of this molecule, indicating a value for the Cl—Sb—Cl bond angle.    (2)

**b**    Antimony(III) oxide is used as a fire retardant. It is made from antimony(III) chloride which is itself produced by heating antimony(III) sulphide with calcium chloride in the presence of oxygen. This reaction is reversible; the forward reaction is exothermic. The equation for the reaction is:

$$Sb_2S_3(s) + 3CaCl_2(s) + 6O_2(g) \rightleftharpoons 2SbCl_3(g) + 3CaSO_4(s)$$

   **i**   The reaction is carried out at 773 K. How would the yield of antimony(III) chloride be affected by increasing the temperature? Justify your answer.    (2)

  **ii**   Apart from changing the temperature, what other change could improve the yield? Justify your answer.    (2)

  **iii**   Suggest the formula of antimony(III) oxide.    (1)

  **iv**   Copy, complete and balance the following equation for the formation of antimony(III) oxide from antimony(III) chloride.

$$SbCl_3(s) + H_2O(l) \longrightarrow \text{antimony(III) oxide(s)} + HCl(aq)$$    (1)

**(10 marks)**

# Organic chemistry: hydrocarbons

Figure 8.1 **Crude oil is the source of most of our organic compounds, especially plastics and synthetic fibres**

This second topic on organic chemistry begins by considering some of the reasons for the great diversity of carbon compounds, and more of the rules necessary for naming them. The results of experiments on two different types of hydrocarbon compounds will be considered. This will help you to understand the different ways in which carbon compounds react. You will also meet the important reactions of these carbon compounds and learn something of their social and industrial importance.

As we discussed in Topic 2, we get most of our carbon compounds from oil, gas and coal, especially crude oil, but some complex compounds are still obtained more easily and cheaply from plants. You will be extracting a compound called limonene from oranges, the same source as used by the chemical industry.

This topic contains a number of ideas that will be new to you. However, the remaining topics on organic chemistry contain a further exploration of these ideas to consolidate your learning. It is important, therefore, that you learn these foundation ideas about the types of organic reaction.

It is also important that you:

- relate the work in this topic to your work in Topic 2
- learn the new displayed and structural formulae carefully
- learn the details of the reactions, such as colour changes.

## 8.1 The variety of molecular structure in organic compounds

---

### REVIEW TASK

Working in groups, list from your work on Topic 2:

1 The names of the first five alkanes.

2 The molecular, structural and displayed formulae of propane, and work out the molar mass.

3 The structural formulae of the isomers having molecular formular $C_4H_{10}$.

---

Although the chemistry of carbon can be studied as a part of Group 4 of the Periodic Table, carbon also has a special chemistry of its own, a chemistry that has been able to flourish in the conditions on this planet. If we compare carbon compounds with those of silicon, as silicon is the nearest neighbour to carbon in Group 4 of the Periodic Table, two major differences can be identified:

**1   Carbon compounds frequently contain long chains of carbon atoms,**

$$-\overset{|}{\underset{|}{C}}-\overset{|}{\underset{|}{C}}-\overset{|}{\underset{|}{C}}-\overset{|}{\underset{|}{C}}-$$

whereas silicon compounds commonly contain chains made up of silicon and oxygen,

$$-O-\overset{|}{\underset{|}{Si}}-O-\overset{|}{\underset{|}{Si}}-$$

**2   Carbon atoms never bond to more than four other atoms.**

At a simple level the first of these differences between carbon and silicon chemistry can be interpreted as due to differences in bond energies (look again at Topic 7 if necessary).

| | |
|---|---|
| $E(C—C)$ | $347 \, kJ \, mol^{-1}$ |
| $E(C—H)$ | $413 \, kJ \, mol^{-1}$ |
| $E(C—O)$ | $358 \, kJ \, mol^{-1}$ |

For single bonds these are all high values of similar magnitude, which means that the bonds can be classified as strong bonds of about the same strength. Thus, there will be no strong tendency for a C—C bond or a C—H bond to be replaced by a C—O bond (under standard conditions).

Now look at the corresponding values for silicon:

| | |
|---|---|
| $E(Si—Si)$ | $226 \, kJ \, mol^{-1}$ |
| $E(Si—H)$ | $318 \, kJ \, mol^{-1}$ |
| $E(Si—O)$ | $466 \, kJ \, mol^{-1}$ |

The Si—Si bond can be classified as a weak bond with a strong tendency to be replaced by Si—O bonds. **So, on the Earth, silicon is found in silicate rocks** while carbon can be found in a rich variety of carbon–hydrogen compounds, as well as in rocks containing metal carbonates.

The second difference can be described as a difference in possible electron arrangements in Group 4 elements. When carbon atoms have formed four bonds, they have eight electrons in the second electron shell, and this shell is incapable of further expansion. This restricts the possibilities of further chemical attack.

$$H \overset{\overset{\displaystyle H}{\times \bullet}}{\underset{\underset{\displaystyle H}{\bullet \times}}{\overset{\bullet}{\underset{\times}{C}}}} H$$

Silicon atoms, however, can form an outermost electron shell with more than eight electrons because of the availability of an empty 3d energy level. So compounds such as the silicon hydrides, for example, $SiH_4$, are not resistant to chemical attack.

For example, some silicon hydrides ignite at once, just on mixing with air,

$$Si_2H_6(g) \xrightarrow{\text{air}} SiO_2(s)$$

but alkanes do not ignite unless heated.

However, bond strengths in carbon compounds, and the limitation of carbon to form compounds with no more than eight electrons in the outermost shell around the carbon atom, are only part of the reason for the diversity of carbon compounds.

Let us look at the tetrahedral arrangement of groups around the carbon atom more fully. If you make a model of the straight-chain $C_4H_{10}$ molecule, you will find that the model can be twisted into a number of different shapes. Is this property of the model shared by the molecule and, if so, can any of the different shapes be described as different compounds? The different shapes cannot correspond to different compounds because chemists have only found properties corresponding to one straight-chain compound. It follows, therefore, that the different shapes are all shapes of one compound which must twist just as our model can twist. A glance at a model of the ethane molecule, $C_2H_6$, shown in the diagram below, should make this clear. The rotation about the C—C single bond which makes possible the movement seen in the diagram is a property of the molecule. So A and B are merely ethane molecules at different stages of a continuous rotation, not isomers of different structures.

## STUDY TASK

Make models of the molecules and write down the structural formulae of all the isomers with the formula $C_6H_{14}$. You should finish with five isomers. Clearly we need some additional rules in order to name all these isomers.

| Number of carbon atoms in chain | Molecular formula | Name |
|---|---|---|
| 1 | $CH_4$ | methane |
| 2 | $C_2H_6$ | ethane |
| 3 | $C_3H_8$ | propane |
| 4 | $C_4H_{10}$ | butane |
| 5 | $C_5H_{12}$ | pentane |
| 6 | $C_6H_{14}$ | hexane |
| 7 | $C_7H_{16}$ | heptane |
| 8 | $C_8H_{18}$ | octane |
| 9 | $C_9H_{20}$ | nonane |
| 10 | $C_{10}H_{22}$ | decane |
| 11 | $C_{11}H_{24}$ | undecane |
| 12 | $C_{12}H_{26}$ | dodecane |
| 20 | $C_{20}H_{42}$ | eicosane |
| $n$ | $C_nH_{2n+2}$ | general alkane |

# The chemists' toolkit: naming organic compounds

The rules for naming compounds are settled by international agreement through the International Union of Pure and Applied Chemistry. They are usually known as IUPAC rules.

You should remember that **compounds containing carbon and hydrogen with only single bonds between the carbon atoms are known as saturated hydrocarbons**. They occur as three main types.

## 1 Alkanes containing unbranched carbon atom chains

These are hydrocarbons in which the molecules are made up of straight chains of carbon atoms. The general name for these is **alkanes**. Names for individual compounds all have the ending '**-ane**'. For example,

$$CH_3—CH_2—CH_2—CH_2—CH_3 \qquad \text{pentane}$$

For convenience the names of the alkanes given in Topic 2 are repeated here in the margin.

## 2  Alkanes containing branched chains

Hydrocarbons having branched chains of carbon atoms are still known as alkanes, but the rules for the individual names are more complicated. An example is

$$CH_3—CH_2—\underset{\underset{CH_3}{|}}{CH}—CH_3$$

2-methylbutane

| Hydrocarbon | Alkyl group | Formula for alkyl group |
|---|---|---|
| Methane | Methyl | $CH_3—$ |
| Ethane | Ethyl | $C_2H_5—$ |
| Propane | Propyl | $C_3H_7—$ |
| Butane | Butyl | $C_4H_9—$ |
| Pentane | Pentyl | $C_5H_{11}—$ |
| Hexane | Hexyl | $C_6H_{13}—$ |
| *and so on* | | |

In order to name these compounds, groups of atoms known as **alkyl** groups are used. These are derived from hydrocarbons with unbranched carbon chains by removing one hydrogen atom from the end carbon atom of the chain. For example $CH_3—CH_2—CH_3$ (propane) becomes $CH_3—CH_2—CH_2—$ with one bond unoccupied. Alkyl groups are named from the parent hydrocarbon by substituting the ending '**-yl**' for the ending '-ane'. Thus, $CH_3CH_2CH_2—$ is the prop**yl** group. A list of alkyl groups is given in the table in the margin.

Branched chain hydrocarbons are named by combining names of alkyl groups with the name of an unbranched chain hydrocarbon. The simplest is

$$CH_3—\underset{\underset{CH_3}{|}}{CH_2}—CH_3$$

which is called **methyl**propane. The hydrocarbon name is always derived from the longest continuous chain of carbon atoms in the molecule. The position of the alkyl group forming the side chain is obtained by numbering the carbon atoms in the chain. The numbering is done so that the lowest number(s) possible are used to indicate the side chain (or chains). Thus

$$CH_3—\underset{\underset{CH_3}{|}}{CH}—CH_2—CH_2—CH_3$$

is named **2-methyl**pentane, not 4-methylpentane which would be obtained by numbering from the other end of the chain. When there is more than one substituent alkyl group of the same kind, the figures indicating the positions of the groups are separated by commas, for example

$$CH_3—\underset{\underset{CH_3}{|}}{CH}—\underset{\underset{CH_3}{|}}{CH}—CH_3 \qquad \text{is } \textbf{2,3-dimethyl}\text{butane, and}$$

$$CH_3—CH_2—\underset{\underset{CH_3}{\overset{\overset{CH_3}{|}}{|}}}{C}—CH_3 \qquad \text{is } \textbf{2,2-dimethyl}\text{butane.}$$

Different alkyl groups are placed in alphabetical order in the name for a branched chain hydrocarbon, for example,

$$CH_3—CH_2—\underset{\underset{\underset{CH_3}{|}}{CH_2}}{CH}—CH_2—\underset{\underset{CH_3}{|}}{CH}—CH_3 \qquad \text{is named } \textbf{3-ethyl}\text{-5-methylhexane.}$$

## 3 Alkanes containing a ring of carbon atoms

Hydrocarbons having one or more rings of carbon atoms (to which side chains may be attached) are called **cycloalkanes**. For example,

$$CH_2-CH_2 \atop CH_2 \quad CH_2 \atop CH_2$$ cyclopentane

They are named from the corresponding unbranched chain hydrocarbon by adding the prefix '**cyclo-**'.

All the carbon atoms in an unsubstituted cycloalkane ring are equivalent, so far as substitution is concerned, so that if only one alkyl group is added as a substituent there is no need to number the carbon atoms. Thus methyl-cyclohexane is

or

# Names and structures of some functional groups

In this table the structures of the functional groups that you need to know now are printed out in the second column so as to show the atomic linkages. When these structures are repeated in the examples given in the fourth column they are printed on one line only, so as to show this abbreviated method of writing them.

| Class of compound | Structure of the functional group | Example of a compound Name | Formula |
|---|---|---|---|
| Alkene | $\diagdown C=C \diagup$ | propene | $CH_2=CH-CH_3$ |
| Arene | ring structure | benzene | $C_6H_6$ or ⬡ |
| Alcohol | $-OH$ | propanol | $CH_3-CH_2-CH_2-OH$ |
| Amine | $-NH_2$ | propylamine | $CH_3-CH_2-CH_2-NH_2$ |
| Halogenoalkane | $-Cl$ etc. | 1-chloropropane | $CH_3-CH_2-CH_2-Cl$ |
| Aldehyde | $-C{\diagup}^H_{\diagdown\!\!\diagdown O}$ | propanal | $CH_3-CH_2-CHO$ |
| Ketone | $\diagdown C=O$ | propanone | $CH_3-CO-CH_3$ |
| Carboxylic acid | $-C{\diagup}^{O-H}_{\diagdown\!\!\diagdown O}$ | propanoic acid | $CH_3-CH_2-CO_2H$ |
| Carboxylate ion | $-C{\diagup}^{O^-}_{\diagdown\!\!\diagdown O}$ | sodium propanoate | $CH_3-CH_2-CO_2^-\ Na^+$ |

## 8.2 The alkanes

**The alkanes are saturated hydrocarbons; they have only single bonds in their structure (saturated) and are composed only of hydrogen and carbon (hydrocarbons).**

Alkanes are the major components of crude oil. The largest international companies make their living from alkanes and the richest men made their fortunes from alkanes. Countries with crude oil have been able to transform their way of life from that of subsistence farming to one with an increasing contribution from modern technology. The money derived from crude oil has enabled governments to build schools, roads, and hospitals, but it has also disrupted traditional ways of life and been used to buy modern war weapons.

The price of crude oil, and ensuring a supply of crude oil, have come to dominate modern economic thinking and modern industrial planning. Consumption of crude oil varies from year to year but the USA takes about 25% of the total while China uses less than 5%. Total world consumption per year has risen by 65% since the first edition of this book in 1970, yet over the same period known reserves have remained at about 30 years' consumption. So how long will the world's oil reserves last?

Exploration for new oil fields is usually planned to ensure that newly discovered fields can be brought into production by the time they are needed. And that can be a long time: in the North Sea the period from exploration to bringing the first oil ashore in the UK was about 15 years.

Nevertheless, we can be sure that the supply of crude oil is finite so that shortages will develop as oil fields run dry, or as countries restrict output to conserve their source of wealth. It remains to be seen if the world will manage an orderly change to new technologies or whether the rich will outbid the poor in a desperate scramble for oil, and whether cars, aircraft and other transport will come to a halt before adequate alternatives are ready. Without care, the future of oil may prove as dark as its past has proved bright.

But how suitable is crude oil for all the potential uses? The composition of a typical barrel of crude oil and the corresponding demand in the market place are illustrated in figure 8.3. Matching supply to demand is the job of the oil refinery.

Figure 8.2 **Going to work in India. To what extent are activities dependent on fuels from oil?**

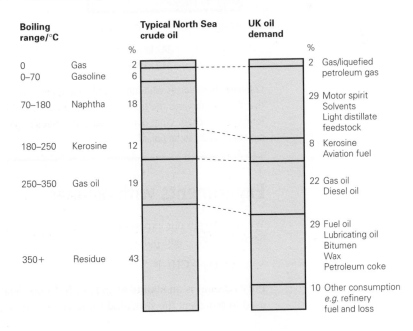

| Boiling range/°C | | Typical North Sea crude oil % | UK oil demand % | |
|---|---|---|---|---|
| 0 | Gas | 2 | 2 | Gas/liquefied petroleum gas |
| 0–70 | Gasoline | 6 | 29 | Motor spirit Solvents Light distillate feedstock |
| 70–180 | Naphtha | 18 | | |
| 180–250 | Kerosine | 12 | 8 | Kerosine Aviation fuel |
| 250–350 | Gas oil | 19 | 22 | Gas oil Diesel oil |
| 350+ | Residue | 43 | 29 | Fuel oil Lubricating oil Bitumen Wax Petroleum coke |
| | | | 10 | Other consumption e.g. refinery fuel and loss |

Figure 8.3 **Matching supply to demand**

This is a complex task because not only must the demand for alkanes be satisfied but also most of the demand for unsaturated hydrocarbons and arene hydrocarbons. We shall return to this question later in the Topic.

One alkane behaves much like another, so we can describe most of the properties we are concerned with by describing ethane, $CH_3—CH_3$. The structure of ethane is illustrated in figure 8.4.

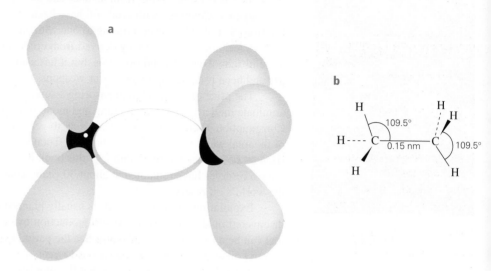

Figure 8.4 **The structure of ethane**
a **A model showing the distribution of the electrons**
b **A diagram showing the bond lengths and bond angles**

Notice that the single bond between the carbon atoms (the σ or sigma bond) is symmetrical, which is consistent with the free rotation about the C—C bond discussed in the previous section.

## QUESTIONS

The average bond energies in alkanes are:

$E(C—C)$    347 kJ mol$^{-1}$
$E(C—H)$    413 kJ mol$^{-1}$

Compare these values with other bond energies in table 4.6 of the *Book of data*, and you will see that they are towards the top of the range. Use a spreadsheet to present some of the data in the form of a bar chart. What does this suggest about the likely reactivity of the alkanes? Are the molecules likely to be polar?

# Experiments with alkanes

We shall begin our experimental investigations with a study of some alkanes: hexane, $C_6H_{14}$, and poly(ethene),

$$-\!\!\left(CH_2—CH_2\right)\!\!-_n$$

**Poly(ethene)** is an alk**ane** in spite of its name. Make a careful note of the method used to represent the structural formulae of polymers.

## EXPERIMENT 8.2

# The properties of some alkanes

Carry out the following tests on a sample of each of your alkanes. Note your observations in tabular form carefully because you will be doing similar tests on other compounds later in this topic and you will be expected to compare the behaviour of the different types of compound.

### SAFETY

Be careful when using hexane as it is volatile, highly flammable and harmful.
Concentrated sulphuric acid is corrosive.
Aqueous bromine is harmful and an irritant.
Avoid inhaling bromine fumes and keep the solution off your skin.
20% potassium hydroxide is very corrosive. Remember to wear eye protection.
Protect your eyes from the light in part 4.

## Procedure

### 1 Combustion

If possible, do this experiment in a fume cupboard. Keep a sample of the liquid alkane in a stoppered boiling tube well away from any flame. Dip a combustion spoon into the sample, so that it is no more than wet with alkane. Set fire to the alkane on the combustion spoon.

✎   **In your notes:** Is the flame clean or sooty? A clean flame is necessary for a substance to be used as a fuel.

### 2 Oxidation

To $0.5 \text{ cm}^3$ of a mixture of equal volumes of 0.01 M potassium manganate(VII) and 1 M sulphuric acid in a test tube add two or three drops of the liquid alkane or two granules of poly(ethene). Shake the contents and try to tell from any colour change if manganate(VII) oxidises the alkane.

✎   **In your notes:** Is there any sign of reaction?

### 3 Action of bromine

To $0.5 \text{ cm}^3$ of bromine water (TAKE CARE) in a test tube add a few drops of the liquid alkane or two granules of poly(ethene).

✎   **In your notes:** What, if anything, happens to the colour of the bromine?

### 4 Action of bromine in sunlight

To $10 \text{ cm}^3$ of hexane in a test tube add several drops of 2% bromine in an inert solvent. Loosely cork the tube and irradiate with sunlight or a photoflood light.

Prepare a second similar tube and leave it in a dark place. Compare the intensity of the bromine colour at intervals.

✎   **In your notes:** Is there any evidence of reaction? Can you identify any fumes evolved? If no fumes are apparent try tipping the contents of the test tube into a beaker.

### 5 Action of sulphuric acid

Put $1–2 \text{ cm}^3$ of concentrated sulphuric acid in a dry test tube held in a rack (TAKE CARE). Add $0.5 \text{ cm}^3$ of the liquid alkane or two or three granules of poly(ethene).

✎   **In your notes:** Is there any sign of reaction?

### 6 Action of alkali

To $0.5 \text{ cm}^3$ of the liquid alkane or two or three granules of poly(ethene) in a test tube add $1–2 \text{ cm}^3$ of 20% potassium hydroxide (TAKE CARE) dissolved in water. Shake the tube gently.

✎   **In your notes:** Is there any sign of reaction?

## 7 Catalytic cracking

Put some 'light paraffin' in a test tube to the depth of 1–2 cm. Light paraffin is a mixture of alkanes, containing molecules with about 12 carbon atoms.

Push in some loosely packed ceramic fibre until all the paraffin has been soaked up. Now add 2–3 cm depth of aluminium oxide granules and clamp the test tube horizontally so that the granules form a layer in the test tube. Connect the test tube for collection of gas over water as shown in figure 8.5.

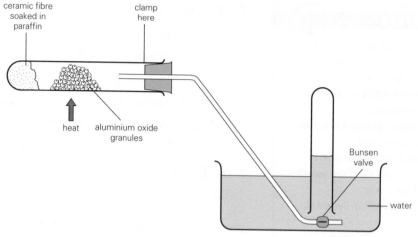

**Figure 8.5** **Apparatus for the catalytic cracking of an alkane**

Heat the aluminium oxide strongly and continuously but be careful not to melt the rubber stopper, nor to allow the delivery tube to become blocked. The paraffin should get hot enough to evaporate without needing direct heat.

Collect three or four tubes of gas (discard the first one: why?), and when the delivery of gas slows down, lift the apparatus clear of the water to avoid it being sucked up into the hot test tube.

Carry out the following two tests on the gas collected.

**a** *Test for flammability.* Any flame will be more visible if the test tube is held upside down.

**b** *Test for reaction with bromine.* Add a little bromine water (TAKE CARE).

✎ **In your notes:** Is the gaseous product an alkane or can different properties be observed?

# An interpretation of the photochemical experiment with alkanes

A lack of positive results when doing experiments with alkanes in the laboratory probably seems disappointing but, **for some uses, the chemical inertness of the alkanes is their greatest asset**. Compounds that are non-corrosive to metals (lubricating oils), harmless to our skin (petroleum jelly), and safe in contact with foods (poly(ethene)), are enormously useful to us.

The reaction of the alkanes that we need to consider here is that of hexane with bromine in sunlight. Since the reaction needs light in order to take place (unless the reactants are heated to over 300 °C), it is known as a **photochemical reaction**. It is a general reaction between alkanes and bromine or chlorine. The

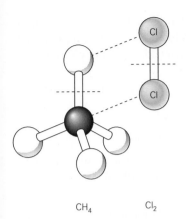

CH₄                Cl₂

**A ball-and-link representation of possible attack by chlorine on methane**

BACKGROUND

To calculate the energy of radiation, $E_{mol}$ in kJ mol$^{-1}$, for 1 mole of photons the relationship used is

$$E_{mol} = Lh\nu$$

where

$L = 6.02 \times 10^{23}$ mol$^{-1}$
    (the Avogadro constant)

$h = 6.62 \times 10^{-37}$ kJ s
    (the Planck constant)

$\nu$ = frequency of the radiation in hertz, s$^{-1}$

According to the *Book of data* table 3.1, an approximate value for the frequency of infrared radiation is $10^{13}$ s$^{-1}$, for visible light is $10^{14}$ s$^{-1}$, and for ultraviolet light is $10^{15}$ s$^{-1}$. If you carry out this calculation you will find that only ultraviolet photons have sufficient energy to be of interest to us.

process by which the reaction takes place must depend on the absorption of the energy of the photons that make up the radiation. Other experiments on the reaction of methane with chlorine have shown that the process does not need many photons: many thousands of product molecules are produced for each photon absorbed. So by what process does this reaction occur? To simplify the equations involved we will consider the methane–chlorine reaction as a typical example of what is involved.

Look at a ball-and-link model, such as the one shown in the margin. You may think that the reaction could begin with the simultaneous breaking of the C—H and Cl—Cl bonds, followed by the making of C—Cl and H—Cl bonds. Calculations using the appropriate bond energies show that this would be an exothermic reaction, with an enthalpy change of about 100 kJ mol$^{-1}$.

$$CH_4 + Cl_2 \longrightarrow CH_3Cl + HCl \qquad \Delta H^{\ominus} = -100 \text{ kJ mol}^{-1}$$

But there are two problems about this proposal. Firstly, the molecules would need to come together with an exact orientation for reaction to happen, and that would be a very rare collision amongst all the collisions occurring. Secondly, the distance between the atoms would have to be reduced to about a bond length and the force of repulsion between the electron clouds would have to be overcome.

How much energy can be provided by the absorption of radiation? When ultraviolet light is absorbed the energy provided is

$$E(\text{ultraviolet photons}) \approx 400 \text{ kJ mol}^{-1}$$

**This is enough energy to break up the chlorine molecule into uncharged chlorine atoms with unpaired electrons,** which are given the symbol Cl·

$$Cl_2 \longrightarrow Cl\cdot + Cl\cdot \qquad \Delta H^{\ominus} = +242 \text{ kJ mol}^{-1}$$

However, it is scarcely enough to break a methane molecule

$$CH_4 \longrightarrow CH_3\cdot + H\cdot \qquad \Delta H^{\ominus} = +435 \text{ kJ mol}^{-1}$$

and certainly not enough to produce ions.

$$Cl_2 \longrightarrow Cl^+ + Cl^- \qquad \Delta H^{\ominus} \approx +1130 \text{ kJ mol}^{-1}$$
$$CH_4 \longrightarrow H^+ + CH_3^- \qquad \Delta H^{\ominus} \approx +1700 \text{ kJ mol}^{-1}$$

We can therefore conclude that the first step in this photochemical reaction is probably the absorption of an ultraviolet photon by a chlorine molecule, resulting in the formation of two chlorine atoms. **These chlorine atoms, each with an odd number of electrons, are known as free radicals.**

Note carefully the difference between breaking a Cl—Cl bond to form free radicals, and the different pattern of breaking that produces ions.

To form a free radical the process is

$$:\!\overset{..}{\underset{..}{Cl}}\!\overset{\times\times}{\underset{\times\times}{Cl}}\!\times \longrightarrow :\!\overset{..}{\underset{..}{Cl}}\!\cdot + \times\!\overset{\times\times}{\underset{\times\times}{Cl}}\!\times$$

**This symmetrical bond breaking is known as homolytic fission; 'homo-' is from ancient Greek, meaning 'same'.**

To form ions the process is

$$:\!\overset{..}{\underset{..}{Cl}}\!\overset{\times\times}{\underset{\times\times}{Cl}}\!\times \longrightarrow \left[:\!\overset{..}{\underset{..}{Cl}}\!\cdot\right]^+ + \left[\times\!\overset{\times\times}{\underset{\times\times}{Cl}}\!\times\right]^-$$

**This asymmetrical bond breaking is known as heterolytic fission, 'hetero-' meaning 'different'.**

How does the reaction proceed? When the chlorine radical attacks a methane molecule there seem to be two possibilities for products. Either a hydrogen radical (we have to have a radical product if we start with an odd number of electrons in the reactants) and chloromethane are produced

$$Cl\cdot + CH_4 \longrightarrow H\cdot + CH_3Cl \qquad \Delta H^{\ominus} = +108\,\text{kJ mol}^{-1}$$

or a methyl radical and hydrogen chloride are produced.

$$Cl\cdot + CH_4 \longrightarrow CH_3\cdot + HCl \qquad \Delta H^{\ominus} = +4\,\text{kJ mol}^{-1}$$

Thus, on the basis of the energy involved, we can conclude that the second step in the reaction is likely to be the formation of a **methyl free radical**. Similar considerations will lead us to the next step.

$$CH_3\cdot + Cl_2 \longrightarrow CH_3Cl + Cl\cdot \qquad \Delta H^{\ominus} = -97\,\text{kJ mol}^{-1}$$

**These two last steps taken together produce the correct end-products, hydrogen chloride and chloromethane in a substitution reaction, but they also link together in an apparently endless chain for as long as methane and chlorine molecules are available** (see figure 8.6).

Is this chain likely to go on indefinitely? Well, not really, because to keep going it depends on free radicals colliding only with ordinary molecules. In

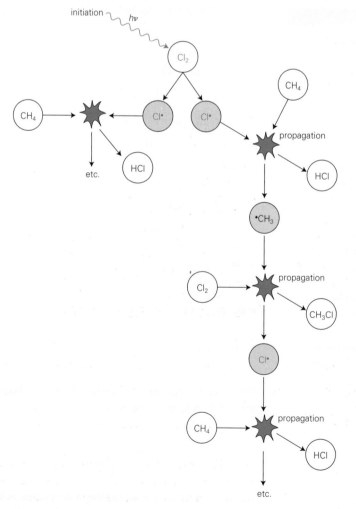

**Figure 8.6    A chain reaction**

practice, free radicals are bound to collide with each other, and if you think about
the possibilities, you should realise there are three:

$$Cl\cdot + Cl\cdot \longrightarrow Cl_2$$
$$CH_3\cdot + CH_3\cdot \longrightarrow CH_3{-}CH_3$$
$$\text{and } Cl\cdot + CH_3\cdot \longrightarrow CH_3Cl$$

**These collisions will all terminate the chain** (see figure 8.7). Experiments
have shown that for each original photon absorbed, on average 10 000 molecules
of chloromethane are produced. So how many links are there on average in a chain
before the chain is terminated?

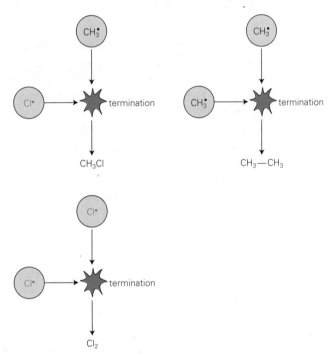

Figure 8.7  **Chain termination**

Free radical chain reactions are also important in the formation of polymers,
such as poly(ethene), and in the combustion of hydrocarbons, especially petrol. We
shall return to these topics later.

# Reactions of the alkanes

## 1 Combustion

**It is the combustion of the alkanes that provides their most important uses.**

$$CH_4 + 2O_2 \longrightarrow CO_2 + 2H_2O \qquad \Delta H_c^{\ominus} = -890\,\text{kJ mol}^{-1}$$
methane

$$C_4H_{10} + 6\tfrac{1}{2}O_2 \longrightarrow 4CO_2 + 5H_2O \qquad \Delta H_c^{\ominus} = -2877\,\text{kJ mol}^{-1}$$
butane

These equations represent very familiar processes although combustion has been
shown to be a free radical chain reaction. The oxygen for combustion normally
comes from the air, while methane is the main component of domestic gas, and
propane and butane are components of bottled gas.

**Figure 8.8** Liquid hydrocarbons are essential fuels for some purposes.

Other industrial products, including petrol, jet fuel (kerosine), diesel oil, paraffin, heating oil, and candlewax are mixtures of saturated and unsaturated hydrocarbons, but the main components are alkanes with appropriate boiling points. In normal use, the alkane fuels have the great advantage of burning with a relatively clean flame and producing non-toxic products. However, if the air supply is restricted, carbon monoxide can be produced:

$$CH_4 + 1\tfrac{1}{2}O_2 \longrightarrow CO + 2H_2O$$

Carbon monoxide is dangerously toxic.

The particular case of the combustion of petrol will be dealt with in more detail in section 8.3.

## 2 Photochemical reactions with halogens

The photochemical reaction of chlorine and bromine with alkanes, e.g.

$$\underset{\text{hexane}}{C_6H_{14}} + Br_2 \longrightarrow \underset{\text{bromohexane}}{C_6H_{13}Br} + HBr$$

is not a useful method of preparing halogenoalkanes. This is because further reaction takes place, forming a mixture of products. Photochemical and free radical organic reactions are important, however, in other contexts.

This photochemical process is a chain reaction involving free radicals in the following sequence (as explained earlier in this section).

$$Cl_2 \xrightarrow{\;h\nu\;} 2Cl\cdot \qquad\qquad\qquad \text{chain \textbf{initiation}}$$

$$\left.\begin{aligned} CH_4 + Cl\cdot &\longrightarrow HCl + CH_3\cdot \\ Cl_2 + CH_3\cdot &\longrightarrow CH_3Cl + Cl\cdot \end{aligned}\right\} \quad \text{chain \textbf{propagation}}$$

$$\left.\begin{aligned} Cl\cdot + Cl\cdot &\longrightarrow Cl_2 \\ CH_3\cdot + CH_3\cdot &\longrightarrow CH_3{-}CH_3 \\ Cl\cdot + CH_3\cdot &\longrightarrow CH_3Cl \end{aligned}\right\} \quad \text{chain \textbf{termination}}$$

The overall reaction is

$$CH_4 + Cl_2 \longrightarrow CH_3Cl + HCl$$

This is followed by reaction with more chlorine in further photochemical chain reactions, producing

$$CH_3Cl + Cl_2 \longrightarrow CH_2Cl_2 + HCl$$
$$CH_2Cl_2 + Cl_2 \longrightarrow CHCl_3 + HCl$$
$$CHCl_3 + Cl_2 \longrightarrow CCl_4 + HCl$$

## 3 Catalytic cracking

**This is an important process in the petrochemical industry** where much of the fraction from the distillation of crude oil with a boiling range 200–300 °C ($C_{10}$ to $C_{20}$ alkanes) is heated to 500 °C in the presence of a silica–alumina catalyst to produce unsaturated hydrocarbons, alkenes, and short-chain alkanes useful for petrol. The high boiling residues are used as fuel oil.

Figure 8.9 Catalytic cracking is the crucial process in changing the distillates from crude oil into useful short-chain hydrocarbons.

## 4 Behaviour with acid and alkali

Alkanes do not react with acids or alkalis normally; some colour changes may occur when impurities are present.

# Review of alkanes

Draw up a summary chart similar to the one below. Add colour and illustrations that you feel might help you learn the properties of the alkanes.

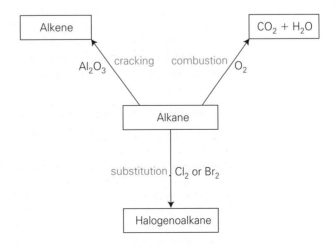

## 8.3     Background reading: octane number of petrol hydrocarbons

### QUESTIONS

Read the passage below and answer these questions based on it.

1   What is meant by pre-ignition?

2   How is octane number related to pre-ignition?

3   Explain the difference between catalytic cracking and catalytic reforming.

4   Suggest an equation for the isomerisation of an unbranched alkane to give a branched chain alkane.

5   Suggest a balanced equation for the cracking of eicosane, $CH_3(CH_2)_{18}CH_3$, with ethene as one of the products.

6   Acids catalyse the process of alkylation. Use the Brønsted–Lowry definition of an acid to suggest how this happens.

7   Write the structural formula of one isomer of $C_8H_{18}$ other than iso-octane (2,2,4-trimethylpentane). Do you think the octane number for your isomer will be about the same, higher, or lower than 100?

8   What is a free radical?

9   What is the effect of chain branching on the reactivity of free radicals?

10  Write a summary in continuous prose, in no more than 100 words, describing the important processes for producing petrol-grade hydrocarbons.

When it is first obtained from the Earth, crude oil is a complex mixture of hydrocarbons with sulphur compounds and inorganic impurities. These hydrocarbons may contain from one to more than 50 carbon atoms, and are mostly alkanes (with straight or branched chains), together with naphthenes and arenes. Petroleum is separated into fractions by distillation, for example, gasoline, naphtha, kerosine, gas oil, and diesel oil.

In general, the percentage of motor gasoline or petrol in crude oils is not enough to meet the heavy demands for motor car use. So it is necessary to devise ways whereby a larger proportion of the hydrocarbons in crude oil can be made use of as petrol. The value of hydrocarbons for use in petrol can be judged from their 'octane number'. Heptane is given an octane number of 0 and 2,2,4-trimethylpentane (iso-octane) is given an octane number of 100. The higher the number, the less the tendency to pre-ignite in a car engine – that is, the less the tendency to explode under compression before the spark is passed. A second explosion when the spark is passed results in the two shock waves producing a characteristic 'knocking' in the engine.

Four processes of importance for producing petrol-grade hydrocarbons are catalytic cracking, catalytic reforming, alkylation, and isomerisation.

### Catalytic cracking

One method of obtaining more petrol is to heat the larger hydrocarbon molecules so that they break down. In early years the process of thermal cracking was used, although much of the petroleum was broken down too extensively. In the 1930s, the higher compression in petrol engines called for fuels with a higher octane rating. The value for the products of thermal cracking was only 70–80. Fortunately, it had been discovered that the cracking of hydrocarbons in the presence of a catalyst (catalytic cracking) gave a petrol containing more branched hydrocarbons and an octane rating of 90–95.

The first catalytic cracking unit was built in 1936 in the US, at New Jersey. It contained a fixed bed of catalyst pellets composed of acid-treated clays. From a knowledge of the chemical composition of clays, various synthetic silica–alumina catalysts were also developed and these are still widely used. More recently, crystalline aluminosilicates, known as zeolites or molecular sieves, have also come into use as cracking catalysts.

## Catalytic reforming

This is now one of the most important processes for the production of motor gasolines. Adding a metallic component to a cracking catalyst gives petrol with an even higher octane number. Platinum is used exclusively as this component and highly purified alumina is used in place of silica–alumina. The process is known as catalytic reforming, but 'platforming' and other commercial names are often used. The improvement in octane number is due largely to the higher percentage of arenes in the product. The process is therefore also a source of arenes for the chemical industry. Some of the chemical reactions which are carried out at the same time by reforming catalysts are:

- dehydrogenation of cyclohexanes to arenes
- dehydrocyclisation of alkanes and alkenes to arenes
- isomerisation of unbranched chain to branched chain alkanes
- hydrocracking to hydrocarbons of lower molar mass.

In a reforming catalyst, the platinum is highly dispersed over the alumina, perhaps as platinum atoms or small groups of atoms. Both the platinum and the alumina play a catalytic role.

## Alkylation

Another means of obtaining high octane blending stocks is to join some of the smaller molecules in the right way, that is, using $C_3$—$C_4$ hydrocarbons. The process of alkylation involves the reaction of a branched chain alkane (for example, 2-methylpropane) and an alkene (for example, propene or butene). The catalysts are, or contain, acids; sulphuric acid, hydrofluoric acid, and phosphoric acid are used.

## Isomerisation

As alkanes with branched chains have a higher octane number than those with straight chains, a process for converting straight $C_5$ or $C_6$ chains to branched chains has been developed. The catalyst used is a specially prepared platinum material kept in an active state by adding an activator to the reactants.

## Octane number and molecular structure

The relationship of octane number to molecular structure can be seen in the tables of $C_7$ alkanes, the cyclic compounds, and the $C_7$ alkenes (overleaf).

You can see that the more branches to the carbon chain, the higher the octane number and hence the value of isomerisation:

$$CH_3-CH_2-CH_2-CH_2-CH_2-CH_2-CH_3 \xrightarrow{\text{isomerisation}} CH_3-CH_2-CH_2-\underset{\underset{CH_3}{|}}{\overset{\overset{CH_3}{|}}{C}}-CH_3$$

octane number 0                                        octane number 89

| $C_7$ alkane | Octane number |
|---|---|
| Heptane | 0 |
| 2-methylhexane | 41 |
| 3-methylhexane | 56 |
| 2,2-dimethylpentane | 89 |
| 2,3-dimethylpentane | 87 |
| 2,4-dimethylpentane | 77 |
| 3,3-dimethylpentane | 95 |
| 3-ethylpentane | 64 |
| 2,3,3-trimethylbutane | 113 |

| Cyclic compound | Octane number |
|---|---|
| (Hexane) | (26) |
| Cyclohexane | 77 |
| Methylcyclohexane | 104 |
| Benzene | 108 |
| Methylbenzene | 124 |

| $C_7$ alkene | Octane number |
|---|---|
| Hept-1-ene | 68 |
| 5-methylhex-1-ene | 96 |
| 2-methylhex-2-ene | 129 |
| 2,4-dimethylpent-1-ene | 142 |
| 4,4-dimethylpent-1-ene | 144 |
| 2,3-dimethylpent-2-ene | 165 |
| 2,4-dimethylpent-2-ene | 135 |
| 2,2,3-trimethylbut-1-ene | 145 |

The conversion of alkanes to cycloalkanes and the dehydrogenation of cycloalkanes by the process of catalytic reforming also enhance the octane number of the petrol fraction from crude oil:

$$CH_3{-}CH_2{-}CH_2{-}CH_2{-}CH_2{-}CH_3 \xrightarrow[\text{reforming}]{\text{catalytic}} \bighexagon + H_2$$

octane number 26      octane number 77

$$\bighexagon \xrightarrow[\text{reforming}]{\text{catalytic}} \benzene + 3H_2$$

octane number 108

If you compare the table of $C_7$ alkenes with the previous one of $C_7$ alkanes, you can see that the formation of an unsaturated compound enhances the octane number of a hydrocarbon:

octane number 89      octane number 144

Why do these changes in molecular structure enhance octane numbers? The answer lies in the process of combustion. The conditions of temperature and pressure in a car engine result in the production of free radicals. The more reactive the free radicals, the greater the chance of an uncontrolled chain reaction such as pre-ignition explosion or knocking in the engine.

$$CH_3{-}CH_2{-}CH_2{-}CH_2{-}CH_2{-}CH_3 \longrightarrow 2CH_3{-}CH_2{-}CH_2{\cdot}$$

octane number 26      reactive radicals

octane number 100      less reactive radicals

## 8.4 The alkenes

If the supply of crude oil ever became seriously restricted, the most obvious effect would be the lack of petrol for cars, of diesel for buses and lorries, and of aviation fuel for aircraft. But another effect would be the lack of alkenes for the synthesis of polymers, detergents, solvents, and many other chemicals.

In Experiment 8.2 (part 7) you did an experiment on the cracking of paraffin to obtain short chain alkanes and alkenes from long chain alkanes (gases from liquids). In the petroleum industry much of the fraction from crude oil boiling in the range 150–300 °C ($C_{10}$ to $C_{20}$ alkanes) is cracked over a catalyst of aluminium and silicon oxides at 500 °C. The products include branched chain alkanes and alkenes which are valuable components of petrol, and the gaseous alkenes which are vital to the chemical industry.

| Alkene | | $T_b$/ °C |
|---|---|---|
| $CH_2{=}CH_2$ | Ethene | $-104$ |
| $CH_3CH{=}CH_2$ | Propene | $-47$ |
| $CH_3{-}CH_2{-}CH{=}CH_2$ | But-1-ene | $-6$ |
| $CH_3{-}CH{=}CH{-}CH_3$ | But-2-ene | $+4$ (*cis*: see below) |
| | | $+1$ (*trans*: see below) |

It is possible to separate but-2-ene into two components with significant differences in boiling point and other physical properties but with no significant differences in chemical reactivity. The explanation is that but-2-ene exists as two **isomers**. Chemists have suggested that **there cannot be free rotation about the double bond** so that

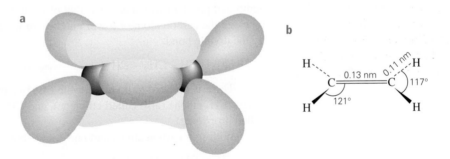

*cis*-but-2-ene    **cannot change to**    *trans*-but-2-ene

The term *cis* means 'on this side of' (from the Latin) and *trans* means 'across'. These isomers are known as **geometric isomers**.

This is quite different from the C—C single bond where free rotation is possible. The difference is due to the difference in the electron clouds making up the single and double bonds, as you will see by comparing figure 8.10 with the similar diagram of ethane in figure 8.4.

a
b

**Figure 8.10   The structure of ethene**
a   A model showing the distribution of the electrons
b   A diagram showing the bond lengths and bond angles

In a C—C single bond (σ bond) the electron cloud is symmetrical about the central axis but in the C=C double bond the geometry is different. The $CH_2{=}CH_2$ molecule is flat and the electron clouds which make up the second bond (π bond) are above and below the plane of the molecule. Note that a double bond consists of a σ bond plus a π bond.

## BACKGROUND

**cis**-retinal

**trans**-retinal

As you read the black print on this page you are using the cells in your eye that detect light and are called 'rods'. There are other cells called 'cones' that enable us to distinguish between colours.

When light photons strike a rod there is a chemical change that converts the energy of the light photon into an electric impulse. This travels via the optic nerve to the brain where we 'see' what our eye was looking at.

The chemical compound that actually interacts with photons is an unsaturated aldehyde, with five alkene groups, called *cis*-retinal. The *cis* molecule bonds onto specific sites on the surface of a large protein molecule (rather like an enzyme). When a *cis* molecule interacts with a photon it changes in shape to the *trans* form. But the *trans* shape no longer fits the sites on the surface of the protein and so the two molecules separate, starting the process that sends an electric impulse to our brain.

So the simple difference between *cis* and *trans* shapes about a double bond has been developed by evolution into the sense of sight.

Breaking a double bond requires more energy than breaking a single bond:

$$CH_3CH_2\text{---}CH_2CH_3 \longrightarrow CH_3CH_2\cdot + \cdot CH_2CH_3 \qquad E(C\text{---}C) = +346\,kJ\,mol^{-1}$$

$$CH_3CH\text{==}CHCH_3 \longrightarrow CH_3CH\text{:} + \text{:}CHCH_3 \qquad E(C\text{==}C) = +610\,kJ\,mol^{-1}$$

But if we consider just the $\pi$ bond we find it is weaker than a $\sigma$ bond. By calculation from the data above, you should be able to confirm that the difference between the two bond energies is only $264\,kJ\,mol^{-1}$.

The rules for naming unsaturated hydrocarbons are similar to those used for the corresponding saturated compounds, explained in section 8.1. The only additional problem which arises is that of locating the double bond. This is done by using the carbon atom of lower number, of the pair of carbon atoms connected by the double bond.

$$CH_2\text{==}CH\text{---}CH_2\text{---}CH_3 \qquad \text{but-1-ene (not but-2-ene or but-3-ene)}$$

There is no need to do this for the first two members of the series, $CH_2\text{==}CH_2$ ethene (also called ethylene), and $CH_3\text{---}CH\text{==}CH_2$ propene (also called propylene).

With four carbon atoms and one double bond, structural isomers are possible:

$$CH_2\text{==}CH\text{---}CH_2\text{---}CH_3 \qquad \text{but-1-ene}$$
$$CH_3\text{---}CH\text{==}CH\text{---}CH_3 \qquad \text{but-2-ene}$$

The same rule is used for compounds containing more than one double bond, for example

$$CH_2\text{==}CH\text{---}CH\text{==}CH\text{---}CH_3 \qquad \text{penta-1,3-diene}$$

(The '**di-**' indicates two double bonds; note also that '**a**' is added to the hydrocarbon root when more than one double bond is present.)

Branched chain alkenes are dealt with as for alkanes, for example

$$CH_2\text{==}\underset{\underset{CH_3}{|}}{C}\text{---}CH_2\text{---}CH_3 \qquad \text{2-methylbut-1-ene}$$

Cycloalkenes follow similar rules to cycloalkanes.

# Experiments with alkenes

H₂
C
CH₃
CH₂
C
CH
CH
CH₃—C
C
H₂
CH₂

Limonene,
obtained from citrus fruits

In the first experiment with alkenes you are going to extract a naturally occurring alkene, limonene, from oranges. Plants are a valuable source of chemical compounds. For thousands of years we have turned to plants for food flavours, perfumes, drugs and dyes. Cooks and chemists have discovered ways to use the different parts of plants as a source of flavours: peppermint from leaves, ginger from roots, mustard from seeds, nutmeg from fruits and cloves from buds.

After extracting limonene you will use it in two simple tests and use the remainder, or a supply from a chemical company, to make a general survey of the reactions of alkenes.

**EXPERIMENT 8.4a**

## Extracting limonene from oranges by steam distillation

Heating plant material directly to distil off the chemicals does not work. The compounds either decompose or burn. Distilling in steam, however, makes it possible to separate plant chemicals without destroying them.

Steam distillation drives off from plant materials oily chemicals which do not mix with water. The oils will distil over in the steam just below 100 °C – well below the boiling point of the oil.

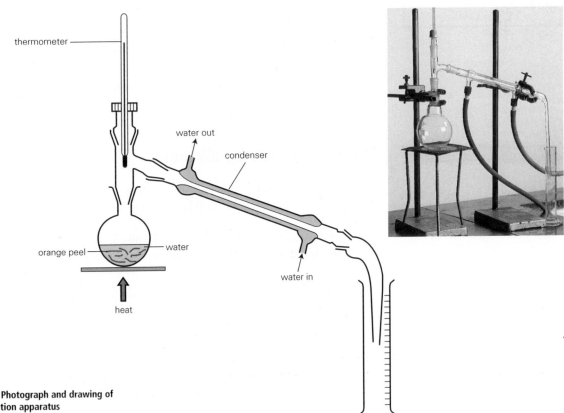

**Figure 8.11 Photograph and drawing of steam distillation apparatus**

## 1 Procedure

Put into a 250 cm³ flask the finely ground or chopped **outer rind** of two oranges and 100 cm³ of water. This is the minimum amount to use but the extraction can be scaled up to suit any size of container. Use only the **outer orange-coloured rind** which needs to be fresh.

Arrange the flask for distillation and heat on a wire gauze as in figure 8.11 (on the previous page). Collect about 50 cm³ of distillate in a measuring cylinder. You should be able to see an oily layer of limonene on top of the water. Use a dropping pipette to remove portions of the oily layer for part **2**.

✎    **In your notes:** Describe how you carried out the steam distillation and what happened.

## 2 Testing limonene

You are now going to compare the limonene from orange peel with another alkene, cyclohexene.

### a Odour

Smell the two liquids **cautiously** by wafting the fumes towards your nose. Do not breathe in directly from their containers.

✎    **In your notes:** Try to describe the odours.

### b Action of bromine

Measure out 1 cm³ of bromine solution in water into two separate test tubes using a dropping pipette. Add a few drops of limonene and cyclohexene to separate test tubes. Shake the tubes gently from side to side.

✎    **In your notes:** What happens to the colour of the bromine in each case?

> **SAFETY** ⚠
>
> Handle cyclohexene with care as it is highly flammable and irritant.
> Bromine solution is harmful and irritant; the fumes are dangerous to your eyes, nose and lungs.

---

**EXPERIMENT 8.4b**

# The reactions of the alkenes

For these experiments we shall repeat most of the reactions carried out with alkanes in section 8.2, but we shall be using unsaturated instead of saturated hydrocarbons.

For this experiment you should use the alkene cyclohexene, and limonene if it is available. Handle cyclohexene with care: it is highly flammable.

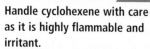

Cyclohexene,
obtained from petroleum

Limonene,
obtained from citrus fruits

Record your results in the form of a table, so that they can be compared with the results of the similar experiments with the alkanes.

## SAFETY

Cyclohexene is highly
flammable and an irritant to
the respiratory system.
Methyl 2-methylpropenoate
is highly flammable and
irritant.
Di(dodecanoyl) peroxide is a
powerful oxidant.
The polymerisation reaction
should be carried out in a
well ventilated laboratory, or
preferably in a fume
cupboard, as irritant fumes
are evolved.
The other reagents which you
will be using are the same as
those in Experiment 8.2, so
you must take the same care.

## Procedure

### 1 Combustion

Keep the liquid alkene in a stopped boiling tube well away from any flame. Dip a combustion spoon into the sample. Set fire to the alkene on the combustion spoon.

✎   **In your notes:** What are the products of combustion? How do they account for the sooty and luminous flame?

### 2 Oxidation

To 0.5 cm$^3$ of a mixture of equal volumes of 0.01 M potassium manganate(VII) solution and 1 M sulphuric acid in a test tube add a few drops of the alkene. Shake the contents and try to tell from any colour change of the manganate(VII) if it oxidises the alkene.

### 3 Action of bromine

To 0.5 cm$^3$ of bromine water (TAKE CARE) in a test tube add a few drops of the alkene.

✎   **In your notes:** What happens to the colour of the bromine?

### 4 Action of sulphuric acid

Put 1–2 cm$^3$ of concentrated sulphuric acid (TAKE CARE) in a test tube held in a test tube rack and add 0.5 cm$^3$ of the alkene. Shake the test tube gently.

✎   **In your notes:** Do the substances mix or are there two separate layers in the test tube?

### 5 Polymerisation

In this experiment you will prepare a sample of poly(methyl 2-methylpropenoate), Perspex.

$$CH_2{=}\underset{\underset{\displaystyle CO_2CH_3}{|}}{\overset{\overset{\displaystyle CH_3}{|}}{C}}$$

methyl 2-methylpropenoate

In a test tube, mix 5 cm$^3$ of methyl 2-methylpropenoate (methyl methacrylate: $T_b$ 100 °C) (TAKE CARE) and 0.1 g of di(dodecanoyl) peroxide to start the reaction. Stand a wooden splint in the reaction mixture as a means of testing the viscosity of the liquid.

Heat a water bath to boiling, remove the Bunsen burner, and place the test tube in the water bath. Allow the test tube to stand in the slowly cooling water bath and try stirring the mixture with the wooden splint every 5 minutes.

✎   **In your notes:** Try to write an equation for the polymerisation of methyl 2-methylpropenoate. Does the product have the same empirical formula as the starting material?

# An interpretation of the experiments with alkenes

You should have seen that the alkenes are readily reactive with reagents such as concentrated sulphuric acid and bromine, whereas the alkanes are unreactive. Furthermore, it can be shown that the reactions are giving only a single product. **Since the reagents are adding to the C=C double bond and not removing any atoms from the alkene, the reactions are known as addition reactions:**

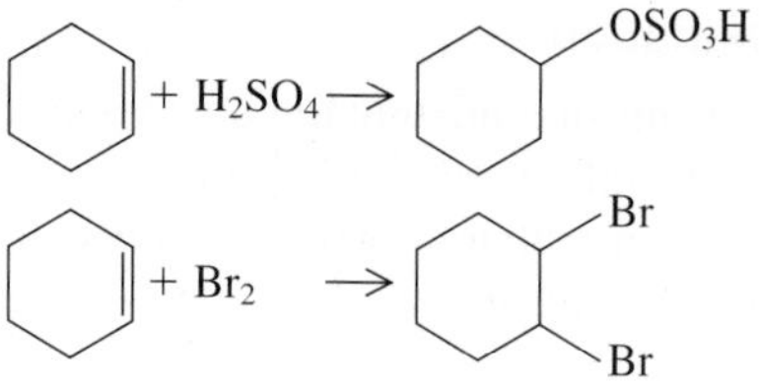

By what process do these reactions occur? From the study of a large number of alkene reactions chemists have proposed a mechanism that is consistent with all the evidence available. The π bond contributes an electron pair to the formation of a new bond with the positively polarised attacking group.

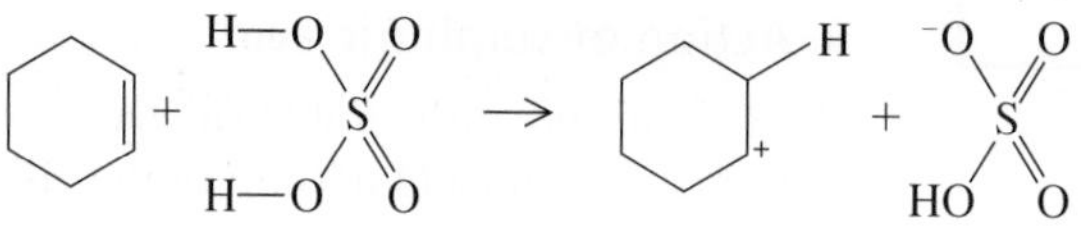

In this and similar reactions the attacking group is called an **electrophile (electron-seeking)**. Electrophiles are commonly acidic compounds, as in the above reaction in which sulphuric acid is reacting as an electrophile. The sulphuric acid donates a proton, $H^+$, to the cyclohexene π bond, which provides an electron pair to form the new bond to the proton.

This is the common pattern of electrophilic reactions.

**An electrophile is an electron-deficient compound that can form a new covalent bond, using an electron pair provided by the carbon compound. The commonest electrophilic reagent is the proton, $H^+$.**

The reaction ends with the addition of a nucleophilic hydrogensulphate ion to the cyclohexyl ion. The cyclohexyl ion is an unstable carbocation, with a positively charged carbon atom, so it reacts with the negative nucleophilic ion.

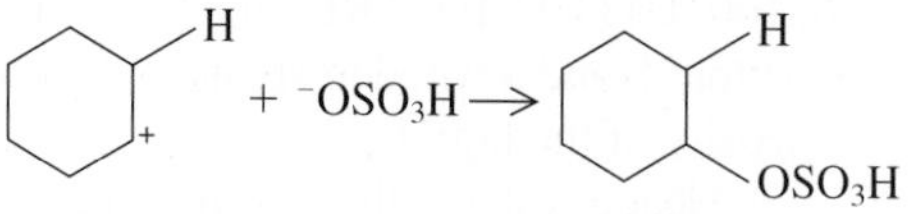

cyclohexyl
hydrogensulphate

**This type of reaction is described as an electrophilic addition.**

The reaction with bromine might not follow the same course because the bromine molecule is not polar and does not have a proton to donate to the double bond. Read the passage quoted below and try to decide whether the results can be explained in terms of the course described for the electrophilic addition of sulphuric acid or whether we shall have to propose a different process for the addition of bromine.

'A 1 dm³ pressure bottle was filled two-thirds full with a saturated salt solution, and sufficient halogen was added to saturate it. The bottle was closed with a cap containing a bicycle valve, and a moderate pressure (4 or 5 atmospheres) of ethene was added from a cylinder. The bottle was well shaken for one minute or until the pressure had become practically atmospheric, and more ethene was added. When the solution had become colourless, more halogen and ethene were introduced. The process was continued until a sufficient amount of oil had been accumulated. This was separated from the aqueous solution, washed with water, dried with calcium chloride, and examined by determination of density, refractive index, or boiling point. In each case a mixture was obtained, and a partial separation was made by fractional distillation.

From ethene, bromine, and sodium chloride solution a mixture of 1,2-dibromoethane and 1-bromo-2-chloroethane was obtained. The product mixture, an oil, contained about 46% of $C_2H_4ClBr$ as estimated from the refractive index, 1.51 (the value for $C_2H_4Br_2$ in the literature is 1.53; for $C_2H_4Cl_2$, 1.44).

1-bromo-2-nitratoethane was obtained from ethene, bromine, and sodium nitrate solution. Before distillation the product mixture was washed with sodium hydrogencarbonate solution to remove any trace of nitric acid. The oil began to boil at 132 °C ($C_2H_4Br_2$) but a portion boiled at 163–5 °C (the boiling point of $C_2H_4BrNO_3$ given in the literature is 164 °C). In the distillation the last trace exploded with evolution of brown fumes of nitrogen dioxide, recognised also by their odour.'

These results were obtained by A. W. Francis, and published in the *Journal of the American Chemical Society* in 1925.

## QUESTIONS

An equation for one reaction carried out by Francis could be written as:

$$CH_2{=}CH_2 + Br_2 + NO_3^- \longrightarrow CH_2Br{-}CH_2ONO_2 + Br^-$$

How might this product have come about?

Consider first the nitrato ($-ONO_2$) group, which is derived from the nitrate ($NO_3^-$) ion.

1   Would you describe the nitrate ion as a free radical, an electron-deficient or an electron-rich species, electrophilic or nucleophilic?

2   So would the nitrate ion be most likely to attack a carbon grouping of the free radical type, a $\pi$ bond, or a carbocation?

Now consider the bromo ($-Br$) group, which is derived from the bromine ($Br_2$) molecule.

3   Can a bromine–bromine bond break to give free radicals, electron-deficient or electron-rich species?

4   Which of these would react with a $\pi$ bond to give a molecule with a charge that the nitrate ion might attack?

5   Finally, does the process you propose give a bromide ($Br^-$) ion as one of the products?

# Reactions of the alkenes

## 1 Addition of halogens

$$CH_3{-}CH{=}CH_2 + Br_2 \longrightarrow CH_3{-}CHBr{-}CH_2Br$$
1,2-dibromopropane

This is an electrophilic addition with the Br—Br molecule being polarised in part by the $\pi$ bond. The reaction needs to be carried out without heat and in the absence of sunlight, to avoid free radical substitution (see section 8.2). It is an important reaction for the preparation of dihalogenoalkanes.

## 2 Addition of hydrogen halides

In normal laboratory conditions the hydrogen halide acts as an electrophile, forming the carbocation intermediate $CH_3 \!\!-\!\! \overset{+}{C}H \!\!-\!\! CH_3$ with the positive charge on the $-CH-$ group.

$$CH_3 \!\!-\!\! CH \!\!=\!\! CH_2 + HBr \longrightarrow CH_3 \!\!-\!\! CHBr \!\!-\!\! CH_3$$
2-bromopropane

In sunlight or with a suitable catalyst the alternative product, 1-bromopropane, is obtained.

## 3 Addition of sulphuric acid

This is an important reaction because the product, an alkyl hydrogensulphate, will take part in further reactions producing alcohols as shown in the following reaction scheme. These reactions are carried out in industry.

$$CH_2 \!\!=\!\! CH_2 \xrightarrow{H_2SO_4} CH_3 \!\!-\!\! CH_2 \!\!-\!\! OSO_3H \xrightarrow{H_2O} CH_3 \!\!-\!\! CH_2 \!\!-\!\! OH$$
ethanol

The addition of sulphuric acid follows the same pattern as the electrophilic addition of hydrogen halides.

## 4 Formation of diols by potassium manganate(VII)

Reaction with cold acidified potassium manganate(VII) produces compounds known as **diols**. The complete balanced equation for this reaction is complicated. As the interest is chiefly centred on the organic compounds, we can write a simplified version in this way:

$$CH_2 \!\!=\!\! CH_2 \xrightarrow{KMnO_4} CH_2OH \!\!-\!\! CH_2OH$$
ethane-1,2-diol

An alternative name for the product is **glycol** (see Topic 2). It is commonly used in antifreeze for car radiators and is manufactured by a more efficient method than manganate(VII) oxidation.

## 5 Reduction with hydrogen

Reduction by hydrogen requires the use of a metal catalyst such as nickel. The metal has to be finely divided, and in the case of nickel the catalyst is made by treating a special nickel–aluminium alloy with sodium hydroxide. This dissolves away the aluminium and leaves the nickel (known as Raney nickel) in a very finely divided state.

$$CH_2 \!\!=\!\! CH_2 + H_2 \xrightarrow{Ni \ catalyst} CH_3 \!\!-\!\! CH_3$$

The reaction is useful for preparing alkanes or for saturating some of the double bonds in natural oils. In this way, liquid fats can be converted to solids for use in margarine, even though saturated fats are considered to be a contributor to heart complaints and unsaturated fats are thought to be safer to eat.

## 6 Polymerisation

Ethene molecules will join together in suitable conditions to form very long chain alkane molecules. The reaction involves **free radicals**:

$$n CH_2{=}CH_2 \xrightarrow{\text{free radicals}} {+}CH_2{-}CH_2{+}_n$$

A variety of substances such as peroxides which yield free radicals are used to initiate the reaction. This reaction allows the formation of side chains and the product has a low density. This is known as an **addition polymerisation** because the unsaturated monomer, ethene, reacts to give the polymer poly(ethene) as the only product.

## Review of alkenes

Draw up a summary chart similar to the one shown below. Add any personal touches that you feel will help you remember and understand the reactions of the alkenes.

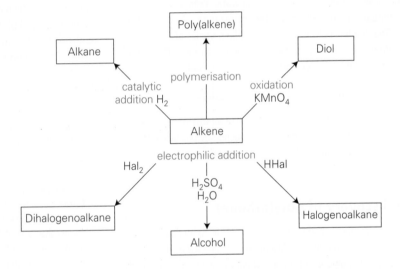

# 8.5 Background reading: polymerisation

### QUESTIONS

Read the passage overleaf, then answer these questions based on it.

1 How many ethene monomer molecules have to polymerise to form a polymer of molar mass $3000\ g\ mol^{-1}$?

2 Sketch a short length of poly(ethene) chain to show the difference between branched and unbranched chains.

3 Suggest why branching occurs in free radical addition polymerisation but not in catalytic polymerisation.

4 Write a summary in continuous prose, in no more than 100 words, summarising the key ideas about addition polymerisation.

Poly(ethene) is manufactured by two distinct processes. In the original process, ethene is polymerised in the liquid state at pressures up to 3000 atmospheres and temperatures up to 300 °C. This reaction allows the formation of side chains and the product has a low density.

$$n\text{CH}_2\text{=CH}_2 \xrightarrow{\text{free radicals}} \text{--}(\text{CH}_2\text{--CH}_2)_n$$

In the 1950s Karl Ziegler developed a process in which ethene could be polymerised at a relatively low pressure and temperature: less than 50 atmospheres and below 100 °C. In the Ziegler process the polymerisation takes place on the surface of catalyst particles to give straight unbranched chains and the product has a higher density. The catalysts used are organometallic complexes, often based on chromium or vanadium.

Poly(chloroethene), PVC, is usually prepared as a suspension in water. Typically, equal quantities of water and chloroethene and a small quantity of a surface active agent are stirred together to produce a suspension of chloroethene in water. Potassium peroxodisulphate(VI) is added and the temperature raised to about 60 °C. The droplets polymerise to form solid particles of poly(chloroethene) which can be recovered by filtration. The water dilutes the reaction mixture and helps to keep it cool.

$$n\text{CH}_2\text{=CHCl} \xrightarrow{\text{free radicals}} \text{--}(\text{CH}_2\text{--CHCl})_n$$

The potassium peroxodisulphate(VI) is called an **initiator** rather than a catalyst. It increases the rate of reaction by producing the free radicals which initiate the reaction, but is decomposed in the process and not re-formed.

## The discovery of poly(ethene)

High pressure studies had been started by ICI in connection with the Haber process but in 1931 attention was directed at the possibility of bringing about organic chemical reactions, particularly those of the condensation type, which at lower pressures require the aid of catalysts. Two research chemists, Gibson and Fawcett, reported in April 1933:

'*Ethene and benzaldehyde*

Attempts have been made to react ethene and benzaldehyde. At 170 °C and 2000 atm pressure, reaction occurred slowly to yield a hard waxy solid containing no oxygen, melting at 113 °C and analysing to $(\text{CH}_2)_n$, apparently an ethene polymer. In some cases during the investigation of this reaction, a violent reaction has occurred with considerable rise in pressure and on opening up the bomb it has been found that complete carbonisation of the charge has taken place. In these experiments (that is, in which carbonisation has occurred) simple decomposition of ethene has apparently taken place.'

By July about half a gram of polymer had been obtained in all, but the explosive carbonisation could not be controlled and work ceased.

To pause on the brink of an important discovery may seem strange but it should be remembered that in 1933 the common plastics, such as Bakelite, were rigid materials while the poly(ethene) obtained was soft and the quantity available was insufficient for technical evaluation. Nor was polymerisation the object of the research, so the high pressure studies were continued using carbon monoxide instead of the explosive ethene. However in 1935 another chemist, Perrin, looked again at the polymerisation of ethene and by good fortune obtained sufficient yields for the importance of the discovery to be realised:

'*December 1935*

In one experiment at 2000 atm and 170 °C where the gas was compressed directly into a steel bomb, the reaction proceeded steadily to give about 8 g in four hours of a white waxy solid polymer of ethene. The molar mass of the polymer is about 3000. The properties of this substance are being studied.

*January 1936*

Further quantities of the polymer have been made. A preliminary figure shows that the electrical volume resistivity of the moulded polymer is greater than $5 \times 10^{14}$ ohm cm$^{-3}$ showing that it falls into the class of good dielectrics. It has been possible to make thin transparent films of the polymer which have considerable strength and toughness.'

# KEY SKILLS

## Communication

Reading about the octane number of petrol and about polymerisation (background reading, sections 8.3 and 8.5) gives you an opportunity to show that you can understand complex lines of reasoning and extract information from text and images.

## IT

In this topic you could use chemical modelling software from a CD-ROM or the Internet to study the shapes and structures of organic molecules including isomers. This would allow you to compare the advantages and limitation of using software,

# TOPIC REVIEW

Remember that this topic builds on the ideas introduced in the first organic chemistry topic. Look back at your Topic 2 review before starting this one. Try to link the two as you go along.

1 **List key words or terms with definitions where necessary**

Illustrate the following by giving suitable **examples** of each:

- geometric isomers
- homolytic fission
- free radical
- chain reaction (initiation, propagation, termination)
- substitution
- elimination
- heterolytic fission
- catalytic cracking
- addition
- nucleophile
- electrophile
- polymerisation.

2 **Summarise the key principles as simply as possible**

You should have already drawn **summary charts** or 'spider diagrams' for the **reactions of alkanes and alkenes** as you worked through this topic. It would be a good idea to file them with this summary. Amongst other things, your review must include details of:

- the rules for naming organic compounds
- the ways in which substitution reactions can occur
- the ways in which addition reactions can occur.

## REVIEW QUESTIONS

* Indicates that the *Book of data* is needed.

**8.1** Using butane as an example, explain the meaning of the terms 'empirical formula', 'molecular formula', 'structural formula' and 'displayed formula'.

**(4 marks)**

**8.2** Draw the displayed formula of each of the following:

a   2-methylbutane (1)
b   2,2-dimethylpropane (1)
c   2,3,3-trimethylpentane (1)
d   2,2,4-trimethylhexane (1)
e   3-ethyl-4,4-dimethylheptane (1)

**(5 marks)**

**8.3** Write down the molecular formula of each of the compounds in question **8.2**.

**(5 marks)**

**8.4** Name the following compounds:

a   $CH_3(CH_2)_3CH_3$ (1)
b   $(CH_3)_2CHCH_2CH_3$ (1)
c   (1)

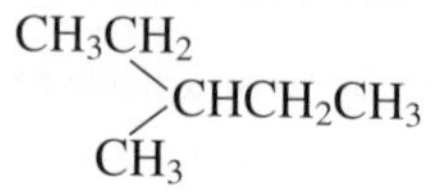

$$CH_3CH_2$$
$$\diagdown$$
$$CHCH_2CH_3$$
$$CH_3$$

d   (1)

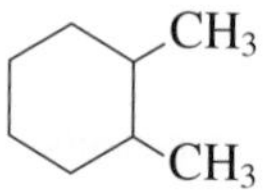

$$\bigcirc\!\!\!-\!CH_3$$
$$-\!CH_3$$

e   $CH_3CH(CH_3)CH(CH_3)CH_2CH_2CH_3$ (1)

**(5 marks)**

**8.5** Ethene, $C_2H_4$, is one product of the cracking of decane, $C_{10}H_{22}$. Assuming there is only one other product in each case, write balanced equations for cracking reactions giving:

a   one mole of ethene per mole of decane (2)
b   two moles of ethene per mole of decane. (2)

**(4 marks)**

**8.6**

   **a**   Write equations showing the sequence of steps in the photochemical reaction between hexane and bromine, identifying them as initiation, propagation and termination stages. (6)

   **b**   Write a balanced equation for the overall reaction, with $C_6H_{13}Br$ as one of the products. (2)

   **c**   In this reaction $C_6H_{14}$ has been converted into $C_6H_{13}Br$. What word describes a reaction of this type? (1)

   **d**   What further reaction(s) might occur? (1)

                                         **(10 marks)**

**\* 8.7**   Follow steps **a** to **d** below to calculate the volume of air, measured at 20 °C and 1 atm, needed for the complete combustion of 1 litre of petrol (assume petrol consists only of octane, $C_8H_{18}$).

   **a**   Write a balanced equation for the complete combustion of octane in air. (2)

   **b**   Look up the density of octane and use it to calculate the mass of 1 litre of the fuel (assume 1 litre = $1000\ cm^3$). (2)

   **c**   Use your answer to **b** and the molar mass of octane to calculate the number of moles of octane in 1 litre. (2)

   **d**   Use your answers to **a** and **c** to calculate the volume of oxygen and hence the volume of air required for complete combustion of the octane (assume that 1 mole of gas at 20 °C and 1 atm has a volume of $24\ dm^3$ and that air is 20% oxygen by volume). (2)

   **e**   In practice, combustion will be incomplete. What are the consequences of this, in terms of atmospheric pollution and the amount of energy produced? (2)

                                         **(10 marks)**

**8.8**   Draw the displayed formulae and give the names of six different compounds having the molecular formula $C_4H_8$. (There are *cis* and *trans* geometric isomers as well as structural isomers.) **(12 marks)**

**8.9**

   **a**   Which of the following can exist as geometric (*cis* and *trans*) isomers? (You may find it helpful to use a molecular model kit, if available.)

          $ClCH{=}CHCl$   $CH_3CH_2CH{=}CHCH_3$   $CH_3CH_2CH{=}C(CH_3)_2$  (2)

   **b**   Draw the displayed formulae of the geometric isomers. (4)

                                         **(6 marks)**

**8.10**   Which of the following reagents form stable addition products with ethene, with or without the use of catalysts?

          $Br_2(l)$   $NaOH(aq)$   $H_2(g)$   $H_2SO_4(l)$   $H_2SO_4(aq)$   $HBr(g)$   $H_2O(l)$
          $NH_3(g)$   $CuSO_4(aq)$

                                           **(5 marks)**

**8.11**

   **a**   Classify the following species as free radicals, electrophiles or neither. Justify your answers by indicating the number of electrons in the outer shell of the significant atom.

          $Br^+$   $OH^-$   $CH_3\cdot$   $H_2O$   $CH_3^+$   $Cl\cdot$   $I^-$   $H^+$   $NH_3$   (3)

   **b**   Why are there no metal cations such as $Na^+$ or $Cu^{2+}$ in the list, although anions of non-metals are represented? (1)

                                         **(4 marks)**

# EXAMINATION QUESTIONS

Questions of the summary and comprehension type are found in the background reading sections (sections 8.3 and 8.5).

**8.12**  **a**  Propane, $C_3H_8$, is used as a feedstock for making ethene using a cracking process. The yield of ethene is about 42%.

    **i**  Write an equation for the cracking of propane to form ethene and one other product using displayed formulae. (2)

    **ii**  Draw a labelled diagram of an ethene molecule, showing the electron density distribution in the $\sigma$ and $\pi$ bonds between the carbon atoms. (2)

**b**  The cracking of propane also produces propene.

$$C_3H_8(g) \longrightarrow C_3H_6(g) + H_2(g)$$

Calculate the standard enthalpy change for this reaction. Use the data, at 298 K:

$$\Delta H_f^{\ominus}[C_3H_8(g)] = -104.5 \text{ kJ mol}^{-1}$$
$$\Delta H_f^{\ominus}[C_3H_6(g)] = +20.2 \text{ kJ mol}^{-1}$$

Your answer should include a sign and units. (2)

**c**  Propene can be used to make a number of important chemical products. The processes involved can be summarised in the diagram:

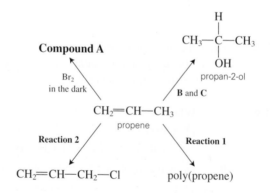

    **i**  Give the displayed formula and name of compound **A**. (2)

    **ii**  State the type of reaction occurring and the type of reagent used in the formation of compound **A**. (2)

    **iii**  Give the formulae of compounds **B** and **C**. (2)

    **iv**  Write a balanced equation for the formation of poly(propene) from propene in **Reaction 1**. (2)

    **v**  Suggest a reagent and condition for **Reaction 2**. (2)

    **vi**  State the type of mechanism in the substitution in **Reaction 2**. (1)

    **vii**  Give the systematic name for $CH_2\!=\!CH\!-\!CH_2\!-\!Cl$. (1)

**(18 marks)**

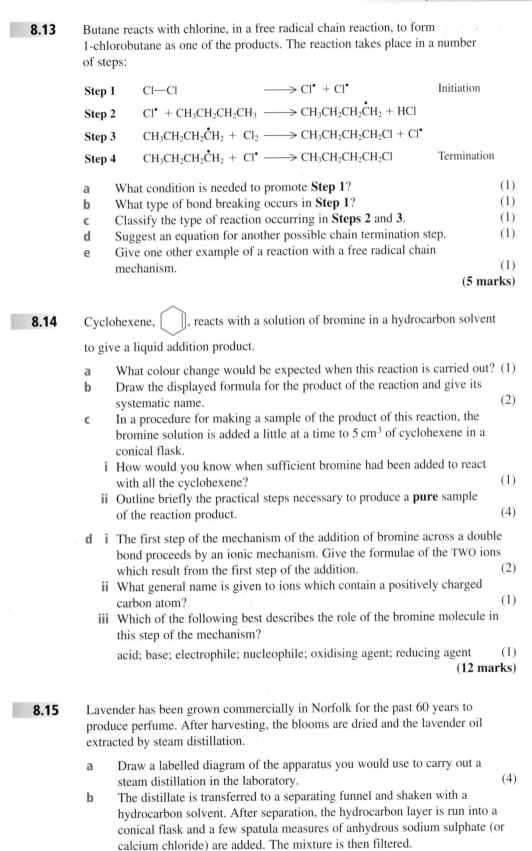

**8.13**  Butane reacts with chlorine, in a free radical chain reaction, to form 1-chlorobutane as one of the products. The reaction takes place in a number of steps:

**Step 1**  $Cl—Cl \longrightarrow Cl^{\bullet} + Cl^{\bullet}$  Initiation

**Step 2**  $Cl^{\bullet} + CH_3CH_2CH_2CH_3 \longrightarrow CH_3CH_2CH_2\overset{\bullet}{C}H_2 + HCl$

**Step 3**  $CH_3CH_2CH_2\overset{\bullet}{C}H_2 + Cl_2 \longrightarrow CH_3CH_2CH_2CH_2Cl + Cl^{\bullet}$

**Step 4**  $CH_3CH_2CH_2\overset{\bullet}{C}H_2 + Cl^{\bullet} \longrightarrow CH_3CH_2CH_2CH_2Cl$  Termination

a  What condition is needed to promote **Step 1**?  (1)
b  What type of bond breaking occurs in **Step 1**?  (1)
c  Classify the type of reaction occurring in **Steps 2** and **3**.  (1)
d  Suggest an equation for another possible chain termination step.  (1)
e  Give one other example of a reaction with a free radical chain mechanism.  (1)
**(5 marks)**

**8.14**  Cyclohexene, [⬡], reacts with a solution of bromine in a hydrocarbon solvent to give a liquid addition product.

a  What colour change would be expected when this reaction is carried out?  (1)
b  Draw the displayed formula for the product of the reaction and give its systematic name.  (2)
c  In a procedure for making a sample of the product of this reaction, the bromine solution is added a little at a time to $5 \, cm^3$ of cyclohexene in a conical flask.
  i  How would you know when sufficient bromine had been added to react with all the cyclohexene?  (1)
  ii  Outline briefly the practical steps necessary to produce a **pure** sample of the reaction product.  (4)

d  i  The first step of the mechanism of the addition of bromine across a double bond proceeds by an ionic mechanism. Give the formulae of the TWO ions which result from the first step of the addition.  (2)
  ii  What general name is given to ions which contain a positively charged carbon atom?  (1)
  iii  Which of the following best describes the role of the bromine molecule in this step of the mechanism?

    acid; base; electrophile; nucleophile; oxidising agent; reducing agent  (1)
**(12 marks)**

**8.15**  Lavender has been grown commercially in Norfolk for the past 60 years to produce perfume. After harvesting, the blooms are dried and the lavender oil extracted by steam distillation.

a  Draw a labelled diagram of the apparatus you would use to carry out a steam distillation in the laboratory.  (4)
b  The distillate is transferred to a separating funnel and shaken with a hydrocarbon solvent. After separation, the hydrocarbon layer is run into a conical flask and a few spatula measures of anhydrous sodium sulphate (or calcium chloride) are added. The mixture is then filtered.

Explain the reasons for using:

i a hydrocarbon solvent (1)

ii anhydrous sodium sulphate or calcium chloride. (1)

c One of the substances present in lavender oil is linalool, $C_9H_{16}O$.

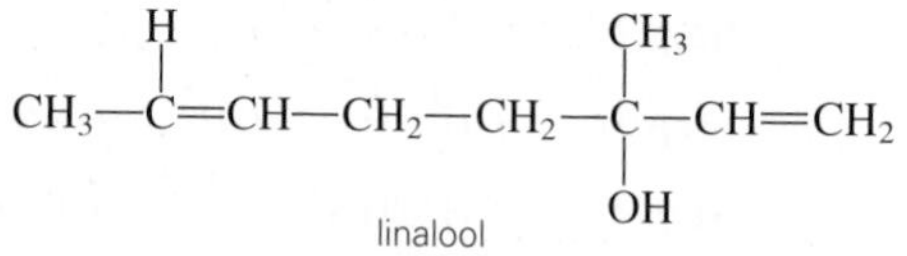

$$CH_3-\overset{\overset{\displaystyle H}{|}}{C}=CH-CH_2-CH_2-\overset{\overset{\displaystyle CH_3}{|}}{\underset{\underset{\displaystyle OH}{|}}{C}}-CH=CH_2$$

linalool

Draw the structural formula of the main organic product formed from linalool in each of the following reactions:

i with sodium, Na (1)

ii with bromine, $Br_2$ (2)

iii with alumina, $Al_2O_3$, at 400 °C. (2)

d Dried lavender flowers only contain a very small proportion of lavender oil. Chemists are often required to find a suitable substitute for naturally occurring plant oils. Suggest THREE factors which must be taken into account when seeking a suitable substitute. (3)

**(14 marks)**

**8.16** The reaction sequence below is used to make one of the chemicals needed to manufacture epoxy resins. Epoxy resins are polymers which are used in heavy-duty adhesives.

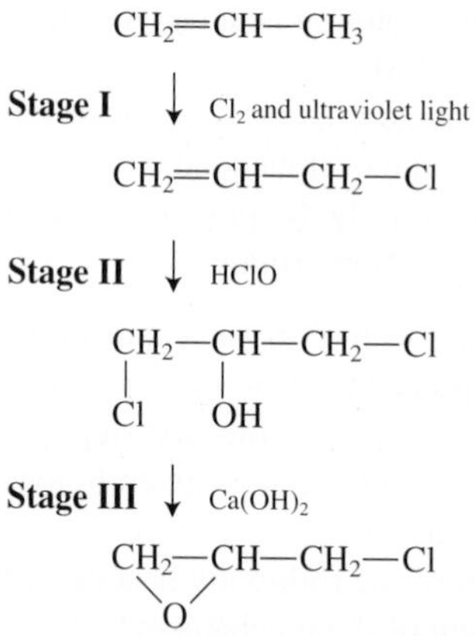

$$CH_2=CH-CH_3$$

**Stage I** $\downarrow$ $Cl_2$ and ultraviolet light

$$CH_2=CH-CH_2-Cl$$

**Stage II** $\downarrow$ HClO

$$CH_2-\overset{}{\underset{\underset{\displaystyle Cl}{|}}{C}}H-CH_2-Cl$$
$$\qquad\;\; \overset{}{\underset{\underset{\displaystyle OH}{|}}{}}$$

**Stage III** $\downarrow$ $Ca(OH)_2$

$$CH_2-CH-CH_2-Cl$$
$$\quad\;\diagdown\!\!O\!\!\diagup$$

a i Name the **type of reaction** and name the **mechanism** that takes place in **Stage I**. (2)

ii What is the reason for using ultraviolet light? (1)

iii Under other conditions a different reaction can occur between propene and chlorine. Write down the name and structural formula of the product of this reaction. (2)

b In **Stage II** the organic molecule, 3-chloropropene, undergoes electrophilic addition with chloric(I) acid. Explain why the 3-chloropropene molecule can undergo electrophilic attack. (2)

c In **Stage III** the reaction taking place is called an **elimination** reaction. Explain why this name can be applied to this reaction. (1)

**(8 marks)**

# Intermolecular forces

When atoms combine with each other and electrons are exchanged to give ions, or shared between the atoms to give molecules, the resulting forces of attraction are very strong and require quite large amounts of energy to break them. Covalent bond energies of most single bonds lie between 200 and 500 kJ mol$^{-1}$.

When a molecular substance melts or boils the covalent bonds normally remain intact, the molecules merely separating from each other:

$$H_2O(l) \longrightarrow H_2O(g)$$

Since the molecules do not break up when the liquid water is boiled, there must be some forces of attraction between the molecules themselves which are broken when the molecules separate from each other. These are called **intermolecular forces**, and they have a vitally important role in many biochemical processes, described later in this topic.

At a practical level, insects can use intermolecular forces to 'walk' on water (see figure 9.1).

In this topic you will:

- be introduced to the three types of intermolecular force
- study some examples of intermolecular forces in chemical and biochemical compounds.

**Figure 9.1 Using intermolecular forces to 'walk' on water. Why do you think these insects have legs this shape?**

## 9.1 Van der Waals forces

Helium, which does not form normal covalent or ionic bonds and has symmetrical atoms, condenses to a liquid and ultimately freezes to a solid at very low temperatures, approaching 0 K. Energy is released in this process, showing that there are cohesive forces operating.

The energy of sublimation of solid helium when it changes from solid to gas is only 0.1 kJ mol$^{-1}$. This should be compared with the dissociation energy of the hydrogen molecule, 436 kJ mol$^{-1}$, required to break the one covalent bond.

**The weak forces of attraction between molecules are known as van der Waals forces.**

Van der Waals forces are considered to be due to continually changing electric charge interactions between atoms, called dipole–dipole interactions.

BACKGROUND

The energy of sublimation is the sum of the enthalpy change of melting and the enthalpy change of vaporisation.

## COMMENT

The noble gases are the only elements which exist as separate single atoms. They can be considered as consisting of monatomic molecules.

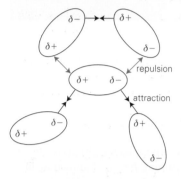

Figure 9.2 **Attractive and repulsive forces between transient dipoles – the overall effect is weak bonding holding the molecules together**

These interactions are thought to arise because the electron charge cloud in an atom is in continual motion. In the turmoil, it frequently happens that rather more of the charge cloud is on one side of the atom than on the other. This means that the centres of positive and negative charge do not coincide, and a fluctuating dipole is set up. This dipole induces a dipole in neighbouring atoms. The sign of the induced dipole is opposite to that of the dipole producing it, and consequently a force of attraction results. These **transient dipole–dipole interactions** produce a **cohesive force** between neighbouring atoms and molecules.

The greater the number of electrons in an atom, the greater will be the fluctuation in the asymmetry of the electron charge cloud and the greater will be the van der Waals attraction set up. The rise in boiling point down Group 7 (fluorine, chlorine, bromine, and iodine) is due to the increasing numbers of electrons in the atoms and the consequent increase in van der Waals attractions, rather than to the increase in the mass of the atoms.

## QUESTIONS

Compare these data by plotting a graph.

| Entity | Number of electrons | Molar mass /g mol$^{-1}$ | Boiling point /K |
|--------|---------------------|--------------------------|------------------|
| $F_2$  | 18                  | 38                       | 85               |
| $Cl_2$ | 34                  | 71                       | 238              |
| $Br_2$ | 70                  | 160                      | 332              |
| $I_2$  | 106                 | 254                      | 457              |

Similarly the increase in boiling point up the homologous series of alkanes (see figure 8.3 page 181) is due to the increased number of electrons in the molecules and the increased total van der Waals attractions and not to the increase in mass or size of the molecules. The difference in boiling point between isomers can also be explained in terms of van der Waals attractions.

## STUDY TASK

The boiling points of pentane and 2,2-dimethylpropane, two isomers of molecular formula $C_5H_{12}$, are 36 °C and 10 °C, respectively.

pentane

2.2-dimethylpropane

Build space-filling models of each of these structures, and compare the shapes of the molecules. Why do the isomers differ in boiling point?

In the case of pentane, the linear molecules can line up beside each other and the van der Waals forces are likely to be comparatively strong, as they can act over the whole of the molecule. In the case of 2,2-dimethylpropane, the spherical molecules can only come close to one another at one point, so the van der Waals forces are likely to be comparatively weak. The isomer with the linear molecules thus has a higher boiling point.

## Van der Waals radii

The normal bonding forces in molecules are concentrated within the molecules themselves; they are **intramolecular**. In molecular crystals individual molecules are held to each other by van der Waals forces. Examples are iodine, solid carbon dioxide, and sulphur. As the forces are weak, the melting points of molecular crystals tend to be low.

In molecular crystals the van der Waals forces draw molecules together until their electron charge clouds repel each other to the extent of balancing the attraction. Thus for argon the atoms are drawn together until the atomic nuclei have a separation of about 0.4 nm (figure 9.3).

The atomic distances **within** simple molecules and **between** simple molecules are not the same.

**The covalent radius is one half of the distance between the nuclei of two atoms in the *same* molecule. The van der Waals radius is one half of the distance between the nuclei of two atoms in *adjacent* molecules (figure 9.4, overleaf).**

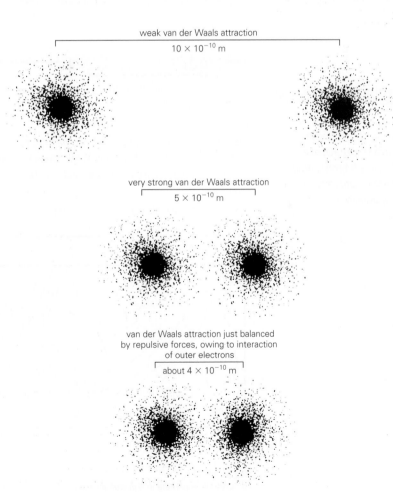

Figure 9.3 **Van der Waals attractions between argon atoms (4 × 10$^{-10}$ m = 0.4 nm)**

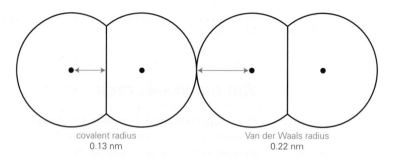

covalent radius
0.13 nm

Van der Waals radius
0.22 nm

**Figure 9.4   The difference between covalent radius and van der Waals radius for $I_2$**

The relative values of these radii for certain elements can be seen in the table.

| Atom | Covalent radius/nm | Van der Waals radius/nm |
|------|--------------------|--------------------------|
| H | 0.037 | 0.12 |
| N | 0.075 | 0.16 |
| O | 0.073 | 0.15 |
| P | 0.110 | 0.19 |
| S | 0.100 | 0.18 |

## COMMENT

Tensile strength is defined as the maximum force that can be applied to a strip or rod of a material before it breaks, divided by its cross-sectional area. It is a commonly used measure of strength.

## STUDY TASK

Although the van der Waals forces between individual atoms, as in helium, give only a small bonding energy, the total van der Waals bonding energy can be significant in large molecules with many contacts between atoms.

Use tables 7.7 and 7.2 in the *Book of data* to compare the tensile strength of a substance such as poly(ethene) that has only van der Waals forces between its molecules and the tensile strengths of metals such as aluminium, copper and iron. Note the change in units between tables 7.7 and 7.2.

The bonding in metals was described in Topic 3.

b

a

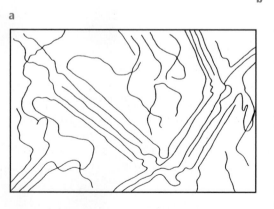

**Figure 9.5**
a  **Crystalline packing in a plastic polymer**
b  **Electron micrograph of poly(ethene) crystals**

## 9.2 Molecules with permanent dipoles

The attraction between the 'flickering dipoles', the van der Waals forces, is universal; all molecules exert some degree of attraction on all other molecules by this means. **In some molecules, however, the dipole is not instantaneous and rapidly changing but permanent.** A good example of this is the molecule of propanone which has a permanent dipole because of its strongly polarised carbonyl bond.

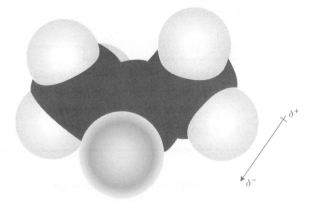

Figure 9.6 **Space-filling model of propanone**

**Molecules with a permanent dipole are called polar molecules.** In Experiment 9.2 you can investigate how permanent dipoles affect the properties of molecules.

---

### EXPERIMENT 9.2

### What is the effect of an electrostatic field on a jet of liquid?

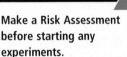

**SAFETY**

Make a Risk Assessment before starting any experiments.
Read the hazard warnings about the liquids selected for investigation and take appropriate precautions. Make sure you have, for instance, a fume cupboard or protective gloves if your Risk Assessment requires it.

You should plan this experiment in groups and produce an agreed list of liquids to test. Organic liquids provide a good range of compounds which have asymmetric molecules; for reasons of safety and cost it is best to confine your attention to hydrocarbons, alcohols and ketones.

Test **one** of the liquids on your list and watch the other tests.

### Procedure

Have your Risk Assessment checked by your teacher before you start the experiment. Fill a burette with a liquid, stand it over a large empty beaker, and turn on the tap so that a stream of the liquid flows into the beaker (figure 9.7, overleaf). Hold a charged plastic rod near the jet of liquid, but do not let it touch the liquid.

A plastic rod (such as a ball-point pen) can be charged by rubbing it vigorously with a piece of cloth, provided both are thoroughly dry.

✎ **In your notes:**

1 What happens to the jet of your liquid?

2 What happens with other liquids?

3 Why does this happen?

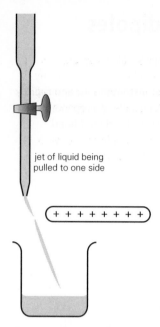

jet of liquid being
pulled to one side

+ + + + + + + +

Figure 9.7 **Apparatus for Experiment 9.2**

|  | Dipole moment /debye |
|---|---|
| Ethane $C_2H_6$ | 0 |
| Hydrogen chloride HCl | 1.1 |
| Ammonia $NH_3$ | 1.5 |
| Water $H_2O$ | 1.8 |
| Chloroethane $C_2H_5Cl$ | 2.0 |

# Interpretation of the experiment

The electrostatic field will be interacting with molecules that have an imbalance in charge distribution, that is, the molecules are **polarised**.

You are detecting the polarisation of **molecules**, but the polarisation of **bonds** can only be inferred from your results. A further complication is that the electrostatic field will create a temporary polarisation in the molecules, so the interpretation of these experiments cannot be precise. Nevertheless, you should have obtained some marked effects.

## QUESTIONS

1 Which liquids seemed to contain strongly polarised molecules?

2 Which bonds in the molecules might be strongly polarised?

3 Can you suggest an order of polarisation for the various bonds involving carbon atoms in the liquids you tested?

The permanent polarisation of molecules can be measured as a dipole moment. The direction of the dipole moment in a molecule is represented by the sign $\longmapsto$ , which is placed to point from the positively charged atom to the negatively charged atom in the molecule, for example:

$$\overset{\delta+}{H}\!\!-\!\!\overset{\delta-}{Cl}$$
$$\longmapsto$$

A difference in electric charge equal to the charge on the electron at a separation of about a bond length (0.1 nm) has a dipole moment of about 5 debyes (a measure of charge $\times$ distance apart).

We can compare this value of 5 debyes with the values for some molecules.

## STUDY TASK

Molecules with permanent dipoles attract each other in a way which is not possible with symmetrical molecules. The extent of this can be seen by comparing the boiling points of polar and non-polar substances with approximately the same number of electrons in their molecules. One pair of examples is given; think of three other examples, work out the number of electrons in the molecules, and look up their boiling points in the *Book of data*.

| Substance | Number of electrons | Boiling point/°C |
|---|---|---|
| Propanone | 32 | 56 |
| 2-methylpropane | 34 | −12 |

# 9.3 Hydrogen bonding

In many molecules there is the possibility of a very special kind of intermolecular force which has certain specific requirements. These are:

**One molecule must have a hydrogen atom which is very highly positively polarised; so highly, in fact, that it is almost ready to be donated as a proton to a base.**

**The other molecule must have one of the small strongly electronegative atoms of the elements nitrogen, oxygen or fluorine and this atom must have available a lone pair of electrons.**

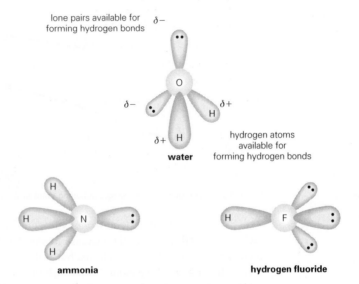

Figure 9.8 **Three molecules in which hydrogen atoms are bonded to highly electronegative atoms and in which there are lone pairs of electrons**

Because of the small size of the hydrogen atom and the comparatively small size of the other atom involved, the two atoms are able to approach one another closely enough for the forces of attraction between them to reach nearly one tenth of the strength of a typical covalent bond. **The resulting force of attraction is known as a hydrogen bond**

Hydrogen bonds are represented by three dots thus:

$$H_3N \cdots H-OH, \qquad H-F \cdots H-F$$

Bond energies of typical hydrogen bonds are around $30\,\text{kJ mol}^{-1}$ or less whereas those of covalent bonds tend to be about $300\,\text{kJ mol}^{-1}$. By contrast van der Waals forces are only of the order of $3\,\text{kJ mol}^{-1}$.

One way of visualising a hydrogen bond is to think of it as being a proton, $H^+$, between two negative charge clouds, the covalent bond on one side and the lone pair of electrons on the other. The angle between the hydrogen bond and the covalent bond to the hydrogen atom is normally 180° for maximum bond strength.

# Evidence for hydrogen bonds

When the boiling points of the four hydrides HF, HCl, HBr and HI are plotted against the halogen period number in the Periodic Table the result is as shown in figure 9.9.

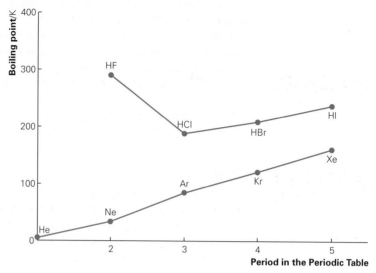

**Figure 9.9**   **Graph showing the changes in boiling point of the Group 7 hydrides and the noble gases**

The rise in boiling point from hydrogen chloride to hydrogen iodide, HCl < HBr < HI, is due to the increase in van der Waals forces because of an increase in the number of electrons; but if this were the only type of intermolecular force, HF would boil at about −90 °C whereas in fact it boils at +20 °C due to hydrogen bonding.

|        | Melting point/K | Boiling point/K |
|--------|-----------------|-----------------|
| $CH_4$   | 91              | 109             |
| $SiH_4$  | 88              | 161             |
| $GeH_4$  | 108             | 185             |
| $SnH_4$  | 123             | 221             |
| $NH_3$   | 195             | 240             |
| $PH_3$   | 140             | 185             |
| $AsH_3$  | 157             | 218             |
| $SbH_3$  | 185             | 256             |
| $H_2O$   | 273             | 373             |
| $H_2S$   | 188             | 212             |
| $H_2Se$  | 207             | 232             |
| $H_2Te$  | 224             | 271             |
| HF     | 190             | 293             |
| HCl    | 158             | 188             |
| HBr    | 185             | 206             |
| HI     | 222             | 238             |

## STUDY TASK

The hydrogen bonds between water molecules are particularly important.

1   Draw a graph for the hydrides of Group 6 of the Periodic Table similar to the one for the hydrogen halides.
Without its hydrogen bonding, what would you predict as the boiling point of water?

2   The molecule of hydrogen fluoride has three lone pairs of electrons but only one hydrogen atom so that each molecule can only use one of its lone pairs on average. The water molecule has two lone pairs and two hydrogen atoms and so can take part in hydrogen bonding to twice the extent.

What feature of the graph you have just drawn arises from this ability?

3   Plot similar graphs for the hydrides of Group 4 and Group 5 and explain the results.

# How strong are the intermolecular forces?

The intermolecular forces in water are largely overcome when the water is vaporised:

$$H_2O(l) \longrightarrow H_2O(g)$$

The next experiment is designed to measure the enthalpy change of vaporisation of water.

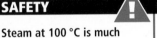

EXPERIMENT 9.3

## Measuring the enthalpy change of vaporisation of water

The aim is to measure the energy required to boil away a known mass of water. The simplest procedure is to use an electric kettle.

### Procedure

Record the power in watts of an electric kettle, fill with about 500 cm³ of water, and weigh with its lid. Remove the lid, plug in and switch on. Start timing when the water starts to boil and steam comes out of the kettle. Boil for a fixed period of time; three minutes is sufficient. Switch off, put the lid on at once and reweigh.
    Work out the electrical energy supplied using the conversion:

$$\text{kilowatts} = kJ\,s^{-1}$$

**SAFETY**

Steam at 100 °C is much more hazardous than water at 100 °C. Take care!

### Calculation

1  Work out the mass of water evaporated. What is this amount in moles?

2  Calculate the enthalpy change of vaporisation from the relationship:

$$\Delta H_{vap}/kJ\,mol^{-1} = \frac{\textbf{electrical energy supplied/kJ}}{\textbf{amount of water evaporated/mol}}$$

A value for the enthalpy change of vaporisation of water from the *Book of data* corresponds to 40.7 kJ mol⁻¹. This would represent the total for all types of intermolecular forces between the water molecules and would include contributions from van der Waals forces and dipole–dipole forces, as well as hydrogen bonding.

STUDY TASK

In this study task you will estimate the hydrogen bonding contribution in water.

1  The enthalpy changes of vaporisation of the hydrides of the Group 6 elements are as follows:

| Compound | $\Delta H_{vap}/kJ\,mol^{-1}$ |
|----------|-------------------------------|
| $H_2O$ | 40.7 |
| $H_2S$ | 18.7 |
| $H_2Se$ | 19.3 |
| $H_2Te$ | 23.2 |

Plot a graph of $\Delta H_{vap}$ on the vertical axis against period number on the horizontal axis. Use it to estimate the value of $\Delta H_{vap}$ for water if there were no hydrogen bonding. Subtract this from the actual $\Delta H_{vap}$ to obtain a measure of the hydrogen bonding contribution.

Divide your answer by two to get an estimate of the strength of 1 mole of hydrogen bonds in water.

2  Make a similar estimation of the hydrogen bond strength in ammonia. Suitable data to 3 sf are:

| Compound | $\Delta H_{vap}$/kJ mol$^{-1}$ |
| --- | --- |
| $NH_3$ | 23.4 |
| $PH_3$ | 14.6 |
| $AsH_3$ | 17.5 |

# Hydrogen bonding in ice

Water molecules have **two** hydrogen atoms and **two** non-bonded electron pairs each and so can form an average of **two** hydrogen bonds each. **There is, therefore, the possibility of water molecules being bound by hydrogen bonds into a three-dimensional lattice.** This is what happens in ice (figure 9.10).

Although this structure accounts for very many of the properties of ice it does not account for all of them, and the structure of ice is not fully understood. The structure of water is even less certain. In water, the strong hydrogen bonding still succeeds in retaining parts of the three-dimensional lattice, and there is a short-range order but no long-range ordered structure.

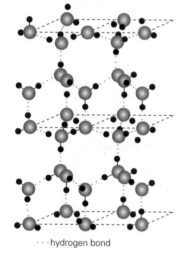

· · · hydrogen bond

Figure 9.10   **Water molecules in ice**

Figure 9.11   **Hoar frost formed by water vapour in the air crystallising on scratches on a glass surface. Why do you think crystals first form where there are scratches?**

## STUDY TASK

What explanation can you offer, in terms of hydrogen bonding, for the high surface tension of water which enables insects to 'walk' on the surface, and causes dew to collect as tiny droplets?

Figure 9.12   **Hydrogen bonding is responsible for some of the properties of water**

# Hydrogen bonding in living organisms

In living processes hydrogen bonds are responsible for a very wide range of structural features and chemical processes, and the full extent is certainly greater than has so far been discovered.

To take one outstanding example, the highly complex shapes of proteins are often maintained by means of hydrogen bonds. Enzymes are proteins, and depend for their action on the retention of highly specific molecular shapes. Consequently, the whole range of enzyme-catalysed reactions upon which life depends is determined by hydrogen bonding.

The double helical structure of DNA (see colour plate C.3 in the *Book of data*) also depends on hydrogen bonds (see figures 9.13 and 9.14).

Van der Waals forces are also important in the helical structure of DNA because of the close packing of the flat nitrogen bases: they appear in the structure like a pile of plates.

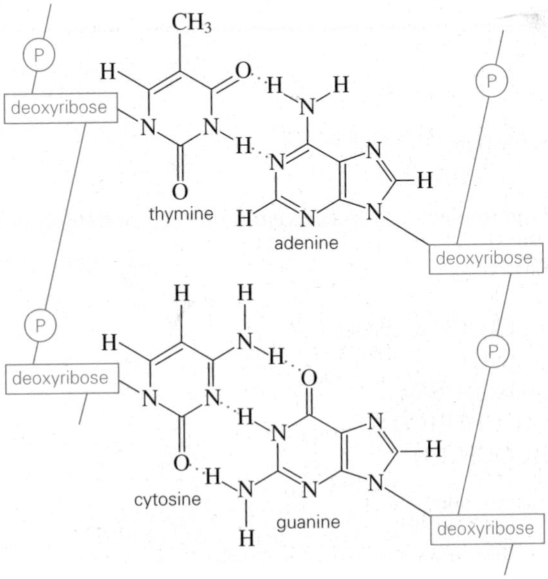

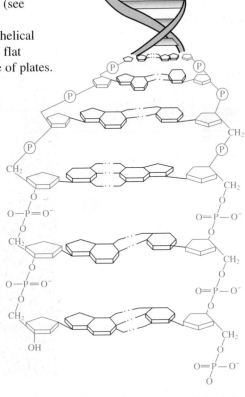

Figure 9.13   **Hydrogen bonds link the nitrogen bases in DNA**

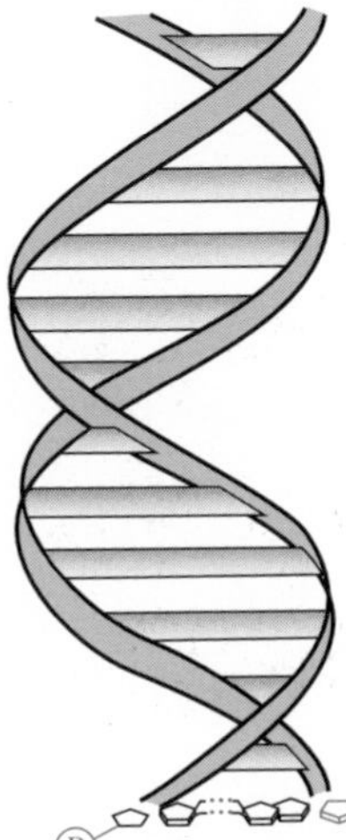

Figure 9.14   **The structure of DNA contains a double helix**

## KEY SKILLS

### Application of number

The study tasks in the topic allow you to obtain relevant information from different sources, to make estimates, to construct and label graphs and to show trends and make comparisons.

## TOPIC REVIEW

1   **List key words or terms with definitions**

- intramolecular forces
- intermolecular forces
- covalent radius
- van der Waals radius
- dipole moment

2   **Summarise the key principles as simply as possible**

- Make sure that you can distinguish between the three types of intermolecular force and that you can give an example of each that will highlight the differences between them.
- Illustrate your understanding by answering some of the questions at the end of the topic.

## REVIEW QUESTIONS

**✱** Indicates that the *Book of data* is needed.

**9.1**   List all the types of intermolecular forces existing in each of the following **liquids**:

| a | liquid helium, He | (1) |
| b | hexane, $C_6H_{14}$ | (1) |
| c | 1-chlorobutane, $CH_3CH_2CH_2CH_2Cl$ | (1) |
| d | liquid ammonia, $NH_3$ | (1) |
| e | liquid sulphur dioxide, $SO_2$ | (1) |
| f | propan-2-ol, $CH_3CHOHCH_3$ | (1) |
| g | butanone, $CH_3COCH_2CH_3$ | (1) |

**(7 marks)**

**✱ 9.2**    Consider the three organic liquids:

- butan-1-ol, $CH_3CH_2CH_2CH_2OH$
- 1-chloropropane, $CH_3CH_2CH_2Cl$
- pentane, $CH_3CH_2CH_2CH_2CH_3$

a    Which of the three liquids have permanent dipoles?    (2)

b    Write down all the types of intermolecular forces you think are present in each liquid.    (3)

c    Using the *Book of data*, tabulate the molar masses, the number of electrons per molecule and the boiling points of the three liquids.    (3)

d    What does the information you have tabulated suggest about the strengths of the various types of intermolecular forces in the three liquids?    (2)

**(10 marks)**

**9.3**    Arrange the following compounds in the order you would expect for their boiling points, putting the one with the highest boiling point first:

A    $CH_3$—$CH_2$—$CH_2$—$CH_3$

B    $CH_3$—$\overset{\displaystyle CH_3}{\underset{\displaystyle CH_3}{\overset{|}{\underset{|}{C}}}}$—H

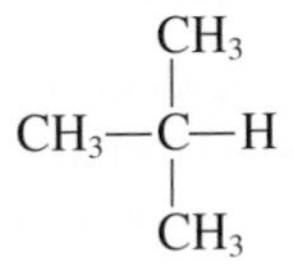

C    $CH_3$—$CH_2$—$CH_2$—$CH_2Cl$

D    $CH_3$—$\overset{\displaystyle CH_3}{\underset{\displaystyle CH_3}{\overset{|}{\underset{|}{C}}}}$—Cl

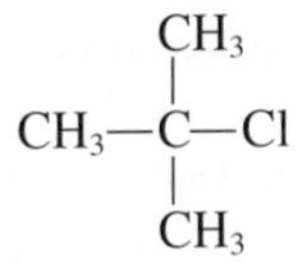

Give reasons for your answer.    **(8 marks)**

**9.4**    Heptane and 2-methylhexane are isomers with the molecular formula $C_7H_{16}$. Which would have the higher boiling point? Explain your answer.    **(3 marks)**

**9.5**    Classify the following mixtures of liquids into:

i    those with only van der Waals forces between the two kinds of molecules

ii    those with van der Waals forces **and** dipole–dipole attractions between the two kinds of molecules

iii    those with van der Waals forces, dipole–dipole attractions **and** hydrogen bonding between the two kinds of molecules.

a    propan-1-ol and butan-1-ol    (2)

b    hexane and cyclohexane    (2)

c    hexane and iodine    (2)

d    ethanol and water    (2)

e    ethanol and hexane    (2)

f    propanone and butanone    (2)

**(12 marks)**

**9.6**    Arrange each of the following groups of substances in the order you would expect for their boiling points, putting the substance with the highest boiling point first. Give reasons for your choice in each case.

a    neon, helium, argon                                                              (2)
b    propane, butane, pentane                                                          (2)
c    hydrogen chloride, hydrogen fluoride, hydrogen iodide                             (2)
d    ammonia, $NH_3$; hydrazine, $N_2H_4$; disilane, $Si_2H_6$.                        (2)
                                                                              **(8 marks)**

**✳ 9.7**    The structural formula of urea is:

$$O=C\begin{array}{c} NH_2 \\ | \\ | \\ NH_2 \end{array}$$

Despite being a molecular substance, urea is a solid because of hydrogen bonding between its molecules. Urea is soluble in water due to the formation of hydrogen bonds between its molecules and water molecules.

a    Draw displayed formulae showing:
   i    a hydrogen bond between two molecules of urea                                  (2)
   ii   a hydrogen bond between a water molecule and a urea molecule                   (2)
   iii  a hydrogen bond between the same two molecules as in ii but between different atoms.                                                                     (2)

b  i    Work out the number of electrons in a molecule of urea and in a molecule of propan-1-ol.                                                                 (2)
   ii   Use the *Book of data* to find the dipole moments of urea and propan-1-ol. (1)
   iii  Are there likely to be more opportunities for hydrogen bonding between molecules of urea than between molecules of propan-1-ol? Explain your answer.                                                                            (3)
   iv   Use your answers to i, ii and iii to explain why urea is a solid at room temperature whereas propan-1-ol is a liquid.                                   (3)
                                                                             **(15 marks)**

# EXAMINATION QUESTIONS

**9.8**    The table below gives the molar masses and boiling points of three carbon compounds.

|  | Molar mass /g mol$^{-1}$ | Boiling point /°C |
|---|---|---|
| Butanone, $CH_3CH_2COCH_3$ | 72 | 80 |
| Pentane, $CH_3(CH_2)_3CH_3$ | 72 | 36 |
| 2-methylbutane, $CH_3CH(CH_3)CH_2CH_3$ | 72 | 28 |

a    What is the main type of interaction between molecules in:
   i    pure butanone                                                                  (1)
   ii   pure pentane?                                                                  (1)

b    Draw a diagram to illustrate the main interaction between two molecules of
     butanone.                                                                    (2)
c    Explain why pentane and 2-methylbutane have different boiling points
     despite having the same molecular formula and molar mass. You may find
     drawing a diagram helpful.                                                   (2)
                                                                          **(6 marks)**

9.9    Some organic compounds having molecules containing eight carbon atoms are
       listed below with their molar masses and boiling points.

| Compound | Structural formula | Molar mass /g mol$^{-1}$ | Boiling point /°C |
|---|---|---|---|
| Octane | $CH_3(CH_2)_6CH_3$ | 114 | 125 |
| 2,2,4-trimethylpentane | $CH_3C(CH_3)_2CH_2CH(CH_3)CH_3$ | 114 | 98 |
| Octan-1-ol | $CH_3(CH_2)_6CH_2OH$ | 130 | 194 |
| Octanoic acid | $CH_3(CH_2)_6CO_2H$ | 144 | 227 |

a  i  What type of intermolecular force is present in all of these compounds?    (1)
   ii 2,2,4-trimethylpentane has a lower boiling point than its isomer, octane.
      Suggest a reason for this. You may find it helpful to draw a diagram.       (2)

b  i  Suggest ONE reason why octanoic acid has a higher boiling point than
      octan-1-ol.                                                                 (1)
   ii Estimate the boiling point of octanal and justify your estimate.
      (Molar mass of $CH_3(CH_2)_6CHO = 128$ g mol$^{-1}$.)                       (2)
                                                                          **(6 marks)**

9.10   The boiling points of four compounds which have hydrogen bonds between their
       molecules are shown below.

| Compound | Formula | Molar mass /g mol$^{-1}$ | Boiling point /°C |
|---|---|---|---|
| Water | $H_2O$ | 18 | 100 |
| Methanol | $CH_3OH$ | 32 | 65 |
| Ethanol | $CH_3CH_2OH$ | 46 | 79 |
| Butan-1-ol | $CH_3(CH_3)_2CH_2OH$ | 74 | 117 |

a    Draw a diagram showing the position of a hydrogen bond between two
     molecules of methanol.                                                       (1)

b    By considering the structures and intermolecular forces involved, explain:
   i  why water has a higher boiling point than ethanol                          (2)
   ii why methanol has a lower boiling point than ethanol.                       (2)

c    Butan-1-ol has an isomer named ethoxyethane, $C_2H_5OC_2H_5$.
     Explain why there are no hydrogen bonds between ethoxyethane
     molecules.                                                                   (1)
                                                                          **(6 marks)**

**9.11**    **a**    Why is energy needed to convert a liquid into a gas?    (2)

**b**    The enthalpy change of vaporisation of water can be found by using an electric kettle. In such an experiment, an electric kettle was used with a power of 1.5 kW. 80 g of water evaporated when the water in the kettle boiled for 2 minutes. Using the conversion, $1\,kW = 1\,kJ\,s^{-1}$, calculate the enthalpy change of vaporisation of water per mole.    (3)

**c**    The enthalpy of vaporisation of the hydrides of three other Group 6 elements is given below.

|  | $\Delta H_{vap}$/kJ mol$^{-1}$ |
| --- | --- |
| Hydrogen sulphide, $H_2S$ | 18.7 |
| Hydrogen selenide, $H_2Se$ | 19.3 |
| Hydrogen telluride, $H_2Te$ | 23.2 |

**i** Plot a graph of $\Delta H_{vap}$ of these hydrides against the atomic number of the Group 6 element.    (2)

**ii** Assuming the structure of water is the same as that of the other Group 6 hydrides, use your graph to predict $\Delta H_{vap}$ for water.    (1)

**iii** Why is your prediction in **c ii** so different from your answer in **b**?    (1)

**(9 marks)**

**9.12**    Van der Waals forces are relatively unimportant in water but in poly(ethene) they are much more significant.

**a**    What feature of poly(ethene) molecules makes these forces so significant?    (1)

**b**    Suggest ONE physical property of poly(ethene) which results from its strong van der Waals forces.    (1)

**c**    What are the strongest intermolecular forces present in water?    (1)

**d**    Explain the origin of these strong forces in water. You may find it helpful to draw a diagram.    (2)

**(5 marks)**

# Organic chemistry: halogenoalkanes

In the whole field of *naturally* occurring materials, there are practically no organic halogen compounds. Thus, almost all of them must be produced synthetically. Those few which do occur in nature are found in rather obscure situations. Examples include the iodine compound thyroxine, a hormone produced by the thyroid gland, a shortage of which causes goitre and cretinism; the bromine compound Tyrian purple (mentioned in Topic 6), present in the sea-snail, *Murex brandaris*, which was extracted and used by the Romans for dyeing their statesmen's robes; and the chlorine compound chloromethane, produced by some marine algae.

**Owing to the considerable reactivity of the halogen atoms in organic compounds many of these compounds are manufactured as 'intermediates', that is, for conversion into other substances.** There is also a range of organic halogen compounds which are important products of industry, for example

$+CH_2-CHCl+_n$      the polymer PVC, poly(chloroethene)
$CHFCl-O-CHF_2$      an anaesthetic, Isoflurane

In this topic you will:

- study the reactions of halogenoalkanes and learn how to interpret them
- survey the reactions and reagents you have met in organic chemistry so that you understand how they are classified and the pattern of their behaviour.

Figure 10.1 **Spraying insecticide onto a field of cotton**

TOPIC 10

## 10.1 Physical properties of halogenoalkanes

When hydrogen atoms in alkanes are replaced by halogen atoms, we have compounds of the type known as **halogenoalkanes**. These are named by using the name for the alkane from which they are derived and adding '**chloro-**', '**bromo-**', or '**iodo-**'. For example,

$CH_3Cl$      chloromethane

$CH_3—CH_2Br$      bromoethane

Two mono-substituted compounds can be derived from propane. They are distinguished by numbering the carbon atoms as for the branched chain alkanes:

$CH_3—CH_2—CH_2Cl$   1-chloropropane

$CH_3—CHCl—CH_3$   2-chloropropane

Halogenoalkanes with side chains are named in the same way as the corresponding alkanes:

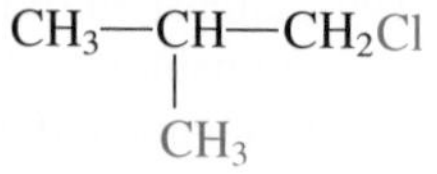

$CH_3—CH—CH_2Cl$   1-chloro-2-methylpropane 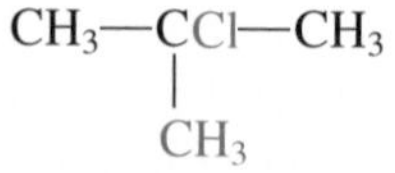
        |
       $CH_3$

$CH_3—CCl—CH_3$   2-chloro-2-methylpropane
        |
       $CH_3$

For halogenoalkanes with more than one halogen atom the full name of the alkane is used, preceded by the number of the carbon atom to which the halogen atoms are attached, with '**di-**', '**tri-**', etc., to indicate the total number of halogen atoms. For example,

$CH_2Br—CH_2Br$      1,2-dibromoethane

In considering the possible reactivity of the halogenoalkanes, we should first look at the strength of the bonds. We shall use the bond energies:

$CH_3Cl \longrightarrow CH_3\cdot + Cl\cdot$      $E(C—Cl) = 351 \, kJ \, mol^{-1}$

$CH_3Br \longrightarrow CH_3\cdot + Br\cdot$      $E(C—Br) = 293 \, kJ \, mol^{-1}$

$CH_3I \longrightarrow CH_3\cdot + I\cdot$      $E(C—I) \;\; = 234 \, kJ \, mol^{-1}$

So,   $E(C—Cl) > E(C—Br) > E(C—I)$

If we change the molecular structure of the alkyl group, we find that the bond energy also changes:

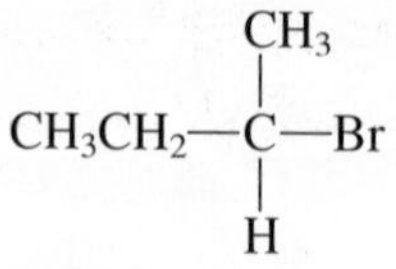

          $CH_3$
          |
$CH_3CH_2—C—Br$   $E(C—Br) = 284 \, kJ \, mol^{-1}$ 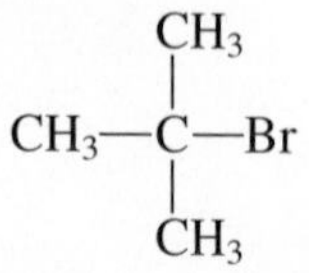
          |
          H

          $CH_3$
          |
$CH_3—C—Br$   $E(C—Br) = 263 \, kJ \, mol^{-1}$
          |
          $CH_3$

| | Dipole moment/D |
|---|---|
| 1-chlorobutane | 2.16 |
| 1-bromobutane | 1.93 |
| 1-iodobutane | 1.88 |

Secondly, we can look at the polarity of some molecules, which is measured by a quantity called the **dipole moment** (in units called debyes, symbol D).

The existence of dipole moments in molecules is due to bond polarisation (see section 9.2). They can however only be a guide to the polarity of individual bonds, since a dipole moment must be a sum of all the bond polarities, but we can suggest that:

$$C^{\delta+}—Cl^{\delta-} > C^{\delta+}—Br^{\delta-} > C^{\delta+}—I^{\delta-}$$

## QUESTION

On the basis of these data and your knowledge of halogen chemistry, what reagents might attack halogenoalkanes?

The mass spectrum of 1-chlorobutane is shown in figure 10.2. See Topic 21 for an account of how mass spectra are obtained.

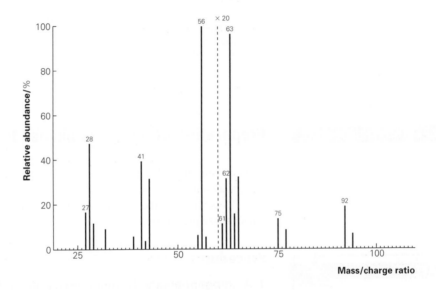

Figure 10.2 A reading from a mass spectrometer giving the mass spectrum of 1-chlorobutane

## QUESTIONS

1 Why are there two peaks at 92 and 94, and also at 75 and 77, in the mass spectrum of 1-chlorobutane, shown in figure 10.2?

2 Why are the peaks at 94 and 77 lower than the peaks at 92 and 75?

## 10.2    Reactions of halogenoalkanes

In these experiments, we shall concentrate on reactions that are likely to occur with the halogen atom, remembering that ionic reagents are likely to be favoured. We shall compare the three halogenoalkanes

$$CH_3—CH_2—CH_2—CH_2—Cl$$
1-chlorobutane

$$CH_3—CH_2—CH_2—CH_2—Br$$
1-bromobutane

$$CH_3—CH_2—CH_2—CH_2—I$$
1-iodobutane

and also look at the influence of the structure of the alkyl group.

The structures are known as **primary**, **secondary**, or **tertiary** on the basis of the number of alkyl groups joined to the carbon atom which is bonded to the halogen atom in the compound:

$$CH_3—CH_2—CH_2—CH_2Cl$$
1-chlorobutane
(primary, one group)

$$CH_3—CH_2—CH—CH_3$$
$$|$$
$$Cl$$
2-chlorobutane
(secondary, two groups)

$$\begin{array}{c} CH_3 \\ | \\ CH_3—C—CH_3 \\ | \\ Cl \end{array}$$
2-chloro-2-methylpropane
(tertiary, three groups)

---

**EXPERIMENT 10.2a**

## Preparation of halogenoalkanes from alcohols

Replacement of the hydroxyl group in an alcohol by a halogen is fairly easy with tertiary alcohols, but more difficult with secondary and primary alcohols.

Depending on the availability of materials you should be able to carry out one of these preparations.

### Procedure

#### 1  A halogenoalkane from a primary alcohol

Place about 5 cm³ of ethanol in a small round-bottomed flask and cautiously, in amounts of 0.5 cm³ at a time, add about 5 cm³ of concentrated sulphuric acid (TAKE CARE). Ensure that the contents of the flask are well mixed, and cool them by holding the flask under a running cold water tap.

Quickly add 6 g of powdered potassium bromide and arrange the apparatus as shown in figure 10.3 (opposite).

Heat the flask, with a low Bunsen burner flame, to distil the halogenoalkane which forms. Collect the product under ice-cold water to ensure complete condensation. Do not remove the flame without first removing the delivery tube, or water may be sucked up into the hot flask.

Next, take the conical flask, tip off the bulk of the water, and remove as much as possible of what remains, using a dropping pipette.

✎    **In your notes:** Write down what you see and smell. What is the evidence that you have changed ethanol into something new? Your product is bromoethane. Write an equation for the reaction and work out which bond was broken in the ethanol.

**SAFETY**

Ethanol is highly flammable.
Concentrated sulphuric acid is corrosive.
Bromoethane is harmful.

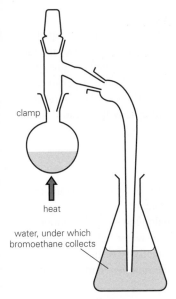

clamp

heat

water, under which
bromoethane collects

Figure 10.3   **Apparatus for the
preparation of a halogenoalkane**

## 2  A halogenoalkane from a tertiary alcohol

You can use 2-methylpropan-2-ol (tertiary butanol) to prepare 2-chloro-2-methylpropane. The product is a volatile liquid with a distinctive odour, and a boiling point, $T_b$, of 50 °C. A yield of 85% can be achieved.

$$(CH_3)_3COH \xrightarrow{\text{concentrated HCl}} (CH_3)_3CCl$$

Place 20 cm³ (0.21 mole) of 2-methylpropan-2-ol and 70 cm³ of concentrated hydrochloric acid in a large conical flask. Stopper and shake at intervals, releasing any pressure after each shaking, until a top layer of 2-chloro-2-methylpropane is fully formed. This usually takes about 20 minutes.

Add about 6 g of powdered anhydrous calcium chloride, shake until dissolved and transfer to a separating funnel (see figure 2.13). Allow to separate and discard the lower aqueous layer.

Add about 20 cm³ of 0.1 M sodium hydrogencarbonate to the tertiary chloride in the funnel. Shake the funnel carefully, releasing the pressure of carbon dioxide frequently. Allow the layers to separate and discard the lower aqueous layer again. Repeat the washing with sodium hydrogencarbonate solution until no more carbon dioxide is formed.

Transfer the tertiary chloride to a small conical flask, add a little anhydrous sodium sulphate and cork securely. Shake occasionally for about 5 minutes to dry the chloride.

Meanwhile set up the apparatus for distillation (see figure 2.12). Filter the product directly into the distillation flask through a small funnel fitted with a plug of cottonwool. Distil the liquid and collect the fraction boiling between 50 °C and 52 °C. You can use your product for the next set of experiments.

Weigh your product and calculate the yield based on the moles of alcohol used.

Using the same molar proportions, 2-methylbutan-2-ol gives 2-chloro-2-methylbutane, $T_b$ 86 °C.

**SAFETY**    ⚠

2-methylpropan-2-ol is highly flammable and harmful.
Concentrated hydrochloric acid is corrosive and its vapour is an extreme irritant.
2-chloro-2-methylpropane is highly flammable and has a harmful vapour.
Powdered calcium chloride is an irritant.

EXPERIMENT 10.2b

# The reactions of the halogenoalkanes

Except where otherwise stated, use 2-chloro-2-methylpropane for the experiments, as it is much the cheapest of the halogenoalkanes you will be using.

## Procedure

### 1 Combustion

Keep the halogenoalkane in a stoppered boiling tube well away from any flame. Dip a combustion spoon into it. Set fire to the halogenoalkane on the combustion spoon and note how readily it burns.

**SAFETY**    ⚠

Halogenoalkanes are flammable and most have toxic vapours.

**SAFETY**

2-chloro-2-methylpropane is
highly flammable.
20% potassium hydroxide in
ethanol is highly flammable
and highly corrosive.
2 M nitric acid is corrosive.
1-chlorobutane is highly
flammable.
1-bromobutane is flammable
and irritant.
1-iodobutane is flammable.
2-chlorobutane is highly
flammable.

## 2 Reaction with aqueous alkali

To 1 cm$^3$ of 20% potassium hydroxide in ethanol (TAKE CARE) add an equal
volume of water followed by 0.5 cm$^3$ of 2-chloro-2-methylpropane. Shake the tube
from side to side for a minute. To test for chloride ions add an equal volume of 2 M
nitric acid to neutralise the potassium hydroxide (test with indicator paper to ensure
that your solution is acidic) and then add a few drops of 0.02 M silver nitrate. If
chloride **ions** are present a white precipitate of silver chloride will appear.

✎   **In your notes:** What new organic compound has been formed?

## 3 A comparison of halogenoalkanes

**a**   Arrange three test tubes in a row and add three drops of halogenoalkane in the
sequence 1-chlorobutane, 1-bromobutane, 1-iodobutane.

Add 4 cm$^3$ of 0.02 M silver nitrate to each halogenoalkane. Without
delay, put all three test tubes simultaneously in a hot water bath. Note the order
in which precipitates appear and try to relate the reactivity of the
halogenoalkanes to their dipole moments and to the halogen–carbon bond
energies.

✎   **In your notes:** Which factor appears to be the more important when considering the
rates of reaction?

**b**   Repeat the experiment in a further three test tubes using the halogenoalkanes
1-chlorobutane (primary), 2-chlorobutane (secondary), and 2-chloro-
2-methylpropane (tertiary).

✎   **In your notes:** Comment on your results as you did for part **a**.

## 4 Reaction with alcoholic alkali

To 2 cm$^3$ of 20% potassium hydroxide in ethanol (TAKE CARE) add 0.5 cm$^3$ of
2-chloro-2-methylpropane. Push a loose plug of ceramic fibres into the mixture
and arrange the test tube for collection of gas (see figure 10.4). Heat gently and
collect two to three test tubes of gas. Test the gas for flammability; also test it with
bromine water.

✎   **In your notes:** What new gaseous compound has been formed? What type of reaction
has taken place?

An oily film may appear on the water surface. Suggest what it is and how it got there.

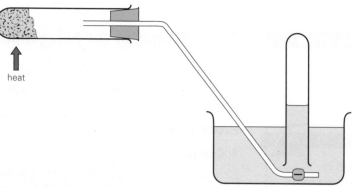

**Figure 10.4    Apparatus for collecting a gas
over water**

# An interpretation of the halogenoalkane experiments

We can write an equation for the reaction in part **2** of Experiment 10.2b, between 2-chloro-2-methylpropane and potassium hydroxide in aqueous solution:

$$(CH_3)_3C—Cl + K^+OH^- \longrightarrow (CH_3)_3C—OH + K^+Cl^-$$

This reaction tells us a great deal about organic halogen reactions in general. **Firstly, we can see that an —OH group has been exchanged for a chlorine atom. Because of this, the reaction is known as a substitution reaction.** Secondly, we need to consider the process by which the reaction occurred. We need to consider what species leaves the organic molecule, the **leaving group**, and what species attacks, the **attacking group**.

1   During the reaction a chloride ion has left the molecule. Being a chloride **ion** it will have taken with it the electron pair that formed the covalent bond:

$$(CH_3)_3C\ \vdots\overset{\bullet\bullet}{\underset{\bullet\bullet}{Cl}}\vdots \longrightarrow (CH_3)_3C^+ + \left[\vdots\overset{\bullet\bullet}{\underset{\bullet\bullet}{Cl}}\vdots\right]^- \text{ (charged)}$$

You should contrast this with the process that would produce a free radical:

$$(CH_3)_3C\ \vdots\overset{\bullet\bullet}{\underset{\bullet\bullet}{Cl}}\vdots \longrightarrow (CH_3)_3C^\bullet + \bullet\overset{\bullet\bullet}{\underset{\bullet\bullet}{Cl}}\vdots \text{ (uncharged)}$$

2   Since the chlorine atom takes away the bonding electrons, the group that attacks the tertiary chlorobutane molecule will need to have an unshared pair of electrons available for bonding to the carbon atom, for example:

$$\vdots O—H^-$$

3   Because of the polarity of the carbon atom, $C^{\delta+}$, it will be an advantage for the attacking group to be negatively charged.

**Attacking groups with an unshared pair of electrons available for forming a new covalent bond are known as nucleophiles.**

In addition, they are often negatively charged. The suffix '-phile' is derived from ancient Greek and means 'loving'; so 'nucleophile' means 'nucleus-loving'. The electron pair is not attacking the nucleus, but an electron-deficient carbon atom which is positively charged.

So far we have used the idea of bond polarity to interpret the process by which a halogenoalkane might react.

Is polarity also a guide to the relative ease of reaction? Look at your results for part **3** of Experiment 10.2b, on the reaction between silver nitrate and five different halogenoalkanes.

What are the leaving groups?

What are the possible attacking groups? Can this be described as a 'nucleophilic substitution reaction'?

If so, it follows that the discussion about the reaction between potassium hydroxide and 2-chloro-2-methylpropane is also applicable to these reactions.

Now compare bond polarities (listed in section 10.1) with the relative ease of formation of the silver halide precipitates. Finally, compare bond energies (also listed in section 10.1) with the relative ease of formation of the precipitates.

✎ **In your notes:** Which factor, bond polarity or bond strength, is the best guide to ease of reaction in this particular case?

The reaction in part **4** of Experiment 10.2b is of a different type. The gaseous product was an unsaturated hydrocarbon, which means that **both halogen and hydrogen have been lost from the 2-chloro-2-methylpropane molecule**.

$$CH_3-\underset{\underset{Cl\ \ H}{|\ \ \ |}}{\overset{\overset{CH_3}{|}}{C}}-CH_2 \longrightarrow CH_3-\overset{\overset{CH_3}{|}}{C}=CH_2 + HCl$$

**This is known as an elimination reaction**. Chemists think that the hydroxide ion, a powerful base, extracts a proton from the halogenoalkane and a chloride ion separates from the molecule. Notice that elimination does not occur by the departure of hydrogen and chlorine as hydrogen chloride in the same step in the reaction process. The overall reaction can be written as:

$$CH_3-\underset{\underset{Cl}{|}}{\overset{\overset{CH_3}{|}}{C}}-CH_3 + K^+OH^- \longrightarrow CH_3-\overset{\overset{CH_3}{|}}{C}=CH_2 + K^+Cl^- + H_2O$$

# Reactions of the halogenoalkanes

## 1 Substitution by a hydroxyl group

$$CH_3-CH_2-CH_2-CH_2Br + K^+OH^- \longrightarrow CH_3-CH_2-CH_2-CH_2OH + K^+Br^-$$

This equation can be written more briefly as

$$CH_3(CH_2)_3Br + OH^- \longrightarrow CH_3(CH_2)_3OH + Br^-$$

The hydroxide ion is a strong **nucleophile**, attacking the terminal carbon atom and substituting for the bromine atom. **The reaction is, therefore, described as a nucleophilic substitution**.

The reaction is not used to prepare the common alcohols because they are more readily and cheaply available by other reactions (for example, the reaction of alkenes with sulphuric acid, Topic 8) but the reaction may be useful when chemists want to substitute a hydroxyl group into a complex compound.

A similar reaction happens just with water but much more slowly:

$$CH_3(CH_2)_3Br + H_2O \longrightarrow CH_3(CH_2)_3OH + HBr$$

This reaction uses water (hydro-) to split apart (-lysis) a molecule. It is an example of **hydrolysis**.

## 2 Substitution by an amine group

$$CH_3(CH_2)_3Br + 2:NH_3 \longrightarrow CH_3(CH_2)_3NH_2 + NH_4^+Br^-$$
butylamine

In this reaction **ammonia** uses an unshared pair of electrons and therefore functions as a **nucleophile**. An alcoholic solution of ammonia is needed, and heating is carried out under pressure to give an adequate concentration of ammonia but yields are not good.

## 3 Elimination in the synthesis of alkenes

$$\underset{\substack{\text{2-bromo-2-}\\\text{methylpropane}}}{(CH_3)_3CBr} + K^+OH^- \longrightarrow \underset{\text{methylpropene}}{CH_3\overset{\overset{\displaystyle CH_3}{|}}{C}{=}CH_2} + K^+Br^- + H_2O$$

**This is a good method of introducing double bonds into complex molecules.** The reagent, concentrated potassium hydroxide (a strong base), is the same as the one used to substitute for halogen (in reaction **1**). But because the solvent is changed from ethanol and water to ethanol alone, and because the reaction is carried out at a higher temperature, **elimination** becomes the more favoured reaction. The hydroxide ion here acts as a strong **base**, in contrast to its behaviour as a nucleophile in reaction **1**.

# Preparation of halogenoalkanes from alcohols

Heating an alcohol with a mixture of sodium bromide and concentrated sulphuric acid replaces the —OH group with —Br. This is another example of a **nucleophilic substitution reaction**. A mixture of sodium bromide and concentrated sulphuric acid produces hydrogen bromide. Bromine forms as well so the mixture turns orange-brown.

$$\underset{\text{bromoethane}}{CH_3CH_2OH + HBr \longrightarrow CH_3CH_2Br + H_2O}$$

The reaction is rather easier with tertiary alcohols, and concentrated hydrochloric acid can sometimes be used. The alcohol molecule is first protonated (see below) and this activated form will then react with nucleophiles to form the substitution product.

$$CH_3CH_2{-}O{-}H \xrightarrow[\text{protonation}]{H^+} CH_3CH_2{-}\overset{+}{\underset{\underset{\textstyle H}{\diagdown}}{O}}{\overset{\diagup H}{}} \xrightarrow[\text{nucleophile}]{Br^-} CH_3CH_2{-}Br + H_2O$$

A proton is transferred to the alcohol and then water is displaced by the nucleophile.

# 10.3 Background reading: anaesthetics

Read the passage below and answer the questions based on it.

1 Why is it surprising that increasing the substitution of hydrogen atoms by fluorine atoms can lead to a lowering of the boiling point?

2 Suggest why the flammability of alkanes is reduced by substituting halogen atoms for hydrogen atoms.

3 Draw the structural formula of ether, including electron lone pairs, to show the shape of the molecule. Suggest a bond angle for the C—O—C bond.

4 Draw displayed formulae for Enflurane and Isoflurane.

5 Write a summary of the desired properties of an anaesthetic, using continuous prose and not more than 100 words.

Knowledge of the exact way in which a drug works can be of help to the chemist in synthesising new compounds; the way a drug works can often suggest the chemical groupings which should be introduced into a molecule in order to produce the desired effect. However, we know little of the mode of action of anaesthetics, even though they have been in use for over a century.

Various suggestions have been made about the type of compound required for anaesthetic activity, but the contribution of the industrial scientist, James Ferguson, has probably been of most use to chemists. Anaesthetics vary widely in *potency*, a term which is usually expressed as the minimum concentration of gas required to produce a loss of consciousness in most patients.

At one time chemists thought that the chlorine atom possessed some special property of conferring high anaesthetic potency on a compound. The potency of chloroform, $CHCl_3$, seemed to support this when compared to ether and nitrous oxide, two other older anaesthetics (see the table below). But Ferguson suggested that gases and volatile liquids which are not toxic will, regardless of their chemical structure, produce anaesthesia when administered at the required concentrations.

 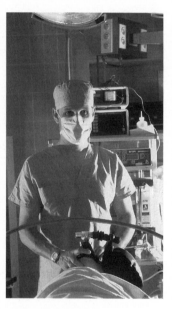

Figure 10.5 Operating without anaesthetic – and a modern anaesthetist. Modern anaesthetics are organic halogen compounds

| Substance | Anaesthetic concentration/ % by volume |
| --- | --- |
| Halothane | 0.8 |
| Chloroform | 0.5 |
| Isoflurane | 1.2 |
| Enflurane | 1.7 |
| Ether | 2 |
| Nitrous oxide | 100 |

An implication of the theory for the design of new anaesthetic compounds was that the higher the boiling point of a compound the greater would be its anaesthetic potency. Compounds boiling within the range 25–75 °C could be expected to have the desired level of potency.

With this background, the problem facing the chemist was defined as the synthesis of new compounds which could be expected to be both volatile, and unreactive. It is especially important that the compounds are not converted in our bodies to different compounds. The greatest risk is that the compounds will be metabolised in the liver to toxic products.

## Fluorinated hydrocarbons

Research was carried out into fluorohydrocarbons, originally prepared as potential refrigerants, because of their boiling range and low toxicity.

| Fluoromethane | Boiling point/°C |
|---|---|
| $CH_3F$ | −78 |
| $CH_2F_2$ | −51 |
| $CHF_3$ | −82 |
| $CF_4$ | −130 |

Flammability is also greatly reduced by the substitution of the hydrogen atoms of alkanes by fluorine. And toxicity was found to be greatly reduced when atoms of fluorine were substituted for hydrogen atoms on a carbon atom already linked to other halogens.

The best compound initially developed was 1-bromo-1-chloro-2,2,2-trifluoroethane, $CF_3CHBrCl$, given the trade name Halothane.

It is a colourless, mobile, heavy liquid with a pleasant smell, boiling at 50 °C, non-explosive and non-flammable at all concentrations in air or oxygen. The compound proved to have a high potency as an anaesthetic and a low toxicity.

After its introduction in 1956, Halothane rapidly became the most commonly administered, volatile anaesthetic agent. Unfortunately, in widespread use Halothane was found to have serious toxic side effects. About 20% of the Halothane administered to a patient is metabolised in the liver and can cause hepatitis, but in about one case in 35 000 the damage is massive and life threatening.

## Ethers

Anaesthetics have now been introduced based on ether. Ether (ethoxyethane) may be thought of as a water molecule in which the hydrogen atoms have been replaced by ethyl groups:

$$C_2H_5-O-C_2H_5$$
ethoxyethane

Ether was first described in 1540. The intoxicating effects it produces following inhalation were known for many years before its usefulness as an anaesthetic for general surgery was demonstrated in 1846. Ether is highly flammable, but the properties required of a modern anaesthetic can be achieved by replacing the hydrogen atoms by halogen atoms.

Two examples are Enflurane, $F_2CH-O-CF_2-CHFCl$, and Isoflurane, $F_3CCHCl-O-CHF_2$. Only 2% and 0.2% are metabolised in the liver so they are most unlikely to cause hepatitis.

Two other halogenated ethers were introduced in 1995 as anaesthetic agents and are believed to be even safer than their predecessors, Sevoflurane, $FCH_2-O-CH(CF_3)_2$ and Desflurane, $F_2CH-O-CHF-CF_3$.

# KEY SKILLS

## Communication

Reading about anaesthetics (background reading, section 10.3) and summarising the information gives you an opportunity to develop your skills of selecting and synthesising information from a document.

## IT

You could use IT to tackle the summary of organic reactions in the topic review. This would give you the chance to use IT to search for and select information, develop the information into a consistent form (with text and images) and present the information in a form which you will find helpful for revision. You could set up a data base for the information with fields such as organic starting material, reagents, conditions, products, type of reaction, mechanism and so on which you could use later for revision.

## TOPIC REVIEW

This topic reinforces the ideas that were introduced in Topics 2 and 8. It is important, at the end of it, that you understand the different types of reaction that can occur in organic chemistry and the way that these may be brought about using different reagents.

1   **List key words or terms with definitions where necessary**

Give suitable **examples** to illustrate the following:

● halogenoalkane, primary, secondary and tertiary
● hydrolysis

2   **Summarise the key principles as simply as possible**

Throughout this review the emphasis must be on **patterns or types of behaviour** that you can apply to other, new situations. Remember the specific detail of the work covered should be reflected in the notes you have made during the topic. Make a **summary chart** or 'spider diagram' showing **reactions of the halogenoalkanes** part of this review.

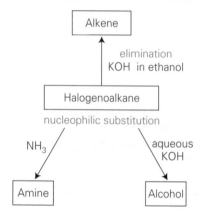

The topics on organic chemistry have introduced you to a number of important ideas that you need to understand as a linked set, so they are summarised opposite, at the mid-point of this course. You also need to learn the particular reagents, and conditions, for each reaction introduced in the organic chemistry topics. When this basic information has been learned you should make sure you understand the interpretations of the reactions.

These lists should be treated as statements to be understood, not definitions to be memorised. You should find an example of your own choice for each item, to help you to understand the ideas involved.

# Bond breaking

**Homolytic bond breaking** involves the breaking of a bond to form atoms with unpaired electrons, called free radicals.

$$Cl:Cl \longrightarrow Cl\cdot + Cl\cdot$$

**Heterolytic bond breaking** involves the breaking of a bond so that the electrons both go to one of the atoms resulting in the formation of two ions.

$$H:Cl \longrightarrow H^+ + :Cl^-$$

# Types of reaction

A **substitution reaction** is a reaction in which one group replaces another in a molecule.

$$CH_3CH_2Br + NaOH \longrightarrow CH_3CH_2OH + NaBr$$

An **addition reaction** is one in which one or more groups are added onto a molecule, to give a single product.

$$CH_2{=}CH_2 + Br_2 \longrightarrow CH_2Br{-}CH_2Br$$

An **elimination reaction** is one in which one or more groups are removed from a molecule.

$$CH_3{-}CH_2Br \longrightarrow CH_2{=}CH_2 + HBr$$

Notice that this is the reverse of an addition reaction.

A **polymerisation reaction** is one in which molecules with a small molar mass join up to become molecules with a very large molar mass.

$$nCH_2{=}CH_2 \longrightarrow +CH_2{-}CH_2+_n$$

A **chain reaction** is one in which molecules of product are produced at each cycle of a process that usually repeats itself a large number of times.

$$CH_4 \xrightarrow{Cl\cdot} \cdot CH_3 + HCl \longrightarrow CH_3Cl + \cdot Cl \longrightarrow \text{and so on}$$

This process includes the stages of initiation, propagation, and termination.

# Types of reagent

**Nucleophiles** are attacking groups with a pair of electrons available for forming a new covalent bond. They are often negatively charged.

$$:OH^-  \quad :NH_3$$

**Electrophiles** are attacking groups with a vacancy for a pair of electrons; a new covalent bond results when the vacancy is filled. Electrophiles are often positively charged.

$$H^+ \quad Br^+$$

**Free radicals** are uncharged attacking groups with an odd number of electrons, so they possess only one of the electron pair needed for the formation of a new covalent bond.

$$\cdot Cl \quad \cdot CH_3$$

TOPIC 10

# REVIEW QUESTIONS

✱ Indicates that the *Book of data* is needed.

**10.1**   Draw the displayed formulae and name all four compounds with the molecular formula $C_4H_9Br$. **(8 marks)**

**10.2**   Draw the displayed formulae and name all four compounds with the molecular formula $C_3H_6Cl_2$. **(8 marks)**

**10.3**   Write the structural formulae of the following compounds:

a   2-bromo-2-methylpropane (1)
b   1,3-dichlorobutane (1)
c   2-bromo-3-iodopentane (1)
d   3,3-dichloro-4-ethylhexane (1)
e   1,2-dichlorocyclohexane (1)
**(5 marks)**

**10.4**   Name the compounds having the following formulae:

a
$$CH_2Cl$$
$$|$$
$$CH_2Cl$$   (1)

b
$$CH_2Br$$
$$|$$
$$CH_2Cl$$   (1)

c   $CH_3CH_2CHICH_3$   (1)

d
$$CH_3CH_2CHCH_2Br$$
$$|$$
$$CH_3$$
(1)

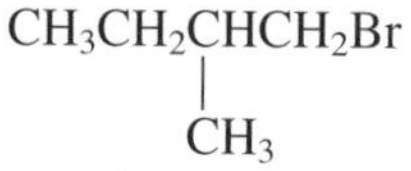

e
$$Cl$$
$$|$$
$$CH$$
$$CH_2 \quad CH_2$$
$$CH_2—CH_2$$
(1)

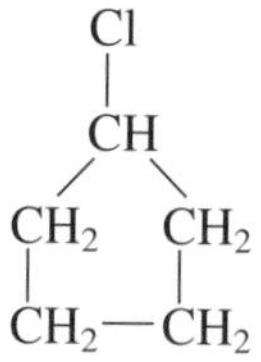

**(5 marks)**

✱ **10.5**   a   The 'parent ion' peak in the mass spectrum of ethanol is at mass/charge ratio 46. Explain the meaning of the term 'parent ion' and what important information can be deduced from it. (2)

b   Suggest the formulae of the ions having mass/charge ratios of 45 and 29, both present in the mass spectrum of ethanol. (2)
**(4 marks)**

✱ **10.6**   a   Explain why there are two 'parent ion' peaks, at mass/charge ratios 108 and 110, in the mass spectrum of bromoethane. (2)

b   The two peaks are of equal heights. Deduce the molar mass of bromoethane and explain how you reached your answer. (2)

c   Confirm that your answer is consistent with that given in the *Book of data*. (1)
**(5 marks)**

**10.7**  a  Draw the electronic structure (outer shell only) of the water molecule, $H_2O$. (2)

b  Draw the electronic structures of the *atom* and *free radical* that would be obtained if one of the O—H bonds in a water molecule underwent *homolytic fission*. (2)

c  Draw the electronic structures of the *ions* that would be obtained if one of the O—H bonds in a water molecule underwent *heterolytic fission*. (2)

d  Explain why the $OH^-$ ion is classed as a nucleophile. (2)

e  What similar type of name is used to describe the $H^+$ ion? (1)

**(9 marks)**

**10.8**  Choose from the following list those reagents which you think might be classed as nucleophiles:

$$H^+, \ CN^-, \ CH_3{}^{\cdot}, \ OH^-, \ Cu^{2+}, \ H_2O, \ NH_3, \ Br^{\cdot}, \ Br^-, \ Na^+$$

**(5 marks)**

**10.9**  When bromoethane reacts with dilute aqueous KOH,

a  What is the formula of the organic product of the reaction? (1)

b  What is the attacking group? (1)

c  What is the leaving group? (1)

d  What type of reaction occurs? (1)

e  What kind of reagent (electrophile, free radical or nucleophile) is involved? (1)

**(5 marks)**

**10.10**  Give the structural formula and the name of the organic product of each of the following reactions:

a  1-chloropropane with ammonia (2)

b  2-bromopropane with aqueous KOH (2)

c  2-chlorobutane with concentrated KOH in ethanol (2)

d  bromoethane with warm aqueous silver nitrate solution (2)

e  1,2-dibromoethane with aqueous KOH. (2)

**(10 marks)**

**10.11**  Give the formula of a halogenalkane, together with the necessary reagent(s) and conditions, which could be used to make each of the following:

a  butan-1-ol, $CH_3CH_2CH_2CH_2OH$ (3)

b  propan-2-ol, $CH_3CHOHCH_3$ (3)

c  propene, $CH_3CH{=}CH_2$ (3)

d  but-2-ene, $CH_3CH{=}CHCH_3$ (3)

e  2-methylbut-1-ene, $CH_3CH_2\underset{\underset{\displaystyle CH_3}{|}}{C}{=}CH_2$ (3)

**(15 marks)**

## EXAMINATION QUESTIONS

Questions of the summary and comprehension type are found in the background reading section (section 10.3).

**10.12** You have used 1-iodobutane in some of your experiments.

a Construct a Hess cycle for the atomisation of 1-iodobutane and use the data below, at 298 K, to show by calculation that the value of $\Delta H^\ominus_{at}$ for $CH_3CH_2CH_2CH_2I(g)$ is $+4987.6\,kJ\,mol^{-1}$.

$$\Delta H^\ominus_f\,[CH_3CH_2CH_2CH_2I(g)] \quad = \quad -52.0\,kJ\,mol^{-1}$$
$$\Delta H^\ominus_{at}\,[C(graphite)] \quad = \quad +716.7\,kJ\,mol^{-1}$$
$$\Delta H^\ominus_{at}\,[\tfrac{1}{2}H_2(g)] \quad = \quad +218.0\,kJ\,mol^{-1}$$
$$\Delta H^\ominus_{at}\,[\tfrac{1}{2}I_2(s)] \quad = \quad +106.8\,kJ\,mol^{-1} \qquad (3)$$

b i Draw a 'dot and cross' diagram for the electronic structure of 1-iodobutane, showing outer shell electrons only. (2)

ii Calculate the energy of the C—I bond in 1-iodobutane. Use the standard enthalpy change of atomisation of 1-iodobutane, and the data below:

$$E(C—H) = +413\,kJ\,mol^{-1}$$
$$E(C—C) = +347\,kJ\,mol^{-1} \qquad (3)$$

c Three drops of 1-iodobutane are added to a test tube containing $2\,cm^3$ of hot aqueous silver nitrate solution. A reaction occurs immediately.
i What would you observe? (1)
ii Write an ionic equation, including state symbols, for your observation. (2)
iii Name the organic product of this reaction. (1)

d When the experiment in c is repeated with 1-chlorobutane it is very slow. Explain why the rates of the two reactions are different. (2)

e The experiment in c is repeated using 2-chloro-2-methylpropane.
i Draw a displayed formula of 2-chloro-2-methylpropane. (1)
ii Describe what you would expect to see. (1)
iii Explain why this reaction is more rapid than the reaction when 1-chlorobutane is used. (2)

**(18 marks)**

**10.13** a This part of the question is about the hydrolysis of halogenoalkanes. Three test tubes are taken. Three drops of 1-chlorobutane are added to the first, three drops of 1-bromobutane to the second, and three drops of 1-iodobutane to the third test tube.
$2\,cm^3$ portions of hot aqueous silver nitrate solution are added to each test tube.
A precipitate forms immediately in the third test tube, slowly in the second test tube and extremely slowly in the first test tube.
In each reaction the precipitate is formed by silver ions, $Ag^+(aq)$, reacting with the halide ions formed by hydrolysis of the halogenoalkane.
i The same organic product forms in each reaction. Name this organic product. (1)
ii Copy and complete the equation for the hydrolysis of 1-bromobutane.

$$C_4H_9Br + H_2O \longrightarrow$$

(2)

iii What is the colour of the precipitate in the third test tube? (1)

iv Name the precipitate which forms extremely slowly in the first test tube and write the ionic equation, including state symbols, for its formation. (3)

v Ammonia solution is added to the precipitate formed in the first test tube. Describe and explain what you would observe. (2)

vi Explain why the rates of hydrolysis of the three halogenoalkanes are different. (2)

b 1-bromobutane reacts with an alcoholic solution of potassium hydroxide at high temperature to form but-1-ene.

i Draw a fully labelled diagram to show an apparatus for carrying out this reaction in the laboratory and collecting the gaseous but-1-ene. (3)

ii Suggest a chemical test for an alkene such as but-1-ene. You should name the reagent to be used and state the colour change you would observe. (2)

**(16 marks)**

**10.14** This question is about the primary alcohol pentan-1-ol, $C_5H_{11}OH$, and some related compounds.

a Give the structural formula and systematic name of another primary alcohol which is an isomer of pentan-1-ol. (2)

b One method of preparing 1-bromopentane is to put pentan-1-ol, water and sodium bromide into a flask and add concentrated sulphuric acid slowly from a tap funnel. The resulting mixture then needs to be heated for some time in order to obtain a reasonable yield.

i Draw a labelled diagram of the apparatus you would use for carrying out this process in the laboratory. (2)

ii The reaction mixture often goes yellow or orange at this stage in the preparation. Name the substance likely to be responsible for this coloration and explain how it forms. (2)

iii This preparation normally gives a yield of 60%. Calculate the minimum mass of pentan-1-ol you would need to produce 15g of 1-bromopentane by this method. (2)

c Dehydration of pentan-1-ol yields pent-1-ene. Copy the diagram below and add a sketch showing the electron density distribution in the carbon–carbon double bond.

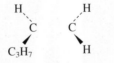

(2)

**(10 marks)**

# How fast? Rates of reaction

What actually takes place during a chemical reaction? Why do some reactions take longer than others to go to completion? What factors influence the rate of a reaction? **Chemical kinetics**, the study of the rates of chemical reactions, is concerned with all of these questions.

From your previous work in chemistry you should remember that **the rate of a chemical reaction can depend on any or all of the following general factors:**

- **the concentration of the reactants (or pressure for gases)**
- **the temperature**
- **the presence of catalysts.**

In this topic you will be developing your knowledge of these three factors and making a quantitative study of the first two.

In particular cases the rate may also depend on the state of subdivision of a solid reactant or the influence of visible or ultraviolet light. This topic is not initially concerned with these other factors, not because they are unimportant (see, for example, the account of the effect of ultraviolet radiation on the rate of halogenation of alkanes in section 8.2), but because there are definite reasons for studying the general factors.

Figure 11.1 **Trying to change the rate of chemical reactions – what factors are at work in these reactions?**

Platinum-rhodium gauze (shown folded up) used as a catalyst for the oxidation of ammonia to make nitric acid

# 11.1   Rates of reactions: why study them?

Rates of reaction are studied for three main reasons. The first reason is curiosity: observing that reactions can take place at very different rates is enough to challenge the curiosity of chemists and encourage them to investigate rates. Secondly, chemists would like to understand how to change the rate of reaction if they want to. In industry, knowledge of rates of reaction is essential when considering the economics of a manufacturing process.

A third reason why a study of reaction kinetics is worthwhile is that a knowledge of the effects of concentration and temperature on the rate of a reaction provides important evidence about the mechanisms of the reaction – the individual steps by which a reaction takes place. The mechanisms of some organic reactions have already been described in Topics 8 and 10.

## The effect of concentration on the rate of a reaction

Firstly it is important to decide what is meant by the **rate of a reaction**. In a reaction which takes place between two substances A and B, it is possible to follow the reaction by observing how quickly substance A is used up. For a reaction in solution, a chemist would probably measure the concentration of A (denoted by [A]), at various times, to see how it changes. **In such a case, the measure of the rate of the reaction would be the rate of change of concentration of A, symbol $r_A$.**

The chemist might have chosen to do his or her measurements on substance B, and obtained a value of $r_B$, the rate of change of concentration of B. This might well have a different numerical value, so it is obviously essential to specify the substance by writing $r_A$ or $r_B$.

In a reaction of the type

$$xA + yB \longrightarrow \text{products}$$

the rate of change of concentration of substance A will be found by experiment to follow a mathematical expression of the form:

$$r_A = k[A]^a[B]^b[C]^c$$

**An expression of this kind is called a rate equation.** Substance C is included in this general expression as well as A and B, because rate equations sometimes include concentrations of substances that do not appear as reactants in the equation for the reaction. An example of this appears in Experiment 11.2b.

It is important to understand the significance of each part of such a rate equation, so consider each part in turn.

### 1 Rate of reaction, $r_A$

The meaning of this has already been explained. The normal units are $\text{mol dm}^{-3}\,\text{s}^{-1}$, but some other units may be more convenient.

Minutes might be used instead of seconds, or some property which is *proportional* to the concentration might be used instead of the concentration itself. We shall meet an example of this in Experiment 11.2a, the first experiment.

## 2 Concentrations [A], [B], [C]

The use of square brackets in this context denotes 'concentration in moles per decimetre cubed (mol dm$^{-3}$)'.

Again, in particular cases it may be more convenient to use a quantity which is proportional to the concentration instead of the concentration itself.

## 3 The indices *a*, *b*, *c*

**The index 'a' is called the order of the reaction with respect to the reactant A, 'b' is the order of the reaction with respect to the reactant B, and so on. The sum of all the indices is called the overall order of the reaction.**

So, the overall order $= a + b + c$. In our work we will only meet reactions in which orders of reaction are whole numbers having the values 0, 1, or 2.

When we want to speak of orders of reaction we say that a reaction is 'first order with respect to A' or 'zero order with respect to B' or perhaps 'second order overall'.

**Note that the orders of a reaction are experimental quantities; they cannot be deduced from the chemical equation for the reaction.**

## 4 The constant *k*

***k* is a constant of proportionality called the rate constant.** The units of $k$ depend on the order of the reaction, and can be worked out from the rest of the rate equation. For example, if the rate equation for the change of concentration of a substance in a particular reaction is

$$r_A = k[A]^1[B]^1$$

then, substituting the units of the various quantities,

$$\text{mol dm}^{-3}\,\text{s}^{-1} = k\,(\text{mol dm}^{-3})^1\,(\text{mol dm}^{-3})^1$$

from which the units of $k$ are $\text{dm}^3\,\text{mol}^{-1}\,\text{s}^{-1}$.

A knowledge of the rate constant has a practical use. It is often used to compare rates of reaction at different temperatures or for comparing the rates of different reactions with similar rate equations.

When studying the dependence of rate on reactant concentration you are usually asked to identify the orders of reaction and perhaps the rate constant.

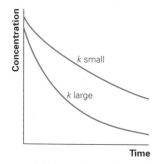

Figure 11.2 **The graphs show how concentration alters depending on the value of the rate constant, *k***

## 11.2 Measuring rates of reaction

In designing an experiment or series of experiments to investigate the rate of a reaction there are several problems which have to be overcome.

One problem is that usually all the reactant concentrations vary at the same time and it is difficult to discover the effect of a particular reactant. This problem can be overcome by making the concentrations of all the reactants which are not being studied much larger than the concentration of interest. The effect of this is that only this one concentration varies significantly and it is possible to see what the effect of this variation is on the rate of the reaction. In Experiment 11.2b, method 1, for example, propanone will be reacting with iodine in the presence of an acid. There are two reactants and a catalyst, but as you want to find the order of the reaction with respect to only one of them, the iodine, it is arranged that the propanone and acid concentrations are much higher than the iodine concentration. Effectively, the iodine concentration is the only one of the three concentrations which varies. The other two concentrations do change, of course, but only very slightly.

A second problem with experimental design is that there is usually no easy way of finding directly the rate of a reaction at a particular time from the start of the reaction, since the rate itself may be changing as reactant concentration changes. In practice, it is usual to measure reactant concentrations at various times from the start of the reaction, and from the shape of a graph of reactant concentration against time it is possible to deduce what the order is without needing to determine actual values for the rate.

A third problem is the very wide variation in the rates themselves. The time needed for a simple electron transfer between atoms to take place is about $5 \times 10^{-16}$ second, whereas the time needed to bring about the change of half of a sample of one isomer of aspartic acid to a different isomer of aspartic acid in fossil bones at ordinary temperatures is about $3 \times 10^{12}$ seconds (which is about 100 000 years), probably the slowest known reaction. Such very fast or very slow reactions can only be studied by using special techniques. The reactions that you will study have been chosen with care, so that they have rates that are measurable by techniques available in a school laboratory.

**EXPERIMENT 11.2a**

## The kinetics of the reaction between calcium carbonate and hydrochloric acid

$$CaCO_3(s) + 2HCl(aq) \longrightarrow CaCl_2(aq) + CO_2(g) + H_2O(l)$$

In this experiment the problem is to find the order of the reaction with respect to hydrochloric acid. The calcium carbonate is in the form of marble. Fairly large pieces are used so that the surface area does not change appreciably during the reaction. On the other hand the hydrochloric acid is arranged to be in such quantity and concentration that it is all used up during the reaction.

Two methods are described; which one you use will depend on the apparatus available.

### Procedure: Method 1

Put all the following items on the pan of a direct-reading, top-pan balance:

- a small conical flask containing about 10 g of marble in six or seven lumps
- a measuring cylinder containing 20 cm³ of 1 M hydrochloric acid
- a plug of cottonwool for the top of the conical flask.

Adjust the balance so that it is ready to weigh all these items. Pour the acid into the conical flask, plug the top with the cottonwool, and replace the measuring cylinder on the balance pan.

Allow a few seconds to pass so that the solution is saturated with carbon dioxide; then start timing and taking mass readings.

Record the mass of the whole reaction mixture and apparatus at intervals of 10 seconds at the start, increasing to 30 seconds, until the reaction is over and the mass no longer changes. Record the final mass as well.

Record your results in the form of a table like the one shown below and work out the total loss of mass at the end of each time interval. This loss of mass is due to the carbon dioxide escaping into the atmosphere.

| Time $t$/s | Total mass $m$/g | Mass of $CO_2$ $m_t$/(g) | $(m_{final} - m_t)$/g |
|---|---|---|---|
|  |  |  |  |
|  |  |  |  |

The fourth column in the table needs a little thought. When the reaction is over, the total mass of carbon dioxide evolved ($m_{final}$) is proportional to the concentration of the hydrochloric acid at the moment when timing started. Thus ($m_{final} - m_t$) is proportional to the concentration of hydrochloric acid at each time $t$.

✎    **In your notes:** Plot a graph of ($m_{final} - m_t$) against $t$, putting $t$ on the horizontal axis.

## Procedure: Method 2

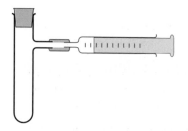

Figure 11.3   **Apparatus for Experiment 11.2a, method 2**

Set up the apparatus as in figure 11.3.

Place about 10 g of marble in six or seven lumps in the test tube and have ready 10 cm³ of 1 M hydrochloric acid. Put the acid into the test tube and allow a few seconds for the solution to become saturated with carbon dioxide.

Put the stopper in place and start timing.

Take readings of volume every 30 seconds until the reaction is over and the volume no longer changes. Record the final volume as well.

Record your results in the form of a table:

| Time $t$/s | Volume of $CO_2$ $V_t$/cm³ | $(V_{final} - V_t)$/cm³ |
|---|---|---|
|  |  |  |
|  |  |  |

The third column in the table needs a little thought. When the reaction is over, the total volume of carbon dioxide collected ($V_{final}$) is proportional to the concentration of hydrochloric acid at the moment when timing started, so ($V_{final} - V_t$) is proportional to the concentration of hydrochloric acid at each time, $t$.

✎    **In your notes:** Plot a graph of ($V_{final} - V_t$) against $t$, putting $t$ on the horizontal axis.

## Discussion of results

Consider the rate equation in the form,

$$r_{HCl} = k[HCl]^a$$

where $r_{HCl}$ is the rate of change of concentration of hydrochloric acid. Note that [$CaCO_3$] is not needed in the rate equation: because calcium carbonate is a solid, its **concentration** does not vary even though its mass is decreasing.

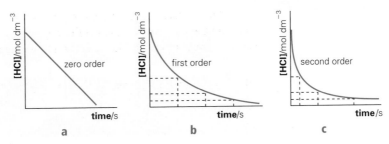

Figure 11.4  **Graphs of concentration against time have different shapes depending on the order of the reaction**

The problem is: 'What is the order of reaction, $a$?'
Let us consider the various possibilities:

**a**  If $a = 0$ **(zero order)** the graph will be a straight line (see figure 11.4a) since the rate of the reaction is the *gradient* of the graph of concentration against time, which is constant and $a$ is therefore zero.

In such cases the reaction proceeds at the same rate, whatever the concentration, until there is no reactant left. Then the reaction stops.

$r_{HCl} = k[HCl]^0$ is the same as $r_{HCl} = k$

**b**  If $a = 1$ **(first order)** the graph will be a curve such that the time it takes for the concentration of the reactant to be halved (**the 'half-life'**) is constant whatever value of the concentration you start from (see figure 11.4b).

**c**  If $a = 2$ **(second order)** the graph will again be a curve but as a second-order curve is much 'deeper' than a first-order one, the half-life is not constant but will increase dramatically as the reaction proceeds (see figure 11.4c).

Compare your results with the descriptions given for the various orders and identify the value of $a$.

Notice that this method assumes that the order is one of the three possibilities 0, 1, or 2.

Now that you have used one method of 'following' a reaction so as to investigate its order you are in a better position to appreciate other possible methods. The account which follows mentions several methods and you will be using one of these in the next experiment.

COMMENT

For any number $x$
$x^0 = 1$

# Methods of 'following' a reaction

## 1  By titration

A reaction mixture is made up and samples are withdrawn from it, using a pipette. Some means is then found of 'quenching' the reaction – slowing it abruptly at a measured time from the start of the reaction, perhaps by rapid cooling in ice or by removing the catalyst. The samples can then be titrated in some way which depends on what is in the reaction mixture. This is the principle of the method which is going to be used in Experiment 11.2b (method 1).

## 2  By colorimetry

If one of the reacting substances or products has a colour, the intensity of this colour will change during the reaction. The intensity can be followed using a colorimeter (see figure 11.5, overleaf).

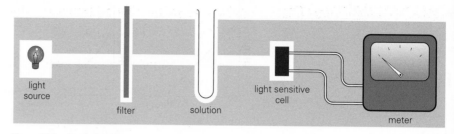

Figure 11.5   A colorimeter

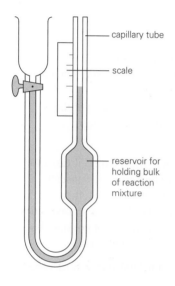

capillary tube

scale

reservoir for
holding bulk
of reaction
mixture

Figure 11.6   A dilatometer

### 3 By dilatometry

In some reactions in the liquid phase the volume of the whole mixture changes slightly during the reaction. If it does, the change of volume can be followed by using an apparatus fitted with a capillary tube. This type of apparatus is called a dilatometer (see figure 11.6).

### 4 By measurements of electrical conductivity

If the total number of ions in solution changes during a reaction it may be possible to follow the reaction by measuring the changes in electrical conductivity of the solution, using a conductivity meter (see figure 11.7). This uses alternating current so that electrolysis of the solution is avoided.

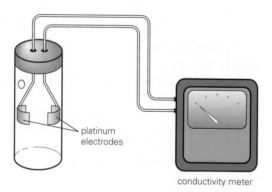

platinum
electrodes

conductivity meter

Figure 11.7   Measurement of the conductivity of a solution

### 5 By measuring a gaseous product

If a gas is given off it can be collected and its volume or mass measured. This was the principle behind the method used in Experiment 11.2a (method 2).

### 6 By measurements of any other property which shows significant change

Possible properties not already discussed include pH and chirality (see Topics 14 and 18).

Now you can try another determination of reaction order by experiment.

**EXPERIMENT 11.2b**

**SAFETY** ⚠

1 M sulphuric acid is an irritant.
Propanone is highly flammable.
Iodopropane (one of the products) is strongly irritating to the eyes and should be disposed of immediately.

# The kinetics of the reaction between iodine and propanone in acid solution

The reaction between iodine and propanone follows the overall equation:

$$CH_3COCH_3(aq) + I_2(aq) \longrightarrow CH_3COCH_2I(aq) + H^+(aq) + I^-(aq)$$

The reaction is acid catalysed and is first order with respect to propanone, and also first order with respect to hydrogen ions.

This reaction can be studied by using a colorimeter to measure the rate at which the iodine is being decolorised, but the methods described below use different approaches.

## Procedure: Method 1

This experiment is designed to determine the order of reaction with respect to iodine. For convenience the solutions you will be using have been given letters to help you identify them.

**A** is a 0.02 M solution of iodine, $I_2$, in potassium iodide
**B** is an aqueous solution of propanone (1.0 M)
**C** is sulphuric acid (1.0 M)
**D** is a solution of sodium hydrogencarbonate (0.5 M)
**E** is a solution of sodium thiosulphate (0.010 M)

1   Collect 7 conical flasks, which you should label **1**, **2**, **T3**, **T4**, **T5**, **T6**, and **T7**.

2   To conical flask **1** add 50 cm³ of **A** using a measuring cylinder.

3   To conical flask **2** add 25 cm³ of **B**, followed by 25 cm³ of **C**, using a different clean, dry measuring cylinder for each solution.

4   To each of the conical flasks **T3** to **T7** add 10 cm³ of **D**, again using a clean, dry measuring cylinder.

5   Place solution **E** in a burette.

6   The reaction starts when the contents of flasks **1** and **2** are mixed. Therefore, pour the contents of flask **2** into flask **1**, and immediately start timing. Shake well.

7   Continue shaking for about 1 minute and then withdraw 10 cm³ of the reaction mixture, using a pipette and safety filler. Run the contents of the pipette into flask **T3**, **noting the time**. Shake until bubbling ceases: the sodium hydrogencarbonate in solution **D** neutralises the acid catalyst and quenches the reaction.

8   Withdraw four more samples at further intervals of between 5 and 10 minutes. In each case, note the exact time of withdrawal. Each sample should be added immediately to the sodium hydrogencarbonate solution in flasks **T4**, **T5**, **T6** and **T7**, used in turn.

9   When convenient, titrate the contents of each of the flasks **T3** to **T7** using the burette you filled with solution **E**.

✎   **In your notes:** Draw up a table for your results and plot a graph of the **titres of E** against **time** from the start of the reaction.

From your graph deduce the order of the reaction with respect to iodine.

## Procedure: Method 2

In this method an attempt is made to estimate the rate of change of concentration of iodine, $r_{\text{iodine}}$, at the start, the **initial rate**. When the reactants are first mixed, the concentration of a reactant will decrease almost linearly with time, whatever the order of the reaction; it is only later that any differences become significant. In this method, therefore, the concentrations of each of the three reactants are varied systematically in the four 'runs' and a direct estimate of $r_{\text{iodine}}$ made from:

$$r_{\text{iodine}} \propto \frac{\text{volume of iodine solution used}}{\text{time for iodine colour to disappear}}$$

The procedure is as follows:

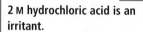

**SAFETY**

2 M hydrochloric acid is an irritant.

1   Make up four mixtures in conical flasks of hydrochloric acid, propanone solution, and water according to the table below, using burettes. Label the flasks **A**, **B**, **C**, and **D**.

|  | Run A | Run B | Run C | Run D |
|---|---|---|---|---|
| Volume of 2 M HCl/cm³ | 20 | 10 | 20 | 20 |
| Volume of 2 M propanone/cm³ | 8 | 8 | 4 | 8 |
| Volume of water/cm³ | 0 | 10 | 4 | 2 |
| Volume of 0.01 M iodine/cm³ | 4 | 4 | 4 | 2 |
| Time for colour to disappear/s |  |  |  |  |
| Rate (as indicated above)/cm³ s⁻¹ |  |  |  |  |

2   Measure out into four test tubes from a burette the volumes of iodine solution required for each run. Label the tubes **a**, **b**, **c**, and **d**.

3   Start the first run by adding the contents of test tube **a** to flask **A**. At the same time start the timer and measure the time taken in seconds for the colour of iodine to disappear.

4   Repeat step **3** for the other three runs.

## QUESTIONS

1   Why was water added to some of the reaction mixtures?

2   If you compare the mixtures for runs A and B you will see that the concentrations of propanone and of iodine are the same in both but the concentration of acid in run B is half of what it is in run A.

   What is the effect on the rate of change of concentration of iodine of halving the concentration of acid?

3   What, then, is the order of the reaction with respect to hydrogen ions?

4   Using similar arguments, what are the orders of the reaction with respect to propanone and to iodine?

# 11.3    Kinetics and reaction mechanism

You will have seen that in Experiment 11.2b the order of the reaction with respect to iodine is zero or, to put it plainly, the rate of change of concentration of iodine, $r_{iodine}$, does not depend on the iodine concentration at all. Putting together all the kinetic evidence we have about the reaction gives the rate equation:

$$r_{iodine} = k[\text{propanone}]^1[\text{hydrogen ion}]^1[\text{iodine}]^0$$

so the reaction is second order overall.

We can omit the iodine from the rate equation altogether:

$$r_{iodine} = k[\text{propanone}]^1[\text{hydrogen ion}]^1$$

At first sight it seems strange that a substance which appears in the chemical equation for the reaction does not affect its rate, whereas a substance which does not appear in the chemical equation as a reactant does appear in the rate equation.

**In organic chemistry, however, you have already met the idea that an organic reaction can occur in a number of successive steps. These steps are known as the mechanism of the reaction** and there is no reason to suppose that all the steps take place at the same rate; in fact, it would be rather surprising if they did. When we realise this, it is clear that the whole reaction goes at the rate of the slowest of the steps in the mechanism. **This slowest step is called the rate-determining step.**

Quite a useful way of visualising the idea of a rate-determining step is to imagine that a teacher has prepared some pages of notes and wants to collect them into sets with the help of some students. The notes are arranged in ten piles and one student collects a page from each of the piles (**step 1**). A second student takes the set of ten pages and tidies them ready for stapling (**step 2**). A third student staples the set of notes together (**step 3**).

It is not hard to see that in this situation the overall rate of the process (the rate at which the final sets of notes are prepared) depends on the rate of **step 1**, the collecting of the sheets of notes, since this is by far the slowest step. It does not matter, within reason, how quickly the tidying or stapling is done; for the most part, the second and third students will be doing nothing while they wait for the

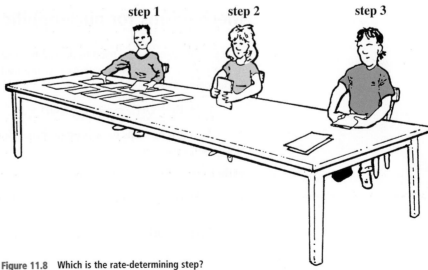

**Figure 11.8**   Which is the rate-determining step?

first student to collect pages. The mechanism of the 'reaction' may thus be refined to

**step 1**   Student 1 collects pages       (slow)
**step 2**   Student 2 tidies set of pages   (fast)
**step 3**   Student 3 staples pages         (fast)

In order to speed up the process, the teacher could offer to help. It would be of no value at all if this additional help were given to either student 2 or student 3 but more people at a time collecting up the pages in **step 1** would clearly make the whole process faster. **Step 1** is the **rate-determining step**.

Returning now to the reaction which was investigated in Experiment 11.2b, various mechanisms might be proposed for the reaction, including this one:

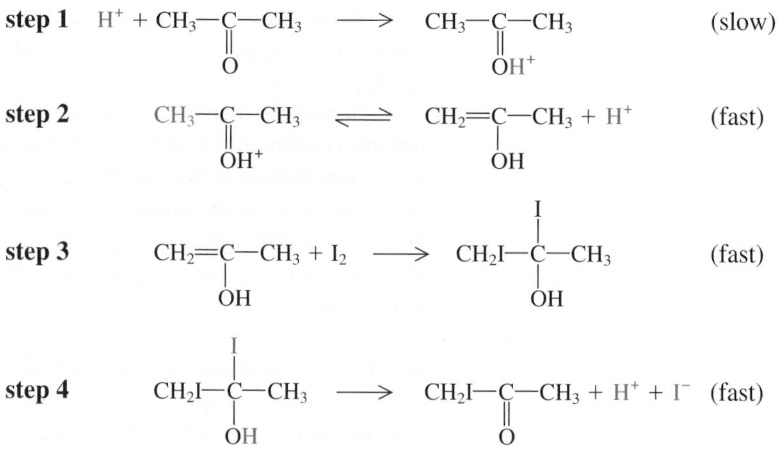

**step 1**   $H^+ + CH_3-\underset{\underset{O}{\|}}{C}-CH_3 \longrightarrow CH_3-\underset{\underset{OH^+}{\|}}{C}-CH_3$   (slow)

**step 2**   $CH_3-\underset{\underset{OH^+}{\|}}{C}-CH_3 \rightleftharpoons CH_2{=}\underset{\underset{OH}{\|}}{C}-CH_3 + H^+$   (fast)

**step 3**   $CH_2{=}\underset{\underset{OH}{\|}}{C}-CH_3 + I_2 \longrightarrow CH_2I-\underset{\overset{\overset{I}{\|}}{\underset{OH}{\|}}}{C}-CH_3$   (fast)

**step 4**   $CH_2I-\underset{\overset{\overset{I}{\|}}{\underset{OH}{\|}}}{C}-CH_3 \longrightarrow CH_2I-\underset{\underset{O}{\|}}{C}-CH_3 + H^+ + I^-$   (fast)

As the iodine molecules are not involved in this proposed mechanism until after the rate-determining step, the overall rate of the reaction would not depend on the concentration of iodine. This is consistent with the outcome of Experiment 11.2b.

It is important to realise that the mechanism suggested was not deduced from the kinetic evidence; the evidence was merely shown to be consistent with the suggestion.

## Mechanisms for nucleophilic substitution

Kinetic data can also be used to decide between possible mechanisms for the hydrolysis of various bromoalkanes, using hydroxide ions. The general pattern of these reactions is:

$$C_4H_9Br + OH^- \longrightarrow C_4H_9OH + Br^-$$

Two mechanisms have been proposed for this type of nucleophilic substitution reaction.

**Either:**

$$C_4H_9Br \rightleftharpoons C_4H_9^+ + Br^-$$   (slow: one molecule in the rate-determining step)

$$C_4H_9^+ + OH^- \longrightarrow C_4H_9OH$$   (fast)

**This mechanism is known as S$_N$1:**

- **S** to represent a substitution reaction
- **N** to represent a nucleophilic reaction
- **1** means that only one particle is involved in the rate-determining step.

(In this example the reaction takes place in two steps.)

**Or:**

$$HO^- + \quad \underset{/}{\overset{\backslash}{C}}-Br \longrightarrow \left[ HO\text{-----}\overset{|}{\underset{|}{C}}\text{-----}Br \right]^- \longrightarrow HO-\overset{//}{\underset{\backslash}{C}} + Br^-$$

This mechanism is effectively a one-step process in which, for an instant of time, both the incoming hydroxide ion and the outgoing bromide ion are equally associated with the hydrocarbon group. **This mechanism is known as S$_N$2:** a nucleophilic substitution reaction with two particles involved in the rate-determining step.

In either of the two mechanisms, water molecules can replace hydroxide ions as the nucleophiles.

Here are some kinetics data about the hydrolysis of some bromoalkanes. Determine which of the two mechanisms is the more appropriate in each case, and answer the questions, recording the answers in your notes in such a way as to make it clear what each question was.

# Case A: The hydrolysis of 1-bromobutane

Equimolar quantities of 1-bromobutane and sodium hydroxide were mixed at 51 °C and the concentration of hydroxide ions was determined at various times with the following results:

| Time/hours | [OH$^-$]/mol dm$^{-3}$ | Time/hours | [OH$^-$]/mol dm$^{-3}$ |
|---|---|---|---|
| 0.04 | 0.241 | 12.0 | 0.084 |
| 0.5 | 0.225 | 14.0 | 0.077 |
| 1.5 | 0.195 | 22.0 | 0.058 |
| 2.5 | 0.172 | 27.0 | 0.050 |
| 3.5 | 0.155 | 33.0 | 0.044 |
| 4.5 | 0.140 | 38.0 | 0.040 |
| 6.5 | 0.118 | 47.0 | 0.035 |
| 9.0 | 0.099 | 59.0 | 0.028 |

## QUESTIONS

1   How might the results have been obtained practically?

2   From a suitable graph of the results, determine the order of the reaction.

3   Is this an overall order or an order with respect to a particular reactant?

4   Which mechanism is operating? Give reasons for your answer.

# Case B: The hydrolysis of 1-bromobutane

In this case, a method was found of estimating the rate of change of concentration of 1-bromobutane, $r_B$, directly and the initial rate was found at various initial concentrations of hydroxide ions, and of 1-bromobutane.

Remember that the rate equation is of the general form:

$$r_B = k[C_4H_9Br]^a[OH^-]^b \quad \text{where } a \text{ and } b \text{ are orders of reaction.}$$

| | Initial concentrations/mol dm$^{-3}$ | | Initial rate/mol dm$^{-3}$ s$^{-1}$ |
|---|---|---|---|
| | [OH$^-$] | [C$_4$H$_9$Br] | |
| A | 0.10 | 0.25 | $3.2 \times 10^{-6}$ |
| B | 0.10 | 0.50 | $6.6 \times 10^{-6}$ |
| C | 0.50 | 0.50 | $3.3 \times 10^{-5}$ |

## QUESTIONS

1 a What is the effect on $r_B$ when the concentration of 1-bromobutane is doubled?
  b What is the order of the reaction with respect to 1-bromobutane?

2 a What is the effect on $r_B$ when the concentration of hydroxide ions is increased five times?
  b What is the order of the reaction with respect to hydroxide ions?

3 Which mechanism is operating?

# Case C: The hydrolysis of tertiary halogenoalkanes

## The hydrolysis of 2-chloro-2-methylpropane using water

In this example the nucleophile is water so that the products of the reaction include a solution of hydrogen ions and chloride ions. Since the original mixture contains almost no ions, the conductivity of the solution increases as the reaction proceeds.

The results shown on the graphs (see figure 11.9, opposite) were obtained by using a conductivity meter to measure the conductivity of the solution, with the data being logged and displayed by computer.

The solvent used was 15 cm$^3$ of ethanol/water in equal volumes. The upper graph (**b**) was obtained by using 1.0 cm$^3$ of 2-chloro-2-methylpropane; the lower graph (**a**) was obtained by using 0.50 cm$^3$ of the compound in the same conditions.

## QUESTIONS

1 Use the graphs in figure 11.9 to estimate the initial rate of the reaction corresponding to each of the concentrations.

2 What is the effect on the rate of the reaction of doubling the concentration of the halogenoalkane?

3 What is the order of the reaction?

4 Is this an overall order of reaction or an order with respect to one reactant?

5 Do you have enough information to say which mechanism is the more appropriate? Explain how you arrived at your answer.

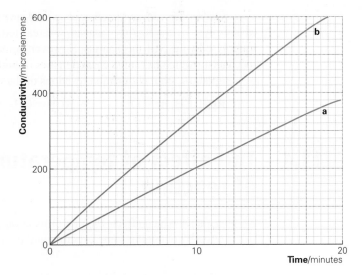

Figure 11.9 Variation in conductivity during the hydrolysis of a tertiary halogenoalkane, 2-chloro-2-methylpropane

**a** 0.5 cm$^3$ 2-chloro-2-methylpropane in 15 cm$^3$ solvent

**b** 1.0 cm$^3$ 2-chloro-2-methylpropane in 15 cm$^3$ solvent

## The hydrolysis of 2-bromo-2-methylpropane using sodium hydroxide solution

Here are the results from another experiment with 2-bromo-2-methylpropane which provide some further kinetics data, this time using hydroxide ions as the nucleophile.

In this experiment the concentration of 2-bromo-2-methylpropane remains the same but in successive runs of the experiment, the concentration of the hydroxide ions is increased. A few drops of an acid–alkali indicator are added to each mixture and a record is kept of the time taken for the indicator to change colour when the hydroxide ions are neutralised. The results are as follows:

| Experiment number | $[C_4H_9Br] \times 10^2$/mol dm$^{-3}$ | $[OH^-] \times 10^3$/mol dm$^{-3}$ | Time/s |
|---|---|---|---|
| 1a | 2.5 | 1.25 | 9 |
| 1b | 2.5 | 1.25 | 8 |
| 2a | 2.5 | 2.50 | 17 |
| 2b | 2.5 | 2.50 | 18 |
| 3a | 2.5 | 3.75 | 26 |
| 3b | 2.5 | 3.75 | 26 |
| 4a | 2.5 | 5.00 | 37 |
| 4b | 2.5 | 5.00 | 39 |

## QUESTIONS

1 What effect does doubling the concentration of hydroxide ions have on the time taken for the indicator to change colour?

2 What is the effect of an increase of hydroxide ion concentration on the rate of the reaction?

3 What is the order of the reaction with respect to hydroxide ions?

4 Which mechanism is the more appropriate in this case?

Overall we can say that there is a tendency for straight chain halogenoalkanes to hydrolyse by the $S_N2$ mechanism, whereas tertiary halogenoalkanes tend to hydrolyse by the $S_N1$ mechanism. However, some halogenoalkanes hydrolyse by a mechanism which has some characteristics of both of those described; and there can be competition from elimination reactions of the type:

$$RCH_2CH_2Br + OH^- \longrightarrow RCH{=}CH_2 + Br^- + H_2O$$

## 11.4 The effect of temperature on the rate of reaction

Another factor which affects the rate of reactions is temperature. We shall begin this section by obtaining some experimental data for this effect.

### EXPERIMENT 11.4

## The effect of temperature on the rate of a reaction

The reaction we are going to investigate is between sodium thiosulphate and hydrochloric acid. The reaction between thiosulphate ions and hydrogen ions follows the equation

$$S_2O_3^{2-}(aq) + 2H^+(aq) \longrightarrow SO_2(aq) + S(s) + H_2O(l)$$

### SAFETY ⚠

**Sulphur dioxide is formed in this reaction.
This gas is toxic and corrosive by inhalation.
Do not stand over the apparatus or inhale the gas.
Dispose of each solution as soon as you have finished taking readings, if possible by pouring down a sink in a fume cupboard.**

### COMMENT

If you muddle up the two measuring cylinders, sulphur precipitates will start to form in them, making the experimental results invalid.

### Procedure

1 Attach a piece of paper marked with a dark ink spot to the outside of a $400 \text{ cm}^3$ beaker. Fill the beaker with water and clamp two boiling tubes, labelled **A** and **B**, vertically in the beaker so that they are about half immersed.

Position the beaker and the tube **A** so that you can see the ink spot through both the beaker and the tube **A**.

2 Add $10 \text{ cm}^3$ of 0.10 M sodium thiosulphate solution to tube **A** and $10 \text{ cm}^3$ of 0.50 M hydrochloric acid to tube **B**. Use labelled measuring cylinders to measure these liquids, and make quite certain that the two are not confused.

Allow time for both boiling tubes to come to the same temperature as the water and then quickly add the acid from **B** to the thiosulphate in **A**.

Stir well with a thermometer and record the steady temperature.

Measure the time from the mixing of the solutions to the point when the dark spot just becomes completely obscured by the formation of a precipitate of sulphur.

3 Repeat the experiment at several different temperatures, say at 25, 30, 40, 50 and 60 °C, using the same concentrations of solution and the same technique of observation.

In these particular circumstances it is possible to get a satisfactory measure of the initial rate of the reaction directly from the experimental results. In each experiment the initial rate of precipitation is given by:

$$\text{rate} = \frac{\text{amount of sulphur}}{\text{time to obscure spot}}$$

The quantity 'amount of sulphur' is impossible to evaluate but as it is the same in each experiment we can say that the rate of the reaction is proportional to the reciprocal of the time taken for the spot to be obscured:

$$\text{rate} \propto \frac{1}{\text{time to obscure spot}}$$

✎ **In your notes:** You will need the following columns in your results table:

| Temperature /°C | Temperature $T$ /K | Time $t$ /s | $1/t$ /s$^{-1}$ |
|---|---|---|---|
|  |  |  |  |
|  |  |  |  |

Plot a graph of **rate** on the vertical axis against **temperature** on the horizontal axis. Label the rate axis $1/t$ /s$^{-1}$ and the temperature axis $T$/K.

Your graph should show that the rate of reaction between sodium thiosulphate and hydrochloric acid increases rapidly with increasing temperature. The same type of result can be obtained for many reactions. But for a fuller interpretation of the experimental results it is necessary to find a qualitative relationship between rate, temperature and a specific property of the reaction system.

COMMENT

$1/t$ is proportional to the rate of the reaction.

# The collision theory of reaction kinetics

One model which has been used to account for the dependence of rate of reaction on temperature is the **collision theory**.

In the collision theory, we can picture the reactant particles as moving towards each other and colliding in such a way that bonds are broken and new bonds formed. The product particles then move away from the site of the reaction.

**In many reactions between gases it is the energy of the colliding particles which controls the rate of the reaction.** For a collision which results in a reaction, the kinetic energy possessed by the colliding particles must be more than a certain minimum energy, $E_{min}$, otherwise bond-breaking will not take place and the reaction will not start.

The distribution of energy amongst gaseous molecules at different temperatures can be measured and the proportion of molecules with more than a minimum value, $E_A$, is found to increase rapidly with increasing temperature (see figure 11.10). So as the temperature rises the proportion of collisions which result

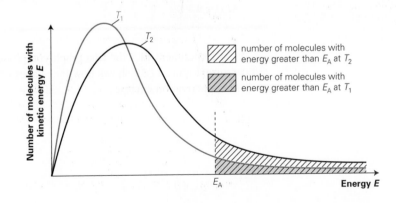

Figure 11.10 **The distribution of energy amongst molecules at two different temperatures, $T_2$ being more than $T_1$**

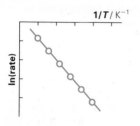

Figure 11.11  **A graph plotted using the Arrhenius equation**

in chemical change also increases markedly, thus increasing the rate of reaction.

When molecules with an energy of $E_A$ or greater collide, they are likely to react and it can be shown that the rate of reaction at a temperature $T$ for a mole of colliding particles can be found from:

$$\text{In(rate of reaction)} = \text{In(collision rate)} - \frac{E_A}{R}(1/T)$$

We can rewrite this relationship in a form that is more useful and is called the **Arrhenius equation**:

$$\ln k = \text{constant} - \frac{E_A}{R}(1/T)$$

where $k$ is the rate constant of the reaction
$R$ is the gas constant, $8.31 \text{ J K}^{-1}\text{mol}^{-1}$
$E_A$ is called the **activation energy** of the reaction, in $\text{J mol}^{-1}$
$T$ is the temperature in kelvins

A typical graph plotted using the Arrhenius equation is shown in figure 11.11.

We can now return to the results of Experiment 11.4 and use them to determine the activation energy of the reaction between sodium thiosulphate and hydrochloric acid.

## STUDY TASK

1  Copy your results for Experiment 11.4 into a new table and calculate the new values you will need to plot a graph using the Arrhenius equation.

| Temperature /°C | Temperature $T$ /K | $1/T$ /$K^{-1}$ | Time $t$ /s | $1/t$ /$s^{-1}$ | In(rate/$s^{-1}$) |
|---|---|---|---|---|---|
| | | | | | |
| | | | | | |
| | | | | | |

2  Plot a graph of **In(rate)** on the vertical axis against **1/T** on the horizontal axis, labelling the axes correctly. Draw a 'best-fit' straight line.

3  Measure the gradient of your straight line and record your value together with its sign and units.

4  According to the Arrhenius equation,

gradient of the graph $= -E_A/R$

Use this relationship to determine your value for $E_A$. A generally accepted value is $+47 \text{ kJ mol}^{-1}$.

## BACKGROUND

The standard form for a straight line graph is

$$y = c + mx$$

$y$ and $x$ are the variables
$m$ is the gradient of the straight line

$$m = \frac{\Delta y}{\Delta x}$$

$c$ is a constant
The gradient of the graph usually has units.

For Experiment 11.4 the first graph you plotted was of rate against temperature. Figure 11.12 shows how the shapes of similar graphs vary according to different activation energies.

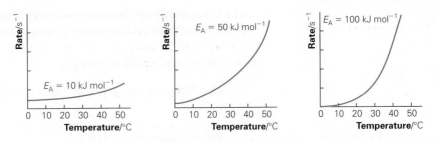

**Figure 11.12 How the rate of reaction varies with temperature and activation energy**

## 11.5 Catalysis

**The essential feature of a catalyst is that it increases the rate of a chemical reaction without itself becoming permanently involved in the reaction. It does, however, become temporarily involved, by providing a route from reactants to products which has a lower activation energy.**

This can be illustrated by an energy diagram (figure 11.13). Before the usual chemical reaction can take place the reactant molecules must be raised to a state of higher energy. They are said to be **activated** or to form an **activated complex**. Reactants and products are both at stable minima, while the activated complex is the transition state at the top of the energy barrier. A catalyst provides a new path in which the energy barrier is lower.

We can distinguish two types of catalysis, homogeneous and heterogeneous.

**When the catalyst and the reactants are all in one phase** (for example all dissolved in the same solvent) **the catalysis is described as homogeneous.**

**When the catalyst is in a different phase from the reactants** (for example two reacting gases in contact with a solid catalyst) **the catalysis is described as heterogeneous.**

The acid hydrolysis of esters is an example of **homogeneous** catalysis, with all the reactants and the catalyst of hydrogen ions dissolved in water.

$$CH_3CO_2CH_3(aq) + H_2O(l) \overset{H^+(aq)}{\rightleftharpoons} CH_3CO_2H(aq) + CH_3OH(aq)$$

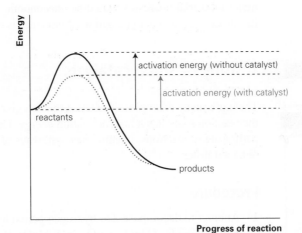

**Figure 11.13 The effect of a catalyst on the activation energy of a reaction**

The synthesis of ammonia is an example of **heterogeneous** catalysis because it involves the reaction of the gases hydrogen and nitrogen on a solid catalyst of iron.

$$3H_2(g) + N_2(g) \overset{Fe(s)}{\rightleftharpoons} 2NH_3(g)$$

The Arrhenius equation is useful in considering how catalysts work. From the equation

$$\ln k = \text{constant} - \frac{E_A}{R}(1/T)$$

you should see that the rate constant $k$, and hence the rate of reaction, will be greater when the activation energy is lower; this assumes, of course, that the constant is the same in both the catalysed and non-catalysed reactions.

An example of this which occurs in homogeneous catalysis is the decomposition of ethanal catalysed by iodine. Ethanal decomposes without a catalyst at about 700 K to produce methane and carbon monoxide:

$$CH_3CHO(g) \longrightarrow CH_4(g) + CO(g) \qquad E_A \approx +200\,\text{kJ mol}^{-1}$$

The addition of a small portion of iodine increases the rate of this reaction by several thousand times, with the activation energy falling to about $130\,\text{kJ mol}^{-1}$. A series of gas reactions has occurred, involving free radicals thus:

$$
\begin{aligned}
I_2 &\rightleftharpoons I\cdot + I\cdot \\
CH_3CHO + I\cdot &\longrightarrow CH_3CO\cdot + HI \\
CH_3CO\cdot &\longrightarrow CH_3\cdot + CO \\
CH_3\cdot + I_2 &\longrightarrow CH_3I + I\cdot \\
CH_3\cdot + HI &\longrightarrow CH_4 + I\cdot \\
CH_3I + HI &\longrightarrow CH_4 + I_2 \\
\hline
CH_3CHO &\longrightarrow CH_4 + CO \qquad \text{overall reaction}
\end{aligned}
$$

As a catalyst the iodine has formed some relatively stable intermediates and a reaction path or mechanism with a lower activation energy is created before the iodine is regenerated. In many homogeneous reactions, however, the intermediates are very reactive species, often present in very low concentrations, and difficult to identify.

The significance of catalysis is that, without the use of a catalyst, many major industrial processes would be uneconomic or impossible to realise while, in life-processes, the catalytic action of enzymes is crucial.

---

**EXPERIMENT 11.5a**

## A study of some catalysts

**SAFETY** ⚠

2 M hydrogen peroxide is an irritant.
2 M sodium hydroxide is corrosive.
Manganese(IV) oxide and copper(I) oxide are harmful.

There are many examples of reactions which give products only slowly because the reaction route has a high activation energy. Catalysts are substances which participate in reactions, opening new pathways of lower energy; the products are obtained faster.

### Procedure

1    Attempt to decompose 2 M hydrogen peroxide by the addition of small portions of metal oxides ($MnO_2$, $CuO$, $ZnO$, $MgO$). Repeat the experiment with a small piece of liver.

✎ **In your notes:** Do the oxides with catalytic activity have any common features? Consult a biochemistry textbook about the significance of the result with liver.

2 Mix 10 cm$^3$ of 0.5 M potassium sodium tartrate (Rochelle salt) with 10 cm$^3$ of 2 M hydrogen peroxide in a 250 cm$^3$ beaker. Bring to the boil carefully and note any signs of a reaction. Stop heating and add 1 cm$^3$ of a 0.1 M solution of any cobalt(II) salt.

✎ **In your notes:** What happens? Confirm that cobalt(II) ions do not change colour with either of the reagents separately.

3 Mix equal volumes of 2 M urea, $CO(NH_2)_2$, and 2 M sodium hydroxide and divide into two portions. Add a small portion of urease-active meal to one of the portions. Wipe the test tube mouths free of sodium hydroxide and place across each mouth a piece of moist red litmus paper. Heat the tubes in a hot water bath, with the mouths well separated.

✎ **In your notes:** Write the equation for the hydrolysis of urea. The activation energy has been measured and is 37 kJ mol$^{-1}$ for the catalysed reaction, and 137 kJ mol$^{-1}$ for the uncatalysed reaction.

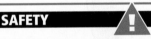

INVESTIGATION 11.5b

# The rate of reaction of metals with acid

## Student brief

A range of acids react with both zinc and magnesium and the kinetics of these reactions can be investigated in a number of ways. A suitable investigation could attempt to answer questions such as:

- What effect does the type of acid (strong or weak) or the type of metal used have on the activation energy of the reaction?
- Is the reaction order the same with monobasic and dibasic acids?
- Does the order of the reaction change as the concentration is varied?
- What effects does agitation have on the activation energy/rate of the reaction?

This is not intended to be a complete list; there are numerous other aspects of the reaction which could yield appropriate investigations.

You will need to consider and select an appropriate method for measuring the rate of the reaction (this could be either an 'initial rate' method or a method where concentrations vary continuously). Suitable quantities of reagents will need to be chosen and a pilot exercise might be appropriate. A quantitative error analysis is important and a good investigation would need to consider at least two variables.

**SAFETY**

You must carry out a Risk Assessment before starting any experimental work on your investigation. Your Risk Assessment must be checked, amended if necessary, approved and signed by your teacher.

# 11.6 Background reading: light and chemical change

## QUESTIONS

Read the passage, then answer the following questions.

1  Which atoms, molecules, and ions are involved in the formation of carbohydrates in chloroplasts?

2  What two processes were involved in the original production of the ozone layer?

3  Explain why one chlorine radical can turn many thousands of ozone molecules into oxygen. You should include appropriate equations in your answer.

4  Write a summary in continuous prose, in no more than 150 words, about the importance of the ozone layer and how it is being depleted.

Chemistry is all about energy and molecules: energy can help to make molecules, change them and break them. Photochemistry is all about exciting the electrons of molecules with discrete packages of light energy called **photons**, thereby making them jump from a lower to a higher energy state. Photons of ultraviolet and visible light can do this. Our eyes rely on such photochemical changes in the molecules of the retina to enable us to see. General interest in photochemistry has been awakened by the realisation that we are being exposed to higher levels of ultraviolet radiation due to the depletion of ozone in the upper atmosphere and the discovery in 1985 by the British Antarctic Survey of the 'ozone hole'.

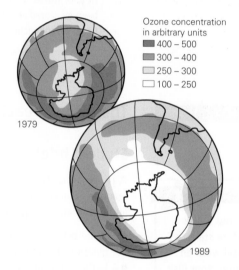

| Ozone concentration in arbitrary units |
| --- |
| ■ 400 – 500 |
| ■ 300 – 400 |
| □ 250 – 300 |
| □ 100 – 250 |

1979

1989

Figure 11.15   The Antarctic ozone hole, mapped by satellite in October 1979 and again in October 1989

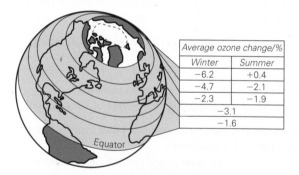

| Average ozone change/% | |
| --- | --- |
| Winter | Summer |
| −6.2 | +0.4 |
| −4.7 | −2.1 |
| −2.3 | −1.9 |
| −3.1 | |
| −1.6 | |

Equator

Figure 11.14   Ozone trends for the Northern Hemisphere in the last two decades of the twentieth century

Shorter wavelengths of light have more energy and cause bigger electron jumps. Light may even have enough energy to strip out an electron completely and turn a molecule into an ion. However, photochemists are more interested in light which excites electrons rather than light which ejects them. They study the remarkable behaviour of molecules once they have captured a photon of light. What happens next depends on the molecule: it may break apart, possibly to form highly reactive free radicals; or react chemically with another molecule; or rearrange itself into another isomer; or emit light.

Nearly all molecules respond to ultraviolet and visible light but some molecules are particularly sensitive. The best-known naturally photosensitive substance is chlorophyll, which enables plants to make carbohydrates with energy trapped from sunlight. Perhaps the best-known artificial photosensitive material is photographic film. Other examples include thin films, liquid crystals, and microelectronic devices that we now use to detect light, to count photons, and even to change the wavelength of light.

Light which produces photochemical changes generally has wavelengths of 200 to 740 nm (1 nm = $10^{-9}$ m). This range includes both visible and ultraviolet light.

When a molecule absorbs a photon of radiation and is excited, how can we study the excited state and follow what happens next? The excited state may last a few seconds but more likely it will last for only a microsecond ($10^{-6}$ s), or just a few femtoseconds ($10^{-15}$ s). We can carry out such studies thanks to the pioneering work of George Porter, the British chemist and Nobel prize winner, who developed a technique known as **flash photolysis**.

Chemists have used femtosecond flash photolysis to study photosynthesis. Chloroplasts, which occur in some cells of green plants, have a reaction centre with two chlorophyll molecules. The chloroplast absorbs a photon of light and in about one picosecond ($10^{-12}$ s) this causes an electron to be transferred out of the reaction centre leaving the system with enough energy to oxidise water in the cell to oxygen, which is released into the air:

$$2H_2O(l) \longrightarrow O_2(g) + 4H^+(aq) + 4e^-$$

The hydrogen ions and the electrons released in the cell then bind to carbon dioxide to form carbohydrate molecules such as starch or cellulose. The process is complex but we know the oxidation takes place at a cluster of four magnesium atoms situated on one of the chlorophyll molecules. Photosynthesis enables an energetically unfavourable change to take place

$$6CO_2(aq) + 12H^+(aq) + 12e^- \longrightarrow C_6H_{12}O_6(aq)$$

which is the basis of plant life on Earth and its atmosphere of oxygen.

## Shielding life on Earth

In the Cambrian period of geological time, about 600 million years ago, only 1% of the atmosphere was oxygen. Life-threatening ultraviolet radiation from the Sun could reach the surface of the planet, so life only survived where it was shielded, in stagnant water for example. But as marine plants released more and more oxygen to the atmosphere, life on the surface became less hazardous, thanks primarily to the formation of a protective shield of ozone in the upper atmosphere, or stratosphere.

When molecular oxygen, $O_2$, is exposed to short wavelength ultraviolet, it is converted into ozone by a photochemical reaction. Light splits the oxygen molecule into two atoms of oxygen, $O\cdot$, each of which can then combine with another molecule of oxygen to form ozone, $O_3$. This process occurs in the stratosphere where there is now an estimated $3.5 \times 10^9$ tonnes of ozone. But the photochemistry does not stop there, because the ozone is also capable of absorbing longer wavelength ultraviolet. When it does, it throws off one oxygen atom and reverts to $O_2$. The result is that only a little ultraviolet of wavelength shorter than 300 nm reaches the surface of the Earth. But some does, and this is life-threatening.

Ozone in the stratosphere also reacts with nitrogen monoxide, the hydroxyl radical and chlorine free radicals (figure 11.16). The

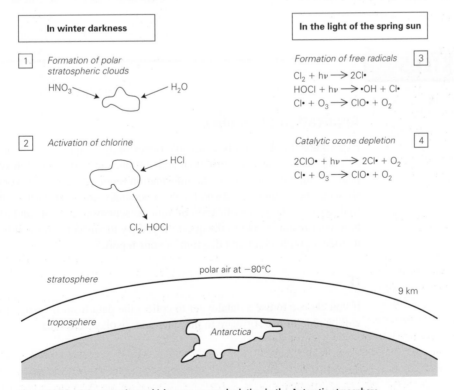

Figure 11.16   **Some reactions which cause ozone depletion in the Antarctic atmosphere**

reactions with nitrogen monoxide and the hydroxyl radical arise from natural causes, such as the dinitrogen monoxide given off from the soil, but the concentration of chlorine has increased rapidly in the second half of the twentieth century. This is mainly due to the chlorofluorocarbons (CFCs) that used to be widely used as solvents, as the coolant liquid in refrigerators, and in aerosol cans, before the damaging consequences were recognised by research.

Once released from their CFC the chlorine radicals reduce ozone concentration by the chain reaction

$$Cl\cdot + O_3 \longrightarrow ClO\cdot + O_2$$
$$ClO\cdot + O\cdot \longrightarrow Cl\cdot + O_2$$

(the dots represent unpaired electrons)

In this chain reaction one chlorine radical can turn many thousands of ozone molecules into oxygen molecules before the chain is terminated.

There are other processes which can reduce ozone concentration. For instance, the detection of the 'ozone hole' over the Antarctic led to research which identified a set of reactions which occur on the surface of ice crystals in Antarctic stratospheric clouds. In these reactions hydrogen chloride is converted into the photochemically active species ClO. A concentration of 1 part per $10^9$ of ClO can destroy nearly all the Antarctic stratospheric ozone in two to three weeks and can be directly attributed to the release of CFCs. This was a surprising and alarming result because 99% of the atmospheric chlorine is in the form of hydrogen chloride and other species which do not normally take part in photochemical reactions.

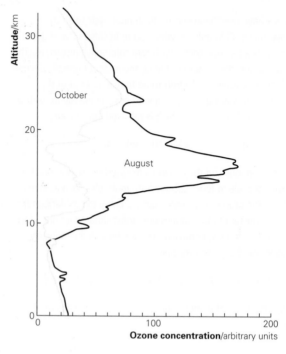

Figure 11.17   **Ozone destruction in the Antarctic during September**

**KEY SKILLS**

### Application of number

Experiment 11.5b could be a suitable opportunity to apply your application of number skills. This is a substantial and complex activity for which you will need a plan for obtaining and using the information required, records of your calculations showing the methods used and levels of accuracy, together with a report on your findings including a justification of your presentation methods and explanations of how your results relate to the question you try to answer. You will be able to include a graph, chart and diagram in your report.

### IT

If you choose to use a datalogger to collect the data from Investigation 11.5b you will be able to use software to interpret and display your data.

# TOPIC REVIEW

1   **List key words or terms with definitions where necessary**

   - [A] with units
   - $r_A$
   - rate equation
   - order of reaction
   - rate constant (including the units used)
   - half-life
   - $E_A$
   - rate-determining step
   - collision theory
   - distribution of molecular kinetic energies

2   **Summarise the key principles as simply as possible**

   You will have detailed practical records of the actual experiments carried out but it is a good idea to have an **overview** of the **ways of following rates**, the kind of **data collected** as well as the **graphs** that might be **drawn** and what you can **deduce from the shape** of each graph:

   - the practical techniques for following the rate of a reaction
   - the procedure for processing experimental data to find:
      **a**   half-life
      **b**   order of reaction
      **c**   rate equation
      **d**   the activation energy
   - the development of a possible mechanism from the rate equation for a reaction.

# REVIEW QUESTIONS

**✱** Indicates that the *Book of data* is needed.

**11.1**   Information about the effect of changes of concentration on the rates of some reactions is given below. For each example, use the information to write the rate equation for the reaction.

**a** 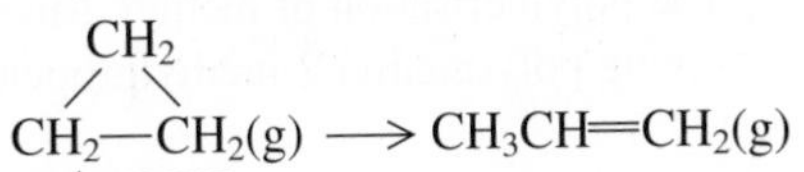
$$CH_2 \diagup\diagdown$$
$$CH_2 \!-\! CH_2(g) \longrightarrow CH_3CH\!=\!CH_2(g)$$
cyclopropane

The rate is proportional to the concentration of cyclopropane.                    (1)

**b**   $2N_2O(g) \longrightarrow 2N_2(g) + O_2(g)$

The rate is proportional to the concentration of nitrogen(I) oxide.                (1)

**c**   $H_2(g) + I_2(g) \longrightarrow 2HI(g)$

The rate is proportional to the concentration of hydrogen and to the concentration of iodine.                                                        (1)

**d**  $2HI(g) \longrightarrow H_2(g) + I_2(g)$

The rate is proportional to the square of the concentration of hydrogen iodide.

(1)

**e**  $C_{12}H_{22}O_{11}(aq) + H_2O(l) \xrightarrow{H^+} 2C_6H_{12}O_6(aq)$
sucrose                                          glucose

The rate is proportional to the concentration of sucrose and to the concentration of hydrogen ions.

(1)

**(5 marks)**

**11.2**  Is it possible to write the rate equation for a reaction if you know only the stoichiometric (chemical) equation for the reaction? Refer to your answers to question **11.1** to support your answer to this question. **(3 marks)**

**11.3**  Write down the overall order of each of the reactions in question **11.1**. **(5 marks)**

**11.4**  What are the units of the rate constant for each reaction in question **11.1**? **(5 marks)**

**11.5**  Indicate a suitable method of collecting rate data for each of the following reactions, justifying your choice in each case. (You are *not* expected to give practical details.)

**a**  The effect of heat on a solution of 2,4,6-trinitrobenzoic acid.

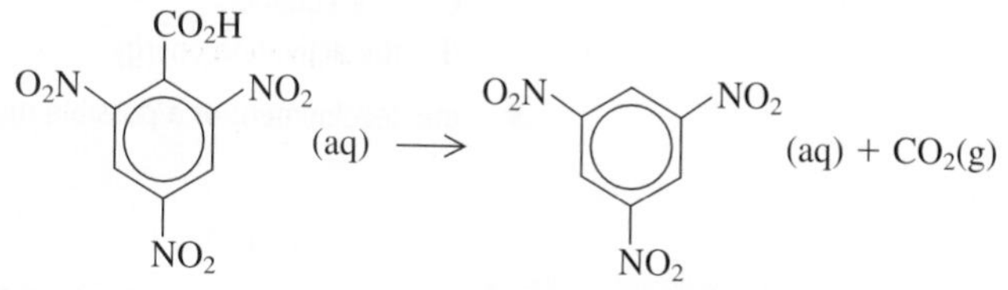

(2)

**b**  The hydrolysis of 2-bromo-2-methylpropane in 80% aqueous alcohol.

$(CH_3)_3CBr(aq) + H_2O(l) \longrightarrow (CH_3)_3COH(aq) + H^+(aq) + Br^-(aq)$ (2)

**c**  The reaction between peroxodisulphate (persulphate) ions and iodide ions in aqueous solution.

$S_2O_8^{2-}(aq) + 2I^-(aq) \longrightarrow 2SO_4^{2-}(aq) + I_2(aq)$ (2)

**d**  The polymerisation of methyl 2-methylpropenoate (methyl methacrylate) giving poly(methyl 2-methylpropenoate), 'Perspex'.

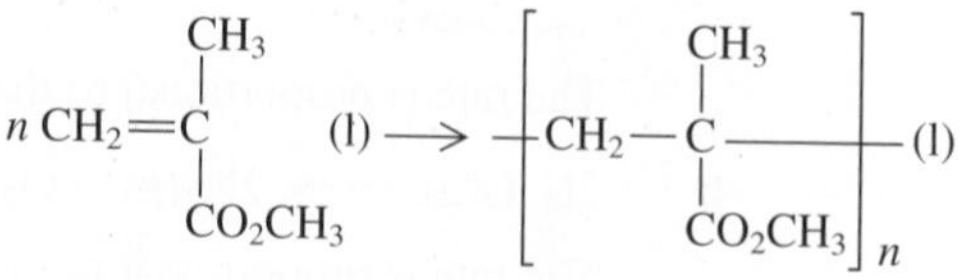

(2)

**(8 marks)**

**11.6**   When hydrogen peroxide solution reacts with iodide ions in aqueous acid, iodine is liberated.

$$H_2O_2(aq) + 2H^+(aq) + 2I^-(aq) \longrightarrow 2H_2O(l) + I_2(aq)$$

The following table gives some experimental results for the reaction.

| Run | Initial reactant concentration /mol dm$^{-3}$ | | | Initial rate of formation of I$_2$ /mol dm$^{-3}$ s$^{-1}$ |
|---|---|---|---|---|
| | [H$_2$O$_2$] | [I$^-$] | [H$^+$] | |
| 1 | 0.010 | 0.010 | 0.10 | $1.75 \times 10^{-6}$ |
| 2 | 0.020 | 0.010 | 0.10 | $3.50 \times 10^{-6}$ |
| 3 | 0.030 | 0.010 | 0.10 | $5.25 \times 10^{-6}$ |
| 4 | 0.030 | 0.020 | 0.10 | $1.05 \times 10^{-5}$ |
| 5 | 0.030 | 0.020 | 0.20 | $1.05 \times 10^{-5}$ |

a   i   Use the results of runs 1, 2 and 3 to deduce the order of reaction with respect to H$_2$O$_2$(aq), and explain how you arrived at your answer.   (2)

   ii   Use the results of runs 3 and 4 to deduce the order of reaction with respect to I$^-$(aq), giving an explanation as in i.   (2)

   iii  Use the results of runs 4 and 5 to deduce the order of reaction with respect to H$^+$(aq), giving an explanation as before.   (2)

   iv   What is the rate equation for the reaction?   (1)

   v   Calculate two values for the rate constant, $k$, by substituting the numerical data for any two runs into the rate equation.   (2)

   vi   What are the units of the rate constant?   (1)

b   A proposed mechanism for this reaction is:

$$H_2O_2 + I^- \longrightarrow H_2O + IO^- \quad \text{(slow)}$$
$$H^+ + IO^- \longrightarrow HIO \quad \text{(fast)}$$
$$HIO + H^+ + I^- \longrightarrow I_2 + H_2O \quad \text{(fast)}$$

Is this mechanism consistent with the rate equation for the reaction? Give your reasons, discussing each of the reactants in turn.   (5)

**(15 marks)**

**11.7**   In acid solution, bromate(V) ions slowly oxidise bromide ions to bromine.

$$BrO_3^-(aq) + 5Br^-(aq) + 6H^+(aq) \longrightarrow 3Br_2(aq) + 3H_2O(l)$$

The following experimental data were obtained for this reaction:

| Mixture | [BrO$_3^-$] /mol dm$^{-3}$ | [Br$^-$] /mol dm$^{-3}$ | [H$^+$] /mol dm$^{-3}$ | Relative rate of formation of bromine |
|---|---|---|---|---|
| 1 | 0.05 | 0.25 | 0.30 | 1 |
| 2 | 0.05 | 0.25 | 0.60 | 4 |
| 3 | 0.10 | 0.25 | 0.60 | 8 |
| 4 | 0.05 | 0.125 | 0.60 | 2 |

a   i   What is the rate equation for the reaction? Explain how you arrived at your answer.   (4)

ii What are the units of the rate constant? (1)

b A proposed mechanism for the reaction is:

$$H^+ + Br^- \longrightarrow HBr \qquad \text{(fast)}$$
$$H^+ + BrO_3^- \longrightarrow HBrO_3 \qquad \text{(fast)}$$
$$HBr + HBrO_3 \longrightarrow HBrO + HBrO_2 \qquad \text{(slow)}$$
$$HBrO_2 + HBr \longrightarrow 2HBrO \qquad \text{(fast)}$$
$$HBrO + HBr \longrightarrow H_2O + Br_2 \qquad \text{(fast)}$$

Is this mechanism consistent with the rate equation for the reaction? Give your reasons, discussing each of the three reactants in turn. (5)

**(10 marks)**

**11.8** Use the 'collision theory' of reactions to give two reasons for each of the following:

a The rate of a reaction increases if the temperature is increased. (2)

b Reaction does not occur after *every* collision between two reactant molecules. (2)

**(4 marks)**

**\* 11.9** The rate equation for the reaction

$$2HI(g) \longrightarrow H_2(g) + I_2(g)$$

is rate of change of $[HI] = k[HI]^2$

The value of the rate constant, $k$, varies with temperature as shown in the following table:

| Temperature/K $1/x$ | Rate constant/$10^{-5}$ dm$^3$ mol$^{-1}$ s$^{-1}$ | $\ln$ data |
|---|---|---|
| 556   1.79 | 0.0352 | -3.3467 |
| 647   1.54 | 8.58 | 2.149 |
| 700   1.428 | 116 | 4.753 |
| 781   1.280 | 3960 | 8.284 |

a Using graph paper, plot a graph of ln(rate constant), on the vertical axis, against 1/temperature, on the horizontal axis. Choose sensible scales and label your axes. (4)

b Your graph should be a straight line; its gradient is equal to $-E_A/RT$. Measure the gradient and use it to find the activation energy of the reaction. (You will find the value and units of the gas constant, $R$, in table 1.6 in the *Book of data*.) (3)

**(7 marks)**

**\* 11.10** The rate constant for the first-order reaction

$$C_6H_5N_2^+Cl^-(aq) + H_2O(l) \longrightarrow C_6H_5OH(aq) + N_2(g) + H^+(aq) + Cl^-(aq)$$

varies with temperature as in the following table:

| Temperature/K | 1/T (×10⁻³) | Rate constant/10⁻⁵ s⁻¹ | ln rate |
|---|---|---|---|
| 278 | 3.517 | 0.15 | −1.89 |
| 298 | 3.355 | 4.1 | 1.410 |
| 308 | 3.247 | 20 | 2.99 |
| 323 | 3.0959 | 140 | 4.94 |

Find the activation energy of the reaction, using the method described in question **11.9**.

**(7 marks)**

# EXAMINATION QUESTIONS

Questions of the summary and comprehension type are found in the background reading section (section 11.6).

**11.11** Equimolar amounts of 1-chlorobutane and sodium hydroxide in solution were mixed at 29 °C and the concentration of hydroxide ions was determined at various times.

The following results were obtained.

| Time/min | [OH⁻]/mol dm⁻³ |
|---|---|
| 0 | 0.25 |
| 60 | 0.21 |
| 120 | 0.17 |
| 180 | 0.15 |
| 240 | 0.13 |
| 360 | 0.11 |
| 480 | 0.09 |
| 720 | 0.07 |
| 1080 | 0.05 |

**a** Plot a graph of the concentration of hydroxide ion on the vertical axis against time on the horizontal axis. (3)
**b** Find TWO successive values for the half-life. (2)
**c** What is the order of the reaction? Give a reason for your answer. (2)
**d** Why is your answer to **c** the overall order for this reaction? (1)
**e** Suggest an equation for the rate-determining step of the reaction between 1-chlorobutane and sodium hydroxide which is consistent with your answer to **d**. (1)

**(9 marks)**

**11.12**   **a**   Peroxodisulphate ions, $S_2O_8^{2-}$, react with iodide ions in aqueous solution to form iodine and sulphate ions, $SO_4^{2-}$. The effect of peroxodisulphate ion concentration on the rate of this reaction can be measured as follows.

Some starch solution and a small measured quantity of sodium thiosulphate solution are added to potassium peroxodisulphate solution. Potassium iodide solution is added and the time measured for the solution to change colour. This occurs when all the sodium thiosulphate is used up and the starch reacts with the iodine. The reaction is repeated using different concentrations of potassium peroxodisulphate.

**i**   What is the final colour of the reaction mixture?   (1)

**ii**  Why is the concentration of iodide ions constant until the reaction mixture changes colour?   (1)

**b**   The rate of reaction is measured by taking the reciprocal of the time for the colour of the reaction mixture to change.

Typical results are shown in the table below.

| $[S_2O_8^{2-} (aq)]$/mol dm$^{-3}$ | Time/s | $(1/\text{time})/\text{s}^{-1}$ |
|---|---|---|
| 0.0100 | 480 | $2.08 \times 10^{-3}$ |
| 0.0090 | 533 | $1.88 \times 10^{-3}$ |
| 0.0075 | 640 | $1.56 \times 10^{-3}$ |
| 0.0060 | 800 | $1.25 \times 10^{-3}$ |

**i**   Plot a graph of 1/time on the vertical axis against concentration of peroxodisulphate ions on the horizontal axis.   (3)

**ii**  Use your graph to deduce the order of the reaction with respect to peroxodisulphate ions. Justify your answer.   (2)

**c**   **i**   The reaction is first order with respect to iodide ions. Use this information and your answer to **b ii** to write the overall rate equation for the reaction.   (1)

**ii**  What are the units of the rate constant for the reaction?   (1)

**(9 marks)**

**11.13**   **a**   Hydrogen iodide decomposes at high temperature to form hydrogen and iodine gases. The rate-determining step of this second-order reaction is:

$$2HI(g) \longrightarrow H_2(g) + I_2(g)$$

**i**   Write the rate equation for the reaction.   (1)

**ii**  What are the units of the rate constant for this reaction, assuming that time is measured in seconds (s)?   (1)

**b**   The rate constant $k$ was measured at different temperatures. In the table below the data have been converted into values of 1/temperature and ln $k$.

| $(1/\text{temperature})/\text{K}^{-1}$ | ln $k$ |
|---|---|
| $1.27 \times 10^{-3}$ | $-4.00$ |
| $1.34 \times 10^{-3}$ | $-5.50$ |
| $1.38 \times 10^{-3}$ | $-6.50$ |
| $1.43 \times 10^{-3}$ | $-7.60$ |
| $1.48 \times 10^{-3}$ | $-8.80$ |

   i Plot a graph of ln $k$, on the vertical axis, against 1/temperature, on the horizontal axis. (3)

   ii Measure the gradient of your graph. (2)

   iii The gradient of your graph is related to the activation energy of the reaction, $E_A$, by

$$\text{gradient} = -\frac{E_A}{R}$$

where $R = 8.31\,\text{J K}^{-1}\,\text{mol}^{-1}$.

Use this relationship to calculate the activation energy, $E_A$, for the reaction. (2)

   iv The presence of nichrome wire greatly increases the rate of decomposition of hydrogen iodide at high temperature. Suggest how the nichrome wire might be acting as a catalyst. (2)

**(11 marks)**

**11.14**    a    The equation for the reaction between thiosulphate ions and hydrogen ions is

$$S_2O_3^{2-}(aq) + 2H^+(aq) \longrightarrow SO_2(g) + S(s) + H_2O(l)$$

The effect of temperature on the rate of this reaction was investigated. Solutions of sodium thiosulphate and hydrochloric acid were heated to the same temperature. The time for the reaction to produce a fixed amount of sulphur was measured, and the reaction repeated at different temperatures.

   i How could you heat the solutions to ensure that both reactants are at the same temperature? (1)

   ii How could you measure the time for the reaction to produce a fixed amount of sulphur? (2)

   iii How could you obtain a measure of the rate of reaction from your measurement of time? (1)

   b    The results obtained from a series of experiments are tabulated below. Most measurements have been converted into values of 1/temperature and ln (rate).

| Temperature/K | (1/temperature)/K$^{-1}$ | Rate | ln (rate) |
|---|---|---|---|
| 293 | $3.41 \times 10^{-3}$ | $7.08 \times 10^{-3}$ | $-4.95$ |
| 303 | $3.30 \times 10^{-3}$ | $1.23 \times 10^{-2}$ | $-4.40$ |
| 313 | $3.19 \times 10^{-3}$ | $2.13 \times 10^{-2}$ | $-3.85$ |
| 323 | | $3.34 \times 10^{-2}$ | |
| 333 | $3.00 \times 10^{-3}$ | $5.50 \times 10^{-2}$ | $-2.90$ |

   i Complete the table by calculating the missing values. (2)

   ii Plot a graph of ln (rate) on the vertical axis, against 1/temperature on the horizontal axis. (3)

   iii Calculate the activation energy, $E_A$, for the reaction, using your graph and the relationship:

$$\ln (\text{rate}) = \text{constant} - \frac{E_A}{R}(1/T)$$

where $R = 8.31\,\text{J K}^{-1}\,\text{mol}^{-1}$.

Remember to include a sign and units in your answer. (3)

**(12 marks)**

# Arenes: benzene and phenol

This topic considers the unique properties of the series of hydrocarbons known as **arenes**, of which benzene is the best known member. The behaviour of the arenes will be contrasted with the alkane and alkene hydrocarbons studied in Topic 8.

When a hydroxyl group, —OH, is attached to an arene ring a new series of compounds known as **phenols** is obtained. Phenol itself (benzene with a hydroxyl group) was the first antiseptic and several phenolic compounds are the basis of important pharmaceutical preparations such as aspirin.

 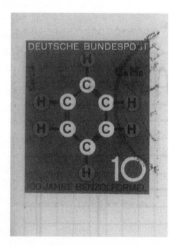

Figure 12.1 **These stamps were issued to commemorate the centenary of Kekulé's proposal of a ring structure for benzene**

This topic, therefore:

- considers the special features associated with the structure of benzene
- investigates the reactions of arenes and looks at how to interpret them
- investigates the reactions of phenols
- looks at the preparation of aspirin from 2-hydroxybenzoic acid.

## 12.1 Benzene and some substituted benzene compounds

The structure of benzene, $C_6H_6$, provided chemists with a major problem. The principal difficulty was the absence of isomers of monosubstituted derivatives of benzene. An acceptable structure must therefore be one in which all six hydrogen atoms would occupy equivalent positions.

A major step towards the solution to the problem was taken by Kekulé, Professor of Chemistry at Ghent in Belgium, in 1865. He later described how he came to propose the structure illustrated below.

'I turned my chair to the fire and dozed. Again the atoms were gambolling before my eyes. This time the smaller groups kept modestly in the background. My mental eye, rendered more acute by repeated visions of this kind, could now distinguish larger structures, of manifold conformation; long rows, sometimes more closely fitted together; all twining and twisting in snake-like motion. But look! What was that? One of the snakes had seized hold of its own tail, and the form whirled mockingly before my eyes. As if by a flash of lightning I awoke.'

*Translation from FINLAY, 100 years of chemistry*

This dream has been described as one of the most important in history. The snake biting its own tail gave Kekulé the clue to the discovery which has been called 'the most brilliant piece of prediction to be found in the whole range of organic chemistry', and which, in fact, is one of the cornerstones of modern science.

Kekulé was not actually the first scientist to propose ring structures for organic compounds. An Austrian schoolteacher, Josef Loschmidt, had published a booklet in 1861 but the ideas were not clearly explained; we know that Kekulé had read the booklet but dismissed it as confused. Perhaps that is the real origin of Kekulé's dream in 1865.

Loschmidt structure

Kekulé structure

The modern evidence for the symmetry of the benzene ring is based on X-ray diffraction studies. The unusual nature of the bonding is seen from a comparison of the bond lengths of benzene with those of cyclohexane and cyclohexene.

| | |
|---|---|
| Carbon–carbon single bond in cyclohexane | 0.15 nm |
| Carbon–carbon double bond in cyclohexene | 0.13 nm |
| Carbon–carbon bonds in benzene | 0.14 nm |

**The bonding in benzene cannot therefore be described as three double bonds plus three single bonds, but must be considered as a delocalised electron charge cloud spread out over the whole ring, as in figure 12.2 (overleaf).**

When drawing a structure to indicate the molecule of benzene certain difficulties arise; a single line is normally used to represent two electrons, and two

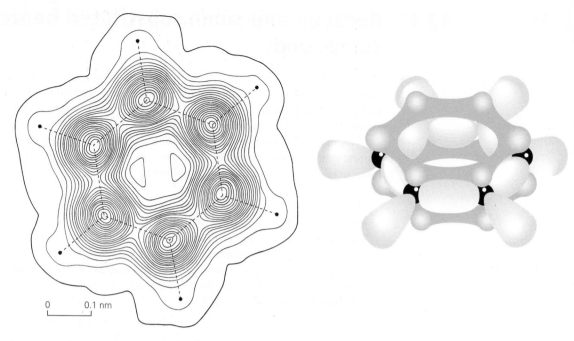

Figure 12.2 **Electron density map of benzene and a model showing the delocalised electron cloud in benzene**

lines to represent four electrons. As neither of these is appropriate for the carbon–carbon bonds in benzene, this representation is often used:

Displayed    or    Structural

The unique nature of the bonding in benzene can be seen in its infrared spectrum (see figure 12.3c, opposite). Infrared spectra provide a unique fingerprint of a compound and are discussed in Topic 21. Each bond shows a characteristic absorption peak at the particular frequency at which the absorption takes place. The frequencies are shown on a scale of wavenumbers, in units of $cm^{-1}$, and are given in the *Book of data* in table 3.3.

The infrared spectra of an alkane and an alkene are shown in figures 12.3a and b to contrast with the spectrum of benzene.

The infrared spectrum of benzene shows that the carbon–carbon bonds are not the normal C=C or C—C bond types.

**STUDY TASK**

Use table 3.3 in the *Book of data* to identify the origin of the main absorptions in the infrared spectra of benzene, decane and oct-1-ene.

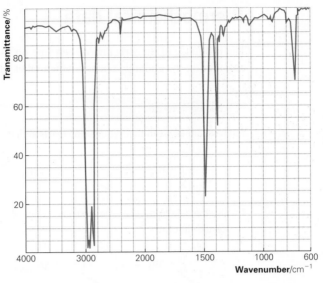

Figure 12.3a **The infrared spectrum of an alkane (decane)**

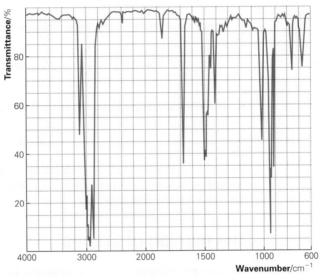

Figure 12.3b **The infrared spectrum of an alkene (oct-1-ene)**

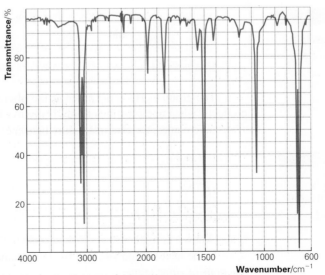

Figure 12.3c **The infrared spectrum of an arene (benzene)**

# Thermochemical data

The influence of the structure of benzene on its reactions can be looked at by considering the enthalpy change which takes place when hydrogen is added.

---

### STUDY TASK

You have already seen that cyclohexene reacts with hydrogen to form cyclohexane.

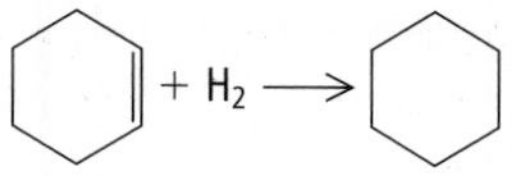

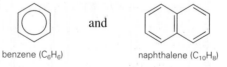

$$\Delta H^{\ominus}_{reaction} = -120 \text{ kJ mol}^{-1}$$

1   Use the data to calculate the enthalpy change of hydrogenation for a molecule with the Kekulé structure:

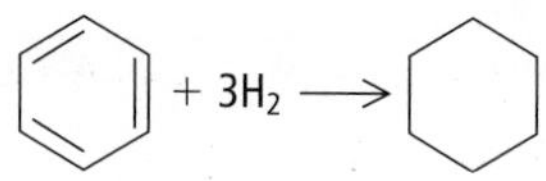

+ 3H$_2$ ⟶      $\Delta H^{\ominus}_{reaction} = ?$

2   Compare your results with the known value for benzene.

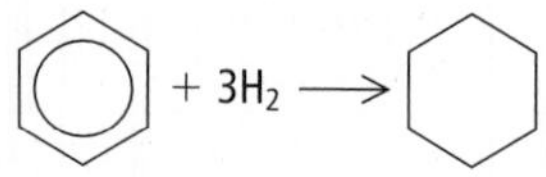

+ 3H$_2$ ⟶      $\Delta H^{\ominus}_{reaction} = -208 \text{ kJ mol}^{-1}$

3   Which structure is more stable, the one with the larger or smaller negative value for $\Delta H^{\ominus}_{reaction}$?

---

On the basis of your result, it is reasonable to deduce that the benzene ring is more stable than expected and is therefore less likely to take part in addition reactions than other unsaturated compounds would be.

# The naming of arenes

Arenes were originally called the **aromatic hydrocarbons**. Two examples are:

benzene (C$_6$H$_6$)    and    naphthalene (C$_{10}$H$_8$)

COMMENT

Where a group is attached to a benzene ring a hydrogen atom has been removed.

The group C$_6$H$_5$— is known as the **phenyl group**. Many substitution products, when one substituent only is involved, are commonly known by non-systematic names, for example methylbenzene

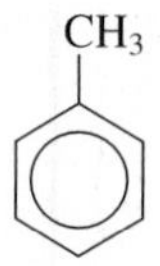

COMMENT

| | |
|---|---|
| phenylamine | C$_6$H$_5$NH$_2$ |
| phenylethene | C$_6$H$_5$CH=CH$_2$ |
| phenol | C$_6$H$_5$OH |

CH$_3$

is also known as toluene.

In the next section you will be doing some experiments to compare the reactions of some arenes.

## 12.2 Reactions of arenes

Benzene has been shown to be toxic and carcinogenic and its use in experiments for teaching is prohibited. We shall therefore need to do our experiments with various derivatives of benzene such as methylbenzene and methoxybenzene, which are safe.

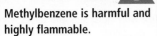

methylbenzene (toluene)     methoxybenzene (anisole)

The hazards of benzene have not been recognised for long and in older books you may find suggestions for experiments involving benzene itself. Use of benzene, or mixtures containing more than 0.1% benzene, is now illegal in the UK for educational purposes.

Although safer than benzene itself, the substitutes used in Experiment 12.2 are highly flammable and have a harmful vapour. Take care when handling them.

Record your results in such a way that you can compare them with those of the experiments you did with alkanes and with alkenes in Topic 8. The experiments with methylbenzene will enable you to compare the reactivity of arenes with that of alkanes and alkenes.

In the experiments with methoxybenzene you will be able to consider the nature of the reactions of arenes. The methyl group and the methoxy group are unreactive in the conditions of the experiments, so any reactions you observe are likely to be reactions of the benzene ring.

---

**EXPERIMENT 12.2**

## Experiments with arenes

This experiment is in two parts: first the reactions of methylbenzene, then of methoxybenzene.

### Procedure for methylbenzene

#### 1 Combustion

Keep a sample of liquid methylbenzene in a stoppered boiling tube well away from any flame. Dip a combustion spoon into the sample and replace the stopper. Set fire to the methylbenzene on the combustion spoon.

✎ **In your notes:** Note the luminosity and sootiness of the flame, which is characteristic of compounds with a low hydrogen to carbon ratio.

#### 2 Oxidation

To 0.5 cm³ of a mixture of equal volumes of 0.01 M potassium manganate(VII) solution and 0.4 M sulphuric acid in a test tube add a few drops of methylbenzene. Shake the contents of the tube and try to tell from any colour changes of the manganate(VII) whether it oxidises the methylbenzene.

#### 3 Action of bromine

To 1–2 cm³ of 2% bromine (TAKE CARE) dissolved in an inert solvent in a test tube add a few drops of methylbenzene.

✎ **In your notes:** What happens to the colour of the bromine?

**SAFETY** ⚠

Methylbenzene is harmful and highly flammable.
Bromine at this concentration is toxic and corrosive; the solvent is highly flammable and harmful. The vapour is particularly dangerous if inhaled. Avoid all skin contact with any bromine solution.
Concentrated sulphuric acid is corrosive.
Remember that products of reactions may also be hazardous.

### 4 Action of sulphuric acid

Place 1–2 cm$^3$ of concentrated sulphuric acid (TAKE CARE) in a dry test tube held in a test tube rack and add 0.5 cm$^3$ of the methylbenzene. Shake the test tube gently.

 **In your notes:** Do the substances mix or are there two separate layers in the test tube?

---

**STUDY TASK**

Compare your results with those obtained with alkanes and with alkenes.

---

## Procedure for methoxybenzene

Methoxybenzene has a benzene ring that is fairly reactive, so by using appropriate reagents you should be able to observe some typical reactions of the benzene ring.

### 1 Bromination

To 0.5 cm$^3$ of 2% bromine (TAKE CARE) in an inert solvent in a test tube add a few drops of methoxybenzene.

 **In your notes:** What happens to the colour of the bromine? What are the fumes that are evolved? (Test them with ammonia.) Did alkenes give off fumes in this reaction? Has an addition reaction occurred, since two products were formed?

### 2 Sulphonation

To 0.5 cm$^3$ of methoxybenzene in a dry test tube add 1 cm$^3$ of concentrated sulphuric acid (TAKE CARE). Shake the test tube **gently** to mix the contents (does the tube get hot?), then **cautiously** add 4 cm$^3$ of water.

 **In your notes:** Is there a product which is soluble in water?

### 3 Friedel–Crafts reaction

To 1 cm$^3$ of methoxybenzene in a test tube add a small spatula measure of **anhydrous** aluminium chloride (TAKE CARE) followed by 1 cm$^3$ of 2-chloro-2-methylpropane. If necessary, warm the mixture in a beaker of hot water.

 **In your notes:** What are the fumes that are evolved? Test with moist indicator paper.

### 4 Nitration

To 1 cm$^3$ of water add 1 cm$^3$ of concentrated nitric acid (TAKE CARE). Then add a few drops of methoxybenzene to the mixture. Warm in a water bath and observe the formation of coloured products.

---

**SAFETY**

Methoxybenzene is flammable.
Anhydrous aluminium chloride dust is corrosive and causes severe burns in contact with moisture.
Concentrated sulphuric and nitric acids are corrosive.

---

# An interpretation of the substitution reactions of the benzene ring

**REVIEW TASK**

You should look again at the chart you drew in Topic 8.

The difference between alkene reactions and benzene ring reactions can be seen most clearly in the bromination reaction. An alkene such as cyclohexene undergoes an addition reaction with bromine:

But when a benzene ring reacts, hydrogen bromide is produced and this means that a hydrogen atom has been displaced from the benzene ring:

The product will react with more bromine to give

with more hydrogen bromide being produced.

**These reactions of the benzene ring are substitution reactions.**

We now consider how the bromine substitution reaction of the benzene ring takes place.

You have seen that the substitution takes place quite easily with methoxybenzene but not with methylbenzene. Methylbenzene **will** undergo such a reaction but a catalyst (iron is suitable) is needed.

The major product is the monobromo compound, although the yields of dibromo- and tribromo-methylbenzene can be increased by heating.

## QUESTIONS

It has been found that the reaction of iodine monochloride, I—Cl, with methoxybenzene produces only iodine substitution products.

1  What is the attacking atom in this reaction? What polarisation would you expect in I—Cl? So what is the charge on the attacking atom in the reaction?

2  Now consider the leaving group. What atom is lost from the benzene ring in the reaction? Will this atom more easily carry a positive or a negative charge when it leaves the benzene ring? Is this consistent with the charge which, you have suggested, the attacking atom will bring to the benzene ring?

You should now have an idea about the charge on the attacking agent in a benzene ring substitution and also about the nature and charge of the leaving group. We can see if your idea is consistent with the relative ease of attack on methylbenzene and methoxybenzene.

## QUESTIONS

1  What polarisation of the benzene ring is required to facilitate attack by the iodine atom of iodine monochloride? The polarisation of the benzene ring caused by substituents will be indicated by the dipole moment of the molecules.

| Molecule | Direction of dipole | Dipole moment/D |
|---|---|---|
| $\bigcirc$—$OCH_3$ | $\Leftarrow\!\!\!+\!^{\delta+}$ | 1.38 |
| $\bigcirc$—$CH_3$ | $\Leftarrow\!\!\!+\!^{\delta+}$ | 0.36 |
| $\bigcirc$ | | 0.0 |

2  Do the dipole moments change in parallel with the reactivity of the benzene ring?

If you examine an electron charge cloud model of methoxybenzene you will see that the p electrons on the oxygen are available to interact with the delocalised $\pi$ electrons in the benzene ring. This electron shift is considered to be the source of the greater reactivity of methoxybenzene. Check that this theory is consistent with your hypothesis about the nature of the attacking group.

Finally, let us look at the function of the iron catalyst. Iron reacts with bromine to form iron(III) bromide:

$$2Fe + 3Br_2 \longrightarrow 2FeBr_3$$

This in turn induces polarisation in other bromine molecules:

$$FeBr_3 + Br_2 \longrightarrow Br^{\delta+}\!\!-\!Br^{\delta-}.FeBr_3$$

Reaction of this last compound with methylbenzene regenerates the iron(III) bromide, and the catalyst is therefore iron(III) bromide and not iron.

Thus, the function of the catalyst is to provide a bromine atom carrying the correct charge for attack on the benzene ring.

# Reactions of the benzene ring

The special reactions of the benzene ring can be described as electrophilic substitutions with electron-deficient reagents attacking the benzene ring. The benzene ring can donate a pair of electrons to the attacking group. This theory can be enlarged to interpret the positions on the benzene ring that are attacked, but this is not essential learning at Advanced Level.

## 1 Halogenation

Bromine, usually in the presence of a catalyst such as iron(III) bromide to make the bromine molecules more electrophilic, substitutes a bromine atom for a hydrogen atom.

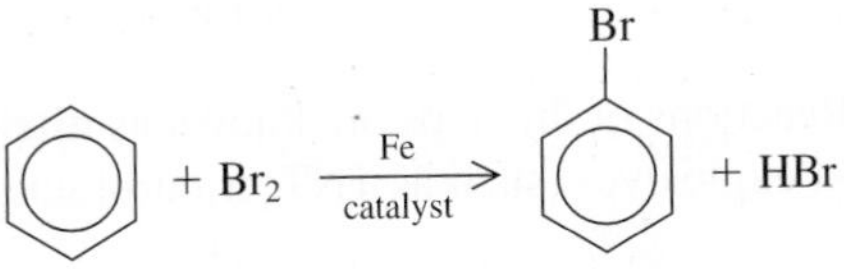

$$\text{benzene} + Br_2 \xrightarrow[\text{catalyst}]{Fe} \text{bromobenzene (Br)} + HBr$$

bromobenzene

## 2 Sulphonation

Fuming sulphuric acid, a solution of sulphur trioxide in concentrated sulphuric acid, is used for sulphonation, giving products which are often water-soluble. Refluxing for several hours is often necessary. **The electrophile is considered to be sulphur trioxide, $SO_3$.**

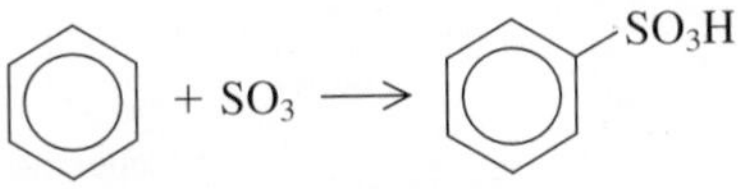

$$\text{benzene} + SO_3 \longrightarrow \text{benzenesulphonic acid } (SO_3H)$$

benzenesulphonic acid

In this reaction, benzene gives benzenesulphonic acid. This compound, like sulphuric acid, ionises in water.

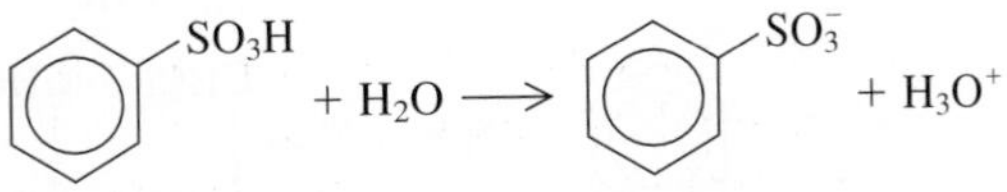

$$\text{(} SO_3H \text{)} + H_2O \longrightarrow \text{(} SO_3^- \text{)} + H_3O^+$$

Sulphonation is used in the manufacture of a wide range of substances including sulphonamide drugs, detergents, and dyestuffs.

## 3 Alkylation by the Friedel–Crafts reaction

Chloroalkanes, RCl, in the presence of aluminium chloride, will form a complex, $R^+AlCl_4^-$, in which $R^+$ acts as an electrophile (R represents any alkyl group). For example, if R is $CH_3CH_2$, the equation is

$$CH_3CH_2Cl + AlCl_3 \longrightarrow CH_3CH_2^+AlCl_4^-$$

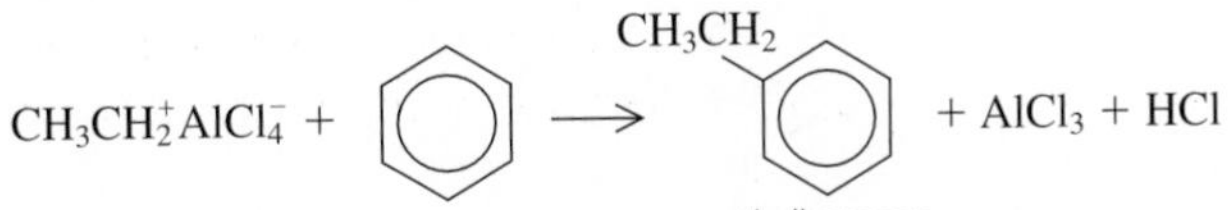

$$CH_3CH_2^+AlCl_4^- + \text{(benzene)} \longrightarrow \text{(} CH_3CH_2 \text{)} + AlCl_3 + HCl$$

ethylbenzene

**The aluminium chloride is a catalyst** so only small quantities are needed to carry out the reaction.

## 4 Nitration

Nitric acid in the presence of concentrated sulphuric acid produces **the electrophile $NO_2^+$**. The reaction of benzene with the electrophile $NO_2^+$ substitutes a nitro group, $NO_2$, for a hydrogen atom.

$$HNO_3 + 2H_2SO_4 \longrightarrow NO_2^+ + 2HSO_4^- + H_3O^+$$

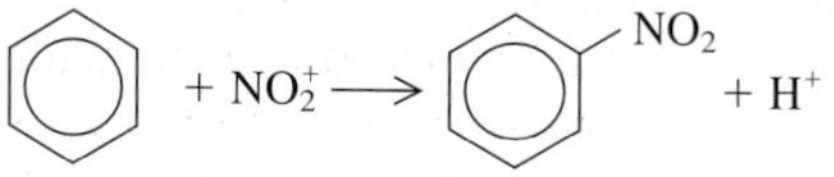

nitrobenzene

Reactions of this type are known as **nitrations**. They are used in the manufacture of explosives (such as TNT, trinitrotoluene) and dyestuffs.

## 5 Addition reactions of benzene

**Severe conditions are needed before benzene will undergo any addition reactions.** Thus hydrogen in the presence of a nickel catalyst will react with benzene to form cyclohexane. A temperature of 200 °C is necessary, and a pressure of 30 atmospheres is used to keep the benzene in the liquid phase. This reaction is the main source of the high purity cyclohexane needed for the manufacture of nylon.

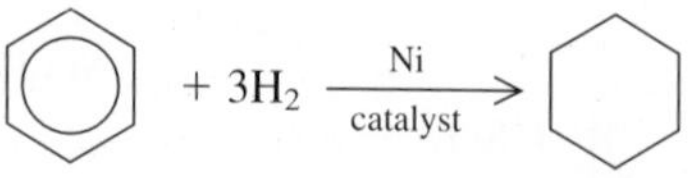

cyclohexane

Chlorine will also add to benzene when irradiated with ultraviolet light, and this is another example of a free radical reaction.

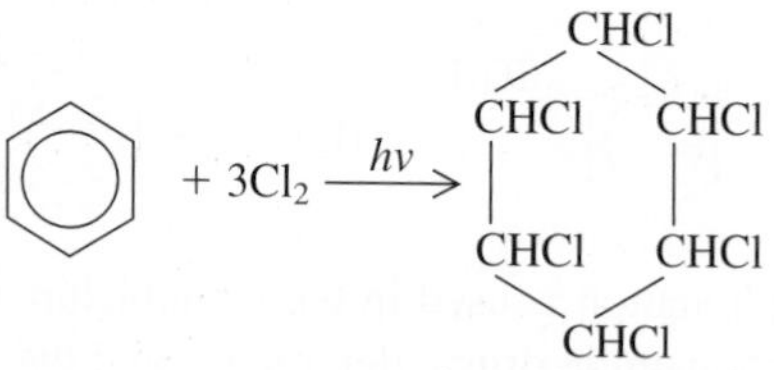

1,2,3,4,5,6-
hexachlorocyclohexane

Hexachlorocyclohexane, known as BHC, is an insecticide which has been particularly useful in controlling the devastation of crops caused by locusts.

# 12.3   Background reading: benzene

QUESTIONS

Read the passage straight through, and then more carefully, in order to answer the following questions.

1   a   Draw the displayed formula for benzene.
   b   Write a balanced equation for the dehydrogenation of cyclohexane, $C_6H_{12}$, to benzene, $C_6H_6$.
   c   Suggest ONE reason why 'platforming' might be preferred to using aluminium oxide.

2   Classify the following reactions as substitution, elimination or addition reactions.
   a   The reaction between benzene and chlorine to form 1,2,3,4,5,6-hexachlorocyclohexane.
   b   The reaction between benzene and chloroethane to form ethylbenzene.

3   Name the chemical used to produce dodecylbenzenesulphonic acid from dodecylbenzene.

4   Write a summary in continuous prose, in no more than 100 words, describing the production of benzene from petroleum.

---

Benzene was first discovered by Michael Faraday in London in 1825. By this time gas lighting was becoming common in London. The Portable Gas Company was producing gas by heating whale oil in a furnace. When they compressed the gas to put it in cylinders an oily liquid separated out. They told Faraday about this and he set about identifying the liquid. He distilled it and collected a fraction which boiled at 80 °C and condensed to a clear liquid. We now know this as benzene.

In 1834 Mitscherlich discovered that the same colourless liquid could be obtained by heating benzoic acid with lime.

In 1845 Hofmann demonstrated the presence of benzene in coal naphtha, the lowest boiling fraction obtained by the distillation of coal tar, and in 1848 Mansfield succeeded in isolating benzene from coal naphtha.

Now most benzene is produced from petroleum. Petroleum is fractionally distilled to separate the crude oil into fractions on the basis of their boiling points. A typical crude oil composition is 2% butane, 11% petrol, 14% naphtha, 17% furnace oil, 39% gas oil and 17% residue. The naphtha fraction, which contains hexane, is used to produce benzene.

The naphtha fraction is purified to remove sulphur compounds which would poison the catalyst used in the process. Sulphur compounds are removed by reduction to form hydrogen sulphide. This is known as hydrodesulphurisation (HDS) and leaves a very low concentration of sulphur in naphtha. The hydrogen sulphide produced is used to manufacture sulphur and sulphuric acid. This treatment was originally only used in the production of sulphur-free fuels but it is now used to reduce the sulphur content of most crude oil fractions.

Purified naphtha is now heated to about 500 °C. It then passes into a reactor where one of two processes may be used, depending on the catalyst.

An aluminium oxide catalyst may be used with the reactants at a pressure of 40 atmospheres. Hexane first reacts to form cyclohexane and hydrogen. Then cyclohexane is dehydrogenated to form benzene. Other aromatics (arenes) like methylbenzene and dimethylbenzenes are also produced. The mixture of products is dissolved in a suitable solvent. The aromatic products are separated from the solvent by further distillation in fractionating towers. Residual impurities are removed, for example, by passing through an active clay catalyst. A final fractionation is then used to separate and purify benzene.

The second process is called 'platforming' because it uses the metal platinum. In platforming the same chemical reactions are involved. The difference is that a platinum catalyst is used, in spite of the extra expense, and a lower pressure of 15 atmospheres is sufficient.

Benzene is the starting material for a large number of useful chemicals and materials.

The insecticide BHC, benzenehexachloride (systematic name, 1,2,3,4,5,6-hexachlorocyclohexane) is made by passing chlorine through benzene irradiated by ultraviolet light. BHC is particularly valuable in the fight against the locust.

Benzene is the starting material for the manufacture of many plastics.

By reacting benzene with chloroethane in the presence of an aluminium chloride catalyst at 80 °C, ethylbenzene is formed. This is dehydrogenated by heating to 600 °C with a zinc oxide catalyst

TOPIC 12

to produce phenylethene (styrene) which polymerises to form polystyrene.

Benzene is also the starting material for making many soapless detergents.

Benzene reacts with dodec-1-ene in the presence of a suitable catalyst to produce dodecylbenzene.

The dodecylbenzene is then sulphonated to produce dodecylbenzenesulphonic acid which can then be neutralised to produce sodium dodecylbenzenesulphonate, a biodegradable soapless detergent.

So it can be seen that from Faraday's discovery a vast and vital range of chemicals has developed.

## 12.4 Phenols

In alcohols the hydroxyl group is attached to an alkyl group. In phenols it is attached to an arene ring.

**A lone pair of electrons on the oxygen atom is now delocalised with the $\pi$ electron charge cloud of the arene ring and this results in some modification of the behaviour of both the hydroxyl group and the arene ring.** The dipole moment of the functional group is reversed by lone pair interaction with the ring.

The introduction of some $\pi$ bond character also increases the strength of the C—O bond.

---

### STUDY TASK

1 Reactions in which the O—H bond might break.
   a Do you think the displacement of the lone pair of electrons towards the ring will assist or hinder the ionisation of the O—H bond?
   b Do you think phenol might therefore be more likely to react with the strong base, sodium hydroxide, than ethanol?
   c If so, write an equation for the reaction you might expect. Do you think phenol might react with the weak base sodium carbonate?

2 Reactions in which the C—O bond might break.
   a Will the delocalisation help or hinder the breaking of this bond?
   b What kind of reagents are generally used to attack arene rings?
   c What kind of reagents are used to effect substitution reactions in alcohols?
   d Do you think that phenol is likely to participate in nucleophilic substitution reactions and elimination reactions?

3 Reactions of the arene ring.
   a What kind of reagents and what kind of reactions normally take place with arene rings?
   b Will it be easier or harder for phenol to participate in reactions of this type on account of the delocalisation of the lone pair?

## EXPERIMENT 12.4

# The reactions of the phenolic functional group

There is a microscale alternative to this experiment

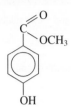

methyl 4-hydroxybenzoate

In these experiments your principal objective will be to find out how the properties of the —OH group are modified by being attached to a benzene ring. You will thus see some of the characteristic features of the chemistry of phenolic compounds.

Because of the toxic and corrosive nature of many phenols it is suggested that methyl 4-hydroxybenzoate is used as an example of a phenolic compound.

## Procedure

### 1 Solubility in water

Put about 5 cm$^3$ of water in a test tube and add a small quantity of your phenolic compound, methyl 4-hydroxybenzoate. Heat to boiling and allow to cool slowly.

✎  **In your notes:** Does the compound dissolve in water?

Test the solution with Full-range Indicator.

✎  **In your notes:** What is the pH of the solution?

Compare the results with the effect of an ethanol–water and an ethanoic acid–water mixture on Full-range Indicator.

### 2 Phenolic compounds as acids

**a**  *Action of sodium*   Place a small amount of your phenolic compound in a **dry** test tube and warm until molten. Add a small cube (2–3 mm side) of sodium (TAKE CARE: wear eye protection) and watch carefully. **Do not heat the tube continuously**. What do you observe? Dispose of the contents with care: do **not** pour down the sink in case some sodium remains but carefully add 1–2 cm$^3$ of ethanol to the **cool** test tube, wait until all bubbling has ceased, and then pour away.

✎  **In your notes:** What bond has been broken in your phenolic compound, a C—H, a C—O or an O—H bond?

Compare this reaction with that of ethanol and sodium.

**b**  *Action of sodium hydroxide*   To about 5 cm$^3$ of 2 M sodium hydroxide solution in a test tube add a small amount of your phenolic compound and warm. Compare the solubility in alkali with the solubility in water. Now add about 2 cm$^3$ of concentrated hydrochloric acid.

✎  **In your notes:** What do you observe and what does this tell you? Compare this reaction with that of ethanoic acid.

**c**  *Action of sodium carbonate*   To about 5 cm$^3$ of 1 M sodium carbonate solution add a small amount of your phenolic compound.

✎  **In your notes:** Is there an effervescence of carbon dioxide gas? Does this suggest that your phenolic compound is a strong or a weak acid?

### 3 Reaction with an organic acid

Organic acids react with alcohols to make compounds known as **esters**, which you will study in Topic 15. Organic acids also react with phenol but the rate of the reaction is extremely slow. So, in this experiment you will use ethanoic anhydride,

### SAFETY

**Full-range Indicator is flammable.**
**Ethanol is highly flammable.**
**2 M ethanoic acid is an irritant.**
**Metallic sodium is corrosive and highly flammable.**
**2 M sodium hydroxide is corrosive.**
**Concentrated hydrochloric acid is corrosive.**
**Ethanoic anhydride is corrosive and flammable; it causes severe burns and severely irritates all tissues.**
**0.05 M bromine water is harmful and an irritant.**
**2 M nitric acid is corrosive.**

which is more reactive and forms the same product. A molecule of ethanoic anhydride, $(CH_3CO)_2O$, is formed from two molecules of ethanoic acid, $CH_3CO_2H$, by the loss of a water molecule.

ethanoic acid

ethanoic anhydride

### COMMENT

The reaction between inorganic acids and bases (hydroxides), which are ionic and water soluble,

$$acid + hydroxide \longrightarrow salt + water$$

has a parallel in the reaction between organic acids and alcohols, which are covalent and mostly insoluble in water:

$$acid + alcohol \longrightarrow ester + water$$

Place about 0.5 g of your phenolic compound in a test tube and add $4\,cm^3$ of 2 M sodium hydroxide to dissolve the phenolic compound. Add $1\,cm^3$ of ethanoic anhydride, cork the test tube, and shake it for a few minutes.

An emulsion of the product should form. Cool in an ice bath to obtain the crystalline product.

### 4 Properties of the benzene ring

**a**  *Combustion*    Set fire to a small amount of your phenolic compound on a combustion spoon.

✎  **In your notes:** What sort of flame do you see? Is a similar flame obtained when ethanol and ethanoic acid are burnt?

Compare these results with your results for the combustions of alkanes in Topic 8 and arenes in section 12.2. Does the presence of a hydroxyl group alter the result?

**b**  *Bromine*    Shake a small amount of your phenolic compound with $5\,cm^3$ of water and add bromine water.

✎  **In your notes:** How readily does a reaction occur?

**c**  *Nitric acid*    To a small amount (0.04 g) of your phenolic compound add $4\,cm^3$ of 1 M nitric acid. Heat to boiling, allow to cool, then chill rapidly in an ice bath.

✎  **In your notes:** How readily do coloured products appear?

Compare the conditions you have used with those normally required for the bromination and nitration of an arene ring.

What type of reactions are these? Do these results confirm your predictions?

### COMMENT

The product from **4c** can be examined by chromatography in 1:1 hexane/ethoxyethane on a silica thin layer; view the result in ultraviolet light. Make a Risk Assessment if you attempt this experiment.

# Interpretation of the experiments: comparison of phenols with ethanol

We will consider first the reactions of phenolic compounds together with the corresponding reactions of alcohols. The simplest compound, phenol itself, is a good example.

phenol

## Solubility in water

Like ethanol, **phenol interacts with water forming hydrogen bonds** but the solubility of phenol is much less, due to the hydrocarbon arene ring. Solubility is sufficient to show acidity with Full-range Indicator.

## Reactions of the —OH group

**Phenol is a very weak acid** (it was formerly known as carbolic acid). The pH of its solution in water is only slightly less than 7, but, unlike ethanol, there is some ionisation in aqueous solution.

$$\text{C}_6\text{H}_5\text{—OH(aq)} \rightleftharpoons \text{C}_6\text{H}_5\text{—O}^-\text{(aq)} + \text{H}^+\text{(aq)}$$

It is suggested that the phenoxide ion is formed because one of the lone pairs of electrons on the oxygen atom in phenol can join the delocalised electrons of the benzene ring. In this way, the negative charge of the ion is stabilised by being spread out over the whole structure. Nevertheless the delocalisation in phenol is not as effective as the stabilisation of the charge in a carboxylic acid functional group (see Topic 15).

The ethoxide ion, $\text{C}_2\text{H}_5\text{O}^-$, cannot form a delocalised system and so cannot gain the same stability as the phenoxide ion. There is, therefore, no ionisation of ethanol in water.

Ethanol will only form the salt sodium ethoxide, $\text{C}_2\text{H}_5\text{O}^-\text{Na}^+$, by reaction with sodium metal, but the weak acid phenol is neutralised by the strong base sodium hydroxide.

$$\text{C}_6\text{H}_5\text{—OH} + \text{Na}^+\text{OH}^- \longrightarrow \text{C}_6\text{H}_5\text{—O}^-\text{Na}^+ + \text{H}_2\text{O}$$

sodium phenoxide

**Phenol is, however, too weakly acidic to react with sodium carbonate solution.**

## Reaction of the lone pair of electrons

Alcohols are themselves nucleophilic, on account of the lone pair of electrons on the oxygen atom. They will react with the electrophilic carbon atom of the carboxyl group of a carboxylic acid to make an ester. The reactions are usually performed with an acid catalyst and the overall result is the elimination of a water molecule between the two reactants.

$$\text{CH}_3\text{—C}\overset{\text{O}}{\underset{\text{OH}}{\Big<}} + \text{HOC}_2\text{H}_5 \longrightarrow \text{CH}_3\text{—C}\overset{\text{O}}{\underset{\text{OC}_2\text{H}_5}{\Big<}} + \text{H}_2\text{O}$$

carboxylic acid        alcohol                    ester              water

The interaction of a lone pair of electrons on the oxygen atom of phenol with the benzene ring means that phenol forms esters much less readily than ethanol. Instead of using a carboxylic acid with an acid catalyst, as in the case of ethanol, the more reactive acid anhydride is used. In the case of phenol, the reactivity of phenol itself can be enhanced by the addition of sodium hydroxide to form the phenoxide ion which is a more reactive nucleophile.

ethanoic anhydride → phenyl ethanoate

These reactions will be used in section 12.5.

## Reactions of the C—O bond

**a** **Phenol will not undergo nucleophilic substitution of the hydroxyl group to form halogenoarenes,** whereas ethanol readily reacts with the nucleophile HBr to form bromoethane.

$$CH_3CH_2OH + HBr \longrightarrow CH_3CH_2Br + H_2O$$

In phenol the interaction of the lone pair of electrons on the oxygen atom with the benzene ring makes it more difficult to break the C—O bond.

The elimination of water from phenol would involve breaking a C—H bond as well as the C—O bond and the introduction of a further π bond into the arene ring. This reaction does not take place.

**b** Oxidation of the hydroxyl group in phenol to a carbonyl group cannot be carried out because that would involve disruption of the stable benzene ring.

## Phenol as an arene

**The delocalisation of electrons from the oxygen in phenol into the benzene ring makes phenol more susceptible than benzene to substitution reactions with electrophilic reagents such as bromine and nitric acid.** The reactions occur so readily that multiple substitution often occurs.

2,4,6-tribromophenol

2-nitrophenol and 4-nitrophenol

2,4,6-trinitrophenol
(picric acid)

BACKGROUND

Phenol was the first antiseptic substance to be used in surgery, by Lister in 1857. Although it limits the growth of bacteria in open wounds, it also makes the wounds difficult to heal. The antibacterial properties of phenol can be improved by chlorination and at the same time the healing properties of the antiseptic are also improved. Dettol and TCP are examples of this development from Lister's original discovery.

4-chloro-3,5-dimethylphenol (Dettol)          2,4,6-trichlorophenol (TCP)

The effectiveness of germicides relative to phenol in killing the bacterium *Salmonella typhosa* are given below.

| Germicide | Relative effectiveness |
| --- | --- |
| Phenol | 1 |
| TCP | 23 |
| Dettol | 280 |

In addition to its use for antiseptics, phenol was historically important as a component of carbolic soaps in the nineteenth century and in the manufacture of plastics such as Bakelite in the twentieth century.

The major industrial uses of phenol at the present time include the manufacture of synthetic polymers or fibres, and non-ionic detergents.

# 12.5   Aspirin

Compounds like 2-hydroxybenzoic acid in which the hydroxyl —OH is attached to a benzene ring are phenolic compounds.

## EXPERIMENT 12.5

## Preparations using 2-hydroxybenzoic acid

There is a microscale alternative to the first part of this experiment

2-hydroxybenzoic acid (salicylic acid) can be converted by straightforward reactions into two products, both of which find application as medicines. Ethanoylation of the phenolic group produces aspirin

2-hydroxybenzoic    ethanoic                    aspirin
acid                anhydride

and methylation of the carboxylic group produces oil of wintergreen

$$\underset{\text{methanol}}{\text{(CO}_2\text{H, OH)} + \text{CH}_3\text{OH} \xrightarrow{\text{catalyst}} \underset{\text{oil of wintergreen}}{\text{(CO}_2\text{CH}_3\text{, OH)}} + \text{H}_2\text{O}}$$

Aspirin is described as having analgesic (pain killing), anti-inflammatory, and antipyretic (fever reducing) actions. Oil of wintergreen has the same properties, but is applied as an ointment for the relief of pain in lumbago, sciatica, and rheumatism as the oil is readily absorbed through the skin.

The preparation of aspirin uses the same compounds as the industrial method of production.

## Procedure

### 1 Preparation of aspirin

Add to a $50\,\text{cm}^3$ pear-shaped flask 2.0 g of 2-hydroxybenzoic acid and $4\,\text{cm}^3$ of ethanoic anhydride.

To this mixture add 5 drops of 85% phosphoric(V) acid and swirl to mix. Fit the flask with a reflux condenser and heat the mixture on a boiling water bath for about 5 minutes. Without cooling the mixture, carefully add $2\,\text{cm}^3$ of water in one portion down the condenser. The excess ethanoic anhydride will hydrolyse and the contents of the flask will boil.

When the vigorous reaction has ended, pour the mixture into $40\,\text{cm}^3$ of cold water in a $100\,\text{cm}^3$ beaker, stir and rub the sides of the beaker with a stirring rod if necessary to induce crystallisation and, finally, allow the mixture to stand in an ice bath to complete crystallisation.

Collect the product by suction filtration and wash it with a little water. The product should be recrystallised from hot water and its melting point determined.

 **In your notes:** What other compounds might have been used to prepare aspirin? Compare their cost with the cost of the compounds actually used. Why do you think ethanoic anhydride and phosphoric(V) acid are used? What further reaction do you think would be necessary to obtain 'soluble aspirin' from aspirin (2-ethanoyloxybenzoic acid)?

### 2 Determination of the melting point

This method is a general one that can be used to determine the melting point of any solid organic compound.

Put a sample into a small thin walled capillary tube sealed at one end, and by gentle tapping, or rubbing with the milled edge of a coin, transfer it to the closed end. Slowly heat the tube in the apparatus provided so as to maintain an even rise of temperature. Watch the crystals in the melting-point tube carefully, and the moment they melt, note the temperature.

Repeat the process with a fresh melting-point tube containing another portion of the compound, in order to obtain a more accurate value for the melting point. The temperature may now be raised rapidly to within $10\,°C$ of the melting point previously obtained, but must then be raised very slowly (about $2\,°C$ rise per minute) until the crystals melt. Note the temperature at which the crystals first melt and also the temperature at which melting is complete. For pure substances these temperatures are close together and the melting point is called 'sharp'.

Figure 12.4 **An early aspirin bottle**

**SAFETY** !

Ethanoic anhydride is corrosive and flammable.
2-hydroxybenzoic acid is harmful.
Phosphoric(V) acid is corrosive.

If the compound under examination is recrystallised and dried, and the melting point again determined, it may be a little higher than before. This is because the melting point of a pure compound is always lowered by the presence of impurities. The compound can be made completely pure by repeated recrystallisation until the melting point is constant.

### 3 Preparation of oil of wintergreen

Add to a $50 \, \text{cm}^3$ pear-shaped flask 9 g of 2-hydroxybenzoic acid, $15 \, \text{cm}^3$ of methanol, and $2 \, \text{cm}^3$ of concentrated sulphuric acid. Fit the flask with a reflux condenser and boil the mixture for about an hour.

Cool the mixture to room temperature and pour it into a separating funnel that contains $30 \, \text{cm}^3$ of cold water. Rinse the flask with $15 \, \text{cm}^3$ of ethyl ethanoate (an organic solvent) and add this to the separating funnel.

Mix the contents of the separating funnel and allow them to settle; if an emulsion forms try adding a little more solvent. Run the lower aqueous layer into a conical flask.

**SAFETY**

2-hydroxybenzoic acid is harmful.
Methanol is toxic and highly flammable.
Concentrated sulphuric acid is corrosive.
Ethyl ethanoate is highly flammable.

**COMMENT**

Always run layers from a separating funnel into conical flasks. It is easy to make a mistake and pour away the layer you want to keep.

Wash the organic solvent extract in the separating funnel with $30 \, \text{cm}^3$ of 0.5 M aqueous sodium carbonate, carefully releasing the pressure in the separating funnel frequently as there is likely to be considerable evolution of carbon dioxide. Separate the aqueous and organic layers by running into separate small conical flasks. The aqueous layer can be discarded.

Dry the organic solvent extract with solid anhydrous sodium sulphate. Leave to dry for about 10 minutes while you set up an apparatus for distillation. Then remove the sodium sulphate by filtering, using a plug of cottonwool.

Remove the organic solvent by distillation (ethyl ethanoate boils at $77 \, ^\circ\text{C}$). Complete the distillation, collecting the distillate boiling above $220 \, ^\circ\text{C}$ as oil of wintergreen, methyl 2-hydroxybenzoate.

✎ **In your notes:** Note the characteristic odour of your product and compare it with a sample of oil of wintergreen.

What is the reason for adding an organic solvent to the reaction mixture?

What is the reason for washing the organic solvent layer with sodium carbonate solution?

**STUDY TASK**

Examine the infrared spectra of 2-hydroxybenzoic acid, aspirin, and oil of wintergreen (see figure 12.5, overleaf) and account for the major differences in the spectra.

Figure 12.5a  The infrared spectrum of 2-hydroxybenzoic acid

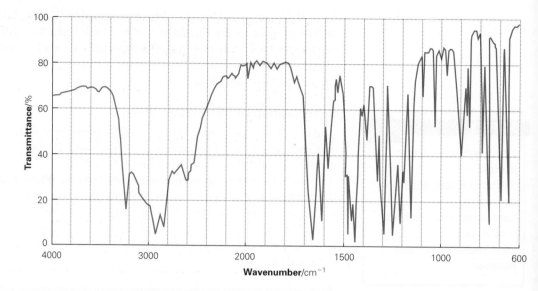

Figure 12.5b  The infrared spectrum of aspirin

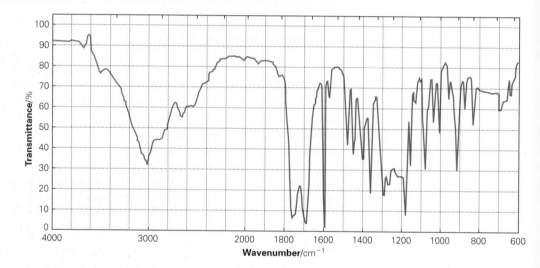

Figure 12.5c  The infrared spectrum of oil of wintergreen

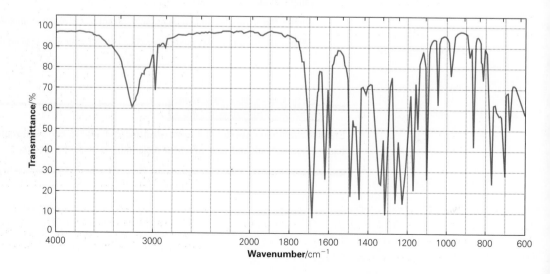

# 12.6 Background reading: aspirin, from herbal remedy to modern drug

## QUESTIONS

Read the passage, then answer the following questions.

1 What confused the understanding of the use of herbal remedies?

2 What is the active chemical ingredient in the bark and leaves of willow and poplar?

3 What unsound reasoning led Edmund Stone to the use of willow bark as a treatment?

4 Classify the reaction used to make aspirin in the Hofmann process.

5 Write a summary in continuous prose, in no more than 100 words, describing Kolbe's synthesis of 2-hydroxybenzoic acid. Your summary should include a classification of the reactions involved and not include formulae or equations.

Herbal remedies are included in the earliest medical writings from ancient Egypt and ancient China but the use of medicines was confused until quite recent times by the inclusion of aspects of magic and religion, together with theories that we now know were unsound. Nevertheless, there were many sound remedies, some better known to peasants than to the medical profession, and it has become common practice for the pharmaceutical industry to check all 'old wives' tales' for possible validity (see figure 12.6). For example, the dried roots of the *Rauwolfia* shrub had been used in Indian folk medicine for over 2000 years but were virtually unknown to Western medical science until 1952; now an alkaloid, reserpine, is extracted from the plant and used in the treatment of hypertension, making it one of the most effective drugs for the relief of high blood pressure.

The commonest drug of all, aspirin, has a typical history. The use of aspirin as a drug derives from the use of the bark and leaves of willow and poplar trees in a variety of ancient remedies. The active ingredient of the bark and leaves is salicin, the glucoside of 2-hydroxybenzoic acid (salicylic acid).

salicin

2-hydroxybenzoic acid

This was not known until 1826 although the bark and leaves had been in use for over 2000 years. From the writings of Hippocrates, the ancient Greek 'Father of Medicine', to those of the Renaissance, willow and poplar extracts had been recommended

Figure 12.6 This 16th century woodcut illustrates the medieval method of preparing drugs. On the right a woman is selecting herbs; at the bottom left an apothecary is distilling a herbal extract; at the top left a physician is inspecting a herbal extract

**Figure 12.7 Willow bark, used to treat 'fevers'**

as remedies in a variety of illnesses – for the eye diseases, for the removal of corns, as a diuretic, and in the treatment of sciatica and gout – although such treatments were mainly based on false hopes. In 1763, the Revd. Edmund Stone of Chipping Norton was the first to describe the value of a willow bark in treating fevers. Even he applied this treatment on the basis of false reasons:

'As this tree delights in a moist or wet soil, where agues (fevers) chiefly abound, I could not help applying the general maxim, that many remedies lie not far off from their causes.'

Natural extract of willow bark was replaced after 1874 by a synthetic process developed by the German chemist, Kolbe:

$$\underset{\text{phenol}}{\text{OH}} \xrightarrow{\text{NaOH}} \underset{\substack{\text{sodium} \\ \text{phenoxide}}}{\text{O}^-\text{Na}^+} \xrightarrow{\text{CO}_2} \underset{}{\text{O}^-\text{Na}^+ \text{CO}_2^-\text{Na}^+} \xrightarrow{\text{H}^+} \underset{\substack{\text{2-hydroxy-} \\ \text{benzoic acid}}}{\text{OH} \quad \text{CO}_2\text{H}}$$

It was also about this time that the value of willow bark in treating rheumatism was reported by doctors. Although this was new to European medicine, it seems that the Hottentots in Africa had long been familiar with the remedy. However, prolonged treatment of rheumatism by 2-hydroxybenzoic acid has unpleasant side effects and the German chemist, F. Hofmann, supplied his father with a variety of derivatives to try for his rheumatism. This led in a short time to the recognition of the merits of 2-ethanoyloxybenzoic acid (aspirin) and its marketing by the Bayer company in 1899.

The synthetic process developed by Hofmann is still used to manufacture aspirin today, and is based on the reaction between 2-hydroxybenzoic acid and ethanoic anhydride.

$$\underset{\substack{\text{2-hydroxybenzoic} \\ \text{acid}}}{\overset{\text{CO}_2\text{H}}{\bigcirc}\text{—OH}} + \underset{\substack{\text{ethanoic} \\ \text{anhydride}}}{(\text{CH}_3\text{CO})_2\text{O}} \xrightarrow{\text{catalyst}} \underset{\text{aspirin}}{\overset{\text{CO}_2\text{H}}{\bigcirc}\text{—O}_2\text{C—CH}_3} + \underset{\substack{\text{ethanoic} \\ \text{acid}}}{\text{CH}_3\text{CO}_2\text{H}}$$

Aspirin is one of the most widely used medicines, with 4000 million tablets produced each year in the United Kingdom. It is mainly taken for feverish colds, headaches, and rheumatism. It has also been found that people at risk from heart attacks and some strokes benefit from a low, regular dose of aspirin.

## Disadvantages of aspirin

Aspirin is not without its hazards; some 200 people a year die of aspirin poisoning due to deliberate or accidental overdose, with children under 5 years forming a large proportion of those who die accidentally through eating the tablets. And it has been recognised that aspirin causes internal bleeding. Consumption of aspirin causes a loss of blood of up to 6 cm$^3$ a day in 70% of patients examined and may be the precipitating factor in 50% of patients with gastroduodenal haemorrhage. It has been suggested, since safer drugs are available for headaches and feverish colds, that aspirin should only be available on prescription. And aspirin is not suitable for children under 12 years old.

Paracetamol is one possible alternative to aspirin. It is both a useful pain-reducing and fever-reducing drug but lacks some of the side effects shown by aspirin. The physiologically active compound is 4-aminophenol but the potential toxicity of the —NH$_2$ group must be reduced by conversion to an ethanoyl derivative. An overdose of paracetamol can cause fatal liver damage.

$$\underset{\text{paracetamol}}{\overset{\text{OH}}{\underset{\text{NHCOCH}_3}{\bigcirc}}}$$

## KEY SKILLS

### Communication

This topic includes complex lines of reasoning and information in text and images. Studying this topic will help you to develop your skills in selecting and synthesising information. To develop or demonstrate your communication skills you might choose to organise the material in the topic into a concise and coherent summary which you would find helpful for revision.

## TOPIC REVIEW

**1   List key words or terms with definitions where necessary**

Illustrate the following with **examples** wherever possible:

- infrared spectrum
- delocalisation
- arene, benzene, phenyl group, phenol
- Friedel–Crafts reaction
- electrophilic substitution
- ester.

**2   Summarise the key principles as simply as possible**

Draw **summary charts** or 'spider diagrams' of the **reactions of benzene** and **phenol** which include **reactants** (with formulae), **conditions**, **type of reaction** and **products** (with formulae).

You should know:

- how delocalisation influences the behaviour of benzene and phenol
- how the reactions of the arenes compare and contrast with those of the alkanes and alkenes
- how the reactions of phenol compare with those of alcohols.

# REVIEW QUESTIONS

✳ Indicates that the *Book of data* is needed.

**12.1**   Write down (or draw, if appropriate) the following formulae of benzene:

a    empirical formula                                                                            (1)
b    molecular formula                                                                           (1)
c    structural formula (use a circle to represent delocalised electrons)    (1)
d    displayed formula (use a circle as in c).                                            (1)

**(4 marks)**

**12.2**   On the displayed formula you drew in question **12.1 d**, mark the C—C—C
and the H—C—C bond angles.                                                           **(2 marks)**

✳ **12.3**   a    Draw the Kekulé formula for benzene, showing all the atoms and all the
bonds.                                                                                                  (1)
b    Mark on your Kekulé formula the carbon–carbon bond lengths you would
expect if this formula were correct.                                                      (2)
c    How do the bond lengths you have suggested in b differ from those obtained
experimentally since Kekulé's work was published?                            (1)

**(4 marks)**

✳ **12.4**   a    Copy and complete the following table showing the wavenumbers of the
principal peaks in the infrared spectra of cyclohexane, cyclohexene and
benzene (use table 3.3 in the *Book of data*).                                     (8)

| | cyclohexane 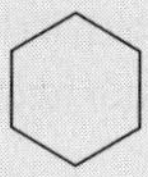 | cyclohexene 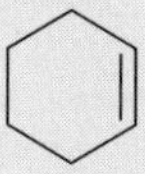 | benzene 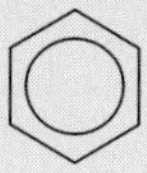 |
|---|---|---|---|
| C—H stretching/cm$^{-1}$ | | | |
| C—H bending/cm$^{-1}$ | | | |
| C=C stretching/cm$^{-1}$ | | | |

b    How does the infrared spectrum of benzene support the modern view of the
structure of the compound rather than the Kekulé formula?                (2)

**(10 marks)**

**12.5**   The standard enthalpy change of hydrogenation of ethene, $CH_2=CH_2$, is
$-120 \text{ kJ mol}^{-1}$ whilst that of benzene, $C_6H_6$, is $-208 \text{ kJ mol}^{-1}$.

a    Write balanced equations, including state symbols, for the two reactions.  (2)
b    Explain why the enthalpy change of hydrogenation of benzene is not three
times that of ethene.                                                                           (2)

**(4 marks)**

**12.6** Copy and complete the following table showing the products of some reactions of benzene.

| Product | Formula of product | Reagent | Conditions | Type of reaction |
|---|---|---|---|---|
| Nitrobenzene | | Nitric acid, $HNO_3$ | Conc $HNO_3$ + conc $H_2SO_4$ | Electrophilic substitution |
| Chlorobenzene | | | | |
| | 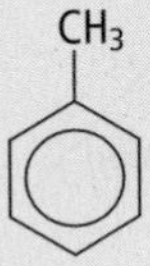 CH₃ ⬡ | | | |
| | | Hydrogen, $H_2$ | | |

**(13 marks)**

**12.7** The Friedel–Crafts reaction is used for alkylation of the benzene ring.

a   What is meant by the term 'alkylation'? (2)

b   What type of reaction (addition, substitution etc.) is alkylation? (1)

c   What reagents and conditions would be needed to convert benzene into the following compounds?

  i  $CH_3$—$CH$—$CH_3$ ⬡

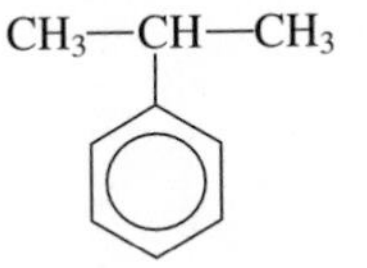

  ii  $CH_2$—$CH_2$—$CH_3$ ⬡

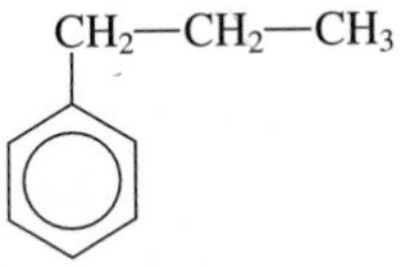

(3)

d   What are the molecular formulae of the two compounds in c? (2)

**(8 marks)**

**12.8** a   Draw the displayed formula of phenol, using a circle to represent delocalised electrons. (1)

b   Draw a 'dot and cross' diagram of the phenol molecule, again using the circle to represent delocalised electrons. (2)

c   On your displayed formula, mark the C—O—H and C—C—O bond angles. (1)

**(4 marks)**

**12.9**   Which of the following compounds are phenols? Justify your answer.

a   CH$_3$

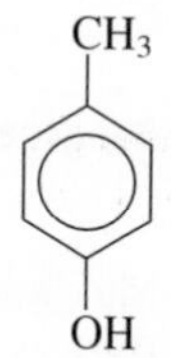

b   CH$_2$OH

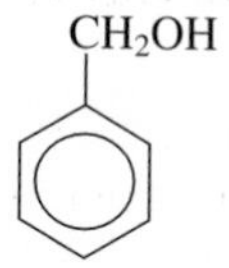

c   OH

OH

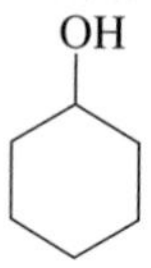

**(4 marks)**

**12.10**   Give the reagents and conditions needed to carry out reactions 1–5 of phenol shown below.

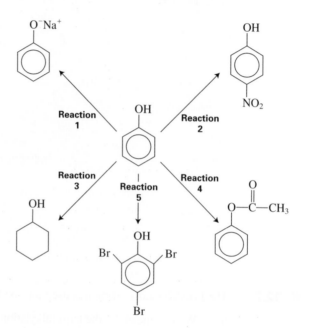

**(10 marks)**

**12.11**   The formula of aspirin can be drawn in the following way:

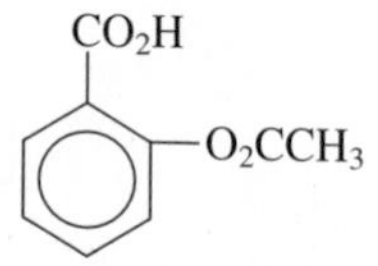

CO$_2$H

O$_2$CCH$_3$

a   Draw the displayed formula of aspirin. (The benzene ring may be drawn as shown.)   (2)

b   What is the molecular formula of aspirin?   (1)

c   Draw the displayed formula and give the name of the reagent which is used to make aspirin from 2-hydroxybenzoic acid.   (3)

d   What type of reaction occurs in c? Justify your answer.   (2)

**(8 marks)**

# EXAMINATION QUESTIONS

Questions of the summary and comprehension type are found in the background reading sections (sections 12.3 and 12.6).

**12.12**  Some important reactions of benzene can be summarised in a flow chart:

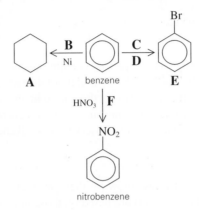

**a**  Name substances **A** to **F**.  (6)

**b  i**  The reactions to form **E** and nitrobenzene are electrophilic substitutions. Give the formula and charge of the electrophile in each reaction.  (2)

  **ii**  In the reaction to form nitrobenzene it is important to keep the temperature below 55 °C. Suggest a reason for this.  (1)

  **iii**  Suggest ONE use for compounds formed by the nitration of arenes.  (1)

**c  i**  State the conditions for the reaction to form **A** from benzene.  (2)

  **ii**  Benzene reacts with chlorine to form 1,2,3,4,5,6-hexachlorocyclohexane, which has been used as an insecticide.
Write a balanced equation for this reaction.  (1)

**(13 marks)**

**12.13**  Three reactions of methylbenzene can be summarised on a flow chart.

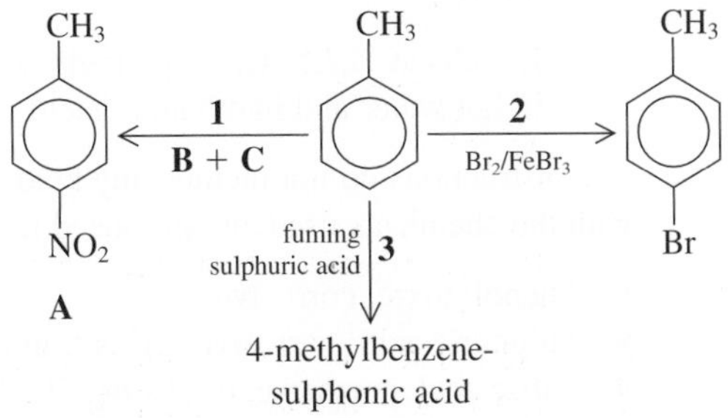

CH$_3$    CH$_3$    CH$_3$

**1**    **2**
**B + C**    Br$_2$/FeBr$_3$

NO$_2$    fuming **3**    Br
sulphuric acid
**A**

4-methylbenzene-
sulphonic acid

**a**  Name substance **A** and the reagents **B** and **C**.  (3)

**b  i**  Draw the structural formula for 4-methylbenzenesulphonic acid.  (1)

  **ii**  State the formula of the molecule which attacks the benzene ring in **Reaction 3**.  (1)

  **iii**  Name an important group of industrial products that is made from benzenesulphonic acids.  (1)

**c** **i** Write an equation to show how the catalyst iron(III) bromide induces polarisation of a bromine molecule in **Reaction 2**. (1)

**ii** Classify **Reaction 2** as fully as possible. (2)

**d** A student suggested making 4-methylcyclohexanol by the following route:

**i** Suggest reagents and conditions for each step. (4)

**ii** In practice, the final yield of 4-methylcyclohexanol made by this route is rather low. This is thought to be due to the formation of some 4-methylcyclohexene. Suggest a chemical test and the colour change you would expect to observe for an alkene such as 4-methylcyclohexene. (2)

**(15 marks)**

**12.14** The instructions below for the conversion of phenol to 2,4,6-trinitrophenol (often called picric acid) are based on those in an old textbook of practical organic chemistry. Read the instructions carefully and then answer the questions which follow.

**Under no circumstances should this preparation be carried out in the laboratory.**

10 g of phenol are dissolved in 20 g of concentrated sulphuric acid by warming in a porcelain basin. The product is cooled and then added to 50 g of concentrated nitric acid in a 500 $cm^3$ round-bottomed flask. A considerable amount of heat is generated during this operation and oxides of nitrogen are abundantly evolved. After the reaction has moderated, the mixture is heated at 100 °C for 2 hours. On cooling, picric acid separates as a yellow crystalline mass. The liquid is diluted with water and the crystals are filtered off at the pump, well washed with cold water and recrystallised from hot water, the picric acid then being obtained in the form of yellow needles.

It melts at 122.5 °C, is sparingly soluble in cold water, but dissolves readily in hot water and in ethanol. Yield, 15 g.

The instructions do not include any kind of risk assessment but hazards associated with the chemicals used and produced in the experiment are as follows:

- Phenol: toxic, corrosive
- Sulphuric acid: corrosive, irritant; more than 1.5 M can cause severe burns
- Nitric acid: corrosive, oxidising; 20–70% causes severe burns
- Oxides of nitrogen: very toxic by inhalation and skin contact
- Picric acid: explosive when dry; toxic; contact may cause yellowing of the skin.

a  Draw the structural formula for 2,4,6-trinitrophenol.    (1)

b  State TWO specific safety precautions you would take if performing this experiment, giving reasons for the precautions you suggest.    (2)

c  Draw a labelled diagram of the apparatus you would use for 'heating the mixture at 100 °C for 2 hours'.    (2)

d  Draw a labelled diagram of the apparatus you would use to 'filter off the crystals at the pump'.    (2)

e  Explain why recrystallisation is necessary and how it would be carried out.    (4)

f  The worker is expected to obtain a yield of 15 g. What percentage is this of the theoretical yield?
(Molar masses: phenol = 94 g mol$^{-1}$; picric acid = 229 g mol$^{-1}$)    (2)

**(13 marks)**

# TOPIC 13

# Entropy

Figure 13.1 **Demolishing a building in Newark, New Jersey, USA. The explosion which started the collapse is a spontaneous change even though a detonator was needed to set it off.**

Figure 13.2 **Drilling for oil: gas flare behind protective water curtain. Combustion is a spontaneous reaction.**

You may not have thought about it so far, but most of the chemical reactions you have met have taken place readily. The laboratory gas, once lit, will burn on and on, as does the surplus gas at oil fields; as soon as a torch is switched on, the chemicals in its batteries will react to produce an electric current.

Sometimes addition of a catalyst has speeded up a reaction. Sometimes we have heated the reagents to start the reaction, but once started the reaction continued until the reagents were used up, without any further intervention by us. The reactions all 'go'.

There are many examples of events that happen naturally: cyclists can freewheel downhill; ice-cream melts in a warm room; the smell of cooking spreads through a building as the molecules diffuse naturally by their random chance mixing with the air.

**Changes that tend to 'go' naturally are called spontaneous changes**; once started they will go. A spontaneous change can be quite slow, spontaneity is not a matter of speed.

The reason why a chemical reaction 'goes' can be stated in a very short principle:

**A reaction occurs when it is overwhelmingly probable by chance alone.**

Chance in chemistry operates predictably and quantitatively, which is extremely helpful. By knowing the rules by which chance operates in chemistry it is possible to tell whether a reaction will 'go' or not. There is no gamble; if the probability is favourable then provided the conditions are right the product can be made.

In this topic you will be introduced to:

- what is meant by order and disorder in chemical reactions
- entropy as a way of describing the extent of disorder
- the importance of considering both the system and the surroundings (see Topic 5) when thinking about entropy changes.

# 13.1 How does chance operate in chemistry?

**If energy is to be shared by some molecules it will be shared, and in all possible ways.** Take a very simple case: an assembly of vibrating atoms making up a crystal. Assume that each vibrating atom has one quantum of energy. This makes things simple and calculations show that it is a fairly accurate assumption at room temperature.

Start with a system of 2 atoms and 2 quanta of energy: there are only 3 ways of arranging the quanta (see figure 13.3). For 3 atoms sharing 3 quanta there are 10 ways. Use figure 13.3 as a guide to draw your own diagram for 3 atoms sharing 3 quanta.

What about a system with a larger number of atoms and quanta? 36 atoms sharing 36 quanta will do. An arrangement that only exists in one way is to have one quantum on each atom. Rearranging the energy by chance – on the throw of dice – will eventually produce an arrangement that can exist in many ways (see figure 13.4).

The energy goes on moving around but the pattern of numbers of atoms with different energy stays much the same (see figure 13.5). This makes the pattern a *probable* arrangement whereas the initial arrangement can be described as *improbable* (it will only occur very rarely as the quanta move around).

The number of ways of arranging the energy will be many, many more if we have more energy levels for each atom than the simple vibrating atoms of our example.

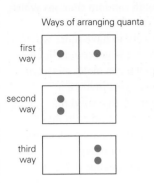

Ways of arranging quanta

first way

second way

third way

**Figure 13.3 Ways of arranging quanta (·) on atoms (□)**

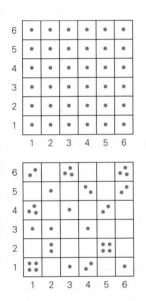

**Figure 13.4 The initial arrangement and a more probable arrangement, after 100 moves**

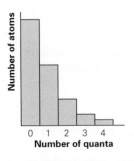

**Figure 13.5 The pattern of atoms with differing numbers of quanta**

## BACKGROUND INFORMATION FOR MATHEMATICIANS

To take our example any further we need a general mathematical formula. One is available that you may meet in a mathematics course. Using $W$ to represent the number of ways of arranging the energy, $N$ to represent the number of atoms, and $q$ to represent the number of quanta of energy, the formula is:

$$W = \frac{(N + q - 1)!}{(N - 1)! \, q!}$$

So that for three atoms sharing three quanta of energy:

$$W = \frac{(3 + 3 - 1)!}{(3 - 1)! \, 3!} = \frac{5!}{2! \, 3!} = \frac{5 \times 4 \times 3 \times 2 \times 1}{2 \times 1 \times 3 \times 2 \times 1} = 10$$

You can check this calculation and try out others with even larger numbers of atoms and quanta by using the factorial button, $x!$, on your calculator.

For 100 atoms sharing 100 quanta:

$$W = \frac{199!}{99! \, 100!} = 8 \times 10^{59}$$

A chemical system behaves in the same way: it will change from a system with a limited number of ways of arranging its energy to a system with the most ways of arranging that energy. This will happen inevitably through random changes which occur by chance. The change occurs spontaneously.

Can we predict what type of chemical system is likely to have more ways of arranging its energy than another type? The answer is that it is not too difficult to make shrewd predictions about some systems. For example, gas molecules can move from place to place, vibrate and rotate. All these energies involve a considerable number of quantised energy levels. By contrast, in a solid the particles will be restricted to mainly vibrational energy levels. And a liquid or solution is likely to have an intermediate number of ways of arranging its energy.

So chemical reactions which involve the spreading out of energy, as crystalline solids change to liquids or solutions, are probable changes. Reactions which produce gases are even more probable.

**The trend is from order to disorder.**

'Order' means few arrangements, 'disorder' means many arrangements. Let us see how these ideas might apply to some real reactions.

---

**EXPERIMENT 13.1**

# Chance in chemical reactions

You are going to examine some chemical reactions. You are asked to estimate whether the possible arrangements of the product particles represent a more ordered or a less ordered system than the original reagents. You should also classify the reactions as exothermic or endothermic.

An increase in temperature is a quite common observation when a chemical change occurs, but decreases in temperature during spontaneous reactions are less frequently observed. Some of the examples are unusual but thinking about unusual examples is often the making or breaking of a chemical theory.

**SAFETY**

Ammonium nitrate is oxidising.
Ethanoic acid is flammable and corrosive.
Ammonium carbonate is harmful.
Magnesium ribbon is highly flammable.
Ammonium chloride is harmful.
Sodium nitrite and soluble barium salts are toxic.

## Procedure

### 1 Dissolving

Measure 5 cm³ of water into a test tube and record the temperature of the water. Add 5 g of solid ammonium nitrate, stir and note the change in temperature as the ammonium nitrate dissolves.

 **In your notes:** Consider the surroundings. Did the surroundings gain or lose energy as the chemicals returned to room temperature after dissolving? Consider the ammonium nitrate–water system. Are the particles in ammonium nitrate solid, $NH_4^+ NO_3^-$, likely to be arranged in an orderly or disorderly way?

Are the particles in a solution normally arranged in a regular or a random way?

### 2 A neutralisation reaction

Measure 5 cm³ of pure ethanoic acid into a test tube and record the temperature of the acid. Add 3 g of solid ammonium carbonate, stir and note the change in temperature as carbon dioxide is produced.

 **In your notes:** Write a balanced equation for the reaction.

Consider the surroundings. Did the surroundings gain or lose energy as the chemicals returned to room temperature?

Consider the acid–base system. Do you think the product particles can be classified as more or less ordered than the reagent particles?

## 3 A combustion reaction

Hold a short length of magnesium ribbon in crucible tongs and light it in a Bunsen burner flame. CAUTION: Do not look directly at the burning magnesium. Does it continue to burn when removed from the flame?

✎ **In your notes:** Write a balanced equation for the reaction. Is the reaction exothermic or endothermic?

Do you think the product, ionic $Mg^{2+}O^{2-}$, can be classified as more or less ordered than the reagents, metallic Mg and gaseous $O_2$?

## 4 A redox reaction

Mix roughly equal small amounts of solid ammonium chloride, $NH_4Cl$, and solid sodium nitrite, $NaNO_2$, in a small beaker. Add sufficient water to cover the solids and warm gently to dissolve them. Remove the Bunsen burner when an effervescence starts.

✎ **In your notes:** What are the products? Hint: the gas evolved is inert.

What changes are occurring in this reaction?

Why is this reaction classified as a redox reaction?

## 5 An acid–base reaction

Mix 3 g of solid hydrated barium hydroxide, $Ba(OH)_2.8H_2O$, with 1 g of solid ammonium chloride, $NH_4Cl$. Note the temperature change.

✎ **In your notes:** What changes are occurring in this reaction?

Why is this reaction classified as an acid–base reaction?

## 6 A thermal decomposition

Heat a small amount of zinc carbonate. Test for the evolution of carbon dioxide and try to estimate the temperature at which decomposition can be detected.

✎ **In your notes:** What changes are occurring in this reaction?

## QUESTIONS

1   Draw up a table in your notes listing all the experiments and classify them as either tending to go or not taking place **at room temperature** (spontaneous or non-spontaneous). Reactions which are slow at room temperature but are helped by a catalyst or 'started off' by heating can be classified as spontaneous. Reactions which only go when **kept** at a high temperature should be classified as non-spontaneous.

2   Write a description of the spontaneous changes, comparing the degree of order in the reagents to the degree of order in the products.

3   State whether energy is transferred to the surroundings (an exothermic reaction) or to the reagents – the system (an endothermic reaction).

4   Can you find a pattern that describes all the spontaneous changes, or are there exceptions to any rule you propose?

# Counting numbers of ways

The importance of energy distribution as the key to whether changes are spontaneous or not was first recognised by the German physicist Clausius and he introduced the term **entropy** as the unit by which energy distribution is measured.

But it was the Austrian scientist Boltzmann who worked out how to convert the **number of ways** atoms can share energy into **entropy units**. For an ideal gas it is possible to count the number of ways, but what matters most to chemists are *changes* in the number of ways and measuring the amount of change in convenient units.

**Boltzmann demonstrated that**

$$S = k \ln W$$

**where $S$ is called the entropy of a substance**
 **$k$ is the Boltzmann constant**
 **$\ln W$ is the natural logarithm of the number of possible arrangements**

By making entropy, $S$, proportional to the natural logarithm of the number of ways, Boltzmann made the amount of entropy *directly proportional* to the amount of substance in a system. Thus doubling the number of moles of a substance doubles $\ln W$ and doubles the amount of entropy.

The constant, $k$, is made equal to $1.381 \times 10^{-23}$ J K$^{-1}$ so that $\ln W$ is converted to joules and changes in entropy are made *inversely proportional* to temperature (as was deduced from experimental results). When calculating entropies chemists consider moles of substances.

**The units of entropy per mole are therefore J mol$^{-1}$ K$^{-1}$.**

The relationship gives manageable values for entropies. For example, for a mole of atoms sharing $10^{23}$ quanta the entropy is

$$S = 11.4 \, \text{J mol}^{-1} \, \text{K}^{-1}$$

For a particular physical or chemical situation, the greater the number of possible arrangements, $W$, the more likely the situation is to come about. For any physical or chemical change which happens spontaneously, of its own accord, $W$ must increase. **This in turn means that entropy must always increase in spontaneous changes.** Another way of putting this is to say that for any spontaneous change, the entropy change, $\Delta S$, must be positive.

This is one of the cornerstones of our present understanding of how energy behaves and is referred to as the **Second Law of Thermodynamics**:

 **Spontaneous reactions go in the direction of increasing entropy.**

# Entropy and our experiments

To apply the Second Law correctly to chemical reactions, we need to be clear about the idea of a closed system and its surroundings, an idea we have already met in Topic 5. It may be helpful to repeat the main features again.

A **closed system** will consist of reactants and, after a reaction, products. A closed system is a theoretical model and does not change in temperature or pressure as a result of a reaction. Energy can transfer in or out, but no matter can transfer – it is 'closed' to matter (figure 13.6).

The **surroundings** can transfer energy to or from the system, and are so large that this takes place without the surroundings altering in temperature or pressure.

---
**QUESTION**
---

Our example of 100 atoms sharing 100 quanta is now more manageable; $\ln W$ is only 138.

Check that $\ln(8 \times 10^{59})$ equals 138 by using the 'ln' button on your calculator.

---

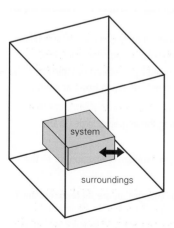

**Figure 13.6** **A closed system and its surroundings. Only energy transfers take place, and only between the system and its surroundings**

We should now be able to see why it was so difficult to see any pattern to describe all the spontaneous changes that were identified in Experiment 13.1.

## Changes in the system

Molar amounts of solids, liquids and gases at the same temperature will, in general, follow a trend of increasing entropy, with a perfect crystal having relatively few ways of arranging its atoms and energy, a liquid having more ways and a gas having the most ways.

**So the chance of a spontaneous reaction is increased when:**

solute and solvent $\longrightarrow$ solution

solid $\longrightarrow$ liquid $\longrightarrow$ gas

few gas molecules $\longrightarrow$ many gas molecules

**QUESTION**

List the results of Experiment 13.1 and decide whether the entropy change in each *system* was positive or negative.

## Changes in the surroundings

Most of the entropy changes in the systems of Experiment 13.1 were positive but for the combustion of magnesium (a common type of reaction) it looks likely that the entropy change in the system was negative. But nevertheless the combustion occurred. Why?

**QUESTION**

List the results of Experiment 13.1 and decide whether the entropy change in the *surroundings* was positive or negative.

The clue to the answer lies in the enthalpy change for the combustion: the reaction is exothermic. When the combustion occurred, energy was given out and passed to the **surroundings** – the air, container, or whatever.

Now, this energy will have had an effect on the entropy of the surroundings. Extra quanta of energy were being made available, and of course this increases the number of ways energy quanta can be arranged among the molecules in the surroundings. In other words, an exothermic change increases the entropy of the surroundings, and the change is positive. As we shall see later, entropy changes in the surroundings can be calculated.

To summarise:

1   When a reaction is **exothermic** energy is transferred **to** the surroundings. This increases the number of ways of arranging the energy and corresponds therefore to an **increase in entropy**. This increases the probability of a change occurring spontaneously.

2   When a reaction is **endothermic** energy is transferred **from** the surroundings. This reduces the number of ways of arranging the energy and corresponds to a **decrease in entropy**. This decreases the probability of a change occurring spontaneously.

**So, the chance of a spontaneous reaction is increased when reactions are exothermic.**

COMMENT

The surroundings are so large that they will always have more ways of arranging energy than any system. Clausius recognised the ultimate size of the surroundings in his remark:

**The entropy of the universe tends to increase.**

## The total entropy change

You should now have realised that **the pattern that describes our spontaneous changes is that they all corresponded to an increase in the number of ways of arranging energy and particles in the system and surroundings taken together.** In other words, there was always an overall increase in entropy.

When we want to consider the total entropy change of any process, we will always have to take into account what happens to the surroundings, $\Delta S_{\text{surroundings}}$, as

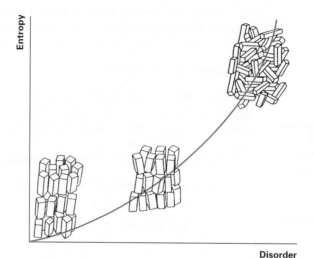

**Figure 13.7   Increasing disorder means increasing entropy**

well as the entropy change of the chemicals themselves, $\Delta S_{system}$. In other words

$$\Delta S_{total} = \Delta S_{system} + \Delta S_{surroundings}$$

This is a useful way of looking at changes in entropy when we are interested in chemical reactions. For **spontaneous** changes the criterion is:

$\Delta S_{total}$ **is positive**

For reactions that do not 'go' the opposite is true and $\Delta S_{total}$ is **negative**.

**Figure 13.8   Building a dry stone wall in the Cotswolds. How can the total entropy change be positive in the process of transforming this heap of stones from disorder to order?**

## 13.2   Measuring entropy

Before we can make progress in our use of the idea of entropy we need to know how to calculate entropy changes in the surroundings and in systems.

### Calculating the entropy change in the surroundings

Chemical reactions usually involve quite large enthalpy changes. Therefore, in most reactions $\Delta S_{surroundings}$ is quite substantial and certainly cannot be ignored. But how can we calculate its value? We cannot possibly count all the ways, $W$, of sharing the energy among the surroundings – for one thing, the surroundings are impossible to define exactly.

Fortunately, there is a simple relation which enables us to calculate $\Delta S_{\text{surroundings}}$ exactly. It is

$$\Delta S_{\text{surroundings}} = \frac{-\Delta H_{\text{reaction}}}{T}$$

where $T$ is the temperature of the surroundings in **kelvins** and $\Delta H$ is in **joules** (not kJ in this case). Clausius proposed a form of this relationship on the basis of experimental measurements but its application to reactions is due to the work of Gibbs.

**When a reaction is exothermic a quantity of energy, $\Delta H_{\text{reaction}}$, is passed to the surroundings: and the more energy is passed to the surroundings, the greater the increase in the number of ways of sharing energy, and so the greater the entropy change.**

But why divide by $T$? Well, when $T$ is high the surroundings are already hot, so giving them more energy will not make much difference to the entropy – there is already plenty of energy to share.

But when $T$ is low the surroundings are cold, so passing energy to them will make a bigger difference to the entropy, and will greatly increase the sharing possibilities. In other words, the **entropy change** will vary **inversely with temperature**. That is why we divide by $T$.

After all, someone on a low income appreciates a £10 rise more than someone on a high one. But both would prefer a £20 rise to a £10 one.

Let us apply this relationship to the combustion of magnesium that we looked at in Experiment 13.1, part **3**:

$$2Mg(s) + O_2(g) \longrightarrow 2MgO(s)$$

The standard enthalpy change of formation at 298K is

$$\Delta H_f^{\ominus}[MgO] = -601.7 \, \text{kJ mol}^{-1}$$

therefore     $\Delta H_{\text{reaction}}^{\ominus} = -2 \times 601.7 \, \text{kJ mol}^{-1}$

and     $\Delta S_{\text{surroundings}}^{\ominus} = \dfrac{-\Delta H_{\text{reaction}}^{\ominus}}{T} = \dfrac{-(-2 \times 601.7 \times 1000)}{298} \, \text{J mol}^{-1} \, \text{K}^{-1}$

$$= +4038 \, \text{J mol}^{-1} \, \text{K}^{-1}$$

This large positive value makes it likely that $\Delta S_{\text{total}}^{\ominus}$ will be positive and the reaction will be spontaneous at 298 K once started, as we actually found.

## Standard entropy of substances

Before we start calculating entropy changes in systems we need to look at the entropy values of some substances.

It has been said that the best way to become acquainted with birds is to look at some birds. And a good way to become acquainted with entropy is to look at some values. The list in the margin gives some typical standard entropies at 298 K.

What useful comments can be made about the entropy values in the table?

Notice that hard structures generally have smaller entropies than soft structures:

- $S^{\ominus}[C, \text{diamond}]$ is less than $S^{\ominus}[C, \text{graphite}]$
- $S^{\ominus}[Mg]$ is less than $S^{\ominus}[Pb]$.

| Entity | $S^{\ominus}$/J mol$^{-1}$ K$^{-1}$ |
|---|---|
| C (diamond) | 2.4 |
| C (graphite) | 5.7 |
| Mg(s) | 32.7 |
| Pb(s) | 64.8 |
| MgO(s) | 26.9 |
| MgCO$_3$(s) | 65.7 |
| H$_2$O(l) | 69.9 |
| C$_2$H$_5$OH(l) | 160.7 |
| He(g) | 126.0 |
| NH$_3$(g) | 192.3 |
| O$_2$(g) | 205.0 |

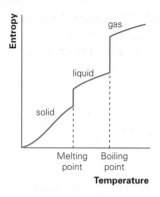

Figure 13.9 **The entropy of a substance increases as the temperature rises; and increases in a jump when a substance melts or boils**

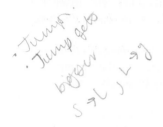

Simple substances generally have smaller entropies than complex substances:

- $S^{\ominus}[MgO]$ is less than $S^{\ominus}[MgCO_3]$.

Solids have smaller entropies than liquids, which are generally smaller than gases:

- $S^{\ominus}[MgO]$ is less than $S^{\ominus}[H_2O]$, which is less than $S^{\ominus}[O_2]$.

In hard solids the crystals have rigid structures with stiff bonds and the thermal motion of the atoms is very restricted: the entropy is correspondingly small. In soft solids there is rather more thermal disorder and entropy is larger.

For liquids and gases there is much more disordered motion and entropy values are much larger.

## BACKGROUND

There are two possible approaches to determining the entropy content of a substance. A statistical approach is to count the actual number of ways, but this approach is only possible for very simple substances. A thermodynamic approach is to measure the effect of transferring energy to the substance. In order to do this we have to have a starting point and this is provided by the **Third Law of Thermodynamics**.

**All perfect crystals have the same entropy at absolute zero.**

The convention adopted by chemists is that this entropy value is zero. So our starting point is one mole of a perfect crystal at absolute zero. A close approach to this situation would be a flawless diamond weighing 12 g cooled in solid helium:

$$S_0[C, \text{diamond}] = 0$$

By how much does the entropy increase as the diamond warms up from zero K to 298 K, the standard temperature? This is actually quite easy in principle because we can apply Clausius's relationship to the process:

$$\Delta S[C, \text{diamond}] = \frac{q}{T}$$

where $q$ is the energy transferred reversibly from the surroundings.

We need to know the energy transferred from the surroundings to the diamond at each stage of the warming process. We have to monitor continuously the temperature rise and the joules being transferred: 1 joule transferred at 10 K has a much greater effect on the number of arrangements than 1 joule transferred at 100 K.

Figure 13.10 **A rough diamond crystal (12 g is 1 mol)**

## Calculating the entropy change in the system

It now becomes possible to calculate entropy changes in the system for chemical reactions, $\Delta S^{\ominus}_{\text{system}}$.

As an example we will again use the reaction of magnesium with oxygen. Once ignited, the magnesium burnt spontaneously in air. A mole of oxygen molecules, $O_2$, was used up for every two moles of $Mg^{2+}O^{2-}$ formed. There are fewer possible arrangements of the energy in the solid product than in the gaseous reactant, so we might expect the entropy to decrease, giving a negative value for $\Delta S^{\ominus}_{\text{system}}$.

$$2Mg(s) + O_2(g) \longrightarrow 2MgO(s)$$

To work out the exact value of the entropy change of the system for this reaction, we need to look up the standard entropy values of the reactants and products in tables 5.2 and 5.3 of the *Book of data*.

The standard entropy values at 298 K are:

$$S^{\ominus}[Mg(s)] = +\ 32.7\ \text{J mol}^{-1}\,\text{K}^{-1}$$
$$S^{\ominus}[\tfrac{1}{2}O_2(g)] = +102.5\ \text{J mol}^{-1}\,\text{K}^{-1}$$
$$S^{\ominus}[MgO(s)] = +\ 26.9\ \text{J mol}^{-1}\,\text{K}^{-1}$$

Notice that the values quoted for elements in table 5.2 are **per mole of atoms**. Notice also how much higher the standard entropy of the gas, oxygen, is than that of the solids, magnesium and magnesium oxide.

We can calculate $\Delta S^{\ominus}_{\text{system}}$ for the reaction in much the same way as we found $\Delta H^{\ominus}$ values using an energy cycle in Topic 5.

$$2Mg(s) + O_2(g) \longrightarrow 2MgO(s)$$
$$2 \times 32.7 \quad 2 \times 102.5 \quad 2 \times 26.9$$

$$\Delta S^{\ominus}_{\text{system}} = S^{\ominus}_{\text{products}} - S^{\ominus}_{\text{reactants}}$$

Therefore, $\Delta S^{\ominus}_{\text{system}} = 2S^{\ominus}[MgO(s)] - 2S^{\ominus}[Mg(s)] - 2S^{\ominus}[\tfrac{1}{2}O_2(g)]$
$$= +\ (2 \times 26.9) - (2 \times 32.7) - (2 \times 102.5)$$
$$= -\ 216.6\ \text{J mol}^{-1}\,\text{K}^{-1}$$

$\Delta S^{\ominus}_{\text{system}}$ is indeed negative, showing that the entropy of the reaction system has decreased. The reaction nevertheless goes spontaneously. Why? Because there is also the entropy change in the surroundings to be considered.

## The total entropy change

We know from experiments that the combustion of magnesium is spontaneous but do our calculations say the same? We can find out by using the relationship

$$\Delta S^{\ominus}_{\text{total}} = \Delta S^{\ominus}_{\text{system}} + \Delta S^{\ominus}_{\text{surroundings}}$$

with the values we have already calculated for the burning of magnesium:

$$\Delta S^{\ominus}_{\text{system}} = -216.6\ \text{J mol}^{-1}\,\text{K}^{-1}$$
$$\Delta S^{\ominus}_{\text{surroundings}} = +4038\ \text{J mol}^{-1}\,\text{K}^{-1}$$

Therefore, $\Delta S^{\ominus}_{\text{total}} = (-216.6 + 4038)\ \text{J mol}^{-1}\,\text{K}^{-1}$
$$= +3821.4\ \text{J mol}^{-1}\,\text{K}^{-1}$$

**The reaction should go spontaneously at 298 K.**

This positive value for $\Delta S^{\ominus}_{\text{total}}$ tells us that the reaction should happen spontaneously. The example warns us of one limitation of 'spontaneous', namely that a spontaneous reaction may be very slow at 298 K.

> **COMMENT**
>
> The appropriate answer for the total entropy change is $3820\ \text{J mol}^{-1}\,\text{K}^{-1}$ (to 3 SF)

# The entropy change of an endothermic reaction

You should now be able to calculate the entropy change at 298 K for another reaction you carried out in Experiment 13.1 (part **5**).

$$2NH_4Cl(s) + Ba(OH)_2(s) \longrightarrow BaCl_2.2H_2O(s) + 2NH_3(g)$$

You will have to start by looking up the $S^\ominus$ and $\Delta H_f^\ominus$ values at 298 K for all the reactants and products. You then have to work out $\Delta S_{system}^\ominus$ for the reaction using the relationship:

$$\Delta S_{system}^\ominus = S_{products}^\ominus - S_{reactants}^\ominus$$

You should get the value:

$$\Delta S_{system}^\ominus = +298.6 \, J \, mol^{-1} \, K^{-1}$$

$\Delta H_{reaction}^\ominus$ is calculated using a similar energy cycle:

$$\Delta H_{reaction}^\ominus = \Delta H_{f\,products}^\ominus - \Delta H_{f\,reactants}^\ominus$$

You should get the value:

$$\Delta H_{reaction}^\ominus = +21.2 \, kJ \, mol^{-1}$$

From $\Delta H_{reaction}^\ominus$ you calculate $\Delta S_{surroundings}^\ominus$ using the relationship:

$$\Delta S_{surroundings}^\ominus = \frac{-\Delta H_{reaction}^\ominus}{T}$$

You should get the value:

$$\Delta S_{surroundings}^\ominus = -71.1 \, J \, mol^{-1} \, K^{-1}$$

Finally obtain a value (to 3 SF) for $\Delta S_{total}^\ominus$ by using the relationship:

$$\Delta S_{total} = \Delta S_{system} + \Delta S_{surroundings}$$

With the values you should have obtained:

$$\Delta S_{total}^\ominus = (+298.6 - 71.1) \, J \, mol^{-1} \, K^{-1}$$
$$= +228 \, J \, mol^{-1} \, K^{-1}$$

**The reaction will go spontaneously at 298 K.**

The experiment you did matches this theoretical prediction. You have demonstrated that entropy calculations match your practical experience, which is a test all scientific theories must pass.

Notice that the production of ammonia gas with its large entropy plays a major role in making this reaction go spontaneously.

# The decomposition of carbonates

You studied the decomposition of zinc carbonate in Experiment 13.1 (part **6**).

$$ZnCO_3(s) \longrightarrow ZnO(s) + CO_2(g)$$

When you do the necessary calculations you should be able to confirm that:

$$\Delta S_{system}^\ominus = +175 \, J \, mol^{-1} \, K^{-1}$$

and $$\Delta S_{surroundings}^\ominus = -238 \, J \, mol^{-1} \, K^{-1}$$

so that $$\Delta S_{total}^\ominus = -63 \, J \, mol^{-1} \, K^{-1}$$

**The reaction will not go spontaneously at 298 K.** But you may remember that most carbonates decompose when heated. How does this happen when we have confirmed that the entropy change is negative? We will leave this question until we next consider entropy.

## QUESTIONS

1 Carry out the complete calculation for the endothermic reaction of barium hydroxide with ammonium chloride in order to confirm the values quoted in the text.

2 Carry out the complete calculation for the decomposition of zinc carbonate in order to confirm the values quoted in the text.

3 In Topic 1 you studied the thermal decomposition of hydrated cobalt chloride and in Topic 5 you calculated the standard enthalpy change at 298 K for:

$$CoCl_2.6H_2O(s) \longrightarrow CoCl_2(s) + 6H_2O(l) \qquad \Delta H^\ominus_{reaction} = +88.1 \text{ kJ mol}^{-1}$$

Which entropy values are mainly responsible for this reaction being spontaneous when heated, in spite of it being endothermic? What are the differences between the molecules that might account for this entropy effect?

## BACKGROUND

Chemists were not measuring heating and cooling changes in reactions properly until after the work of Hess, published in 1840. A Dutchman, van't Hoff, was the first chemist whose work on the energy relationships in chemistry, published in 1894, was widely understood and accepted. His theories had already been published by other chemists, especially by the American Willard Gibbs in the period 1876–78, but the subtlety of the ideas resulted in them being not understood and therefore neglected. Gibbs's work became more widely known after being translated into French by Le Chatelier in 1899.

Finally the Austrian scientist Ludwig Boltzmann was able to show how atomic theory and energy theory could be combined to produce an overall interpretation of the direction of spontaneous change.

Many distinguished scientists in that period, such as Kelvin, regarded aspects of atomic theory as useful fictions, not to be taken too seriously. It was Einstein's explanation of Brownian motion, confirmed experimentally by Perrin, that provided support for the atomic theory. Perrin's book on Brownian motion, published in 1913, was perhaps the first scientific best-seller, 30 000 copies being sold.

We will meet the ideas of some of these scientists again in other topics, as their work is commemorated in the Boltzmann constant and Le Chatelier's Principle.

Figure 13.11 **Boltzmann and his tombstone**

# TOPIC REVIEW

Concentrate on the essential principles rather than on details as you review this topic. Once these principles are clear, you can learn the equations and tackle the quantitative examples in the end-of-topic questions.

**1 List key words or terms with definitions where necessary**

Illustrate the following with suitable **examples**:

- entropy
- system
- surroundings
- Second Law of Thermodynamics
- $\Delta S^{\ominus}_{\text{total}}$
- spontaneous change.

**2 Summarise the key principles as simply as possible**

You should know:

- the relative values of the entropies of solids, liquids and gases
- what happens to the entropy of the surroundings during
  **a** an exothermic change
  **b** an endothermic change
- when a +ve sign is appropriate for $\Delta S^{\ominus}_{\text{total}}$ and when to use a −ve sign.

The best way to **test yourself** is to do some of the end-of-topic questions, paying particular attention to the signs and the units involved.

# REVIEW QUESTIONS

✱ Indicates that the *Book of data* is needed.

**✱ 13.1** **a** Arrange the following substances in increasing order of standard entropy ($S^{\ominus}$) at 298 K. Predict the order first, then check it using the *Book of data*, quoting the actual values: benzene, $C_6H_6$(l); calcium hydroxide, $Ca(OH)_2$(s); carbon dioxide, $CO_2$(g); gold, Au(s); hexane, $C_6H_{14}$(l); iron, Fe(s); methane, $CH_4$(g); neon, Ne(g); octane, $C_8H_{18}$(l); sodium chloride, NaCl(s). (6)

**b** Comment on any differences between your predictions and the actual values. (3)

**(9 marks)**

**✱ 13.2** Consider the reaction:

$$C(s) + O_2(g) \longrightarrow CO_2(g)$$

**a** Use the *Book of data* to find the standard molar entropies of C(s), $O_2$(g) and $CO_2$(g). Use these data to calculate the standard molar entropy change, $\Delta S^{\ominus}_{\text{system}}$, for the reaction. (2)

**b** Use the *Book of data* to find the standard enthalpy change, $\Delta H^{\ominus}(298)$, for the reaction. Use your answer to calculate the standard molar entropy change in the surroundings, $\Delta S^{\ominus}_{\text{surroundings}}$, at 298 K for the reaction. (3)

**c** Calculate the total entropy change, $\Delta S^{\ominus}_{\text{total}}$, for the reaction. (1)

**d** Does your answer to **c** suggest that this reaction will be spontaneous at 298 K? Give a reason for your answer. (2)

**(8 marks)**

**✳ 13.3** Calculate $\Delta S^{\ominus}_{\text{surroundings}}$ at 298 K for the following reactions. You may still have the values for the enthalpy changes, $\Delta H^{\ominus}$, that you calculated in Topic 5, question **5.6a, b, d** and **e**; if not, you will need to work them out again.

**a** $N_2O(g) + Cu(s) \longrightarrow CuO(s) + N_2(g)$ (3)

**b** $NH_4Cl(s) \longrightarrow NH_3(g) + HCl(g)$ (3)

**c** $Mg(s) + \frac{1}{2}O_2(g) \longrightarrow MgO(s)$ (3)

**d** $CO_2(g) + 2Mg(s) \longrightarrow 2MgO(s) + C(s)$ (3)

**e** $2Al(s) + Fe_2O_3(s) \longrightarrow 2Fe(s) + Al_2O_3(s)$ (3)

**f** $H_2(g) + S(s) \longrightarrow H_2S(g)$ (3)

**g** $Na(s) + \frac{1}{2}Cl_2(g) \longrightarrow NaCl(s)$ (3)

**(21 marks)**

**13.4** Predict whether the value of $\Delta S^{\ominus}_{\text{system}}$ at 298 K will be positive, negative or little changed for each of the reactions in question **13.3**. Give reasons for your predictions.

**(14 marks)**

**✳ 13.5** Use the *Book of data* to calculate $\Delta S^{\ominus}_{\text{system}}$ at 298 K for the reactions in question **13.3**.

**(14 marks)**

**13.6** Use your answers to questions **13.3** and **13.5** to calculate $\Delta S^{\ominus}_{\text{total}}$ at 298 K. Which reactions will be spontaneous at 298 K?

(You may find it useful to check the precise meaning of *spontaneous* on pages 302 and 306 of this book.)

**(14 marks)**

**✳ 13.7** Carry out similar calculations to those in questions **13.3**, **13.5** and **13.6** to predict whether each of the following reactions could occur spontaneously at 298 K.

**a** $CuO(s) \longrightarrow Cu(s) + \frac{1}{2}O_2(g)$ (4)

**b** $C_2H_4(g) + H_2O(l) \longrightarrow C_2H_5OH(l)$ (4)

**c** $CH_4(g) + Cl_2(g) \longrightarrow CH_3Cl(g) + HCl(g)$ (4)

**d** $CaCO_3(s) \longrightarrow CaO(s) + CO_2(g)$ (4)

**e** $(NH_4)_2SO_4(s) \longrightarrow 2NH_3(g) + H_2SO_4(l)$ (4)

**(20 marks)**

**\* 13.8**    The enthalpy change, $\Delta H^{\ominus}$, for the reaction

$$Ni^{2+}(aq) + Zn(s) \longrightarrow Ni(s) + Zn^{2+}(aq)$$

at 298 K is $-100\,kJ\,mol^{-1}$.

a    Calculate $\Delta S^{\ominus}_{\text{surroundings}}$ at 298 K.    (1)
b    With the help of the *Book of data*, calculate $\Delta S^{\ominus}_{\text{system}}$ at 298 K.    (2)
c    Suggest why your value for $\Delta S^{\ominus}_{\text{system}}$ is small.    (1)
d    Calculate $\Delta S^{\ominus}_{\text{total}}$ at 298 K and comment on the significance of your value. (2)
    **(6 marks)**

**\* 13.9**    When 1 mole of rubidium chloride is dissolved in water at 298 K to form a
solution of concentration $1.0\,mol\,dm^{-3}$, the enthalpy change is $+19\,kJ\,mol^{-1}$.

$$RbCl(s) + aq \longrightarrow Rb^{+}(aq) + Cl^{-}(aq) \qquad \Delta H^{\ominus} = +19\,kJ\,mol^{-1}$$

a    Calculate the entropy change in the surroundings when this process takes
    place.    (1)
b    With the help of the *Book of data*, calculate the standard entropy change of
    the system at 298 K.    (2)
c    Use the results of your calculations to explain why rubidium chloride
    dissolves readily in water despite this being an endothermic process.    (2)
    **(5 marks)**

# EXAMINATION QUESTIONS

**13.10**    Phosphorus pentachloride, $PCl_5$, is prepared by passing chlorine gas through
phosphorus trichloride, $PCl_3$.

$$PCl_3(l) + Cl_2(g) \longrightarrow PCl_5(s)$$

a    Use the following data to calculate the enthalpy change at 298 K for the
    production of 1 mole of phosphorus pentachloride from the trichloride. Your
    answer should include a sign and units.

| Compound | $\Delta H^{\ominus}_f$/kJ mol$^{-1}$ |
| --- | --- |
| $PCl_3(l)$ | $-319.7$ |
| $PCl_5(s)$ | $-443.5$ |

    (2)

b    Use your answer from **a** to calculate the entropy change in the surroundings
    at 298 K. Your answer should include a sign and units.    (3)

c    The standard entropy change of the system for this reaction is
    $-215.6\,J\,mol^{-1}\,K^{-1}$.
    i  Suggest TWO reasons why $\Delta S^{\ominus}_{\text{system}}$ has a negative value.    (2)
    ii Calculate the total entropy change, $\Delta S^{\ominus}_{\text{total}}$, for the reaction.    (1)
    iii Will the reaction proceed spontaneously at 298 K? Explain your answer.    (1)

d    In practice the apparatus used in this reaction is ice-cooled. How does the
    yield of phosphorus pentachloride change when the temperature is allowed
    to rise? Explain your answer in terms of entropy.    (2)
    **(11 marks)**

**13.11**   The gases hydrogen sulphide, $H_2S$, and sulphur dioxide, $SO_2$, react according to the equation:

$$2H_2S(g) + SO_2(g) \longrightarrow 3S(s) + 2H_2O(l)$$

**a**   Which of the four substances in the equation would you expect to have the lowest entropy at 298 K? Justify your answer. (2)

**b**  **i**   Would you expect $\Delta S^{\ominus}_{\text{system}}$ for the reaction to have a positive or negative value? Justify your answer. (2)

**ii**   The reaction is known to be spontaneous at 298 K. What can you deduce about $\Delta S^{\ominus}_{\text{surroundings}}$? (2)

**iii**   What can you deduce about $\Delta H^{\ominus}$? (1)

**(7 marks)**

**13.12**   Methanol can be manufactured using the reaction shown below:

$$CO(g) + 2H_2(g) \longrightarrow CH_3OH(l) \qquad \Delta H^{\ominus}(298) = -128.6 \, \text{kJ mol}^{-1}$$

**a**  **i**   Use the value of $\Delta H^{\ominus}$ (298) to calculate the entropy change of the surroundings when one mole of methanol forms at 298 K. Quote your answer to three significant figures and include a sign and units. (3)

**ii**   Calculate the entropy change in the system when one mole of methanol forms at 298 K. Use the following data:

$$S^{\ominus}[CO(g)] = 197.6 \, \text{J mol}^{-1} \, \text{K}^{-1}$$
$$S^{\ominus}[H_2(g)] = 130.6 \, \text{J mol}^{-1} \, \text{K}^{-1}$$
$$S^{\ominus}[CH_3OH(l)] = 239.7 \, \text{J mol}^{-1} \, \text{K}^{-1}$$

(2)

**iii**   Your answer to **ii**, for the entropy change in the system, should include a sign. Is the sign the one you would have predicted from the equation for the reaction? Give TWO reasons to justify your answer. (2)

**b**   In industry the reaction producing methanol is carried out at around 300 to 400 °C at high pressure, and an equilibrium mixture containing methanol vapour is produced.

**i**   What is the value of $\Delta S^{\ominus}_{\text{total}}$ when this system is at equilibrium? (1)

**ii**   State ONE advantage and ONE disadvantage to the manufacturer of carrying out the reaction at high pressure. (2)

**(10 marks)**

**13.13**   Zinc is extracted commercially by heating its oxide with coke in a furnace. The equation for the reaction is:

$$ZnO(s) + C(s) \longrightarrow Zn(s) + CO(g)$$

Some data for this reaction at 298 K are given below:

$$\Delta H^{\ominus} = +237.5 \, \text{kJ mol}^{-1}$$
$$\Delta S^{\ominus}_{\text{system}} = +190 \, \text{J mol}^{-1} \, \text{K}^{-1}$$

**a**   Explain why $\Delta S^{\ominus}_{\text{system}}$ has a positive value. (1)

**b**   The reaction is spontaneous at temperatures greater than 1250 K. Show that this statement is correct by appropriate calculation of $\Delta S^{\ominus}_{\text{surroundings}}$ and $\Delta S^{\ominus}_{\text{total}}$. (Assume $\Delta S^{\ominus}_{\text{system}}$ is unaffected by temperature change). (3)

**c**   The boiling point of zinc is 1180 K. What difference is this likely to make to the entropy change of the system at 1250 K? Explain your reasoning. (1)

**d**   How will the difference predicted in **c** affect the temperature required for spontaneous reaction? Explain your reasoning. (1)

**(6 marks)**

# How far? Reversible reactions

In this important topic we shall be extending the ideas which were introduced in section 7.7 on reversible reactions and their ability to reach a state of dynamic equilibrium. In Topic 7 we also introduced **Le Chatelier's Principle** as a summary of the ways in which equilibrium systems respond to changes of concentration, pressure or temperature. We shall now be making the study of equilibrium systems quantitative and will be exploring more fully the ideas underlying Le Chatelier's Principle.

The aims of the topic are therefore to:

- introduce and use the Equilibrium Law and the concept of the equilibrium constants $K_c$ and $K_p$
- study the underlying entropy changes in equilibrium processes
- apply the Equilibrium Law to acid–base reactions
- introduce buffer solutions and extend your understanding of pH indicators.

## 14.1 Reversible reactions

Figure 14.1 **The manufacture of ammonia is a reversible reaction carried out on a very large scale**

Many important reactions, used in the chemical industry, are reversible. Two examples are the production of ammonia for fertilisers and of esters for perfumes and solvents. The success of the chemical industry depends on a good understanding of how to arrange conditions so that such processes can be operated most efficiently.

$$N_2(g) + 3H_2(g) \rightleftharpoons 2NH_3(g)$$

The reaction of nitrogen with hydrogen is one of many reactions which, when allowed to start, does not proceed to completion. As a result, not all the starting materials are changed into new products.

A mixture of a solid and its saturated solution helps to explain what happens when a reversible reaction reaches a state of equilibrium.

When a small volume of a solvent is added to solid potassium nitrate, for example, some of the solid dissolves. No more solid will dissolve once the solution is saturated. At this point a state of equilibrium has been reached between solid potassium nitrate and the solution of the salt. The state of equilibrium can be represented by this equation:

$$KNO_3(s) + aq \rightleftharpoons KNO_3(aq)$$

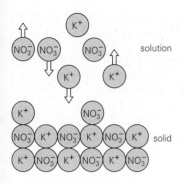

Figure 14.2 **Potassium ions and nitrate ions at equilibrium**

As explained in Topic 7, in such an equation the same equilibrium state can be approached from either direction. From the left (as shown in the equation) by dissolving potassium nitrate crystals in water at a particular temperature; or from the right by cooling a hot saturated solution of potassium nitrate to the same temperature.

**At equilibrium the system is dynamic.** Potassium and nitrate ions are continuously moving from the solid into solution, while other ions are moving from the solution to the crystal lattice. *Overall* there is no change.

## Features of the equilibrium state

We often use the term **position of equilibrium** to describe the equilibrium state attained under a particular set of conditions. It is reached when the reactions are taking place at the same speed in both directions, so the substances present do not vary in amount. When there are more reactants than products, then we say the position of equilibrium lies to the left. Similarly when the amounts of products are greater than those of the reactants, the equilibrium is described as lying to the right.

In such an equation the reaction going from left to right is termed **the forward reaction** and the opposite reaction is the **backward reaction**.

For example:

$$CO_2(aq) + H_2O(l) \rightleftharpoons HCO_3^-(aq) + H^+(aq)$$

forward reaction →
reactants        products
← backward reaction

So to summarise some important features of the equilibrium state:

1  **A stable state of equilibrium is only possible in a closed system** – one that cannot exchange matter with its surroundings. In a system which allows matter to enter or leave, a stable equilibrium is not possible.

In practice there are many such systems that can be studied in open test tubes or flasks because no gases are involved which would otherwise escape. There is no interaction with the constituents of the air and during the time-scale of the experiment any evaporation is insignificant.

2  **The equilibrium state can be approached from either direction** – that is, the products can be used as reactants and the reaction will still take place. Reactions of this kind are called **reversible reactions**.

3  **Equilibrium is a dynamic state** in that change is continually taking place in opposite directions on the molecular level.

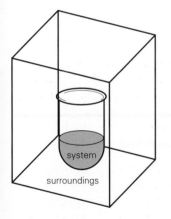

Figure 14.3 **A closed system**

4  **The dynamic aspect of equilibrium means that it is stable under fixed conditions but sensitive to alteration in these conditions.** The existence of an equilibrium state can be recognised by taking advantage of its sensitivity to changes in conditions. For example, when a change in temperature, pH, or concentration leads to an obvious change in a system it is likely to have been at equilibrium before the change took place.

## 14.2    The Equilibrium Law

From many quantitative investigations of equilibrium reactions, the following general statement applies. For any system at equilibrium, there is a simple relationship between the concentration of the substances present:

$$mA + nB \rightleftharpoons pC + qD$$

When a reaction at equilibrium is represented by the equation above, the expression

$$\frac{[C]_{eqm}^{p} [D]_{eqm}^{q}}{[A]_{eqm}^{m} [B]_{eqm}^{n}}$$

is a constant at a given temperature $= K_c$.

**This is known as the Equilibrium Law and $K_c$ is called the equilibrium constant.** The subscript $c$ indicates that it is expressed in concentrations measured in $mol\,dm^{-3}$. This is indicated by the use of square brackets [ ] and can be applied to liquids, solutions and gases.

By convention, the concentrations of the substances on the right-hand side of the equation are always put at the top of the fraction of the equilibrium constant and those of the substances on the left-hand side at the bottom.

The equilibrium constant $K_c$ for the reaction

$$2SO_2(g) + O_2(g) \rightleftharpoons 2SO_3(g)$$

is therefore given by

$$K_c = \frac{[SO_3(g)]^2}{[SO_2(g)]^2[O_2(g)]}$$

while that for the reaction

$$Co^{2+}(aq) + 4Cl^-(aq) \rightleftharpoons CoCl_4^{2-}(aq)$$

is given by

$$K_c = \frac{[CoCl_4^{2-}(aq)]}{[Co^{2+}(aq)] [Cl^-(aq)]^4}$$

### COMMENT

The correct form for concentrations at equilibrium is [ ]$_{eqm}$ but eqm will not be used in all examples. This is to simplify the appearance of an otherwise visually confusing expression – the expression given above for $K_c$ therefore simplifies to read:

$$\frac{[C]^p [D]^q}{[A]^m [B]^n}$$

### QUESTIONS

Now try writing a few equilibrium constant expressions for yourself. What would be the expressions for $K_c$ in the following cases?

1    $Ce^{4+}(aq) + Fe^{2+}(aq) \rightleftharpoons Ce^{3+}(aq) + Fe^{3+}(aq)$

2    $CO(g) + 2H_2(g) \rightleftharpoons CH_3OH(g)$

3    $N_2(g) + 3H_2(g) \rightleftharpoons 2NH_3(g)$

Chemists can draw some important conclusions from this law:

1    When $K_c$ is large the equilibrium mixture will contain a high proportion of products; that is, the reaction has gone nearly to completion (figure 14.4, opposite).

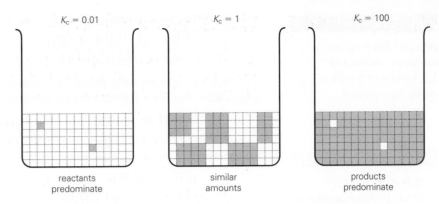

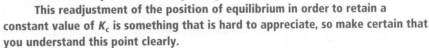

Figure 14.4 **Proportions of reactants (in white) and products (in green) for different values of $K_c$**

2  When $K_c$ is small, the reaction does not proceed very far at the temperature concerned and the concentration of products is low.

3  The value of $K_c$ is not altered by the addition of more reactants or more products to an equilibrium mixture kept at a constant temperature.

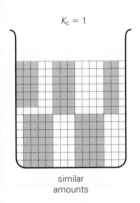

Figure 14.5 **Doubling the amounts does not alter the ratios**

On the addition of more reactants, the equilibrium will move in the forward direction until the concentrations again satisfy the value for $K_c$.

Similarly, on addition of more products, the equilibrium will move in the reverse direction and the concentrations of reactants will increase.

Consider a reaction represented by the equation

$$A(aq) + B(aq) \rightleftharpoons C(aq) + D(aq)$$

for which $\quad K_c = \dfrac{[C(aq)]\,[D(aq)]}{[A(aq)]\,[B(aq)]}$

If we add more B, the value of the bottom part of the expression would increase and the value of the expression would no longer equal $K_c$. The reaction, however, readjusts itself. Some of the extra B reacts with A to form more C and more D. The reaction continues until the new values of all the concentrations are such that the value of the expression once again equals $K_c$.

**This readjustment of the position of equilibrium in order to retain a constant value of $K_c$ is something that is hard to appreciate, so make certain that you understand this point clearly.**

A similar situation arises when a reactant or a product is removed from an equilibrium mixture kept at a constant temperature.

However, it is also important to stress that the equilibrium constant only has a constant value at a particular temperature. Change the temperature and the value of the equilibrium constant will change.

4  **When $K_c$ for a reaction is known, the relative proportions of reactants and products at equilibrium can be calculated for any mixture of reactants used initially.**

When stating the value of $K_c$ for a particular reaction, it is important to indicate the equation on which the constant is based. For example, in the reaction between ethanoic acid and ethanol to form ethyl ethanoate and water, we can write the equation in the form:

$$CH_3CO_2H(l) + C_2H_5OH(l) \rightleftharpoons CH_3CO_2C_2H_5(l) + H_2O(l)$$
$$\text{ethanoic acid} \qquad \text{ethanol} \qquad \text{ethyl ethanoate} \qquad \text{water}$$

COMMENT

Remember that these are equilibrium concentrations. $[\ ]_{eqm}$ is not used in order to simplify the expression.

COMMENT

In this example, water is a reactant or product depending on whether one is looking at the forward reaction or the reverse reaction. It is not a solvent present in large amounts. So $[H_2O]$ appears in the expression for $K_c$.

The appropriate form of the equilibrium expression is:

$$K_c = \frac{[CH_3CO_2C_2H_5(l)]\ [H_2O(l)]}{[CH_3CO_2H(l)]\ [C_2H_5OH(l)]}$$

for which the experimentally determined value of $K_c = 3.7$ at a particular temperature. But if we approach the equilibrium from the other direction:

$$CH_3CO_2C_2H_5(l) + H_2O(l) \rightleftharpoons CH_3CO_2H(l) + C_2H_5OH(l)$$
$$\text{ethyl ethanoate} \qquad \text{water} \qquad \text{ethanoic acid} \qquad \text{ethanol}$$

the appropriate form of the equilibrium expression is

$$K_c = \frac{[CH_3CO_2H(l)]\ [C_2H_5OH(l)]}{[CH_3CO_2C_2H_5(l)]\ [H_2O(l)]}$$

and $K_c = 0.27$ (which is 1/3.7) at the same temperature as before.

For reactions in which the number of particles on each side of the equation is the same, as in the example above, the concentration units cancel and $K_c$ has no units.

In this example

$$K_c \text{ is } \frac{\text{mol dm}^{-3} \times \text{mol dm}^{-3}}{\text{mol dm}^{-3} \times \text{mol dm}^{-3}}$$

which cancels to no units.

For other reactions this may not be the case and units for $K_c$ must be stated. Thus in the equilibrium

$$2NO_2(\text{solvent}) \rightleftharpoons N_2O_4(\text{solvent})$$

$$K_c = \frac{[N_2O_4]}{[NO_2]^2}$$

and the units of $K_c$ are $\text{mol}^{-1}\ \text{dm}^3$.

## QUESTIONS

What are the units for $K_c$ for these systems?

1    $2SO_2(g) + O_2(g) \rightleftharpoons 2SO_3(g)$

2    $Co^{2+}(aq) + 4Cl^-(aq) \rightleftharpoons CoCl_4^{2-}(aq)$

# Relative concentrations at equilibrium

COMMENT

The chemistry of esters is explored in more detail in Topic 15.

The reaction of esters with water, for example the reaction of ethyl ethanoate with water, involves an equilibrium state:

$$CH_3CO_2C_2H_5(l) + H_2O(l) \rightleftharpoons CH_3CO_2H(l) + C_2H_5OH(l)$$
$$\text{ethyl ethanoate} \qquad \text{water} \qquad \text{ethanoic acid} \qquad \text{ethanol}$$

Equilibrium is reached very slowly indeed at ordinary temperatures in this system. It is reached more rapidly by heating the reagents or by using a catalyst such as concentrated hydrochloric acid in the mixture. A mixture of ethyl ethanoate and water alone would take several years to reach equilibrium at room temperature, so the catalyst has a remarkable effect.

The equilibrium can be studied by a simple titration technique but has to be set up with special care and even with a catalyst needs at least a week for the reaction to reach equilibrium.

---

## QUESTION

Some experiments on this ester equilibrium led to the following equilibrium concentrations being obtained.

### Concentrations at equilibrium/mol dm$^{-3}$

| Ethyl ethanoate | Water | Ethanoic acid | Ethanol |
| --- | --- | --- | --- |
| 15.4 | 5.27 | 4.33 | 4.33 |
| 13.6 | 7.87 | 5.47 | 5.47 |
| 10.0 | 17.4 | 7.00 | 7.00 |
| 6.00 | 35.4 | 7.60 | 7.60 |

When this ester equilibrium is represented by

$$CH_3CO_2C_2H_5(l) + H_2O(l) \rightleftharpoons CH_3CO_2H(l) + C_2H_5OH(l)$$

$$K_c = \frac{[CH_3CO_2H(l)]\ [C_2H_5OH(l)]}{[CH_3CO_2C_2H_5(l)]\ [H_2O(l)]}$$

Use your calculator to check that the Equilibrium Law is satisfied and that there is a constant numerical relationship between the equilibrium concentrations of the reactants and products within the limits of experimental error.

---

Take care in questions of this kind that you are clear as to the units which should be quoted. For example, you might be told that in a particular experiment the number of moles of each substance present was as follows:

| Substance | Number of moles |
| --- | --- |
| ethyl ethanoate | 0.61 |
| water | 0.35 |
| ethanoic acid | 0.25 |
| ethanol | 0.25 |

But you may not be given any indication of the total volume of the mixture. In such a case, you would state that the total volume was $V\,dm^3$ and then use the following values in mol dm$^{-3}$ before insertion into the equilibrium expression:

$$[\text{ethyl ethanoate}] = \frac{0.61}{V}\ \text{mol dm}^{-3} \qquad [\text{water}] = \frac{0.35}{V}\ \text{mol dm}^{-3}$$

$$[\text{ethanoic acid}] = \frac{0.25}{V}\ \text{mol dm}^{-3} \qquad [\text{ethanol}] = \frac{0.25}{V}\ \text{mol dm}^{-3}$$

In this case, the $V$ terms all cancel when substituted into the equilibrium expression, so you may wonder why you should bother to put them in. Realise, however, that the concentration terms in the equilibrium expression should always be in units of mol dm$^{-3}$, so do not take short cuts.

Moreover the $V$ terms only cancel out because there are the *same number* of concentration terms on the top and bottom of the equilibrium expression. In many cases this is not so, and you would need to know the total volume of the equilibrium mixture before you could attempt any sensible calculation.

As another example let us look at some results from a study of the equilibrium:

$$2NO_2(\text{solvent}) \rightleftharpoons N_2O_4(\text{solvent})$$

Equilibrium mixtures can be in an organic solvent at temperatures near 0 °C. The composition of the equilibrium mixture can be calculated from the intensity of colour of the solution because dinitrogen tetraoxide, $N_2O_4$, is colourless but nitrogen dioxide, $NO_2$, is brown.

## QUESTION

In a solution of this kind, at 10 °C, the equilibrium concentrations in a set of mixtures were:

| $[NO_2]_{\text{eqm}}$/mol dm$^{-3}$ | $[N_2O_4]_{\text{eqm}}$/mol dm$^{-3}$ |
|---|---|
| 0.0012 | 0.13 |
| 0.0016 | 0.28 |
| 0.0019 | 0.32 |
| 0.0021 | 0.42 |
| 0.0028 | 0.78 |

For each pair of concentrations, calculate the value of $K_c$ for this reaction at 10 °C using an appropriate expression for $K_c$: with a calculator the work should not take long. Include the correct units. Are the values constant?

## STUDY TASK

An equilibrium that has been widely investigated is that involving hydrogen, iodine and hydrogen iodide, all as gases.

$$H_2(g) + I_2(g) \rightleftharpoons 2HI(g)$$

Known amounts of mixtures of hydrogen and iodine, or pure hydrogen iodide, were sealed in glass containers and heated at constant temperature for a considerable time until equilibrium was reached.

The reaction was then cooled rapidly to 'freeze' the equilibrium in the condition it was in at the high temperature. Then the glass container was opened under potassium iodide solution to dissolve the iodine and hydrogen iodide.

Portions of the solution were then titrated with sodium thiosulphate solution to determine how much iodine was present in the equilibrium mixture.

Here are some results of equilibrium concentrations at 400 °C.

a    Results obtained by heating hydrogen and iodine in sealed containers:

| $[H_2(g)]$ /$10^{-3}$ mol dm$^{-3}$ | $[I_2(g)]$ /$10^{-3}$ mol dm$^{-3}$ | $[HI(g)]$ /$10^{-3}$ mol dm$^{-3}$ |
|---|---|---|
| 4.56 | 0.74 | 13.54 |
| 3.56 | 1.25 | 15.59 |
| 2.25 | 2.34 | 16.85 |

**b**   Results obtained by heating hydrogen iodide in sealed containers:

| $[H_2(g)]$ $/10^{-3}\,mol\,dm^{-3}$ | $[I_2(g)]$ $/10^{-3}\,mol\,dm^{-3}$ | $[HI(g)]$ $/10^{-3}\,mol\,dm^{-3}$ |
|---|---|---|
| 0.48 | 0.48 | 3.53 |
| 0.50 | 0.50 | 3.66 |
| 1.14 | 1.14 | 8.41 |

**1**   Use each of these sets of results to determine the values of these possible expressions for $K_c$:

$$\frac{[HI(g)]}{[H_2(g)]\,[I_2(g)]} \quad \text{and} \quad \frac{[HI(g)]^2}{[H_2(g)]\,[I_2(g)]}$$

**2**   Which of these expressions has a more constant value?

**3**   Which of these expressions is in accordance with the Equilibrium Law?

The Equilibrium Law is an empirical law, that is, a law established from the results of large numbers of experimental results. So it is important to link the value of the equilibrium constant to a specific chemical equation. For example, the chemical equation for the reaction we are studying could, just as validly, be written as:

$$\tfrac{1}{2}H_2(g) + \tfrac{1}{2}I_2(g) \rightleftharpoons HI(g)$$

**4**   What expression is used to calculate $K_c$ from this equation?

**5**   Is the value the same as the constant value obtained earlier?

**6**   If not, how are the two sets of constant values related?

# Heterogeneous equilibria

All the systems for which you have met $K_c$ expressions so far are examples of **homogeneous equilibria**. This means that the substances involved in the system are all in the *same phase*: all are gases, or all are liquids, or all are aqueous solutions.

However, many equilibria involve substances which are not all in the same phase. These equilibria are referred to as **heterogeneous equilibria**. For example when calcium carbonate is decomposed by heating strongly the equation is:

$$CaCO_3(s) \rightleftharpoons CaO(s) + CO_2(g)$$

Concentrations are measured, as usual, in units of $mol\,dm^{-3}$. But for a solid the concentration does not alter, and the equilibrium constant for the reaction is therefore written:

$$K_c = [CO_2(g)]$$

You will be meeting another example of a heterogeneous equilibrium in Experiment 14.2. You will be determining an equilibrium constant in this experiment.

# Measurement of an equilibrium constant, $K_c$

There is a microscale alternative to this experiment

### COMMENT

[Ag(s)] does not appear in the expression for $K_c$ because the mass of solid silver present does not alter the concentration of solid silver, which therefore remains constant.

Silver ions and iron(II) ions react in a slow redox reaction. This reaches an equilibrium in which both ions are present in measurable concentrations.

$$Ag^+(aq) + Fe^{2+}(aq) \rightleftharpoons Ag(s) + Fe^{3+}(aq)$$

The concentration of silver ions can be measured by titration with potassium thiocyanate. The equilibrium constant can then be calculated from the relationship:

$$K_c = \frac{[Fe^{3+}(aq)]}{[Ag^+(aq)] \times [Fe^{2+}(aq)]}$$

When titrating the reaction mixture with potassium thiocyanate, KCNS, the first reaction is the precipitation of silver thiocyanate.

$$KCNS(aq) + AgNO_3(aq) \longrightarrow AgCNS(s) + KNO_3(aq)$$

When all the silver ions have been removed from solution, thiocyanate ions react with the iron(III) ions in the equilibrium mixture to give a deep red colour. This acts as an indication of the end-point of the titration.

$$CNS^-(aq) + Fe^{3+}(aq) \longrightarrow Fe(CNS)^{2+}(aq)$$

This procedure should be successful because the equilibrium changes quite slowly.

## Procedure

Using separate clean pipettes transfer $25.0 \, cm^3$ each of $0.10 \, M$ silver nitrate solution and $0.10 \, M$ iron(II) sulphate solution into a dry $100 \, cm^3$ conical flask, stopper it so that it is air-tight and allow to stand undisturbed overnight.

During this time the equilibrium is established. There should be a precipitate of silver, which settles to the bottom of the flask.

Using a pipette, transfer $10.0 \, cm^3$ of the solution into another conical flask, disturbing the silver precipitate as little as possible. Titrate the sample with $0.020 \, M$ potassium thiocyanate. The end-point is marked by the first permanent brown/red colour. Take care: it is easy to 'overshoot' the end-point.

Repeat the titration (twice if possible) and calculate the average of your 'good' titres.

✎  **In your notes:**

1  Why is it necessary to keep the mixture in an air-tight flask and leave it overnight before doing the titration?

2  Calculation. When you mix equal volumes of two solutions you are effectively diluting both of them by half so the initial concentrations are:

$$[Fe^{2+}]_{initial} = 0.05 \, mol \, dm^{-3} \text{ and } [Ag^+]_{initial} = 0.05 \, mol \, dm^{-3}$$

The equation for the titration reaction is:

$$KCNS(aq) + AgNO_3(aq) \longrightarrow AgCNS(s) + KNO_3(aq)$$

Use it to calculate the concentration of $[Ag^+]_{eqm}$ from your titration results.

Since          $[Fe^{2+}]_{initial} = [Ag^+]_{initial}$
it follows that     $[Fe^{2+}]_{eqm} = [Ag^+]_{eqm}$
so           $[Fe^{2+}]_{eqm} = $ your answer to **2**
and           $[Fe^{3+}]_{eqm} = [Fe^{2+}]_{initial} - [Fe^{2+}]_{eqm}$

**Figure 14.6   Microscale apparatus for Experiment 14.2**

Using   $K_c = \dfrac{[Fe^{3+}(aq)]_{eqm}}{[Ag^+(aq)]_{eqm} \times [Fe^{2+}(aq)]_{eqm}}$

calculate $K_c$ and give its correct units in your result.

3   Explain why $[Fe^{3+}]_{eqm} = [Fe^{2+}]_{initial} - [Fe^{2+}]_{eqm}$. If you are unsure, imagine starting with 5 ions of each reagent and letting 2 react. Work it out with labelled pieces of paper.

## 14.3   The equilibrium constant for reactions involving gases, $K_p$

Although it is possible to measure the concentration of a gas in moles per cubic decimetre (mol dm$^{-3}$) and determine a value of $K_c$ for a gaseous equilibrium, it is often more convenient to measure the pressure of a gas and to use an equilibrium constant expressed in terms of gas pressures.

The possibility of using a pressure relationship for an equilibrium constant arises from the fact that the total pressure of a mixture of gases is the sum of the separate pressures, called partial pressures, of each of the gases in the mixture. **The partial pressure of a gas in a mixture is the pressure that the gas would have if it alone occupied the volume occupied by the whole mixture.**

For example, for three gases in a mixture with a total pressure of $P$ atmospheres, the individual gases can be described as exerting external partial pressures of $p_1, p_2$ and $p_3$. So the total pressure, $P$, is

$$P = p_1 + p_2 + p_3$$

This law was first established by Dalton in 1801 and is known as the **Law of partial pressures**.

**At constant temperature the pressure of a gas is proportional to its concentration.**

This relationship is particularly helpful in dealing with equilibrium mixtures of gases, because it allows us to use **an equilibrium constant determined in terms of gas pressures and which is given by the symbol $K_p$.** So, it is acceptable to use $K_p$ or $K_c$ for reactions, depending on the most convenient approach.

In a mixture of gases each gas exerts a partial pressure which depends on what proportion of it there is in the mixture. The partial pressure of each gas can be worked out from the relationship:

partial pressure = mole fraction $\times$ total pressure

The mole fraction of a particular gas in a mixture is in turn determined from the relationship:

$$\text{mole fraction} = \frac{\text{number of moles of a particular gas}}{\text{total number of moles of gas in the mixture}}$$

## Writing $K_p$ expressions

This is done in the same way as for $K_c$ except that only gases appear in the expression, any solids or liquids being omitted. Moreover, since there are no concentrations measured in mol dm$^{-3}$, square brackets [ ] are not used.

Instead we use the symbol $p$ to indicate the partial pressure of a gas, followed by the formula of the gas as a subscript.

Thus, for the reaction:

$$2NO_2(g) \rightleftharpoons N_2O_4(g)$$

$$K_p = \frac{p_{N_2O_4}}{p_{NO_2}^2}$$

and for the reaction:

$$C(s) + CO_2(g) \rightleftharpoons 2CO(g)$$

$$K_p = \frac{p_{CO}^2}{p_{CO_2}}$$

# Evaluating $K_p$

Here is an example of how to calculate a value for $K_p$. There are other examples for you to try in the questions at the end of this topic.

A mixture of 1.0 mole of ammonia, 3.6 moles of hydrogen and 13.5 moles of nitrogen (total 18.1 moles of gases) is at equilibrium at a total pressure of 200 atmospheres, and at a constant temperature. Calculate a value for $K_p$.

$$N_2(g) + 3H_2(g) \rightleftharpoons 2NH_3(g)$$

and    $$K_p = \frac{p_{NH_3}^2}{p_{N_2} p_{H_2}^3}$$

Partial pressure of ammonia, $p_{NH_3} = \dfrac{1.0}{18.1} \times 200$ atm

$$= 11 \text{ atm}$$

Partial pressure of hydrogen, $p_{H_2} = \dfrac{3.6}{18.1} \times 200$ atm

$$= 40 \text{ atm}$$

Partial pressure of nitrogen, $p_{N_2} = \dfrac{13.5}{18.1} \times 200$ atm

$$= 149 \text{ atm}$$

## COMMENT

You will notice that the same reaction has been used for calculations involving $K_c$ and $K_p$. The two terms are in fact related by a simple equation:

$$K_p = K_c(RT)^n$$

where $n$ is the number of molecules on the right-hand side of the chemical equation for the system minus the number of molecules on the left-hand side.

Therefore,    $$K_p = \frac{(11 \text{ atm})^2}{(149 \text{ atm})(40 \text{ atm})^3}$$

$$= 1.3 \times 10^{-5} \text{ atm}^{-2}$$

You will note that we started to work with partial pressures only when we knew the quantities in moles which were present at equilibrium.

It is generally best, when evaluating $K_p$, to keep everything in moles for as long as possible.

# 14.4 Entropy and equilibrium reactions

When we first encountered the idea of equilibrium, in Topic 7, we examined the way in which an equilibrium responded to changes in concentration, pressure and temperature. We summed up the effects in terms of Le Chatelier's Principle. We are now going to try and explain the effects of the changes in terms of the changes in entropy which occur.

In Topic 13 on entropy we found out how to calculate the total entropy change for a reaction

$$\Delta S_{total} = \Delta S_{system} + \Delta S_{surroundings}$$

and concluded that **for all spontaneous changes $\Delta S_{total}$ is positive**

But in this topic we have been looking at reactions that are spontaneous in *both* directions:

$$acid + alcohol \longrightarrow ester + water$$

is spontaneous but so is

$$ester + water \longrightarrow acid + alcohol$$

How can the total entropy change be positive in both directions? The paradox is resolved by looking for the differences between the *theoretical* world of a system plus its surroundings and the *real* world of the laboratory.

To calculate **standard** entropy changes, some assumptions about the change from the initial state to the final state have been made:

1. Pure reactants changed to pure products with no intermediate mixing.

2. The temperature remained constant at 298 K.

3. The pressure remained constant at 1 atmosphere.

What is the effect on the total entropy changes when we do real experiments in conditions that are not the standard conditions?

Let us remind ourselves of an experiment we first saw in Topic 7. It will be useful to see the experiment again.

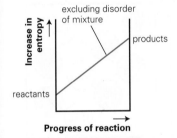

Figure 14.7 **Entropy change as a reaction progresses, excluding the effect of the mixing of products with reactants**

---

| EXPERIMENT 14.4 | The $N_2O_4 \rightleftharpoons 2NO_2$ equilibrium |

**SAFETY** ⚠

Nitrogen oxides are severely irritant and toxic; this experiment must be carried out in a fume cupboard.

The nitrogen dioxide produced from the thermal decomposition of lead(II) nitrate can be trapped in an ice bath and small amounts sealed in a glass tube if sufficient care is taken. Otherwise samples can be collected in a gas syringe.

## Procedure

Have two beakers of water available, one cooled to less than 10 °C with ice and the other warmed to about 50 °C.

Note the colour of the gas mixture at room temperature, and what the changes are on cooling and warming.

**COMMENT**

Sudden changes in pressure are approximately 'adiabatic' which means that no energy is exchanged with the surroundings.

If your sample of gas is in a gas syringe note the colour change when the pressure is suddenly altered, both increased and decreased.

 **In your notes:** Remembering that pure $N_2O_4$ is colourless and $NO_2$ is brown, how do you interpret the changes in colour? The colour changes with pressure change are not so easy to interpret because the volume change will alter the colour anyhow.

# The effect of product concentration on entropy change

Consider the conversion of dinitrogen tetraoxide to nitrogen dioxide. The molecules of pure dinitrogen tetraoxide will be disordered to a certain extent. The disorder will increase when some molecules decompose because there will be two types of molecule instead of one. The disorder will increase further when more molecules decompose, but not by so much because there are already some nitrogen dioxide molecules present.

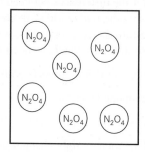 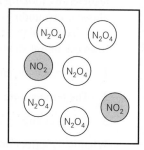 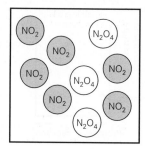

Figure 14.8 **Increasing molecular disorder as a reaction progresses**

So in the early stages of the reaction we get proportionately greater positive entropy changes in the system than at later stages. You could think of this as an example of the 'law of diminishing returns'. Each increase is not as great as the previous increase.

We can therefore expect that at some stage of the reaction there will be so many product molecules that producing any more will actually reduce the extent of disorder in the system. At this stage the entropy change of the system for the forward reaction will have become negative and as far as the system is concerned the reaction might as well 'stop'.

The amount of entropy change in the surroundings also depends on how much reaction has actually occurred; and the same arguments will apply to the reverse reaction. So we can deduce that at the position of dynamic equilibrium for the **total** entropy change (system and surroundings):

$$\Delta S_{\text{total(forward)}} = \Delta S_{\text{total(reverse)}}$$

This means that at equilibrium the overall entropy change is *zero*.

There is a simple relationship between standard entropy change and extent of reaction:

$$\Delta S^{\ominus}_{\text{total}} \propto \ln K$$

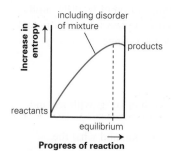

Figure 14.9 **Entropy change as a reaction progresses, *including* the effect of mixing of products with reactants**

COMMENT

The relationship between entropy change and extent of reaction can be stated quantitatively as

$$\Delta S^{\ominus}_{total} = R \ln K$$

where $R = 8.31 \text{ J K}^{-1} \text{ mol}^{-1}$

You will not be expected to use this relationship.

Figure 14.10 **Skaters making use of the variation of entropy with pressure. Ice melts under pressure and the water lubricates the skater**

COMMENT

high pressure $\longrightarrow$

more molecules $\rightleftharpoons$ fewer molecules

$\longleftarrow$ low pressure

Notice that the equilibrium constant has been written in this proportionality as $K$ rather than as $K_c$ or $K_p$. This is because in the case of equilibrium systems which do not involve gases, $K_c$ is used but in such systems when gases are involved, $K_p$ is used instead.

We can, therefore, deduce from our discussions and this expression that all reactions are reversible to some extent.

When a reaction has a value for its total standard entropy change in the range of about $+40$ to $-40 \text{ J mol}^{-1} \text{ K}^{-1}$, the reaction will produce a mixture of products and reactants that can be regarded as an equilibrium.

When a reaction has a total standard entropy change of $+200 \text{ J mol}^{-1} \text{ K}^{-1}$ or more, the concentration of reactants at 'equilibrium' will be less than the concentration of the traces of impurities that are present in all laboratory reagents, so we regard the reaction as 'complete'.

When a reaction has a total standard entropy change of $-800 \text{ J mol}^{-1} \text{ K}^{-1}$ or less, the concentration of products at 'equilibrium' will be so small that normal analytical procedures would not detect their presence, so we would normally say that the reaction 'does not go'.

## The effect of pressure on entropy change

We should not expect the effect of pressure to be significant for solids and liquids (the melting point of ice changes from 0 °C to only $-8$ °C even when the pressure is increased to 1000 atmospheres). But the number of ways gas particles can be arranged alters a lot with a change of pressure.

When the pressure on a gas is reduced the volume increases and this increases the number of ways of arranging the gas particles, which is an increase in the entropy of the gas.

So a reaction like

$$ZnCO_3(s) \rightleftharpoons ZnO(s) + CO_2(g)$$

will go further in the forward direction when the pressure is reduced.

**In general you need to lower the pressure to shift a reaction in the direction of more molecules, and raise the pressure to shift a reaction in the direction of producing fewer molecules.** For example:

high pressure $\longrightarrow$

$$N_2(g) + 3H_2(g) \rightleftharpoons 2NH_3(g)$$

$\longleftarrow$ low pressure

### STUDY TASK

Apply these ideas to the equilibrium

$$N_2O_4(g) \rightleftharpoons 2NO_2(g)$$

Do your conclusions agree with your observations made in Experiment 14.4?

# The effect of temperature on entropy change

We have already established in Topic 13 that the entropy change in the surroundings is:

$$\Delta S_{\text{surroundings}} = \frac{-\Delta H_{\text{reaction}}}{T}$$

What happens to the value of the entropy change if the apparatus is cooled in an ice bath, or heated in boiling water, or even in an electric furnace? The entropy change will no longer be a standard entropy but $\Delta H^{\ominus}(298)$ can still be used to estimate a value for the entropy change, because $\Delta H^{\ominus}$ does not vary much with temperature.

The thermal decomposition of zinc carbonate from Experiment 13.1 part **6** provides an example:

$$ZnCO_3(s) \longrightarrow ZnO(s) + CO_2(g)$$

For this reaction

$$\begin{array}{cccc} \Delta S^{\ominus}_{\text{total}} = & \Delta S^{\ominus}_{\text{system}} & + & \Delta S^{\ominus}_{\text{surroundings}} \\ -63 & +175 & & -238 \end{array} \quad \text{J mol}^{-1}\,\text{K}^{-1}$$

and    $\Delta H^{\ominus}_{\text{reaction}}(298) = +71\,000\,\text{J mol}^{-1}$

It is possible to calculate the effect on the entropy change of raising the temperature, for example to 500 K, by using

$$\Delta S_{\text{surroundings}} = \frac{-\Delta H_{\text{reaction}}}{T}$$

so        $\Delta S_{\text{surroundings}}(500) = -71\,000 \div 500 = -142\,\text{J mol}^{-1}\,\text{K}^{-1}$

Since $\Delta S^{\ominus}_{\text{system}}$ does not normally vary significantly with temperature,

$$\Delta S_{\text{total}}(500) = +175 - 142 = +33\,\text{J mol}^{-1}\,\text{K}^{-1}$$

By prediction, the reaction is spontaneous. This matches our experience that zinc carbonate decomposes quite readily when heated.

# How to make reactions go the way you want

The position of equilibrium can be shifted in favour of more product using these general guidelines:

1   raise the pressure when there are fewer product molecules than reactant molecules

2   lower the pressure when there are more product molecules than reactant molecules

3   raise the temperature when the reaction is endothermic

4   lower the temperature when the reaction is exothermic.

The appropriate procedure is to do the opposite to the natural effect of the reaction:

- A reduction in molecules causes a pressure drop, so compress it.
- An endothermic reaction cools the apparatus, so heat it.

These guidelines are in fact part of Le Chatelier's Principle, which was introduced in Topic 7.

**When a system in equilibrium is subjected to a change, the processes which take place are such as to tend to counteract the change.**

When the principle was first introduced, it was based on observation alone with no explanation in terms of energy or the behaviour of molecules. Now you should have some understanding of the chemistry underlying Le Chatelier's Principle.

## 14.5 Acid–base equilibria

When an egg is first laid by a hen, the yolk is slightly acidic and the white is slightly alkaline, but as the egg ages the contents become much more alkaline and the egg becomes 'runnier'. The yolk is much more likely to break as you cook your egg. In this, and hundreds of other ways, we meet subtle acid–base changes in our daily lives.

In Topic 4 we introduced the Brønsted–Lowry theory of acids and bases. In this theory, an acid is a substance which can *provide* protons (hydrogen ions) in a reaction; a base is a substance which can *combine with* protons.

We shall now take the theory a little further and look at its quantitative applications.

So far you will have studied mainly the reactions of strong acids, such as sulphuric acid, and the weathering they can cause (see figure 14.11). In this topic you will study mainly the behaviour of weak acids in reactions which are reversible. Their behaviour is best summarised as:

$$acid_1 + base_2 \rightleftharpoons base_1 + acid_2$$

We shall also explain pH values and how they can be calculated. Finally, we shall explain how solutions which resist changes in pH, that is buffer solutions, work. They have a vital role in living systems, maintaining a steady pH in your blood and all your body cells.

Figure 14.11 **Weathering of stone sculpture by acid rain on a building in Oxford**

| EXPERIMENT 14.5 |
| --- |

# What is an acid?

Start by collecting data on the pH of some aqueous solutions. **Record the results for all these experiments with particular care. You will need to refer to them while working through the remainder of this topic.**

**SAFETY** ⚠

All acidic and alkaline solutions should be handled with care; the majority are corrosive depending on the concentration.

## Procedure

1 Using Full-range Indicator solution, test the pH of dilute solutions of the following sets of compounds:

$H_2SO_4$,    $NaHSO_4$,    $Na_2SO_4$
$H_3PO_4$,    $NaH_2PO_4$,    $Na_2HPO_4$,    $Na_3PO_4$

Classify the compounds into three groups using their **formulae**:

- those that you would expect to donate protons
- those that you would expect to accept protons
- those that you would expect both to **donate** protons and to **accept** protons.

✎ **In your notes:** Which is more helpful to acid–base classification: the pH value of the solution or the ability to donate or accept protons?

2 a Measure the pH of 0.1 M ethanoic acid and of 0.1 M solutions of the following salts: sodium carbonate, ammonium chloride and sodium ethanoate.

 b Add pieces of clean magnesium ribbon to the solutions. Record any signs of reaction.

3 Record the colours of the following indicators in both acidic and alkaline solution: methyl orange, phenolphthalein, bromothymol blue and bromophenol blue.

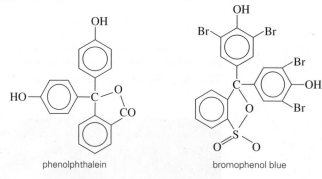

phenolphthalein            bromophenol blue

# Interpretation of acid–base reactions

**COMMENT**

An acid is a proton donor; a base is a proton acceptor.

The chemistry of acid–base systems is concerned with equilibria between ionically-bonded species and covalently-bonded species. Equal sharing of electrons (a true covalent bond) occurs only between like atoms, as in $H_2$, $Cl_2$, etc. Bonding between unlike atoms always results in unequal sharing and polar bonds, for example:

$$\overset{\delta+}{H}\!-\!\overset{\delta-}{Cl}$$

The degree of electron sharing in polar molecules is changed when they are dissolved in polar solvents. This results in the formation of ions. It happens when hydrogen chloride reacts with water

$$HCl(g) + H_2O(l) \longrightarrow H_3O^+(aq) + Cl^-(aq)$$

a process which can be seen as two stages:

$$HCl(g) \longrightarrow H^+ + Cl^-$$
$$H^+ + Cl^- + H_2O(l) \longrightarrow H_3O^+(aq) + Cl^-(aq)$$

**COMMENT**

$H_3O^+(aq)$ can be referred to as the **conjugate acid** of $H_2O(l)$; and $Cl^-(aq)$ can be referred to as the **conjugate base** of $HCl(g)$

The hydrogen ion, $H^+$, is a single proton, with no electrons. Thus it is some 50 000 times smaller than the next smallest cation, $Li^+$. The possibility of very close approach between the free proton and the oxygen atom in the water molecule results in a strong bond being formed by a lone pair of electrons on the oxygen atom. Many other substances react with water in this way.

One consequence of the Brønsted–Lowry theory of acids and bases is that when an acid donates a proton in a neutralisation reaction it becomes a substance that can, in turn, accept a proton. It becomes, in effect, another base. For example, the equilibria involved in the reaction of hydrogen chloride with water are

**STUDY TASK**

Use the Brønsted–Lowry theory to interpret the results of Experiment 14.5.

$$\underset{\text{acid}_1}{HCl(aq)} \rightleftharpoons \underset{\text{base}_1}{Cl^-(aq)} + H^+$$

and

$$\underset{\text{base}_2}{H_2O(l)} + H^+ \rightleftharpoons \underset{\text{acid}_2}{H_3O^+(aq)}$$

These can be combined to give:

$$\underset{\text{acid}_1}{HCl(aq)} + \underset{\text{base}_2}{H_2O(l)} \rightleftharpoons \underset{\text{base}_1}{Cl^-(aq)} + \underset{\text{acid}_2}{H_3O^+(aq)}$$

In this reaction, water behaves as a base by accepting a proton.

Similarly by accepting a proton a base becomes a substance that can donate a proton: it becomes an acid. In aqueous ammonia, for example, the acid–base equilibrium is

**COMMENT**

Ammonium chloride, $NH_4Cl$, is not usually called an acid, but when it dissolves in water the solution is weakly acidic. The Brønsted–Lowry theory copes with this because it views the ammonium ion as a weak acid:

$$NH_4^+(aq) + H_2O(l) \rightleftharpoons$$
$$NH_3(aq) + H_3O^+(aq)$$

The ammonium ion donates a proton to a water molecule. The equilibrium **lies to the left** but there are sufficient hydrogen ions in solution to make it noticeably acidic.

$$\underset{\text{base}_1}{NH_3(aq)} + \underset{\text{acid}_2}{H_2O(l)} \rightleftharpoons \underset{\text{acid}_1}{NH_4^+(aq)} + \underset{\text{base}_2}{OH^-(aq)}$$

In this reaction water acts as an acid by donating a proton.

$$\begin{array}{c} H \\ | \\ H\!-\!N\!\cdots\!H \\ | \\ H \end{array}^{+}$$

**A reaction between an acid and a base is essentially a competition for protons.**

# pH and the equilibrium constant for the ionisation of water

In practical laboratory situations acids are generally used in aqueous solutions, and we must therefore take into account some of the properties of water.

You have seen that water is able to function both as a base, accepting protons

$$H^+ + H_2O \longrightarrow H_3O^+$$

and as an acid, donating protons

$$H_2O \longrightarrow H^+ + OH^-$$

As a consequence, an equilibrium exists in water, with some of the molecules acting as an acid and some as a base

$$2H_2O(l) \rightleftharpoons H_3O^+(aq) + OH^-(aq)$$

or more simply

$$H_2O(l) \rightleftharpoons H^+(aq) + OH^-(aq)$$

and we say that the water is **ionised**. The equilibrium constant for this ionisation, $K_c$, is given by

$$K_c = \frac{[H^+(aq)]\,[OH^-(aq)]}{[H_2O(l)]}$$

Rearranging the expression, we get:

$$K_c \times [H_2O(l)] = [H^+(aq)]\,[OH^-(aq)]$$

We can treat the concentration of water molecules, $[H_2O(l)]$, as constant because the proportion of water molecules that ionises is very small. The lefthand side of this equation is therefore a constant. It is known as the ionisation constant for water, and given the symbol $K_w$.

**At 298 K, $K_w = [H^+(aq)]\,[OH^-(aq)] = 1 \times 10^{-14}\,mol^2\,dm^{-6}$**

In pure water, and in any absolutely **neutral** solution

$$[H^+(aq)] = [OH^-(aq)]$$

and so the value of each is $\sqrt{1 \times 10^{-14}} = 1 \times 10^{-7}\,mol\,dm^{-3}$. This small value shows that our assumption that $[H_2O(l)]$ can be treated as constant was correct.

## EXAMPLE

- In 0.1 M HCl in water

$$[H^+(aq)] = 10^{-1} \text{ mol dm}^{-3}$$

and since in water

$$[H^+(aq)] [OH^-(aq)] = K_w = 10^{-14} \text{ mol}^2 \text{ dm}^{-6}$$

we can deduce that the concentration of hydroxide ions in 0.1 M HCl is

$$[OH^-(aq)] = 10^{-14} \div 10^{-1} = 10^{-13} \text{ mol dm}^{-3}$$

Therefore even in a strong acidic solution there is a very small equilibrium concentration of hydroxide ions.

- In 0.01 M NaOH

$$[OH^-(aq)] = 10^{-2} \text{ mol dm}^{-3}$$

Therefore by the same type of calculation

$$[H^+(aq)] = 10^{-14} \div 10^{-2} = 10^{-12} \text{ mol dm}^{-3}$$

and we find that in a strongly alkaline solution there is a very small equilibrium concentration of hydrogen ions.

Because the range of possible hydrogen ion concentrations in solution is very large, from about $10 \text{ mol dm}^{-3}$ to $10^{-15} \text{ mol dm}^{-3}$, chemists find it convenient to use a logarithmic scale. This is the origin of the **pH scale**, and the relationship between the pH value of a solution and the hydrogen ion concentration is

$$pH = -\log_{10} [H^+(aq)]$$

where $[H^+(aq)]$ is measured in $\text{mol dm}^{-3}$. The minus sign is introduced to make pH values positive in almost all cases.

A few examples should help to make the relationship clearer. When

$$[H^+(aq)] = 1 \times 10^{-3} \text{ mol dm}^{-3} \qquad pH = 3$$
$$[H^+(aq)] = 1 \times 10^{-8} \text{ mol dm}^{-3} \qquad pH = 8$$
$$[H^+(aq)] = 5 \times 10^{-4} \text{ mol dm}^{-3} \qquad pH = 3.3$$

When, with concentrations in $\text{mol dm}^{-3}$:

$$[OH^-(aq)] = 10^{-2} \qquad [H^+(aq)] = 10^{-12} \qquad pH = 12$$
$$[OH^-(aq)] = 10^{-4} \qquad [H^+(aq)] = 10^{-10} \qquad pH = 10$$
$$[OH^-(aq)] = 5 \times 10^{-1} \qquad [H^+(aq)] = 2 \times 10^{-12} \qquad pH = 11.7$$

The range of pH values you will actually encounter in aqueous systems varies between just less than zero (concentrated acid) and a little over 14 (concentrated alkali). Your teacher may give you some more examples on how to work out logarithms.

## COMMENT

Memorise the relationship

$$pH = -\log_{10} [H^+(aq)]$$

## BACKGROUND

The pH scale is a logarithmic scale using logarithms **to base 10**, symbol '$\log_{10}$' or just 'log'. In other topics the logarithms that are used are 'natural logarithms' (common logarithms) to base $e$, where $e = 2.718...$, symbol 'ln'.

## STUDY TASK

Use your calculator to check the pH examples; do the calculations from pH to concentration as well.

## 14.6 The strengths of acids and bases

## COMMENT

Two species which differ in formula by $H^+$ are known as a conjugate pair. HA for example, is an acid but $A^-$ is its conjugate base.

When an acid, represented by HA, is dissolved in water, an equilibrium is established

$$HA(aq) \rightleftharpoons A^-(aq) + H^+(aq)$$

where HA is an acid and $A^-$ is its conjugate base.

In examples where HA loses protons readily, a high concentration of $H^+$

TOPIC 14

ions will be produced when the system has reached equilibrium. In this case HA is functioning as a strong acid.

On the other hand, where HA is a weak acid with no pronounced tendency to part with protons to water, the concentration of $H^+$ ions will be smaller.

In effect, the $H^+$ ion can be used as a standard against which to compare the relative strengths of acids. The problem now becomes one of measuring the hydrogen ion concentration, $[H^+]$, in aqueous solutions of different acids.

When we measure pH values for progressively diluted hydrochloric acid, we find that there is an increase of about one pH unit per tenfold dilution. For example:

pH of 1.0 M    HCl(aq) is approximately 0
pH of 0.1 M    HCl(aq) is approximately 1
pH of 0.01 M   HCl(aq) is approximately 2
pH of 0.001 M  HCl(aq) is approximately 3

These observations can be accounted for if we assume that when the gas dissolves in water it is almost completely ionised at all concentrations, so that the equilibrium

$$HCl(g) \rightleftharpoons HCl(aq) \rightleftharpoons H^+(aq) + Cl^-(aq)$$

lies almost completely over to the right. A tenfold dilution will then reduce the value of $[H^+(aq)]$ by $\frac{1}{10}$ and the pH will have increased by 1 unit ($-\log \frac{1}{10} = 1$).

A few other acidic solutions behave in the same way. For most acidic solutions, however, the increase in pH for a dilution factor of ten is less than one unit, and the pH values for comparable concentrations are always greater than for hydrochloric acid solutions. This means that dissociation into ions is incomplete and a considerable proportion of reactants remains when the equilibrium

$$HA(aq) \rightleftharpoons H^+(aq) + A^-(aq)$$

is reached. Thus the hydrogen ion concentration will be smaller than would be expected for complete dissociation and the pH value higher.

**Acids which ionise nearly completely at moderate dilutions (e.g. 0.1 M or 0.01 M) are called strong acids.**

**Those which ionise slightly, or exist mainly as the covalently bonded form at moderate dilutions (e.g. 0.1 M or 0.01 M) are called weak acids.**

There is no sharp dividing line between strong and weak acids but rather a spectrum of acidic properties. $H^+(aq)$ ions catalyse the hydrolysis of sugars in solution. The rate of reaction is a measure of the concentration of $H^+(aq)$ ions (figure 14.12).

In the Brønsted–Lowry definition, the strength of an acid is measured by the extent to which protons are released and the strength of a base by the extent to which protons are accepted. The strength of an acid, represented by HA, is given by the equilibrium constant, $K_c$, for the following reaction

$$HA(aq) \rightleftharpoons H^+(aq) + A^-(aq)$$

where HA is an acid and $A^-$ is the conjugate base. We will use $H^+(aq)$ rather than $H_3O^+(aq)$ to simplify the expressions, so for this equilibrium:

$$K_c = \frac{[H^+(aq)]\,[A^-(aq)]}{[HA(aq)]}$$

When dealing with acid–base equilibria the symbol $K_a$ is often used instead of $K_c$.

$$\frac{[H^+(aq)]\,[A^-(aq)]}{[HA(aq)]} = K_a \text{ (the dissociation constant of the acid)}$$

---

**COMMENT**

Instruments known as pH meters can be used to determine the pH of a solution with greater accuracy than can be achieved by using indicators; a glass electrode is immersed in the solution whose pH is to be determined and the value is read off a meter. The pH meter is described in more detail in Topic 21.

---

**COMMENT**

| Acid | $K_a$ value/mol dm$^{-3}$ |
|---|---|
| Ethanoic | $1.7 \times 10^{-5}$ |
| Carbonic | $4.5 \times 10^{-7}$ |
| Phenol | $1.3 \times 10^{-10}$ |

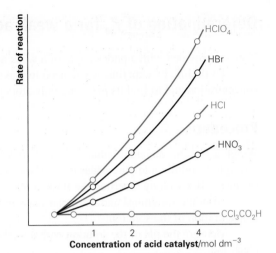

Figure 14.12   **The rate of hydrolysis of sugar depends on acid strength. The graph shows that hydrochloric acid is a strong acid, perchloric(VII) acid, HClO$_4$ is the strongest and trichloroethanoic acid the weakest of the acids tested**

Table 6.5 in the *Book of data* shows the relative strengths of various acids as represented by their equilibrium constants. The Brønsted–Lowry definition covers almost all the common acid and base reactions and is the one most generally used.

## Converting $K_a$ values to pH values

As an example, we will calculate the value of the pH of a 0.01 mol dm$^{-3}$ solution of methanoic acid, HCO$_2$H, at 25 °C. The value of $K_a$ from table 6.5 in the *Book of data* is $1.6 \times 10^{-4}$ mol dm$^{-3}$.

$$HCO_2H(aq) \rightleftharpoons HCO_2^-(aq) + H^+(aq)$$

$$K_a = \frac{[HCO_2^-(aq)]\,[H^+(aq)]}{[HCO_2H(aq)]}$$

Neglecting the hydrogen ions which arise from ionisation of the water, since the concentration of these will be very small compared with the concentration of those from the acid, we can say that:

$$[H^+(aq)] = [HCO_2^-(aq)]$$

and   $[HCO_2H(aq)] = (0.01 - [H^+(aq)])$ mol dm$^{-3}$

We will also assume that the concentration of hydrogen ions is small compared to the concentration of methanoic acid.

So   $[HCO_2H(aq)] \approx 0.01$ mol dm$^{-3}$

$$K_a = \frac{[H^+(aq)]^2}{0.01 \text{ mol dm}^{-3}} = 1.6 \times 10^{-4} \text{ mol dm}^{-3}$$

$$[H^+(aq)]^2 = (1.6 \times 10^{-4} \text{ mol dm}^{-3}) \times (0.01 \text{ mol dm}^{-3})$$
$$= 1.6 \times 10^{-6} \text{ mol}^2 \text{ dm}^{-6}$$

$$[H^+(aq)] = 1.26 \times 10^{-3} \text{ mol dm}^{-3}$$

and   $pH = -\log[H^+(aq)]$

so   $pH = -\log(1.26 \times 10^{-3})$

and using your calculator

$$pH = 2.90$$

When the calculation is carried out *without* the assumptions, the pH value is 2.87. So you can see that making the assumptions still produces a satisfactory answer.

QUESTION

The pH of a solution of a weak acid for any molarity can be found if the value of $K_a$ for the acid is known. Calculate the pH of a 0.001 M solution of chloric(I) acid, HClO, given $K_a = 3.7 \times 10^{-8}$ mol dm$^{-3}$

**EXPERIMENT 14.6a**

# Determination of $K_a$ for a weak acid

You are provided with a pure sample of a weak acid.

To find $K_a$ by experiment you need to make a dilute solution of known concentration and to find its pH using indicators or a pH meter.

### SAFETY

Make a Risk Assessment for the acid you are going to use.

## Procedure

Weigh a $100\ cm^3$ standard volumetric flask. Add 1 drop of the weak acid and reweigh. Carefully add pure water to the flask until it is full to the 'ring-mark' on the neck. Mix well by inverting the flask at least 5 times.

From the weighings and the molar mass of the acid, calculate the concentration of the solution.

Measure the pH of the solution with a well washed and calibrated pH electrode.

If a pH meter is not available, pour some of the solution into each of two beakers. Test the contents of the first beaker with Full-range Indicator to get a rough idea of its pH. Then select a suitable narrow-range indicator and use it to test the contents of the second beaker. Record the pH as accurately as you can.

### COMMENT

Amount/mol

$$= \frac{\text{mass/g}}{\text{molar mass/g mol}^{-1}}$$

then concentration/mol dm$^{-3}$

$$= \frac{\text{amount/mol}}{\text{volume/dm}^3}$$

✎ **In your notes:**

1   You should be able to recall from which it follows that and

$$pH = -\log [H^+(aq)]$$
$$\log [H^+(aq)] = -pH$$
$$[H^+(aq)] = 10^{-pH}$$

Enter the pH of the solution into your calculator and, by using suitable functions, change its sign to '−' and find the value of $[H^+(aq)]$.

### COMMENT

[HA(aq)] is the concentration of the acid you calculated from the weighings.

2   Calculate a value for $K_a$ from the expression:

$$[H^+(aq)] = \sqrt{K_a \times [HA(aq)]}$$

State the correct units of $K_a$.

3   Check your answer against the value given in the *Book of data*. Which of your measurements is likely to have been the least accurate?

---

**EXPERIMENT 14.6b**

# Comparing some weak acids

Why is one acid weaker than another? What will be the effect on their reactions? The next brief experiment is designed to explore these two questions.

### SAFETY

Phenols and the chloroethanoic acids are toxic and corrosive. You will use a phenol provided by your teacher, but use the equivalent data for phenol itself from the *Book of data*.

## Procedure

Measure the pH of 0.1 M solutions of the following acids: ethanoic acid, chloroethanoic acid, dichloroethanoic acid and trichloroethanoic acid (TAKE CARE).

Find out whether dilute solutions of the following acids will react with sodium carbonate solution producing carbon dioxide gas: ethanoic acid, benzoic acid and a phenol (TAKE CARE). Use warm water to make your solution of benzoic acid.

### COMMENT

It is often convenient to use the logarithmic form of $K_a$.

$$pK_a = -\log K_a$$

**In your notes:**

**1** Use table 6.5 in the *Book of data* to complete this table:

| Name of acid | Equation with conjugate base | $K_a$ | $pK_a$ |
|---|---|---|---|
| Ethanoic | | | |
| Chloroethanoic | | | |
| Dichloroethanoic | | | |
| Trichloroethanoic | | | |
| Phenol | | | |
| Benzoic | | | |
| Carbonic | | | |

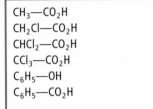

**2** Arrange carbonic, benzoic and ethanoic acids and phenol in order of acid strength, putting the strongest acid first.

Which of these acids would you expect to displace carbonic acid (carbonic acid readily decomposes into carbon dioxide and water) from a carbonate, and which would not?

**3** Write structural formulae for the first four of the acids in the list in the margin.

Can you suggest why the acids get stronger? *Hint*: look at the text on dipole-dipole interactions.

**4** Use the data to interpret the results of your experiment.

---

## 14.7 Acid–base titrations

When a base is added to an acid the reaction

$$H^+(aq) + OH^-(aq) \rightleftharpoons H_2O(l)$$

takes place. As we have already seen, this equilibrium lies far to the right. As a base is added to an acid the hydrogen ion concentration grows progressively less, that is, the pH value of the resulting solution grows progressively greater.

In the following experiment we will investigate, using a pH meter, how the pH changes on addition of a base.

### EXPERIMENT 14.7a

## The change of pH during an acid–base titration

There are four different combinations of acid and base possible, namely:

- strong acid and strong base
- strong acid and weak base
- weak acid and strong base
- weak acid and weak base.

The best procedure is to use a computer with a datalogger to capture and process the data.

**SAFETY** !

1.0 M acids and 1.0 M alkalis are likely to be corrosive.

## Procedure

Using a pipette and pipette filler, or a burette, put 25.0 cm³ of the 1.0 M acid that you are using in a 100 cm³ beaker. If a magnetic stirrer is available, stand the beaker on it, and place the stirrer bar in the beaker.

Fill a burette with 1.0 M alkali (TAKE CARE), and clamp it so that the alkali can be run into the acid in the beaker.

Connect the electrode to the computer via a suitable pH meter or other device, and put it in the acid in the beaker. Clamp it gently in position; if you are using a magnetic stirrer, make sure that the electrode is in a position where it cannot be struck by the stirrer bar when the stirrer is switched on.

Next, switch on the magnetic stirrer, start the computer procedure and run the alkali from the burette as a steady flow into the acid. You should add a total of 35 cm³ of alkali in this way.

Use the computer to plot the results as a graph of pH against time (which will approximate to volume of alkali added).

**COMMENT**

pH ranges of indicators are listed in table 6.6 of the *Book of data*.

 **In your notes:** Are the shapes of the graphs as you expected?

Use your results to select an appropriate indicator for each titration. You looked at the colour change of some indicators in Experiment 14.5.

## The theory of indicators

You will have used acid–base indicators such as methyl orange and phenolphthalein in previous work. They are used to test for alkalinity and acidity, and for detecting the end-point in acid–base titrations. A particular indicator cannot be used in all circumstances; some are more suitable for use with weak acids and others with weak bases. From a study of the titration curves that you obtained in Experiment 14.7a you will see that there is a rapid change of pH in the neutralisation reaction near its end-point.

However, this rapid change of pH occurs at a comparatively low pH during a titration of a strong acid against a weak base, and at a comparatively high pH during a titration of a weak acid against a strong base.

Different indicators change colour at different values of pH. Phenolphthalein, for example, changes colour over the range pH 8–10, and so is suitable for a titration involving a weak acid and a strong base, whose end-point occurs within this range.

Methyl orange, however, changes colour over the range pH 3–5, and so can be used to find the end-point in a titration involving a strong acid and a weak base.

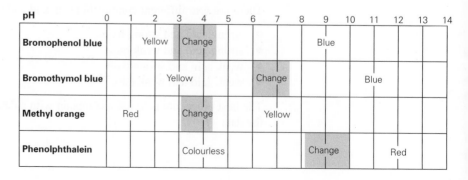

Figure 14.13 Colour change and pH range for some indicators

Phenolphthalein would be unsuitable for this type of titration, as it would only change colour when an excess of alkali was present, and then only gradually, instead of sharply on the addition of one drop of extra alkali.

**An indicator may be considered as a weak acid, for which either the acid or the corresponding base, or both, are coloured.** We can represent this in a general way, using HIn for the acid form, as

$$\text{HIn(aq)} \rightleftharpoons \text{H}^+(\text{aq}) + \text{In}^-(\text{aq})$$
colour A                    colour B

Addition of acid displaces the equilibrium to the left and increases the intensity of colour A. Addition of base, for example, $NH_3(aq)$, removes hydrogen ions

$$NH_3(\text{aq}) + \text{H}^+(\text{aq}) \longrightarrow NH_4^+(\text{aq})$$

with the result that the equilibrium moves to the right to restore the value of $K_a$ for the indicator and increase the intensity of colour B.

Therefore, when an indicator is added to a solution the colour of the system will depend on the relative concentrations, [HIn(aq)] and [In$^-$(aq)], which in turn depend on the pH of the solution.

## QUESTION

What colour is the HIn form of methyl orange and the In$^-$ form of phenolphthalein?

---

## INVESTIGATION 14.7b

# An analysis of vinegars

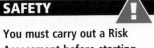

**SAFETY**

You must carry out a Risk Assessment before starting any experimental work and this must be checked, amended if necessary, approved and signed by your teacher.

Vinegar is a solution of ethanoic acid together with other acids and flavour components. A suitable investigation could attempt to answer questions such as:

- How does the concentration of ethanoic acid vary between vinegars and how accurate is the information provided by the manufacturer?
- What is the concentration of ethanoic acid in a particular vinegar and what are the concentrations of the other organic acids which are often found in vinegar?
- How can various components of a vinegar be separated and identified?

You may need to research methods for discovering whether a particular vinegar contains any other acids or not. If other acids are confirmed as being present separation is crucial if the concentration of the ethanoic acid alone is to be determined.

The determination of any acid concentration could well involve more than one technique.

This is not intended to be a complete list; you may wish to consider other aspects of the task.

A quantitative analysis of any concentrations calculated should be an important facet of an investigation.

## 14.8 Buffer solutions

Ethanoic acid is a weak acid, being only slightly ionised in solution
($K_a = 1.7 \times 10^{-5}$ mol dm$^{-3}$). In an aqueous solution of ethanoic acid the
equilibrium

$$CH_3CO_2H(aq) \rightleftharpoons CH_3CO_2^-(aq) + H^+(aq) \qquad (1)$$

acid                  corresponding
base

lies well over to the left, and the hydrogen ion concentration is relatively small.
There is a second equilibrium involving hydrogen ions in this system:

$$H^+(aq) + OH^-(aq) \rightleftharpoons H_2O(l) \qquad (2)$$

What happens when extra ethanoate ions are added to the solution? They can
be introduced by adding a soluble salt of ethanoic acid, such as sodium ethanoate,
which is highly ionised in solution.

**EXPERIMENT 14.8**      **Buffer solutions**

In a 100 cm$^3$ beaker take about 50 cm$^3$ of 0.1 M ethanoic acid and add a small
spatula measure of solid sodium ethanoate. Stir to dissolve and then add Full-range
Indicator solution, sufficient to give a recognisable colour.

Determine the pH by comparison with the colour charts provided with the
Indicator or by using a pH meter. Stand this beaker on a white tile or piece of
white paper.

Label the beaker **buffer solution of pH =**

Take a second beaker and put into it 1 drop of 1 M hydrochloric acid and
50 cm$^3$ of pure water. Add some Full-range Indicator solution and find the pH of
this solution. Now dilute the contents of this beaker with pure water and add more
indicator as necessary until you have a solution of hydrochloric acid which has the
same appearance (and therefore pH) as the first beaker.

Label the second beaker **unbuffered solution of pH =**

Now add 1 drop of 0.1 M sodium hydroxide to each of the beakers and
observe what happens. Follow this with further drops of sodium hydroxide and
then drops of 0.1 M hydrochloric acid.

 **In your notes:**

1   Which solution does not change much in pH?

2   Which solution changes very easily indeed?

## Interpretation of buffer behaviour

The mixture of ethanoic acid and sodium ethanoate contains a relatively high
concentration of ethanoic acid molecules, and a relatively high concentration of
ethanoate ions. It therefore contains both an acid and its conjugate base.

When more hydrogen ions are added to this system by adding a small
volume of a solution of a strong acid, these hydrogen ions will combine with
ethanoate ions to form more acid molecules. Equilibrium (1) (above) moves to the

left, removing nearly all the added hydrogen ions. The concentration of hydrogen ions, and thus the pH of the solution, will alter a little, but not very much.

Adding a strong base, for example sodium hydroxide, to the system disturbs equilibrium (2) so that $OH^-$ ions combine with $H^+$ ions to form $H_2O$ molecules. This reduces the hydrogen ion concentration, and more $CH_3CO_2H$ molecules ionise to restore it to near its original value.

The two equilibria adjust themselves in this way until nearly all the added hydroxide ions are removed. The pH value of the system will rise a little in consequence, but not very much.

The changes in pH resulting from additions of acid or base are much smaller than they would be if the mixture of weak acid and its salt were not present.

**Solutions of this kind, containing a weak acid and its conjugate base, thus provide a 'buffer' against the effects of adding strong acid or strong base. They are therefore known as buffer solutions.** Essentially they are solutions possessing readily available reserve supplies of both an acid and its conjugate base.

Another example of a buffer solution contains a mixture of ammonium chloride (highly ionised) and ammonia (present mainly as $NH_3$ molecules). The equilibria present are

$$\underset{\text{acid}}{NH_4^+(aq)} \rightleftharpoons \underset{\substack{\text{conjugate} \\ \text{base}}}{NH_3(aq)} + H^+(aq)$$

and   $H^+(aq) + OH^-(aq) \rightleftharpoons H_2O(l)$

The addition of more $H^+$ ions results in their reacting with the base $NH_3$ to form $NH_4^+$ ions. When more $OH^-$ ions are added the following changes occur

**QUESTION**

Use this information about buffers to interpret the titration curves you obtained in Experiment 14.7a.

$$H^+(aq) + OH^-(aq) \longrightarrow H_2O(l)$$

and   $$NH_4^+(aq) \longrightarrow NH_3(aq) + H^+(aq)$$

until the two equilibria are again restored. Again, the pH value remains nearly constant.

## Calculations involving buffer solutions

When the relative concentrations of acid and base in a buffer solution are known, the pH of the mixture can be calculated. Alternatively, the composition of the mixture needed to make a buffer solution of a given pH value can be found.

A general relationship for the calculation of the pH of a buffer solution can be obtained from the expression you met in section 14.6.

$$\underset{\text{acid}}{HA(aq)} \rightleftharpoons H^+(aq) + \underset{\text{conjugate base}}{A^-(aq)}$$

for which

$$K_a = \frac{[H^+(aq)]\,[A^-(aq)]}{[HA(aq)]}$$

Converting to logarithms and rearranging the expression, so that $[H^+(aq)]$ becomes pH, we can arrive at the important general relationship

$$\textbf{pH} = -\textbf{log}\,\boldsymbol{K_a} - \textbf{log}\left(\frac{\textbf{[acid]}}{\textbf{[base]}}\right)$$

Three points are worth noting from this equation.

1 The pH of a buffer solution depends on the *ratio* of the concentrations of acid and base, not on the actual values of these concentrations.

2 When [acid] = [base], pH = $-\log K_a$. This means that the $K_a$ value of an acid can be found by measuring the pH value of a solution of the acid which has been half-neutralised by a strong base.

The expression $pK_a$ is often used instead of $-\log K_a$.

3 $pK_a$ values are quoted in the *Book of data* so they do not usually need to be calculated from $K_a$ values.

Two examples will show how the equation can be used.

## Example 1

What is the pH of a solution which is 0.05 M with respect to ethanoic acid and 0.20 M with respect to sodium ethanoate? (For ethanoic acid, $pK_a = 4.8$.)

In this, and all similar calculations, we are dealing with systems for which $K_a$ is small. We can, therefore, simplify the calculations by assuming that the ethanoic acid is un-ionised and that all the ethanoate ions come from the sodium ethanoate.

By doing this we can write

$$[acid] = [CH_3CO_2H(aq)] = 0.05 \text{ mol dm}^{-3}$$

and $[base] = [CH_3CO_2^-(aq)] = 0.20 \text{ mol dm}^{-3}$

Therefore $pH = 4.8 - \log\left(\dfrac{0.05}{0.20}\right)$

Using your calculator, $\log\left(\dfrac{0.05}{0.20}\right) = \log 0.25 = -0.6$

so $pH = 4.8 - (-0.6) = 4.8 + 0.6$
$= 5.4$

## Example 2

In what proportions must 0.1 M solutions of ammonia and ammonium chloride be mixed to obtain a buffer solution of pH 9.8? ($pK_a$ for the ammonium ion is 9.3.)

Here the acid is $NH_4^+(aq)$ and the base $NH_3(aq)$.

$$9.8 = 9.3 - \log\left(\dfrac{[NH_4^+(aq)]}{[NH_3(aq)]}\right)$$

$$0.5 = -\log\left(\dfrac{[NH_4^+(aq)]}{[NH_3(aq)]}\right)$$

or $\log\left(\dfrac{[NH_4^+(aq)]}{[NH_3(aq)]}\right) = -0.5$

Using your calculator, inverse log $(-0.5) = 0.316$

so, $\dfrac{[NH_4^+(aq)]}{[NH_3(aq)]} = 0.32$

The solutions must, therefore, be mixed in the proportions, 0.32 volume of 0.1 M ammonium chloride to 1 volume of 0.1 M ammonia solution.

Therefore, to make up 1 $dm^3$ of the buffer solution $(0.32 \div 1.32) \times 1000 \, cm^3$ of 0.1 M $NH_4Cl$ (which is 242 $cm^3$) and $(1 \div 1.32) \times 1000 \, cm^3$ of 0.1 M $NH_3$ (which is 758 $cm^3$) are required.

## KEY SKILLS

### Application of number

Experiment 14.7b could be a suitable opportunity to apply your application of number skills. This is a substantial and complex activity for which you will need a plan for obtaining and using the information required, records of your calculations showing the methods used and levels of accuracy, together with a report on your findings including a justification of your presentation methods and explanations of how your results relate to the question you try to answer. You will be able to include a graph, chart and diagram in your report.

### IT

A spreadsheet is a powerful tool for exploring the Equilibrium Law quantitatively. A pH probe, datalogger and computer can help to record measurements and display the changes in pH during titrations.

## TOPIC REVIEW

This topic is quantitative in nature. If you are concerned about the maths you must make sure that you get lots of practice and include worked examples in this review. If the same errors recur, annotate your notes to remind yourself of the pit-falls.

**1   List key words or terms with definitions where necessary**

Illustrate the following with suitable **examples**. Make sure that you can identify the units for the physical quantities.

- dynamic equilibrium
- position of equilibrium
- Equilibrium Law
- $K_c$, $K_p$
- heterogeneous equilibria
- partial pressure
- $K_w$
- $K_a$
- indicator
- buffer solution

TOPIC 14

**2 Summarise the key principles as simply as possible**

The common thread throughout this topic is the **Equilibrium Law**. All values of $K$ are specific to the kind of substances under scrutiny ($K_a$ for acids, $K_p$ for gases etc). It follows, therefore, that the maths does not vary much either, so get one set of calculations right and you should be able to do the others.

You must know, understand and be able to show:

- the features of the equilibrium state
- how to use the Equilibrium Law to get specific answers
- how the entropy of a system is influenced by changes of condition
- how the pH and $K_a$ for a given acid are related.

A good way of illustrating your review is by including worked examples from the end-of-topic questions.

## REVIEW QUESTIONS

✱ Indicates that the *Book of data* is needed.

**14.1** For each of the following reversible reactions,

a Write a balanced equation, including state symbols. (The first-named substance(s) should be on the left-hand side of each equation.)

b Write the expression for the equilibrium constant, $K_c$. You need not use the subscript 'eqm' after each concentration, but remember that all concentrations in these expressions are those at equilibrium.

c Deduce the units of $K_c$ for each reaction.

 i hydrogen and chlorine in equilibrium with hydrogen chloride (all gases) (3)

 ii hydrogen iodide in equilibrium with hydrogen and iodine (all gases) (3)

 iii sulphur dioxide and oxygen in equilibrium with sulphur trioxide (all gases) (3)

 iv ozone ($O_3$) gas in equilibrium with oxygen ($O_2$) gas (3)

 v carbon monoxide and steam in equilibrium with carbon dioxide and hydrogen (3)

 vi methanol and ethanoic acid in equilibrium with methyl ethanoate and water (all liquids) (3)

 vii nitrogen and hydrogen in equilibrium with ammonia (all gases) (3)

 viii nitrogen and oxygen in equilibrium with nitrogen(II) oxide (all gases) (3)

 ix iron(III) ions and tin(II) ions in equilibrium with iron(II) ions and tin(IV) ions (all in aqueous solution) (3)

 x propanone and hydrogen cyanide in equilibrium with 2-hydroxy-2-methyl-propanenitrile,

$$CH_3 - \underset{\underset{CH_3}{|}}{\overset{\overset{OH}{|}}{C}} - CN$$

(all in solution in ethanol, which can be represented by the subscript '$C_2H_5OH$'). (3)

**(30 marks)**

**14.2** The equilibrium

$$N_2O_4 \rightleftharpoons 2NO_2$$

can be established in solution in a suitable organic solvent at low temperatures. The composition of the equilibrium mixture can be calculated from the density of colour of the solution as $N_2O_4$ is virtually colourless and $NO_2$ is brown. In a solution of this kind, at 10 °C, the concentration of $NO_2$ molecules was found to be 0.0014 mol dm$^{-3}$ and the concentration of $N_2O_4$ molecules, 0.19 mol dm$^{-3}$. Calculate the value of $K_c$ for the reaction at 10 °C.

**(4 marks)**

**14.3** Pent-1-ene ($C_5H_{10}$) reacts with ethanoic acid to produce pentyl ethanoate, the equilibrium

$$C_5H_{10} + CH_3CO_2H \rightleftharpoons CH_3CO_2C_5H_{11}$$

being established. When a solution of 0.02 mol of pentene and 0.01 mol of ethanoic acid in 600 cm$^3$ of an inert solvent was allowed to reach equilibrium at 15 °C, 0.009 mol of pentyl ethanoate was formed.

a How many moles of pentene were present in the solution at equilibrium? (1)

b How many moles of ethanoic acid were present in the solution at equilibrium? (1)

c Write down the expression for the equilibrium constant, $K_c$, for the above reaction. (1)

d Calculate the concentrations, in mol dm$^{-3}$, of the three substances at equilibrium. (3)

e Use your answers to c and d to calculate the value of $K_c$ at 15 °C, giving its units. (2)

**(8 marks)**

**14.4** The equilibrium between hydrogen, iodine and hydrogen iodide can be investigated by sealing hydrogen iodide in glass tubes and maintaining them at known temperatures until equilibrium is reached.

At 698 K, the equilibrium constant, $K_c$, for the reaction

$$2HI(g) \rightleftharpoons H_2(g) + I_2(g)$$

is 0.019.

The tubes are rapidly cooled and then opened under potassium iodide solution, in which the iodine and hydrogen iodide dissolve.

a i Why are the tubes rapidly cooled? (1)

ii Describe how the appearance of the contents of a tube would change as it was cooled. (1)

iii What practical procedure could be used to measure the amount of iodine dissolved from a tube? (3)

b i Write an expression for the equilibrium constant, $K_c$. (1)

ii The concentration of iodine in a sample tube was found to be $4.8 \times 10^{-4}$ mol dm$^{-3}$. Using the equation, deduce the equilibrium concentration of hydrogen, $[H_2(g)]_{eqm}$. (1)

iii Calculate the equilibrium concentration of hydrogen iodide. (2)

**(9 marks)**

**14.5**   For the seven **gas phase** reactions in question **14.1**, write the expressions for $K_p$, the equilibrium constant in terms of partial pressures, and deduce the units of $K_p$ in each case.   (2 marks for each example)
**(14 marks)**

**14.6**   Assume that air consists only of nitrogen, $N_2(g)$, and oxygen, $O_2(g)$, and that there are 4 molecules of $N_2$ to 1 molecule of $O_2$. If the total pressure of air is 1 atm, calculate the partial pressures of two gases, showing your reasoning.
**(4 marks)**

**14.7**   Equilibrium was established for the reaction

$$2NO_2(g) \rightleftharpoons 2NO(g) + O_2(g)$$

A particular equilibrium mixture had the composition 0.96 mol $NO_2(g)$, 0.04 mol $NO(g)$ and 0.02 mol $O_2(g)$ at 700 K. The total pressure was 0.2 atm.

**a**   Calculate the partial pressure of each gas.   (6)
**b**   Write the expression for the equilibrium constant, $K_p$, for this reaction.   (1)
**c**   Calculate the value of $K_p$ and give its units.   (2)
**(9 marks)**

**✳ 14.8**   Table 6.8 in the *Book of data* gives the values of $K_p$ for the reaction

$$N_2(g) + 3H_2(g) \rightleftharpoons 2NH_3(g)$$

over a range of temperatures.

**a**   What do the values tell you about the proportion of ammonia at equilibrium as the temperature increases? Explain your answer.   (2)
**b**   Deduce whether the forward reaction is exothermic or endothermic and explain your answer.   (2)
**c**   A temperature of around 450 °C is used industrially for the production of ammonia by this reaction. What would be the consequence of using
**i**   a higher temperature
**ii**   a lower temperature?   (2)
Explain your answers.   (2)
**(8 marks)**

**✳ 14.9**   This question is concerned with the equilibrium

$$2SO_2(g) + O_2(g) \rightleftharpoons 2SO_3(g) \qquad \Delta H = -197 \, \text{kJ mol}^{-1}$$

**a**   Calculate the entropy change $\Delta S^{\ominus}_{\text{system}}$ for this reaction under standard conditions ($S^{\ominus}[SO_3(g)] = 256.1 \, \text{J mol}^{-1} \, \text{K}^{-1}$).   (2)
**b**   Calculate $\Delta S^{\ominus}_{\text{surroundings}}$ for the reaction at 298 K.   (1)
**c**   Calculate $\Delta S^{\ominus}_{\text{total}}$ and hence comment on the position of equilibrium at 298 K.   (2)
**d**   Calculate $\Delta S^{\ominus}_{\text{surroundings}}$ at 700 K and at 1100 K; use these values to calculate $\Delta S^{\ominus}_{\text{total}}$ at these temperatures, assuming that the value of $\Delta S^{\ominus}_{\text{system}}$ is unaffected by changes of temperature.   (2)
**e**   By comparing your three values for $\Delta S^{\ominus}_{\text{total}}$, comment on the effect of increased temperature on the position of equilibrium.   (1)
**f**   Use the *Book of data*, table 6.8, to find the values of $K_p$ at 298 K, 700 K and 1100 K. Are they consistent with your answer to **e**?   (2)

**g** Calculate the temperature at which $\Delta S^{\ominus}_{total} = 0$. What can you say about the position of equilibrium in this case? (2)

**(12 marks)**

**14.10** Calculate the pH of each of the following solutions. They are strong acids and bases and are assumed to be completely ionised.

| | | | | | |
|---|---|---|---|---|---|
| **a** | 0.02 M HCl | (1) | **d** | 0.75 M NaOH | (1) |
| **b** | 0.05 M $HNO_3$ | (1) | **e** | 0.04 M KOH | (1) |
| **c** | 0.001 M HBr | (1) | **f** | 4.0 M KOH | (1) |

**(6 marks)**

**14.11** Write the expression for the acid dissociation constant, $K_a$, for each of the following weak acids:

**a** benzoic acid, $C_6H_5CO_2H$ (1)
**b** phenol, $C_6H_5OH$ (1)
**c** butanoic acid, $CH_3(CH_2)_2CO_2H$ (1)
**d** hydrocyanic acid, HCN (1)

**(4 marks)**

**✱ 14.12** Use the expressions you have written in question **14.11** together with numerical values of $K_a$ from the *Book of data* to calculate the pH of:

| | | | | | |
|---|---|---|---|---|---|
| **a** | 0.001 M benzoic acid | (3) | **c** | 0.0025 M butanoic acid | (3) |
| **b** | 0.0005 M phenol | (3) | **d** | 0.15 M HCN | (3) |

**(12 marks)**

**14.13** Calculate the values of $K_a$ for the following acids:

**a** HA, of which a 0.100 M solution has pH 5.1 (3)
**b** HX, of which a 0.025 M solution has pH 4.9 (3)

**(6 marks)**

**14.14** Sketch curves showing how the pH changes during a titration when:

**a** NaOH is added to ethanoic acid (3)
**b** $NH_3$ (a weak base) is added to HCl (3)
**c** $NH_3$ is added to ethanoic acid (3)
**d** Why does no indicator show a satisfactory end-point in titration **c**? (1)

**(10 marks)**

**✱ 14.15** Calculate the pH of the following buffer solutions:

**a** a solution 0.05 M with respect to propanoic acid and 0.075 M with respect to sodium propanoate (4)
**b** a solution 0.001 M with respect to boric acid and 0.002 M with respect to sodium dihydrogenborate, $NaH_2BO_3$ (4)
**c** a solution 0.01 M with respect to boric acid and 0.02 M with respect to sodium dihydrogenborate. (2)
**d** Compare your answers to **b** and **c** and comment. (2)

**(12 marks)**

**\* 14.16**    **a**    In what proportions must the following solutions be mixed to obtain buffer solutions of the stated pH?

    **i**  1.0 M ethanoic acid and 1.0 M sodium ethanoate to give pH 4.9     (3)

    **ii**  0.5 M ammonia and 0.5 M ammonium chloride to give pH 9.6     (3)

    **b**    What volumes of the solutions should be mixed to make 1 dm$^3$ of each buffer solution?     (4)

                                                    **(10 marks)**

# EXAMINATION QUESTIONS

**14.17**    Many carbonyl compounds exist in two isomeric forms in dynamic equilibrium. For example:

However, this conversion between **A** and **B** is very slow unless a catalyst is present.

**a**    What is meant by the term 'dynamic equilibrium'?     (2)

**b**    In order to measure the equilibrium constant, $K_c$, for this reaction at 20 °C, about 1 g of the liquid from a stock bottle was dissolved in an inert solvent. The solution was rapidly titrated with 0.200 M bromine solution, $Br_2$, dissolved in the same inert solvent.

    1 mole of bromine, $Br_2$, reacts with 1 mole of **B** but does not react with **A**.

    **i**  Suggest how you would weigh out accurately about 1 g of a volatile organic liquid.     (1)

In such an experiment, 0.980 g of the liquid was used and this reacted with 38.7 cm$^3$ of the 0.200 M bromine solution.

    **ii**  Calculate the number of moles of the compound present in the 0.980 g used.     (2)

    **iii**  Calculate the number of moles of **B** present in the sample.     (1)

    **iv**  Hence calculate the number of moles of **A** present in the sample.     (1)

    **v**  Write an expression for $K_c$ for this reaction and calculate its value.     (2)

                                                    **(9 marks)**

**14.18**    **a**    A solution of iodine in a hydrocarbon solvent was shaken with water until equilibrium was reached. The mixture was allowed to settle and then 5 cm$^3$ of the hydrocarbon solvent layer and 50 cm$^3$ of the aqueous layer were removed and titrated separately with sodium thiosulphate solution of concentration 0.0100 mol dm$^3$.

    The following results were obtained.

| Solvent | Volume of solution used /cm$^3$ | Volume of 0.0100 mol dm$^{-3}$ sodium thiosulphate solution used/cm$^3$ | $I_2$ concentration /mol dm$^{-3}$ |
|---|---|---|---|
| Hydrocarbon | 5 | 76 | ? |
| Water | 50 | 8.9 | $8.9 \times 10^{-4}$ |

    **i** Which indicator, if any, would you use for this titration and what would the colour change be at the end-point? (3)

    **ii** The equation for the reaction between iodine and sodium thiosulphate is

$$I_2(aq) + 2Na_2S_2O_3(aq) \longrightarrow 2NaI(aq) + Na_2S_4O_6(aq)$$

Calculate the concentration of iodine molecules, $I_2$, in mol dm$^{-3}$ in the hydrocarbon layer. (2)

    **iii** When a solution of iodine in a hydrocarbon solvent is shaken with water the following equilibrium occurs:

$$I_2(\text{hydrocarbon}) \rightleftharpoons I_2(\text{water})$$

Write down an expression for $K_c$ for this equilibrium and calculate its value. (2)

    **iv** Suggest TWO improvements to this titration procedure which would increase its accuracy. Assume that the results table is a complete record of all the practical work carried out. (2)

    **v** How would you expect the value of $K_c$ to change when the concentration of iodine molecules, $I_2$, in the hydrocarbon solvent at the start is doubled? (1)

**b** The experiment was repeated using potassium iodide solution instead of water. The following equilibrium was set up in the aqueous layer:

$$I_2(aq) + I^-(aq) \rightleftharpoons I_3^-(aq)$$

How would you expect this to affect the volume of sodium thiosulphate solution used in the titration of the aqueous layer? Justify your answer. (2)

**(12 marks)**

**14.19** This question is concerned with boric acid, $H_3BO_3$, which is a weak acid. When it is dissolved in water several equilibria are established, one of them being

$$H_3BO_3(aq) \rightleftharpoons H^+(aq) + H_2BO_3^-(aq)$$

**a** Write the expression for the acid dissociation constant, $K_a$, for the equilibrium shown above. (1)

**b** Using a pH meter, a student finds the pH of a 0.1 M solution of boric acid to be 5.1.
Assuming that this equilibrium makes the only significant contribution to the hydrogen ion concentration, calculate the value of $K_a$ for this equilibrium. (3)

**c** Write equations for TWO other equilibria likely to be established in an aqueous solution of boric acid. (2)

**d** Unlike many acids, boric acid does not react with sodium carbonate to produce carbon dioxide gas. Suggest the reason for this. (2)

**e** Suggest the formula of a compound which would make a buffer solution when added to an aqueous solution of boric acid. (1)

**(9 marks)**

**14.20** When ammonium salts are dissolved in water the following equilibrium is set up:

$$NH_4^+(aq) \rightleftharpoons NH_3(aq) + H^+(aq)$$

**a** Write the full expression for the dissociation constant, $K_a$, for this equilibrium. (2)

**b** The pH of a solution of ammonium chloride is 5.6.
    **i** Calculate the hydrogen ion concentration in this solution, showing the mathematical relationship you use. (2)

**ii** What will happen to the concentration of ammonium ions in solution when hydrochloric acid is added to the ammonium chloride? Explain your answer. (2)

**c** A mixture of ammonium chloride and ammonia solution acts as a buffer.
**i** What is meant by a buffer solution? (2)
**ii** Explain the changes which occur when a solution containing hydroxide ions, $OH^-$, is added to this buffer. (2)

**d** The equilibrium involving ammonium ions and ammonia can be written showing the water molecules:

$$NH_4^+(aq) + H_2O(l) \rightleftharpoons NH_3(aq) + H_3O^+(aq)$$

Use the Brønsted–Lowry theory to explain whether water is acting as an acid or a base in this equilibrium. (1)

**(11 marks)**

**14.21** The conversion of sulphur dioxide to sulphur trioxide is a vital step in the industrial manufacture of sulphuric acid. The equation for this reaction is

$$2SO_2(g) + O_2(g) \rightleftharpoons 2SO_3(g) \qquad \Delta H^\ominus = -197\,kJ\,mol^{-1}$$

To achieve the conversion, a mixture of sulphur dioxide and air is passed through a catalyst bed at 700 K. The emergent gases are cooled and passed through a second catalyst bed, again at 700 K, to increase the yield of sulphur trioxide. These operations are repeated twice more so that a minimum of 99.5% conversion is achieved.

**a** **i** Write the full expression for the equilibrium constant, $K_p$, for the reaction, including its units. (2)
**ii** Why are the gases cooled between successive passes through the catalyst beds? (2)
**iii** Suggest TWO conditions, other than temperature control, which will help to maximise the amount of sulphur dioxide converted to sulphur trioxide. (2)
**iv** For what reason must the escape to the environment of these oxides of sulphur be rigorously prevented? (1)

**b** **i** Predict whether there will be an increase or a decrease in the entropy of the system during the formation of sulphur trioxide in this reaction. Give a reason for your answer. (1)
**ii** Calculate the entropy change of the surroundings, assuming the reaction occurs at 700 K. Include the sign and units in your answer. (2)
**iii** In the light of your answer to **b ii**, what can you deduce about the numerical value of the entropy change of the system? (1)

**c** **i** Calculate the pH of a 0.075 mol dm$^{-3}$ solution of sulphuric acid, assuming it to be fully ionised according to the equation

$$H_2SO_4(aq) \rightleftharpoons 2H^+(aq) + SO_4^{2-}(aq)$$ (2)

**ii** A total of 25.0 cm$^3$ of ammonia solution was added in small portions from a burette to 10.0 cm$^3$ of 0.075 M sulphuric acid. The pH of the solution was followed as the ammonia was added.
Sketch a graph showing how the pH changed, assuming that 20.0 cm$^3$ of the ammonia solution was sufficient to neutralise the fully ionised sulphuric acid. (3)
**iii** Calculate the concentration in mol dm$^{-3}$ of the ammonia solution. (2)
**iv** Not all indicators are suitable for this titration. Explain why some indicators cannot be used. (1)

**(19 marks)**

**14.22** Ethanol can be manufactured by the direct hydration of ethene with steam over a catalyst of phosphoric acid:

$$C_2H_4(g) + H_2O(g) \rightleftharpoons C_2H_5OH(g)$$

The proportion of ethene converted into ethanol at equilibrium under different conditions is given in the table:

| Mole ratio of reactants ethene:steam | Temperature /°C | Pressure /atm | % ethene converted |
|---|---|---|---|
| 1:1 | 290 | 50 | 31 |
| 1:2 | 290 | 50 | 38 |
| 1:3 | 290 | 50 | 46 |
| 1:2 | 290 | 60 | 42 |
| 1:2 | 290 | 70 | 46 |
| 1:2 | 260 | 50 | 40 |
| 1:2 | 320 | 50 | 36 |

a   Write down the expression for the equilibrium constant, $K_p$, for the reaction. (1)

b   Using your answer to **a** and the data table above, explain the effect on the proportion of ethene converted of increasing the proportion of steam in the reaction mixture. (1)

c   i Copy and complete the table below for the equilibrium at 290 °C and 70 atmospheres.

| | Ethene | Steam | Ethanol |
|---|---|---|---|
| Initial moles | 1.00 | 2.00 | 0 |
| Moles at equilibrium | | | 0.46 |
| Partial pressures at equilibrium | | | |

(5)

   ii Calculate the equilibrium constant, $K_p$, using your expression in **a** and the partial pressures from the table. Remember to include units. (2)

d   The actual operating conditions used are similar to those in **c** above, but only 9% conversion of ethene to ethanol is achieved by a single pass of the reactants over the catalyst.
    Explain why a relatively high temperature is used when a lower temperature should give a better yield of ethanol. (1)

e   The production cost of ethanol is about £450 per tonne, of which raw materials (ethene, steam and phosphoric acid) account for £300.
    Suggest TWO other factors which contribute to the production cost of ethanol. (2)

**(12 marks)**

# Oxidation products of alcohols

When you oxidised primary alcohols in Topic 2 you obtained **aldehydes** containing the **carbonyl** functional group, $\diagdown C{=}O$ , and **carboxylic acids** with the functional group $-\overset{\displaystyle O}{\underset{\displaystyle O-H}{C}}$

The oxidation of secondary alcohols leads to the formation of a closely related group of carbonyl compounds known as **ketones**.

Carbonyl compounds occur in many important natural products such as carbohydrates. Carboxylic acids, and the derivatives that can be made from them, are important in understanding many aspects of biochemistry.

Figure 15.1 The French biochemist Louis Pasteur proved that the spoiling of wine by an unwanted change to 'vinegar' was not due to 'germs', but to a chemical reaction. The ethanol in the wine was being oxidised by oxygen from the air and converted to ethanoic acid

In this topic you will:

- investigate the reactions of carbonyl compounds and learn how to interpret them
- investigate the reactions of carboxylic acids and consider their special features
- investigate the compounds that can be made from carboxylic acids and compare their behaviour with that of the acids themselves.

## 15.1  Carbonyl compounds

**Compounds with one alkyl group and one hydrogen atom attached to the carbonyl group are known as aldehydes.** They are named after their parent alkane, with the terminal 'e' replaced by '**-al**': propane becomes propanal.

**Compounds with two alkyl groups attached to the carbonyl group are known as ketones.** They are named in the same manner, but with the terminal 'e' replaced by '**-one**': propane becomes propan**one**.

Examples of these two types of compound are:

|  | **Aldehyde** | **Ketone** |
|---|---|---|
| Displayed formulae | $\begin{array}{ccc} H & H & O \\ | & | & \diagdown \\ H-C-C-C \\ | & | & \diagdown \\ H & H & H \end{array}$ | $\begin{array}{ccccc} H & H & O & H & H \\ | & | & \| & | & | \\ H-C-C-C-C-C-H \\ | & | & & | & | \\ H & H & & H & H \end{array}$ |
| Structural formulae | $CH_3-CH_2-CHO$ <br> propanal | $CH_3-CH_2-CO-CH_2-CH_3$ <br> pentan-3-one |

Since aldehydes and ketones have an unsaturated functional group, $\diagup C{=}O$, we should start by comparing their properties with the properties of alkenes, which also have an unsaturated group, $\diagup C{=}C \diagdown$.

As you should remember from Topic 8, the characteristic reactions of the alkenes are addition reactions. In the case of the alkenes, we calculated that the $\pi$ bond was weaker than the $\sigma$ bond.

$$E(C{-}C) = +347 \text{ kJ mol}^{-1}$$
$$E(C{=}C) = +612 \text{ kJ mol}^{-1}$$

so $E$ for the $\pi$ bond $= +265$ kJ mol$^{-1}$.

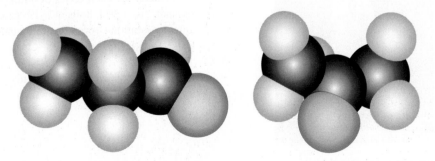

Figure 15.2  **Models of the molecules of propanal and propanone**

If you look at similar data for carbonyl compounds:

$$E(\text{C—O}) = +358 \text{ kJ mol}^{-1}$$
$$E(\text{C=O}) = +736 \text{ kJ mol}^{-1} \text{ in aldehydes}$$
$$+749 \text{ kJ mol}^{-1} \text{ in ketones}$$

you can calculate that the carbon–oxygen bonds are similar in strength, so addition to C=O bonds may not occur as readily as to C=C bonds.

The dipole moments of symmetrical alkenes are zero as, for example, in ethene where the C=C bond is symmetrical. However, the carbon–oxygen bond is polarised, $C^{\delta+}$—$O^{\delta-}$. This means that carbonyl compounds usually have dipole moments and they are larger than those of the corresponding alcohols.

The carbon–oxygen double bond must therefore be strongly polarised:

$$\diagdown \underset{\diagup}{C}^{\delta+}=O^{\delta-}$$

Thus, we can expect an electron pair to transfer readily from the double bond to the oxygen atom, giving the oxygen atom a negative charge, during reactions:

$$\diagdown \underset{\diagup}{C}^{+}\text{—}O^{-}$$

The infrared spectra of carbonyl compounds have a characteristic peak due to the C=O stretching vibration. In the case of aldehydes the peak is found at $1740\text{–}1720 \text{ cm}^{-1}$, and in the case of ketones it is found at $1727\text{–}1705 \text{ cm}^{-1}$ (see figure 15.8).

|  | Dipole moment/D |
|---|---|
| propan-1-ol | 1.66 |
| propanone | 2.95 |

## QUESTIONS

1 Is the carbon atom on the carbonyl group likely to be attacked by nucleophiles or electrophiles?

2 Is this the same as or different from the usual pattern of attack on alkenes?

3 What type of reactions would you expect carbonyl compounds to undergo?

# Experiments with aldehydes and ketones

The first few members of each series of compounds are gases or very volatile liquids. Methanal, H—CHO, boils at $-19\,°\text{C}$ and is commonly supplied as a 40% w/v aqueous solution ('formalin'); ethanal, $CH_3$—CHO, boils at $+20\,°\text{C}$; propanal, $CH_3CH_2$—CHO, boils at 48 °C; and propanone, $CH_3$—CO—$CH_3$, boils at 56 °C.

For our experiments we shall need only one aldehyde and one ketone, and we shall use propanal and propanone, which are relatively easy to handle.

Figure 15.3 **Specimen of a crab preserved in methanal ('formalin')**

**EXPERIMENT 15.1**

# An investigation of the reactions of aldehydes and ketones

## Procedure

### 1 Solubility in water

To 1 cm$^3$ of propanone in a test tube add 1 cm$^3$ of water. Do the two liquids mix? Repeat with propanal.

 **In your notes:** What type of interaction would you predict between carbonyl groups and water molecules?

### 2 Oxidation with sodium dichromate(VI)

**a** To a few cm$^3$ of dilute sulphuric acid in a boiling tube add a few drops of sodium dichromate(VI) solution. Next add 2 drops of propanal and heat the mixture until it *just* boils. Try to tell from any colour change of the dichromate(VI) whether the propanal has been oxidised.

**b** Repeat the test using propanone instead of propanal.

 **In your notes:** Is there any difference in the behaviour of aldehydes and ketones?

### 3 Oxidation with Benedict's solution

**a** Add a few drops of propanal to 2.5 cm$^3$ of water in a boiling tube and add 2.5 cm$^3$ of Benedict's solution and 2.5 cm$^3$ of 0.04 M sodium hydroxide solution. Heat in a water bath. Note the colour of any precipitate.

**b** Repeat the test using propanone instead of propanal.

 **In your notes:** Note the colour of any precipitate and any substance which does not react. Does Benedict's solution distinguish between aldehydes and ketones?

### 4 Reaction with Brady's reagent

To a few drops of a carbonyl compound in a test tube add 5 cm$^3$ of Brady's reagent. Note the formation of a coloured crystalline solid.

Brady's reagent contains a nucleophile, 2,4-dinitrophenylhydrazine, dissolved in a mixture of methanol, water, and concentrated sulphuric acid.

2, 4-dinitrophenylhydrazine

**SAFETY**

Propanone is highly flammable.
Propanal is also highly flammable and irritates the respiratory system, eyes and skin.
Sodium dichromate(VI) is toxic.
1 M sulphuric acid is an irritant.
Brady's reagent is highly flammable, toxic and corrosive: **gloves must be worn when using this solution**.

**COMMENT**

Liquid propanal is the pure compound so two drops is a large amount compared to a dilute solution.

# Reactions of aldehydes and ketones

## 1 With water

Carbonyl compounds with small alkyl groups mix readily with water owing to hydrogen bonding. The oxygen atom has two unshared pairs of electrons available and the possibility of hydrogen bonding is enhanced by the polarity of the bond.

As well as hydrogen bonding, water (which is a nucleophile) will add to the double bond:

$$CH_3-\overset{\overset{\displaystyle H}{|}}{C}=O + H_2O \rightleftharpoons CH_3-\overset{\overset{\displaystyle H}{|}}{\underset{\underset{\displaystyle OH}{|}}{C}}-OH$$

ethanal            'ethanal hydrate'

Methanal is almost totally hydrated in aqueous solution, and ethanal to the extent of 58%, but the presence of two methyl groups in propanone reduces its hydration to a very small proportion. The reaction is readily reversible and hydrates can only be isolated in exceptional cases.

## 2 Oxidation

The dichromate(VI) ion and other mild oxidising agents convert aldehydes to carboxylic acids; ketones cannot be oxidised without breaking a carbon–carbon bond.

$$3CH_3CHO + Cr_2O_7^{2-} + 8H^+ \longrightarrow 3CH_3CO_2H + 4H_2O + 2Cr^{3+}$$

ethanal                      ethanoic acid

Most aldehydes reduce the Cu(II) ions in Benedict's solution to Cu(I) ions, resulting in the precipitation of the brick-red coloured copper(I) oxide. Ketones do not react as they are not so readily oxidised.

Both aldehydes and ketones can be reduced back to their alcohols by the use of suitable reducing agents.

## 3 Nucleophilic reactions

The reaction you performed with Brady's reagent, 2,4-dinitrophenylhydrazine, involves a nucleophilic addition to a carbonyl group, but this is immediately followed by an elimination reaction to give the coloured, crystalline solid obtained.

ethanal 2,4-dinitrophenylhydrazone

You are not expected to remember the details of this reaction, but a familiarity with the steps of this type of mechanism will help you to appreciate the behaviour of the carboxylic acids studied in the next section.

## 15.2 Carboxylic acids

alcohol —OH

carbonyl $>$C$=$O

carboxylic acid $-\overset{\displaystyle O}{\underset{\displaystyle OH}{C}}$

Carboxylic acids are manufactured on a large scale because they are used in foods and to produce other products as diverse as flavours, perfumes, solvents and polymers.

We have studied the reactions of the hydroxyl group in alcohols in Topic 2 and reviewed them in Topic 12: the reactions of alcohols were compared with the reactions of phenol. Some modification of the behaviour of the —OH group in phenol was observed on account of the interaction of the lone pair of electrons with the benzene ring by delocalisation.

We now consider what happens when the hydroxyl group is part of the carboxyl group of **carboxylic acids**. Again, we might expect some changes in the behaviour of the individual groups, particularly if there is any interaction between the lone pair of electrons of the hydroxyl group and the double bond of the carbonyl group.

Consider the possible reactions of the carboxyl group. **When the hydroxyl group ionises, the resulting anion is stabilised by delocalisation** (see page 367) and we would therefore expect to find some acidic behaviour.

$$CH_3-\overset{\displaystyle O}{\underset{\displaystyle OH}{C}} + H_2O \rightleftharpoons CH_3-\overset{\displaystyle O}{\underset{\displaystyle O}{C}} + H_3O^+$$

The large dipole of the carbonyl group means that the carbon atom of the carboxyl group is electrophilic in nature and should be susceptible to nucleophilic attack. Very weak nucleophiles, such as ethanol $CH_3CH_2\ddot{O}H$, will react, attacking the carbon atom, but only when catalysed by $H^+$ ions. Reagents such as ammonia, however, react as bases forming a salt

$$CH_3-CO_2H + NH_3 \longrightarrow CH_3-CO_2^- + NH_4^+$$

rather than acting as nucleophiles and attacking the carbon atom.

## Experiments with ethanoic acid

Pure ethanoic acid is sometimes known as **glacial** ethanoic acid because it freezes at 17 °C and its ice-like crystals were often observed in unheated laboratories. An alternative name for ethanoic acid is acetic acid (from the Latin *acetum* or vinegar). In these experiments use pure, that is, glacial, ethanoic acid.

TOPIC 15

# The reactions of ethanoic acid

## Procedure

### 1 Solubility and pH

To 1 cm³ of pure ethanoic acid in a test tube, add water in drops. Do they mix in all proportions? Add a few drops of Full-range Indicator. Finally add sodium carbonate solution.

✎ **In your notes:** When ethanoic acid and water were mixed, what type of molecular interaction was helping the ethanoic acid to dissolve?

Is it a strong enough acid to displace carbon dioxide from carbonates?

Write the equation of the reaction.

Look up the $K_a$ values of some of the carboxylic acids (in the margin overleaf). Is ethanoic acid a strong or a weak acid?

### 2 Formation of salts

To 10 cm³ of 0.1 M ethanoic acid in a beaker add a few drops of Full-range Indicator (or use a pH meter); then add, while stirring, 3 cm³ portions of 0.1 M sodium hydroxide until you have added a total of 15 cm³. Note the pH after each addition. Also measure the pH of a solution of sodium ethanoate.

✎ **In your notes:** Explain what happens. Write an equation for the reaction.

### 3 Formation of esters

Put 1 cm³ of pure ethanoic acid in a test tube and add 2 cm³ of ethanol and two or three drops of concentrated sulphuric acid (TAKE CARE).

Warm the mixture gently in a hot water bath for 5 minutes, when an ester will be formed.

What does the product smell like? How does this compare with the smells of the starting materials? Pour the contents of the test tube into a small beaker of sodium carbonate solution, to neutralise any excess of acid. Stir well and smell again. Is it like the smell of ethyl ethanoate from the bottle?

Cautiously smell a range of esters if they are available.

✎ **In your notes:** Write down what you see and smell. Which ester smells do you recognise? Which esters smell fruity?

You can also attempt to prepare one of the esters listed in the table below using the same procedure.

| Flavour | Alcohol | | Carboxylic acid | |
|---|---|---|---|---|
| Banana | Pentan-2-ol | 0.01 mole | Ethanoic acid | 0.03 mole |
| Peach | Benzyl alcohol | 0.01 mole | Ethanoic acid | 0.03 mole |
| Pear | Propan-1-ol | 0.02 mole | Ethanoic acid | 0.04 mole |
| Pineapple | Ethanol | 0.015 mole | Butanoic acid | 0.025 mole |

### SAFETY

Concentrated ethanoic acid is corrosive and flammable; it has a pungent odour and will cause painful blisters if left in contact with the skin; you should use gloves when handling this liquid.

0.1 M sodium hydroxide is an irritant.

Ethanol is highly flammable.

Concentrated sulphuric acid is corrosive.

Ethyl ethanoate (formed in reaction 3) is highly flammable.

# Carboxylic acids: acid properties involving the O—H bond

## 1 Solubility and pH

The carboxylic acids $C_1$ to $C_4$ mix with water in all proportions but at $C_5$ and thereafter solubility rapidly reduces. All carboxylic acid molecules will hydrogen bond to each other as well as to water molecules.

**The carboxylic acids are only weak acids in water** as can be seen from their $K_a$ values (see the table in the margin).

$$RCO_2H(aq) \rightleftharpoons H^+(aq) + RCO_2^-(aq)$$

They are usually less than 1% ionised in water and do not readily produce hydrogen by reaction with metals.

The infrared spectrum of a carboxylic acid such as ethanoic acid shows a broad absorption due to hydrogen bonding of the O—H group around $3100\,cm^{-1}$ (figure 15.6). Ethanol has a less pronounced broad absorption also due to hydrogen bonding (figure 15.7).

The infrared spectrum of a carboxylic acid also shows the characteristic absorption at $1740\,cm^{-1}$ due to the C=O group, which is again a broader peak. But the hydrogen atoms in propanone are not sufficiently polar to form hydrogen bonds so the infrared spectrum of pure propanone does not have broadened peaks (figure 15.8).

| Compound | $K_a$ /$10^{-5}\,mol\,dm^{-3}$ |
|---|---|
| Methanoic acid | 16 |
| Ethanoic acid | 1.7 |
| Propanoic acid | 1.3 |
| Butanoic acid | 1.5 |

## 2 Formation of salts

The carboxylic acids are strong enough acids to displace carbon dioxide from sodium carbonate and will neutralise sodium hydroxide, forming a sodium salt.

$$2CH_3CO_2H + Na_2CO_3 \longrightarrow 2CH_3CO_2Na + H_2O + CO_2$$
$$CH_3CO_2H + NaOH \longrightarrow CH_3CO_2Na + H_2O$$

You will have noticed that a sodium ethanoate–ethanoic acid mixture changes only slightly in pH on the addition of a strong acid or a strong base: the mixture is behaving as a **buffer**, which was described in Topic 14.

# Nucleophilic reactions involving the C=O bond

## 1 Formation of esters

**Carboxylic acids react with alcohols to form esters.** Alcohols have lone pairs of electrons on their oxygen atom and can therefore act as nucleophiles. The reaction is slow unless the mixture is warmed and an acid is present to act as a catalyst: concentrated sulphuric acid is suitable. The reaction is reversible.

benzoic acid    methanol    methyl benzoate

---

### REVIEW TASK

Re-read your notes on hydrogen bonding from Topic 9.

Figure 15.4   **The infrared spectrum of ethanoic acid, showing broad absorptions for both O—H and C=O due to hydrogen bonding**

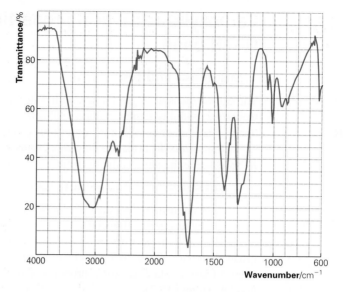

Figure 15.5   **The infrared spectrum of ethanol, showing an absorption at 3300 cm$^{-1}$ that is broadened by hydrogen bonding**

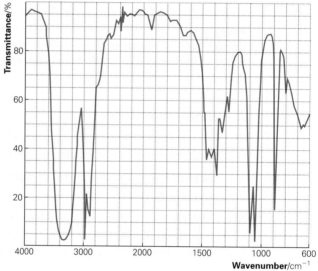

Figure 15.6   **The infrared spectrum of propanone, showing a characteristic sharp absorption at 1740 cm$^{-1}$**

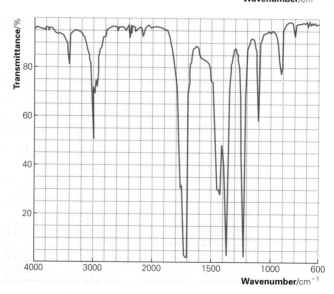

COMMENT

The structural formulae of esters can be confusing because the formula of the alcohol component is reversed from the usual convention: $CH_3CH_2OH$ becomes $-CH_2CH_3$.

From the equation below you can see that the water produced may have derived its oxygen atom from either the acid or the alcohol. Check the structural formulae and notice that both reactant molecules have an O—H group. In 1938 two American chemists, Roberts and Urey, found out which compound provided the oxygen for the water, by using methanol containing a high proportion of the isotope $^{18}O$.

$$\text{either} \quad \text{Ph—}\overset{\overset{\displaystyle O}{\|}}{C}\text{—}^{18}OCH_3 + H_2O \quad (1)$$

$$\text{Ph—}\overset{\overset{\displaystyle O}{\|}}{C}\text{—OH} + CH_3{}^{18}OH$$

$$\text{or} \quad \text{Ph—}\overset{\overset{\displaystyle O}{\|}}{C}\text{—}OCH_3 + H_2{}^{18}O \quad (2)$$

Using a mass spectrometer to determine the masses of the products they were able to establish that the $^{18}O$ isotope appears in the ester (equation (1)) and not the water (equation (2)). Thus the new bond was formed between the C atom in the acid and the $^{18}O$ atom in the alcohol, with the loss of the —OH group from the acid and not from the alcohol. This confirms that the reaction was a nucleophilic attack by the alcohol. Chemists consider that the first step in an acid-catalysed esterification is the addition of a proton to the C=O group of the acid:

$$\text{Ph—}\overset{\overset{\displaystyle O^{\delta-}}{\|}}{\underset{}{C^{\delta+}}}\text{—OH} \xrightleftharpoons[\text{protonation}]{H^+} \left[\text{Ph—}\overset{\overset{\displaystyle OH}{|}}{\underset{\underset{\displaystyle OH}{|}}{C^+}}\right] \xrightleftharpoons[\text{addition}]{CH_3OH} \left[\text{Ph—}\overset{\overset{\displaystyle OH}{|}}{\underset{\underset{\displaystyle OH\ H}{|}}{C}}\text{—O—CH}_3\right]^+$$

$$\text{Ph—}\overset{\overset{\displaystyle O}{\|}}{C}\text{—O—CH}_3 \xrightleftharpoons[\text{deprotonation}]{-H^+} \left[\text{Ph—}\overset{\overset{\displaystyle OH}{|}}{\underset{+}{C}}\text{—O—CH}_3\right] \xleftarrow[\text{elimination}]{-H_2O}$$

This is an addition–elimination reaction in which the overall process is substitution of the —OH group by the $CH_3O—$ group. You are not expected to learn this set of equations.

Figure 15.7   Molecular modelling by computer is a powerful research tool

## 2 Reduction

Carboxylic acids can be reduced to alcohols by lithium tetrahydridoaluminate, $LiAlH_4$.

$$\langle\bigcirc\rangle\!\!-CO_2H \xrightarrow{\text{LiAlH}_4} \langle\bigcirc\rangle\!\!-CH_2OH + H_2$$

benzoic acid                                phenylmethanol

The reaction proceeds by a nucleophilic attack on the carboxylate ion by the hydride ion, $:H^-$. The same reagent will also reduce aldehydes and ketones to alcohols.

## 3 Structure of functional groups and delocalisation

Methanoic acid (formic acid) is one of the components of the venom injected by stinging ants and caterpillars: it has the structural formula

$$H\!-\!C\underset{O\!-\!H}{\overset{O}{\diagdown}}$$

Electron diffraction studies of methanoic acid vapour have shown it to have the bond lengths given in the margin. The shortening of the C—O bond suggests some double bond character. This implies the interaction of the lone pair of electrons on the oxygen atom of the hydroxyl group with the $\pi$ bond of the carbonyl group.

Figure 15.8  An ant bite involves the injection of methanoic (formic) acid

STUDY TASK

Use table 4.6 in the *Book of data* to predict the bond lengths of the C—H, C=O, C—O and O—H bonds.

0.109 nm   O
          //  0.123 nm
H—C
  0.136 nm  \
              O—H
             0.097 nm

QUESTIONS

Sodium methanoate has the formula $HCO_2^-Na^+$ and the methanoate ion is $HCO_2^-$.

1    What bond lengths would you predict for C=O and C—O?

2    Are alternative arrangements possible?

          O
        // 0.127 nm
H—C
        \ 0.127 nm
          O

Structural investigations show that both bonds have the same length, as shown in the diagram on the left.

Where equivalent alternative bond structures can be drawn for a compound the actual situation is neither of these. The bond lengths in these situations often prove to be equal and the available electrons must therefore be equally distributed among the atoms concerned.

This is another case of electron **delocalisation** which we observed in the benzene ring and in phenol. **Delocalisation occurs when single and double bonds alternate or when an atom with a lone pair of electrons is bonded through a single bond to an atom with a double bond attached.** The lone pair of electrons in a p orbital are delocalised with the $\pi$ electron cloud above and below the plane of the molecule. Delocalisation is, therefore, present in all carboxylic acid molecules and their ions.

          O
        /
H—C     ⊖
        \
          O

or

          O
        /
H—C  ⊖
        \
          O

the methanoate ion

## 15.3 Carboxylic acid derivatives

The derivatives of the carboxylic acids are considered to be those compounds in which another group appears in the $-CO_2H$ group in the place of the $-OH$. In this section, we shall be concerned with esters, acyl chlorides, and amides.

ethyl ethanoate     ethanoyl chloride     ethanamide
(an ester)     (an acyl chloride)     (an amide)

Figure 15.9 **Formulating food and drink flavours using esters**

---

**EXPERIMENT 15.3**

## Some reactions of carboxylic acid derivatives

Some of these experiments will be demonstrated to you; you should be able to carry out the first experiment yourself.

### Procedure

#### 1 Hydrolysis of an ester

Place 2 cm³ of methyl benzoate and 15 cm³ of 2 M sodium hydroxide solution in a 50 cm³ pear-shaped flask fitted with a condenser. Reflux for about half an hour. Cool the mixture and acidify with 2 M hydrochloric acid.

    What is the precipitate that forms?

    If you have time, you can confirm the identity of the precipitate by collecting it by suction filtration, recrystallising from water, drying and determining its melting point.

✎    **In your notes:** Write an equation showing the structures of the compounds, identifying the nucleophile and the bond which breaks in the ester.

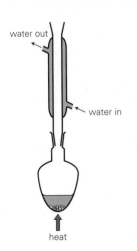

Figure 15.10 **Reflux apparatus**

## SAFETY

Methyl benzoate is
flammable.

2 M sodium hydroxide is
corrosive.

2 M hydrochloric acid is an
irritant.

Ethanoyl chloride is highly
flammable and corrosive; it
can cause severe burns and is
severely irritant to all tissues;
it is a pungent liquid and
fumes in moist air. **Eye
protection must be worn
during this experiment,
even if it is carried out as
a demonstration, which
must be done in a fume
cupboard.**

Ethanol is highly flammable.

8 M ammonia is corrosive.

## BACKGROUND

Some insect sex attractants are
unsaturated esters. They are
examples of pheromones,
compounds used by animals to
communicate with each other. An
example is *cis*-7-dodecenyl
ethanoate, used by the cabbage
looper moth. This is given out by
female insects in order to attract
males.

**Figure 15.11** Cabbage looper moths
use an ester aroma, a pheromone, to
communicate with each other

## 2 Demonstration of the reactions of an acyl chloride

Be prepared for vigorous reactions.

**a** Put 5 cm³ of water in a small (100 cm³) beaker and very carefully add a little ethanoyl chloride one drop at a time. Note the vigour of the reaction.

**b** Put 1 cm³ of ethanol in a small beaker and carefully add 1 cm³ of ethanoyl chloride one drop at a time. When the reaction has subsided, cautiously add sodium carbonate solution to neutralise any acids present and then see if you can detect the presence of an ester by its smell.

**c** Put 1 cm³ of 8 M ammonia in a small beaker and add 5 drops of ethanoyl chloride. Note the fumes produced, then evaporate off the water; a solid product should be obtained.

**In your notes:** For each of the experiments, write an equation showing the structures of the compounds, name the nucleophile involved, and identify the bond which breaks in the ethanoyl chloride.

# Reactions of carboxylic acid derivatives

## Nucleophilic reactions

The hydrolysis of the carboxylic acid derivatives amounts to a nucleophilic substitution:

$$CH_3-C \overset{O}{\underset{W:}{\diagdown}} + :OH^- \longrightarrow CH_3-C \overset{O}{\underset{OH}{\diagdown}} + :W^-$$

where — W: and :W⁻ can be  —Cl and Cl⁻

or  —OCH₃ and OCH₃⁻

or  —NH₂ and NH₂⁻.

The ease with which the substitution occurs is related to the power of —W: to attract electrons.

If —W: is strongly electron-attracting then the acid derivative can be hydrolysed by a weak nucleophilic reagent such as water; if —W: is only weakly electron-attracting, then the hydrolysis of the acid derivative will need a strong nucleophilic reagent such as hydroxide ions.

The relative electron-attracting powers of —W: can be summarised as

$$-Cl > -OH > -OCH_3 > -NH_2$$

**Acyl chlorides** which mix with water react rapidly, and often violently, to give the parent acid:

$$CH_3-COCl + H_2\overset{..}{O} \longrightarrow CH_3-CO_2H + HCl$$

Other nucleophiles such as alcohols, ammonia, and amines (see Topic 18) also react readily with acyl chlorides and this is an excellent method of preparing esters and amides.

$$CH_3—COCl + CH_3\ddot{O}H \longrightarrow CH_3—CO_2—CH_3 + HCl$$
methyl ethanoate

$$CH_3—COCl + NH_3 \longrightarrow CH_3—CO—NH_2 + HCl$$
ethanamide

**Esters** react quite slowly with water and an acid or base catalyst is necessary:

$$\langle \bigcirc \rangle—CO_2CH_3 + H_2O \underset{}{\overset{H^+}{\rightleftharpoons}} \langle \bigcirc \rangle—CO_2H + CH_3OH$$

When a base is used as a catalyst the product is the anion of the carboxylic acid. The anion is resistant to attack by weak nucleophiles such as alcohols, so the reaction is not reversible and goes to completion:

$$\langle \bigcirc \rangle—CO_2CH_3 + NaOH \longrightarrow \langle \bigcirc \rangle—CO_2^-Na^+ + CH_3OH$$

Figure 15.12   Harvesting olives – how do they extract the oil?

## BACKGROUND

Naturally occurring fats and oils are commonly esters of the alcohol propane-1,2,3-triol (glycerol), $CH_2OH—CH(OH)—CH_2OH$, and long chain carboxylic acids such as stearic acid $CH_3—(CH_2)_{16}—CO_2H$. A typical fat molecule therefore has the structure

$$CH_2—O—CO—(CH_2)_{n_1}—CH_3$$
$$|$$
$$CH—O—CO—(CH_2)_{n_2}—CH_3$$
$$|$$
$$CH_2—O—CO—(CH_2)_{n_3}—CH_3$$

where $n_1$, $n_2$, and $n_3$ may be the same, or different, but are almost always **even** numbers.

| Number of C atoms | Naturally occurring compound | Common name | Common source |
|---|---|---|---|
| 8 | $CH_3(CH_2)_6CO_2H$ | caprylic acid | coconut oil |
| 10 | $CH_3(CH_2)_8CO_2H$ | capric acid | coconut oil |
| 12 | $CH_3(CH_2)_{10}CO_2H$ | lauric acid | coconut oil |
| 14 | $CH_3(CH_2)_{12}CO_2H$ | myristic acid | nutmeg seed fat |
| 16 | $CH_3(CH_2)_{14}CO_2H$ | palmitic acid | palm oil |
| | $CH_3(CH_2)_{14}CH_2OH$ | cetyl alcohol | sperm whale oil |
| 18 | $CH_3(CH_2)_{16}CO_2H$ | stearic acid | animal fats |
| | $CH_3(CH_2)_7CH=CH(CH_2)_7CO_2H$ | oleic acid | olive oil |
| | $CH_3(CH_2)_7CH=CH(CH_2)_7CH_2OH$ | oleyl alcohol | sperm whale oil |
| | $CH_3(CH_2)_5CH(OH)CH_2CH=CH(CH_2)_7CO_2H$ | ricinoleic acid | castor oil |

## 15.4   Background reading: citric acid manufacture

Figure 15.13   **Laboratory-scale fermentation**

### QUESTIONS

Read the passage, then answer the following questions

1   Citric acid is often referred to as 'nature's acidulant'. Explain this term.

2   Draw up a table to compare the lime/sulphuric acid and solvent extraction processes for producing citric acid

3   Why is calcium hydroxide preferred to calcium carbonate in the modern version of the lime/sulphuric acid process?

4   What damage might result from releasing into the environment the untreated filtrate after recovering the calcium citrate during the lime/sulphuric acid process? How can manufacturers limit the damage?

5   Which uses of citric acid depend on:
   a   its acid properties in solution,
   b   its ability to form salts,
   c   its ability to form complex ions?

6   Draw the displayed formula of the ester triethyl citrate and suggest reasons why it is suitable for use as a plasticiser for pvc.

## Citric acid in nature

Citric acid occurs widely in nature as an acid, complex-forming agent and a buffer. Citric acid plays a vital role in the metabolism of humans and animals during the production of energy from food by respiration. In human metabolism the body produces and metabolises up to 1.5 to 2 kg of citric acid every day via the use of the Krebs Cycle.

Citric acid gives a refreshing, tart taste to citrus fruits; hence its name. Other fruits, vegetables, plants and even milk contain measurable quantities of citric acid either as the free acid or as citrate salts.

| | |
|---|---|
| Lemon | 5.0 |
| Lime | 3.0 |
| Orange | 1.0 |
| Strawberry | 0.7 |
| Tomato | 0.3 |
| Milk | 0.1 |

The natural occurrence (% w/w) of citric acid in fruits and milk

Citric acid is a white crystalline solid. It can be isolated either as a monohydrate or in an anhydrous form. Direct crystallisation is not possible after evaporation of natural sources such as lemon juice because of the high solubility of the acid and its salts.

**Figure 15.14** **Industrial fermentation tank**

## Isolating citric acid from natural sources

In 1874, the Swedish chemist Carl Wilhelm Scheele was the first person to isolate pure citric acid crystals from a natural source. He successfully precipitated insoluble calcium citrate by adding calcium carbonate to hot lemon juice. After filtering and washing the calcium citrate with water, Scheele released the citric acid by adding sulphuric acid, which at the same time removed the calcium ions as a precipitate of calcium sulphate. He then evaporated the solution and crystallised citric acid by cooling to obtain the monohydrate.

$$\text{hot lemon juice} \xrightarrow{\text{CaCO}_3} \text{calcium citrate} + \text{CO}_2 \xrightarrow{\text{H}_2\text{SO}_4} \text{citric acid solution} + \text{CaSO}_4$$

Citric acid monohydrate

$$\begin{array}{c} \text{CH}_2\text{---CO}_2\text{H} \\ | \\ \text{HO---C---CO}_2\text{H.H}_2\text{O} \\ | \\ \text{CH}_2\text{---CO}_2\text{H} \end{array}$$

Citric acid anhydrous

$$\begin{array}{c} \text{CH}_2\text{---CO}_2\text{H} \\ | \\ \text{HO---C---CO}_2\text{H} \\ | \\ \text{CH}_2\text{---CO}_2\text{H} \end{array}$$

**Figure 15.15** **The structure of citric acid. The systematic name is 2-hydroxypropane-1,2,3-tricarboxylic acid.**

In 1823 John & E. Sturge of Birmingham commercialised Scheele's lime/sulphuric process for the production of citric acid and its salts from Italian lemon juice. The company supplemented its supplies with calcium citrate produced from its own lime groves on the West Indian island of Montserrat.

## Fermentation processes

In 1923, the company Pfizer took commercial advantage of Carl Wehmer's discovery (in 1893) that certain moulds produced citric acid from sugar. This observation was confirmed by J. N. Currie in 1917 who studied the formation of citric acid when sugars ferment with the fungus *Aspergillus niger*.

By the 1930s the production of citric acid from fruit juice had been substantially replaced by commercial applications of Currie's *Aspergillus niger* surface fermentation. In this technology the fungus grows on the surface of a liquid aqueous media containing sucrose and various nutrient salts. Oxygen for respiration diffuses

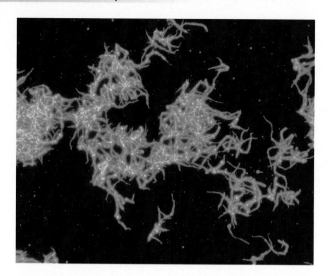

Figure 15.16 **Filamentous mycelia of the fungus** *Aspergillus niger* ($\times$ 100)

into the solution from the atmosphere. Commercialisation of this technology was undertaken by several manufacturers including Citrique Belge (now Hoffman–La Roche), Pfizer (now ADM) and John & E. Sturge (now Tate & Lyle Citric Acid).

The last fifty years has seen the development of the submerged aerobic citric acid fermentation technology using glucose syrups, sucrose and/or beet/cane molasses. *Aspergillus niger* strains have been developed by conventional mutation and selection techniques to provide highly efficient submerged fermentations. Similarly some manufacturers have developed strains of yeast to perform efficient citric acid conversions.

Typically a submerged fermentation comprises a two-stage process under sterile conditions.

● Stage 1: growth of the fungus *Aspergillus niger* to the verge of citric acid production in a small stainless steel vessel

● Stage 2: citric acid fermentation in the main stainless steel fermentation vessels (typically 50 to 600 $m^3$).

The large fermentation vessel has a cooling system to maintain temperature around 35 °C. Compressors inject air to provide a stream of air bubbles supplying oxygen and removing fermentation by products such as carbon dioxide.

In airlift fermenters the stream of air bubbles also suspends the pelleted *Aspergillus niger* in the solution and provides effective mixing. Sometimes the fermenting mixture is too thick for air mixing to work and then the vessel requires a multi-bladed agitator to ensure efficient mixing and oxygen transfer during the fermentation. This is necessary when the manufacturers use the fungus in a filamentous form or choose to ferment sugars produced directly in the vessel by the hydrolysis of starch from sweet potato, cassava, maize or wheat.

The progress of the main fermentation can be monitored by a simple acid–base titration of the citric acid. Fermentation time varies from 3 to 8 days from the start of stage 2. Typically the concentration of citric acid in the solution at the end of stage 2 is between 10 and 25 per cent.

## Purification and recovery processes

More than 75 per cent of the world's current citric acid production is still based on the process developed by Scheele in 1784. Obviously during the past 200 years of operation various modifications in process technology have taken place.

● Fermentation processes using natural, renewable raw materials such as molasses, sugar and cereal-based glucose syrups have replaced fruit juices as the source of citric acid.

● The waste mycelia from fermentation are used as an animal feed supplement and soil improver.

● Calcium carbonate has been largely replaced by calcium hydroxide for the primary precipitation of calcium citrate – calcium hydroxide has a higher solubility so that the precipitation of calcium citrate occurs in solution, avoiding the co-precipitation of unreacted calcium carbonate. Also no carbon dioxide forms when the hydroxide neutralises the citric acid, which avoids foaming.

● To avoid pollution, the organic wastes are now used to produce biogas thus producing fuel and cutting pollution.

Figure 15.17 **Citric acid: packing the finished product**

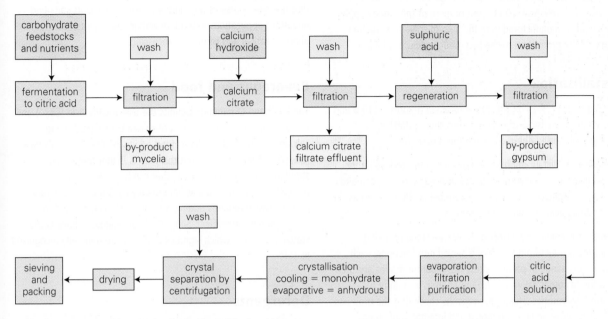

Figure 15.18a   **Citric acid production by the lime/sulphuric acid process**

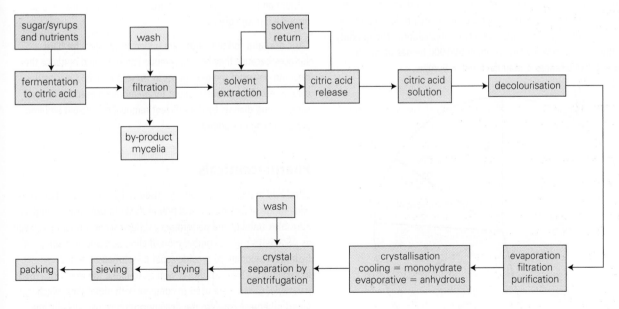

Figure 15.18b   **Citric acid production by the solvent extraction process**

Solvent extraction is an alternative to the lime/sulphuric acid process, when the citric acid is formed by fermenting pure solutions of sugars such as cane sugar or glucose, made by the hydrolysis of starch. Now 20 per cent or more of the world supply of citric acid is manufactured with the help of solvent extraction. This avoids the production of the by-product calcium sulphate.

## Crystallisation

Following on from these purification processes (figures 15.19 a and b) the solution of citric acid is evaporated and crystallised. Centrifugation and washing complete the separation.

The process of crystallisation can be controlled to produce either the monohydrate or anhydrous crystals depending on the demand – the acid crystallises as the monohydrate below 36.6 °C and as the anhydrous acid at higher temperatures.

The product is commonly air-dried. To ensure stability during storage, the product from the drier is sieved into fractions, each with a narrow range of particle sizes. The separate grades are then packed for customer delivery following analysis in quality assurance laboratories. The analysis results check that the products are fit for purpose and meet national and international quality standards.

Citric acid is commonly sold to customers in quantities ranging from 25 kg bags to 20 tonne bulk tankers. The acid may be supplied as crystals or in solution. Manufacturers also supply commercial quantities of calcium citrate, citrate esters, potassium citrate, sodium citrate and zinc citrate which are produced and sold alongside citric acid for a wide variety of applications. The quantity of citric acid used worldwide is about 900 000 tonnes of which about 300 000 tonnes is manufactured in Europe.

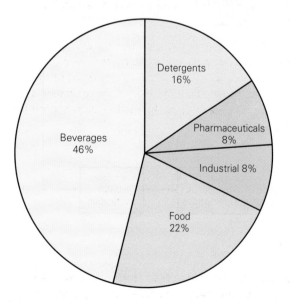

Figure 15.19    **Uses of citric acid**

## Uses of citric acid

Two centuries of the widespread use of citric acid in food show that it is safe to use as an additive. Citric acid and its salts find numerous applications in food, beverage, detergents, pharmaceutical and technical processing.

## Beverages and food

The European Community permits the use of citric acid (E330) and its salts sodium citrate (E331), potassium citrate (E332) and calcium citrate (E333) salts as food additives. The chemicals have 'Quantum Satis' status. What this means is that there is no stipulated limit to the amounts that can be added to food products. In fact their use is limited only by Good Manufacturing Practice which requires adding only as much as is needed to achieve the desired effect. Similarly these chemicals have GRAS status in the USA which signifies that they are generally recognised as safe.

## Detergents

Sodium citrate is used in both liquid and powder laundry detergents as a builder. Builder systems containing citrate are used as environmentally acceptable alternatives for phosphates, with the added advantage that citric acid and citrate ions are totally biodegradable. Citrates soften water by forming complexes with calcium and magnesium water-hardness ions. They also help to disperse dirt and grease.

Citric acid and sodium citrate are added to cleaners for hard surfaces because they help to remove limescale and enhance the cleaning power of the detergents in these products. Citric acid is also an excellent cleaning agent for membranes used for reverse osmosis and dialysis by the efficient removal of calcium and iron scale-forming compounds.

## Pharmaceuticals

Citric acid and its citrate salts are used to buffer (pH 2.5 to 6.5) a wide range of pharmaceutical preparations to optimise pH and so maximise stability and performance. Effervescent formulations such as Alka-Seltzer use a combination of citric acid and sodium hydrogencarbonate to provide rapid dissolution of active ingredients such as aspirin, as well as to make the medicines more palatable. Citrates are used to complex with metal ions which might otherwise catalyse the decomposition of oxygen-sensitive ingredients. The complexing power of citrates is used to prevent the coagulation of blood products. Calcium and iron(III) ammonia citrates also make good dietary supplements effective in the treatment of osteoporosis and anaemia, because they are easily absorbed into the blood stream from the gut.

| Food product/application | Citric acid/salt | Purpose | Typical level |
|---|---|---|---|
| Soft drinks | Citric acid | Imparts tangy flavour. Chelates metal ions to improve storage | 0.25 to 0.4% |
| Soft drinks | Sodium citrate | Agreeable cooling, saline taste. Forms a valuable pH buffer with citric acid to improve $CO_2$ retention and stabilise colour and flavour | 0.1% |
| Wine | Citric acid | Prevents or dissolves iron(III) turbidity produced by tannin-iron or phosphate-iron complexes | 0 to 0.3% |
| Confectionery | Citric acid | Flavour enhancer for berries and fruits. Promotes sucrose inversion | 0.5% |
| Canned fruits and vegetables | Citric acid | Permits use of lower cooking temperatures. Preserves flavour, appearance, texture and prevents discoloration | 0.1% |
| Jams and jellies | Citric acid/ sodium citrate | pH adjustment/buffering for optimum pectin gelling | 0 to 0.3% |
| Gelatin deserts | Citric acid/ sodium citrate | pH adjustment/buffering for optimum setting. Flavour enhancer and colour stabiliser | 2 to 3% |
| Processed cheese | Sodium citrate | Emulsion stabiliser for fats. Complexes calcium ions and improves microbiological stability | 3 to 4% |
| Dried ingredient blends | Calcium citrate | Anti-caking agent | 1 to 2% |
| Mineral supplements | Calcium citrate | Dietary supplement | 0.1 to 0.2% |
| Antioxidant | Citric acid | Promotes product stability by chelating copper and iron impurities in seafoods, etc. | 0.02% |

## Industrial uses

Citric acid and its salts are used to provide elements needed for healthy growth of both animals and plants. The essential elements are added as complexes with citrate ions to animal feed or to high performance fertilisers.

Partially neutralised citric acid forms the basis of many industrial descalents and metal cleaners which promote rapid rates of scale removal particularly deposits of compounds of calcium or iron. In the oil industry citric acid is used to prevent the formation of plugs of iron(III) hydroxide which can block the flow of oil in limestone rocks. Aluminium citrate can help to enhance oil recovery.

Citric acid/sodium citrate buffers can be used to remove sulphur dioxide from flue gases at pH 4.5. Citric acid finds many applications as a complexing agent for metal ions in metal plating, textile preparations, the control of discoloration in paper, and the manufacture of cosmetics. Citric acid and citrates are also used to modify the setting rates of concrete, grouts and mortars in the building industry.

Esters of citric acid are replacing phthalates as plasticisers in pvc-based products used to wrap or contain food. These plasticisers provide good heat and light stability with excellent flexibility at low temperatures. Phthalates are being phased out from these uses because they may be harmful – they can mimic the action of hormones.

## KEY SKILLS

### Communication

Reading about the manufacture of citric acid (background reading, section 15.4) and summarising the information gives you an opportunity to develop your skills of selecting and synthesising information from a document.

## TOPIC REVIEW

1   **List key words or terms with definitions where necessary**

Illustrate the following with suitable **examples**:

- nucleophilic addition
- addition–elimination reaction
- ester
- acyl chloride

2   **Summarise the key principles as simply as possible**

The **summary chart** or 'spider diagram' below summarises the main reactions in this topic. You may prefer to split this large chart up into several smaller ones each dealing with a new functional group. Remember that, **eventually**, you will have to know how to convert one substance into another, which may involve several stages (Topic 20). For this reason, **this over-view is essential knowledge**. As before you must include **reactants, conditions, type of reaction** and **products** on the chart(s).

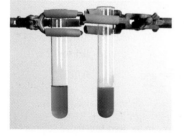

Figure 15.20   **Which oxidation products of alcohols react with Benedict's solution? What is the red precipitate?**

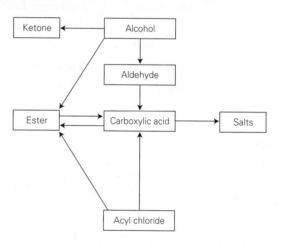

## REVIEW QUESTIONS

✶ Indicates that the *Book of data* is needed.

**15.1**   a   Draw displayed formulae for THREE isomeric carbonyl compounds of molecular formula $C_4H_8O$. (3)

b   Name these three compounds. (3)

**(6 marks)**

**15.2**   a   Give the structural formulae of THREE isomeric ketones which have the molecular formula $C_5H_{10}O$. (3)

b   Name the three ketones. (3)

**(6 marks)**

**15.3**   The following compounds can all be made by the oxidation of an appropriate alcohol. Give the structural formula and name of the alcohol in each case.

a   ethanoic acid, $CH_3CO_2H$                                                                (2)
b   propanone, $CH_3COCH_3$                                                                 (2)
c   propanal, $CH_3CH_2CHO$                                                                  (2)
d   hexan-2-one, $CH_3(CH_2)_3COCH_3$                                                        (2)
e   cyclohexanone,                                                                           (2)

f   benzoic acid,   $CO_2H$                                                                  (2)
                                                                                    **(12 marks)**

**15.4**   Hydrazine, $NH_2$—$NH_2$, is a compound which reacts with aldehydes and ketones, attacking the carbon atom of the carbonyl group.

a   Draw a 'dot and cross' diagram of a molecule of hydrazine (outer electron shells only).                                                                      (2)
b   What kind of attacking reagent do you expect hydrazine to be? Justify your answer.                                                                           (2)
c   Use structural formulae to show the first stage of the reaction which might occur between hydrazine and propanone.                                            (1)
                                                                                     **(5 marks)**

**15.5**   a   What type of reaction takes place between butanal and the following reagents?
   i   sodium dichromate and sulphuric acid                                                  (1)
   ii  Benedict's solution                                                                   (1)
   iii Brady's reagent.                                                                      (1)
b   Draw the structural formulae of the organic products of reactions i and ii. (2)
c   Which of the reagents would you expect to react with butanone? Justify your answer.                                                                           (2)
                                                                                     **(7 marks)**

**15.6**   Write balanced equations, including state symbols, for the reactions between methanoic acid, $HCO_2H$, and

a   sodium metal                                                                            (2)
b   sodium hydroxide solution                                                               (2)
c   sodium carbonate solution                                                               (2)
d   sodium hydrogencarbonate solution.                                                      (2)
                                                                                     **(8 marks)**

**15.7**   a   Draw displayed formulae of the organic products of the reactions of ethanoic acid (in the presence of an acid catalyst) with
   i   ethanol          (2)          iii  propan-2-ol          (2)
   ii  propan-1-ol      (2)          iv   cyclohexanol         (2)
b   Name the four compounds whose formulae you have drawn.                                  (4)
                                                                                    **(12 marks)**

**15.8**  **a**  Draw displayed formulae of the organic products of the reactions of ethanol with

    **i** ethanoic acid with an acid catalyst (such as concentrated $H_2SO_4$) (2)
    **ii** benzoyl chloride, $C_6H_5COCl$ (2)
    **iii** propanoyl chloride (2)
    **iv** hexanoic acid with an acid catalyst as in **i**. (2)

    **b**  Name the four compounds whose formulae you have drawn. (4)

          **(12 marks)**

**✳ 15.9**  **a**  Both ethanoic acid and propanone absorb infrared radiation at around $1740\ cm^{-1}$. Which bond is responsible for this absorption? (1)

    **b**  Which of the two compounds has a broadened trough (peak) at this wavenumber? Justify your answer. (2)

    **c**  Would you expect the infrared spectrum of ethyl ethanoate to show absorption at around $1740\ cm^{-1}$? Give a reason for your answer and suggest whether the trough (if formed) is likely to be broadened. (2)

          **(5 marks)**

**✳ 15.10**  **a**  Draw a displayed formula for benzoic acid, $C_6H_5CO_2H$. (1)

    **b**  Mark on your displayed formula the bond lengths for all the different bonds present in the benzoic acid molecule. (6)

    **c**  Draw a displayed formula for the benzoate ion, $C_6H_5CO_2^-$. (1)

    **d**  What difference would you expect in any of the bond lengths in the benzoate ion, compared with the benzoic acid molecule? (2)

    **e**  Justify your answer to **d**. (2)

          **(12 marks)**

**15.11**  Give the structural formulae of the organic product(s) of the following reactions:

    **a**  ethyl methanoate and aqueous sodium hydroxide (2)
    **b**  methyl ethanoate and aqueous sodium hydroxide (2)
    **c**  propanoic acid and lithium tetrahydridoaluminate, $LiAlH_4$ (1)
    **d**  ethanoyl chloride and propan-1-ol (1)
    **e**  propanoyl chloride and ammonia (1)

          **(7 marks)**

# EXAMINATION QUESTIONS

Questions of the summary and comprehension type are found in the background reading section (section 15.4).

**15.12**  This question is about propanoic acid and some of its reactions.

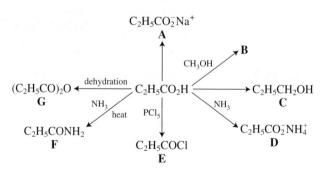

**a  i** What is the name of substance **A**?                                              (1)

**ii** Substance **A** can be made by reacting propanoic acid with sodium hydroxide. Name TWO other substances which would react with propanoic acid to form **A**.                                              (2)

**b  i** Draw a displayed formula for substance **B** formed from propanoic acid and methanol.                                              (2)

**ii** What additional substance and what conditions are necessary to speed up this reaction?                                              (2)

**c  i** What is the name for the type of reaction which produces **C** from propanoic acid?                                              (1)

**ii** Name a suitable reagent to bring about this reaction.                                              (1)

**d  i** Which one of the substances, **A** to **G**, reacts rapidly with water to form two different acids?                                              (1)

**ii** What type of reagent is water in this reaction?                                              (1)

**(11 marks)**

**15.13**   **a**   The scheme below shows three reactions of benzoyl chloride.

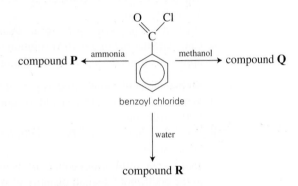

**i** Copy and complete the displayed formulae of **P**, **Q** and **R**.                                              (3)

**ii** What type of attacking reagents are ammonia, water and methanol?                                              (1)

**iii** Explain why ammonia molecules can behave in this way but ammonium ions cannot.                                              (1)

**b**   Another compound which can be prepared from benzoyl chloride is the ester phenyl benzoate, $C_6H_5CO_2C_6H_5$. Name the other organic compound required for this reaction and state the necessary conditions.                                              (2)

**c** **i** Phenyl benzoate prepared by the reaction in **b** is first seen as off-white 'lumps' of solid. This solid is filtered off and is then purified by recrystallisation. This technique involves dissolving the impure phenyl benzoate in the minimum quantity of a hot solvent. Pure phenyl benzoate crystallises out when the solution is cooled. Explain why the final product is of higher purity than the original off-white solid. (2)

**ii** How could you check the purity of the recrystallised phenyl benzoate? (2)

**d** Many esters are fragrant liquids and some of them are used as constituents of perfumes. Suggest TWO properties (apart from smell and safety in use) an ester needs if it is to be suitable for this use. (2)

**(13 marks)**

**15.14** This question is concerned with methanoic acid, $HCO_2H$, an acid present in red ants. Aqueous solutions of methanoic acid are sometimes sold for removing calcium carbonate scale from kettles.

**a** Write a balanced equation, including state symbols, for the reaction between aqueous methanoic acid and calcium carbonate. (2)

**b** The acid dissociation constant, $K_a$, of methanoic acid is $1.6 \times 10^{-4}\ mol\ dm^{-3}$.

**i** Write the expression for $K_a$ for methanoic acid. (2)

**ii** Calculate the pH of a 0.10 M solution of methanoic acid, making the usual approximations during your calculation. (2)

**c** Methanoic acid can be used as part of a buffer solution.

**i** What substance would you add to aqueous methanoic acid to make a buffer solution? (1)

**ii** Write equations for the TWO equilibria involving hydrogen ions in your buffer solution. (2)

**iii** Using your equilibrium equations, explain how this buffer solution responds to the addition of a small quantity of sodium hydroxide solution. (2)

**d** **i** What organic compound reacts with methanoic acid to form an ester of molecular formula $C_3H_6O_2$? (1)

**ii** Name and draw the displayed formula of another ester which has the same molecular formula, $C_3H_6O_2$. (2)

**(14 marks)**

# The Born–Haber cycle, structure and bonding

## COMMENT

| Period 3 elements | Atomic number |
|---|---|
| Na | 11 |
| Mg | 12 |
| Al | 13 |
| Si | 14 |
| P | 15 |
| S | 16 |
| Cl | 17 |
| Ar | 18 |

In this topic you will be mainly concerned with a study of periodicity of properties across the elements of the third period of the Periodic Table, the elements sodium to argon.

One aspect of this study will be to look again at ionic and covalent bonding. The two types of bonding have been presented as distinct types in previous topics (3 and 7), but now we are going to look at compounds which illustrate that there is a *transition* in bonding, rather than an abrupt change. The chlorides and oxides of the Period 3 elements will be the basis of this work.

Your study of bonding will start by looking at the enthalpy changes when ionic solids are formed from their elements. This can be done by using a special application of Hess's Law called the Born–Haber cycle.

## REVIEW TASK

You should reread Topic 5 on energy changes and reactions.

In this topic you will:

- investigate the energy changes which occur when an ionic solid is formed from its elements and when it is dissolved in water
- look at the factors which govern whether a simple compound is ionic or covalent, summarised in Fajans' rules
- explore in more detail the periodic behaviour of some Period 3 compounds towards water.

## 16.1 The formation of ions and enthalpy changes

We saw in Topic 13 that *spontaneous change* in a process is possible when the total entropy change for that process is *positive*. The dominant component of most total entropy changes is the entropy change in the surroundings, $\Delta S^{\ominus}_{\text{surroundings}}$.

When this is positive, a reaction is highly likely. Applying this idea to the formation of a positive ion, such as $Na^+(g)$, has a surprising result:

for the reaction      $Na(s) \longrightarrow Na^+(g) + e^-$

$$\Delta H^\ominus = +60.3 \text{ kJ mol}^{-1}$$

and      $\Delta S^\ominus_{\text{surroundings}} = -\Delta H^\ominus/T$

$$= -\frac{603000}{298}$$

$$= -2020 \text{ J mol}^{-1} \text{ K}^{-1}$$

Given this large negative entropy change, it is hardly sensible to suggest that sodium atoms ionise easily; they may ionise more easily than the atoms of other elements, but the process cannot happen spontaneously.

So, why is sodium so reactive?

To find an answer **we have first to realise that the ionisation of sodium does not happen in isolation; the sodium reacts with something.** Changes happen to another substance as well. We must look at the whole reaction and include all the enthalpy changes which take place.

This we do in a **Born–Haber cycle**, which is the name given to a Hess cycle applied to the formation of an ionic compound from its elements. To use this new cycle we shall need to define some more standard enthalpy changes which were not included in Topic 5.

# Enthalpy changes of atomisation, electron affinity and ionisation

These are energy changes for which the data are regularly needed when constructing Born–Haber cycles. The appropriate data are collected together in tables in the *Book of data*.

**The standard enthalpy change of atomisation of an element, symbol $\Delta H^\ominus_{\text{at}}$, is the enthalpy change that takes place when one mole of gaseous atoms is made from the element in its standard physical state under standard conditions.**

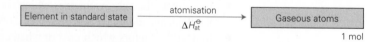

| Equation | Enthalpy change of atomisation/kJ mol$^{-1}$ |
|---|---|
| $Mg(s) \longrightarrow Mg(g)$ | $\Delta H^\ominus_{\text{at}}[Mg(s)] = +148$ |
| $Na(s) \longrightarrow Na(g)$ | $\Delta H^\ominus_{\text{at}}[Na(s)] = +107$ |
| $\frac{1}{2}O_2(g) \longrightarrow O(g)$ | $\Delta H^\ominus_{\text{at}}[\frac{1}{2}O_2(g)] = +249$ |
| $\frac{1}{2}H_2(g) \longrightarrow H(g)$ | $\Delta H^\ominus_{\text{at}}[\frac{1}{2}H_2(g)] = +218$ |

More values are listed in table 5.2 in the *Book of data*.

**The energy change which takes place when one mole of gaseous atoms of an element acquire electrons and form single negatively charged ions is known as the electron affinity, $E_{\text{aff}}$, of that element.**

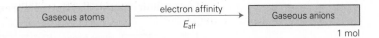

Values are listed in table 5.10 in the *Book of data*. Some examples are given below.

| Equation | Electron affinity $E_{aff}$ /kJ mol$^{-1}$ |
|---|---|
| $Cl(g) + e^- \longrightarrow Cl^-(g)$ | $-349$ |
| $Br(g) + e^- \longrightarrow Br^-(g)$ | $-325$ |
| $I(g) + e^- \longrightarrow I^-(g)$ | $-295$ |

The opposite change is the loss of an electron from a gaseous atom to form a single positively charged ion. This enthalpy change was introduced in Topic 3 and is known as the **ionisation energy,** $E_{mj}$, of an element.

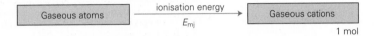

Values are listed in table 4.1 in the *Book of data*. Some examples are:

| Equation | Ionisation energy $E_{mj}$ /kJ mol$^{-1}$ |
|---|---|
| $Li(g) - e^- \longrightarrow Li^+(g)$ | $+520$ |
| $Na(g) - e^- \longrightarrow Na^+(g)$ | $+496$ |
| $K(g) - e^- \longrightarrow K^+(g)$ | $+419$ |

## 16.2 The Born–Haber cycle: lattice energies

When ions form crystals the bonding which occurs is very strong, so ionic compounds are not easily decomposed to their elements. The energy given out when ions come together to form a crystalline solid is called the **lattice energy** of the compound. Lattice energies *always* have negative values.

**The lattice energy of an ionic crystal is the standard enthalpy change of formation of one mole of the crystal lattice from its constituent ions in the gas phase.**

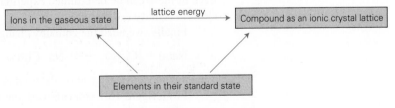

$$Na^+(g) + Cl^-(g) \longrightarrow Na^+Cl^-(s) \qquad \Delta H^{\ominus}_{lattice}(298) = \text{lattice energy}$$

The direct determination of lattice energies is not possible, but values based on experimental measurements can be calculated from an energy cycle, known as a **Born–Haber cycle**.

For sodium chloride the Born–Haber cycle is:

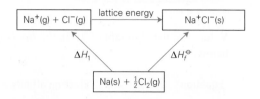

The standard enthalpy change of formation of sodium chloride can be measured directly, by the reaction of sodium with chlorine in a calorimeter. The energy required to convert sodium metal into gaseous ions, and chlorine molecules into gaseous ions, can be obtained, so $\Delta H_1$ will be known, and it is then possible to obtain a value for the lattice energy.

$\Delta H_1$ has to be obtained in stages. Taking the sodium first,

$$\text{Na(s)} \xrightarrow[\substack{\text{standard enthalpy} \\ \text{change of atomisation}}]{} \text{Na(g)} \xrightarrow[\substack{\text{ionisation} \\ \text{energy}}]{-e^-} \text{Na}^+\text{(g)}$$

The two energy values required are the **standard enthalpy change of atomisation** of sodium, for the conversion of solid sodium into gaseous sodium consisting of separate atoms,

$$\text{Na(s)} \longrightarrow \text{Na(g)} \qquad\qquad \Delta H^{\ominus}_{\text{at}} = +107.3\,\text{kJ mol}^{-1}$$

and the **ionisation energy**, for the conversion of gaseous atoms into gaseous ions,

$$\text{Na(g)} \longrightarrow \text{Na}^+\text{(g)} + e^- \qquad\qquad E_{\text{m1}} = +496\,\text{kJ mol}^{-1}$$

Taking the chlorine we have:

$$\tfrac{1}{2}\text{Cl}_2\text{(g)} \xrightarrow[\substack{\text{standard enthalpy} \\ \text{change of atomisation}}]{} \text{Cl(g)} \xrightarrow[\substack{\text{electron} \\ \text{affinity}}]{+e^-} \text{Cl}^-\text{(g)}$$

The two energy values required are the **standard enthalpy change of atomisation** of chlorine, for the conversion of gaseous chlorine molecules into gaseous chlorine atoms,

$$\tfrac{1}{2}\text{Cl}_2\text{(g)} \longrightarrow \text{Cl(g)} \qquad\qquad \Delta H^{\ominus}_{\text{at}} = +121.7\,\text{kJ mol}^{-1}$$

and the **electron affinity**, which is the energy change occurring when a chlorine atom accepts an electron and becomes a chloride ion,

$$\text{Cl(g)} + e^- \longrightarrow \text{Cl}^-\text{(g)} \qquad\qquad E_{\text{aff}} = -348.8\,\text{kJ mol}^{-1}$$

Each of these can be determined experimentally, although the determination of electron affinity is difficult.

Finally, we need the enthalpy change of formation of sodium chloride:

$$\text{Na(s)} + \tfrac{1}{2}\text{Cl}_2\text{(g)} \longrightarrow \text{Na}^+\text{Cl}^-\text{(s)} \qquad \Delta H^{\ominus}_{\text{f}} = -411.2\,\text{kJ mol}^{-1}$$

Then the lattice energy can be determined.

From figure 16.1 you can work out the lattice energy by substituting the appropriate values:

$$\Delta H^{\ominus}_{\text{lattice}} = \Delta H^{\ominus}_{\text{f}}[\text{NaCl(s)}] - \{\Delta H^{\ominus}_{\text{at}}[\text{Na(s)}] + \Delta H^{\ominus}_{\text{at}}[\tfrac{1}{2}\text{Cl}_2\text{(g)}] + E_{\text{m1}}[\text{Na(g)}] + E_{\text{aff}}[\text{Cl(g)}]\}$$

$$= -411.2 - \{+107.3 + 121.7 + 496 - 348.8\}\,\text{kJ mol}^{-1}$$

$$\Delta H^{\ominus}_{\text{lattice}} = -787\,\text{kJ mol}^{-1}$$

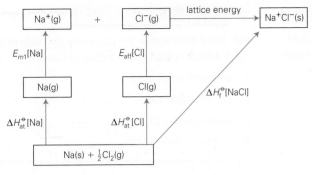

Figure 16.1 **The Born–Haber cycle for sodium chloride**

# Other Born–Haber cycles

When you want to use a Born–Haber cycle to calculate the lattice energies of other ionic substances, the basic procedure is always the same as in figure 16.1 but there are additional points which you have to remember.

- **When there are two ions of one kind in the formula** – you will have to count its enthalpy change of atomisation and its ionisation energy or electron affinity *twice*.

  For example, magnesium chloride has two chloride ions in its formula so the enthalpy change of atomisation of chlorine is $2 \times +122\,kJ\,mol^{-1}$ plus twice the electron affinity $2 \times -349\,kJ\,mol^{-1}$.

- **When the metal forms ions with more than one positive charge** – you will need to use the appropriate number of ionisation energies.

  For example, magnesium ions are $Mg^{2+}$ so when ionising the gaseous magnesium atoms in the Born–Haber cycle you must use $(+738\,kJ\,mol^{-1})$ $+ (+1451\,kJ\,mol^{-1})$.

- **When the anion has two negative charges** you will need two electron affinities.

  For example, for oxygen you must use not only $O(g)$, which has a negative value, but also the electron affinity of $O^{-}(g)$, which has a positive value.
  Your Born–Haber cycle will therefore include $(-141\,kJ\,mol^{-1})$ $+ (+798\,kJ\,mol^{-1})$. The electron affinity of $O^{-}(g)$ is endothermic because negatively charged electrons have to overcome a force of repulsion from the negative ion which they are joining.

| Enthalpy change | | Value/kJ mol$^{-1}$ |
|---|---|---|
| $\frac{1}{2}Cl(g)$ | $\longrightarrow Cl(g)$ | +122 |
| $Cl(g) + e^{-}$ | $\longrightarrow Cl^{-}(g)$ | +349 |
| $Mg(g)$ | $\longrightarrow Mg^{2+}(g) + 2e^{-}$ | +2189 |
| $O(g) + e^{-}$ | $\longrightarrow O^{-}(g)$ | −141 |
| $O^{-}(g) + e^{-}$ | $\longrightarrow O^{2-}(g)$ | +798 |

## COMMENT

The state symbols for the various species are very important. Make sure you are using the correct ones and are remembering to write them in.

## QUESTIONS

You should now calculate the lattice energy of each of the following using the methods described above and information from the *Book of data*.

1 potassium bromide, KBr

2 calcium iodide, $CaI_2$

3 lithium oxide, $Li_2O$

4 aluminium fluoride, $AlF_3$

## 16.3 Lattice energy values and reactivity

We started by asking the question, 'Why is sodium so reactive?'

The answer is quite complicated because much depends on the reaction which is supposed to be taking place. We cannot answer the question as it stands. So, let us ask more specifically:

'Why is sodium so reactive towards chlorine?'

A good answer is: because the lattice energy of sodium chloride, taken with the electron affinity of chlorine, is sufficiently large numerically as to make the sodium atoms vaporise and ionise *and* leave some energy over. This gives $\Delta S^{\ominus}_{\text{surroundings}}$ a positive value.

The value of the lattice energy has a considerable influence on the reactivity of the elements in a compound. The most important single contributing factor as to why sodium is reactive towards chlorine is that the lattice energy of sodium chloride has a large negative value.

## Factors affecting lattice energies

It is important, therefore, to understand the factors which affect the values of lattice energies. There are three principal factors:

### 1 The sizes of the ions

The larger the ions, the further apart their charges can be considered to be and the less negative the lattice energy becomes.

### 2 The charges on the ions

A doubly charged ion has a greater attraction for an oppositely charged ion than a singly charged ion has, giving a more negative lattice energy.

### 3 The structure of the solid

The way the ions are arranged in the solid does not make a big difference between lattice energies but it is important to realise its existence when two dissimilar structures are being compared.

BACKGROUND

There is a problem when comparing the values of negative numbers. Mathematically, $-100$ is a larger number than $-200$ but this is unhelpful when speaking or writing about lattice energies. The use of the expressions 'more negative' and 'less negative' will help to make your meaning clearer.

## QUESTIONS

Use table 5.9 in the *Book of data* to answer the following questions about trends in lattice energies.

1    How do the lattice energies of the Group 1 fluorides vary down the group?

2    How do the lattice energies of the Group 1 chlorides differ from the lattice energies of the Group 2 chlorides?

3    How do the lattice energies of the Group 2 chlorides differ from the lattice energies of the Group 2 oxides?

4    Try to suggest explanations for the trends you have found.

# The solubility of ionic compounds

In this short experiment you are going to look at the enthalpy change when some ionic solids dissolve.

**EXPERIMENT 16.3**

## 16.3 Enthalpy changes of solution

You are supplied with the following **anhydrous solids**:

potassium chloride, calcium chloride and iron(III) chloride

These solutes absorb moisture from the atmosphere so the stock bottles should be securely stoppered after use.

**SAFETY**

Anhydrous calcium chloride is an irritant.
Anhydrous iron(III) chloride is harmful if swallowed and irritating to skin.

### Procedure

Put about $5\,cm^3$ of water in a test tube and measure its temperature. Add one of the solutes heaped on a spatula. Replace the thermometer and stir, noting the temperature of the solution.

Repeat the experiment with the other two solutes, recording the temperature before and after dissolving.

In each case work out the temperature change.

✎    **In your notes:** Interpret your results in terms of the three factors listed in the introduction to this section.

# Interpretation of the experiment

When an ionic solid dissolves in water, the crystal lattice breaks down and the ions separate. It takes a large amount of energy to separate the ions. The energy needed is equal to the lattice energy (but opposite in sign because the ions are separating rather than coming together). For sodium chloride the energy needed to separate the ions is $+780\,kJ\,mol^{-1}$.

The overall energy change when sodium chloride dissolves in water is small. So where does the energy come from to separate the ions? The answer is that there is a strong attraction between the ions and polar water molecules. The $\delta-$ oxygen

**COMMENT**

In water, ions are 'hydrated' by water molecules as they dissolve. In other solvents chemists use the term 'solvated' to describe the state of ions in solution.

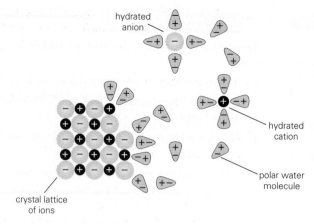

Figure 16.2    **Water molecules dissolving an ionic solid**

atoms in water molecules attract positive sodium ions. The $\delta+$ hydrogen atoms attract negative chloride ions. The ions are hydrated (see figure 16.2) and the total energy released as the water molecules hydrate the ions is about the same as the lattice energy.

The hydration energy given out when a positive ion is hydrated varies with the charge on the ion. So the hydration energy of iron(III) ions is greater than the hydration energy of calcium ions, which in turn is greater than the hydration energy of potassium ions.

# The transition from ionic to covalent bonding

We suggested previously that the three principal factors which affect the size of lattice energies are:

● the radii of the ions
● the charges on the ions
● the type of crystal lattice.

It is possible, using these three factors, to calculate a value for the lattice energy of an ionic solid. In doing this calculation it is assumed that the ions are perfectly spherical and have their charges distributed evenly. We can describe such a structure as a **purely ionic model**. Lattice energies calculated in this way are referred to as **theoretical lattice energies**.

When the theoretical lattice energies for many compounds are compared with the values from the Born–Haber cycle, which are based on experimental data, the agreement is close. Since the Born–Haber cycle makes no assumptions about the nature of the attraction between ions, this is good evidence that the purely ionic model accurately describes the structures of many compounds.

Here are some examples of this agreement, all values being given in kJ mol$^{-1}$:

| Compound | Theoretical value | Experimental value (Born–Haber cycle) | Difference |
|---|---|---|---|
| NaCl | −770 | −780 | 10 |
| NaBr | −735 | −742 | 7 |
| NaI | −687 | −705 | 17 |

There are compounds, however, where the agreement is not nearly as impressive. Consider, for example, the halides of the next element to sodium in Period 3, magnesium (again all values are in kJ mol$^{-1}$).

| Compound | Theoretical value | Experimental value (Born–Haber cycle) | Difference |
|---|---|---|---|
| MgCl$_2$ | −2326 | −2526 | 200 |
| MgBr$_2$ | −2097 | −2440 | 343 |
| MgI$_2$ | −1944 | −2327 | 383 |

It seems that the purely ionic model is not such a good representation of the structure of the magnesium halides.

It is thought that the cause of this disagreement is that the ions of magnesium are smaller than those of sodium and have two positive charges instead of one. The ionic radii are

$$Mg^{2+} \quad 0.07 \, nm \qquad Na^+ \quad 0.10 \, nm$$

COMMENT

1 nm = 1 × 10$^{-9}$ m

The small magnesium ion is very intensely charged and can approach the negative ion more closely than can the sodium ion. This intense charge pulls the electron cloud of the negative ion out of shape, creating a region of negative charge between the ions – effectively a partial covalent bond.

This makes a value for the lattice energy which is rather greater numerically than that expected from the purely ionic model, since the calculation makes no allowance for the extra attraction caused by the distortion of the negative ion. Figure 16.3 illustrates the effect, which is known as the 'polarisation' of the negative ion by the positive ion.

The extent of polarisation of the negative ion by the positive one is described by a series of rules known as **Fajans' rules**:

**There is a tendency towards increasing covalency when:**

- **the positive ion is small**
- **the positive ion has multiple positive charges**
- **the negative ion is large**
- **the negative ion has multiple negative charges.**

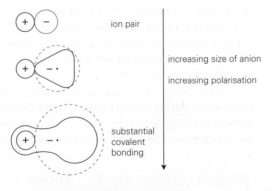

Figure 16.3    **The polarisation of large anions by a small cation (the green circles show the size of the unpolarised ions)**

**STUDY TASK**

Table 5.9 in the *Book of data* gives values for the theoretical and experimental lattice energies of a range of compounds. Choose examples from the table to investigate the validity of Fajans' rules, relating any difference in lattice energies to ionic sizes and charges.

## 16.4 Periodicity of the structures and properties of the chlorides and oxides of the Period 3 elements

**Figure 16.4** Kasimir Fajans was a Polish-born chemist. He was an academic chemist in Germany before moving to the US in 1936 where he became a professor. He formulated his 'rules' in 1923–4

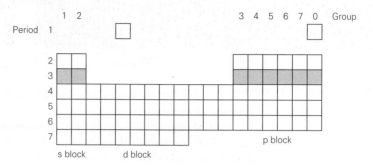

**Figure 16.5** The position of the Period 3 elements in the Periodic Table (short form)

Using Fajans' rules, when the differences in the ionic radii and in the ionic charges become very large, you should notice that covalent bonding can become the main type of bonding present, and the bond then becomes essentially covalent with some ionic character.

The *Book of data* gives estimates of ionic radius and charge for some very surprising ions in table 4.4. When we list these for some of the elements of the third period, we get the following:

| Element | Cation | Ionic radius/nm |
|---|---|---|
| sodium | $Na^+$ | 0.10 |
| magnesium | $Mg^{2+}$ | 0.07 |
| aluminium | $Al^{3+}$ | 0.05 |
| silicon | $Si^{4+}$ | 0.04 |
| phosphorus | $P^{5+}$ | 0.02 |

The radius of a chloride ion, $Cl^-$, is given as 0.18 nm, much larger than any of the positive ions given in the list above.

According to Fajans' rules, therefore, we might reasonably expect that the bonding between chlorine and each of the elements of Period 3 from sodium to phosphorus would become increasingly covalent and less ionic in character as we go across the period.

This should be reflected in the melting points of the chlorides since **ionic compounds, having strong forces of attraction between the ions, have high melting points**. On the other hand, **molecular compounds, with only relatively weak intermolecular forces, have low melting points**. The data bear this out.

| Compound | Melting point/K | Structure type | Bond type |
|---|---|---|---|
| NaCl | 1074 | ionic | ionic |
| $MgCl_2$ | 987 | ionic | ionic |
| $AlCl_3$ | 463 | molecular | covalent |
| $SiCl_4$ | 203 | molecular | covalent |
| $PCl_3$ | 161 | molecular | covalent |

sodium

magnesium

aluminium

Figure 16.6 **Some elements from the third period of the Periodic Table**

---

### STUDY TASK

Apply the principles of this section to examine the chlorides of the period which begins with potassium. Miss out the transition elements so that you can see whether the pattern of the chlorides in Period 3 is reproduced in Period 4.

---

When the chlorides of metals are added to water they dissolve. The chlorides of non-metals are not ionic and they dissolve much less readily. Recalling the ideas about intermolecular forces from Topic 9, the principal reason is that the dipole–dipole and van der Waals forces, which might serve to attract non-metal chlorides to water, are much weaker than the hydrogen bonding between water molecules which would have to be broken.

**Non-metal chlorides often do react with water, however. The reaction with water is called hydrolysis and the products often include hydrochloric acid.** The following table shows what happens to the chlorides of the elements of the third period of the Periodic Table when they are added to water. Notice that aluminium chloride hydrolyses – aluminium is behaving like a non-metal here.

| Formula | Effect of adding the chloride to water | Equation | Other known chlorides |
|---|---|---|---|
| $NaCl(s)$ | Dissolves readily | $NaCl(s) + aq \longrightarrow$ $Na^+(aq) + Cl^-(aq)$ | – |
| $MgCl_2(s)$ | Dissolves readily with very slight hydrolysis | $MgCl_2(s) + aq \longrightarrow$ $Mg^{2+}(aq) + 2Cl^-(aq)$ | – |
| $AlCl_3(s)$ | Hydrolyses | $AlCl_3(s) + 3H_2O(l) \longrightarrow$ $Al(OH)_3(s) + 3H^+(aq) + 3Cl^-(aq)$ | – |
| $SiCl_4(l)$ | Hydrolyses | $SiCl_4(l) + 4H_2O(l) \longrightarrow$ $SiO_2(s) + 4H^+(aq) + 4Cl^-(aq)$ | many |
| $PCl_3(l)$ | Hydrolyses | $PCl_3(l) + 3H_2O(l) \longrightarrow$ $H_3PO_3(aq) + 3H^+(aq) + 3Cl^-(aq)$ | $PCl_5, P_2Cl_4$ |
| $S_2Cl_2(l)$ | Hydrolyses | $S(s)$, $H^+(aq)$, and $Cl^-(aq)$ are amongst the products | $SCl_2, SCl_4$ |
| $Cl_2(g)$ | Hydrolyses | $Cl_2(g) + H_2O(l) \rightleftharpoons$ $HClO(aq) + H^+(aq) + Cl^-(aq)$ | – |

# The behaviour of oxides towards water

While discussing the behaviour of oxides towards water, you should recall and compare the reactions of the oxides of the Group 2 elements, magnesium to barium, which you studied in Topic 4.

When oxides are mixed with water they never simply dissolve. Many undergo no change at all, particularly those of the transition elements. The oxides of Period 3 follow a pattern.

**Metal oxides tend to react with water to give hydroxides which are alkaline. Non-metal oxides react with water to give acids.**

The table below shows what happens to some of these oxides.

| Formula | Effect of adding the oxide to water | Equation |
|---|---|---|
| $Na_2O$ | Exothermic reaction Soluble product | $Na_2O(s) + H_2O(l) \longrightarrow 2Na^+(aq) + 2OH^-(aq)$ |
| $MgO$ | Reaction occurs Product is only slightly soluble | $MgO(s) + H_2O(l) \longrightarrow Mg(OH)_2(s)$ |
| $Al_2O_3$ | No sign of reaction | |
| $SiO_2$ | No sign of reaction | |
| $P_2O_5$ | Reacts vigorously Exothermic | $P_2O_5(s) + 3H_2O(l) \longrightarrow 2H_3PO_4(aq)$ |
| $SO_3$ | Reacts vigorously Exothermic | $SO_3(s) + H_2O(l) \longrightarrow H_2SO_4(aq)$ |
| $Cl_2O$ | Reacts with water Acidic product | $Cl_2O(g) + H_2O(l) \longrightarrow 2HOCl(aq)$ |

Although metal oxides do not always give alkaline mixtures with water, they are basic oxides, containing the base $O^{2-}$ and so will react with acids.

**Aluminium oxide is capable of reacting with both acids and alkalis; it is, for this reason, described as amphoteric.** Equations for its reactions with sulphuric acid and with sodium hydroxide are given below but the structure of aluminium oxide is so tightly held together that these reactions are difficult to demonstrate.

$$Al_2O_3(s) + 3H_2SO_4(aq) \longrightarrow Al_2(SO_4)_3(aq) + 3H_2O(l)$$
$$Al_2O_3(s) + 2NaOH(aq) \longrightarrow 2NaAlO_2(aq) + H_2O(l)$$
sodium aluminate

## 16.5 Background reading: the elements of Period 3

### QUESTIONS

Read the following passage and then answer the questions.

1  a  State the elements with the highest and lowest melting point.
   b  State the elements with the highest and lowest boiling point.
   c  There is an interesting anomaly in your answers to parts **a** and **b**. Suggest reasons for this.

2   a   Which is the most reactive element?

   b   The least reactive element has some important uses. What is this element? Explain how it is useful.

3   Write a summary in continuous prose, in not more than 100 words, stating which elements are important in the diet and how they are used within the body.

# Sodium

- Melting point 98 °C.
- Boiling point 883 °C.
- Discovered by Humphry Davy in London in 1807.
- The name is derived from the English soda, and the chemical symbol comes from the Latin *natrium*.
- A soft metal that tarnishes within minutes of being exposed to the air, and which reacts vigorously with water. The liquid metal is used as a heat exchanger in some nuclear reactors, and as a reagent in the chemicals industry. Sodium salts such as sodium chloride and sodium carbonate are more important than the metal itself.
- Sodium is an essential element for all living things, including humans. Sodium performs several functions within the body, such as the transmission of electrical impulses and the regulation of water content in tissues and blood. Our bodies contain about 100 g, and as this is continually being lost in various ways, it needs to be replaced. The sodium that comes from our food provides all we need. The average person consumes about 10 g of salt a day even though all that is needed is about 3 g. Any excess may contribute to high blood pressure.

Figure 16.7   **Cubic crystals of sodium chloride ($\times$60)**

Figure 16.8   **Dolomite, $MgCO_3.CaCO_3$. Limestone peaks like these in the Dolomites show evident signs of weathering. What chemical reaction causes the normally insoluble calcium carbonate to dissolve?**

# Magnesium

- Melting point 649 °C.
- Boiling point 1107 °C.
- Recognised as an element by Joseph Black of Edinburgh in 1755 and first isolated as the metal by Humphry Davy in 1808.
- The element is named after Magnesia, a district in Thessaly in Greece, where it was first found.

- A silvery white metal that can be made to burn with a bright light and was formerly used in flash bulbs. It is now used to provide lightweight frames for bicycles, car seats and luggage. It is also used as sacrificial anodes on iron structures like boats and bridges to help reduce corrosion (see the Special Study, *Materials science*).

- The sea is the source of most of the 350 000 tonnes of metal produced annually.

- It is an essential element for all living things. Humans take in 300 mg each day, and we each have about 20 g in our bodies.

# Aluminium

- Melting point 661 °C.

- Boiling point 2467 °C.

- Discovered by Hans Oersted in Copenhagen in 1825.

- The name comes from *alumen*, the Latin name for the mineral alum.

- The most abundant of metals. A lot of energy is needed to extract it from its ores: however, this is worthwhile because it does not corrode except to form a surface protective layer and it is easy to recycle. It is lightweight but tough, and is widely used for window frames, aircraft parts, engines, kegs, cooking foil and drinks cans. Aluminium hydroxide is a fire retardant; when heated it decomposes endothermically to form aluminium oxide and steam, thereby hindering the fire.

- There may be a link between aluminium in the diet and Alzheimer's disease, but only a small amount of what we take in with our food is absorbed by our bodies. Foods with above average amounts of aluminium are tea, processed cheese, lentils and sponge cakes. Cooking in aluminium pans does not greatly increase the amount in our diet except when cooking acid foods such as rhubarb. Some indigestion tablets are pure aluminium hydroxide.

**Figure 16.9   Corundum, Al₂O₃ (×7). Why is aluminium oxide so hard and durable? What is the connection between aluminium oxide and the fact that aluminium is corrosion-resistant despite its apparent reactivity?**

# Silicon

- Melting point 1410 °C.

- Boiling point 2355 °C.

- Discovered by J.J. Berzelius in Stockholm in 1824.

- The name is derived from the Latin *silicis*, 'flint'.

- The second most abundant element on the surface of the Earth after oxygen. Sand and flint are silicon dioxide, as are semi-precious stones such as rock crystal and rhinestone. The element itself, when ultra pure, is blue-grey and is one of those unusual elements which fall between being a metal and a non-metal, and is classified as a semi-conductor. It is used in silicon chips. Every year 5000 tonnes of semi-conductor silicon and 500 000 tonnes of metallurgy-grade silicon are produced.

- Silicon is essential for some species and perhaps humans, in whom it is found in connective tissue and skin.

**Figure 16.10   Pure silicon crystals. In what way is the structure of silicon similar to that of diamond?**

# Phosphorus

- Melting point of white phosphorus 44 °C.

- Boiling point 280 °C.

- Discovered by Hennig Brand in Hamburg in 1669.

Figure 16.11   **Phosphorus is extracted from phosphate rocks. Why should sodium and phosphorus not be stored next to each other in chemical store-rooms?**

- The name is derived from the Greek *phosphoros*, 'bringer of light', because it glows in the dark.
- There are several forms of phosphorus. White phosphorus is manufactured industrially, glows in the dark, is spontaneously flammable when exposed to the air and is a deadly poison. Red phosphorus, made by heating white phosphorus, does not glow, is stable and is not poisonous. This is the material stuck on the side of boxes of safety matches on which the matches must be struck to light them.
- Phosphorus itself is essential to all forms of life since it is part of DNA, although there are many phosphorus compounds that are essential in the living cell. So phosphoric acid is a safe additive for foods that need to be kept acidic. We take in about 1 g of phosphate a day, and we store about 750 g in our bodies, since our bones are mainly calcium phosphate.
- In the environment and in living things, phosphorus is present as phosphate. Phosphates are used in fertilisers and detergents and in metal coatings to prevent corrosion.

# Sulphur

Figure 16.12   **Sulphur crystals (×0.5) (compare with figure 3.6)**

- Melting point 113 °C.
- Boiling point 444 °C.
- Known to ancient civilisations. The name may have one of two derivations: the Sanskrit *sulvere* or Latin *sulphurium*, both meaning 'sulphur'.
- Occurs in large deposits as yellow crystals. It is stable in air and water but will burn if ignited, giving off the acrid gas, sulphur dioxide, which is used to make sulphuric acid, the single most important industrial chemical. Sulphur dioxide is also produced when coal and oil are burned and it is responsible for acid rain.
- Sulphur is essential to all living things, and there is a sulphur cycle in nature. The average human contains 140 g and takes in about 1 g a day.

# Chlorine

Figure 16.13   **Chlorine is extracted from sea water**

- Melting point −101 °C.
- Boiling point −34 °C.
- Discovered by C.W. Scheele in Uppsala, Sweden, in 1774.
- The name is derived from the Greek *chloros*, 'pale green'.
- A yellow-green, dense gas, with a choking smell. It is very poisonous and was used as a weapon during the First World War. The gas is made on a large scale from sodium chloride, and is used in the manufacture of bleach and chloroethene for the plastics industry (to make pvc), and to purify drinking water and disinfect swimming pools.
- Our daily intake is about 6 g, mainly as salt, but we could manage with half this amount.

# Argon

**Figure 16.14** **Light bulbs are filled with argon**

- Melting point −189 °C.
- Boiling point −186 °C.
- Discovered by Lord Rayleigh and Sir William Ramsay in 1894.
- The name comes from the Greek *argos*, 'inactive'.
- The third most abundant gas, making up 1% of the atmosphere. The quantity has increased since the Earth was formed because radioactive potassium turns into argon as it decays.
- Argon is a colourless, odourless gas that is totally inert to all other substances, and for this reason it is ideal for use in electric light bulbs.

## KEY SKILLS

### IT

The use of a chemical database on a CD-ROM with static images and videos will allow you both to explore trends and patterns in numerical data and to study the behaviour of elements and compounds which can be hazardous to work with in a school or college laboratory.

## TOPIC REVIEW

Much of the specific vocabulary met in this topic has been included in earlier reviews. Make sure that you remember what each term means as you go over the topic. List any particular words or terms with which you still have difficulty.

1. **List key words or terms with definitions where necessary**

   - $\Delta H^\ominus_{\text{lattice}}$ (298)
   - hydration
   - hydrolysis
   - purely ionic model

2. **Summarise the key principles as simply as possible**

   Draw up a table to **summarise properties** of the **elements** of **Period 3**. Make sure that your notes contain the following.

   - examples of the use of data to calculate lattice energies using the Born–Haber cycle
   - an explanation of the differences in value between lattice energies for different compounds
   - an explanation of the changes involved when ionic substances dissolve
   - an explanation of the relationship of bond type and structure to the physical and chemical properties of the chlorides and oxides in Period 3.

# REVIEW QUESTIONS

✱ Indicates that the *Book of data* is needed.

✱ **16.1**   A student was attempting to calculate the lattice energy of potassium chloride. He looked up the value of the standard enthalpy change of formation of this compound but failed to find values for the enthalpy changes accompanying the two conversions:

$$K(s) \longrightarrow K^+(g) + e^-$$
$$\tfrac{1}{2}Cl_2(g) + e^- \longrightarrow Cl^-(g)$$

   a   What data should the student have used to find the values for these enthalpy changes?   (2)

   b   Set out the appropriate Born–Haber cycle and calculate the lattice energy yourself. Compare your value with that in the *Book of data*.   (8)
   **(10 marks)**

✱ **16.2**   This question is concerned with aluminium oxide, $Al_2O_3$.

   a   Set out and use a Born–Haber cycle to calculate the lattice energy of aluminium oxide.   (8)

   b   How does the lattice energy help to account for the very low solubility of aluminium oxide in water?   (2)
   **(10 marks)**

✱ **16.3**   Use the *Book of data* to find the radius of the iron(III) ion, $Fe^{3+}$, and the melting point of iron(III) chloride.

   a   What do these data suggest about the bonding in this compound? Justify your answer.   (2)

   b   What other data might help you to make a decision about the type of bonding? Explain your answer.   (3)
   **(5 marks)**

✱ **16.4**   a   Use the *Book of data* to find the radii of the following ions:

   $Li^+$, $Cs^+$, $Be^{2+}$, $Ba^{2+}$, $Zn^{2+}$, $F^-$, $I^-$, $S^{2-}$, $N^{3-}$   (2)

   b   Use these radii together with Fajans' rules to predict whether there is likely to be a significant tendency towards covalent bonding in each of the following compounds:

   $LiI$, $CsF$, $BeF_2$, $BeI_2$, $BaI_2$, $Li_2S$, $ZnI_2$, $Li_3N$   (8)
   **(10 marks)**

✱ **16.5**   a   Use the *Book of data* to find the melting points of the fluorides of the elements of Period 3 (sodium to phosphorus).   (2)

   b   Predict the bond type in each fluoride.   (2)

   c   Compare the patterns of melting point and bond type shown by the fluorides with those of the chlorides. Can you account for any differences?   (2)
   **(6 marks)**

# EXAMINATION QUESTIONS

Questions of the summary and comprehension type are found in the background reading section (section 16.5).

**\* 16.6**    This question is about some boron compounds.

**a**   **i**  Draw a labelled Born–Haber cycle for the formation of boron oxide, $B_2O_3$, assuming it to be ionic.                                                      (5)
    **ii**  Use your cycle to calculate the lattice energy of boron oxide.      (2)
    **iii**  Would you expect your value for the lattice energy of the oxide to be in good or poor agreement with a theoretically derived value? Give TWO reasons for your answer.                                                            (2)

**b**   One mole of the oxide reacts with three moles of water. The product dissolves in water to give a weakly acidic solution. Write a balanced equation, including state symbols, for the reaction between the oxide and water.                                                                                              (1)

**c**   Boron also forms a chloride, $BCl_3$. Use appropriate data to suggest the type of bonding in this chloride and predict its likely behaviour towards water.                                                                                              (2)

**(12 marks)**

**\* 16.7**    This question is about the stability and structure of calcium(II) iodide. Calcium(II) iodide crystals have a layer structure in which the calcium–iodine separation is 0.31 nm and the iodine–iodine separation is 0.43 nm. The usual radii are given below.

| | $r_{cov}$/nm | $r_{ion}$/nm |
|---|---|---|
| Calcium | 0.17 | 0.09 |
| Iodine | 0.13 | 0.22 |

The layer structure can be represented as shown in the margin (not to scale).

**a**   **i**  Construct a labelled Born–Haber cycle for the formation of calcium(II) iodide.                                                                                   (5)
    **ii**  From your Born–Haber cycle, calculate the lattice energy of calcium(II) iodide.                                                                               (2)

**b**   In crystalline calcium(II) iodide, what bonding would you predict? Show how the data in the table of radii support your prediction.                         (3)

**c**   In what other way could the bonding in calcium(II) iodide be confirmed?                                                                                   (1)

**(11 marks)**

Ca
I

# TOPIC 17

# Redox equilibria

In this topic you begin with some simple metal displacement reactions and observe that, as well as an enthalpy change, electrical energy can also be obtained from the reactions. To make your study quantitative you will find out how to measure this electrical energy as the e.m.f. (electromotive force) of electrochemical cells.

Figure 17.1    An electric eel (*Electrophorus electricus*)

You will investigate some oxidation and reduction (redox) reactions which involve the transfer of electrons and see how measurement of the electrical energy involved enables us to understand these reactions more fully. You will also look at some examples of the use of electrical energy data in chemical situations.

An understanding of electrochemistry is essential if we are to control corrosion in metals. Corrosion is an ever-present problem wherever metals are used, for example in ships' hulls, car bodies, steel bridges and pipes for the transport of liquids.

Finally there is a section on the application of these ideas to the design of batteries: from torch batteries to the miniature cells used in watches and hearing aids.

## 17.1 Metal/metal ion systems

REVIEW TASK

Working in groups, write down as much as you can recall about oxidation and reduction. Make as long a list as you can of oxidising agents, with their formulae.

Earlier in the course, you have met a number of oxidation and reduction reactions and have seen, in Topic 6, that these always involve a change of oxidation number of the reacting substances.

Start by looking at some reactions between metal **atoms** and metal **ions**. You may have met these before when studying the reactivity series of the metals. The reactivity series is shown in the table below.

| Element | Reduced form | Oxidised form |
| --- | --- | --- |
| *Most strongly reducing* | | |
| Potassium | K | $K^+$ |
| Sodium | Na | $Na^+$ |
| Calcium | Ca | $Ca^{2+}$ |
| Magnesium | Mg | $Mg^{2+}$ |
| Aluminium | Al | $Al^{3+}$ |
| Zinc | Zn | $Zn^{2+}$ |
| Iron | Fe | $Fe^{2+}$ |
| Tin | Sn | $Sn^{2+}$ |
| Lead | Pb | $Pb^{2+}$ |
| (Hydrogen) | $H_2$ | $H^+$ |
| Copper | Cu | $Cu^{2+}$ |
| Mercury | Hg | $Hg_2^{2+}$ |
| Silver | Ag | $Ag^+$ |
| Gold | Au | $Au^+$ |
| *Least strongly reducing* | | |

**EXPERIMENT 17.1a** | **The reactivity series of the metals**

All the following reactions can be carried out in test tubes.

### Procedure

1   Add a small amount of zinc powder to 5 cm$^3$ of 0.5 M copper(II) sulphate solution and shake the mixture gently. Measure the temperature change that occurs. Look for other signs of reaction by examining the solid and solution.

2   Repeat the experiment using any metal powders that are available, such as iron, lead and magnesium. Use similar fine powders if you can.

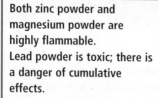

   In your notes:

   1   Was heat evolved or absorbed in the reactions?

   2   Try to arrange the metals in order of reactivity based on your estimates of the enthalpy changes of the reactions.

3   Repeat part **1**, but this time adding magnesium powder to 0.5 M zinc sulphate solution.

SAFETY

Both zinc powder and magnesium powder are highly flammable.
Lead powder is toxic; there is a danger of cumulative effects.

COMMENT

Some hydrogen may be produced when magnesium powder is used but this is not the effect we are interested in.

**QUESTION**

Write ionic equations for the reactions you have observed.

**In your notes:**

1 Write down the oxidation numbers of the reactants and the products in each of the reactions in **1**, **2** and **3**.

2 Which of the reactants has been oxidised and which reduced in each reaction?

# Oxidation and reduction by electron transfer

You should have realised from the equations you have just written that **reactions between metals and metal ions involve the transfer of electrons from one reactant to another**; and that the reactivity series appears to be connected to the energy change involved in this transfer of electrons.

We described 'half-reactions' in Topic 6 and for the zinc–copper reaction the half-reactions are

$$Zn(s) \longrightarrow Zn^{2+}(aq) + 2e^-$$
$$2e^- + Cu^{2+}(aq) \longrightarrow Cu(s)$$

and you can see that the overall reaction will involve the transfer of electrons.

In the first half-reaction, the oxidation number of zinc increases (0 to $+2$) so that an **oxidation** is involved; in the second half-reaction the oxidation number of copper decreases ($+2$ to 0) thus involving a **reduction**. In the complete reaction zinc is the reducing agent and copper(II) ions the oxidising agent:

$$Zn(s) + Cu^{2+}(aq) \longrightarrow Zn^{2+}(aq) + Cu(s)$$

| 0 | $+2$ | $+2$ | 0 |
| reducing agent | oxidising agent | | |

**QUESTION**

Write half-reaction equations for the magnesium/zinc sulphate reaction. Which species is the oxidising agent and which the reducing agent in this reaction?

In Experiment 17.1a you will have seen that zinc can act as either an oxidising agent, $Zn^{2+}(aq)$, or a reducing agent, $Zn(s)$. Each half-reaction can be treated as an equilibrium, so that we have:

$$Zn(s) \rightleftharpoons Zn^{2+}(aq) + 2e^-$$

When electrons are added to this system, the equilibrium will move towards the left; removal of electrons will have the opposite effect.

Thus in the presence of a metal whose tendency to lose electrons and form ions is greater than that of zinc, the reaction moves towards the left and zinc is produced. This is the case with magnesium, which dissolves to form magnesium ions.

In the presence of copper ions the reverse is the case and zinc metal atoms lose electrons to become hydrated ions, while metallic copper is precipitated.

**QUESTION**

Write equilibrium half-reaction equations for magnesium and copper.

EXPERIMENT 17.1b

# Electrical energy from a redox reaction

When you keep the reactants of the last experiment apart you can get the electrons to transfer from the metal to the ions via an external wire rather than directly in the test tube.

COMMENT

E.m.f. (electromotive force) is a measure of the transformation of the energy of a chemical reaction into electrical energy. It is measured in volts (V).

## Procedure

Set up an electrochemical cell similar to the one in figure 17.2.

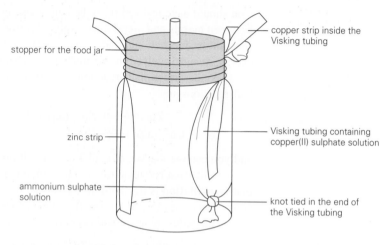

Figure 17.2 **A simple cell made from a food jar**

Clean the metal strips by rubbing with emery paper if necessary.

Soak the Visking tubing in water for 2 minutes until it is soft enough for you to tie the knot. You will find it easier to fill the knotted tubing with copper(II) sulphate solution, using a dropping pipette, before you insert the copper metal strip.

Connect the metal strips to a high resistance voltmeter and measure the e.m.f. of your electrochemical cell.

Can you get useful work, such as lighting a bulb or LED, from your cell?

 **In your notes:**

1 Which metal was the negative connection in the circuit? Can you explain why?

2 Draw a circuit diagram of your apparatus.

# Measuring the tendency of a metal to form ions in solution

When an equilibrium is set up between a piece of metal foil and an aqueous solution of its ions

$$M(s) \rightleftharpoons M^{z+}(aq) + ze^-$$

you can expect the metal to become negatively charged, by electrons building up on it as metal cations are released into the solution. The solution will become positively charged because of the excess of cations.

Thus there should be an **electric potential** between solution and ions. If the

Figure 17.3 **A metal becomes negatively charged as cations are released into solution**

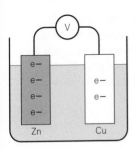

Figure 17.4 **The difference in potential between two metal/metal ion systems can be found by incorporating them into a cell**

equilibrium position differs for different metals, the potentials set up will differ also. These potentials (called **absolute potentials**) **cannot** be measured but the **difference** in potential between two metal/metal ion systems can be found by incorporating them into an electrochemical cell and measuring the voltage between the metal electrodes.

## Cell diagrams

It is convenient to have an agreed method of representing electrochemical cells and the e.m.f. which they produce. **This is called a cell diagram and may be illustrated by the Daniell cell, for which the cell diagram is:**

$$\text{Zn(s)} \,|\, \text{Zn}^{2+}\text{(aq)} \,\vdots\, \text{Cu}^{2+}\text{(aq)} \,|\, \text{Cu(s)} \qquad E = +1.1 \text{ V}$$

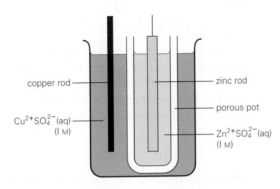

copper rod

zinc rod

porous pot

$\text{Cu}^{2+}\text{SO}_4^{2-}\text{(aq)}$ (I M)

$\text{Zn}^{2+}\text{SO}_4^{2-}\text{(aq)}$ (I M)

Figure 17.5 **A Daniell cell, named after its inventor John Daniell who produced the first reliable source of electric current in 1836. This drawing of the apparatus corresponds to the cell diagram for the Daniell cell**

The solid vertical lines in the cell diagram represent boundaries between solids and solutions in each electrode system and the two vertical broken lines represent the porous partition (or other device to ensure a conducting path through the cell). The e.m.f. of the cell is represented by the symbol $E$, and the value is given in volts, with a sign (+ or −) preceding it which indicates the polarity of the **righthand electrode** in the cell diagram. In the example above the copper rod is the positive terminal of the cell.

Obviously the cell diagram can be written in the reverse order but it is still the righthand electrode whose polarity is indicated. The Daniell cell can thus be written in the alternative form:

$$\text{Cu(s)} \,|\, \text{Cu}^{2+}\text{(aq)} \,\vdots\, \text{Zn}^{2+}\text{(aq)} \,|\, \text{Zn(s)} \qquad E = -1.1 \text{ V}$$

This is the basic pattern for all cell diagrams. Additional conventions are required for more complicated cells. These will be dealt with as they arise.

BACKGROUND

We are using the convention agreed by the International Union of Pure and Applied Chemistry (IUPAC).

## Contributions made by separate electrode systems to the e.m.f. of a cell

Measurement of the potential of a single electrode system is impossible because two such systems, or **half-cells**, are needed to make a **complete cell** before an e.m.f. can be measured.

We can, however, assess the **relative** contributions of single electrode systems to cell e.m.f.s by choosing one system as a standard against which all other systems are measured. The standard system is then arbitrarily assigned zero potential and the potentials of all other systems referred to this value. **By international agreement the hydrogen electrode is the standard reference electrode**

## A hydrogen electrode

From redox reactions such as

$$Mg(s) + 2H^+(aq) \rightleftharpoons Mg^{2+}(aq) + H_2(g)$$

it is clear that an equilibrium can be set up between hydrogen gas and its ions in solution

$$H_2(g) \rightleftharpoons 2H^+(aq) + 2e^-$$

By an arrangement such as the one shown in figure 17.6 this reaction can be used in a half-cell. This half-cell is called a **hydrogen electrode**. Essentially it consists of a platinum surface which is coated with finely divided platinum (usually called 'platinum black') which dips into a solution of hydrogen ions. A slow stream of pure hydrogen is bubbled over the platinum black surface. The equilibrium

$$H_2(g) \rightleftharpoons 2H^+(aq) + 2e^-$$

is established rather slowly. The platinum black acts as a catalyst in this process and, being porous, it retains a comparatively large quantity of hydrogen. The platinum metal also serves as a convenient route by which electrons can leave or enter the electrode system. **The hydrogen electrode is represented by:**

$$Pt[H_2(g)] \,|\, 2H^+(aq)$$

The potential of the hydrogen electrode under specified conditions, described after the next experiment, is taken as zero. **The electrode potential of any other**

**SAFETY**

Hydrogen is extremely flammable; you should wear eye protection and avoid naked flames.

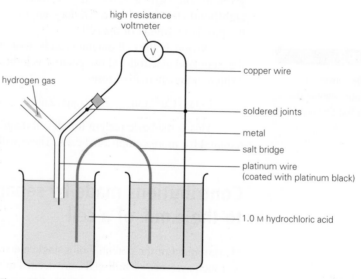

Figure 17.6  **A hydrogen electrode**

metal is taken as the difference in potential between the metal electrode and the standard hydrogen electrode with the hydrogen electrode always on the left:

$$Pt[H_2(g)] \mid 2H^+(aq) \mathbin{\|} M^{z+}(aq) \mid M(s)$$

If the metal electrode is negative with respect to the hydrogen electrode, the standard electrode potential is given a negative sign. If the metal electrode is positive with respect to the hydrogen electrode, the standard electrode potential is given a positive sign.

Some values for **standard** electrode potentials, $E^\ominus$, are given below. The conditions of temperature and concentration under which these are measured are specified after the next experiment.

$$Pt[H_2(g)] \mid 2H^+(aq) \mathbin{\|} Mg^{2+}(aq) \mid Mg(s) \qquad E^\ominus = -2.37\ V$$
$$Pt[H_2(g)] \mid 2H^+(aq) \mathbin{\|} Ag^+(aq) \mid Ag(s) \qquad E^\ominus = +0.80\ V$$

## COMMENT

When you look at table 6.1 in the *Book of data* under the heading Standard Electrode Potentials you will see that the hydrogen electrode is not included on the left,

| | |
|---|---|
| $Pb^{2+}(aq) \mid Pb(s)$ | $-0.13\ V$ |
| $2H^+(aq) \mid [H_2(g)]Pt$ | $0.00\ V$ |
| $Cu^{2+}(aq) \mid Cu(s)$ | $+0.34\ V$ |

but each of these values refers to the e.m.f. of a real cell with a standard hydrogen electrode as the lefthand half.

---

## EXPERIMENT 17.1c

# To measure the e.m.f. of some electrochemical cells

The apparatus for this experiment is shown in figure 17.7.

Several types of cell can be used. The one shown in figure 17.7b uses metal strips as electrodes; they dip into solutions of metal ions contained in 50 or 100 cm³ beakers. Each beaker contains a half-cell and electrical connection between them is made by a strip of filter paper moistened with saturated potassium nitrate solution (the 'salt bridge').

Connections to the metal electrodes are made with crocodile clips.

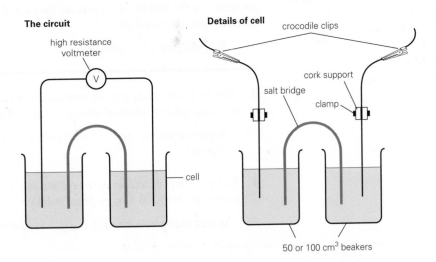

Figure 17.7   The apparatus for Experiment 17.1c

**SAFETY** ⚠

1.0 M copper(II) sulphate is harmful.

## Procedure

**1** Set up the cell

$$Cu(s)\,|\,Cu^{2+}(aq)\,\|\,Zn^{2+}(aq)\,|\,Zn(s) \tag{1}$$

using $1.0\,M\,ZnSO_4(aq)$ and $1.0\,M\,CuSO_4(aq)$ as the electrode liquids.

Clean the metal strips with emery paper before using them. Put a $10\,cm \times 1\,cm$ strip of filter paper in place and then wet it with saturated potassium nitrate solution using a dropping pipette. Connect the cell to the voltmeter and measure the e.m.f.

You should be able to forecast which is the positive pole of this cell, and make the voltmeter connections accordingly.

**2** Repeat the measurements for the following cells, using a fresh salt bridge each time a half-cell is changed:

$$Mg(s)\,|\,Mg^{2+}(aq)\,\|\,Cu^{2+}(aq)\,|\,Cu(s) \tag{2}$$

$$Mg(s)\,|\,Mg^{2+}(aq)\,\|\,Zn^{2+}(aq)\,|\,Zn(s) \tag{3}$$

For the magnesium half-cell use magnesium ribbon.

✎ **In your notes:**

**1** Compare the results of this experiment with the results of the reactivity series reactions in Experiment 17.1a.

Is the system with the greatest tendency to lose electrons and form ions the positive or negative pole of each cell?

**2** Is the e.m.f. for cell (**3**) what you would expect from the values obtained for cells (**1**) and (**2**)?

You could obtain the equivalent of cell (**3**) by connecting cells (**1**) and (**2**) together as follows:

$$Mg(s)\,|\,Mg^{2+}(aq)\,\|\,Cu^{2+}(aq)\,|\,Cu(s) \quad Cu(s)\,|\,Cu^{2+}(aq)\,\|\,Zn^{2+}(aq)\,|\,Zn(s)$$

The two copper half-cells would then cancel each other.

### QUESTION

You should now realise that the e.m.f. of other cells can be deduced from a list of electrode potentials. Use the *Book of data* to work out the value of the e.m.f., and the sign of the righthand electrode, for the cell:

$$Ag(s)\,|\,Ag^+(aq)\,\|\,Cu^{2+}(aq)\,|\,Cu(s)$$

**3** Test the effect of changes in concentration on the e.m.f. of the zinc–copper cell by using a 0.1 M solution instead of one of the 1 M solutions.

✎ **In your notes:** Does the e.m.f. change when the concentration of one half-cell is changed?

**4** Test the effect of temperature on the e.m.f. of the zinc–copper cell by heating a sample of the 0.1 M zinc sulphate solution to boiling before setting up a cell.

✎ **In your notes:** Does the e.m.f. change when the temperature changes?

# Standard electrode potentials

In the last experiment you saw that the value of $E$ for an electrode system varies with the concentration of the solution. You also saw that $E$ varies with the temperature. Thus, standardised conditions of temperature and concentration must be used if electrode potential measurements are to be compared.

**The conditions chosen are:**

- **an ion concentration of one mole per cubic decimetre**
- **a temperature of 298 K (25 °C).**

**The value of an electrode potential relative to the standard hydrogen electrode under these conditions is called the standard electrode potential. Standard electrode potentials are denoted by the symbol $E^{\ominus}$.**
By definition, the standard hydrogen electrode consists of hydrogen gas at one atmosphere pressure bubbling over platinised platinum in a solution of hydrogen ion concentration one mole per cubic decimetre, at 298 K.
A series of $E^{\ominus}$ values is given in the *Book of data* in table 6.1.

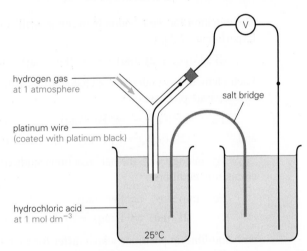

hydrogen gas
at 1 atmosphere

salt bridge

platinum wire
(coated with platinum black)

hydrochloric acid
at 1 mol dm$^{-3}$

25°C

Figure 17.8   **The standard hydrogen electrode with hydrogen gas at 1 atmosphere, hydrochloric acid at 1 mol dm$^{-3}$ and the solutions at 25 °C**

## 17.2   Redox equilibria extended to other systems

So far in this topic you have been mainly concerned with redox systems involving a metal in equilibrium with its ions in solution. Earlier in the course, however, you have encountered redox systems of other kinds. Examples of these are

$$2Br^-(aq) \rightleftharpoons Br_2(aq) + 2e^-$$

and   $MnO_4^-(aq) + 8H^+(aq) + 5e^- \rightleftharpoons Mn^{2+}(aq) + 4H_2O(l)$

in which the half-cells involve non-metal species or ionic species. There are other reactions in which the reacting species are ions only:

$$Fe^{3+}(aq) \rightleftharpoons Fe^{2+}(aq) + e^-$$

You will now see how reactions of this kind can be fitted into the pattern of electrode potentials which we have developed in section 17.1. To begin with you will investigate a reaction in which there is no solid metal involved.

EXPERIMENT 17.2a

# The reaction between iron(III) ions and iodide ions

COMMENT

Check the behaviour of potassium hexacyanoferrate(III) solution with iron(II) by adding some to a solution containing $Fe^{2+}(aq)$ ions.

To about $2\,cm^3$ of a solution 0.1 M with respect to $Fe^{3+}(aq)$ ions, add an equal volume of 0.1 M potassium iodide solution, noting any changes that you see.

Test separate portions of the original solutions and the final mixture with

1 starch solution
2 potassium hexacyanoferrate(III) solution.

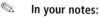 **In your notes:**

On the basis of your observations write an equation for the reaction.

# Interpretation of the reaction between iron(III) ions and iodide ions

The equation for the reaction between iron(III) ions and iodide ions, studied in Experiment 17.2a, is:

$$2Fe^{3+}(aq) + 2I^-(aq) \longrightarrow 2Fe^{2+}(aq) + I_2(aq)$$

Each element has undergone a change of oxidation number, which we can write as two separate processes:

$$Fe^{3+}(aq) + e^- \longrightarrow Fe^{2+}(aq) \qquad \textit{reduction}$$
and $$2I^-(aq) \longrightarrow I_2(aq) + 2e^- \qquad \textit{oxidation}$$

By analogy with the half-reactions studied earlier we might expect two competing equilibria:

$$Fe^{3+}(aq) + e^- \rightleftharpoons Fe^{2+}(aq)$$
$$2I^-(aq) \rightleftharpoons I_2(aq) + 2e^-$$

with equilibrium positions which differ for each reaction.

When the two systems are brought together the tendency for the iodide/iodine system to lose electrons is greater than that of the iron(II)/iron(III) system. Thus the iodide/iodine equilibrium moves to the right and $I_2(aq)$ is produced.

Gain of electrons by the iron(II)/iron(III) equilibrium causes this to move to the right as well and $Fe^{2+}(aq)$ ions are produced. This process will continue until the two systems are in equilibrium with each other.

COMMENT

The equilibrium position for the overall reaction

$$2Fe^{3+}(aq) + 2I^-(aq) \rightleftharpoons 2Fe^{2+}(aq) + I_2(aq)$$

lies well over to the righthand side so that we can say the reaction is almost complete.

$$K_c \doteqdot \frac{[Fe^{2+}(aq)]^2_{eqm}\,[I_2(aq)]_{eqm}}{[Fe^{3+}(aq)]^2_{eqm}\,[I^-(aq)]^2_{eqm}} = 10^5\,dm^3\,mol^{-1}\ \text{at }25\,°C$$

It should be possible to use this reaction in an electrochemical cell. The only problem is how the electrons will leave and enter the electrode systems. The solution is to use inert platinum electrodes.

COMMENT

The oxidation numbers of the species in the half-cells are:

$Fe^{3+}(aq), Fe^{2+}(aq) \mid Pt$
   +3          +2

and   $I_2(aq), 2I^-(aq) \mid Pt$
        0        -1

We need to extend our conventions for writing cell diagrams in order to deal with systems such as these. **The accepted convention is to put the species with the lower oxidation number nearest to the electrode, and separate it from the species with the higher oxidation number by a comma.** The following electrode systems can therefore be set up and their $E$ values determined by using a reference electrode:

$$Fe^{3+}(aq), Fe^{2+}(aq) \mid Pt$$

and $$I_2(aq), 2I^-(aq) \mid Pt$$

## EXPERIMENT 17.2b

## To measure some electrode potentials

You are going to measure the electrode potentials for the $Fe^{3+}(aq)/Fe^{2+}(aq)$ equilibrium and the $2I^-(aq)/I_2(aq)$ equilibrium.

In order to allow the half-cell reactions to proceed in either direction, you must have both the oxidised and reduced forms present in the half-cells. The righthand half-cell must therefore contain a solution in which both $Fe^{3+}(aq)$ ions and $Fe^{2+}(aq)$ ions are present for the first e.m.f. measurement, and $I^-(aq)$ ions and $I_2$ molecules for the second e.m.f. measurement.

The $Cu(s) \mid Cu^{2+}(aq)$ system is used as a reference electrode.

SAFETY !

1.0 M copper(II) sulphate is harmful.

### Procedure

Set up the following cells and measure their e.m.f. The circuit to be used is shown in figure 17.9.

$$Cu(s) \mid Cu^{2+}(aq) \mathbin{\vdots\!\vdots} Fe^{3+}(aq), Fe^{2+}(aq) \mid Pt$$

and $$Cu(s) \mid Cu^{2+}(aq) \mathbin{\vdots\!\vdots} I_2(aq), 2I^-(aq) \mid Pt$$

Keep the same cells for the third measurement.

From the results deduce the e.m.f. of the cell:

$$Pt \mid 2I^-(aq), I_2(aq) \mathbin{\vdots\!\vdots} Fe^{3+}(aq), Fe^{2+}(aq) \mid Pt$$

Check your deduction by measuring the e.m.f. of this cell. A second platinum electrode will be needed for this.

COMMENT

The platinum electrode need not function as a catalyst, so smooth platinum is suitable. Copper can be used as a substitute for platinum.

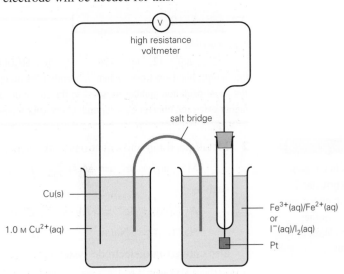

**Figure 17.9** **The cell for Experiment 17.2b**

# Concentration effects on ion/ion systems

From the results of Experiment 17.2b you will have seen that ion/ion systems and non-metal/non-metal ion systems can be used in cell reactions in exactly the same way as metal/metal ion systems.

The equilibrium position is affected by ion concentrations. The greater the relative concentration of $Fe^{3+}(aq)$ ions, the more the equilibrium

$$Fe^{3+}(aq) + e^- \rightleftharpoons Fe^{2+}(aq)$$

moves to the right. This will change the e.m.f. of the cell.

As with metal/metal ion systems, temperature also has an effect on ion/ion equilibria. It is therefore necessary to specify both concentration and temperature conditions for standard electrode potentials involving equilibria between ions. **The conditions chosen are:**

- **equal molar concentrations of the reduced and oxidised forms of ion**
- **a temperature of 298 K (25 °C)**

# Some further notes on standard potentials

You should now be in a position to appreciate all the information given in table 6.1 in the *Book of data*, the table of standard electrode potentials. The following notes may, however, be helpful in using this and other similar tables of $E^\ominus$ values.

1   It sometimes happens that the reduced and oxidised parts of an electrode system contain more than one chemical species (ion or molecule) taking part in the cell reaction. For example, the manganate(VII) ion generally exerts its oxidising power in the presence of hydrogen ions, and water molecules are formed amongst the products of oxidation. These ions and molecules must be included in the oxidised and reduced forms of the equilibrium mixture.

$$MnO_4^-(aq) + 8H^+(aq) + 5e^- \rightleftharpoons Mn^{2+}(aq) + 4H_2O(l)$$

The half-cell diagram for this system is written:

$$[MnO_4^-(aq) + 8H^+(aq)], [Mn^{2+}(aq) + 4H_2O(l)] \,|\, Pt$$

---

## QUESTION

Try converting
$$2IO_3^-(aq) + 12^+(aq) + 10e^- \rightleftharpoons I_2(aq) + 6H_2O(l) \qquad E^\ominus = +1.19\,V$$
into a right-hand electrode system. Remember the accepted practice is to put the species with the lower oxidation number **nearest** to the electrode, and separate it from the species with the higher oxidation number by a comma. Check your answer in the *Book of data*.

---

COMMENT

The square brackets in this and similar diagrams do **not** stand for 'the concentration of' but are used to bracket together the oxidised and reduced forms of the equilibrium mixture.

2   Metal/metal ion half-equations of the general form
$$M^{z+}(aq) + ze^- \rightleftharpoons M(s) \qquad E^\ominus = \pm x\,V$$
such as
$$Al^{3+}(aq) + 3e^- \rightleftharpoons Al(s) \qquad E^\ominus = -1.66\,V$$
$$Na^+(aq) \rightleftharpoons Na(s) \qquad E^\ominus = -2.76\,V$$
also convert into electrode systems:
$$Al^{3+}(aq) \,|\, Al(s)$$
$$Na^+(aq) \,|\, Na(s)$$

STUDY TASK

Try converting the reaction

$$Ag^+(aq) + Fe^{2+}(aq) \rightleftharpoons Ag(s) + Fe^{3+}(aq)$$

into a cell diagram.

## 17.3 The chemists' toolkit: some uses of $E^{\ominus}$ values

You will now look at three important uses of tables of $E^{\ominus}$ values.

### 1 Predicting whether a reaction is likely to take place

$E^{\ominus}$ values in order of **increasing negative values** are also in order of increasing tendency for the electrode system to lose electrons. $E^{\ominus}$ values are listed in the table below from the most negative value to the least negative value (which is the same as the most positive value). Notice that the table is arranged with the highest oxidation number on the left, and the highest positive electrode potential at the bottom.

| Electrode system | $E^{\ominus}$/volts | |
|---|---|---|
| $Mg^{2+}(aq) \mid Mg(s)$ | $-2.37$ | increasing tendency |
| $Zn^{2+}(aq) \mid Zn(s)$ | $-0.76$ | for electrode to |
| $S(s), S^{2-}(aq) \mid Pt$ | $-0.48$ | release electrons |
| $Fe^{2+}(aq) \mid Fe(s)$ | $-0.44$ | |
| $Sn^{2+}(aq) \mid Sn(s)$ | $-0.14$ | |
| $2H^+(aq) \mid [H_2(g)]Pt$ | $0.00$ | |
| $Cu^{2+}(aq) \mid Cu(s)$ | $+0.34$ | |
| $I_2(aq), 2I^-(aq) \mid Pt$ | $+0.54$ | |
| $Fe^{3+}(aq), Fe^{2+}(aq) \mid Pt$ | $+0.77$ | |
| $Br_2(aq), 2Br^-(aq) \mid Pt$ | $+1.09$ | decreasing tendency |
| $Cl_2(aq), 2Cl^-(aq) \mid Pt$ | $+1.36$ | for electrode to |
| $[MnO_4^-(aq) + 8H^+(aq)], [Mn^{2+}(aq) + 4H_2O(l)] \mid Pt$ | $+1.51$ | release electrons |

STUDY TASK

Ox, **Rd** $\mid$ Pt

**Ox,** Rd $\mid$ Pt

Explain what this diagram represents and give an example of your own choice.

As we go down the series, the oxidising power of the oxidised forms in the electrode systems increases and the reducing power of the reduced forms decreases.

This change in oxidising and reducing power can be illustrated by the $Fe^{3+}(aq)$, $Fe^{2+}(aq)$ and $I_2(aq)$, $2I^-(aq)$ reaction studied earlier. Write down the electrode systems with the more negative or less positive value on top:

$$I_2(aq), 2I^-(aq) \mid Pt \qquad E^{\ominus} = +0.54 \text{ V}$$
$$Fe^{3+}(aq), Fe^{2+}(aq) \mid Pt \qquad E^{\ominus} = +0.77 \text{ V}$$

Note that $+0.54$ counts as 'more negative' than $+0.77$.

The iodine system will release electrons to the iron system,

$$2I^-(aq) - 2e^- \longrightarrow I_2(aq)$$

and in the half-cell the reaction will go from right to left:

$$I_2(aq), 2I^-(aq) \,|\, Pt$$
$$\longleftarrow$$

For the iron system the opposite is true:

$$Fe^{3+}(aq) + e^- \longrightarrow Fe^{2+}(aq)$$

and $\quad Fe^{3+}(aq), Fe^{2+}(aq) \,|\, Pt$
$$\longrightarrow$$

**This is the general situation for all reactions of this kind and can be summed up in a simple procedure:**

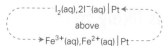

1 **Write down the reaction in the form of two electrode systems in the order in which they occur in the standard electrode potential series, that is from most negative to most positive.**

2 **The reaction will go in an anti-clockwise pattern.**

Another convenient procedure for predicting the direction a reaction will go in is to write the half-equations for the electrodes in the form of figure 17.10. Note that the diagram is constructed with the values on both axes **increasing** in the directions they would be **decreasing in a normal graph**.

The difference in $E^\ominus$ values is no guarantee that the reaction will proceed quickly. **Although we can use $E^\ominus$ values to tell us something about the position of equilibrium for a given change, they can never tell us how long it will take for this equilibrium to be attained.** Another example is the reaction of aluminium with acids: although the $E^\ominus$ value is large this is quite a slow reaction in many cases.

COMMENT

A mnemonic that will help you to remember the anti-clockwise rule is LORA, Left Oxidises Right Above.

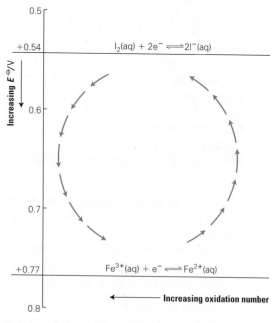

Figure 17.10 **A procedure to predict the direction of a reaction**

We have to experiment to find out the rate of a given reaction and, if it is slow, look for a catalyst if we want to make use of the reaction. A table of $E^{\ominus}$ values enables us to predict whether a search for a catalyst is worth while.

## 2 Calculating the e.m.f. of electrochemical cells

You have already done this in Experiment 17.1c. Now we want to be clear about the general procedure.

$E^{\ominus}$ values in order of increasing negative values are also in order of increasing tendency for the electrode system to lose electrons, as we explained above. Hence when we link two half-cells to form an electrochemical cell, the system which is more negative will become the negative pole and the other system will become the positive pole.

As an example, we will calculate the e.m.f. of the magnesium–lead cell. The cell diagram can be written

$$Mg(s)\,|\,Mg^{2+}(aq)\,\vdots\,Pb^{2+}(aq)\,|\,Pb(s)$$

1 Look up the $E^{\ominus}$ values in the *Book of data* and write them down with the more negative value first.

$$Mg^{2+}(aq)\,|\,Mg(s) \qquad E^{\ominus} = -2.37\ \text{V}$$
$$Pb^{2+}(aq)\,|\,Pb(s) \qquad E^{\ominus} = -0.13\ \text{V}$$

2 The e.m.f. is the difference between the two values.

$$\text{e.m.f.} = 2.24\ \text{V}$$

3 The more negative half-cell will be the negative side of the cell.

$$Mg^{2+}(aq)\,|\,Mg(s)\ \text{will be the negative side of the cell.}$$

Therefore, the lead electrode will be the positive pole and the e.m.f. of the cell as written above will be $+2.24$ V, under standard conditions.

## 3 Writing equations from cell diagrams

It is often useful to be able to deduce the actual reaction that will take place when the compounds used to make a cell are mixed in a test tube. Which of the compounds will be the reactants and which the products?

The general procedure is described below. Let us take as our example the cell illustrated in the margin.

1 Look up, in the *Book of data*, the electrode systems and $E^{\ominus}$ values for the compounds you are studying.

$$Ni^{2+}(aq)\,|\,Ni(s) \qquad E^{\ominus} = -0.25\ \text{V}$$
$$Fe^{3+}(aq),\,Fe^{2+}(aq)\,|\,Pt \qquad E^{\ominus} = +0.77\ \text{V}$$

2 Combine the two electrode systems in a cell diagram so that the $E_{cell}$ has a **positive** sign (positive e.m.f.).

$$Ni(s)\,|\,Ni^{2+}(aq)\,\vdots\,Fe^{3+}(aq),\,Fe^{2+}(aq)\,|\,Pt \qquad E_{cell} = +1.02\ \text{V}$$

3 The reaction that will take place corresponds to the transfer of electrons from left to right in the cell (the anti-clockwise rule) so the reactants are on the **left** in each of the electrode systems. It follows that the products are on the right.

**BACKGROUND**

Non-standard concentrations or temperatures may alter the equilibrium position and lead to a partial reversal of the predicted reaction. When the difference in $E^{\ominus}$ values for the electrodes concerned is greater than about 0.6 V, this is unlikely to happen.

**QUESTION**

Use table 6.1 in the *Book of data* to work out the e.m.f. of a lithium–silver cell.

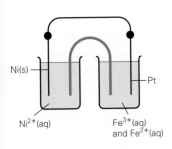

Ni(s)

Pt

Ni²⁺(aq)

Fe³⁺(aq) and Fe²⁺(aq)

Figure 17.11   **Example cell**

So the reactants in our example are $Ni(s)$ and $Fe^{3+}(aq)$; and the products are $Ni^{2+}(aq)$ and $Fe^{2+}(aq)$.

4  To produce a balanced equation, convert the electrode systems into two half-reaction equations, starting with the reactants.

$$Ni(s) \longrightarrow Ni^{2+}(aq) + 2e^-$$

and  $Fe^{3+}(aq) + e^- \longrightarrow Fe^{2+}(aq)$

Then combine the two half-equations into a balanced equation, making sure that the number of electrons released equals the number taken up.

$$Ni(s) + 2Fe^{3+}(aq) \longrightarrow Ni^{2+}(aq) + 2Fe^{2+}(aq)$$

Reactions normally go to completion when $E_{cell}$ is more positive than 0.6 V.

However in some cases it would be more appropriate to use the equilibrium sign $\rightleftharpoons$, as the $E_{cell}$ value tells us that the reaction does not go to completion. This is the case when $E_{cell}$ value is in the range $+0.6$ V to $-0.6$ V.

An example is

$$Pt \,|\, Fe^{2+}(aq), Fe^{3+}(aq) \,\|\, Ag^+(aq) \,|\, Ag(s) \qquad E_{cell} = +0.03 \text{ V}$$

and the appropriate balanced equation is

$$Fe^{2+}(aq) + Ag^+(aq) \rightleftharpoons Fe^{3+}(aq) + Ag(s)$$

If you write an equation for a cell with a large negative $E_{cell}$ value you are writing the equation of a reaction that does not take place.

## 17.4 Entropy changes when metal ions go into solution

COMMENT

Entropy $S$ is related to the number of ways of arranging the particles, and quanta of energy, in a system.

In the last three sections we have looked at redox reactions in cells, particularly cells involving metal/metal ion electrodes. In this section we shall consider changes that take place in these cells, and how they lead to a better understanding of cell reactions.

Consider the reaction:

$$Cu(s) \longrightarrow Cu^{2+}(aq) + 2e^-$$

A simplified picture of just one Cu atom becoming a $Cu^{2+}$ ion and entering pure water is shown in figure 17.12.

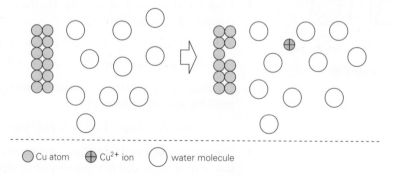

&#9711; Cu atom    &#8853; $Cu^{2+}$ ion    &#9711; water molecule

Figure 17.12  **One copper atom becomes an ion in water**

Which has the greater number of possible arrangements – the Cu atom in the solid lattice, or the $Cu^{2+}$ ion in solution?

There are more ways of arranging the $Cu^{2+}$ ion, since it could go anywhere among the water molecules.

Ions in solution have a lot of freedom to move about, so the number of arrangements, and therefore the entropy, of ionic solutions is high – much higher than for solid lattices. In fact, ions in solution behave in many ways like molecules in gases.

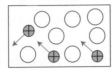
**Ionic solution**
Ions are free to move anywhere among the water molecules

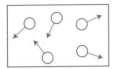
**Gas**
Molecules are free to move anywhere in the container

**Figure 17.13  Ions in solution behave like molecules of gas**

Of course, this is greatly simplified. For one thing it ignores any interactions between the ions and the water molecules, whereas there are in fact strong attractions (see figure 17.14). Nevertheless, it is a useful approximate model to think of ions in solutions, especially dilute ones, as behaving like gases.

With this in mind, it is quite clear that whenever a copper atom turns into a copper ion and goes into solution, there must be an increase in the number of arrangements – an entropy increase.

When a second copper atom becomes an aqueous ion there will be a further entropy increase. But the increase will not be quite as large as last time, because this time there is an ion already present; this slightly reduces the number of arrangements available to the new ion. As more and more ions go into solution, the entropy increases each time – but each time by a little less.

So if you have a metal electrode surrounded by a solution already containing lots of ions – a concentrated solution – metal atoms turning into aqueous ions will give only a fairly small entropy increase. But if the surrounding solution is dilute, the entropy increase will be bigger.

To summarise, there are two things to bear in mind when considering metal/ion reactions:

1  **There is always an entropy increase when metal atoms go into solution as metal ions.**

2  **The more concentrated the solution of ions surrounding the metal, the smaller the entropy increase when new ions go into solution.**

**Figure 17.14  Copper(II) ions in water are $Cu(H_2O)_4^{2+}$ entities**

**COMMENT**

When there are only a few molecules (or quanta) present, adding one more makes a big difference to the entropy. When there are lots of molecules or quanta present, adding one more makes a smaller difference. It is the same with money, for that matter: when you are poor an extra pound makes a bigger difference to you than when you are rich.

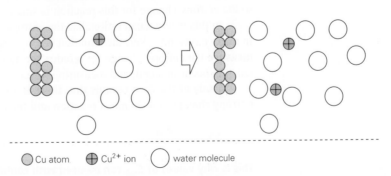

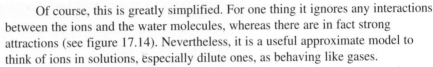
○ Cu atom    ⊕ $Cu^{2+}$ ion    ○ water molecule

**Figure 17.15  What is the entropy change when a second copper atom becomes an aqueous ion?**

# Entropy changes in redox reactions

So far we have looked at the changes that occur when metal atoms turn into ions. This is the kind of change that occurs at a metal electrode in a cell. But to make a cell you need *two* electrodes. What happens when the entropy changes at **both** electrodes are taken into account?

Consider these two simple reactions:

$$2Ag^+(aq) + Cu(s) \longrightarrow 2Ag(s) + Cu^{2+}(aq) \tag{1}$$

$$Cu^{2+}(aq) + Zn(s) \longrightarrow Zn^{2+}(aq) + Cu(s) \tag{2}$$

We can use the *Book of data* to look up the entropy changes needed to calculate the entropy changes in the system for these reactions. At standard conditions:

For reaction (1)   $\Delta S^{\ominus}_{\text{system}} = -193.0 \, \text{J K}^{-1} \, \text{mol}^{-1}$

For reaction (2)   $\Delta S^{\ominus}_{\text{system}} = -20.9 \, \text{J K}^{-1} \, \text{mol}^{-1}$

---

## BACKGROUND

Collecting standard molar entropy data from tables 5.2 and 5.6 in the *Book of data*, with values in $\text{J K}^{-1} \, \text{mol}^{-1}$ at 298 K:

$$2Ag^+(aq) + Cu(s) \longrightarrow 2Ag(s) + Cu^{2+}(aq)$$
$$\phantom{2Ag^+}2(+72.7)\phantom{aq}+33.2\phantom{xxx}2(+42.6)\phantom{x}-99.6$$

so

$$\Delta S^{\ominus}_{\text{system}} = -193.0 \, \text{J K}^{-1} \, \text{mol}^{-1}$$

and

$$Cu^{2+}(aq) + Zn(s) \longrightarrow Zn^{2+}(aq) + Cu(s)$$
$$\phantom{Cu^{2+}}-99.6\phantom{xx}+41.6\phantom{xxxx}-112.1\phantom{xx}+33.2$$

so

$$\Delta S^{\ominus}_{\text{system}} = -20.9 \, \text{J K}^{-1} \, \text{mol}^{-1}$$

---

We can use the ideas already discussed to try to explain these values. In the $Ag^+/Cu$ reaction, the solution gets only one $Cu^{2+}$ ion but loses **two** $Ag^+$ ions. We can be sure that the entropy will **decrease** on this account, because aqueous ions have higher entropy than atoms in a solid.

In the $Cu^{2+}/Zn$ reaction, one ion enters and one leaves. Furthermore, Cu and Zn are very alike as atoms and ions, even down to having similar mass. The entropy of the reactants and the entropy of the products are therefore very similar, so the entropy change for this reaction is small.

In this way we can rationalise the entropy change for some redox reactions. In many cases, however, the situation is too complex. But in any case we can **measure** the entropy change for a redox reaction quite easily, by making the reaction occur in a cell, and measuring its e.m.f.

**Study of the data reveals that there is a relationship between the total entropy change of a chemical reaction and the e.m.f. of the corresponding cell.**

$$\Delta S_{\text{total}} \propto \frac{E_{\text{cell}}}{T}$$

**This is why values of $E_{\text{cell}}$ can be used with confidence to predict whether reactions are likely to take place or not.**

## 17.5  Predicting whether reactions will take place: $\Delta S^{\ominus}_{total}$, $K_c$ and $E_{cell}$

Chemists are often involved in predicting whether a chemical reaction will 'go' of its own accord, and if not, what can be done to make it go. In Topic 13 on entropy we saw that **reactions are always possible if $\Delta S_{total}$ is positive**, taking into account the surroundings as well as the reacting system itself.

But what does it mean to say a reaction 'goes'? If you put zinc into copper sulphate solution, there is certainly a reaction:

$$Zn(s) + Cu^{2+}(aq) \rightleftharpoons Zn^{2+}(aq) + Cu(s)$$

The equilibrium lies well over to the right and the reaction appears to go to completion. This is the Daniell cell reaction, for which $K_c = 1.9 \times 10^{37}$, a large value.

In section 14.4 on equilibria we arrived at the relationship

$$\Delta S_{total} \propto \ln K_c$$

and for the Daniell cell we can work out that $\Delta S_{total}$ is $+707 \, J \, K^{-1} \, mol^{-1}$, a value that confirms that the reaction goes well over to the righthand side of the equilibrium.

A reaction is usually described as 'going to completion' if $K_c = 10^{10}$ or greater. This corresponds to a value of $\Delta S_{total}$ of about $+200 \, J \, K^{-1} \, mol^{-1}$ or a greater positive value. Even with $K_c = 10^{10}$, though, there will always be a very small proportion of reactants left unreacted – the reaction will never go *fully* to completion.

Similarly, if $K_c$ has a value less than $10^{-10}$, the reaction is considered not to go at all, even though there must in fact be a tiny amount of product formed (otherwise $K_c$ would be zero). When $K_c$ is less than $10^{-10}$, $\Delta S_{total}$ will be more negative than $-200 \, J \, K^{-1} \, mol^{-1}$.

A reaction in equilibrium with **equal amounts** of reactants and products and for which $K_c$ has no units but is equal to 1 corresponds to $\Delta S_{total} = 0$.

This topic has now provided us with a third way of predicting whether reactions can 'go': using $E^{\ominus}$ values. In general, if $E^{\ominus}$ for a reaction is positive, the reaction 'goes'. As we stated in the previous section, $E^{\ominus}$ is related directly to $\Delta S_{total}$.

So $E^{\ominus}$ will have a value of about $+0.6 \, V$, or larger, for reactions that go to completion. Use the chemists' toolkit (section 17.3) to deduce the reaction corresponding to the cell diagram for which $E_{cell}$ is positive. All this can be summarised as follows (units not included):

| Reaction 'does not go' | Reactants predominate in an equilibrium | Equal amounts of products and reactants | Products predominate in an equilibrium | Reaction goes to completion |
| --- | --- | --- | --- | --- |
| $K_c < 10^{-10}$ | $K_c \approx 0.01$ | $K_c = 1$ | $K_c \approx 100$ | $K_c > 10^{10}$ |
| $E^{\ominus} < -0.6$ | $E^{\ominus} \approx -0.1$ | $E^{\ominus} = 0$ | $E^{\ominus} \approx +0.1$ | $E^{\ominus} > 0.6$ |
| $\Delta S^{\ominus}_{total} < -200$ | $\Delta S^{\ominus}_{total} \approx -40$ | $\Delta S^{\ominus}_{total} = 0$ | $\Delta S^{\ominus}_{total} \approx +40$ | $\Delta S^{\ominus}_{total} > +200$ |

A final word of warning. Many reactions with high $K_c$ values which should apparently go to completion do not do so at room temperature. This is because the rate of reaction is very slow as a result of a high activation energy barrier.

$E^\ominus$, $\Delta S^\ominus_{total}$ and $K_c$ only tell us whether a reaction is feasible. They tell us nothing about how fast it will go.

The following table shows data for some reactions at 298 K.

| Reaction | $\Delta S^\ominus_{total}$ /J K$^{-1}$ mol$^{-1}$ | $E^\ominus$ /V | $K_c$ |
|---|---|---|---|
| $Cu^{2+}(aq) + Zn(s) \longrightarrow Cu(s) + Zn^{2+}(aq)$ | +707 | +1.10 | $10^{37}$ |
| $Zn(s) + 2H^+(aq) \longrightarrow Zn^{2+}(aq) + H_2(g)$ | +487 | +0.76 | $10^{26}$ |
| $Pb^{2+}(aq) + Zn(s) \longrightarrow Zn^{2+}(aq) + Pb(s)$ | +417 | +0.63 | $10^{21}$ |
| $2Ag^+(aq) + Cu(s) \longrightarrow 2Ag(s) + Cu^{2+}(aq)$ | +298 | +0.46 | $10^{15}$ |
| $Tl(s) + H^+(aq) \longrightarrow Tl^+(aq) + \frac{1}{2}H_2(g)$ | +107 | +0.34 | $10^5$ |

## 17.6 Background reading: cells and batteries

### QUESTIONS

Read the passage below, and answer the questions based on it.

1 Why does the battery industry have to manufacture a wide range of cells?

2 Write an equation for the reaction at the anode in an alkaline manganese cell.

3 Write a conventional cell diagram for a button cell.

4 Which type of button cell has the largest capacity per cm$^3$?

5 Suggest applications where it is important to choose cells with a high energy output per cm$^3$.

6 Suggest applications where it is important to choose cells with a high energy output per kilogram.

7 Does it matter that secondary cells have a lower energy output per kilogram than primary cells?

8 What, in your view, should be the priorities for research and development to improve cells and batteries?

Batteries and cells are available with a bewildering variety of shapes, sizes and names – dry cells, button cells, car batteries, alkaline manganese, mercury, lithium, nickel–cadmium (Ni–Cad). The terms battery and cell are often used interchangeably, although the term **cell** is preferred for a single anode–cathode system and **battery** for a set of anodes and cathodes.

There are two main types of cells. **Primary cells** can be discharged once only and then have to be thrown away. Their active reagents are irreversibly converted to products as electrical current is produced. The other type is **secondary cells**, which can be recharged by supplying a current to the cell in the reverse direction to the discharge current. In this group the chemical reaction can be reversed. Car batteries and Ni–Cad cells are familiar examples.

A battery provides electric power from a chemical reaction; the ones we can buy in shops (which are not rechargeable) are sealed for convenience and safety. These work on the same principles as redox cells such as the Daniell cell, with two electrodes, a salt bridge and an electrolyte.

$$Zn(s) \,|\, Zn^{2+}(aq) \,\|\, Cu^{2+}(aq) \,|\, Cu(s) \qquad E = +1.1 \text{ V}$$

Standard electrode potentials are measured using a voltmeter that takes little or no current from the cell being tested. But a practical battery has to be designed to produce an electric current to light a flashbulb, operate a calculator, a hearing aid, or heart pace-maker. So there are some important differences between laboratory cells for measuring electrode potentials and commercially-produced batteries. In a laboratory cell the electrolyte used in the salt bridge is selected so that it takes no part in the cell reaction. But in a commercial battery the electrolyte may play an important part in the reactions: not only does it connect the negative half-cell to the positive half-cell but it may also be expected to absorb the products of the reaction in such a way that the cell can operate efficiently for most of its life.

Most of the disposable batteries we buy are variants of a type of cell in which the negative electrode is zinc and the positive electrode consists of a mixture which includes the oxidant manganese(IV) oxide. Changing the electrolyte modifies the characteristics of the cell. 'Heavy duty' or long-life batteries contain an electrolyte of zinc chloride while in the 'alkaline manganese' battery the electrolyte is concentrated potassium hydroxide electrolyte.

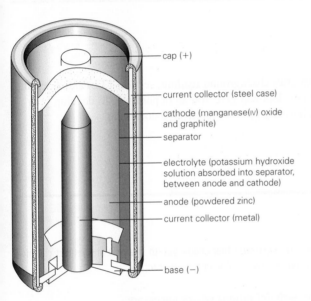

Figure 17.16  **The alkaline manganese cell**

The theoretical voltage available ranges from 1.5 to 1.7 volts depending on the reactions that take place with the electrolyte, for example forming $Zn(OH)_2$ or ZnO. By connecting the cells in series or in parallel, batteries of different capacity and voltage are manufactured, ranging from 1.5 to about 500 volts.

Miniature cells are usually used in applications where a very steady voltage is required for the life of the cell. 'Button cells' are manufactured with a wide variety of redox systems, but the most commonly available are based on zinc–mercury(II) oxide, zinc–silver(I) oxide, lithium–manganese(IV) oxide and lithium–iodine.

The reactions in a typical button cell are

$$Zn(s) + Ag_2O(s) \longrightarrow ZnO(s) + 2Ag(s) \qquad E = +1.60\,V$$

and in a lithium–manganese(IV) oxide cell

$$2Li(s) + 2MnO_2(s) \longrightarrow Li_2O(s) + Mn_2O_3(s) \qquad E = +3.0\,V$$

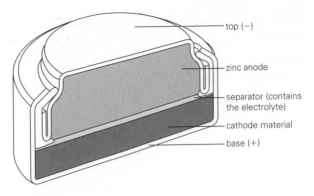

Figure 17.17  **A typical button cell**

Lithium cells use organic solvents because of the reactivity of lithium, and a typical electrolyte is lithium chlorate(VII).

The lithium–iodine cell is a special type because it is a solid-state cell which operates without the need for an electrolyte

$$Li(s) + \tfrac{1}{2}I_2(s) \longrightarrow LiI(s) \qquad E = +2.8\,V$$

The cell does not short-circuit internally because a thin layer of lithium iodide forms during the manufacture of the cell where the two electrodes are in direct contact.

As well as the voltage of the cell, there are other technical features which need to be considered when thinking about batteries. Their **capacity** depends on the amount of reactive chemicals which can be packed into the battery and the number of moles of reaction that will produce a useful flow of electric current; it is measured as **current × time** over the life of the battery. Their **power rating** is the power the battery can deliver in normal working conditions and is measured in watts, **current × voltage**.

For a torch the mass and volume of the batteries we use does not matter too much and in a car there is room for the large and heavy lead–acid battery. But we now use batteries in a wide range of applications with quite different requirements. One way of comparing batteries is the ratio of their energy output to their mass.

|  | Energy output/ watt-hours kg$^{-1}$ |
|---|---|
| *Primary cells* | |
| Zn–MnO$_2$ (alkaline) | 100 |
| Zn–HgO | 100 |
| Li–MnO$_2$ | 260 |
| Li–I$_2$ | 290 |
| *Secondary cells* | |
| Pb–acid | 20 |
| Cd–NiO | 25 |
| Zn–Ag$_2$O | 40 |

| Feature of a button cell | Zn–Ag$_2$O | Li–MnO$_2$ | Zn–HgO |
|---|---|---|---|
| Voltage/V | 1.5 | 3.0 | 1.35 |
| Capacity/mA h | 130 | 70 | 400 |
| Volume/cm$^3$ | 0.56 | 0.49 | 1.2 |
| Mass/g | 1.9 | 1.8 | 4.8 |

For any battery or cell we can work out what is theoretically possible knowing the amounts of reactants in the battery and the standard electrode potential of the cell reaction, but what can actually be achieved depends on a great deal of attention to the way the battery is constructed. Research into the working of the family of zinc–manganese(IV) oxide cells followed by technical development resulted in the capacity being doubled every decade of the last century.

Batteries represent a remarkable technical achievement. Developing a practical battery at a competitive price takes years, and there is always more work being done to improve the design.

# KEY SKILLS

## Communication

Reading about cells and batteries (background reading, section 17.6) and assessing priorities for research and development give you an opportunity to develop your skills of selecting and synthesising information from a document.

# TOPIC REVIEW

This topic is important because it includes ideas that enable you to interpret and predict chemical behaviour, some of which has been observed and learnt in other topics.

1   **List key words or terms with definitions where necessary**

Include in this list any particular relevant words or terms, met previously, with which you still have difficulty. Where appropriate give **equations** or **specific notation**.

- half-cell
- hydrogen electrode
- standard electrode potential
- $E^{\ominus}_{\text{cell}}$

2   **Summarise the key principles as simply as possible**

It is important that by the end of this topic you can confidently **manipulate information** as follows:

- use standard electrode potentials to predict and interpret redox reactions
- combine equations for half-reactions into equations for complete reactions
- convert an equation into a suitable cell diagram
- deduce the e.m.f. of a cell from data
- draw a suitable apparatus for making a cell
- use values of $E^{\ominus}_{\text{cell}}$, $K_c$ and $\Delta S^{\ominus}_{\text{total}}$ to predict whether a reaction is likely to 'go' and how far.

# REVIEW QUESTIONS

✻ Indicates that the *Book of data* is needed.

**17.1**  State which of the reactants is the oxidising agent and which is the reducing agent in each of the following reactions:

a    $Fe(s) + Cu^{2+}(aq) \longrightarrow Fe^{2+}(aq) + Cu(s)$    (1)
b    $Al(s) + 3H^+(aq) \longrightarrow Al^{3+}(aq) + 1\frac{1}{2}H_2(g)$    (1)
c    $Zn(s) + Pb^{2+}(aq) \longrightarrow Zn^{2+}(aq) + Pb(s)$    (1)
d    $2Fe^{3+}(aq) + Sn^{2+}(aq) \longrightarrow 2Fe^{2+}(aq) + Sn^{4+}(aq)$    (1)
**(4 marks)**

**✻17.2**  Calculate the $E^\ominus$ value of each of the following cells. Make sure each value has the correct sign.

a    $Pt[H_2(g)]\,|\,2H^+(aq) \,\vdots\, Fe^{2+}(aq)\,|\,Fe(s)$    (2)
b    $Ni(s)\,|\,Ni^{2+}(aq) \,\vdots\, 2H^+(aq)\,|\,[H_2(g)]Pt$    (2)
c    $Zn(s)\,|\,Zn^{2+}(aq) \,\vdots\, Ni^{2+}(aq)\,|\,Ni(s)$    (2)
d    $Al(s)\,|\,Al^{3+}(aq) \,\vdots\, Cr^{3+}(aq)\,|\,Cr(s)$    (2)
**(8 marks)**

**✻17.3**  $E^\ominus_{cell}$ is $+0.62$ volt for the cell:

$$Co(s)\,|\,Co^{2+}(aq) \,\vdots\, Cu^{2+}(aq)\,|\,Cu(s)$$

Confirm that this value is consistent with the $E^\ominus$ values for the two standard half-cells.

**(2 marks)**

**✻17.4**  $E^\ominus_{cell}$ is $+1.61$ volt for the cell:

$$Zn(s)\,|\,Zn^{2+}(aq) \,\vdots\, Hg^{2+}(aq)\,|\,Hg(l)$$

Calculate the standard electrode potential for:

$$Hg^{2+}(aq)\,|\,Hg(l)$$    **(2 marks)**

**✻17.5**  For each of the following cells, calculate $E^\ominus_{cell}$. Also, construct the two half-reaction equations and the whole equation to represent the changes which take place when the cell terminals are connected by a conductor.

a    $Al(s)\,|\,Al^{3+}(aq) \,\vdots\, Sn^{2+}(aq)\,|\,Sn(s)$    (3)
b    $Ag(s)\,|\,Ag^+(aq) \,\vdots\, Pb^{2+}(aq)\,|\,Pb(s)$    (3)
c    $Pt[H_2(g)]\,|\,2H^+(aq) \,\vdots\, Mg^{2+}(aq)\,|\,Mg(s)$    (3)
**(9 marks)**

**✻17.6**  Arrange the following groups of ions in order of their ability to oxidise. Put the one with the greatest ability to oxidise first (assume that they are all at $1.0\,M$ concentration).

a    $Cu^{2+}(aq),\ Ag^+(aq),\ Pb^{2+}(aq),\ Cr^{3+}(aq)$    (2)
b    $Mg^{2+}(aq),\ Zn^{2+}(aq),\ Fe^{3+}(aq),\ Sn^{2+}(aq)$    (2)
**(4 marks)**

**＊17.7**  The equilibrium constant, measured by an analytical method, for the reaction

$$Ag^+(aq) + Fe^{2+}(aq) \rightleftharpoons Fe^{3+}(aq) + Ag(s)$$

is $3.2 \, dm^3 \, mol^{-1}$ at 25 °C.

**a**  Does this value for $K_c$ suggest that, under standard conditions, the reaction between solutions of silver(I) ions and iron(II) ions is likely to:

 **i**  go to completion

 **ii**  reach an equilibrium at which there are significant quantities of both reactants and products

 **iii**  not go at all?

Justify your answer. (2)

**b**  Does the value of $K_c$ tell you anything about the probable rate of the reaction? (1)

**c**  The reaction could be carried out using a suitable electrochemical cell. Write the cell diagram for this cell. (2)

**d**  Draw a fully labelled diagram of the apparatus and materials you would use to measure the standard e.m.f. of this cell. (3)

**(8 marks)**

**＊17.8**  Use the anti-clockwise rule to predict whether the following reactions are likely to occur under standard conditions. You should draw diagrams similar to figure 17.10 in each case.

**a**  $2Fe^{3+}(aq) + Cu(s) \longrightarrow 2Fe^{2+}(aq) + Cu^{2+}(aq)$ (3)

**b**  $Ni^{2+}(aq) + 2I^-(aq) \longrightarrow Ni(s) + I_2(aq)$ (3)

**c**  $H_2O_2(aq) + Cu^{2+}(aq) \longrightarrow 2H^+(aq) + O_2(g) + Cu(s)$ (3)

**(9 marks)**

**＊17.9**  When an aqueous solution of bromine is added to a solution of potassium iodide, the following reaction takes place:

$$Br_2(aq) + 2I^-(aq) \longrightarrow I_2(aq) + 2Br^-(aq)$$

**a**  Write two half-equations, one for each half-cell reaction. (2)

**b**  Write down a cell diagram for an electrochemical cell in which this reaction could occur. (2)

**c**  Use the values of the appropriate standard electrode potentials given in the *Book of data* to calculate the standard e.m.f. of your cell. (2)

**d**  Is the position of equilibrium in favour of reactants or products? Justify your answer. (2)

**(8 marks)**

**＊17.10**  The reaction

$$Mg(s) + 2H^+(aq) \longrightarrow Mg^{2+}(aq) + H_2(g)$$

takes place spontaneously under standard conditions. It is an exothermic reaction.

**a**  Predict the signs of $\Delta S_{system}$, $\Delta S_{surroundings}$ and $\Delta S_{total}$ for the reaction. Justify your predictions. (6)

**b**  Using data from tables 5.2 and 5.6 in the *Book of data*, calculate values for

 **i**  $\Delta S^{\ominus}_{system}$

 **ii**  $\Delta H^{\ominus}_{reaction}$

iii  $\Delta S^{\ominus}_{\text{surroundings}}$
iv  $\Delta S^{\ominus}_{\text{total}}$
    for the reaction.                                                                    (4)
    Are the values in line with the predictions you made in **a**?                        (1)
  c  Is the numerical value of $K_c$ for the reaction likely to be closest to $10^{20}$,
     $10^2$, $10^{-2}$ or $10^{-20}$? Justify your answer.                                (2)
                                                                                **(13 marks)**

# EXAMINATION QUESTIONS

Questions of the summary and comprehension type are found in the background
reading section (section 17.6).

**17.11**  Some standard electrode potentials for iron and vanadium are:

$$Fe^{2+}(aq)\,|\,Fe(s) \qquad E^{\ominus} = -0.44\,\text{V}$$
$$Fe^{3+}(aq),\, Fe^{2+}(aq)\,|\,Pt \qquad E^{\ominus} = +0.77\,\text{V}$$
$$V^{3+}(aq),\, V^{2+}(aq)\,|\,Pt \qquad E^{\ominus} = -0.26\,\text{V}$$

  a  i  Write out the conventional cell diagram of a cell to be used to measure the
        electrode potential for the $Fe^{3+}(aq)/Fe^{2+}(aq)$ system with a standard
        hydrogen electrode as the reference electrode.                               (2)
    ii  Which would be the positive electrode in your cell?                           (1)
  b  i  In which oxidation state will iron reduce $V^{3+}(aq)$ to $V^{2+}(aq)$?        (1)
    ii  Write an equation for the reaction from **b i**.                              (2)
   iii  What e.m.f. would you expect if the reaction were set up as a cell, using
        standard conditions?                                                         (1)
                                                                                **(7 marks)**

**✱ 17.12**  The diagram shows a calomel electrode, which is often used for measuring
standard electrode potentials in preference to a hydrogen electrode.

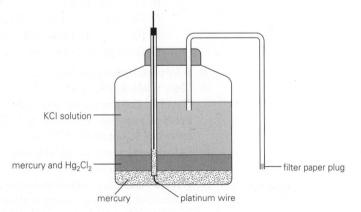

It consists of mercury in contact with a solution of potassium chloride saturated
with $Hg_2Cl_2$. Notice that it contains its own salt bridge in the side tube.

  a  i  What is the oxidation number of mercury in $Hg_2Cl_2$?                        (1)
    ii  What is the purpose of the filter paper plug?                                 (1)
   iii  What do you think are the relative merits of the calomel electrode and the
        hydrogen electrode for measuring standard electrode potentials? State ONE
        advantage and ONE disadvantage for each electrode.                           (2)

**b  i** Draw a diagram to show how you would use a calomel electrode to measure the standard e.m.f. of the cell:

$$Pt \,|\, [2Hg(s) + 2Cl^-(aq)], Hg_2Cl_2(s) \,\|\, Cu^{2+}(aq) \,|\, Cu(s)$$

State the concentration of any solution you would use and the experimental conditions. You need only draw the calomel electrode in outline. (2)

**ii** Predict the e.m.f. of your cell using standard electrode potentials. (2)

**(8 marks)**

**✳ 17.13    a  i** Use the *Book of data* to find the standard electrode potentials for the following half-cells:

$$Fe^{2+}(aq) \,|\, Fe(s)$$
$$Sn^{2+}(aq) \,|\, Sn(s)$$
(2)

**ii** Calculate the standard electrode potential of the following cell. Include a sign and unit in your answer.

$$Sn(s) \,|\, Sn^{2+}(aq) \,\|\, Fe^{2+}(aq) \,|\, Fe(s)$$
(2)

**iii** Which is the better reducing agent, iron or tin? Explain your answer in terms of the way electrons would flow if the cell delivered a current. (2)

**b** Cans which are used to hold acidic fruit juice are often made from iron coated with tin. The tin surface inside the can is often coated with a layer of lacquer. Use standard electrode potential data to explain what would happen if both the tin and the lacquer coating were scratched, exposing the iron. (2)

**(8 marks)**

**✳ 17.14** Rusting is an electrochemical process which involves iron, air and water.

**a  i** Copy the following list of half-cells and add the standard electrode potential for each one.

**A** $Fe(OH)_3(s), [Fe(OH)_2(s) + OH^-(aq)] \,|\, Pt$
**B** $Fe^{2+}(aq) \,|\, Fe(s)$
**C** $Fe(CN)_6^{3-}(aq), Fe(CN)_6^{4-}(aq) \,|\, Pt$
**D** $[O_2(g) + 2H_2O(l)], 4OH^-(aq) \,|\, Pt$
**E** $Fe^{3+}(aq), Fe^{2+}(aq) \,|\, Pt$
(2)

**ii** Why is platinum included in all of the half-cells except for **B**? (1)

**iii** Draw a labelled diagram to show how the cell made up from half-cells **C** and **E** could be set up in the laboratory to measure its e.m.f. Label all materials, apparatus and solutions clearly and state the conditions necessary to obtain the $E^{\ominus}$ value. (4)

**iv** Calculate the e.m.f. of this cell under standard conditions corresponding to the diagram you have drawn in **iii**. Include a sign and units in your answer. (2)

**v** Write a balanced equation including state symbols to show the reaction which results when a current is allowed to flow through the external circuit in this cell, made up from half-cells **C** and **E**. (2)

**b  i** State ONE of the half-cells that would not be involved in the normal rusting process. Justify your choice. (1)

**ii** Rust contains iron in oxidation state +3. Use the $E^{\ominus}$ values of half-cells **A** to **E** to suggest the reactions which take place when Fe(0) is converted into Fe(+3). You are not required to write equations for the reactions you suggest. (3)

**(15 marks)**

# Natural and synthetic polymers

Figure 18.1 **Steel wire of the same mass would be weaker than the filaments of this spider's web, made from a natural protein polymer**

This topic is about some of the very large molecules or 'macromolecules' whose size depends upon the ability of carbon atoms to link together in long chains. Some of these polymers are artificial, such as the plastics. Other polymers have been made by living organisms for millions of years, for example proteins.

**Amino acids** are the building blocks from which proteins are made. They contain the **carboxyl** group, which you studied in Topic 15 and the **amine** group which is introduced here. Many natural products have interesting three-dimensional structures which we will also consider.

In this topic you will:

- investigate the reactions of amines and learn how to interpret them
- consider the shapes of carbon compounds
- investigate the behaviour of amino acids and proteins
- consider the different types of synthetic polymers.

There is more background information than usual in this topic to help you appreciate the importance of these complex substances, but when learning the topic you should concentrate on the reactions involved.

## 18.1  Amines

Amines contain nitrogen. You can think of the amines as derived from ammonia, with one or more of the hydrogen atoms replaced by an alkyl group.

$$CH_3NH_2 \qquad \text{methylamine,} \qquad \text{a primary amine}$$
$$(CH_3)_2NH \qquad \text{dimethylamine,} \quad \text{a secondary amine}$$
$$(CH_3)_3N \qquad \text{trimethylamine,} \quad \text{a tertiary amine}$$

You should note the differences between these structures and the structures of primary, secondary, and tertiary halogenoalkanes and alcohols (see Topics 2 and 10).

Phenyl groups may also replace the hydrogen atoms:

$\langle\!\bigcirc\!\rangle$ — $\overset{\cdot\cdot}{N}H_2$  phenylamine, also known as aniline

Amines, like ammonia, have a **lone pair of electrons** on the nitrogen atom.

A comparison with ammonia suggests that **amines should similarly be basic, be good nucleophiles, and form complex ions with metal cations**. In the next experiment we shall be testing these expectations.

The N—H bond absorbs in the infrared in the region 3500–3300 cm$^{-1}$; the peak is broadened by hydrogen bonding when it occurs (see figure 18.2).

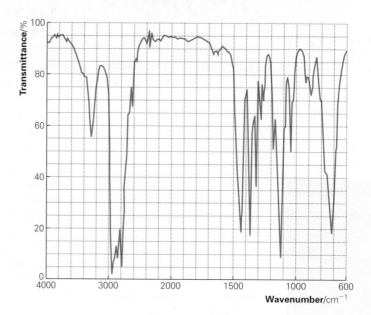

**Figure 18.2 The infrared absorption spectrum of diethylamine**

---

## EXPERIMENT 18.1

# The reactions of amines

In these experiments, you will be looking at the reactions of ammonia, butylamine, and an aryl amine. The simplest aryl amine, phenylamine, is toxic, so we suggest that you use ethyl 4-aminobenzoate, which is the anaesthetic benzocaine.

Before starting the experiments, make sure that you are familiar with the formulae of the three compounds and the shapes of their molecules, if possible by building models.

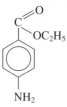

ethyl 4-aminobenzoate

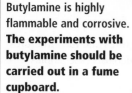

**SAFETY**

**Butylamine is highly flammable and corrosive. The experiments with butylamine should be carried out in a fume cupboard.**
2 M hydrochloric acid is an irritant.
Ethyl 4-aminobenzoate is an anaesthetic.

## Procedure

### 1 Solubility and pH

Prepare or obtain dilute aqueous solutions of the three compounds, warming if necessary. Add drops of Full-range Indicator.

✎ **In your notes:** Are the compounds readily soluble or only sparingly soluble? What type of molecular interaction will be helping them dissolve?

Are the compounds acidic or basic, strong or weak?

### 2 Formation of salts

Add small quantities of the three compounds, warming the aryl amine, to separate portions of 2 M hydrochloric acid.

✎ **In your notes:** Are the amines more soluble in hydrochloric acid than in water? Could they be reacting with the hydrochloric acid? Write down equations representing any reactions which you consider to be taking place. How might you recover the butylamine or

aryl amine from their mixture with 2 M hydrochloric acid?
Test your suggestion experimentally, checking with your teacher first.

### 3 Reaction with transition metal ions

Add small quantities of the three compounds, warming the aryl amine, to separate portions of 0.1 M copper(II) sulphate solution until present in excess.

✎ **In your notes:** Are somewhat similar results obtained with the three compounds? What type of reaction do you think is taking place?

### 4 Nucleophilic reactions of amines with acid derivatives

The reaction with ethanoyl chloride may be demonstrated by your teacher.

Carefully add 0.2 cm³ of ethanoyl chloride (TAKE CARE) to 0.2 cm³ of your amine in separate test tubes, in a fume cupboard. A solid compound should be obtained whose melting point is characteristic of the original amine.

✎ **In your notes:** Write an equation for the reaction. Which electrophilic centre is attacked? Which bond breaks?

**SAFETY** ⚠

Ethanoyl chloride is highly flammable and corrosive; it has a violent reaction with water; **carry out experiments involving this substance in a fume cupboard.**

# Interpretation of the reactions of amines

## 1 Basic properties

The simpler amines such as methylamine are readily soluble in water. Solubility is assisted by hydrogen bonding through a lone pair of electrons on the nitrogen atom:

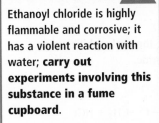

**Amines are quite strong bases,** as can be seen from the $K_a$ values of their conjugate acids.

$$CH_3NH_2(aq) + H_2O(l) \rightleftharpoons CH_3NH_3^+(aq) + OH^-(aq)$$

Phenylamine is an exception; electron pair interaction with $\pi$ bonds in the arene ring of this compound much reduces the acceptance of protons by the $NH_2$ group. Compare this interaction with the interaction that occurs in phenol.

In the presence of strong acids the equilibrium is shifted towards the $RNH_3^+$ ions and the amines form soluble salts:

COMMENT

If an acid is weak, its conjugate base (see section 14.5) is strong.

| Ions of compound | $K_a$ /mol dm⁻³ |
|---|---|
| Phenylammonium | $2.0 \times 10^{-5}$ |
| Ammonium | $5.6 \times 10^{-10}$ |
| Ethane-1,2-diammonium | $1.3 \times 10^{-10}$ |
| Butylammonium | $0.15 \times 10^{-10}$ |

$K_a$ values of the conjugate acids of some amines; they refer to $K_a$ for the equilibrium
$RNH_3^+(aq) \rightleftharpoons H^+(aq) + RNH_2(aq)$.

⬡—NH₂(aq) + H⁺(aq) ⇌ ⬡—NH₃⁺(aq)

phenylamine                              phenylammonium ion

## 2 Complex ions

**The lone pair of electrons on the nitrogen atom of amines allows them to form complex ions with metal cations,** parallel with the deep blue-coloured complex ion formed between ammonia and copper(II) cations

$$4NH_3 + Cu(H_2O)_4^{2+} \rightleftharpoons Cu(NH_3)_4^{2+} + 4H_2O$$

but the stoichiometry of the reaction may be different:

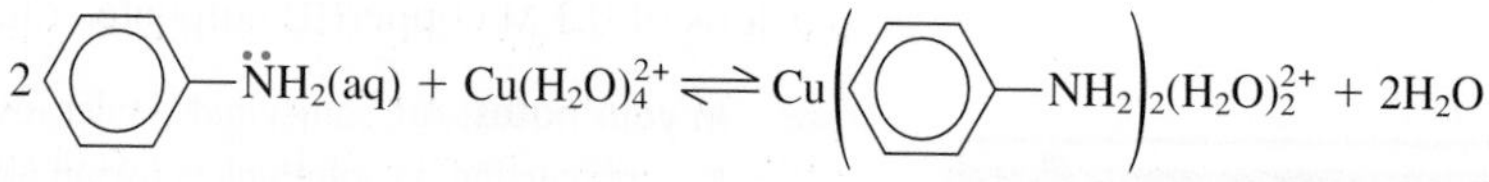

### 3 Nucleophilic reactions

Amides form when amines react with acyl chlorides: **the nucleophilic amine** attacks the electrophilic carbon atom of the acyl chloride.

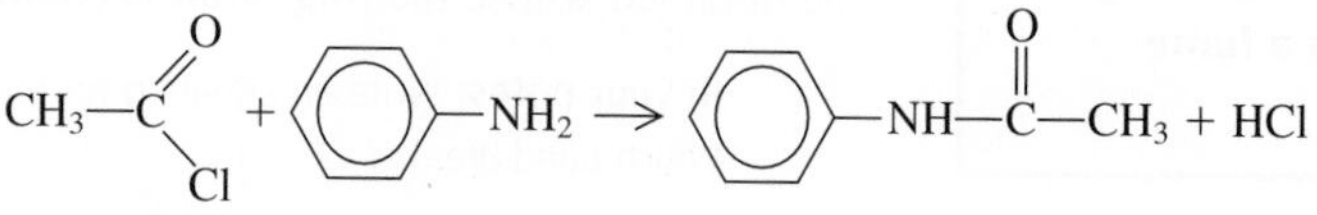

ethanoyl chloride    phenylamine    *N*-phenylethanamide

Amines will also react with the electrophilic carbon atom of halogenoalkanes to give secondary and tertiary amines:

$$CH_3CH_2NH_2 + CH_3CH_2Cl \rightarrow CH_3CH_2{-}NH{-}CH_2CH_3 + HCl$$

diethylamine

and then

$$CH_3CH_2{-}NH{-}CH_2CH_3 + CH_3CH_2Cl \rightarrow CH_3CH_2{-}N(CH_2CH_3){-}CH_2CH_3 + HCl$$

When chloroethane and ammonia react, ethylamine is produced (see Topic 10), but a mixture of products is obtained because the ethylamine will react with more chloroethane, according to the above sequence of reactions.

## 18.2 The shape of carbon compounds

You are going to smell the contents of three tubes labelled **A**, **B** and **C** and try to decide whether all the tubes have the same smell, or whether the tubes differ in smell from each other.

Remove a stopper and smell the tube, breathing in gently. Try to describe the smell to yourself. Replace the stopper.

Repeat the process with a second tube, and then with the third tube. Does one tube have a different smell? Ignore any differences in the strength of smell.

You can smell a tube again to help you decide, but only open one tube at a time. Record the answer you think is correct:

- **A** is different from the other two
- **B** is different from the other two

- **C** is different from the other two
- all the tubes smell the same
- the tubes all have different smells.

Write a short sentence in which you try to describe what you have smelt.

What is odd is that when chemists extract the aroma compounds responsible for the two smells, they seem to find only one compound. Both aroma compounds have the molecular formula $C_{10}H_{14}O$, both have a carbonyl group, both decolorise bromine water because they have double bonds, and they have the same mass spectrum and infrared spectrum.

They have the same structural formula:

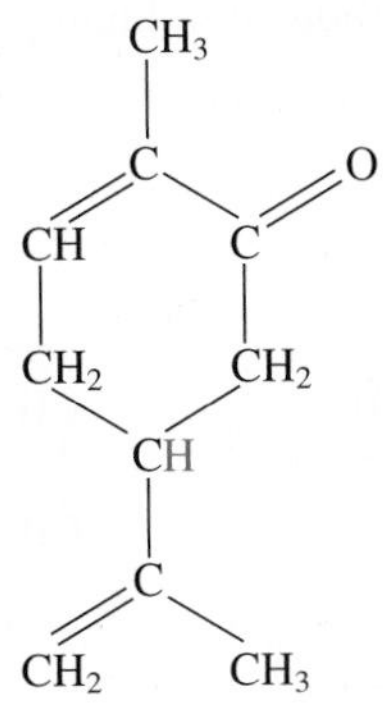

## STUDY TASK

1 Use a ball-and-spoke model kit to build a model of the aroma compound shown above. Collect model atoms representing five carbon atoms that are singly bonded (tetrahedral) and five carbon atoms that are double bonded (trigonal), plus one double bonded oxygen and one hydrogen atom. Using only one hydrogen atom makes the structure easier to understand.

Build a model representing the molecular structure, using the hydrogen atom where it is shown in green in the diagram.

Compare your model with models built by other students. Are they all identical? With the rings more or less flat and the solitary hydrogen sticking up, are the oxygen atoms on the left or right when you look at the models?

2 Build a model of 1-bromo-1-chloroethane, $CH_3$—$CHBrCl$.

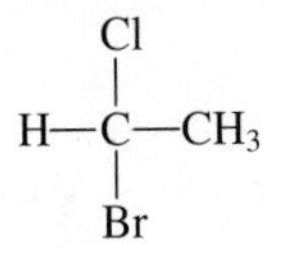

What do you see when you view your model in a mirror?

Compare your model with your neighbour's model. You should find that some models are mirror images of other models. Thus 1-bromo-1-chloroethane can exist as two isomers:

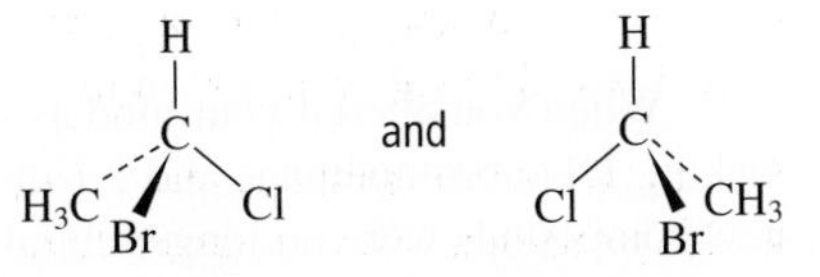

If you exchange halogen atoms between models so that two groups are identical, for example making 1,1-dibromoethane and 1,1-dichloroethane, you will find that the new compounds no longer form mirror-image isomers.

Figure 18.3 **A left hand glove won't fit the right hand**

The clue to the strange behaviour of the aroma molecules is the arrangement of atoms around the carbon atom highlighted in green below. **It has four different groups attached:**

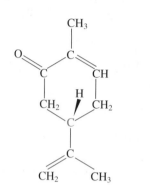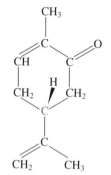

**This results in two molecular shapes which are mirror images of each other and called optical isomers. The carbon atom is called a chiral centre, pronounced** *kiral*.

Our sense of smell works by identifying the exact shape of molecules and therefore responds differently to these two molecules, whereas many chemical tests are 'blind' to this type of molecular difference.

**The most common reason for a carbon compound to be a chiral compound is the presence in the molecule of a carbon atom attached to four *different* atoms or groups of atoms.**

The molecules of 1-bromo-1-chloroethane, $CH_3$—$CHBrCl$ also exist as two isomers which are mirror images. Thus 1-bromo-1-chloroethane is a chiral compound.

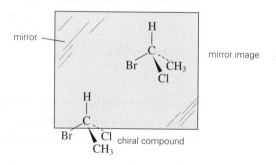

When you altered your models so that two groups were identical, for example making 1,1-dibromoethane and 1,1-dichloroethane, you should have found that the new compounds were no longer chiral (they are **achiral**, as are most compounds).

## BACKGROUND

Chiral is from the ancient Greek for 'hand': a left hand is a mirror image of a right hand. Find a mirror and check this claim.

Many naturally occurring compounds have very complex structures so it is perhaps not surprising that they are often chiral compounds, sometimes with several chiral centres (see figure 18.4). The amino acids, studied in the next section, are usually chiral.

Chiral compounds can be detected by an instrument called a **polarimeter**. Plane-polarised light (as produced when sunlight is reflected) is affected by having its plane of polarisation rotated by chiral compounds and this effect is detected by a polarimeter.

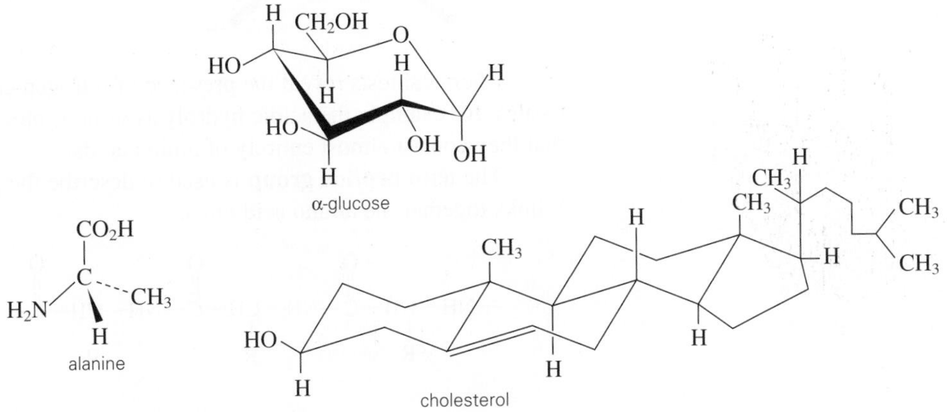

**Figure 18.4**  **Examples of chiral compounds. Alanine is an amino acid with one chiral centre; glucose has four chiral centres and cholesterol eight. Try to identify them**

# 18.3  Amino acids and proteins

Amino acids possess two of the functional groups that you have already studied, namely the amino group, $-NH_2$, and the carboxylic acid group, $-CO_2H$. The simplest amino acid is glycine (aminoethanoic acid):

$$NH_2-CH_2-CO_2H \qquad \text{glycine (gly)}$$

As we shall only be concerned with amino acids that occur naturally, we shall be using the non-systematic names that are favoured by biochemists. These names are often abbreviated to a 3-lettered 'code', which usually consists of the first three letters of the name. **The amino acids that occur naturally are all 2-amino acids with the amino group on the carbon atom adjacent to the acid group**

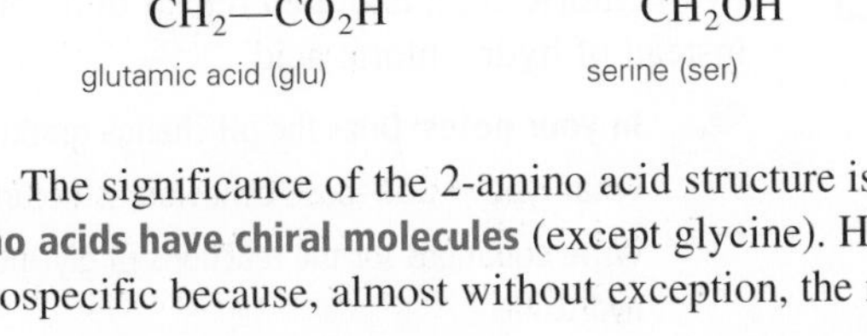

glutamic acid (glu)

serine (ser)

The significance of the 2-amino acid structure is that the **naturally occurring amino acids have chiral molecules** (except glycine). However, nature appears to be stereospecific because, almost without exception, the naturally occurring amino acids in living material have the *same* configuration. After death a slow conversion from one form to the other occurs until eventually an equilibrium mixture results.

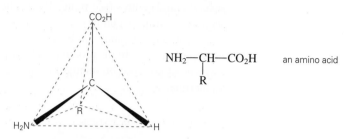

an amino acid

Chemical tests reveal the presence of nitrogen compounds in most animal tissues, for example the acidic hydrolysis of hair, blood, and muscle tissue shows that they consist almost entirely of amino acids.

The term **peptide group** is used to describe the group —CO—NH— when it links together the amino acid units.

$$-NH-CH-\overset{\overset{\displaystyle O}{\|}}{C}-NH-CH-\overset{\overset{\displaystyle O}{\|}}{C}-NH-CH-\overset{\overset{\displaystyle O}{\|}}{C}-$$

part of a protein

R   peptide   R   R
group

When a number of amino acid residues are connected by peptide groups the molecules are known as **polypeptides** or **proteins**. The determination of the amino acid sequence of a protein is considered in the next section.

# Experiments with amino acids and proteins

Glycine and glutamic acid can be used in these experiments as examples of simple amino acids and, as an example of a mixture, casein hydrolysate (containing the free amino acids from the protein milk) might also be used. Fresh milk, egg (white and yolk), or the derived extracts casein and albumin can be tested. Other possibilities are pepsin and trypsin, which are digestive enzymes; or gelatin, from the hydrolysis of the connective tissue of animals.

---

**EXPERIMENT 18.3a**

## Protein materials

### SAFETY ⚠

Ninhydrin is harmful and irritant; wear gloves and avoid inhaling the spray; ninhydrin spray is highly flammable.
Spray in a fume cupboard.

### Procedure

Make solutions in water of your samples of protein materials and amino acids, warming if necessary, and use them for the following tests.

### 1 Acidity and basicity

To 2 $cm^3$ of 0.01 M hydrochloric acid add a few drops of Full-range Indicator and note the effect on the pH of adding 0.01 M sodium hydroxide in 0.5 $cm^3$ portions. Repeat the experiment, using a solution of 0.01 M glycine in place of the hydrochloric acid; and then repeat in reverse, adding 0.01 M sodium hydroxide instead of hydrochloric acid.

 **In your notes:** Does the pH change gradually or sharply?

What type of acid–base behaviour is occurring?

Write equations for the reactions of glycine with hydrochloric acid and with sodium hydroxide.

## 2 Ninhydrin test

On a piece of chromatography paper place small drops of your solution and allow to dry. Spray lightly with 0.02 M ninhydrin solution in propanone (TAKE CARE: **spray in a fume cupboard**) and again allow to dry. Avoid getting the spray on your fingers by wearing gloves. Heat for 10 minutes in an oven at 110 °C. Red to blue coloured spots will develop if proteins or amino acids are present. Make a note of any unexpected coloured areas.

Ninhydrin is a reagent used as a specific colour test for amino acids. You do not need to be concerned with the formula of the compound (which is complicated) nor with the details of the chemical reaction which produces the colours.

## 3 Chirality

You will need a polarimeter for this optional experiment. Figure 18.5 shows how the instrument is constructed.

Use a concentrated solution of sodium glutamate for the experiment.

**Half fill** the specimen tube from the polarimeter. **Without** placing the specimen tube in position, adjust the polarimeter by rotating the centre of the analyser until, on looking through the analyser and polariser, you see that the source of light is extinguished. Note the position of the pointer on the scale.

Put the specimen tube in position and look through the instrument once more. Do you have to alter the setting of the analyser to extinguish the light, and if so, by how much?

Now fill the specimen tube so as to double the length of liquid through which the light passes. Is a further adjustment of the analyser necessary for extinction of the light?

**Compounds which rotate the plane of polarised light are said to be optically active** and this is the standard property by which chiral compounds can be recognised in the laboratory. The two isomers of a chiral compound will produce the same amount of rotation but in opposite directions.

The property can be indicated by adding a prefix to their names: for example, (+) glutamic acid and (−) glutamic acid.

BACKGROUND

Rotation of the plane of polarisation in the clockwise sense, as viewed by an observer looking towards the source of light, is given a (+) sign.

COMMENT

The (+) isomer rotates the plane of polarised light clockwise. The (−) isomer has the opposite effect.

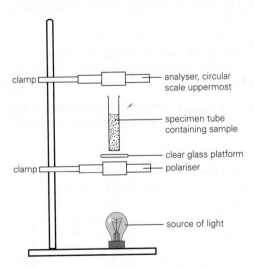

Figure 18.5   **A simple polarimeter**

**EXPERIMENT 18.3b**

# The chromatographic separation of amino acids

The experiment is designed to give you experience and understanding of an important method. To isolate, separate and identify naturally occurring amino acids from a protein by paper chromatography would require an effort spread over about three days, so this brief experiment can only suggest the potential of the method.

To obtain satisfying results you will have to work with care and keep the experimental materials scrupulously clean. Touch the chromatography papers only on their top corners and never lay them down except on a clean sheet of paper.

## Procedure

Put spots of 0.01 M amino acids in aqueous solution 1.5 cm from the bottom edge of the chromatography paper cut to the dimensions shown in figure 18.6. To do this, dip a **clean** capillary tube in the stock solution and apply a **small** drop to the chromatography paper, using a quick delicate touch.

Practise on a piece of ordinary filter paper until you can produce spots not more than 0.5 cm in diameter. Apply spots of individual amino acids and also mixtures, making identification marks in **pencil** at the top of the paper. Allow the spots to dry.

Meanwhile prepare a fresh solvent mixture of butan-1-ol (12 cm³), pure ethanoic acid (3 cm³), and water (6 cm³) in a covered 1 dm³ beaker (TAKE CARE). Cover the beaker to produce a saturated atmosphere.

Now roll the chromatography paper into a cylinder and secure it with a plastic paper clip. Stand the cylinder in the covered solvent beaker and leave it for the solvent to rise to nearly the top of the paper. As 20 minutes are needed to complete the experiment after removing the paper from the beaker, you may not have time to allow the solvent to rise the full distance.

Remove the chromatography paper from the beaker, and mark the solvent level. Dry the paper (without unfastening it), in an oven if possible, but **not** over a Bunsen flame, because the solvent is both pungent and flammable.

Detect the amino acids by spraying the paper sparingly with 0.02 M ninhydrin solution in a fume cupboard (TAKE CARE) and then heating in an oven at 110 °C for 10 minutes. Purple spots should appear at the positions occupied by the amino acids.

Preserve the spots by spraying with a mixture made up of methanol (19 cm³), 1 M aqueous copper(II) nitrate (1 cm³), and 2 M nitric acid (a drop), and then expose **in a fume cupboard** to the fumes from 8 M ammonia (TAKE CARE). Determine the $R_f$ value of the amino acid samples using the expression

$$R_f \text{ value} = \frac{\text{distance moved by amino acid}}{\text{distance moved by solvent}}$$

**SAFETY**

Ninhydrin is harmful and irritant; wear gloves and avoid inhaling the spray. Use a fume cupboard. The ninhydrin and fixing sprays are both highly flammable. Methanol in the fixing spray is toxic and highly flammable.
1 M copper nitrate is harmful.
2 M nitric acid is corrosive.
8 M ammonia is corrosive and pungent.
The chromatography solvent mixture is flammable and harmful, and has an irritant vapour.

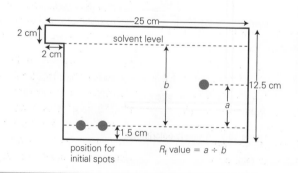

Figure 18.6 Apparatus for simplified chromatography of amino acids

## 18.4 Background reading: the chemical and structural investigation of proteins

### QUESTIONS

Read the passage below in order to answer these questions based on it.

1 Draw a structural formula for the tripeptide gly-val-ser.

2 Show how two tripeptides can be held together by hydrogen bonds.

3 How would Sanger have separated the 17 amino acids in the hydrolysate from insulin?

Proteins have remarkably complex molecules, with molar masses of 1000 or more; but at the same time they illustrate how in nature complex ends are often achieved through the infinitely varied use of simple means. All the different naturally occurring proteins are built, not, as might be expected, from many hundreds of different amino acids, but from only about two dozen. The most important of these, together with their structures, are listed in figure 18.8 (overleaf).

| Protein | Occurrence (examples) | Function | Molar mass | Approximate number of amino acid units |
|---|---|---|---|---|
| Insulin | animal pancreas | governs sugar metabolism | 5700 | 51 |
| Haemoglobin | blood | oxygen carrier | 66 000 | 574 |
| Urease | soya beans | converts urea to ammonia | 480 000 | 4500 |

Since there are many proteins and few amino acids in nature it is apparent that proteins will be characterised by the sequence in which their amino acids are linked:

-gly-val-ser-

or -val-gly-ser-

or -val-ser-gly- etc.

If the correct molecular formula of a substance is to be established it must be available pure, and the necessary experimental techniques must be available. Frederick Sanger, working at Cambridge, was the first chemist to establish the structural formula of a protein. When he started work in 1944, he had to develop new experimental techniques because the problems of protein composition were unsolved at that time, and the only simple protein available pure was insulin. Ten years' work was necessary to establish the correct amino acid sequence for insulin.

Figure 18.7 Frederick Sanger was awarded a Nobel Prize in 1958 for his work on insulin and a second Nobel Prize in 1980 for his work on DNA. You can read more about his work in the Special Study *Biochemistry*

### The amino acid composition of proteins

The molar mass of insulin is about 5700 and its formula is $C_{254}H_{377}N_{65}O_{75}S_6$! As is the case with any protein, the first stage in the investigation of insulin was to discover the nature, and number, of the amino acid units present.

Hydrolysis of a protein by heating in a sealed tube with 6 M hydrochloric acid for 24 hours produces the free amino acids. Quantitative separation of the hydrolysate will determine which amino acids are present and their relative amounts. Sanger, using chromatography, found that the insulin molecule contains 17 different amino acids ranging from six molecules of cysteine and leucine to one molecule of lysine, the molecular formula being

| Formula | Name | Abbreviation | Nature of side chain | $R_f$ value in butan-1-ol/ ethanoic acid/ water |
|---|---|---|---|---|
| $H_2NCHCO_2H$<br>$\vert$<br>H | glycine | gly | non-polar | 0.26 |
| $H_2NCHCO_2H$<br>$\vert$<br>$CH_3$ | alanine | ala | non-polar | 0.38 |
| $H_2NCHCO_2H$<br>$\vert$<br>$CH_2$<br>$\vert$<br>$CH(CH_3)_2$ | leucine | leu | non-polar | 0.73 |
| $H_2NCHCO_2H$<br>$\vert$<br>$CHC_2H_5$<br>$\vert$<br>$CH_3$ | isoleucine | ile | non-polar | 0.72 |
| 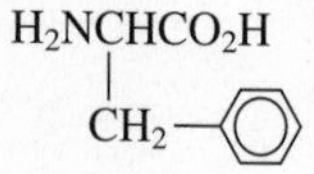 $H_2NCHCO_2H$<br>$\vert$<br>$CH_2$—◯ | phenylalanine | phe | non-polar | 0.68 |
| $H_2NCHCO_2H$<br>$\vert$<br>$CH_2OH$ | serine | ser | polar | 0.27 |
| $H_2NCHCO_2H$<br>$\vert$<br>$CHOH$<br>$\vert$<br>$CH_3$ | threonine | thr | polar | 0.35 |
| $H_2NCHCO_2H$<br>$\vert$<br>$CH_2SH$ | cysteine | cys | polar | 0.08 |
| $H_2NCHCO_2H$<br>$\vert$<br>$CH_2$<br>$\vert$<br>$CH_2CONH_2$ | glutamine | gln | polar | — |
| 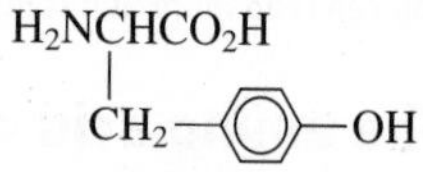 $H_2NCHCO_2H$<br>$\vert$<br>$CH_2$—◯—OH | tyrosine | tyr | polar | 0.50 |
| $H_2NCHCO_2H$<br>$\vert$<br>$(CH_2)_3$<br>$\vert$<br>$CH_2NH_2$ | lysine | lys | basic | 0.14 |
| $H_2NCHCO_2H$<br>$\vert$<br>$CH_2CO_2H$ | aspartic acid | asp | acidic | 0.24 |
| $H_2NCHCO_2H$<br>$\vert$<br>$CH_2$<br>$\vert$<br>$CH_2CO_2H$ | glutamic acid | glu | acidic | 0.30 |

**Figure 18.8** Some examples of naturally occurring amino acids

accounted for by a total of 51 amino acid units. Using other techniques Sanger was able to establish the amino acid sequence in insulin (see figure 18.9).

```
phe            gly
 |              |
val            ile
 |              |
asp            val
 |              |
gln            glu
 |              |
his            gln
 |              |
leu            cys
 |              |
cys—S—S—cys
 |              |
gly            thr
 |              |
ser            ser
 |              |
his            val
 |              |
leu            cys
 |              |
val            ser
 |              |
glu            leu
 |              |
ala            tyr
 |              |
leu            gln
 |              |
tyr            leu
 |              |
leu            glu
 |              |
val            asp
 |              |
cys—S          tyr
 |               \
gly              S—cys
 |              |
gly            asp
 |
arg
 |
gly
 |
phe
 |
phe
 |
tyr
 |
thr
 |
pro
 |
lys
 |
thr
```

**Figure 18.9   The amino acid sequence of insulin from a sheep**

Mass spectrometry is becoming increasingly important in the determination of the amino acid sequence of proteins. The advantages of the mass spectrometer are speed, the small amount of sample needed (only $5–30 \times 10^{-9}$ mol are required) and the fact that the polypeptides produced by partial hydrolysis need not be completely separated from each other, because analysis is possible on a mixture of two to five peptides.

## The shapes of protein molecules

There are countless possibilities for the shape of a large molecule of a protein such as insulin. These possibilities arise because of the rotation that can take place at the single bonds in the polypeptide chain. A given protein molecule may actually adopt several of these possible shapes, or **conformations**, as they are called. The three-dimensional shape of insulin as determined by X-ray diffraction techniques is shown in figure 18.10.

Hydrogen bonds between the peptide groups play a major role in maintaining the conformation usually adopted by the insulin molecule.

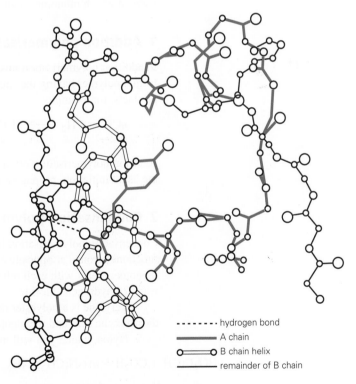

- - - - - - - hydrogen bond
━━━━ A chain
o━━━o B chain helix
──── remainder of B chain

**Figure 18.10   The shape of the insulin molecule**

## 18.5    Synthetic polymers

Most technological innovations have been inspired or made possible by the emergence of a new material. Although we tend to take our materials for granted, terms like Stone Age, Bronze Age and Iron Age suggest how significant they have been in our history.

Nowadays synthetic polymers play such an important part in our lives that we could be said to be living in the 'Polymer Age'. It is these materials and their astonishing variety of properties and uses which we shall study in this section.

## The formation of polymers

When Hermann Staudinger, the pioneer of polymer chemistry in the 1920s, first suggested that rubber was a giant molecule with a molar mass of about 100 000, his ideas were ridiculed. He was advised to purify his products properly and obtain an acceptable value. He persisted with his researches however, and established that **polymers are very long chain molecules formed by combining a large number of small units or 'monomers'.** His views are now accepted and in 1953 he was awarded the Nobel Prize for chemistry.

Wallace Carothers, who discovered nylon in 1935, showed that there are two ways in which monomers can be combined.

### 1 Addition polymerisation

In addition polymerisation unsaturated monomer molecules add to each other to form a polymer having the same empirical formula as the monomer with no other products, for example:

$$n\text{CH}_2{=}\text{CH}_2 \longrightarrow {+}\text{CH}_2{-}\text{CH}_2{+}_n$$

ethene                 poly(ethene)

Addition polymerisation often follows a free radical chain mechanism involving the usual initiation, propagation and termination stages (see Topic 8).

### 2 Condensation polymerisation

Condensation polymerisation involves two different monomers each having two functional groups at opposite ends of their molecules. Molecules of the two monomers react with each other with the elimination of a small molecule such as water or hydrogen chloride.

Terylene is a polyester made by the polymerisation of the acid benzene-1,4-dicarboxylic acid and the alcohol ethane-1,2-diol.

Nylon, which you will make in the next experiment, is another example.

$$n\text{HO}_2\text{C(CH}_2)_4\text{CO}_2\text{H} + n\text{H}_2\text{N(CH}_2)_6\text{NH}_2 \longrightarrow {+}\text{OC(CH}_2)_4\text{CONH(CH}_2)_6\text{NH}{+}_n + (2n-1)\text{H}_2\text{O}$$

## Classification of polymers

Synthetic polymers can be hard, rigid glasses or soft rubbery solids; they can be made into strong, resilient fibres or tough flexible films. It is not surprising that they have come to be recognised as some of the most useful materials known. You are probably wearing or using something made from a synthetic polymer at this very moment; and if you have recently been to a supermarket, played almost any kind of sport, listened to a tape or CD or watched a video, or travelled by bicycle or car you have been using polymers.

Perhaps more important than any one property is the *versatility* of polymers. The same polymer, PVC, is used to make rigid window frames, credit cards and cling film.

**The properties of all materials depend on their structure and on the bonding which holds that structure together.** It may help to appreciate the distinctive properties of polymers if we fit them into the spectrum:

methane – poly(ethene) – diamond

Methane consists of small separate molecules able to move with complete freedom because only weak, non-directional van der Waals forces act between them.

At the other extreme there is no independent movement at all in diamond, because all the atoms are held in one giant structure by strong covalent bonds.

In poly(ethene) the atoms are covalently bonded into long molecular chains. They, therefore, have less freedom than methane molecules but much greater freedom than the atoms in diamond, since only van der Waals forces act between the chains. Furthermore, although the covalent bonds in the linear chains of poly(ethene) are directional, rotation about a bond is still possible. The chains are thus flexible and can slither about in tangled coils like freshly cooked spaghetti. This tangling reduces the freedom of the chains, since any large-scale movement of one chain affects others. Breaking a piece of poly(ethene) therefore involves pulling chains from an entangled mass, which gives the polymer greater strength than it would have simply from van der Waals forces between short sections of neighbouring chains.

Two different forms of poly(ethene) are available depending upon the method of manufacture. The two forms have different properties since the chains have different degrees of alignment. Areas of regular alignment lead to **crystalline** packing and irregular areas are known as **amorphous**. Low density poly(ethene) has numerous short side chains branching off from the main chain; these obstruct the alignment of the chains, and the material is only about 75% crystalline. The catalytic process used to make high density poly(ethene), however, produces a regular chain with no branching which can give almost 100% crystallinity. High density poly(ethene) is therefore harder, stronger and less flexible than low density poly(ethene).

The wide field of polymeric materials can be divided into three broad categories on the basis of their response to heating and to an applied force.

1   Some polymers soften on heating; they can then be shaped and the new shape is retained on cooling. **These are thermoplastic polymers.**

2   Some polymers that soften on heating show rubber-like elasticity rather than plastic behaviour; **these are elastomers.**

3   At the other extreme come **the thermosetting polymers** (or resins), which are hardened by heating into a brittle mass. Subsequent heating does not soften them so they can only be shaped by moulding before the heat treatment (or 'curing').

Figure 18.11 **Rock climbing with a polymer rope**

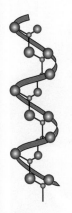

Figure 18.12 **The regular structure of poly(propene); the chain makes one complete turn every three monomer units**

# Polymerisation reactions

You should be able to carry out at least one of the reactions described, but look at them all to identify the common features. Wear gloves to do these experiments and do the work in a fume cupboard if possible.

## Procedure

### 1 Preparation of poly(phenylethene)

Mix thoroughly 5 cm³ of phenylethene and 0.2 g of di(dodecanoyl) peroxide in a test tube. Plug the test tube with some cottonwool and place in a beaker of boiling water in a fume cupboard for about 30 minutes.

phenylethene

Test the viscosity of the mixture by stirring with a wooden splint from time to time. Allow to cool in the water bath when the polymerisation nears completion.

✎ **In your notes:** What type of polymerisation was involved here?
Write an equation for the polymerisation reaction using structural formulae.

**SAFETY** ⚠

Phenylethene (styrene) gives off harmful and irritant fumes and is flammable. Di(dodecanoyl) peroxide (lauroyl peroxide) is an oxidant.

This experiment should be carried out in a well-ventilated laboratory, or preferably in a fume cupboard.

Figure 18.13   Polystyrene foam blocks being used in Norway as the foundation of a road. Normal road foundations would freeze in the winter, making the road surface likely to break up

### 2 The 'nylon rope trick'

Prepare a solution of 0.5 cm³ of decanedioyl dichloride (TAKE CARE) in 15 cm³ of hydrocarbon solvent and, separately, a solution of 0.7 g of hexane-1,6-diamine (TAKE CARE) and 2 g of sodium carbonate in 15 cm³ of water in a 100 cm³ beaker.

Clamp the beaker, and alongside it clamp a pair of glass rods as shown in figure 18.16. If possible allow a drop of about 1 metre from the rod to the receiver.

**SAFETY** ⚠

Decanedioyl dichloride (sebacoyl dichloride) is corrosive and irritating to the respiratory system. Hexane-1,6-diamine is corrosive.

You must wear gloves when handling these chemicals and when carrying out the entire 'nylon rope trick'.

Figure 18.14   The 'nylon rope trick'

Now pour the hydrocarbon solution carefully onto the aqueous solution and, using crucible tongs, pull the interfacial film out, over the rods, and down towards the receiver. When a long enough rope has formed, the process should go on of its own accord until the reagents are used up, but the rope may need to be pulled out gently, using the tongs. Take care not to get either solvent or reagent on your fingers.

To obtain a dry specimen of nylon polymer, wash it thoroughly in 50% aqueous ethanol and then in water until litmus is not turned blue by the washings. Note that, because of the way in which it is formed, the nylon 'rope' is likely to be a hollow tube, containing solvent and possibly reagent. You should therefore take care when handling it, even after washing in this way.

✎   **In your notes:** Was the reaction an addition or a condensation polymerisation? Write an equation for this polymerisation reaction.

### 3 The preparation of a polyester resin

Wearing protective gloves, mix 3 g of benzene-1,2-dicarboxylic anhydride with 2 cm³ of propane-1,2,3-triol in a test tube. Measure out the propane-1,2,3-triol with a dropping pipette and allow the pipette plenty of time to drain.

Heat to 160 °C and then more slowly to 250 °C in a fume cupboard. When the mixture ceases to bubble allow it to cool. Test the viscosity of your product.

benzene-1,2-dicarboxylic
anhydride

> **SAFETY** ⚠
>
> **Benzene-1,2-dicarboxylic anhydride (phthalic anhydride) is an irritant towards the skin, eyes and respiratory system.**

✎   **In your notes:** Was the reaction an addition or a condensation polymerisation? Write an equation for a possible polymerisation reaction.

### 4 The preparation of a cross-linked polymer

Measure about 25 cm³ of a 4% aqueous solution of poly(ethenol) into a disposable container. Rinse out your measuring cylinder thoroughly. Add about 5 cm³ of 4% sodium borate solution and immediately stir well. Continue stirring as the mixture thickens. Put on disposable gloves and examine the properties of the 'slime' you have produced. Take care as 'slime' sticks to clothing and removes paint.

**In your notes:** What monomer is needed to make poly(ethenol)? The molar mass of the poly(ethenol) used in this experiment is about $10^5$ g mol$^{-1}$. How many monomer units does this involve?

In 'slime' the poly(ethenol) chains have been cross-linked by hydrogen bonds to borate ions, so the links are not permanent.

hydrogen bonding

## STUDY TASK

1   Why are nylons known as polyamides?

2   Try to write an equation for the formation of the polyester formed from ethane-1,2-diol and benzene-1,4-dicarboxylic acid,

$$HO-CH_2-CH_2-OH \quad \text{and} \quad HO_2C-\langle\bigcirc\rangle-CO_2H$$

3   The condensation reaction of phenol with methanal forms a linear polymer at first. These polymers then react with more methanal to form a highly cross-linked product called Bakelite:

What feature of the methanal molecule enables it to react with the benzene ring?

**Soluble laundry bags**

# SOLUBLE
# LAUNDRY BAG

FOR THE SAFE ISOLATION, TRANSPORTATION, DISINFECTION & CLEANING OF FOUL/INFECTED OR CONTAMINATED LINEN

These Hot Water Soluble Laundry Bags have been developed and improved using the experience of the last 15 years, to produce the ultimate in efficient and practical laundry bags.

Only this amount of field testing can produce a consistent quality of material that is free from the problems of blocking and gelling and produces utterly reliable operating parameters, freeing the user from continuous monitoring of performance to ensure trouble free operation.

Manufactured from high grade Polyvinyl Alcohol to exacting standards, the bag has a deep embossed finish to ensure the bag does not cling and complicate filling. The attached cold water soluble Tie Tape offers convenient closure of the bag and allows rapid opening during the initial sluice, essential to prevent the setting of stains by unremoved body waste, blood* etc., that could occur during the following wash cycles.

Bacteriological Tests confirm that the bag material is impermeable to bacteria and thus provides an effective barrier to isolate Foul/Infected linen.

★ Hazard warnings can be printed on the bag to customer specifications.

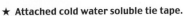

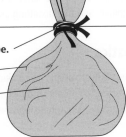

★ **Attached cold water soluble tie tape.**

★ **Embossed for easy handling.**

★ **PROVEN impermeable to bacteria.**

Hospital laundry is often collected in bags which are designed to dissolve in hot water and there are a number of possible variables which can affect the rate and ease of solution.

A suitable investigation could attempt to answer questions such as:

- What effect does the temperature have on rate of solution?
- What effect does the pH of the solution have on the rate of solution?
- What effect does variable agitation have?
- What is the effect of the presence in the solution of other ions/detergent?

This is not intended to be a complete list; there are other areas which could yield appropriate investigations.

You will need to use small pieces of the polymer from which the bags are made and devise a reliable method for measuring the rate at which they dissolve. The investigation should be as quantitative as possible, with particular emphasis

**SAFETY** ⚠

You must carry out a Risk Assessment before starting any experimental work and this must be checked, amended if necessary, approved and signed by your teacher.

being placed on the reproducibility of the results. You may also need to use the information in this book and from any other sources in order to try to explain the results you obtain.

## 18.6 Background reading: the structure and properties of synthetic polymers

### QUESTIONS

Read the following passage, then answer the questions based on it.

1   What are the structural differences between the three main types of thermoplastics?

2   State TWO structural factors which increase the likelihood of crystallinity in a polymer.

3   Explain why it is relatively easy to stretch an elastomer.

4   What is the main structural feature of a thermosetting plastic?

All polymers have long chains but their huge variety of behaviour depends upon their structure and how their chains are aligned with each other. This passage describes the differences between thermoplastics, elastomers and thermosetting polymers.

## 1 Thermoplastics

This group shows the greatest variety, and includes the familiar commercial plastics such as polythene and nylon. We can divide them into three main groups: amorphous polymers, crystalline polymers and fibres.

## Amorphous polymers

These materials are made of linear chains: when molten they are loosely arranged and can move, although their spaghetti-like entanglements make the liquid viscous. When this writhing mass is cooled the disordered arrangement is frozen in to give an amorphous solid. Unlike normal solids, however, some limited movement persists: the chains may be able to twist or even slide past each other segment by segment, like a snake. Consequently, the solid can be bent or stretched: it is rubbery.

On further cooling even this limited movement is lost, and the rubber changes into a rigid, brittle glass-like solid. The glass state differs from the rubber state not in structure but in the freedom of movement of the chains. The temperature at which this change occurs is called the **glass temperature**, $t_g$, and a designer needs

to know when this marked change in behaviour will occur (see the table below).

| Polymer | Repeat unit | Glass temperature, $t_g$/°C |
|---|---|---|
| poly(propene) | $-CH_2-CH-$ $\quad\quad\quad CH_3$ | $-10$ |
| poly(chloroethene) rigid flexible | $-CH_2-CH-$ $\quad\quad\quad Cl$ | 85 $-20$ to $-30$ |
| poly(phenylethene) | $-CH_2-CH-$ ⬡ | 100 |

Data on the physical properties of polymers are listed in table 7.7 in the *Book of data*.

## Crystalline polymers

When some polymers are cooled the jumbled arrangement of the liquid is not retained and the molecular chains become aligned in rows: the polymer has become crystalline. However, the chains are too long and flexible to form the regular crystals found in ionic compounds so the crystalline regions are still surrounded by amorphous regions as shown in figure 18.15.

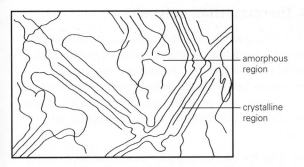

**Figure 18.15   Amorphous and crystalline regions in a crystalline polymer**

In the crystalline regions, sections of the chains are packed in closer 'contact' so there will be greater intermolecular forces. The crystalline regions will, therefore, make the polymers harder than rubbers, but in the amorphous regions the chains can still move relatively easily (above $t_g$) so the polymer will be less brittle (tougher) than glass-like polymers. Toughness is a very desirable property and some of the most useful polymers are partially crystalline.

| | Estimated maximum crystallinity/% |
|---|---|
| Natural rubber | 30 |
| Poly(propene) fibre | 60 |
| Nylon fibre | 60 |
| Polyester fibre | 60 |
| Poly(ethene) – low density | 75 |
| – high density | 95 |

The flexibility of the chains is a second factor which affects the ease with which they can be organised into a regular arrangement in the solid.

In polyester, the chain is regular and not branched, and the polar C=O groups in the ester linkages increase intermolecular forces, encouraging crystallinity. However the planar benzene rings in the chain produce a larger, less flexible repeating unit and, as a result, polyester crystallises rather slowly. It can be cooled below its $t_g$ without crystallising to form the transparent material familiar as large fizzy drinks bottles. But if the polymer is held at a temperature above $t_g$ the molecules have time to wriggle into the crystalline arrangement which is more suitable for a fibre. By contrast, poly(ethene) with its flexible chain crystallises so readily that even very rapid cooling fails to form an amorphous material.

A third way of encouraging crystallisation is by stretching (drawing) the polymer; this both increases the crystallinity in amorphous regions, and also orientates any existing crystalline regions along the direction of draw (see figure 18.16). This in turn increases the strength in that direction but usually at the expense

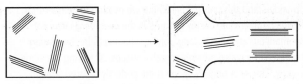

**Figure 18.16   Aligning crystalline regions by 'drawing'**

of strength in other directions. Poly(ethene) bags or tubes made by extrusion show this directional strength.

Drawing the polymer film during manufacture can be used to adjust the properties of the polymer; a large amount of draw produces a high strength nylon ideal for tyre cord, while less draw leads to a softer, more elastic fibre which is more suitable for making clothes.

## Fibres

Fibres are a special case of crystallinity in which the chains are aligned along the fibre axis. This gives the high strength needed for a successful fibre. A good fibre-forming polymer usually possesses some or all of the following features:

- regular linear chains favouring high crystallinity
- strong intermolecular forces, but no actual cross-linking
- some, but not too much, chain flexibility.

Thus poly(propene) forms excellent fibres. 'Acrylic' fibres are based on poly(propenenitrile), which is less regular than poly(propene) but the polar —CN groups compensate for this.

The classic fibre-forming polymers are the polyamides (nylon) and polyesters (Terylene) both of which have regular, linear chains. In nylon crystallinity is further encouraged by hydrogen bonding between adjacent chains.

$$
\begin{array}{c}
\overset{O}{\overset{\|}{-C}}-(CH_2)_4-\overset{H}{\overset{|}{C}}-\overset{}{N}-(CH_2)_6-\overset{}{N}-\overset{O}{\overset{\|}{C}}-(CH_2)_4-\overset{H}{\overset{|}{C}}-\overset{}{N}- \\
\end{array}
$$

For clothing in general, a fibre with reasonable moisture retention is more comfortable and attracts less dirt because it is less prone to static. Nylon has poor moisture retention, but this is improved by grafting on poly(epoxyethene): the chemist tailors the polymer before the tailor cuts the cloth.

## 2 Elastomers

Some rubbery polymers show a quite exceptional elastic behaviour. Natural rubber, for example, can be stretched by 600% and still snap back to its original length when the force is removed. Such a material is an **elastomer**.

To understand this unusual behaviour we need to remember that entropy, rather than energy or force, is the overriding factor for spontaneous changes. A long polymer chain with freely rotating bonds can be coiled into innumerable shapes, all having the same energy. The most unlikely shape is the perfectly ordered straight chain, just as it is most unlikely that a drunken reveller, whose every step is in a randomly chosen direction, will walk straight home.

The natural shape of a chain is that which has the highest entropy: a highly crumpled random tangle in which the two ends may be quite close together. The chain may be readily straightened out by applying a force: and since this involves only bond rotation rather than bond stretching, a relatively small force is needed.

This is why it is easier to stretch a rubber band than a steel wire or a carbon fibre. For this uncoiling to take place, of course, the molecules must have some freedom to move: the polymer must be above its glass temperature. A useful elastomer must, therefore, have a glass temperature well below room temperature, which implies that the interchain forces must be weak.

These factors do not account fully for the essential feature of 'rubberiness'. Such loosely held molecules should slide past each other, untangling as well as uncoiling: but elastomers seem to have a molecular 'memory' which enables them to return to their original arrangement. The reason for this elastic recovery is that the coiled chains in unstretched rubber are actually looped around each other so that they are virtually knotted together. This effect can be greatly enhanced by replacing these knots with cross-links in the form of covalent bonds which permanently anchor the chains at various points.

The key feature of elastomers is thus limited cross-linking which can successfully combine high local movement of chain segments with low overall movement of chains, as shown below.

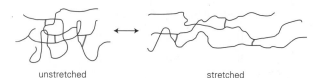

unstretched             stretched

## 3 Thermosetting polymers

When these materials are heated, extensive cross-linking takes place between the polymer chains; this causes the material to harden permanently or 'set'. Like diamond, these cross-linked polymers are hard and brittle. Unlike all the other polymers we have discussed, their properties are not sensitive to temperature since there is no possibility of even local movement of the 'chains'.

One of the first thermosetting polymers was Bakelite, formed by the condensation polymerisation of phenol and methanal. It is brittle, but it is harder and has better wear and temperature resistance than thermoplastics, keeping its shape even when hot. It is also an excellent insulator and Bakelite is still widely used for plug tops, electrical fittings and heat resistant handles and knobs.

Polymerisation of methanal with melamine, rather than phenol, produces the resins familiar as tableware and laminates for table surfaces. Being almost colourless they can be produced in a much wider and more decorative range of colours. This, together with their greater hardness and chemical resistance, justifies the extra cost.

$$NH_2$$

melamine

Polymers are an invaluable and evolving group of materials, continually being adapted to meet new demands. Such developments are based on our growing understanding of the chemistry of polymerisation reactions and of the intimate connection between properties and structure.

## KEY SKILLS

### Application of number

Investigation 18.5b could be a suitable opportunity to apply your application of number skills. This is a substantial and complex activity for which you will need a plan for obtaining and using the information required, records of your calculations showing the methods used and levels of accuracy, together with a report on your findings including a justification of your presentation methods and explanations of how your results relate to the question you try to answer. You will be able to include a graph, chart and diagram in your report.

## IT

Molecular modelling software (from a CD-ROM or the Internet) will help you to explore the shapes of chiral molecules in three dimensions.

## TOPIC REVIEW

This topic introduced the last functional group to be studied, the amine group.

**1   List key words or terms with definitions where necessary**

Illustrate the following with suitable **examples**:

- amine
- amino acid
- chiral compound
- $R_f$ value
- peptide group, protein
- polyester, polyamide
- addition and condensation polymerisation

**2   Summarise the key principles as simply as possible**

The **summary chart** or 'spider diagram' below summarises the reactions of **amines**. Complete the diagram with **reactants**, **conditions**, **type of reaction** and **products**.

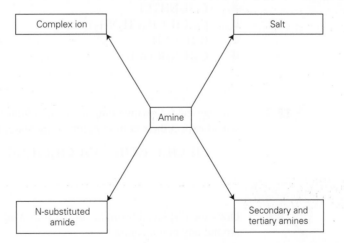

## REVIEW QUESTIONS

**✳** Indicates that the *Book of data* is needed.

**18.1**    Classify the compounds whose formulae are shown below as:

A  primary amines
B  secondary amines
C  tertiary amines
D  amides
E  amino acids

a    $(C_2H_5)_3N$                  (1)

b    $C_6H_5CONH_2$          (1)

c    $C_6H_5CH_2NH_2$        (1)

d    $\underset{\underset{CH_3}{|}}{H_2NCHCO_2H}$          (1)

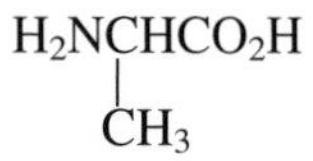

e 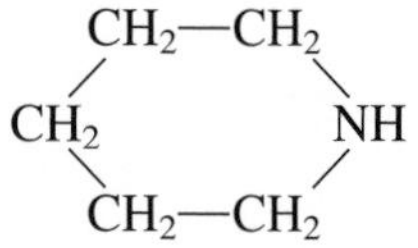    (1)

$$\begin{array}{ccc} CH_2—CH_2 & \\ CH_2 & NH \\ CH_2—CH_2 & \end{array}$$

f    $\underset{\underset{NH_2}{}}{\overset{\overset{NH_2}{|}}{O=C}}$          (1)

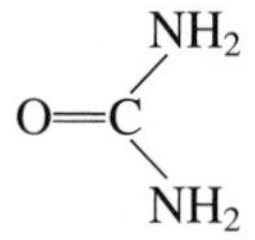

**(6 marks)**

**18.2**    The following ions and molecules can be made by a reaction between a primary amine and another reagent. In each case, give the formula of the amine and identify the other reagent.

a    $C_6H_5NH_3^+Cl^-$                                            (2)
b    $Cu(CH_3CH_2CH_2NH_2)_4^{2+}$                    (2)
c    $(CH_3)_2NH$                                                    (2)
d    $C_4H_9NHCOCH_3$                                       (2)

**(8 marks)**

**18.3**    Arrange the following compounds of similar molar mass in the order in which you would expect their boiling points to increase, giving reasons for your choice:

$CH_3CH_2CH_2CH_3$,   $CH_3CH_2CH_2OH$,   $CH_3CH_2CH_2NH_2$,   $CH_3CONH_2$

**(6 marks)**

**18.4**    Draw the displayed formulae of the following organic compounds, putting a circle around any chiral centres:

a    2-hydroxypropanoic acid                        (2)
b    2-chlorobutane                                          (2)
c    3-methylbutanal                                        (2)
d    2,3-dimethylpentane                                (2)
e    limonene (see page 195)                          (2)

**(10 marks)**

**18.5**     A substance, **A**, of molecular formula $C_5H_{13}N$, exists as two optical isomers. On treatment with hydrochloric acid, **A** forms **B**, $C_5H_{14}NCl$. **A** also reacts with ethanoyl chloride to form **C**, $C_7H_{15}NO$.

a     Give structural formulae which could apply to **A**, **B** and **C**.     (6)

b     Give the structural formulae of two isomers of **A** which are not optically active and name them.     (2)

c     Suggest a method by which one of your suggestions for part **b** could be synthesised starting from the appropriate alcohol containing five carbon atoms.     (4)

**(12 marks)**

**✱ 18.6**     The formula below represents a molecule of alanine:

$$CH_3—CHNH_2—CO_2H$$

a     The infrared absorption spectrum of alanine has some peaks at similar wavenumbers to those of peaks in the infrared spectra of aminoethane, $CH_3CH_2NH_2$, and chloromethane, $CH_3Cl$.

  i     Which bond(s) are responsible for these peaks?     (1)

  ii    What are their approximate wavenumbers?     (2)

b     Alanine can behave both as an acid and as a base.

  i     Draw the structural formula of the anion formed from an alanine molecule on adding a strong base.     (1)

  ii    Draw the structural formula for the cation formed from an alanine molecule on adding a strong acid.     (1)

c     The following questions concern the optical isomers of alanine. What differences, if any, would you expect there to be in

  i     the melting points of the two isomers?     (1)

  ii    the rates of their reaction with ethanoyl chloride?     (1)

  iii   their effect on copper(II) sulphate solution?     (1)

  iv    their effect on plane-polarised light?     (1)

  v     their occurrence in natural proteins?     (1)

**(10 marks)**

**18.7**     This question is concerned with the synthesis and properties of polymers. A polymer, **Z**, is produced by the reaction between the two compounds **X** and **Y** below.

$NH_2(CH_2)_6NH_2$     $ClOC(CH_2)_4COCl$
Compound **X**          Compound **Y**

a     What type of polymerisation reaction occurs between **X** and **Y**?     (1)

b     Draw the formula of the repeat unit of the polymer molecule. You should display the formula apart from the —$CH_2$— groups.     (3)

c     Name the type of linkage which joins **X** and **Y** in the polymer.     (1)

d     Name the polymer produced.     (1)

e     After the reaction, the polymer is warmed to soften it and is then 'drawn' or extruded; it is then much stronger.

  i     Draw a diagram showing the arrangement of molecules of the polymer before and after extrusion. (You can use zigzag lines, /\/\/ , to represent polymer molecules.)     (2)

  ii    Explain why the polymer is stronger after extrusion.     (2)

**(10 marks)**

**18.8** The equation for the formation of poly(ethene) from ethene is

$$n\text{CH}_2{=}\text{CH}_2 \longrightarrow \text{+CH}_2\text{—CH}_2\text{+}_n$$

Write similar equations for the formation of the following addition polymers:

a poly(phenylethene) (1)
b poly(propene) (1)
c poly(chloroethene) (1)
d poly(ethenol) (1)

**(4 marks)**

# EXAMINATION QUESTIONS

Questions of the summary and comprehension type are found in the background reading sections (sections 18.4 and 18.6).

**18.9** The diagram shows a section of the polyamide Kevlar, which can be made from a diamine and a dicarboxylic acid.

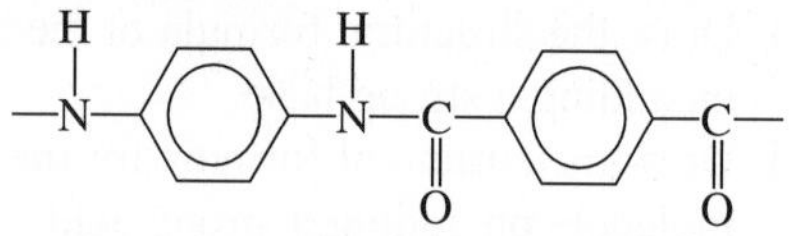

a Explain the term 'polyamide'. (1)

b Draw the structural formulae of the two monomers (the diamine and the dicarboxylic acid) which react to make Kevlar. (2)

c More than one type of intermolecular force occurs between molecules of Kevlar.
  i Which is the strongest type of intermolecular force occurring between molecules of Kevlar? (1)
  ii Copy the diagram below, which shows sections of two Kevlar molecules and draw lines showing where two different patterns of these strong forces might act.

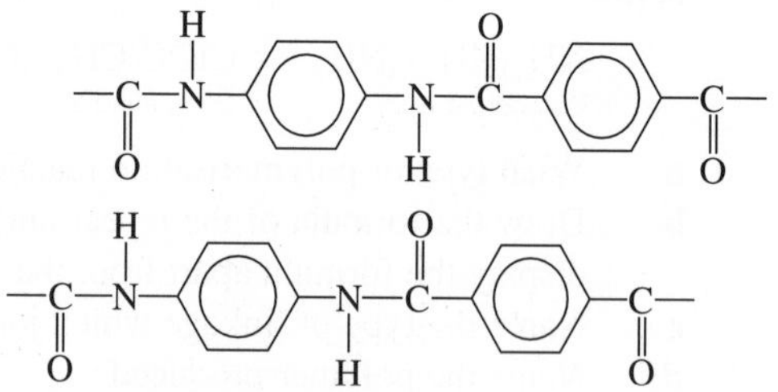

(2)

d Kevlar is a very strong polymer as it contains crystalline regions.
  i How does the arrangement of Kevlar molecules differ in crystalline regions and noncrystalline regions? A sketch may be helpful. The long polymer molecules can be represented by lines. (1)
  ii Explain why the presence of crystalline regions helps to make Kevlar strong. (1)

**(8 marks)**

**18.10**    A naturally occurring dipeptide, **X**, has the molecular formula $C_8H_{17}O_3N_3$. It can be broken down into its two constituent amino acids, **A** and **B**, by heating with moderately concentrated hydrochloric acid. The two amino acids can then be separated by paper chromatography using a mixture of butan-1-ol, ethanoic acid and water as the solvent.

   Amino acid **A** has an $R_f$ value of 0.26 and amino acid **B** has an $R_f$ value of 0.14.

   **a**    Draw a labelled diagram to scale of the resulting chromatogram marking the positions of the original and final spots and the solvent front.    (3)

   **b**  **i**  Only amino acid **B** is optically active. What structural feature must be present in **B**, but absent in **A**, which causes the plane of plane-polarised light to be rotated?    (1)
      **ii**  Draw the displayed formula of the optically inactive amino acid, **A**.    (1)
      **iii**  Deduce the molecular formula and a possible structural formula of **B**.    (2)
      **iv**  Suggest a structural formula for the dipeptide **X**.    (2)

   **c**    Would you expect a solution of **X** in water to be acidic, neutral or alkaline? Justify your answer.    (2)
                                                                **(11 marks)**

**18.11**    One of the constituents of the fabric Lycra, used in making sports clothing, is a polyether with the formula-type:

$$+CH_2-CH_2-O+_n$$

This constituent gives softness and stretchiness to the fabric, whereas another polymer gives Lycra its strength and elasticity. This is a polyurethane constituent with a formula such as:

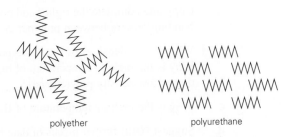

   **a**    Assuming that the polyether is made by loss of water molecules, give the formula of its monomer.    (1)
   **b**    The contrast in physical properties between the two types of polymer is largely due to differences in crystallinity:

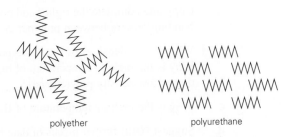

polyether                    polyurethane

   Suggest why, when produced under the same conditions, polyurethane should be more crystalline than polyether.    (3)
   **c**    Polyesters are sometimes used instead of polyethers but are more expensive. Write the formula for a polyester by replacing the ether group, —O—, in the polyether formula by an ester group.    (1)
                                                                **(5 marks)**

**18.12** This question is concerned with the molecular interactions between the polymer chains in various semi-crystalline plastic materials in common use.

| Chain unit of polymer | Melting temperature /°C | Strongest type of bonding between chains |
|---|---|---|
| —CH₂—CH₂—<br>poly(ethene)<br>low density | 115 | . |
| —CH₂—CH₂—<br>poly(ethene)<br>high density | 138 | |
| —O—CH₂—O—CH₂—<br>poly(oxymethene) | 180 | dipole/dipole |
| Terylene | 265 | |
| nylon 66 | 265 | |
| Bakelite | — | covalent |

a Copy and complete the right-hand column to show the strongest type of bonding present between polymer chains. (3)

b i Why are the densities of the two types of poly(ethene) different? (1)

ii Why is the melting temperature of high density poly(ethene) greater than that of low density poly(ethene)? (1)

c Why is the melting temperature of Bakelite not given? (1)

d Suggest FOUR further pieces of data that you would like to see included in the table if you wished to evaluate the suitability of various polymers for use as a rope on board a boat. (4)

**(10 marks)**

# The transition elements

| Element | Electronic structure |
|---------|---------------------|
| (Sc) | $3d^1 4s^2$ |
| Ti | $3d^2 4s^2$ |
| V | $3d^3 4s^2$ |
| Cr | $3d^5 4s^1$ |
| Mn | $3d^5 4s^2$ |
| Fe | $3d^6 4s^2$ |
| Co | $3d^7 4s^2$ |
| Ni | $3d^8 4s^2$ |
| Cu | $3d^{10} 4s^1$ |
| (Zn) | $3d^{10} 4s^2$ |

**The electronic structures of the first row of transition elements: only the outermost energy levels are shown**

In previous work you have probably used the term *transition element* to refer to those elements which come in the d block of the Periodic Table, between Groups 2 and 3. This topic is only concerned with the elements of the first row of that block.

True transition elements and their compounds have a number of characteristic properties, and these properties are usually a consequence of the ions of the elements having d orbitals which are incompletely filled with electrons. This effectively removes both scandium and zinc from the list (in the margin). **Therefore, when referring to transition elements we mean an element which contains an incomplete d orbital in at least one compound.** In the first row, this means the elements Ti to Cu.

Transition metals, like gold, copper and iron, were amongst the earliest materials humans produced. Their importance has not diminished, because these metals have found an ever increasing range of uses as we have learnt more about their properties.

In this topic you will develop:

- the use of electrode potentials to predict the outcome of redox reactions and to interpret the mechanism of some catalytic reactions
- a systematic way of interpreting the formation of complex ions, and their structures.

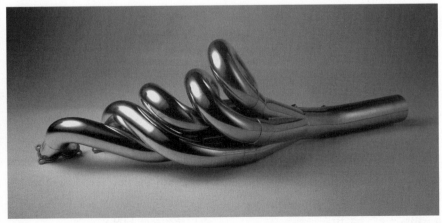 

**Figure 19.1** Nickel exhaust pipes from a Formula One racing car and a bronze cat sculpture. What special properties would be needed in an exhaust system for a high performance car? Can you find data or evidence to suggest that nickel is a good choice? What criteria would you use when choosing the metal for the sculpture?

## 19.1 Variable oxidation number

In this section you are going to investigate some chemical reactions of compounds of the transition elements that involve changes of oxidation number. The diagram below shows the range of oxidation numbers in transition metal compounds and the common ones you are likely to meet (in green).

|   | Ti | V | Cr | Mn | Fe | Co | Ni | Cu |
|---|---|---|---|---|---|---|---|---|
|   |   |   |   | 7 |   |   |   |   |
|   |   |   | 6 | 6 | 6 |   |   |   |
|   |   | 5 | 5 | 5 | 5 | 5 |   |   |
|   | 4 | 4 | 4 | 4 | 4 | 4 | 4 |   |
|   | 3 | 3 | 3 | 3 | 3 | 3 | 3 | 3 |
|   | 2 | 2 | 2 | 2 | 2 | 2 | 2 | 2 |
|   | 1 | 1 | 1 | 1 | 1 | 1 | 1 | 1 |
| Element | Ti | V | Cr | Mn | Fe | Co | Ni | Cu |

You will begin your investigation with a study of iron compounds.

## The redox chemistry of iron

You should be able to recall that iron has two principal oxidation numbers in its compounds, $+2$ and $+3$, as in the ions $Fe^{2+}(aq)$ and $Fe^{3+}(aq)$. The purpose of Experiment 19.1a is to use standard electrode potentials to predict the likelihood of oxidising $Fe^{2+}(aq)$, or reducing $Fe^{3+}(aq)$, and then for you to test your predictions experimentally.

✎ **In your notes:** Begin by copying figure 19.2 onto graph paper, and stick it in your notes.

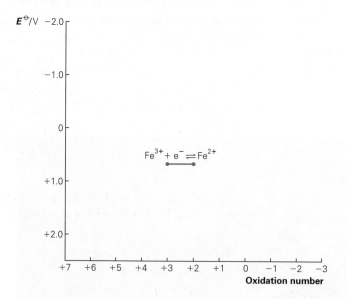

Figure 19.2 **Electrode potential chart for Experiment 19.1a**

Enter on your chart the following equilibria, in the way the $Fe^{2+}/Fe^{3+}$ equilibrium has been entered.

**a** $\frac{1}{2}Br_2 + e^- \rightleftharpoons Br^-$ $\qquad E^{\ominus} = +1.09\ V$

**b** $MnO_4^- + 8H^+ + 5e^- \rightleftharpoons Mn^{2+} + 4H_2O$ $\qquad E^{\ominus} = +1.51\ V$

c $\frac{1}{2}Cl_2 + e^- \rightleftharpoons Cl^-$ $\qquad\qquad\qquad E^\ominus = +1.36\ V$

d $Ag^+ + e^- \rightleftharpoons Ag$ $\qquad\qquad\qquad E^\ominus = +0.80\ V$

e $SO_4^{2-} + 4H^+ + 2e^- \rightleftharpoons SO_2 + 2H_2O$ $\qquad E^\ominus = +0.17\ V$

f $Zn^{2+} + 2e^- \rightleftharpoons Zn$ $\qquad\qquad\qquad E^\ominus = -0.76\ V$

g $\frac{1}{2}I_2 + e^- \rightleftharpoons I^-$ $\qquad\qquad\qquad E^\ominus = +0.54\ V$

Now you are ready to begin the experiment.

| EXPERIMENT 19.1a | |
|---|---|

# The redox reactions of iron

You will need the following solutions, as far as possible of concentration 0.1 M.

| Name | Notes |
|---|---|
| Iron(II) sulphate solution | Contains $Fe^{2+}(aq)$ ions. These ions have a tendency to react with water (hydrolysis) which eventually makes the solution go brown and become cloudy. This has been minimised by adding some sulphuric acid. |
| Iron(III) chloride solution | Contains $Fe^{3+}(aq)$ ions which also have a tendency to react with water. In this case the reaction has been suppressed by using hydrochloric acid. |
| Bromine water | This solution contains $Br_2(aq)$ molecules. |
| Potassium manganate(VII) solution | Contains $MnO_4^-(aq)$ ions, and has been acidified with sulphuric acid. |
| Chlorine solution | This solution contains $Cl_2(aq)$ molecules, but gaseous chlorine escapes from solution. |
| Sodium chloride solution | This solution contains $Cl^-(aq)$ ions. |
| Sulphur dioxide solution | This solution has been made by bubbling sulphur dioxide gas through water. The solution has a strong smell which may be harmful to those who suffer from respiratory complaints such as asthma. |
| Silver nitrate solution | This solution contains $Ag^+(aq)$ ions. |
| Potassium iodide solution | This solution contains $I^-(aq)$ ions. |
| Powdered zinc | Zinc metal is $Zn(0)$. |

Use the chart that you have drawn to predict the likelihood of reactions occurring when the following pairs of substances are mixed, most of which are in solution:

a iron(II) sulphate and bromine water

b iron(III) chloride and zinc

c iron(II) sulphate and silver nitrate

d iron(III) chloride and sodium chloride

e iron(III) chloride and sulphur dioxide solution (with warming)

f iron(II) sulphate and acidified potassium manganate(VII)

g iron(III) chloride and potassium iodide

h iron(II) sulphate and chlorine water.

**COMMENT**

You may find it helpful to revise the method of predicting redox reactions that was introduced in section 17.3.

**SAFETY**

0.01 M bromine water is toxic
and corrosive.
0.01 M chlorine water is
harmful, but the vapour
which escapes is toxic.
Aqueous sulphur dioxide is
toxic by inhalation; its vapour
is corrosive. Asthmatics
should avoid inhaling it.
Powdered zinc is highly
flammable.

# Procedure

For each of the pairs of substances listed, try to confirm your predictions by
experiment. Do this by mixing roughly equal volumes of the two solutions in a test
tube, or by adding a spatula measure of the solid to a few cm$^3$ of solution.

In a number of the reactions it should be easy to tell whether a reaction has
taken place or not because there are coloured reactants or coloured products.

In other cases, however, it may be necessary to test the solution to find out
whether the iron has changed in oxidation number. A suitable test is to add sodium
hydroxide solution. Iron(II) ions give a green precipitate when sodium hydroxide
solution is added, whereas iron(III) ions give a red–brown precipitate.

  **In your notes:** Draw up a table of results using the following headings.

| Substances mixed | Predicted reaction, if any | Observations on mixing |
| --- | --- | --- |
| **a** Iron(II) sulphate and bromine water | | |
| | | |

Mention in the 'Observations' column any confirmatory tests you used.

## QUESTIONS

Use your table of results to write balanced ionic equations for the redox reactions which took
place.

Here is an example of how to do this. In the reaction between $Fe^{2+}$ and $Cl_2$, the ions $Fe^{2+}(aq)$
are oxidised to $Fe^{3+}(aq)$ and the chlorine molecules $Cl_2(aq)$ are reduced to $Cl^-(aq)$. The
equations for the half-reactions are:

$$Fe^{2+}(aq) \rightleftharpoons Fe^{3+}(aq) + e^-$$
$$Cl_2(aq) + 2e^- \rightleftharpoons 2Cl^-(aq)$$

The first equation involves one electron, whereas the second involves two electrons. The first
equation should therefore be doubled throughout, and added to the second, so that the electrons
do not appear in the final equation. This is:

$$2Fe^{2+}(aq) + Cl_2(aq) \longrightarrow 2Fe^{3+}(aq) + 2Cl^-(aq)$$

# The oxidation numbers of vanadium

Whereas iron has only two readily accessible oxidation numbers in its compounds,
vanadium has four: $+5$, $+4$, $+3$, and $+2$. In the next experiment we shall study.
this rather more complicated situation.

**EXPERIMENT 19.1b**

# The reduction of vanadium(V)

The object of the experiment is to start with a solution containing vanadium with oxidation number $+5$, and to selected reducing agents which will reduce it to each of the other oxidation numbers.

The most convenient starting material is solid ammonium vanadate(V), $NH_4VO_3$. When ammonium vanadate(V) is acidified the vanadium becomes part of a positive ion, $VO_2^+(aq)$, in which the vanadium still has an oxidation number of $+5$. You are provided with this solution. The other oxidation numbers of vanadium are included with this one in the table below.

| Ion | Oxidation number of vanadium | Colour of solution |
|-----|------------------------------|--------------------|
| $VO_2^+$ | $+5$ | yellow |
| $VO^{2+}$ | $+4$ | blue |
| $V^{3+}$ | $+3$ | green |
| $V^{2+}$ | $+2$ | mauve |

 **In your notes:** Copy the table and also the chart of electrode potentials and oxidation numbers (figure 19.3).

Enter on the chart the equilibria **a**, **e**, **f**, and **g** from Experiment 19.1a and also the equilibrium

$$Sn^{2+}(aq) + 2e^- \rightleftharpoons Sn(s) \qquad E^{\ominus} = -0.14 \text{ V}$$

Use the chart to select a reducing agent which should reduce vanadium from $+5$ in $VO_2^+$ to $+4$ in $VO^{2+}$, but should not reduce the vanadium any further.

Then select a reducing agent which should reduce vanadium from $+5$ to $+4$ and also from $+4$ to $+3$ but no further.

Finally select a reducing agent which should reduce vanadium all the way from $+5$ to $+2$.

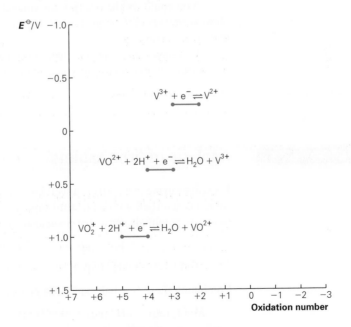

Figure 19.3   **Electrode potential chart for vanadium**

**SAFETY**

You are using most of the same reagents as in Experiment 19.1a so you must take the same precautions.
0.01 M acidic ammonium vanadate(V) solution is toxic and irritant.
50% phosphoric(I) acid is corrosive.
Aqueous sulphur dioxide is toxic by inhalation and its vapour is corrosive.

Record your selections in a table like the one shown below and then try out the reactions and record your observations.

| Desired final oxidation number | Selected reducing agent | Observations |
|---|---|---|
| +4 ($VO^{2+}$)<br>+3 ($V^{3+}$)<br>+2 ($V^{2+}$) | | |

If you decide to use potassium iodide solution as a reducing agent, the iodide will be oxidised to elemental iodine. This will give a colour to the solution which will mask the colour of the vanadium ion. The iodine can be reduced back to colourless iodide by reaction with sodium thiosulphate solution (see Topic 6): add only just enough to discharge the colour due to the iodine. Incidentally, it has been discovered that sodium thiosulphate will itself reduce the $VO_2^+$ ion. If the reaction involved is

$$S_4O_6^-(aq) + 2e^- \rightleftharpoons 2S_2O_3^{2-}(aq) \qquad E^\ominus = +0.09 \text{ V}$$

what oxidation number of vanadium should result?

As a further experiment you might try a very good way of making the vanadium(IV) ion which illustrates a very important limitation of the principle of predicting redox reactions from electrode potentials. For this you will need to enter the following system and its electrode potential into your chart:

$$H_3PO_3 + 2H^+(aq) + 2e^- \rightleftharpoons H_3PO_2(aq) + H_2O(l) \qquad E^\ominus = -0.50 \text{ V}$$

Using this information you would expect phosphoric(I) acid, $H_3PO_2(aq)$, to reduce vanadium from the $+5$ state to the $+2$ state. In fact, what happens is reduction to the $+4$ state only. It is thought that the two further stages leading to the $+2$ state of vanadium are extremely slow – the reactions are 'kinetically hindered'.

You could try the reaction for yourself by adding 3 drops of 50% phosphoric(I) acid to about $10 \text{ cm}^3$ of your solution of $VO_2^+(aq)$. Gentle warming may be necessary.

It is important to realise that you can predict the feasibility of a reaction from electrode potentials but you cannot predict its speed.

---

**EXPERIMENT 19.1c**

## Analysis of 'iron tablets'

Potassium manganate(VII) is a well known oxidising agent, usually used in solutions acidified with a plentiful supply of dilute sulphuric acid. The following electrode potentials show that manganate(VII) ions should oxidise iron(II) ions:

$$Fe^{3+}(aq) + e^- \rightleftharpoons Fe^{2+}(aq) \qquad E^\ominus = +0.77 \text{ V}$$
$$MnO_4^-(aq) + 8H^+(aq) + 5e^- \rightleftharpoons Mn^{2+}(aq) + 4H_2O(l) \qquad E^\ominus = +1.51 \text{ V}$$

Combining these two half-equations gives the overall equation for the reaction:

$$MnO_4^-(aq) + 8H^+(aq) + 5Fe^{2+}(aq) \longrightarrow Mn^{2+}(aq) + 5Fe^{3+}(aq) + 4H_2O(l)$$

so that in acid solution 1 mole of $MnO_4^-(aq)$ reacts with 5 moles of $Fe^{2+}(aq)$.

Solutions containing $MnO_4^-(aq)$ ions have an intense purple colour, whereas those containing $Mn^{2+}(aq)$ ions are almost colourless. Solutions containing $Fe^{2+}(aq)$ ions can be titrated against potassium manganate(VII) solution. The colour of the manganate(VII) is discharged, the end-point of the titration being the point at which the addition of one more drop of potassium manganate(VII) gives a permanent purple colour.

This titration forms the basis of an analytical technique for the estimation of iron which can be used to analyse a popular 'iron tonic'.

## Procedure

**SAFETY**

1 M sulphuric acid is an irritant.

Weigh accurately two 'ferrous sulphate' tablets. Grind up the tablets with a little 1 M sulphuric acid, using a pestle and mortar. Through a funnel, transfer the resulting paste into a $100 \, cm^3$ volumetric flask. Use further small volumes of 1 M sulphuric acid to rinse the ground-up tablets into the flask. During this process, you must take great care to ensure that all the particles of tablet get into the flask.

When this has been done, add sufficient 1 M sulphuric acid to make up the solution to exactly $100 \, cm^3$. Stopper the flask and shake it to make sure that all the contents are thoroughly mixed. They will not all be in solution although the $Fe^{2+}$ ions which were present in the tablets will be dissolved.

Titrate $10.0 \, cm^3$ portions of the solution with 0.0050 M potassium manganate(VII). The end-point is marked by the first permanent purple colour. Brown or red colours should not be allowed to develop; the remedy is to add more 1 M sulphuric acid.

**In your notes:**

1 What are the reasons for using so much 1 M sulphuric acid during this experiment? There are two reasons, one to do with the behaviour of solutions containing $Fe^{2+}$ ions, and the other to do with the equation for oxidations involving potassium manganate(VII).

2 Do your results agree with the analysis of the tablets given by the manufacturers on the bottle label?

3 Write a short account of the theory of this analysis, record the practical procedure used, and calculate the percentage of iron in the tablets from your results.

## 19.2 Complex ion formation

We shall now consider another of the characteristic properties of transition elements, the ability to form complex ions.

**A complex is formed when the ion of a metal is surrounded by ligands. These ligands are either negatively charged ions, or molecules, and in both cases contain a lone pair of electrons which is used to make a dative bond to the central metal.**

Water is a common ligand that you have already met. For example, the water in hydrated salts is often part of a complex ion: $Cu(H_2O)_4^{2+}$ occurs in hydrated copper sulphate. In Topic 6 on the halogens you met the silver–ammonia complex, $(H_3N-Ag-NH_3)^+$ and in Topic 14 on reversible reactions you met one of the complex ions that chloride ions can form, $CoCl_4^{2-}$.

In the next experiment you are going to be introduced to some organic compounds that form very stable complex ions.

**Two bidendate ligands that form two bonds in a complex ion**

2-hydroxybenzoate ion

1,2-dihydroxybenzene

**A hexadentate ligand that forms six bonds in a complex ion**

edta, (from ethylenediaminetetra-acetic acid, recommended name 1,2–bis[bis(carboxymethyl)amino] ethane)

---

**EXPERIMENT 19.2a**

# Some copper(II) complexes

As you write down the answers to the questions in this experiment, you should make it clear what each question was and to which reaction it refers.

## Procedure: Part 1

**SAFETY**

8 M ammonia is corrosive. Concentrated hydrochloric acid is corrosive.

**1** Put five or six drops of 0.5 M copper(II) sulphate solution in a test tube.

✎ **In your notes:** What complex ion is present? Record its colour. *blue*

**2** Add 10 drops of concentrated hydrochloric acid drop by drop.

✎ **In your notes:** Record the colour change of the solution. What ligands do you think are now present in the complex ion? *blue → green*

**3** Keep half of the solution for **4**. Pour the other half into a test tube half full of water.

✎ **In your notes:** What colour is the solution now? What complex ion is now present? In view of what happened in **2** why do you think this reaction occurred?

**4** To the solution kept from **3**, add 8 M ammonia solution (TAKE CARE) drop by drop till there is no further colour change. Save this solution for **6**.

✎ **In your notes:** Record the colour of the solution. What ligands do you think are now present in the complex ion? *goes blue*

What do you think is the order of stability of the complex ions you have seen in these experiments?

**5** To 4 or 5 drops of a solution containing $Cu(H_2O)_4^{2+}$ (aq) in a test tube add a solution of the ligand edta until there is no further colour change.

✎ **In your notes:** Record the colour of the edta–Cu(II) complex. *blue*

**6** Add edta solution drop by drop to the solution obtained in **4** until there is no further colour change. *goes blue*

✎ **In your notes:** Which ligand forms the most stable complex?

*the one*

## Procedure: Part 2

You are going to carry out an experiment in which first a solution of ammonia, then one of sodium 2-hydroxybenzoate, then edta, then 1,2-dihydroxybenzene are added in turn to a solution of copper(II) ions.

First you need to know the colour of the complexes that result.

1  Put five or six drops of copper(II) solution in each of four test tubes. To the first test tube add edta solution drop by drop until there is no further colour change. To the second similarly add 8 M ammonia solution (TAKE CARE); to the third, sodium 2-hydroxybenzoate solution; and to the fourth, 1,2-dihydroxybenzene solution in 0.4 M sodium hydroxide.

✎  **In your notes:** What are the colours of the four complexes?

2  Now add 8–10 drops of 8 M ammonia solution (TAKE CARE) to 4–5 drops of copper(II) solution, followed by 10–15 drops of sodium 2-hydroxybenzoate solution, 10–15 drops of edta solution, and 10–15 drops of 1,2-dihydroxybenzene solution in turn. Add the solutions drop by drop, noting the colours of the mixture.

✎  **In your notes:** What is the order of stability of the complex ions?

**SAFETY**

8 M ammonia is corrosive. Aqueous alkaline 1,2-dihydroxybenzene (catechol) is irritant. 0.4 M sodium hydroxide is irritant.

# Interpretation of the experiments

## Stability constants of copper(II) complexes

**QUESTION**

What shapes would you predict for these complex ions?

The commonest ligand is water, and aqueous solutions of simple compounds of transition elements contain complex ions with formulae such as:

$$Cu(H_2O)_4^{2+} \qquad Ni(H_2O)_6^{2+} \qquad Co(H_2O)_6^{2+}$$

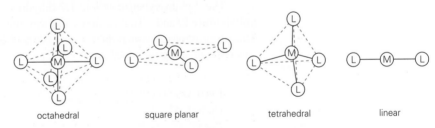

octahedral          square planar          tetrahedral          linear

**Figure 19.4  Possible shapes of transition metal complexes (M = metal; L = ligand)**

When a solution containing a different ligand is added to an aqueous solution containing these hydrated ions, an equilibrium is set up in which the water molecules are replaced by the new ligands. For example, in the case of the copper(II) complexes which you investigated in Experiment 19.2a, the equilibrium in the presence of chloride ions would be:

$$Cu(H_2O)_4^{2+}(aq) + 4Cl^-(aq) \rightleftharpoons CuCl_4^{2-}(aq) + 4H_2O(l)$$

Application of the Equilibrium Law gives an equilibrium constant, $K$, where

$$K = \frac{[CuCl_4^{2-}(aq)]}{[Cu(H_2O)_4^{2+}(aq)][Cl^-(aq)]^4}$$

$[H_2O(l)]$ is constant and is not included in the expression.

**Equilibrium constants such as this are called stability constants**. They enable us to compare the stabilities of complexes of an element with different ligands; the larger the stability constant, the more stable the complex may be said to be, compared with the water complex.

For convenience, the table below gives the logarithms of the values of the stability constants for various complexes of copper(II):

| Ligand | | lg $K$ |
|---|---|---|
| $Cl^-$ | chloride | 5.62 |
| $NH_3$ | ammonia | 13.1 |
| | 2-hydroxybenzoate | 16.9 |
| | 1,2-dihydroxybenzene | 25.0 |
| $edta^{4-}$ | ethylenediaminetetra-acetate | 18.8 |

They are 'overall' stability constants for the complete reaction, for example:

$$Cu(H_2O)_4^{2+}(aq) + 4Cl^-(aq) \rightleftharpoons CuCl_4^{2-}(aq) + 4H_2O(l)$$

The reaction occurs in four separate stages and stability constants can also be found for each stage of the reaction.

The 2-hydroxybenzoate ion, 1,2-dihydroxybenzene, and edta are **polydentate** ligands. That is, they can form more than one link with the metal ion. Thus in solutions in which there is an excess of ligand present, the predominating species containing the metal are:

$Cu(H_2O)_4^{2+}$
$Cu(NH_3)_4^{2+}$     monodentate ligands
$CuCl_4^{2-}$

bidentate ligands

**COMMENT**

edta is usually supplied as a sodium salt, $Na_2Y$, where Y is edta$^{2-}$. As it forms complexes the ligand loses two more protons to become edta$^{4-}$.

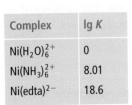

hexadentate ligand

## Entropy considerations

When bidentate ligands replace monodentate ligands in a complex, there will be an increase in the entropy of the system because one molecule of ligand is replacing two molecules, for example:

$$Ni(H_2O)_6^{2+}(aq) + 3NH_2CH_2CH_2NH_2(aq)$$
$$\text{1,2-diaminoethane}$$
$$\rightleftharpoons Ni(NH_2CH_2CH_2NH_2)_3^{2+}(aq) + 6H_2O(l)$$

In this example there are four particles on the left of the equation but seven particles on the right. Because the entropy of the system depends, amongst other things, on the number of particles present, $\Delta S_{system}$ increases when 1,2-diaminoethane molecules replace ammonia molecules.

**COMMENT**

$\Delta S_{total}$ must always be positive if a change is to occur spontaneously; there are two entropy changes to consider, $\Delta S_{system}$ and $\Delta S_{surroundings}$ connected by the expression:

$$\Delta S_{total} = \Delta S_{system} + \Delta S_{surroundings}$$

A similar, but larger, increase of $\Delta S_{system}$ takes place when edta replaces monodentate or bidentate ligands in a complex. For example:

$$Ni(NH_3)_6^{2+}(aq) + edta^{4-}(aq) \rightleftharpoons Ni(edta)^{2-}(aq) + 6NH_3(aq)$$

Comparison of the numbers of particles involved shows a large increase, corresponding to an increase of $\Delta S_{system}$.

Because of this entropy-increasing effect, complexes with a hexadentate ligand such as edta are usually much more stable than those with a monodentate ligand. A good example of this effect is shown by the stability constants of nickel complexes, shown in the margin.

In these complexes the ligands are bonded to the nickel ion by means of lone pairs of electrons on oxygen atoms in water, nitrogen atoms in ammonia, and both oxygen and nitrogen atoms in edta. Ignoring the entropy effect, therefore, the edta complex might be expected to be comparable in stability with the ammonia complex. It is the increase in $\Delta S_{system}$ accompanying its formation which accounts for the high stability of the edta complex compared with the other two.

| Complex | lg $K$ |
|---|---|
| $Ni(H_2O)_6^{2+}$ | 0 |
| $Ni(NH_3)_6^{2+}$ | 8.01 |
| $Ni(edta)^{2-}$ | 18.6 |

Write an account of your experiments involving complex ions, interpreting the results in terms of:

- stability constants, from table 6.13 in the *Book of data*
- whether the ligand is mono-, bi- or hexadentate
- the entropy change.

# The preparation of compounds containing complexes

You should have time to carry out one of the following preparations.

EXPERIMENT 19.2b

## Stabilising an unusual oxidation number: chromium(II) ethanoate, $Cr_2(CH_3CO_2)_4(H_2O)_2$

Chromium(II) ethanoate is a neutral complex of $Cr^{2+}$ ions with $CH_3CO_2^-$ ions and water molecules as ligands.

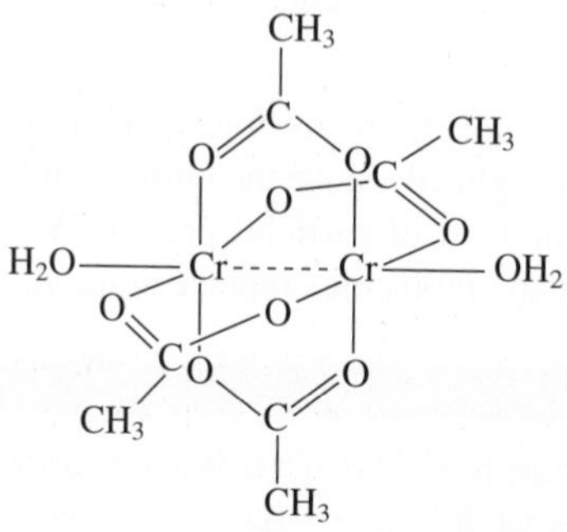

Figure 19.5 **The structure of chromium(II) ethanoate**

This compound is interesting because it is an example of the way in which the formation of a complex can sometimes stabilise an oxidation number which would otherwise be unstable. Chromium(II) ions are normally very readily oxidised to chromium(III) by the oxygen of the air.

The apparatus shown in figure 19.6 can be used, or one which will perform similarly. Zinc in the presence of acid reduces chromium(VI) to chromium(II). Excess zinc also reacts with hydrogen to produce hydrogen gas. The build-up of pressure in the apparatus forces the solution into the complexing reagent.

## Procedure

Dissolve 1 g of sodium dichromate(VI) in 5 cm$^3$ of water, and put it in the 50 cm$^3$ round-bottomed flask. Add 3 g of zinc in equal proportions by mass of powder and granulated. Put a mixture of 20 cm$^3$ concentrated hydrochloric acid and 10 cm$^3$ water in the tap funnel. Put 10 cm$^3$ of saturated sodium ethanoate solution in the boiling tube. The solubility of sodium ethanoate in water is about 30% by mass.

## SAFETY !

The chemicals and procedures used in this experiment are extremely hazardous, so you must take even more care than usual to reduce the risks from them by using suitable control measures.

Solid sodium dichromate(VI) is very toxic and is classed as a category 2 carcinogen; it is an irritant to all tissues; you must wear gloves when handling this solid. Avoid inhaling any tiny crystals.

Zinc powder is highly flammable.

Concentrated hydrochloric acid is corrosive.

The hydrogen evolved is extremely flammable. As hydrogen is evolved, naked flames must be kept well clear.

Throughout this experiment, you must wear eye protection.

## COMMENT

$Cr^{3+}(aq)$ is green and $Cr^{2+}(aq)$ is blue.

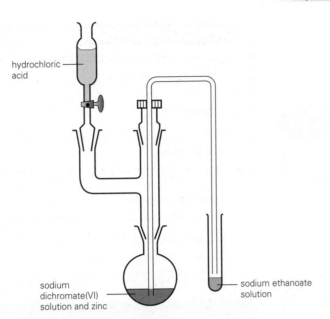

hydrochloric acid

sodium dichromate(VI) solution and zinc

sodium ethanoate solution

**Figure 19.6   Apparatus suitable for the preparation of chromium(II) ethanoate**

Add the hydrochloric acid to the mixture in the flask and leave the tap funnel partially OPEN to allow the hydrogen which is generated to escape. The reduction of the chromium soon reaches a green stage and gradually becomes increasingly blue over 10–20 minutes.

When the solution is distinctly blue and **while hydrogen is still being generated** close the tap on the funnel. The pressure of the hydrogen will force the blue solution over into the saturated sodium ethanoate. A red precipitate of chromium(II) ethanoate should be formed, and the solution will contain dissolved red chromium(II) ethanoate.

Dismantle the apparatus and pour the remaining blue solution containing $Cr^{2+}(aq)$ into another boiling tube. Keep the two boiling tubes unstoppered and side by side in a rack.

**In your notes:** Write an account of the method and answer the questions, recording your answers in such a way as to make it clear what each question was.

1   Show, using electrode potentials, that zinc should reduce chromium from $+6$ in sodium dichromate(VI) to $+2$ in chromium(II) ethanoate.

2   What happens to the colour of the $Cr^{2+}(aq)$ solution when it is allowed to stand open to the air?

3   Over the same period of time does the colour of the chromium(II) ethanoate solution also change?

## Preparation of a complex anion

Iron is usually present in its compounds as a cation. But iron cations will form covalent bonds with ethanedioate (oxalate) anions: the resulting complex ion in this case is an anion.

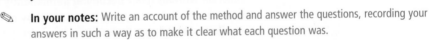

$$FeCl_3(aq) + 3K_2(C_2O_4)(aq) \longrightarrow K_3[Fe(C_2O_4)_3](aq) + 3KCl(aq)$$

Calculate the amounts of hydrated iron(III) chloride, $FeCl_3.6H_2O$, and hydrated potassium ethanedioate, $K_2(C_2O_4).H_2O$, that you need to mix in order to obtain $\frac{1}{100}$ mole of the product, $K_3[Fe(C_2O_4)_3].3H_2O$. Have your calculation checked before you proceed.

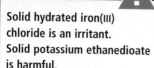

**SAFETY**

Solid hydrated iron(III) chloride is an irritant.
Solid potassium ethanedioate is harmful.

## Procedure

Dissolve the calculated amount of hydrated iron(III) chloride in $5\ cm^3$ of pure water in a test tube.

In another test tube dissolve the calculated amount of hydrated potassium ethanedioate in $10\ cm^3$ of pure water, warming gently.

Mix your solutions in a small beaker, cover and leave to crystallise. The product is called potassium triethanedioatoferrate(III).

**In your notes:** Write an account of the experiment, including all your calculations; record the colour changes you observe.

Leave a sample exposed to sunlight or a powerful light.

### BACKGROUND

The complex ion you have prepared is decomposed by light photons quantitatively so a solution of a known concentration can be used to measure the amount of light falling on the solution. This is valuable information when a chemist wishes to measure the rate of a photochemical change.

## 19.3 Transition elements as catalysts

**The essential feature of a catalyst is that it increases the rate of a chemical reaction without itself becoming permanently involved in the reaction.** It does, however, become temporarily involved, by providing a route from reactants to products which has a lower activation energy (see section 11.5).

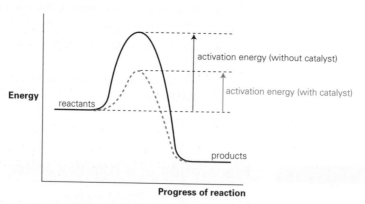

Figure 19.7 **The effect is to provide a route for a reaction with a lower activation energy**

The following experiment is about catalysis, though it treats it in an unusual way. Carry out the instructions and try to answer the questions which follow.

**EXPERIMENT 19.3**

# A kinetic study of the reaction between manganate(VII) ions and ethanedioic acid

Potassium manganate(VII) will oxidise ethanedioic acid (oxalic acid) to carbon dioxide and water, in the presence of an excess of acid:

$$2MnO_4^-(aq) + 6H^+(aq) + 5(CO_2H)_2(aq) \longrightarrow 2Mn^{2+}(aq) + 10CO_2(g) + 8H_2O(l)$$

**SAFETY**

1 M sulphuric acid is an irritant.
Ethanedioic acid is harmful in contact with skin and if swallowed.
Iodine formed in the reaction is harmful.

## Procedure

1 Carry out a trial experiment by mixing one tenth quantities of each of Mixtures 1 and 2, but without adding any water. Record the colour changes you see on adding 5 cm$^3$ of 0.02 M potassium manganate(VII) to each.

| Solution | Mixture 1 | Mixture 2 |
|---|---|---|
| 0.2 M ethanedioic acid | 100 cm$^3$ | 100 cm$^3$ |
| 0.2 M manganese(II) sulphate | – | 15 cm$^3$ |
| 1 M sulphuric acid | 10 cm$^3$ | 10 cm$^3$ |
| Water | 90 cm$^3$ | 75 cm$^3$ |

2 Prepare a reaction mixture according to the table, using measuring cylinders. Some members of your group should use Mixture 1 and some Mixture 2. The results should then be shared.

3 Add 50 cm$^3$ of 0.02 M potassium manganate(VII) and start timing. Shake the mixture for about half a minute to mix it well.

4 After about a minute use a pipette and safety pipette filler to withdraw a 10.0 cm$^3$ portion of the reaction mixture and run it into a conical flask.

5 Note the time and add about 10 cm$^3$ of 0.1 M potassium iodide solution. This stops the reaction and releases iodine equivalent to the residual manganate(VII) ions.

6 Titrate the liberated iodine with 0.01 M sodium thiosulphate, adding a little starch solution near the end-point. Record the titre of sodium thiosulphate.

7 Remove further portions every 3 or 4 minutes and titrate them in the same way. Continue until the titre is less than 3 cm$^3$.

**In your notes:**

1 What set of figures gives a measure of the reactant concentration at the various time intervals?

2 Plot an appropriate graph for each experiment. Refer to Topic 11 if you need help.

3 Try to answer these questions about the graphs:
   a How does the rate of reaction vary with time?
   b What is unusual about the graph for Mixture 1? What explanation can you offer for this abnormal behaviour?
   c Can you suggest an experiment that would test your explanation?

# Homogeneous catalysis

## COMMENT

You should remember from section 11.5 that catalysts can be of two types, *heterogeneous* and *homogeneous*.

Although heterogeneous catalysis is of more widespread significance commercially, homogeneous catalysis is important too and often involves transition element ions, because of their ability to change oxidation number readily. It is sometimes possible to identify a possible catalyst by using electrode potentials. Consider the electrode potential chart below.

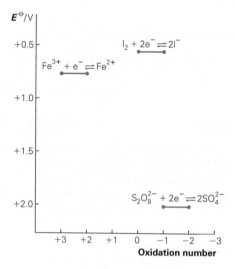

Figure 19.8  **Identifying catalysts by electrode potential**

Peroxodisulphate ions, $S_2O_8^{2-}$ (aq), are capable of oxidising iodide ions, $I^-$ (aq), to iodine, but the reaction is a very slow one.

$$S_2O_8^{2-}(aq) + 2I^-(aq) \longrightarrow 2SO_4^{2-}(aq) + I_2(aq)$$

When iron(II) ions are added to the mixture, these can be oxidised by the peroxodisulphate ions rather more quickly (perhaps because the negative peroxodisulphate ions would then be reacting with positive ions instead of with negative ones). The resulting iron(III) ions can oxidise iodide ions to iodine and the iron(II) ions are re-formed.

Clearly, in order for this catalysis to work, the electrode potential for the reaction involving the catalyst must lie between the electrode potentials involving the two reactants.

This predictive method only shows that catalysis should be possible. It does not guarantee that an increase in the rate of reaction will actually take place.

## STUDY TASK

Throughout this course there are a number of references to catalysis and you should now attempt to make brief notes on all the different situations in which catalysis is important. Apart from the experiment and account given in this section, there are references to catalysis in the following sections:

- section 8.4  – catalysis in the polymerisation of alkenes
- section 11.5 – catalysis and rates of reaction
- section 14.2 – ester hydrolysis

# 19.4 The special properties of the transition elements

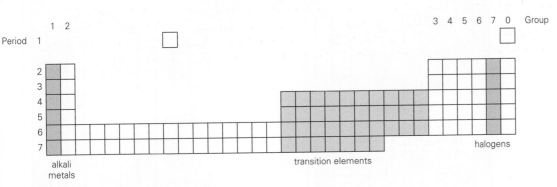

Figure 19.9 **Transition elements in the Periodic Table**

✎ **In your notes:** Write a general account of transition element chemistry in your notes, using the outline below as a basis. You should begin by explaining what a transition element is, and then list the characteristic properties with well selected examples in each case. Use the results from your experiments, together with the *Book of data*, reference books and textbooks as sources of examples.

The special properties regarded as typical of transition elements are as follows.

## 1 Similarity of physical properties

**QUESTION**

Compare the transition element diagrams with the similar diagrams for the Group 2 and Group 7 elements (Topics 4 and 6).

The physical properties of the transition elements, which are all metals, show very little variation across the row. Such properties include melting point, boiling point, density, and first ionisation energy (see figures 19.10, 11 and 12). You could produce your own versions of these diagrams using a spreadsheet program.

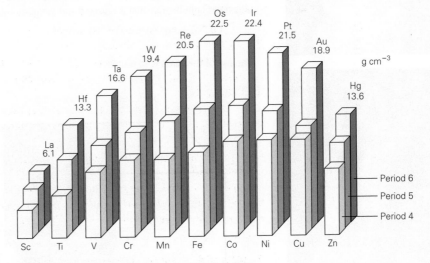

Figure 19.10 **Variation in density of the d-block elements**

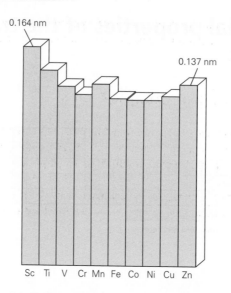

Figure 19.11   **Variation in atomic radius of the first row d-block elements**

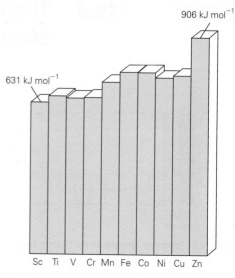

Figure 19.12   **Variation in first ionisation energy of the first row variable elements**

## 2 Variable oxidation number

**Most of the transition elements show a range of oxidation numbers in their compounds.** To review how these numbers vary in the first row transition elements, look again at the chart in section 19.1 of the oxidation numbers known to exist, with the more common ones marked in green.

### BACKGROUND

A novel application of redox equilibria is in photochromic glass. The photochromic glass contains tiny crystals of silver and copper halides: in sunlight high energy ultraviolet light causes clusters of silver atoms to form and the glass darkens. In diffused daylight with reduced ultraviolet light the reaction is reversed and the glass lightens.

$$Cu^+(s) + Ag^+(s) \rightleftharpoons Cu^{2+}(s) + Ag(s)$$

clear glass              dark glass

One use of this glass is in sunglasses.

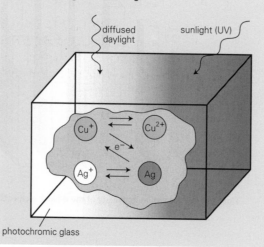

Figure 19.13   **Photochromic sunglasses**

Find examples in the *Book of data* of compounds with the more common oxidation numbers, and add any uncommon examples that you met as you worked through this topic.

# 3 Ability to form complex ions

Ions of the transition elements, and sometimes the atoms themselves, can be surrounded by, and bonded to, a number of molecules or negative ions called **ligands**. The result is a molecule or ion called a **complex**. You looked at complex ions in section 19.2.

These complexes generally have structures in which the ligand molecules or ions are arranged around the ion or atom of the transition element in one of the ways shown in section 19.2.

# 4 Colour

Many of the compounds of the transition elements are coloured, both in the solid state and in solution. The phenomenon is not, of course, confined to the compounds of the transition elements but it is relatively rare for **metal** ions outside the transition series to form coloured solutions.

# 5 Catalytic activity

Many slow reactions are accelerated by the presence of transition elements or their ions. This subject was treated in section 19.3.

# KEY SKILLS

## Communication

The study task in section 19.3 is an opportunity first to skim-read a range of documents to identify relevant material and then to scan and read the material to find specific information about catalysts. You then have to select an appropriate form for presenting the information as a concise summary.

## TOPIC REVIEW

As with the other inorganic topics, the emphasis in this one must be on patterns of behaviour and how a knowledge of them may be useful in predicting the outcome of an unfamiliar reaction.

1   **List key words or terms with definitions where necessary**

Illustrate the following with suitable **examples**:

- complex ion
- ligand, monodentate, bidentate, hexadentate
- stability constant
- transition metals and their characteristic properties
- homogenous catalysis.

2   **Summarise the key principles as simply as possible**

Illustrate the following with suitable **examples**:

- how electrode potential charts can be used to predict reaction feasibility and a mechanism by which transition metal catalysts can function

- how stability constants can be used to interpret competition between ligands and the entropy change involved

- how potassium manganate(VII) can be used in titrations to measure amounts of reducing agents.

## REVIEW QUESTIONS

✱ Indicates that the *Book of data* is needed.

✱ **19.1**    Write out the ground-state electron configuration of each of the following:

a    a chromium atom    (1)
b    a chromium(III) ion, $Cr^{3+}$    (1)
c    a cobalt atom    (1)
d    a cobalt(II) ion, $Co^{2+}$    (1)
e    a nickel atom.    (1)

**(5 marks)**

**19.2**    a    What is the oxidation number of the transition element in each of the following?

i    $MnO_4^-$    (1)          vi    $Hg_2Cl_2$    (1)
ii   $MnO_4^{2-}$    (1)          vii   $OsO_4$    (1)
iii  $VO^{2+}$    (1)          viii  $ReO_3$    (1)
iv   $VO_2^+$    (1)          ix    $Na_2MoO_4$    (1)
v    $CrO_4^{2-}$    (1)          x    $K_2IrCl_6$    (1)

b    Name the transition elements in **a vi** to **x** above.    (5)

**(15 marks)**

**✱ 19.3**   Write balanced equations for the following half-reactions and add the standard electrode potential, $E^{\ominus}$, for each one.

 a   $Fe^{3+}(aq)$ to $Fe^{2+}(aq)$                                              (2)
 b   $Sn^{2+}(aq)$ to $Sn^{4+}(aq)$                                            (2)
 c   $I^{-}(aq)$ to $I_2(aq)$                                                          (2)
 d   $H_2O_2(aq)$ to $H^{+}(aq)$ and $O_2(g)$                      (2)
 e   $MnO_4^{-}(aq)$ in acid solution to $Mn^{2+}(aq)$       (2)
 f   $Cr_2O_7^{2-}(aq)$ in acid solution to $Cr^{3+}(aq)$.      (2)

                                                                                      **(12 marks)**

**19.4**   Using graph paper, construct a chart of standard electrode potential, $E^{\ominus}$, against oxidation number for the systems in question **19.3**.

                                                                                       **(8 marks)**

**19.5**   Use your chart (question **19.4**) to predict which of the following reactions are likely to go to completion. Write balanced equations for any such reactions.

 a   the reduction of aqueous iron(III) ions by aqueous tin(II) ions            (2)
 b   the oxidation of hydrogen peroxide by acidified manganate(VII) ions in
     acid solution                                                                          (2)
 c   the oxidation of iodide ions by acidified dichromate(VI) ions               (2)
 d   the oxidation of manganese(II) ions to manganate(VII) ions by acidified
     dichromate(VI) ions                                                                  (2)
 e   the reduction of aqueous tin(IV) ions by aqueous iodine                    (2)

                                                                                     **(10 marks)**

**✱ 19.6**   2.41 g of a salt containing iron(III) ions was dissolved in dilute sulphuric acid and zinc was added to reduce the $Fe^{3+}(aq)$ to $Fe^{2+}(aq)$. The resulting solution was made up to $100 \, cm^3$ with dilute sulphuric acid and $10.0 \, cm^3$ portions were titrated with $0.0200 \, M$ potassium manganate(VII) solution. Exactly $10.0 \, cm^3$ of the $0.0200 \, M \, KMnO_4$ was required.

 a   Show by using electrode potentials that zinc should reduce $Fe^{3+}(aq)$ to
     $Fe^{2+}(aq)$.                                                                       (3)
 b   Why was the solution made up to $100 \, cm^3$ by using dilute sulphuric acid
     rather than water?                                                                  (1)
 c   Calculate the percentage of iron, by mass, in the original salt.           (5)

                                                                                       **(9 marks)**

**✱ 19.7**   When iron(III) ions, $Fe^{3+}(aq)$, are added to iodide ions, $I^{-}(aq)$, iodine is produced, but if sodium fluoride is first added the reaction does not take place. The complexes $FeF_6^{3-}$ and $FeF_6^{4-}$ both exist.

 a   The atomic number of iron is 26. State the electronic configuration of the
     $Fe^{3+}$ ion.                                                                       (1)
 b   Sketch the shape you would expect the complex $FeF_6^{3-}$ to have.     (2)
 c   What is the oxidation number of iron in $FeF_6^{4-}$?                          (1)
 d   Show by using electrode potentials that iron(III) ions should oxidise
     iodide ions under standard conditions.                                           (3)

                                                                                       **(7 marks)**

**19.8**    The stability constants for some octahedral cobalt(II) complexes are listed in the following table.

| Ligand | lg $K$ (overall) | Colour |
|--------|------------------|--------|
| $Cl^-$ | (no complex) | |
| $H_2O$ | – | pink |
| $NH_3$ | 4.39 | green |
| edta | 16.3 | pink |

a    What colour change, if any, would you expect to see when ammonia solution is added to an aqueous solution of cobalt(II) chloride?    (2)

b    What colour change, if any, would you expect to see when the solution resulting from **a** is added to hydrochloric acid? Give a reason for your answer.    (3)

c    What colour change, if any, would you expect to see when edta solution is added to an aqueous solution of cobalt(II) chloride? Give a reason for your answer.    (3)

d    Complexing by edta involves nitrogen atoms and oxygen atoms just as complexing by ammonia or water does, so why is the stability constant of Co(edta) so much larger than that of $Co(NH_3)_6^{2+}$?    (2)

**(10 marks)**

**✳ 19.9**    a    Use the *Book of data* to find lg $K_c$ (overall stability constant) at 298 K for the following complex ions:

   i   $Cu(NH_3)_4^{2+}$    (1)
   ii  $Co(NH_3)_6^{2+}$    (1)
   iii $Ni(NH_3)_6^{2+}$    (1)
   iv  $Ag(NH_3)_2^+$    (1)

b    Use the values in **a** to deduce the metal ion with which ammonia forms
   i   the most stable complex    (1)
   ii  the least stable complex.    (1)

c    With the help of the *Book of data*, predict whether edta would displace ammonia from the following complexes, justifying your predictions.

   i   $Ni(NH_3)_6^{2+}$    (2)
   ii  $Ag(NH_3)_2^+$    (2)

**(10 marks)**

# EXAMINATION QUESTIONS

**✳ 19.10**    Iron is the world's most used metal, but it rusts easily. Rusting begins as a redox process involving iron, oxygen and water. The relevant standard electrode potentials are those for the systems:

   $Fe^{2+}(aq) \,|\, Fe(s)$

   $[O_2(g) + 2H_2O(l)], 4OH^-(aq) \,|\, Pt$

a    i   Write the cell diagram for a cell using the two redox systems above.    (2)
     ii  What is the $E^\ominus$ of the cell you have written?    (2)

    **iii** Write a balanced equation, including state symbols, for the reaction between iron, oxygen and water in the cell. (2)

    **iv** Suggest TWO ways in which the actual conditions under which iron rusts in winter in the UK are likely to differ from the standard conditions of the cell. (2)

**b** Iron(II) ions are readily oxidised to iron(III) ions, which in aqueous solution form a complex with water molecules: $Fe(H_2O)_6^{3+}$ ions. These ions show acidic properties.

    **i** Draw the structure of the $Fe(H_2O)_6^{3+}$ ion. (1)

    **ii** Write an equation for the equilibrium established when an $Fe(H_2O)_6^{3+}$ ion donates a proton to a molecule of water. (2)

                                                   **(11 marks)**

**19.11** **a** The electron arrangement of copper can be written $[Ar]3d^{10}4s^1$, where $[Ar]$ refers to the electron arrangement of argon.

    **i** Use this notation to write electron arrangements for a $Cu^+$ ion and a $Cu^{2+}$ ion. (1)

    **ii** Explain on the basis of electron arrangements why copper is classed as a transition metal but zinc is not. (1)

**b** When 2-hydroxybenzoate ions are added to a solution containing $Cu(H_2O)_4^{2+}$ ions the following complex forms:

    Is the 2-hydroxybenzoate ion a mono-, bi- or tetradentate ligand? (1)

**c** The table below gives information about the colour and stability constant, $K$, of some copper(II) complexes.

| Ligand | Colour of complex | lg $K$ |
|---|---|---|
| chloride ion | yellow | 5.6 |
| 2-hydroxybenzoate ion | green | 16.9 |
| edta | pale blue | 18.8 |

    What changes in colour, if any, would you expect to see when the following solutions are added to separate test tubes containing the complex produced in **b**?

    **i** edta (1)

    **ii** sodium chloride (1)

    **iii** Justify your answers. (1)

**d** Solutions of copper(II) sulphate and potassium iodide react to form a white precipitate of copper(I) iodide and a brown solution of iodine. The ionic equation for this reaction is:

$$2Cu^{2+}(aq) + 4I^-(aq) \longrightarrow 2CuI(s) + I_2(aq)$$

    **i** Explain why this is classed as a redox reaction. (2)

    **ii** Suggest why the copper(I) iodide which forms is white, while copper(II) compounds are coloured. (2)

                                                   **(10 marks)**

**19.12** The complex compound **A**, with the formula $Na_3Co(NO_2)_6$, may be made by reacting a cobalt(II) salt with excess aqueous sodium nitrite, $NaNO_2$, in the presence of a weak acid.

The first step of the reaction may be represented by the equation:

$$Co^{2+}(aq) + NO_2^-(aq) + X \longrightarrow Co^{n+}(aq) + NO(g) + Y$$

The cobalt ion, $Co^{n+}(aq)$, formed then complexes with more nitrite ions to produce the complex cobalt salt.

a  Write the formula for the complex ion in the compound **A**. (2)

b  Complete the following statement by inserting the appropriate prefix: 'The nitrite ion is a _____ dentate ligand' (1)

c  What are the two missing items, shown as **X** and **Y**, required to balance the equation given above? (2)

d  What is the value of $n$ in the formula $Co^{n+}$ shown in the equation? (1)

e  Suggest TWO observations which would be expected during the addition of the sodium nitrite solution in the procedure described and briefly give a reason for your expectation in each case. (4)

f  What name is given to the shape of the complex ion in the compound **A**? (1)

g  i  The cobalt(II) ion, $Co^{2+}$, forms a complex with the ligand $edta^{2-}$, present in the disodium salt of edta.
What formula would be expected for this compound? (1)

ii  The stability constant for the formation of the edta complex of cobalt(II) is approximately $1 \times 10^{16}$ whereas that for the formation of its ammonia complex is approximately $1 \times 10^4$.
Explain in terms of entropy change why there is such a large difference in stability between the two complexes. (2)

**(14 marks)**

**19.13** Potassium manganate(VII) in acid solution may be used to determine the concentration of iron(II) ions by titration.

a  Copy, complete and balance the equation:

$$MnO_4^-(aq) + \underline{\quad}(aq) + 5Fe^{2+}(aq) \longrightarrow \underline{\quad}(aq) + \underline{\quad}(aq) + \underline{\quad}(l) \quad (2)$$

b  0.350 g of a sample of impure iron wire was reacted with excess sulphuric acid to convert the iron into a solution of iron(II) ions. The impurities may be assumed to be inert.
The solution was made up to exactly $100 \text{ cm}^3$ in a volumetric flask.
$10.0 \text{ cm}^3$ portions of this diluted solution required $11.8 \text{ cm}^3$ of $0.0100 \text{ M}$ potassium manganate(VII) for complete reaction.

i  Explain why this titration is said to be self-indicating. (1)

ii  Calculate the number of moles of $KMnO_4$ used in the titration; the number of moles of $Fe^{2+}(aq)$ used in the titration; the mass of iron in the sample of iron wire and the percentage purity of the iron wire. (4)

**(7 marks)**

**19.14** The complex compound *cis*-dichlorodiammineplatinum(II), also known as '*cis*-diplatin', shows activity against cancer cells.

**a  i** What type of bonding exists between the ammonia molecules and the platinum atom? (1)

**ii** What feature of the ammonia molecule enables this type of bond to form? (1)

**iii** What name is given to molecules such as ammonia when they are involved in forming this type of compound? (1)

**b  i** What is the value of the N—Pt—Cl bond angle in *cis*-diplatin? (1)

**ii** Draw the structural formula of an isomer of *cis*-diplatin which will have similar bond angles. (1)

**c** *Cis*-diplatin reacts to form new complexes with compounds in the nuclei of cells. One such compound is adenine.

$$
\begin{array}{c}
NH_2 \\
| \\
C \\
\end{array}
$$

**i** Which atoms in the adenine molecule are most likely to bond to the platinum atom in these complexes? (1)

**ii** What ions or molecules are likely to be released in this reaction? (1)

**iii** Suggest a reason why *cis*-diplatin shows anti-cancer cell activity, and not the isomer you have drawn in **b**. (2)

**(9 marks)**

# Organic synthesis

The purpose of organic synthesis is the preparation of useful substances from simpler materials which are readily available from natural products or the petrochemical industry. The design of the often complex molecular structures required for use as drugs, pesticides, perfumes or polymers depends upon a knowledge of the reactions of the functional groups of carbon compounds and an understanding of the mechanisms by which they occur.

The search for more effective drugs often requires the synthesis of hundreds of compounds which are variations on a basic structure. For example cocaine is an effective local anaesthetic but has dangerous side effects which prohibit its general use; however other compounds with a similar structure, such as benzocaine, have been developed which are safe enough to be available without prescription.

Figure 20.1 **Researchers developing new medicinal drugs**

In this topic you are going to develop strategies for making new organic compounds. You will therefore be revising the reactions of organic compounds by using them to work out synthetic routes for the conversion of compounds having simple molecules into more complex and useful substances.

There are four main activities in this topic. You will:

- **assemble flow charts of synthetic routes** based upon the summary of reactions you have constructed at the end of each organic topic
- **perform the two-step synthesis** of methyl 3-nitrobenzoate which will remind you of the techniques needed to obtain a reasonable yield of pure product
- **use the results of modern instrumental techniques** to help you identify unknown substances
- **revise the carbon chemistry in the course**, using the examination questions that are available at the end of the topic.

## 20.1 Devising a synthesis

The enormous range of carbon compounds that are known to exist is the result of the ability of atoms of carbon to join together to form extensive chain or ring structures and to establish covalent bonds to atoms of hydrogen, oxygen and nitrogen which are of similar strength to the bonds that they form with each other.

There are over nine million reported organic compounds, but fortunately their behaviour can be understood in terms of the **functional groups** which they contain. These functional groups usually follow the same type of reactions even though they may be attached to different carbon skeletons. For example, the functional groups of an alcohol, an alkene, or a ketone, behave in a characteristic manner whether they are found in simple molecules such as those of ethanol, ethene and propanone or in a complex molecule such as that of the steroid hormone cortisone.

### COMMENT

| Bond | Bond energy /kJ mol$^{-1}$ |
|------|------|
| C—H | 413 |
| C—O | 336 |
| C—N | 286 |
| C—C | 347 |

Use table 4.6 in the *Book of data* to compare these values with other single bond values

$$CH_3—CH_2OH$$
ethanol

$$CH_2{=}CH_2$$
ethene

$$CH_3—CO—CH_3$$
propanone

Figure 20.2   **Russell Marker collected 10 tons of yam plants in the 1930s in order to investigate the properties of female hormones. At that time no one was interested in his work so he had to finance his expedition to the Mexican jungle himself. His work was eventually developed into the first contraceptive pill**

The structure of cortisone was confirmed in 1951 by the American chemist Robert Woodward who completed its synthesis in more than forty steps! This achievement clearly involved a remarkable manipulation of the bond-making and bond-breaking processes of carbon compounds. In order to assemble structures of this degree of complexity, where the basic carbon framework must be built from simpler structures, the synthetic chemist needs to deploy suitable **carbon–carbon bond-forming reactions** as well as **functional group interconversions** which alter the groups attached to the basic carbon skeleton.

# The general approach

The natural starting point for planning a synthesis is an examination of the desired end-product which is called the **target molecule**. Listing its functional groups will enable a plan to be made for its synthesis from simpler and more readily available **starting materials**. Several steps may well be necessary and a number of **intermediates** may have to be formed first before a synthesis of the target molecule can be achieved. However, the strategy always involves **working backwards** in a logical sequence from the target molecule until suitable starting materials can be identified.

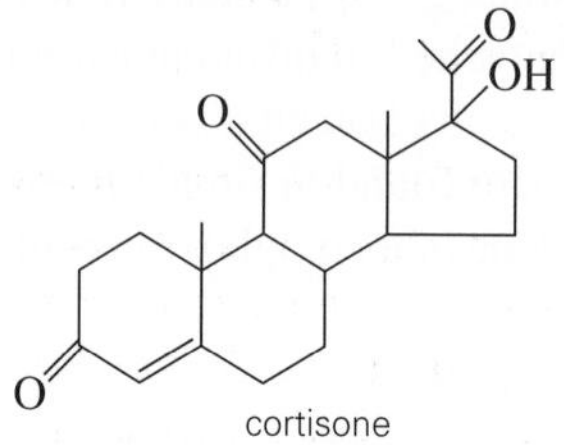

Figure 20.3   **Cortisone (Woodward's target molecule)**

Starting materials must be cheap and easily available. In practice this means that the majority will be derived from the simpler hydrocarbons obtained by petroleum refining, although natural products from plant and animal sources may also be useful.

## BACKGROUND

### The synthesis of complex drugs containing iodine

The X-ray departments of hospitals regularly use iodine compounds when taking X-ray pictures of soft tissue rather than bone (see section 6.8). Inorganic salts containing iodine are not used as any suitable compound has to be soluble in our blood, absorbed by cells, not interfere with our metabolism and be readily excreted without the risk of being converted into toxic by-products by enzyme catalysts.

The search for a suitable organic compound containing iodine started in 1928 and led in 1950 to a triiodobenzene compound ('Urokon'), based on 3-aminobenzoic acid and therefore ionic.

Two years of synthetic effort resulted in a better compound but with a much more elaborate structure ('Conray'). This compound is a relatively low cost product, but can have serious side effects for a few patients.

A better product, 'Omnipaque', with an even more elaborate structure has been produced by further synthetic effort backed by detailed medical studies. One reason for the advantages of this compound is that it is non-toxic.

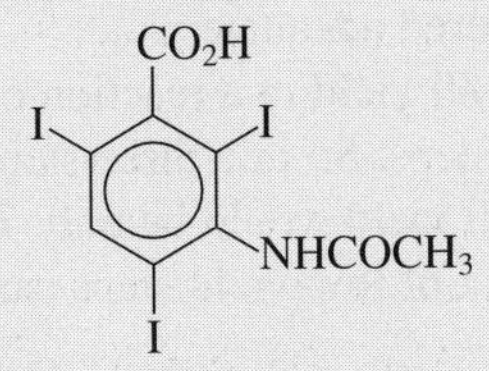

'Urokon'

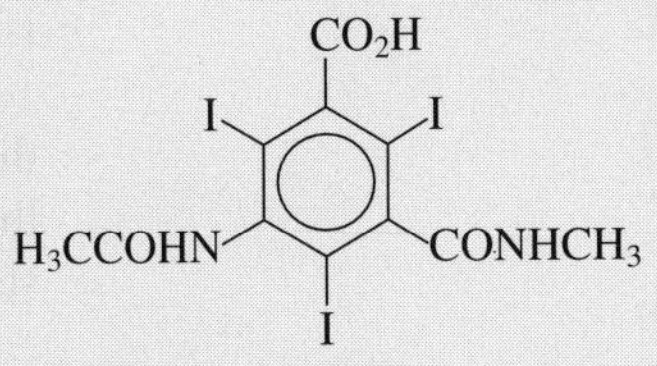

'Conray'

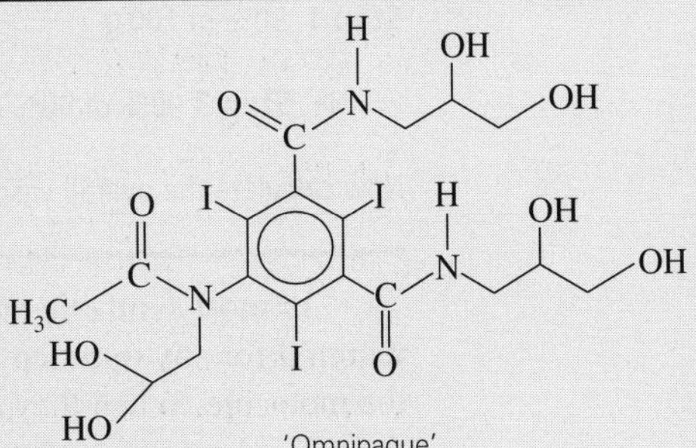

'Omnipaque'

## STUDY TASK

### Some synthetic routes

Use your summary charts from the end of each organic chemistry topic to help you with these questions. When you write down your synthetic route in the final part of each question, use structural formulae and give the reaction conditions over the arrows between compounds, but do not give any details of mechanisms.

1   Some 1,2-dibromobutane has to be made from butan-1-ol.
  a   What functional group does butan-1-ol contain?
  b   Write down the structural formula of the target molecule.
  c   What sort of reaction can place two bromine atoms on neighbouring carbon atoms?
  d   What intermediate compound must you have in order to make 1,2-dibromobutane by reaction c? Write down its name and its structural formula.
  e   Write down your suggested route, using structural formulae.

2   Your problem is to find a way of converting 1-bromobutane into butanoic acid.
  a   What are the structural formulae of these compounds?
  b   Is there the same number of carbon atoms in the target molecule as in the starting material?
  c   What functional group does the target molecule contain?
  d   The target molecule can be prepared by an oxidation reaction. What would be a suitable compound to treat in this manner?
  e   Can this compound d be made from 1-bromobutane, and if so, how?
  f   Write down the synthetic route for the changes you have suggested.

# Problems in devising a synthesis

In more complex syntheses there will often be more than one possible route to the target molecule and choices will have to be made.

The most desirable route is likely to be the one requiring the fewest steps. Most reactions of carbon compounds are accompanied by side reactions which result in the formation of minor products as well as the major product. A reaction yield of 90% would be considered excellent, 80% is extremely good and even 50% is often considered adequate.

The overall yield in a reaction of several steps is the product of the yields of the individual steps. So in a three-step synthesis where each step had a 90% yield the final overall yield would be only 73%. Clearly in complex syntheses of many stages the effect of low-yield steps can be disastrous.

## QUESTION

**Step 1** 90% of 100 g $\longrightarrow$ **Step 2** 90% of 90% of 100 g

$\longrightarrow$ **Step 3** 90% of 90% of 90% of 100 g $= \dfrac{90 \times 90 \times 90}{100 \times 100 \times 100} \times 100\,\text{g} = 73\,\text{g}$

Now calculate the overall yield when each step has a yield of only 50%.

In most synthetic problems it will be essential to check that the reagents required for any one step in the synthesis do not react with other groups present in the molecule. When they do it may be necessary to 'protect' these groups while the desired reaction is carried out. Also, it will often be important to perform the synthesis in a definite ordered sequence, because changing the functional group may result in changes of reactivity that might block the next step.

Another complication can be the presence of chiral centres in the target molecules. The correct isomer has to be synthesised because, especially for drugs, only one of the isomers is an effective product.

Factors associated with health and safety as well as economics will always be important in devising a commercial synthetic route.

There is often no single correct solution to a synthetic problem; several routes may be equally possible. An 'elegant' synthesis will achieve the target molecule by an optimum route which involves the minimum number of steps each with maximum yields, at an acceptable cost.

## STUDY TASK

**Mapping synthetic routes**

You should now prepare three large **flow charts** which summarise all the reactions you have met in carbon chemistry. These will provide you with a map with which you should be able to work out synthetic routes.

The three flow charts should be:

1 **Alkanes, alkenes and halogenoalkanes**

2 **Alcohols, carboxylic acids and their derivatives**

3 **Arenes**

You may choose to link Flow charts 1 and 2 together if you have a large enough sheet of paper.

Use your summary reaction schemes from the end of each organic topic to draw up the flow charts in the following way:

a include the conditions needed for each **functional group interconversion**, which you should write above the arrow; below the arrow you may like to remind yourself of the reaction type, e.g. substitution or oxidation

b illustrate the functional groups in the flow charts by using the structural formula of ethene for Flow chart 1, ethanol for Flow chart 2 and benzene for Flow chart 3

c highlight any **carbon–carbon bond forming reactions** in Flow chart 3.

You may prefer to create these flow charts in your own way, but three possible frameworks are given below.

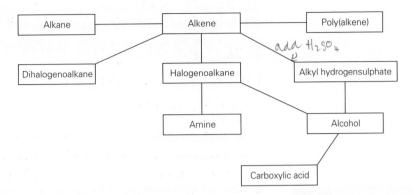

Figure 20.4 **Flow chart 1: alkanes, alkenes and halogenoalkanes**

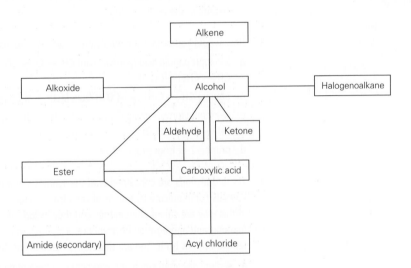

Figure 20.5 **Flow chart 2: alcohols, carboxylic acids and their derivatives**

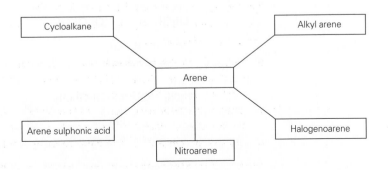

Figure 20.6 **Flow chart 3: arenes**

---

STUDY TASK

## Planning synthetic routes

Here are a selection of synthetic problems for you to try to solve. Use your flow charts to gain familiarity with the synthetic routes available to you, first for simple conversions and then for the more complex syntheses which lead to useful products. In each case write structural formulae for the target molecule, starting material, and any intermediates with the reaction conditions over the arrow.

1   How would you synthesise the following compounds using ethanol alone as the starting material?

   a   ethane

   b   ethyl ethanoate

   c   ethylamine

2   How would you synthesise the following compounds using benzene alone as the starting material?

   a   4-bromo-ethylbenzene

   b   4-amino-propylbenzene
       Assume that the reactions you choose place the new functional group in the position you require in the benzene ring.

BACKGROUND

Definite rules govern the position of substitution in benzene and these can be found in more advanced texts.

3   How would you obtain the following target compounds?

   a   2-oxopropanoic acid (pyruvic acid) $CH_3$—CO—$CO_2H$, from 2-bromopropanoic acid $CH_3$—CHBr—$CO_2H$

   b   alanine $CH_3$—$CHNH_2$—$CO_2H$ from lactic acid $CH_3$—CHOH—$CO_2H$

   c   N-ethanoylpropylamine $CH_3$—$CH_2$—$CH_2$—NH—CO—$CH_3$ from 1-bromopropane $CH_3$—$CH_2$—$CH_2Br$

   d   propan-2-ol from propan-1-ol

4   These questions are concerned with the synthesis of a number of **pheromones**. Many animals communicate by means of chemical signals. Substances used to convey information in this way are called pheromones and they include sex attractants, alarm signals, trail marking and aggregation pheromones. Aggregation pheromones attract either male or female but not both, and are therefore potentially useful in controlling insect populations.

   a   4-methylheptan-3-ol is the aggregation pheromone of the European elm beetle. Suggest how this might be synthesised from 4-methylhept-3-ene which is available from petroleum distillates.

4-methylheptan-3-ol

4-methylhept-3-ene

**b** This question concerns pheromones that have ester groups.

    **i** 3-methylbutyl ethanoate is a component of the alarm pheromone of the honey bee. Write the structural formulae and name the starting materials needed to make this substance in one step.

    **ii** Heptyl butanoate is used as a bait in wasp traps. Suggest a synthesis for this substance in one step.

    **iii** The ester phenylmethyl benzoate is used as an insect repellent. Suggest a synthesis of this substance using benzoic acid as the only starting material.

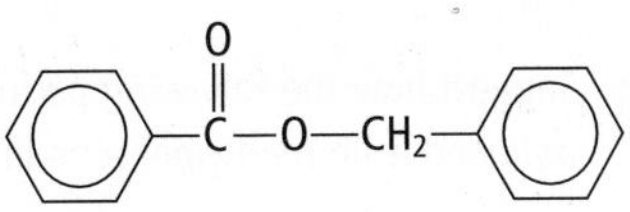

phenylmethyl benzoate

**5** These questions are concerned with substances with pleasant smells used in perfume preparations.

    **a** Diphenylmethane is used to impart a geranium odour to soap. What two starting materials would be needed to make this substance in a one-step synthesis and what catalyst would you use?

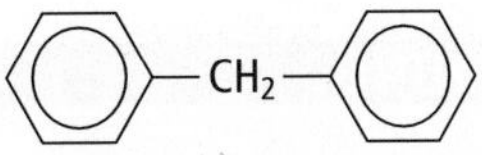

diphenylmethane

    **b** The valuable musk range of perfumes are only available naturally from a small gland in the male musk deer. Musk ambrette (**i**) is a synthetic musk used to enhance and retain the musk odour in perfumes and can be made from the starting material 3-methylmethoxybenzene (**ii**) in a two-step synthesis.

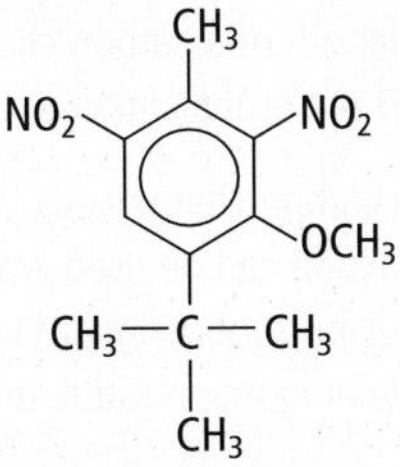

(**i**) musk ambrette 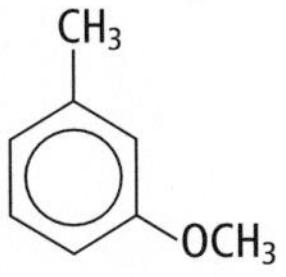    (**ii**) 3-methylmethoxybenzene

    What other carbon compound will be needed for the synthesis? Write down your two-step synthesis assuming that the functional groups are added to the benzene ring in the correct positions.

    **c** 1-phenylethanol has a powerful floral odour and is also used in perfumes. How could it be synthesised from phenylethene in two steps?

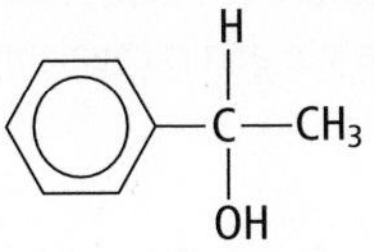

1-phenylethanol 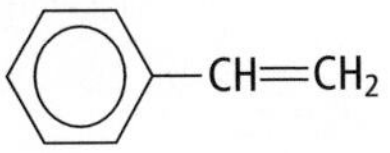    phenylethene

**d** What steps would be necessary to convert the synthetic perfume (**i**) into the appetite suppressant drug, phentamine (**ii**)?

(**i**) a carbinol perfume                    (**ii**) phentamine

**e** Suggest how the following perfume, a constituent of jasmine flower oil, might be obtained from methylbenzene in a multi-step synthesis.

phenylmethyl ethanoate

## BACKGROUND

### Changing the length of the carbon chain

In the synthesis of materials such as detergents, dyes and drugs chemists often need to alter the length of a carbon chain in order to achieve their target product.

One way of increasing the length of a carbon chain in a molecule by one carbon atom is to introduce the nitrile functional group —CN. Nitriles are readily converted to a carboxylic acid or amine.

To decrease the length of a carbon chain, the silver salt of a carboxylic acid can be treated with bromine and the organic molecule will lose a carbon atom as carbon dioxide.

More usually the carbon chain needs to be increased by several carbon atoms and the Friedel–Crafts reaction can be used when benzene rings are involved. When an alcohol functional group is present, Grignard reagents can be used. These are organometallic compounds, containing magnesium, and have to be used in rigorously dry conditions.

Chain lengths may need to be changed so that the target molecule has the most effective shape and size, for example drugs that are required to interact with enzymes have to have exact shapes if they are to fit an active site.

Examples are drugs called 'suicide substrates' which are designed to block the active site on enzymes. Suicide substrates bind irreversibly to an enzyme. You can find out more about the inhibition of enzymes in the Special Study *Biochemistry*.

Figure 20.7 (opposite) shows an enzyme that reduces the vitamin folic acid, and in some cases problems occur because too much folic acid is being reduced. A suicide substrate is shown blocking the active site and is covalently bonded to the amino acid serine.

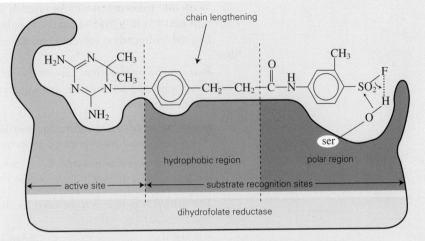

**Figure 20.7   A suicide substrate. You can read about the importance of folic acid on some cereal packets**

# 20.2   A two-step synthesis

You are now going to carry out a full-scale laboratory synthesis in two steps, followed by some simple tests to check the purity of your product. You should calculate your yield at each step, and also your overall yield.

You may be able to carry out a similar two-step synthesis using microscale techniques, from instructions your teacher can provide.

---

**EXPERIMENT 20.2**

## The synthesis of methyl 3-nitrobenzoate in two steps

There is a microscale alternative to this experiment

The first step is the preparation of the intermediate ester, methyl benzoate. You will be using a standard procedure for the preparation of esters.

$$CH_3OH + HO-\overset{\displaystyle O}{\underset{}{C}}-\bigcirc \underset{acid}{\rightleftharpoons} CH_3-O-\overset{\displaystyle O}{\underset{}{C}}-\bigcirc + H_2O$$

methanol      benzoic acid              methyl benzoate

---

**SAFETY**

**Methanol is toxic and highly flammable.
Concentrated sulphuric acid is corrosive.
The hydrocarbon solvent used is flammable.
The product methyl benzoate is harmful.**

## Procedure: Step 1  Formation of the ester, methyl benzoate

To a 50 cm$^3$ pear-shaped flask add 8 g of benzoic acid, 15 cm$^3$ of methanol, and 2 cm$^3$ of concentrated sulphuric acid. Fit the flask with a reflux condenser and boil the mixture for about 45 minutes.

Cool the mixture to room temperature and pour it into a separating funnel that contains 30 cm$^3$ of cold water. Rinse the flask with 15 cm$^3$ of hydrocarbon solvent and pour this into the separating funnel.

Mix the contents of the separating funnel by vigorous shaking, releasing the pressure carefully from time to time, allow them to settle, and run the lower aqueous layer into a conical flask.

Wash the hydrocarbon solvent layer in the separating funnel with 15 cm³ of water and then 15 cm³ of 0.5 M aqueous sodium carbonate solution.

Dry the hydrocarbon solvent extract over anhydrous sodium sulphate, and filter.

Remove the hydrocarbon solvent by careful distillation. Complete the distillation, collecting the distillate boiling above 190 °C as methyl benzoate.

Weigh your product.

**In your notes:** What is the percentage yield, based on the mass of benzoic acid you used in your preparation? The yield should be about 70%.

Which bonds could have broken in the reaction? You should find that two patterns of bond-breaking are possible.

The methyl benzoate is to be used for the next step.

$$\underset{\text{methyl benzoate}}{\text{CO}_2\text{CH}_3} + \text{HNO}_3 \xrightarrow{\text{H}_2\text{SO}_4} \underset{\substack{\text{methyl} \\ \text{3-nitrobenzoate}}}{\text{CO}_2\text{CH}_3} \text{NO}_2 + \text{H}_2\text{O}$$

The nitration of your methyl benzoate is again a standard procedure, but the wrong conditions could reverse the first step and the temperature and concentration of the nitric acid will influence the number and position of the nitro groups substituted into the benzene ring.

## Procedure: Step 2 The nitration of methyl benzoate

1  Measure 9 cm² of concentrated sulphuric acid (TAKE CARE) into a 100 cm³ conical flask and cool it to below 10 °C in an ice bath. Add 4 cm³ of methyl benzoate while swirling the flask. Prepare a mixture of 3 cm³ of concentrated nitric acid with 3 cm³ of concentrated sulphuric acid in another small flask and cool the mixture in the ice bath.

2  Use a dropping pipette to add the nitric acid–sulphuric acid mixture a drop at a time to the methyl benzoate solution. Swirl the conical flask and control the rate of addition so that the temperature stays in the range 5 to 15 °C. The addition should take about 15 minutes.

3  When the addition is complete, remove the flask from the ice bath and allow it to stand at room temperature for 10 minutes. Pour the reaction mixture over 40 g of crushed ice and stir until the product solidifies. Collect the product by suction filtration after waiting until all the ice melts. Wash with three portions of water, sucking dry and disconnecting the suction pump before each addition of washing water.

4  Change the Buchner flask for a smaller clean dry Buchner flask and wash the product with two portions of 5 cm³ of **ice cold** ethanol. **Keep this wash liquid for examination by chromatography**.

5  To recrystallise the product, transfer it to a 100 cm³ conical flask and add about 15 cm³ of ethanol, the minimum value that will dissolve the solid when hot. Heat a water bath to boiling and **turn out the Bunsen burner** before

**SAFETY** ⚠

Concentrated sulphuric acid is corrosive.
Concentrated nitric acid is corrosive and a powerful oxidant.
Methyl benzoate is flammable and harmful.
Ethanol is highly flammable.

putting the conical flask containing the ethanol in the water bath. When the solid has dissolved, it can be recovered by cooling the solution in an ice bath and collecting, by suction filtration, the crystals which form. Methyl 3-nitrobenzoate is a pale yellow solid of melting point 78 °C.

When your product is dry, weigh it.

For **chromatography** evaporate the wash liquid to 1 cm³ in an evaporating basin, either by standing it overnight or by heating it on a hot water bath. Use a fine capillary tube to put a spot of the solution 2 cm from the bottom of a thin layer of silica on an inert support. Some of the product can be dissolved to make a second separate spot on the plate. Allow the solvent to evaporate and develop with an ethoxyethane–hexane mixture containing 1 volume of ethoxyethane to 9 volumes of hexane.

Methyl 2-nitrobenzoate, a minor product, should be visible on the silica sheet as a yellow spot, while methyl 3-nitrobenzoate can be seen under ultraviolet light or by exposing the sheet to iodine vapour.

The **melting point** of your product should now be determined.

**SAFETY**

Ethoxyethane ('ether') is extremely flammable; inhalation of vapour may cause dizziness and unconsciousness.
Hexane is highly flammable and harmful.
Do not look directly at the ultraviolet light.
Iodine is harmful. If iodine is used, take care not to expose yourself to the vapour.

## 20.3 The identification of organic compounds

Knowledge of the composition and structure of organic compounds is now largely based on instrumental methods, making use of mass spectrometers, infrared spectrometers, and nuclear magnetic resonance spectrometers (see Topic 21). Examination by these techniques will give precise information on the composition of a compound and the presence of various functional groups in the molecule. Nevertheless, older-established techniques are still useful and necessary.

### Combustion analysis of organic compounds

**Combustion analysis is used to determine the empirical formulae of organic compounds.** An exact mass of the organic compound is burnt in oxygen, producing carbon dioxide and water from the carbon and hydrogen in the compound.

The mass of carbon dioxide is converted into the number of moles of carbon in the sample in two steps:

mass of carbon dioxide/g $\longrightarrow$ mass of carbon/g
$\longrightarrow$ amount of carbon/mol

The same procedure enables the number of moles of hydrogen in the sample to be determined.

To find out how much oxygen, if any, was present in the sample of the compound, the original mass of the sample must be compared with the combined masses of carbon and hydrogen (and other elements if present), as determined by the combustion analysis. Any original mass of sample not accounted for is attributed to an oxygen content and used to calculate the number of moles of oxygen in the sample of the compound:

(mass of sample/g) − (mass of C, H/g) $\longrightarrow$ mass of oxygen/g
$\longrightarrow$ amount of oxygen/mol

The empirical formula of the compound is then determined as the whole number ratio of the moles of the elements present.

The empirical formula of a compound can only be converted to a molecular formula when the molar mass of the compound is known.

$n \times$ **empirical formula** = **molecular formula**

$n \times$ **empirical mass**     = **molar mass**

The molar mass can be obtained from a low resolution mass spectrum, provided the spectrum contains a peak corresponding to positively charged ions which are complete molecules of the compound, the **parent ion** peak.

## BACKGROUND

One method for the determination of the elemental composition of organic compounds involves their complete combustion in pure, dry oxygen. An exact mass (between 0.1 g and 0.3 g) of the compound is burned in a stream of oxygen diluted with helium gas and the combustion products are passed through a complex sequence of chemicals to ensure that the only gaseous products are carbon dioxide, water vapour, and nitrogen, mixed with helium. The amount of carbon dioxide is used to calculate the carbon content, the amount of water vapour is used to calculate the hydrogen content, and the amount of nitrogen gas to calculate any nitrogen content of the compound.

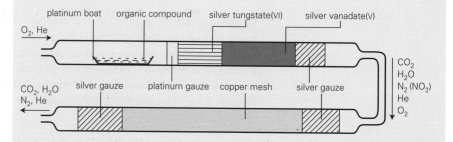

Volatile compounds of phosphorus, sulphur, and the halogens are all removed from the gas stream by reaction with chemicals that convert them to involatile substances, while the excess oxygen is removed by reaction with copper. The copper also serves to reduce any oxides of nitrogen to nitrogen gas. The mass of water vapour in the gas stream is determined by comparing the thermal conductivity of the gas stream before and after passing through 'Anhydrone'. Anhydrone absorbs water vapour.

A similar procedure is used to determine the mass of carbon dioxide in the gas stream, using soda lime to absorb carbon dioxide, while the mass of nitrogen is determined by comparing the thermal conductivity of pure helium with the nitrogen–helium gas stream.

To obtain a pure sample for analysis, or to separate a mixture before analysis, gas chromatography is commonly used when the compounds are sufficiently volatile and stable.

# Sample problem 1

COMMENT

Molar mass of
C = 12 g mol$^{-1}$
H = 1 g mol$^{-1}$

0.205 g of the liquid, **A**, on complete combustion produced 0.660 g of carbon dioxide and 0.225 g of water. The mass spectrometer parent ion peak is at 81.0. What is the molecular formula of **A**?

## Calculation

*Part 1: Determination of the empirical formula of* **A**

0.660 g of carbon dioxide contains $0.660 \times \dfrac{12}{44} g = 0.180$ g of carbon

0.225 g of water contains $\qquad 0.225 \times \dfrac{2}{18} g = 0.025$ g of hydrogen

0.180 g + 0.025 g = 0.205 g which is the mass of the original sample

So **A** consists of carbon and hydrogen only.

0.180 g of carbon is $\dfrac{0.180}{12}$ mol = 0.015 mol of carbon atoms

0.025 g of hydrogen is $\dfrac{0.025}{1}$ mol = 0.025 mol of hydrogen atoms

0.015 mol carbon atoms/0.025 mol hydrogen atoms = 3C/5H

So the empirical formula of **A** is $C_3H_5$.

*Part 2: Determination of the molar mass of* **A**
The parent ion peak from the mass spectrometer indicates

molar mass = 81.0 g mol$^{-1}$

*Part 3: Determination of the molecular formula of* **A**

$$n \times \text{empirical mass} = \text{molar mass}$$
$$n \times (C_3H_5) = 81.0 \text{ g mol}^{-1}$$
$$n \times 41 = 81.0$$
$$\text{so } n = 2, \text{ to the nearest whole number}$$

## Answer

Therefore the molecular formula of **A** is $(C_3H_5)_2$ or $C_6H_{10}$.

# Sample problem 2

COMMENT

Molar masses of C = 12,
H = 1, N = 14,
O = 16 g mol$^{-1}$

0.220 g of the liquid **B** on complete combustion produced 0.472 g of carbon dioxide, 0.080 g of water, and 0.025 g of nitrogen. The mass spectrometer parent ion peak is at 123.0. What is the molecular formula of **B**?

## Answer

You should find that the empirical formula of **B** is the same as the molecular formula and is $C_6H_5NO_2$, nitrobenzene.

| EXPERIMENT 20.3 | # The identification of organic compounds |

You are asked to try to identify three unknown organic compounds.

You will be provided with the three compounds labelled **A**, **B**, and **C**. **A** and **B** contain carbon, hydrogen, and oxygen only.

The problem is to confirm their identity with as much certainty as possible. You should check, therefore, that all the data available are consistent with any identity you propose and not 'jump to conclusions' using only part of the data.

## Procedure: compound A

1   The quantitative analysis of **A** gives C, 68.9%; H, 4.9%; O, 26.2%. Use these data to calculate the empirical formula of **A**.

2   Use the mass spectrum of **A** to deduce the molar mass of **A**, assuming that a parent ion peak is present, and determine the masses of the fragment ions from **A**. Use the molar mass and empirical formula of **A** to calculate the molecular formula of **A**. What are the likely formulae of the seven fragment ions?

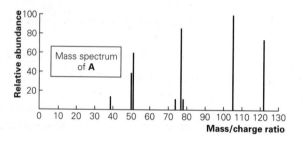

3   Use the infrared spectrum of **A** and table 3.3 in the *Book of data* to identify the functional group(s) and nature of the hydrocarbon group in **A**.

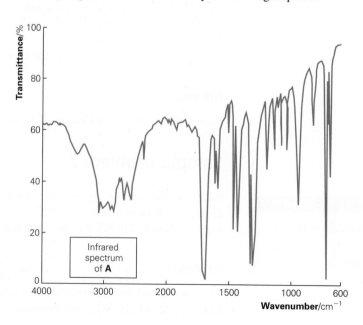

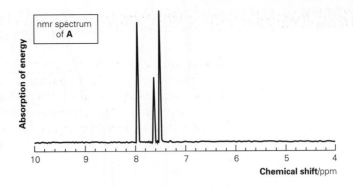

4   Use the nmr spectrum of **A**, together with the chemical shifts for hydrogen in table 3.4 in the *Book of data*, to make suggestions about the molecular environment of the hydrogen atoms in **A**.

5   Carry out the following experiments with **A**.

   **a** Burn a small amount on a combustion spoon. What type of flame is obtained? What can you deduce about **A**?

   **b** Test the solubility of **A** in water by shaking a small amount with 5 cm³ of water. If it does not dissolve in cold water, see if it will dissolve in hot water. What can you deduce about **A**?

   **c** Test a warm solution of **A** with 5 cm³ of 1 M sodium carbonate solution. What can you deduce about **A**?

   **d** Determine the melting point of **A**.

6   What is your conclusion about the identity of **A**?

**SAFETY**   !

The organic substances are flammable.
When you set fire to each of the unknown substances, do so with very small quantities, and remember that the fumes evolved include toxic gases, such as carbon monoxide.

## Procedure: compound B

**1–4** Follow the same procedure as for **A**. The analysis of **B** gives C, 60.0%; H, 13.3%; O, 26.7%. The mass, infrared and nmr spectra are given in the diagrams below.

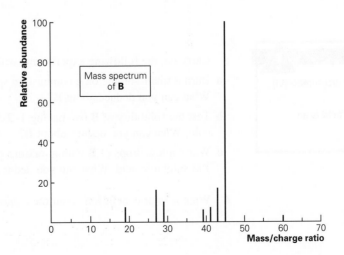

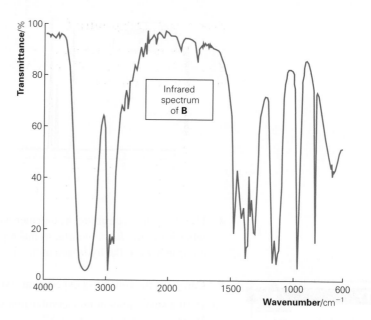

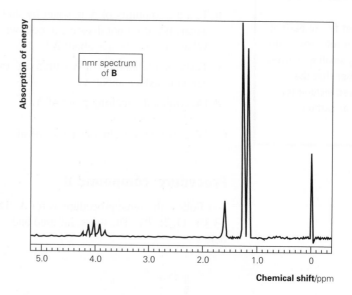

**SAFETY** !

0.1 M sodium dichromate(VI) is toxic.
1 M sulphuric acid is an irritant.

**5** Carry out the following experiments with **B**.

**a** Burn a small volume on a combustion spoon. What type of flame is obtained? What can you deduce about **B**?

**b** Test the solubility of **B** by shaking 1–2 cm³ of **B** with 5 cm³ of water, hot and cold. What can you deduce about **B**?

**c** Warm a few drops of **B** with a mixture of aqueous sodium dichromate(VI) and 1 M sulphuric acid. What can you deduce about **B**?

**6** What is your conclusion about the identity of **B**?

## Procedure: compound C

**1–3** Follow the same procedure as for **A** and **B**. The analysis of **C** gives C, 71.1%; H, 6.7%; O, 11.9%; N, 10.4%, and the mass spectrum and infrared spectrum are given in the diagrams below.

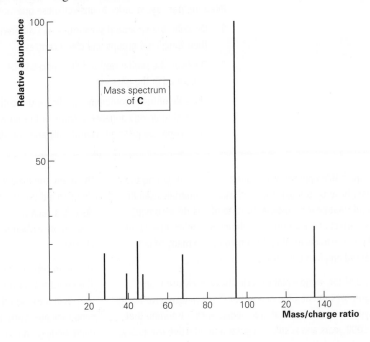

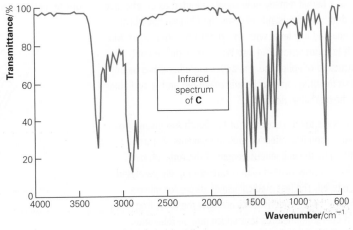

**SAFETY**

0.05 M bromine water is harmful and an irritant. 1 M sulphuric acid is an irritant.

**4**  Carry out the following experiments with **C**.

**a**  Burn a small quantity on a combustion spoon. What type of flame is obtained? What can you deduce about **C**?

**b**  Test the solubility of **C** in water by shaking a small quantity with 5 cm³ of water, cold and hot. Allow to cool slowly. Test the pH of the solution. What can you deduce about **C**?

**c**  To 5 cm³ of bromine water add a small quantity of **C**. What can you deduce about **C**?

**d**  To 5 cm³ of dilute acid or alkali add a small quantity of **C** and warm. Allow to cool slowly. What can you deduce about **C**?

**5**  What is your conclusion about the identity of **C**?

## 20.4 Background reading: drugs

| QUESTIONS |

Read the passage in order to answer these questions.

1 Describe the structural similarities and differences of morphine, codeine and heroin. Refer to their functional groups and chiral centres.

2 Describe the similarities and differences of benzocaine to the other local anaesthetics illustrated in the passage.

3 The sale of items containing alcohol and nicotine is legal to adults over 18; the sale or use of items containing cannabis, cocaine or heroin is illegal for the general public. Can these distinctions be justified scientifically and socially?

The most remarkable applications of organic chemistry during the last 100 years have occurred in the synthesis of materials used in the successful treatment of disease. In spite of this development over three-quarters of the world's population still relies mainly on plants and plant extracts for their health care, and many of our drugs are based on plant derivatives.

About a third of the world's plant species have been used for medicinal purposes at one time or another. The Chinese have been the most systematic users of herbal remedies with a tradition that goes back 5000 years and is still in regular and effective use today. An example of a herbal remedy now widely adopted as an effective drug is ephedrine. For thousands of years the Chinese have been treating asthma and hay fever with an extract from their shrub Ma Huang, but it was not introduced into Western medicine until 1924. The structure of ephedrine, the active ingredient, has been worked out so the drug can now be manufactured and is available pure and in the quantities needed.

Another example is the development of the South American arrow poison, called curare, into effective muscle relaxants. Curare is used for hunting by the indigenous people of the Amazon river. Animals hit by an arrow treated with curare are rapidly paralysed and easily captured. The first medical use of curare for muscle relaxation was in 1942. Its derivatives are now the most frequently used drugs in operating theatres to produce muscle relaxation without the need for high doses of anaesthetics.

The discovery and development of new drugs is a difficult and expensive process. Until recently drug discovery was largely based upon the random screening of numerous chemical compounds obtained from natural sources and by laboratory synthesis; but only one potential drug in 10 000 compounds is likely to survive rigorous testing procedures and become commercially available for medical use.

There have been huge developments in our understanding in recent years of how our bodies work, which has led to a more rational approach to drug design. For example, the study of the structure of

the brain and how it works has led to the successful design of drugs to aid the treatment of people with a wide range of mental disorders such as schizophrenia or clinical depression. These drugs may be prescribed to control some of the symptoms of these illnesses.

The brain consists mainly of two types of cells, neurons and glia. The neurons transmit information; the functions of the glia are still unknown although they comprise 85% of the brain. One neuron communicates with another from specialised nerve endings. At a nerve ending an incoming electrical impulse will trigger the release of chemicals called neurotransmitters.

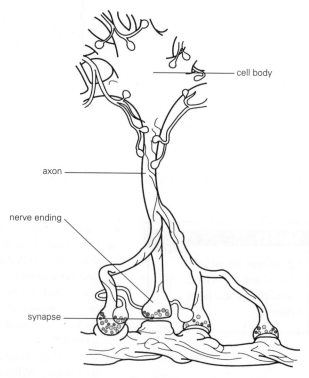

Figure 20.8 **The nerve structure of the brain, first identified by the Spanish scientist Santiago Ramón y Cajal**

The neurotransmitters diffuse to receptors on the next neuron and stimulate its electrical activity. At any stage of the process there may be a problem resulting in the release of excess neurotransmitters and over-stimulation of the neurons, or alternatively there may be a shortage of neurotransmitter molecules.

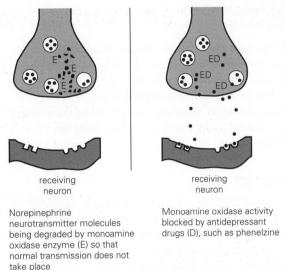

Norepinephrine neurotransmitter molecules being degraded by monoamine oxidase enzyme (E) so that normal transmission does not take place

Monoamine oxidase activity blocked by antidepressant drugs (D), such as phenelzine

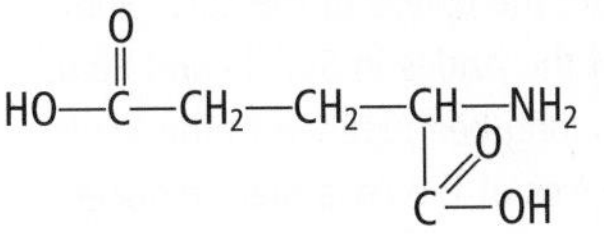

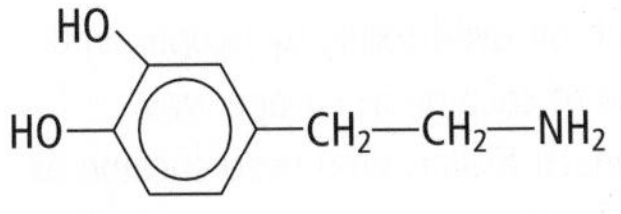

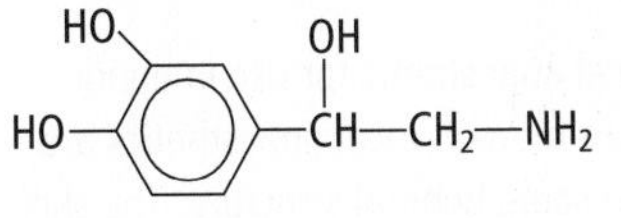

**Figure 20.11**  **Drug intervention in the control of depression**

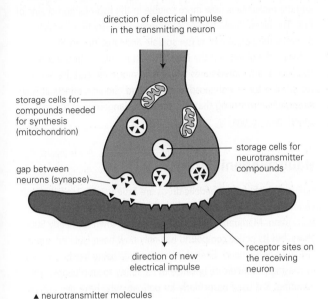

**Figure 20.9**  **Method of communication between neurons in the brain**

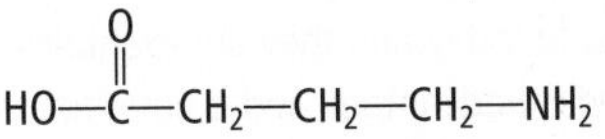

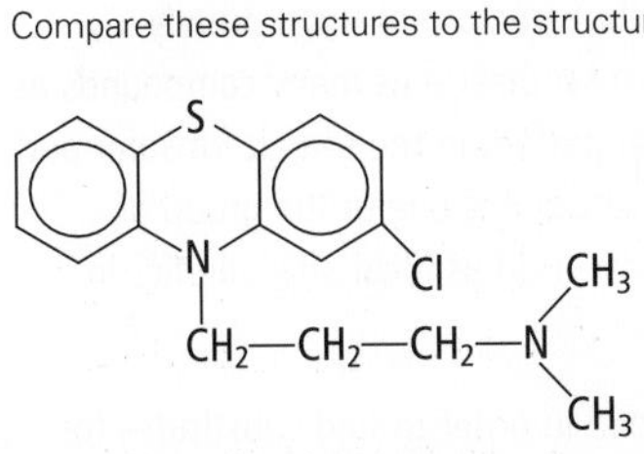

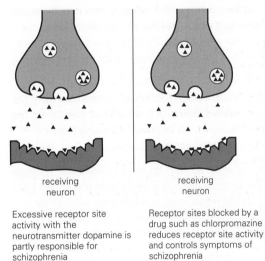

Excessive receptor site activity with the neurotransmitter dopamine is partly responsible for schizophrenia

Receptor sites blocked by a drug such as chlorpromazine reduces receptor site activity and controls symptoms of schizophrenia

**Figure 20.12**  **Drug intervention in the control of schizophrenia**

One aspect of depression is that there are reduced supplies of a particular neurotransmitter because the molecules are being broken down by an enzyme (figure 20.11); a drug is available that blocks the enzyme activity so that normal amounts of the neurotransmitter are available for communication with the next nerve. Other drugs block the return of neurotransmitter molecules to the original neuron and again the supply of the neurons can be at a normal level.

Other drugs that are available can stimulate the release of a neurotransmitter from storage; this again results in more neurotransmitter being available for neuron communication.

Research has shown that sometimes a mental disorder is due to excess receptor site activity (figure 20.12). A method which will

**Figure 20.10**  **Compounds that can act as neurotransmitters**

reduce excess activity is to block some of the receptors on the receiving neuron.

All of these drugs approaches benefit from detailed knowledge of the brain chemicals involved so the drugs of appropriate molecular shape and properties can be synthesised and their effectiveness tested. Nevertheless, most of the original discoveries so far in this area have been due to 'serendipity': research studies that produced totally unplanned results, but the value of the results was nevertheless realised.

## Analgesics

Some chemical molecules are able to relieve pain by modifying the pain signals as they approach the brain. A wide spectrum of substances is available which range from the relatively mild, widely used, aspirin and paracetamol to the powerful drugs of the morphine group: codeine is the mildest of these.

All the powerful analgesics in clinical use are related to morphine, which belongs to a group of naturally occurring substances called alkaloids. They have been available for many years from the opium obtained from poppy plants. The chief medical effects are all due to morphine: it has a remarkable ability to relieve pain. Treatment with morphine does not lead to addiction at the normal doses used to control pain.

The molecular structure looks complex since the nitrogen atom is a part of a six-membered ring which is in a different plane to the rest of the molecule: however, the structural relationship between codeine, morphine and heroin should be clear.

The morphine alkaloids act upon the neuron transmission system in the brain. The action of morphine is related to its ability to fit into and block a specific receptor site: communication between the neurons is blocked and the sensation of pain is removed.

morphine

codeine

heroin

The codeine molecule only differs from morphine by a methyl group and, although it is converted back to morphine in the body, it is significantly less potent.

In heroin the two alcohol groups of morphine have been converted to esters. Esterification of the two alcohol groups reduces solubility in water because the potential for hydrogen bonding is removed, and the molecule is now more soluble in the hydrocarbon chains of fats. The blood–brain barrier is composed of fatty tissue which prevents the passage of water soluble and large molecules between the blood and the brain. Heroin is able to diffuse across this barrier a hundred times faster than morphine and this is responsible for its enhanced analgesic and euphoric effects: it is so strongly habit-forming that it is the most dangerous of the so called 'hard' drugs.

## Hallucinogenic drugs

Hallucinogenic or psychedelic drugs are little used in medicine, but can have a profound effect on the user's mood, memory, or perception. Marijuana (cannabis) has been known for nearly 5000 years, but its active compound has only now been isolated and its structure determined. Cannabis, however, is being used increasingly in medicine because of its ability to stop people from vomiting. It is used particularly for patients who have been given drugs to treat cancer which tend to make people vomit badly. In the UK cannabis cannot be legally prescribed, but its medical value is being evaluated by limited clinical trials.

Cocaine and the amphetamines are perhaps the principal stimulants used in the Western world today and they are examples of drugs which can bring both medical advantage and a potential for abuse. Cocaine is extracted from the leaves of the coca plant which grows on the high slopes of the Andes in Bolivia and Peru. Its potential for altering mood has long been known to the South American Indians. Chewing the leaves of the coca plant reduces fatigue and increases endurance; the practice was known to the ancient Inca civilisation and is still followed today by people who live in the Andes. The medical use of cocaine in Europe was pioneered by a Viennese physician, Dr Koller, who used cocaine as a local anaesthetic in 1884 for operations on the eye.

Cocaine was the first effective local anaesthetic for use in minor surgery, and some of the important modern local anaesthetics are synthetic substitutes based on the same general structure. The skill of chemists is first to establish the structure of the naturally occurring compound and then to synthesise as many compounds as possible with a similar structural pattern in the search for safer and more effective alternatives. Benzocaine is one of the group of similar compounds which are now used as local anaesthetics in preference to cocaine.

These compounds were developed in order to find substitutes for cocaine, which has dangerously addictive properties. Before the

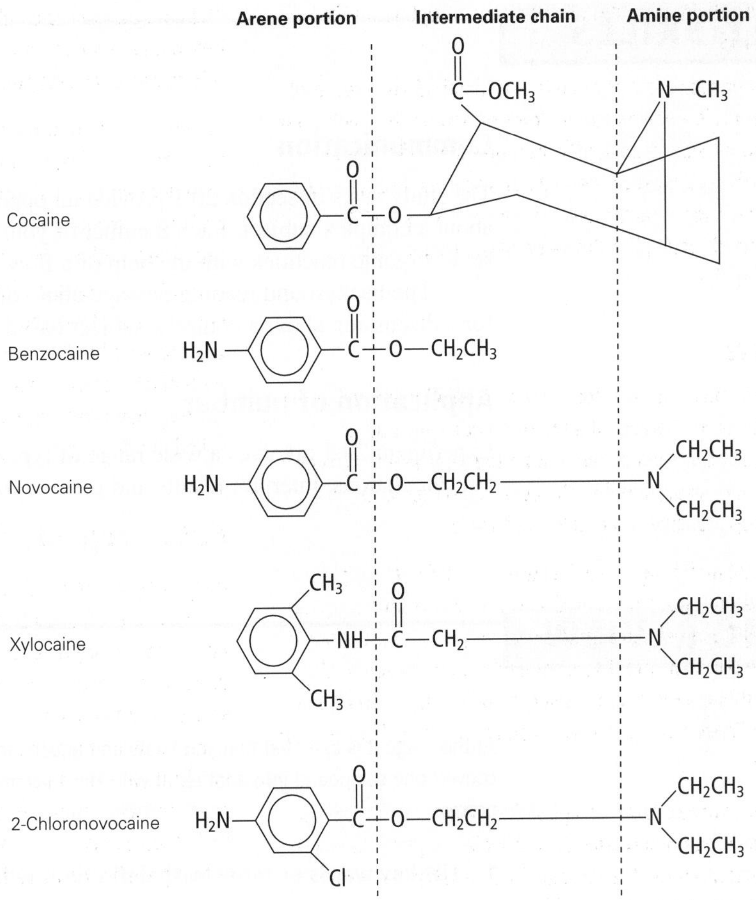

**Arene portion**   **Intermediate chain**   **Amine portion**

Cocaine

Benzocaine

Novocaine

Xylocaine

2-Chloronovocaine

Figure 20.13   **Structural patterns in some local anaesthetics**

danger of addiction to cocaine was recognised coca extracts were used quite casually as a stimulant and in a range of products. Coca Cola was originally marketed with extracts from coca leaves and kola nuts. After much argument between the Coca Cola company and the United States government the company was obliged to leave coca extract out of its drink, which is now an acceptable product.

## Drug dangers and dependence

For as long as we have used chemical substances to relieve pain and cure illness we have used other chemical substances to alter our moods and produce feelings of well-being. The social drugs such as alcohol and caffeine are usually only harmful when used to excess, but it should be remembered that alcoholism is a serious health problem, and that even small amounts of alcohol can cause damage to an unborn child. And smoking, which involves the social drug nicotine, is regarded by the medical profession as harmful in any amount, even to non-smokers by exposure to tobacco smoke. The 'soft' drugs, like cannabis and the amphetamines, may not lead to physical dependence, but an

increase in availability has led to an increase in abuse and has involved some users in serious crime. Addiction is inevitable with the 'hard' drugs of the morphine group: these narcotic drugs lead to complete dependence and eventually physical and mental damage. In order to obtain the desired effect, the addict finds it necessary to continually increase the amount of the drug until it reaches a level which is many times higher than might be administered for medical therapy.

The possibilities of drug abuse should not obscure the enormous advantages to be gained from the careful medical application of chemical substances in the treatment of disease. All drugs carry the risk of possible side effects, for the greater the effect a drug has on one part of the body the more likely it is to affect another part: these risks must be weighed against the advantages, which will vary with the patient and the nature of the illness. No drug or medicine can now be marketed without the approval of the expert Committee on Safety of Medicines, which assesses the evidence in support of the safety and effectiveness of new drugs. Nevertheless some hazards may only be identified when a drug is in widespread use, and then the drug company can be forced to stop selling the drug.

## KEY SKILLS

### Communication

The study tasks in section 20.1 provide an opportunity to make a presentation about a complex subject. Each member of your group or class might talk about one set of organic reactions with the help of a flow chart as the illustrative image.

The background reading passage about drugs (section 20.4) is an opportunity for a discussion about a complex subject based on question **3**.

### Application of number

Experiment 20.3 involves a wide range of types of data and requires you to carry out calculations, interpret results and present your findings.

## TOPIC REVIEW

At this stage it is essential that you know and understand enough organic chemistry to be able to convert one compound into another at will. This may involve a simple reaction or a multi-stage process.

1   **List key words or terms with definitions where necessary**

Illustrate the following with suitable **examples**:

- synthesis
- combustion analysis.

2   **Summarise the key principles as simply as possible**

At the end of this topic you should have constructed for yourself **three flow charts** for mapping **synthetic routes**. Included on these flow charts should be **reactants**, **conditions**, **type of reaction** and **products**. Not only are these charts useful **tools for revision**, but also the very task of **constructing** them **reinforces** your **understanding**.

## REVIEW QUESTIONS

**✱** Indicates that the *Book of data* is needed.

**20.1**   a   Copy the structural formula of cortisone (page 480). Circle the functional groups and name them.                                                                 (5)
           b   Work out the molecular formula of cortisone.                              (2)
                                                                                 **(7 marks)**

**20.2**    Carry out the same exercises as in question **20.1** for the following compounds:

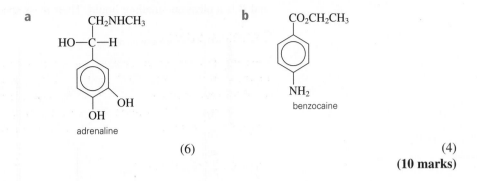

a    adrenaline

(6)

b    benzocaine

(4)

**(10 marks)**

**✳ 20.3**    A method of synthesising aspirin from phenol is shown below:

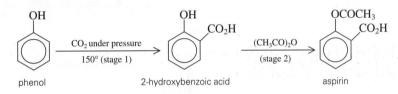

phenol          2-hydroxybenzoic acid          aspirin

a    Calculate the mass of aspirin which would be obtained from 50 g of phenol assuming that the yields for the two stages were 95% and 90% respectively.    (3)
b    What is the overall percentage yield?    (2)
c    Based on this overall percentage yield, what mass of phenol would be needed to make 1 tonne (1000 kg) of aspirin?    (2)

**(7 marks)**

**✳ 20.4**    0.200 g of an organic compound **Q** gave on complete combustion 0.455 g of carbon dioxide and 0.186 g of water. The compound also contained oxygen. The mass spectrometer parent ion peak is at 116.

a    Determine the empirical formula from the combustion analysis data, setting out your method clearly.    (4)
b    Use the mass spectrum data to determine the molar mass; then use this together with the empirical formula to work out the molecular formula.    (2)
c    Suggest TWO possible structural formulae for **Q**.    (2)
d    What instrumental technique could be used to distinguish between the isomers of **Q**? Explain briefly how it would do so.    (3)

**(11 marks)**

★ 20.5

Two organic compounds, **A** and **B**, are isomers with the composition by mass of carbon, 70.5%; hydrogen, 5.9%; oxygen, 23.6%. **A** is moderately soluble in water and **B** is a pleasant-smelling liquid. Their mass spectra are shown below:

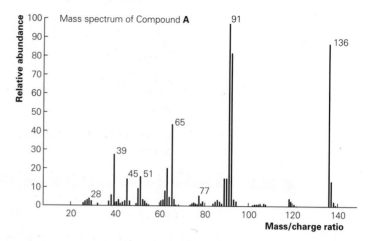

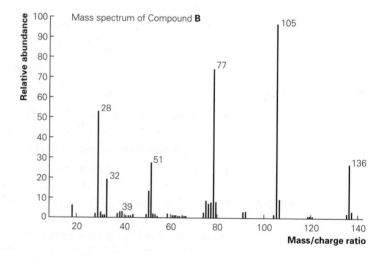

**a**  **i** What is the empirical formula of **A** and **B**? (2)

   **ii** What is the molecular formula of **A** and **B**? (2)

**b**  Suggest the formulae of the molecular fragments corresponding to the peaks with mass/charge ratio 136, 105, 91, 77. (4)

**c**  What structural formulae would you predict for **A** and **B**? (3)

**d**  Describe TWO chemical tests in which the behaviour of **A** and **B** would differ. (2)

**e**  What predictions can you make about the nmr spectra of **A** and **B**? (4)

**(17 marks)**

**20.6** The structures of two female sex hormones, oestrone and oestradiol, are given below. They belong to the class of natural products known as steroids.

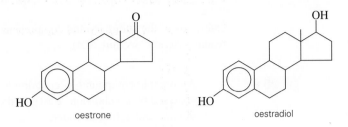

oestrone          oestradiol

a Suggest ONE physical and ONE chemical method of distinguishing between the two structures. (2)

b What reagent could you use to convert oestrone into oestradiol? (1)

c How would you attempt to remove the double bonds in the ring structure of oestradiol? (2)

d The two —OH groups in oestradiol are similar in some reactions but differ in others.
   i Give ONE example of a reaction in which they are similar. (1)
   ii Give examples (one for each group) in which they behave differently. (2)
                                                    **(8 marks)**

**✷ 20.7** A liquid hydrocarbon **X** is found to contain 85.7% carbon by mass, and to have a molar mass of 70 g mol$^{-1}$. The infrared spectrum for this compound includes peaks at 3085 cm$^{-1}$ and 1650 cm$^{-1}$.

a Calculate the molecular formula of **X** from the percentage composition. (2)
b Draw the structural formulae of FIVE possible isomers which might produce these two peaks in the infrared spectrum. (5)
c Suggest the structural formula of another isomer, **Y**, which would not have these two peaks in the infrared spectrum. (1)
d Predict THREE chemical reactions of one of your isomers of **X**. For each prediction write an equation or reaction scheme, and indicate the necessary reaction conditions. (6)
e Comment on whether all the isomers of **X** you have drawn would be expected to have identical physical and chemical properties. (1)
                                                    **(15 marks)**

# EXAMINATION QUESTIONS

Questions of the summary and comprehension type are found in the background reading section (section 20.4).

**20.8**

**a** An organic compound **X**, containing only carbon, hydrogen and oxygen, was analysed by combustion. 2.20 g of the compound produced 4.03 g of carbon dioxide and 1.10 g of water.

An aqueous solution of the compound reacted with sodium carbonate solution producing a gas. The solution also decolorised a solution of bromine.

The principal peaks in the mass spectrum of the compound are shown below.

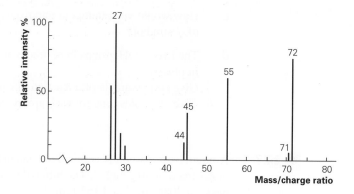

**i** Use the information given above to calculate the empirical and molecular formulae of the compound, making your method clear. (3)

**ii** Deduce the structure of the compound **X** explaining why it reacts with sodium carbonate and bromine. (1)

**iii** Give equations for these two reactions. (2)

**iv** Suggest formulae for the species which cause the peaks in the mass spectrum at 27, 44 and 45 and suggest why the peaks at 55 and 71 occur. (2)

**b** Predict how, and under what conditions, the compound **X** would react with the following substances:

**i** methanol

**ii** hydrogen chloride

**iii** TWO different reducing agents. (4)

**c** The compound can form a polymer. What type of polymerisation would you expect it to undergo? Draw a section of the polymer showing at least two formula units. (2)

**(14 marks)**

**20.9** The reaction scheme below shows a route by which the drug benzedrine may be prepared from benzene.

**a** **i** Give the reagents and conditions for the conversion of benzene to 1-phenylpropane in **Step 1**. Write an equation for the reaction. (2)

**ii** Identify the compound **X** and state the reagents and conditions for its conversion to benzedrine. (2)

**b** The yield of benzedrine produced at the end of this route is low as a number of other unwanted reactions occur. Suggest TWO organic products which may be formed as well as benzedrine and show how they might be produced. (4)

**c** The identity of benzedrine can be confirmed by instrumental methods. Predict the results which benzedrine would give in investigations using TWO different methods, making your reasoning clear. (4)

**(12 marks)**

# Instrumental methods

The chemical and physical properties of materials are strongly influenced by their structure. Therefore, to understand the properties of materials it is necessary to understand their structures. This applies as much to naturally occurring substances, such as rocks and minerals and the constituents of living organisms such as cells, muscles, and bone, as it does to substances such as semi-conductors for computer chips and polymers for 'easy-care' fabrics.

A very wide range of methods is available for obtaining information about the properties and structures of substances; in fact, any property of a material can be made to produce evidence of its structure. The most useful investigations are those in which:

1   **Properties of solutions of substances are measured**: e.m.f., pH, temperature changes.

2   **Matter interacts with an electric or a magnetic field**: mass spectrometry (see Topics 1 and 20).

3   **Electromagnetic radiation is emitted or absorbed by matter**, giving rise to emission or absorption spectra: infrared absorption and nuclear magnetic resonance (see Topics 12, 15 and 20).

4   **Electromagnetic radiation interacts with matter to give diffraction patterns**: X-ray diffraction (see Topics 3 and 7).

Investigation in each of these areas gives different information about a substance and when the evidence from several techniques is added together, it is often possible to obtain a detailed knowledge of its structure.

Descriptions of some of the most important instruments used to obtain structural information now follow. You are not expected to memorise the details of the instruments described in this topic or their method of operation. You should concentrate on the interpretation of the results obtained by the various methods.

## 21.1   The mass spectrometer

**The most accurate method of determining atomic and molar masses is by use of the mass spectrometer.** Figure 21.1 shows how it works. Five main operations are performed by the spectrometer:

1   the sample is vaporised
2   positive ions are produced from the vapour
3   the positive ions are accelerated by a known electric field
4   the ions are then deflected by a known magnetic field
5   the ions are detected.

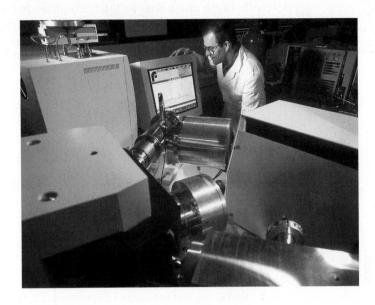

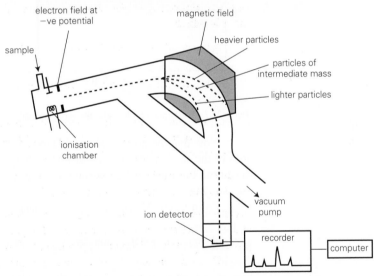

Figure 21.1   A mass spectrometer and
how it works

First let us consider the determination of the molar mass of an element. A stream of the vaporised element enters the main apparatus, which is maintained under high vacuum. The atoms of the element are bombarded by a stream of high-energy electrons which, on collision with the atoms, knock electrons out of them and produce positive ions. In most cases single electrons are removed from atoms of the element:

$$E(g) \longrightarrow E^+(g) + e^-$$

although in some cases more electrons may be removed.

The stream of positive ions passes through holes in two plates to which a known electric field is applied; quadrupole machines have four rods across which the electric field is applied. The ions then enter a region to which a magnetic field is applied.

For given electric and magnetic fields only ions with the same charge and mass reach the detector at the end of the apparatus: all other ions hit the side walls of the instrument. By gradually increasing the strength of the magnetic field, ions of increasing masses are brought successively to the detector. A computer is used to calculate their masses from measurements of the strength of the applied fields; and their relative abundance is found from the relative magnitudes of the current produced in the detector.

A mass spectrum for naturally-occurring lead is shown in figure 21.2. The mass spectrum gives the relative abundance of the various isotopes of the element.

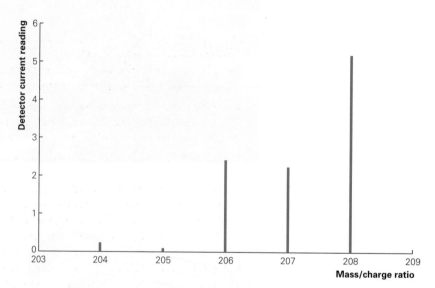

Figure 21.2 **Mass spectrum for naturally-occurring lead**

Note that the horizontal axis is labelled 'Mass/charge ratio'. This is because ions of the same mass but with different charges give separate traces in the mass spectrum. For ions carrying a single charge the mass/charge ratio is equal to the isotopic mass.

From figure 21.2 the relative abundances can be seen to be:

| Isotopic mass | Relative abundance | % relative abundance |
|---|---|---|
| 204.0 | 0.2 | 2 |
| 206.0 | 2.4 | 24 |
| 207.0 | 2.2 | 22 |
| 208.0 | 5.2 | 52 |
| | 10.0 | 100 |

From these values the molar mass of naturally-occurring lead can be worked out as follows.

In 100 atoms of naturally-occurring lead there will be, on average, 2 atoms of isotopic mass 204.0, 24 of 206.0, 22 of 207.0, and 52 of 208.0. By finding the total mass of all these 100 atoms, it is possible to calculate the average mass by dividing by 100.

COMMENT

Molar mass (g mol$^{-1}$)
= a.m.u. (g) $\times$ $L$ (mol$^{-1}$)
($L$ = Avogadro constant)
1 a.m.u. = $1.661 \times 10^{-24}$ g
$L = 6.023 \times 10^{23}$ mol$^{-1}$

| Isotopic mass | Number of atoms in 100 atoms of mixture | Mass of isotope in 100 atoms of mixture |
|---|---|---|
| 204.0 | 2 | 408 |
| 206.0 | 24 | 4 944 |
| 207.0 | 22 | 4 554 |
| 208.0 | 52 | 10 816 |
| | | 20 722 |

Average mass of 1 atom $= \dfrac{20\,722}{100} = 207.2$ atomic mass units (a.m.u.)

### STUDY TASK

1   Use table 2.2 in the *Book of data* to work out the molar masses of naturally-occurring lithium and iron. Record the working, and the result, in your notes.

2   Examine the abundance of the isotopes of tellurium-52, $_{52}$Te, and the molar mass of tellurium. Compare this with the molar mass of $_{53}$I and comment on their positions in the Periodic Table and their relative molar masses. Do the same for $_{18}$Ar and $_{19}$K.

For the determination of its molar mass, the compound under investigation is injected into the instrument as a vapour. High velocity electrons then bombard the molecules and produce a variety of positively charged ions.

The ion detected to have the highest mass, the 'parent ion', normally indicates the molar mass of the compound. Having found the molecular formula, some idea of the structure of the compound can be obtained from the ions of smaller mass, caused by the break-up of some of the original molecules under the electron bombardment.

The spectrometer can be connected directly to a computer which is programmed to determine, not just the molar mass, but also the structural formula of any sample. The computer has access to a database of mass spectra so that it can identify a compound by comparing its spectrum to other spectra until it finds a good match. The computer can also help to determine the structure of newly synthesised substances by identifying fragments in the spectrum. The analyst can then fit these together like the pieces of a jigsaw.

### STUDY TASK

The mass spectrum of the compound **V**, $C_8H_8O$, has a parent ion peak at 120, corresponding to the $C_8H_8O^+$ ion. The molecule also breaks into smaller fragments, such as the peaks at 105 and 77 (see figure 21.3).

1   Try to work out a structural formula for the compound.

2   How many isomers can you find with the formula $C_8H_8O$?

3   What atoms might correspond to the loss of mass represented by the peaks at 120, 105 and 77?

4   Which isomers are unlikely to produce fragments of mass/charge ratio 105 and 77?

5 What structure do you suggest?

6 Compare your answer with the deductions that can be made from the infrared spectrum shown in figure 21.5.

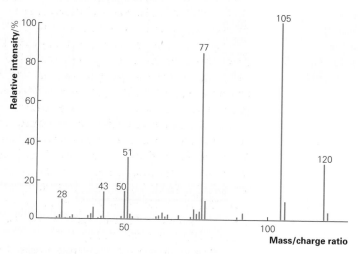

Figure 21.3 Mass spectrum of compound **V**, $C_8H_8O$

## 21.2 Infrared spectroscopy

COMMENT

When describing infrared spectra, the position of peaks is referred not to the frequency of the radiation but to the wavenumber, measured in cm$^{-1}$

An infrared spectrometer passes all the required frequencies simultaneously through the instrument in order to record the infrared spectrum of a compound. The source of infrared radiation is usually a ceramic rod heated to around 1500 °C, which emits infrared radiation covering the whole of the required range of wavenumbers (200 to 4000 cm$^{-1}$).

A liquid sample is usually held as a thin film between two sodium chloride discs; a solid sample is powdered, mixed with potassium bromide, and crushed under considerable pressure to form a disc. The use of alkali halides such as sodium chloride and potassium bromide is necessary because they are transparent

Figure 21.4 Operating an infrared spectrometer

to infrared radiation, whereas glass discs would absorb most of the radiation. This means, of course, that all samples have to be completely dry before their spectra can be recorded.

**Most compounds absorb infrared radiation. The wavelengths they absorb correspond to the natural frequencies at which vibrating bonds in the molecules stretch and bend.** The bonds which absorb strongly as they vibrate are polar covalent bonds such as O—H, C—O and C=O.

Bonds vibrate in characteristic ways and absorb at specific wavelengths. This means that in functional groups one bond affects the vibrations of others close to it. Even comparatively simple molecules can vibrate in many ways. The aldehyde butanal, $CH_3CH_2CH_2CHO$, has over 30 ways of vibrating and although not every possible vibration produces an absorption peak, the spectrum is still complex.

Individual wavenumbers in an infrared spectrum are useful because each peak is characteristic of a vibration of a particular molecular structure. Thus the C—H stretching vibration absorbs at about $2900 \text{ cm}^{-1}$ in alkanes but at about $3050 \text{ cm}^{-1}$ in alkenes. In a benzene ring carbon–carbon vibrations absorb at both $1600 \text{ cm}^{-1}$ and $1500 \text{ cm}^{-1}$. The characteristic absorptions that are useful for the identification of particular groups of atoms in molecules of organic carbon compounds are found in the region from $200 \text{ cm}^{-1}$ to $4000 \text{ cm}^{-1}$. Details are given in table 3.3 of the *Book of data*.

Analysts now have access to computer databases, with infrared spectra stored like 'fingerprints' for a large number of pure compounds. They can identify specimens by matching the absorption spectrum of an unknown with one of the known spectra in a database, and comparing the result with spectra from other techniques such as nuclear magnetic resonance (nmr) and mass spectrometry.

Spectra can also be used to follow the progress of synthetic reactions but interpretation is difficult because all the substances present produce spectra. Matching the infrared spectrum of a product with that of a known pure sample can be used to check that the product is pure and free from traces of solvents or by-products.

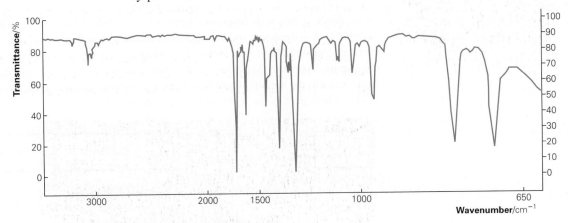

Figure 21.5 **The infrared spectrum of compound V, $C_8H_8O$**

---

**STUDY TASK**

Identify the bonds responsible for the peaks in the infrared spectrum of the compound **V**, $C_8H_8O$, shown in figure 21.5. Hence predict possible structures for the compound and compare your answer with the deductions that can be made from the mass spectrum shown in figure 21.3.

# 21.3  Nuclear magnetic resonance spectroscopy

Figure 21.6    Operating a nuclear magnetic resonance spectrometer

- **Nuclear** refers to the atomic nuclei of those atoms, such as hydrogen or carbon, which the instrument detects.
- **Magnetic** refers to the behaviour of the nuclei of the atoms, which act like small magnets in a strong magnetic field, lining up either in the same direction as the field or in the opposite direction.
- **Resonance** refers to the absorption of radio waves of the resonance frequency corresponding to the energy change as the nuclei flip from one alignment to the other.

Nuclear magnetic resonance (nmr) requires only 10–20 mg of material. The sample is dissolved in a solvent with no hydrogen atoms, such as $CDCl_3$. If the solvent contained hydrogen atoms, it would have absorption peaks of its own. Nuclei of deuterium do not behave like tiny magnets so they are not detected by nmr. Also in the solution there is a reference material, such as tetramethylsilane, TMS, which acts as the standard for measurements.

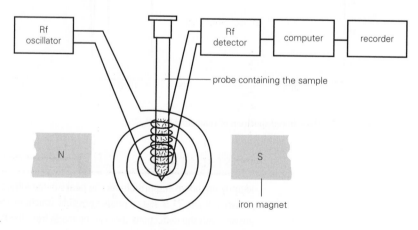

Figure 21.7    Diagram of an nmr spectrometer

The instrument displays an absorption peak whenever the sample absorbs strongly so that there is a drop in the power of the signal from the detector. Each peak corresponds to hydrogen nuclei in a particular molecular environment. The area under the peak is proportional to the number of nuclei in that environment. In ethanol, $CH_3CH_2OH$, for example, hydrogen nuclei occur in three environments, resonating at three different frequencies: three in the —$CH_3$ group, two in the —$CH_2$—, and one in the —OH.

In figure 21.8, the low resolution spectrum has peaks which correspond to the single hydrogen nucleus in the hydroxyl group, H—O, and higher peaks corresponding to the two hydrogen nuclei in the —$CH_2$— group and the three methyl hydrogen nuclei. In the high resolution spectrum it can be seen that the single peak at low resolution is actually made up of three peaks.

Nuclear magnetic resonance can be used to analyse drugs and determine their structure. An nmr spectrum, like an infrared spectrum, can be used as a 'fingerprint' to check that the compound synthesised is the required drug. The nmr spectrum can also help to check for impurities, identify them and work out the scale of contamination. Another medical use is to detect hydrogen nuclei in the human body, mainly those in water and lipids. A computer translates the information from a three-dimensional scan to produce images of soft tissue; the technique is more powerful than X-ray methods, which are generally used to study bones.

**COMMENT**

The positions of the peaks are identified by their chemical shifts (δ in ppm) from the position of the tetramethylsilane peak. By definition the δ value for TMS is zero.

**a  low resolution**

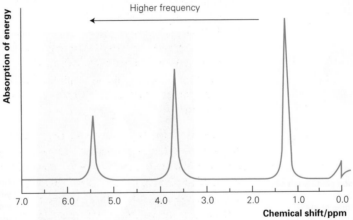

**b  high resolution**

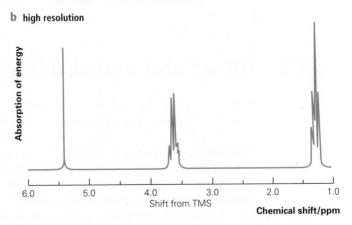

**Figure 21.8   Nuclear magnetic resonance spectra of ethanol**

## 21.4    X-ray diffraction

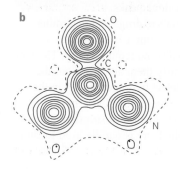

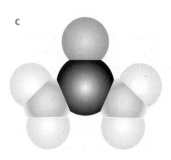

As an example of the interaction of electromagnetic radiation with matter to give diffraction patterns, we shall consider X-ray diffraction. X-rays are to be found in the electromagnetic spectrum beyond the far ultraviolet.

When a beam of X-rays of one particular wavelength, that is a monochromatic beam, falls on a crystalline solid the X-rays are scattered in an orderly manner. This scattering is known as diffraction and gives rise to a diffraction pattern, which can be recorded electronically. A typical X-ray diffraction pattern is shown in figure 21.9a.

**The X-ray diffraction pattern is related to the pattern of the electrons in the solid.** By analysis of the X-ray pattern it is possible to deduce the pattern of the electrons in the solid, and thus the identity of the atoms and their relative positions. The electron pattern is usually presented as an electron density map, such as figure 21.9b. From these maps it is possible to construct a model of the structure of the solid (figure 21.9c). **Because the hydrogen atom has a low electron density which is not easily detected by X-rays, the position of the hydrogen atoms cannot be seen in figure 21.9b.**

Even for a relatively simple structure the calculations which are involved in translating a diffraction pattern into a crystal structure model can be very complex. For structures such as those of proteins and of DNA the quantity of calculation involved is immense and requires huge computing capacity, but modern computers can achieve results very rapidly.

**Figure 21.9**
a   An X-ray diffraction photograph of a single crystal of urea
b   Electron density map of urea
c   A model of the structure of urea ($NH_2CONH_2$)

**Figure 21.10    Professor Dorothy Hodgkin** who won a Nobel Prize in 1964 for her work on X-ray crystallography. Amongst other achievements she discovered the structure of vitamin $B_{12}$ and of penicillin

## 21.5    Ultraviolet and visible spectroscopy

Spectroscopy originally referred to the analysis of substances using visible radiation, but the term now includes the use of ultraviolet and infrared radiation.

When light, either visible or ultraviolet, is absorbed by electrons these electrons are promoted from their normal energy levels to higher levels, with exact energy changes involved. The absorption peaks in an ultraviolet or visible spectrum are, however, broad peaks because there are also vibrational and rotational energy levels available in molecules.

In a typical spectrometer samples are used in solution and are placed in a small silica cell. Two lamps are used: a hydrogen or deuterium lamp for the ultraviolet region and a tungsten/halogen lamp for the visible region. In this way, radiation across the whole range can be scanned by a spectrometer. The spectrometer compares the light passing through the sample with that passing through a reference cell.

**Ultraviolet spectroscopy is particularly valuable for studying colourless organic compounds with unsaturated functional groups such as C=O and C=C** The molecules absorb ultraviolet radiation at frequencies which excite shared electrons in double bonds. The radiation may also excite non-bonding electrons in compounds containing oxygen, nitrogen, sulphur or halogens.

In the pharmaceutical industry scientists use ultraviolet spectroscopy to analyse drugs such as paracetamol which absorb strongly in the UV region. Spectroscopy can be used to check that medicines contain the correct amounts of drugs and that the products have not deteriorated in storage.

## 21.6 Using a pH meter

The hydrogen ion concentration of a solution is usually expressed as a pH number, where:

$$pH = -\log [H^+(aq)]$$

In principle, the simplest method for measuring hydrogen ion concentration is to use a hydrogen electrode (see Topic 17) dipped in the solution of unknown $H^+(aq)$ concentration. However, the hydrogen electrode is not easy to use. It is bulky when the hydrogen generator is taken into account, slow to reach equilibrium, and rather easily 'poisoned' by impurities. The glass electrode is an alternative electrode in common use.

The glass electrode consists of a thin-walled bulb blown from special glass of low melting point. The bulb contains a solution of constant pH (a 'buffer' solution) with a platinum wire dipping into it. When the bulb is immersed in a solution of unknown pH, a potential develops on the platinum wire and the whole arrangement can be used as a half-cell.

Combined with a suitable reference electrode, it is possible to make e.m.f. measurements. The resistance of the glass bulb is high ($10^7$–$10^8$ ohms) and a very sensitive solid-state voltmeter must be used to measure the e.m.f. The reference electrode is usually made of silver/silver chloride.

The theory of the glass electrode is complicated but an arrangement such as

| Pt | solution A of known pH | glass bulb | solution B of unknown pH | reference electrode |

can be attached to a meter calibrated in pH units. An instrument designed on this basis is called a pH meter. In commercial pH meters the glass electrode and the reference electrode are often combined in one unit which can be dipped into the solution under investigation. Simple, reliable and robust pH meters are available which are useful for field work.

A pH meter should first be checked using solutions of reliable pH. Buffer solutions of pH 4 and pH 9 are suitable for checking the acid–base range of a meter. You will not get reliable readings of pH 7 in pure water because the concentration of ions is too low.

When measuring the pH of solutions, the pH electrode must always be rinsed in a large volume of pure water before and between readings. It should never be used in solutions of concentrated acid or alkali.

## KEY SKILLS

### IT

You can search the Internet and chemical data sets on CD-ROMs to discover more about the techniques described in this topic and to find spectroscopic data about compounds you have studied.

# Safety appendix

## Laboratory health and safety

You are more likely to suffer a minor injury – a cut, burn or scald – in a kitchen than in a laboratory. The reason is quite simple; we know there are hazards involved in working in a laboratory so Risk Assessments are made for every experiment and protective measures are taken to control those risks. In chemistry lessons most risks arise from the use of chemicals, but some other practical activities have associated hazards (for example, micro-organisms or electricity).

Laboratory safety is about minimising exposure to risk, as well as protecting yourself from the results of mishaps. When you do an experiment that involves the production of an unpleasant gas like nitrogen dioxide, you should think about using small quantities of reagents and containing the gas in a fume cupboard. You should also think about what you might need to do if the gas was produced unexpectedly fast.

You will be healthy, safe and successful in your laboratory work provided:

- you plan your work taking note of the health and safety information provided
- you wear eye protection and whatever else is recommended
- you carry out all instructions thoughtfully and correctly.

All the experiments in this course have been checked for health and safety implications, but when you are going to do an investigation of your own you will be expected to carry out a Risk Assessment (and have it checked before starting any practical work).

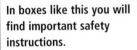

**SAFETY**

In boxes like this you will find important safety instructions.

## Risk Assessments

Risk Assessments are most conveniently made on a standard form; an example is shown overleaf. The procedure is straightforward – always bear in mind that the intention is to protect you from any risks. The steps in making an assessment are:

1  **Write down the procedures** you will be using (chemicals used or made, quantities, concentrations, techniques and any non-chemical hazards).

2  Use reference sources to **identify any hazardous chemicals** you are planning to use or make. The appropriate warning symbol should be on reagent bottles and in suppliers' catalogues.

3  **Record the nature of the hazards** involved and the way you might be exposed to the hazard. There are standard reference sources with this information, such as the 'Hazcards' published by CLEAPSS.

4　**Decide what protective or control measures to take** so that you can carry out your practical work healthily and in safety.

5　Find out how to **dispose** of any hazardous residues from your practical work.

The protective measures you need to take will depend on your laboratory as well as your experiment. The experiments in this course have been assessed for use in a well-lit, well-ventilated and uncrowded laboratory. Where conditions are different, additional protective measures may be necessary.

# Risk Assessment form

| Title of the experiment | | | |
|---|---|---|---|
| **Outline of the procedures** | | | |
| | | | |
| **Hazardous substances being used or made** | **Nature of the hazards (e.g. toxic, flammable)** | **Quantities and concentrations being used or made** | **Control measures (precautions)** |
| | | | |

| Any non-chemical hazards and precautions to be taken | Signed (student) |
|---|---|
| | Signed (teacher) |
| **Disposal of residues** | Date: |

# Good laboratory practice

As well as the specific protective measures to be taken when hazardous chemicals are being used, there are also general procedures to be observed in all laboratories at all times.

COMMENT

Control of Substances Hazardous to Health

- **Long hair** should be tied back and you should not wear 'wet look' hair preparations, which can make hair unusually flammable. Do not let **ties**, **scarves** or **cardigans** hang freely, where they could be a fire hazard. We strongly recommend the wearing of **laboratory coats** to avoid damage to clothing.
- **Eating**, **drinking** and **chewing** are not permitted in laboratories. It is, in fact, contrary to the COSHH regulations (and therefore illegal) to permit eating, drinking or indeed smoking or the application of cosmetics in any area which could be contaminated with hazardous chemicals.
- **Eye protection** should be worn whenever a Risk Assessment requires it, or whenever there is any risk to your eyes. This includes, for example, washing up at the end of the lesson and even when you have finished practical work, as long as other students are still working.
- You should find that the chemicals that you are going to use are in **clearly labelled** stock bottles, with the name of the chemical, any hazards, and the date of acquisition or preparation. When taking liquids from a bottle, remove the stopper with one hand and keep the stopper in your hand whilst pouring from the bottle. This way, the stopper is likely to be replaced at once and to remain uncontaminated. Pour liquids from the opposite side to the label, so that it does not become damaged by corrosive chemicals.
- Study carefully the best techniques for **safely heating** chemicals. Small quantities of solid can be heated in test tubes; liquids present greater problems, because of the risk of 'bumping' and 'spitting'. Boiling tubes are safer than test tubes (because of their greater volume), but should be **less than one-fifth full**. You are likely to point test tubes away from your own face, but do remember the need to do the same for your neighbours. **Use a water bath to heat flammable liquids; NEVER use a naked flame.**
- When testing for the odour of gases, the gas should be contained in a test tube (not a larger vessel) and the test tube held about 10–15 cm from your face, pointing away. Fill your lungs with air by breathing in and then cautiously sniff the contents of the test tube, by using a hand to waft the vapours to your nose. Slowly bring the test tube nearer, if necessary. If you are asthmatic you should not smell gases without a report from other students because gases such as chlorine are harmful.
- You must always **clear up chemical spillages straight away**. Whilst a few spills may need chemical neutralisation or similar treatment, most minor spills can be wiped up using a damp cloth. (Don't forget to rinse it afterwards.)
- In the event of getting a chemical in your eye, or on your skin, **flood the area with large quantities of water at once**. Keep the water running for at least 10 minutes (20 minutes for alkalis in the eye). Rubber tubing on a tap is the most convenient way of doing this. Even if the chemical reacts exothermically with water, provided a large quantity of water is used, the heating effect will be negligible.
- A heat burn from apparatus, scalding liquids or steam is treated by **immersing the area in cool water** for at least 10 minutes. Preferably use running water from rubber tubing, fixed to a tap.
- **Report all accidents at once.**

SAFETY ⚠

The most common mishaps in the laboratory involve splashes from liquids (especially in the eye) and burns from hot apparatus.

# Warning symbols

HARMFUL
or IRRITANT

FLAMMABLE

CORROSIVE

OXIDISING

TOXIC

EXPLOSIVE

DANGER

EYE PROTECTION
MUST BE WORN

DANGEROUS FOR
THE ENVIRONMENT

# Index

# Acknowledgements

## Picture acknowledgements

We are grateful to the following for permission to reproduce photographs:

ADM Ingredients of Cork, pages 370 bottom, 371,372; American Chemical Society, page 479; Heather Angel, pages 116, 209, 425; Art Directors & Trip, pages 78(H.Rogers), 358(A,Lambert), 391 left(A.Lambert), 391 centre(A.Lambert); Bayer, page 290; C.Blackie, page 470; Gareth Boden, pages 3, 4, 8, 11, 14, 17 top, 32, 33, 34, 37, 39, 83, 128, 195, 376; Boltzmann Society, page 313 left; Paul Brierley, page 310; University of Bristol, page 441; The British Petroleum Company plc, pages 176, 189; Ecoscene, page 333(Tony Page); Malcolm Evetts, Burford School, pages 114, 326; Leslie Garland Picture Library, pages 1 left(Jim Gibson), 391 right(Andrew Lambert), 395 top(Andrew Lambert), 395 bottom(Andrew Lambert); GeoScience Features Picture Library, pages 9, 12, 393 bottom; Sonia Halliday & Laura Lushington, page iv top left; David Hoffman, page 19; IACR Rothamsted, page 92; Image Select, pages 40, 234 left; Professor A Keller, University of Bristol, page 212; Kemira, pages 242 right, 318; Andrew Lambert, page 64; Frank Lane Picture Agency, pages 308(R.Lawrence), 399(Ron Austing); Dame Kathleen Lonsdale, page 514 top; Mansell Collection/Time Inc, page 293; NHPA, pages 366(N.A Callow), 368(Anthony Bannister), 294(David Woodfall); Norfolk Lavender, page 26; Office de Tourisme des Congres, Paris, page 53 bottom; Oxford Scientific Films, pages 77(Mills Tandy), 115(Martyn F.Chillmaid), 219(Niall Benvie); Pictor International, page 100; Royal Society of Chemistry, page 390; Science Museum/Science & Society Picture Library, page 453 left; Science Photo Library, pages 1 right(Simon Fraser), 1 centre(NASA), 17 below, 18 left(Maximilian Stock Ltd), 49, 51 top(Eye of Science), 51 bottom(Manfred Kage), 52(Sidney Moulds), 53 top(Northwestern University), 54, 66(Andrew Syred), 68(Lawrence Berkeley National Laboratory), 88(Russ Lappa), 127(Alfred Pasieka), 132, 151(Joseph Nettis), 218(Alfred Pasieka), 225(Debra Ferguson/Agstock), 234 right(BSIP, LECA), 313 right, 356(Custom Medical Stock Photo), 365(US Department of Energy), 393 top(Dr Jeremy Burgess), 394 top(John Walsh), 394 bottom(Alfred Pasieka), 395 centre(Bernhard Edmaier), 435, 440(Dr Jeremy Burgess), 478 left(Robin Laurance), 478 right(R.Maisonneuve, Publiphoto Diffusion), 507(Tek Image), 510(Simon Fraser/Mauna Loa Observatory), 512(James King-Holmes), 514 bottom; R.Sheridan/Ancient Art & Architecture Collection, pages iv top right, iv below, 453 right; Stone, pages title page(Wayne Eastep), 131(Ben Edwards), 181(Paul Harris), 188(Ross Harrison Koty), 242 left(Vince Streano), 302 top(Fred Charles), 302 bottom(James Wells), 331(Soenar Chamid), 369(Robert Frerck), 367(David Joe), 396(Stephen Johnson), 439(Ted Wood); Telegraph Colour Library, page 18 right(V.C.L); G.T & P.J Woods, page 48.

## Other acknowledgements

We are grateful to the following for permission to reproduce copyright material:

Education in Chemistry for an adapted extract from the article 'Growing Diamonds' by Harold Zaugg & 'Burning Diamonds and Squeezing Peanuts by Dr K A Davenport in *CHEMISTRY MATTERS* April, 1990; Macmillan Publishers Ltd for adapted extracts from *AN A-Z OF THE ELEMENTS*, published under the Channel Four Books imprint; The Royal Society of Chemistry for text adapted from 'A Golden Opportunity' by Jack Barrett and Martin Hughes in *CHEMISTRY IN BRITAIN* June 1997 and author's agents PFD for the poem 'Iron' by Roger McGough from *DEFYING GRAVITY* published by Penguin © Roger McGough; Edexcel for permission to reproduce questions from past examination papers.

# Periodic Table

| | 1 | 2 | | 3 | 4 | 5 | 6 | 7 | 0 |
|---|---|---|---|---|---|---|---|---|---|
| 1s | 1 H 1 | | | | | | | | 2 He 4 |
| 2s | 3 Li 7 | 4 Be 9 | 2p | 5 B 11 | 6 C 12 | 7 N 14 | 8 O 16 | 9 F 19 | 10 Ne 20 |
| 3s | 11 Na 23 | 12 Mg 24 | 3p | 13 Al 27 | 14 Si 28 | 15 P 31 | 16 S 32 | 17 Cl 35.5 | 18 Ar 40 |
| 4s | 19 K 39 | 20 Ca 40 | 3d → | | | | | | |
| 5s | 37 Rb 85 | 38 Sr 88 | 4d → | | | | | | |
| 6s | 55 Cs 133 | 56 Ba 137 | 5d → | | | | | | |
| 7s | 87 Fr (223) | 88 Ra (226) | 6d → | | | | | | |

## d-block

| 3d | 21 Sc 45 | 22 Ti 48 | 23 V 51 | 24 Cr 52 | 25 Mn 55 | 26 Fe 56 | 27 Co 59 | 28 Ni 59 | 29 Cu 63.5 | 30 Zn 65.4 |
|---|---|---|---|---|---|---|---|---|---|---|
| 4d | 39 Y 89 | 40 Zr 91 | 41 Nb 93 | 42 Mo 96 | 43 Tc (99) | 44 Ru 101 | 45 Rh 103 | 46 Pd 106 | 47 Ag 108 | 48 Cd 112 |
| 5d | 57 La 139 | 72 Hf 178 | 73 Ta 181 | 74 W 184 | 75 Re 186 | 76 Os 190 | 77 Ir 192 | 78 Pt 195 | 79 Au 197 | 80 Hg 201 |
| 6d | 89 Ac (227) | 104 Rf (261) | 105 Db (262) | 106 Sg (263) | 107 Bh (262) | 108 Hs (265) | 109 Mt (266) | | | |

## p-block (continued)

| | 3 | 4 | 5 | 6 | 7 | 0 |
|---|---|---|---|---|---|---|
| 4p | 31 Ga 70 | 32 Ge 73 | 33 As 75 | 34 Se 79 | 35 Br 80 | 36 Kr 84 |
| 5p | 49 In 115 | 50 Sn 119 | 51 Sb 122 | 52 Te 128 | 53 I 127 | 54 Xe 131 |
| 6p | 81 Tl 204 | 82 Pb 207 | 83 Bi 209 | 84 Po 210 | 85 At (210) | 86 Rn (222) |

## f-block

| 4f | 58 Ce 140 | 59 Pr 141 | 60 Nd 144 | 61 Pm (147) | 62 Sm 150 | 63 Eu 152 | 64 Gd 157 | 65 Tb 159 | 66 Dy 163 | 67 Ho 165 | 68 Er 167 | 69 Tm 169 | 70 Yb 173 | 71 Lu 175 |
|---|---|---|---|---|---|---|---|---|---|---|---|---|---|---|
| 5f | 90 Th 232 | 91 Pa (231) | 92 U 238 | 93 Np (237) | 94 Pu (244) | 95 Am (243) | 96 Cm (247) | 97 Bk (247) | 98 Cf (251) | 99 Es (254) | 100 Fm (257) | 101 Md (258) | 102 No (259) | 103 Lr (260) |

Key

Atomic number
Symbol
Molar mass for stable isotopes /g mol$^{-1}$